THE

# PUBLICATIONS

OF THE

# Northamptonshire Record Society

FOUNDED IN DECEMBER, 1920

---

## VOLUME XXXIV

FOR THE TWO YEARS ENDED 31 DECEMBER 1985

Earl Spencer, 1902

# THE RED EARL

## The Papers of the Fifth Earl Spencer 1835–1910

Edited by PETER GORDON

In two volumes
Vol. II 1885–1910

Northampton
1986

ISBN 0 901275 52 2

Published by the Northamptonshire Record Society,
Delapre Abbey, Northampton NN4 9AW


*The Northamptonshire Record Society
gratefully acknowledges the generous sponsorship of
Mrs Hilda Benham and the Benham Charitable Settlement
which has made possible the publication
of this volume*

Printed by Butler & Tanner Ltd., Frome, Somerset

# CONTENTS

# ILLUSTRATIONS

Acknowledgements and thanks for permission to reproduce the illustrations are due to the Northampton Public Library for the frontispiece and Plates 2, 8 and 9; to the *Northampton Mercury* for Plate 1; to *Punch* for Plate 3; to the John Rylands University Library of Manchester for Plate 4; to the *Illustrated London News* for Plate 5; and to the National Monuments Record for Plates 6 and 7.

# ACKNOWLEDGEMENTS

This volume completes a portrait of the fifth Earl Spencer as seen through memoranda, diaries and a wide range of correspondence to and from political colleagues, family and friends. No biography exists at present. In 1923, the seventh Earl Spencer approached J. A. Spender, on the advice of Rosebery, with a view to writing his uncle's life, but nothing came of the project. (Wilson Hunt, *J. A. Spender* (1946), p. 175). Ten years later, W. Graham Greene, who had served as assistant private secretary to the fifth Earl when he was First Lord of the Admiralty, 1892-5, began a Life, but only a fragment, covering these years, was completed. (Greene Papers, GEE/13(g). National Maritime Museum, Greenwich.)

In 1969, the seventh Earl suggested that an edition of his papers might be undertaken. I was greatly helped by him whilst working at Althorp during the following years: of particular value were the first-hand reminiscences concerning his uncle, along with recollections about many of the leading figures who appear in these pages. I trust that he would have considered that the publication of these volumes represented a step towards a wider recognition of the importance of the fifth Earl in British politics as well as in Northamptonshire affairs. I am also grateful to his son, the present Earl Spencer, for his continuing interest in the project and for facilitating access to the muniment room when the papers were at Althorp.

I should like particularly to thank the following: Dr. Edmund King, the honorary general editor of the Society, for his guidance and helpfulness in many ways over the years; Christopher Howard, for undertaking the task of reading the entire manuscript and saving me from committing a number of errors; Victor Hatley, for making available his unrivalled knowledge of Northamptonshire history; Professor John Vincent for directing my attention to some interesting archival sources; Dr. Nicholas Rodger for his advice on naval records; and Dr. Colin Matthew for providing information on Gladstone. I am also pleased to acknowledge financial assistance from the British Academy and the Leverhulme Trust.

I much appreciate the ready assistance afforded by private owners of papers as well as the national institutions and the county and local record offices which are listed at the beginning of this volume. I wish to acknowledge the gracious permission of Her Majesty the Queen to quote from the papers of Queen Victoria in the Royal Archives and to thank Miss Jane Langton, Registrar, for tracing relevant material. I am grateful to the Duke of Devonshire and the Chatsworth Settlement, the Earl of Crawford and Balcarres, Sir William Gladstone, the late Viscount Harcourt, the Earl of Harrowby, the Earl and Countess of Rosebery, the Marquess of Salisbury the Earl of Shelburne and Lord Shuttleworth for permission to use family papers.

I am pleased to thank Fuz Bagum, Susan Bailey, Pauline Bryant, Lesley

Cornish and Anne Lewtas for the very cheerful and efficient way in which they helped to prepare the typescript for publication.

My deepest debt, however, is to my wife, Tessa, as well as to Pauline and David, who have not only assisted in many practical ways at all stages of the work, but have shared with me the varying fortunes of the Red Earl during his long career. Their patience and understanding has made the editing of the papers a most enjoyable and rewarding experience.

# ABBREVIATIONS

| | |
|---|---|
| AP | Asquith Papers |
| CBP | Campbell–Bannerman Papers |
| CP | Chatsworth Papers |
| EHJ | Edward Hamilton Journal |
| GGP | Glynne-Gladstone Papers |
| GP | Gladstone Papers |
| Gr.P | Granville Papers |
| HGP | Herbert Gladstone Papers |
| HP | Harcourt Papers |
| KP | Kimberley Papers |
| LHJ | Lewis Harcourt Journal |
| RA | Royal Archives |
| Ren.P | Rendel Papers |
| Rip.P | Ripon Papers |
| RP | Rosebery Papers |
| SP | Spencer Papers |
| Crewe | Marquess of Crewe, *Lord Rosebery* (London, 1931), 2 vols. |
| Gardiner | A. G. Gardiner, *The Life of Sir William Harcourt* (London, 1923), 2 vols. |
| Garvin | J. L. Garvin, *The Life of Joseph Chamberlain* (London, 1932–68), 6 vols., last 2 vols. completed by Julian Amery. |
| James | R. Rhodes James, *Rosebery: A Biography of Archibald Philip, Fifth Earl of Rosebery* (London, 1963). |
| LQV | G. E. Buckle (ed.), *Letters of Queen Victoria 1886–1901* (London, 1930–2), 3rd series, 3 vols. |
| Morley, *Gladstone* | J. Morley, *The Life of William Ewart Gladstone* (London, 1903), 3 vols. |
| Morley, *Recollections* | J. Morley, *Recollections* (London, 1917), 2 vols. |
| *A Political Memoir* | C. H. D. Howard (ed.), *Joseph Chamberlain. A Political Memoir* (London, 1953). |
| Ramm | A. Ramm (ed.), *The Political Correspondence of Mr. Gladstone and Lord Granville 1876–1886* (Oxford, 1962), 2 vols. |
| Spender | J. A. Spender, *The Life of the Right Hon. Sir Henry Campbell-Bannerman, G.C.B.* (London, 1923), 2 vols. |
| West | H. G. Hutchinson (ed.), *Private Diaries of the Rt. Hon. Sir Algernon West G.C.B.* (London, 1922). |
| *NH* | *Northampton Herald* |
| *NM* | *Northampton Mercury* |

# MANUSCRIPT COLLECTIONS CONSULTED

| | |
|---|---|
| Acland AHD Papers | Killerton, Devon; Devon Record Office |
| Acland HW Papers | Bodleian Library, Oxford |
| Acland TD Papers | Bodleian Library, Oxford |
| Acton Papers | Cambridge University Library |
| Admiralty Papers | Public Record Office |
| Arnold-Forster Papers | British Library |
| Ashbourne Papers | House of Lords Record Office |
| Asquith Papers | Bodleian Library, Oxford |
| Balfour Papers | British Library |
| Brackenbury Papers | National Maritime Museum, Greenwich |
| Bryce Papers | Bodleian Library, Oxford |
| Cabinet Papers | Public Record Office |
| Cadogan Papers | House of Lords Record Office |
| Campbell-Bannerman Papers | British Library |
| Carnarvon Papers | Public Record Office; British Museum |
| Cartwright Papers | Northamptonshire Record Office |
| Lady Frederick Cavendish Papers | Chatsworth, Derbyshire |
| Cawdor Papers | Carmarthenshire Record Office |
| Chamberlain Papers | Birmingham University Library |
| Courtney Papers | British Library of Economics and Political Science, London |
| Cranbrook Papers | East Suffolk Record Office |
| Crawford Papers | Balcarres, Fife, Scotland |
| Crewe Papers | Cambridge University Library |
| Derby Papers | Liverpool Record Office |
| Devonshire Papers | Chatsworth, Derbyshire |
| Dilke Papers | British Library |
| Dillon Papers | Trinity College, Dublin |
| Dufferin Papers | Public Record Office of Northern Ireland |
| Education Papers | Public Record Office |
| Elliot Papers | National Library of Scotland |
| Ellis Papers | National Library of Wales, Aberystwyth |
| Fisher Papers | Churchill College, Cambridge |
| Fremantle Papers | National Maritime Museum, Greenwich |
| Gardiner Papers | British Library of Economic and Political Science, London |
| Herbert, Viscount Gladstone Papers | British Library |
| Mary Gladstone Papers | British Library |
| W. E. Gladstone Papers | British Library |
| Glansevern Papers | National Library of Wales, Aberystwyth |
| Glynne-Gladstone Papers | St. Deiniol's Library, Hawarden |

| | |
|---|---|
| Gosse Papers | House of Lords Record Office; Brotherton Library, University of Leeds |
| Granville Papers | Public Record Office |
| Greene Papers | National Maritime Museum, Greenwich |
| Haldane Papers | National Library of Scotland |
| Hambleden Papers | W H Smith and Son Ltd., Strand House, Fetter Lane, London |
| Edward Hamilton Papers | British Library |
| Hammill Papers | National Maritime Museum, Greenwich |
| Harcourt Papers | Bodleian Library, Oxford |
| Hardcastle Papers | Duke University Library, North Carolina, USA |
| Harrowby Papers | Sandon Hall, Staffordshire |
| Heneage Papers | Lincolnshire Archives Office |
| Isham Papers | Northamptonshire Record Office |
| James Papers | Hereford and Worcester Record Office |
| Johnstone Papers | National Maritime Museum, Greenwich |
| Kimberley Papers | National Library of Scotland |
| Kitson Papers | Leeds Archives Department |
| Knightley Papers | Northamptonshire Record Office |
| Langham Papers | Northamptonshire Record Office |
| Lansdowne Papers | Bowood House, Wiltshire |
| Lloyd George Papers | House of Lords Record Office |
| Long Papers | British Library |
| MacDonnell Papers | Bodleian Library, Oxford |
| Markham Papers | National Maritime Museum, Greenwich |
| Minto Papers | National Library of Scotland |
| Monck Papers | National Library of Ireland, Dublin |
| Monk Bretton Papers | Bodleian Library, Oxford |
| Monson Papers | Lincolnshire Archives Office |
| Mundella Papers | Sheffield University Library |
| Norris Papers | National Maritime Museum, Greenwich |
| Northamptonshire County Council Papers | County Hall, Northampton |
| O'Hagan Papers | Public Record Office of Northern Ireland |
| Omond Papers | Duke University Library, North Carolina, USA |
| Playfair Papers | Imperial College of Science, University of London |
| Ponsonby, Sir Henry Papers | British Library |
| Ponsonby, 1st Baron Papers | Bodleian Library, Oxford |
| Quickswood Papers | Hatfield House, Hertfordshire |
| Rendel Papers | National Library of Wales, Aberystwyth |
| Richard Papers | National Library of Wales, Aberystwyth |
| Ridley Papers | Northumberland Record Office |
| Ripon Papers | British Library |
| Ritchie Papers | British Library |

| | |
|---|---|
| Rosebery Papers | National Library of Scotland |
| Royal Archives | Windsor Castle |
| Runciman Papers | University of Newcastle upon Tyne Library |
| Rylands Papers | John Rylands University Library, Manchester |
| St. Aldwyn Papers | Gloucestershire Record Office |
| Salisbury Papers | Hatfield House, Hertfordshire |
| Samuel Papers | House of Lords Record Office |
| Sandars Papers | Bodleian Library, Oxford |
| Selborne, 1st Earl of, Papers | Lambeth Palace Library, London |
| Selborne, 2nd Earl of, Papers | Bodleian Library, Oxford |
| Shuttleworth Papers | Cowan Bridge, Lancashire |
| Loe St. Strachey Papers | House of Lords Record Office |
| Strachie Papers | Somerset Record Office |
| Trevelyan Papers | University of Newcastle upon Tyne Library |
| Vivian Papers | National Library of Wales, Aberystwyth |
| Spence Watson Papers | House of Lords Record Office |
| Wolseley Papers | Hove Area Library, East Sussex |

# INTRODUCTION

Spencer had relinquished the post of Lord-Lieutenant of Ireland at the end of June 1885 with few regrets. Five weeks later, he told Sir Richard Cross, the Conservative Home Secretary, 'You have been good enough to look after me in London with a Sergeant of Police since I left office. I am now leaving town and cannot suppose that I shall need protection in the country... I hope they will soon, if they have not already, forgotten me.'[1] This was a somewhat vain wish, for Spencer was already becoming involved in the deliberations within the Liberal Party which would determine its future attitude towards Ireland.

On 6 August, Spencer had called on Gladstone and urged that no 'great scheme' for Ireland should be formulated before the general election. Spencer's own predilections at this stage were for reforms in local government, establishing county boards rather than a central board, the abolition of the Lord-Lieutenancy and an enlightened education policy.[2] Spencer also noticed that Gladstone was already communicating with Parnell on Irish matters.[3]

A Conservative minority government, headed by Salisbury, had held office since June 1885, though there was to be an autumn election, based on the new register of voters. Since May, a section of the Conservative Party had sought to establish closer contact with the Parnellites. On 1 August, Carnarvon and Parnell met at an unoccupied house in London to exchange opinions. Gladstone was concerned that Parnell's support should not depend on the highest bidder and therefore refused to show his hand in the early stages of the election campaign. Commenting on Gladstone's address to his Midlothian constituents, published on 17 September 1885, Spencer told a friend, 'I think Mr. G's manifesto very good and it will clear the air... He is enigmatical about Ireland, but it is well that he is so just now with his inclinations. Suppose we could

1. Get security for the Landlords;
2. Prevent a civil war with Ulster;
3. Make the Irish nation our friends, not enemies

it would be worth while giving them Home Rule, but I don't see my way to the three conditions or any of them being secured.'[4] Further, matters were made more difficult by Hartington's public rejection of home rule on 29 August.

Equally serious was 'the Radical Programme' expounded by Chamberlain in a series of speeches, starting on 8 September. Three proposals were particularly stressed: free education, the introduction of graduated property taxes, and the conferment on local authorities of powers to purchase land compulsorily. Spencer's views on Chamberlain were unequivocal. On a visit to Althorp in Septem-

---

[1] Spencer to Cross, 1 Aug. 1885, Cross Papers, Add. MS. 51274 f. 77.

[2] Spencer had undertaken a course of reading at this time which encompassed Bentham's *Principles of Legislation*, Helps's *Thoughts on Government*, Henry George's *Progress and Poverty*, J. S. Mill's *Principles of Political Economy* and Fawcett's *Manual of Political Economy*. C. Boyle to Spencer, 25 Aug. 1885, SP.

[3] Spencer to Granville, 8 Aug. 1885, Gr. P, PRO 30/29/22A/5. No. **415**.

[4] Spencer to C. Boyle, 20 Sept. 1885, SP (copy). No. **419**.

ber 1885, Edward Hamilton, Gladstone's former private secretary, discussed the
political situation at length with Spencer. Hamilton recorded in his journal:
'Chamberlain is evidently a good deal on his nerves. He cannot swallow the
land proposals; but what I think most grates on his feelings is the appearance of
intrigue which characterizes Chamberlain's proceedings. The curious characteristic of the modern Radical is his want of discretion and reserve on the one
hand, and on the other hand his proneness to underhand and secret wire-pulling.
Lord Spencer moreover regards Chamberlain as wanting in proper loyalty
towards Mr. Gladstone.'[5]

Chamberlain, for his part, regarded Spencer with equal hostility. During a
dinner party at Harcourt's in the following January, at which Chamberlain was
present, a servant announced that Spencer was downstairs. When Harcourt
suggested that it might be useful to have a talk with Spencer, Chamberlain
replied, 'No, I am off. I don't want to see the Red Earl. I attribute our present
difficulties in Ireland entirely to his opposition to and rejection of my National
Council scheme last summer.'[6] Harcourt went to see Spencer whilst Lewis
Harcourt helped Chamberlain on with his coat in the front hall, nearly putting
on Spencer's by mistake. As Chamberlain was leaving, 'Harcourt caught him
and told him to come in as Spencer wanted to see him. There was no escape so
Chamberlain went in damning audibly.'[7]

Politics were not the only worry for Spencer at this time. During his second
spell as Lord-Lieutenant of Ireland, in spite of receiving a salary of £20,000 a
year, he found the expenses of the office required a personal contribution of an
extra £7,000.[8] The depressed state of agriculture throughout the country
affected the Althorp estate like so many others. Prices were unprecedently low,
with wheat at 25s. a quarter and stock only saleable at a loss. He calculated that
his net income was 40 per cent less than it had been ten years previously.[9]
Spencer's solicitor, negotiating a £40,000 mortgage for him at this time, stated
that 'the difficulty of borrowing money on any terms on land is extreme.
People are thoroughly frightened about it, and nothing but the most perfect
security will be looked at.'[10] By August 1886, matters were more serious.
Writing from Althorp, Spencer informed Rosebery, 'We have given up all
travels and mean to live in a hut or corner without servants. We have given
notice to nearly all our servants. It is a great bore but inevitable and it is better
to face it at once than return to narrow means in 6 months.'[11] Financial worries
plagued him during his last three periods in office, leading eventually to a drastic
solution of the problem.

With the growing popularity during the 1880s of public meetings addressed

[5] EHJ, 26 Sept. 1885, Add. MS. 48641 f. 86.
[6] See Spencer Memorandum, 22 June 1885, SP. No. **402**.
[7] LHJ, 11 Jan. 1886, HP, MS. 735 ff. 177–8.
[8] Campbell-Bannerman also told T. L. Omond that, in contrast, 'Lord Carnarvon was a perfect
screw, and is supposed to have made a clear £8000 out of his term of office.' Omond to his mother,
10 May, 1886, Omond Papers.
[9] EHJ, 26 Sept. 1885, Add. MS. 48641 f. 86.
[10] W. S. Forster to Spencer, 15 Oct. 1885, SP. Spencer found some comfort in a note he had
discovered of his uncle, 3rd Earl, which stated that in 1835 he had had to pay £29,000 in interest
on debts and charges. Spencer to Rosebery, 1 Oct. 1885, RP, 10062 f. 13.
[11] Spencer to Rosebery, 29 Aug. 1886, RP, 10062 f. 23.

by leading members of the parties, politicians were obliged to respond to this call, especially at election time. Spencer spoke at Saffron Walden in October on behalf of the local candidate, Herbert Gardner; this was his first public political speech since 1857, when he stood successfully as a member for the Southern division of Northamptonshire. He also addressed a meeting at Dorchester in the following month, where he stressed the need for reconciliation in Ireland.[12]

During Gladstone's Midlothian campaign in November, Lady Spencer stayed with his party at Dalmeny; her husband, though invited, decided to remain at Althorp.[13] She kept him informed of Gladstone's state of mind as displayed in his many conversations with her. On 19 November she reported on one such occasion. 'I see he does not like to believe Ireland is in the bad state it is, that he hardly realises the boycotting, and that he would like to think the Nationalists reasonable men! ... I think one always feels the hopelessness of talking to him on the subject.'[14] Such accounts depressed Spencer and were reinforced by Parnell's manifesto issued on the eve of the general election, which roundly attacked the Liberal Party, making future co-operation very difficult.[15] At this point, Spencer believed that, as neither party would in future be independent of the Irish, the best plan would be to combine with the Conservatives to settle a policy for Ireland, thus presenting a united front against the Parnellites.[16]

Encouraged by the large majority over his Conservative opponent at Midlothian, Gladstone hoped that the Liberal Party would achieve a majority which would make it independent of the Parnellites.[17] Granville, Spencer and Rosebery, whose views Gladstone valued, were invited to come to Hawarden early in December. Granville had gone there on 5 December and departed for Chatsworth two days later, where he met Spencer, who was on his way to Hawarden. According to Morley, Granville told Spencer and Hartington that Gladstone was 'full of Ireland in the direction of some large concession of self-government.'[18] Spencer was joined by Rosebery on 8 December at Hawarden where they both talked at length with Gladstone. In his Journal, Rosebery summed up Gladstone's views:

His mind is:

1. If Tories can come to agreement with Parnell and produce complete scheme, they should be supported.
2. If not, no time should be lost in opposing them.
3. A vote of want of confidence without reference to Ireland would be the best form.
4. But if it must have reference to Ireland it should be moved by Liberal leaders and not Parnell. He leans at present to proceeding by resolution.[19]

[12] The *Sherborne, Dorchester and Taunton Journal*, 5 Nov. 1885, p. 5.

[13] Spencer avoided visits there whenever possible. He later told Lewis Harcourt, 'I never know why but I always feel depressed at Dalmeny. Some air and places have that effect on me.' Spencer to L. Harcourt, 5 Oct. 1890, HP, MS. 429 f. 12.

[14] Lady Spencer to Spencer, 19 Nov. 1885, SP.

[15] C. H. D. Howard, 'The Parnell Manifesto of 21 November 1885 and the Schools Question', *English Historical Review*, lxii (1947), p. 47.

[16] Spencer to Hartington, 29 Nov. 1885, CP, 340. 1838.

[17] Granville to Spencer, 6 Dec. 1885, SP. No. 429.

[18] Morley, *Gladstone*, iii, p. 261.

[19] Rosebery, Journal, 8 Dec. 1885, f. 342.

Reflecting on the meeting seven years later, Spencer ruefully commented, 'whatever Granville, Rosebery ... and I said, Mr. G. had practically made up his mind and it became only a question as to who would agree with him'.[20] However, Gladstone made a point of telling Spencer that he had no definite scheme; the notes which he showed them represented a trial of ideas only.[21]

One matter raised by Spencer and on which he held firm views was the necessity for obtaining proper guarantees for landlords under any proposed scheme.[22] This view was consistently held by him when the Liberals returned to office.

Little comfort could be drawn from the eventual outcome of the election. The Conservatives and Parnellites together had won the same number of seats as the Liberals (333 each), and Salisbury continued in office.

Spencer's attitude towards home rule was not a consistent one, fluctuating as events unfolded during the autumn of 1885. He was astonished at the total disappearance in Ireland of non-Parnellite candidates at the election, and the return of 86 Irish Nationalists. This clearly indicated the mood of Irish opinion.[23] But even before this, Spencer's views were changing. A conversation between Lady Frederick Cavendish and Lady Spencer in July 1886 indicated that the refusal of the Conservatives to renew the Crimes Act, which expired in September 1885, weighed heavily with Spencer:

> Charlotte [Lady Spencer] told me, that as soon as he knew the Tories had dropt the Crimes Act bodily, he said to her, 'There's an end to Coercion.' I said, 'But why?—might not the Liberals on returning to power, have taken up "Spencer's minimum measure", as the Cabinet had agreed just before their defeat?' She replied, 'Well of course it *might* have been done: it might have been dragged thro' Parliament with all the usual friction and exaspera- tion, outrage and fury in Ireland and all-night sittings and suspension of members in the House. It might have been carried; but what then? Matters would have been just back where they were in '80, all the same weary ground to traverse and moreover, by that time the "minimum measure" would have been utterly inadequate: boycotting, which Spencer's steady administration of 3 years had only succeeded in hindering and checking, would have meanwhile spread like a network over the whole country, and no coercion would be of any avail except of such a drastic sort as no Liberal would go for, and as this country would never sanction. The only chance for

---

[20] Spencer to W. V. Harcourt, 15 July 1892, HP, MS. 46.

[21] Spencer to Hartington, 27 Dec. 1885, CP, 340. 1873.

[22] Spencer to Gladstone, 22 Dec. 1885, GP, Add. MS. 44312 ff. 218-20. No. **439**. Spencer had earlier written to T. D. Acland, from Hawarden, 'Whoever is bold enough to try and settle the Parnellites must do so on condition of settling the Land question.' Spencer to T. D. Acland, 9 Dec. 1885, Bodleian Lib., MS. Eng. lett. d. 81.

[23] In one of his rare ventures into print, Spencer declared, 'It was this evidence of want of continuity of policy in 1885, and the startling disclosure of the weakness of the anti-national party in Ireland at the election in the autumn of that year, which finally convinced me that the time had come when we could no longer turn to a mixed policy of remedial and exceptional criminal legislation as the means of winning the constituencies of that country in support of our old system of governing Ireland.' Preface in J. Bryce (ed.), *Handbook of Home Rule*, 3rd edn. (1888), p. xix.

the old policy would be if it had been *continuously* tried. And small enough was that chance.'[24]

Spencer was anxious to consult with his former cabinet colleagues on the situation in order to clarify his own views. Northbrook was at Althorp on 13 December where he discussed with Spencer the comparative strength of feeling in Ireland for home rule or the desire to get possession of the land.[25] Two days later Spencer had a lengthy talk with Goschen, whom he 'frightened and horrified'[26] by putting 'the case for a big measure more strongly than I ought'.[27] On 17 December Hartington, who had entertained Northbrook at Chatsworth after the latter's visit to Althorp, wrote to Gladstone, 'Northbrook I think agrees very much with Spencer, who as I understood would be willing to try a limited Home Rule experiment *if* terms could be obtained for landlords.'[28]

The day Hartington's letter was written saw the publication in the press of the so-called 'Hawarden Kite', which purported to have emanated from Gladstone himself, announcing that he had definitely adopted the policy of Irish home rule. It soon became clear that the 'Kite' was the work of his son, Herbert. Spencer was 'very disgusted' at the statement, adding, 'Although a trial balloon sometimes does good, I can see nothing but harm out of this.'[29] One immediate consequence was the public declaration by Hartington that he would not accept any new policy for Ireland. On Christmas Day, Hartington wrote to Spencer, 'Nothing worse than Home Rule and separation which it will lead to can happen to us in the end; and I am all for making a struggle before it is accepted as inevitable.'[30]

Spencer was now examining in detail some of the problems which would need to be dealt with by a scheme of home rule, particularly those of the police, landowners, tariffs and taxation. He discussed these over Christmas at Althorp with his former Chief Secretary, Campbell-Bannerman.[31]

Gladstone still hoped that something might come out of a Tory-Irish alliance.[32] On 26 December he sketched out for his two most trusted colleagues, Granville and Spencer, the strategies which ought to be pursued by Salisbury's ministry over Ireland and the possible consequences if the government were defeated and the Liberals were to take office. Spencer, who had meanwhile invited Hartington to Althorp for the last days of the old year, was in the uncomfortable position of not being able to make reference to Gladstone's memorandum on parliamentary procedure, but instead spoke generally on the discussions which had taken place at Hawarden earlier in the month on this subject.[33] Reporting on his talks with Hartington, Spencer informed

[24] Lady Frederick Cavendish, Diary, 26 July 1886, CP, vol. xiv ff. 31-2.
[25] Northbrook to Spencer, 18 Dec. 1885, SP.
[26] Spencer to Campbell-Bannerman, 16 Dec. 1885, CBP, Add. MS. 41228 f. 296.
[27] Spencer to Granville, 17 Dec. 1885, Gr. P, PRO 30/29/22A/5. No. **432**.
[28] Hartington to Gladstone, 17 Dec. 1885, CP, 340. 1852 (copy).
[29] Spencer to H. Seymour, 20 Dec. 1885, SP.
[30] Hartington to Spencer, 25 Dec. 1885, SP.
[31] Campbell-Bannerman to Spencer, 27 Dec. 1885, SP. No. **442**.
[32] See A. B. Cooke and J. R. Vincent, *The Governing Passion* (1974), p. 316.
[33] Spencer to Gladstone, 31 Dec. 1885, GP, Add. MS. 44312 f. 246.

Campbell-Bannerman, 'I am in great distraction. My views remain much what they were, but the difficulties and objections accumulate, and I wish myself in Timbuctoo or any other remote place.'[34]

Spencer sounded out a number of Irish landlords on Gladstone's behalf. Some, like Powerscourt, were appalled at the prospect of home rule. 'I trust,' he warned Spencer, 'you are not going to give us all over to the wolves. Our property would be all confiscated, and what would become of us and our children, in Ireland, God only knows!'[35] Others, whose views Spencer respected, adopted a more moderate line. Lord Monck, a former Governor-General of Canada and a Liberal, who had advised Gladstone on the 1870 Land Act, had always upheld the principle of self-government for any country which was ready for it. 'You ask me my views,' he replied to Spencer, 'upon the present condition of things in Ireland ... I do not love Home rule myself. I am in sentiment and opinion a West Briton, and I think it would be much better for my fellow countrymen if they would take my view of the matter, but they evidently think otherwise by a large majority, and I prefer the attempt to attain a modus vivendi with them by peaceful means, rather than continue an unequal contest which is bringing disaster to both parties to it.'[36] Spencer was also impressed by the fact that two prominent former members of his staff when he was Lord-Lieutenant, Sir Robert Hamilton, Under-Secretary, Dublin Castle, and Jenkinson, Assistant Under-Secretary and Head of the Police, were now in favour of home rule.[37]

Spencer drafted a memorandum on Christmas Day headed 'Home Rule', examining the pros and cons of the situation.[38] He was aware that among many leading Liberals opinion was running strongly against such a measure,[39] and calculated that of those colleagues who would follow Gladstone, only Granville, Rosebery, John Morley and himself could be relied on. The prospects of forming a strong government were not bright.[40] Nevertheless, weighing up the alternatives, Spencer considered that there was only one answer. On 31 December, he wrote to Mundella, 'I must confess to you that I look on the old methods and ideas of dealing with Ireland which we long fanned ourselves into believing would bring her people round towards us, as gone and hopeless ... Some solution must be found. There seems nothing but a big measure, Home Rule with proper safeguards, or at no distant day, coercion stronger than we have ever had before. The latter cannot be thought of now.'[41]

Various explanations have been suggested to acount for Spencer's adoption

[34] Spencer to Campbell-Bannerman, 31 Dec. 1885, CBP, Add. MS. 41228 f. 305.

[35] Powerscourt to Spencer, 15 Dec. 1885, SP.

[36] Monck to Spencer, 22 Dec. 1885, SP. Monck later withheld his support from the first Home Rule Bill, though Spencer attempted to enlist his support. E. Batt, *Monck, Governor General* (1976), p. 173.

[37] Hamilton sent 'two curious letters' to Spencer in Dec. in favour of 'a big scheme as the only possible solution'. Spencer to Granville, 29 Dec. 1885, Gr. P, PRO 30/29/22A/5. Jenkinson was slightly less enthusiastic, seeing home rule as 'perhaps the least bad of two alternatives.' Northbrook to Spencer, 18 Dec. 1885, SP.

[38] Memorandum, Home Rule, 25 Dec. 1885, GP, Add. MS. 44312 ff. 232-7.

[39] Spencer to Gladstone, 29 Dec. 1885, GP, Add. MS. 44312 ff. 242-3.

[40] Spencer to Rosebery, 30 Dec. 1885, SP (copy).

[41] Spencer to Mundella, 31 Dec. 1885, Mundella Papers, MP 6P/18.

of home rule, the most common one being that he was persuaded by Gladstone.[42] Morley, in his *Life of Gladstone* refutes this: 'Somebody said to Mr.
Gladstone, people talked about his turning Spencer round his thumb. "It would
be more true," he replied, "that he had turned me round his".'[43] It would
seem, from the evidence here stated and confirmed by Lady Frederick Cavendish, that Spencer adopted the same views as Gladstone without collusion.[44]

When the Conservative government was defeated in the Commons in the
early hours of 27 January 1886, the cabinet decided on resignation. As Lewis
Harcourt, Sir William's son and secretary, wrote in his Journal, 'Never were
victors less triumphant or vanquished less depressed.'[45] Later that morning
Spencer, unhappy at the turn of events, called on W. V. Harcourt, who was a
lukewarm home ruler. Spencer said, '"You and I shall have to go down to
Osborne again" (this referred to the Kandahar row in 1881).[46] "Yes," replied
WVH, "but it's a comfort to think that the Queen will be much more angry
with you than with me and very rightly so".'[47]

Harcourt's prognostication was correct, though surprisingly Spencer did not
appear to have been aware that the Queen strongly disapproved of his conversion to home rule. On the occasion of a visit to Osborne when taking office,
Spencer reported to Gladstone later, 'I rarely knew of a better reception than
that given by the Queen.'[48] A somewhat different picture emerges from Victoria's own detailed description of the meeting:

> Before the 2nd Council at 20 to 3 on Saturday 6th I saw *Ld. Spencer* who
> looked nervous & embarrassed. I began by saying they had undertaken a
> great deal & a most difficult task to which he at once assented and said it was
> extremely difficult, that he thought their position & his opinion had entirely
> changed since last year, when the policy was altered. I observed that this
> Govt. had only waited to see what could be done & that at the last there had
> been difficulties which might have prevented action being taken. I said they
> must be very explicit, & ought to let people know what they really meant,
> & that I thought Ld. Spencer had always been greatly against 'Home Rule'.
> He said Mr. Gladstone never had declared for Home Rule (!!?) that it might
> have come to that, that the time for coercion was past, & that he feared
> concessions must be made—but that it was only intended to examine into
> the state of Ireland to see what could be done... He continued that he

[42] For example, Julia Ady, née Cartwright, recorded in her Journal in April 1886, 'Lord Spencer
no one can understand. St. John [Brodrick, Conservative M.P., Guildford] says he was simply
talked around by Mr. Gladstone at Hawarden.' Julia Cartwright, Journal, 26 April 1886, Cartwright
Papers, X 1200 f. 81.

[43] Morley, *Gladstone*, iii, p. 262.

[44] Lady Frederick Cavendish, Journal, 26 July 1886, CP, vol. xiv f. 27. Derby called on Harcourt
on 11 Jan. 1886 to discuss home rule. Derby afterwards recorded, 'He said (which I find hard to
believe) that Spencer was more in favour of Gladstone's principles than Gladstone himself.' J. R.
Vincent (ed.), *The Later Derby Diaries* (1981), p. 55. Reflecting in 1897 on the events of autumn
1885, Gladstone stated that he had no means of estimating Liberal support for a home rule measure,
but that 'Lord Spencer had indeed declared himself in this sense.' J. Brooke and M. Sorenson (eds.),
*The Prime Minister's Papers: W. E. Gladstone. 1. Autobiographica* (1971), pp. 108-9.

[45] LHJ, 26 Jan. 1886, HP, MS. 735 f. 191.

[46] See No. **194**.

[47] LHJ, 27 Jan. 1886, HP, MS. 735 f. 191.

[48] Spencer to Gladstone, 6 Feb. 1886, GP, Add. MS. 44313 f. 22. No. **463**.

certainly had changed his opinion very much tho' he must confess he had for
some time had a sneaking feeling that 'something of this kind wd have to be
resorted to.' That he had 'certainly changed his opinion very rapidly as last
but that he had been seeing Mr. Gladstone continually.' It is quite clear that
Mr. Gladstone has quite talked him over. Altogether I thought his explanations very unsatisfactory and weak.[49]

Before this, Spencer had been much occupied in the business of advising
Gladstone on candidates for office in the new ministry. The choice was limited
in the first instance by the secession of so many moderate Liberals in both
Houses of Parliament, notably Carlingford,[50] Northbrook, Selborne, Bright,
Goschen and Sir Henry James. Those peers remaining loyal to Gladstone in-
cluded Granville, Kimberley, Ripon and Spencer and among those from the
Commons were Childers, Harcourt, Herschell and John Morley.[51]

An immediate embarrassment faced Gladstone. In the process of cabinet-
building, he relied on the judgement of both Spencer and Granville, but it had
been apparent for some time that the latter, whose ineffectualness and irresolu-
tion as Foreign Secretary had become noticeable during the later stages of
Gladstone's last ministry, could not be offered the post. Gladstone had expressed
his fears to Rosebery on Granville's wishes for this office at the Hawarden
meeting in December. Rosebery recorded, 'Mr. G. appears to know this is
inexpedient.'[52] The Queen had also refused to consider Granville's return to the
Foreign Secretaryship. 'How is Lord G to be approached?' asked Edward Hamilton in his Journal. 'Who would be commissioned to open the subject with
him? I say, Lord Spencer.'[53] As Gladstone was to go to Osborne on 1 February
to accept office, it was essential that the matter should be settled beforehand.
On 31 January, Spencer was given the 'painful duty' of informing Granville
that the Foreign Secretaryship was to be given to Rosebery and not to him.
Some years later, Spencer recounted the interview to Sir Henry James: 'For a
time Granville was unwilling to accept any office, saying he should like me to
present one instance of a man refused the office he wished and yet giving a full
and zealous support to the Ministry from which he was excluded. This view
was combated by pointing out that his refusal to join Mr. Gladstone's Government would be an almost fatal blow to its prospects of success.'[54]

By the following morning, Granville had accepted the Colonial Office, refusing the Lord Presidency of the Council. These manoeuvres affected Spencer's
own choice of office. If Granville had accepted the Lord Presidency, the Colonies could have gone to Ripon and the Admiralty to Spencer, a post much
coveted by him. The position of Lord President was now vacant but Ripon, as
a Catholic, was not offered it, as the post included responsibility for education.

[49] Queen Victoria, Journal, 6 Feb. 1886, RA C37/280b, transcribed by her daughter, Princess
Beatrice.
[50] Carlingford was considered for office as Lord-Lieutenant of Ireland on 4 Feb., but on Granville's and Spencer's testimony of Carlingford's Unionist tendencies, Gladstone ruled him out. J. R.
Vincent (ed.), *Lord Carlingford's Journal. Reflections of A Cabinet Minister* (1971), p. 38.
[51] D. Southgate, *The Passing of the Whigs, 1832–1886* (1962), pp. 408–9.
[52] Rosebery, Journal, 9 Dec. 1885, f. 343.
[53] EHJ, 29 Jan. 1886, Add. MS. 48642 f. 114.
[54] Lord James, Diary, 22 May 1891, James Papers, M 45/1864.

Consequently, as Lewis Harcourt noted, 'the plan now being that poor Spencer, who is too good natured in those things, has given up the Admiralty, which he liked, so that Ripon might have it, and has taken the Presidency of the Council himself which he did not want.'[55]

The difficult task of attempting to fill the remaining posts was done by Gladstone, Granville, Harcourt (now Chancellor of the Exchequer) and Spencer. When it was suggested that Campbell-Bannerman should resume as Chief Secretary for Ireland, Spencer ridiculed the idea and said, 'You might as well send me, for he was nearly as unpopular as I was,' and proposed John Morley.[56] Acting as an intermediary for Gladstone, Spencer saw Northbrook on 3 February, unsuccessfully urging him to take office as Lord-Lieutenant of Ireland.[57] His views on home rule were employed by the prime minister in interviews with possible office holders. Selborne, a former Lord Chancellor, recalled in 1887, 'When Gladstone saw me, at the time when he made his last overture in January 1886, he was for referring me, for satisfaction on that point, to Lord Spencer—not going into it, as if the plan was exactly his own.'[58] Spencer also helped in filling the minor offices, which was a tedious and protracted business.[59] Chamberlain, with some misgivings, took office as President of the Local Government Board after first refusing the Admiralty. Even before this, he complained to a fellow M.P. that Spencer 'swallows Self Government without Coercion. Having strained at a Gnat, he swallows a Camel'.[60]

Although Spencer now held the office of Lord President of the Council, a post which he had previously occupied from 1880 to 1883,[61] his main task was to help in the preparation of Irish legislation. But as was the case throughout Spencer's political life, he accepted his responsibilities as office holder seriously. Even in the few months of the life of the 1886 administration, he became involved in the activities of the Education Department. He much favoured a scheme of reorganizing the work of the officials of the Department. The division of responsibilities between the Examiners, who were mainly university men, and the clerks, who carried out the more routine tasks, had become unclear over the years. The clerks, for their part, urged that they were capable of taking over many of the duties then exercised by the Examiners. The scheme would have involved changing the balance of staff servicing the five Divisions into which England and Wales was then divided, from four Examiners, to two Examiners and two or three clerks.[62] He frequently urged his Vice-President, Playfair, to put his views in writing on the subject.[63] Recalling the issue two

[55] LHJ, 3 Feb. 1886, HP, 735 ff. 207–8.

[56] LHJ, 27 Jan. 1886, HP, MS. 735 f. 193. Morley was appointed Chief Secretary on 6 Feb.

[57] B. Mallet, Thomas George, Earl of Northbrook, A Memoir (1908), p. 228.

[58] Selborne to Sir A. H. Gordon, 18 March 1887, Selborne Papers, MS. 1874 f. 152.

[59] For example, Henry Brand, M.P. for Stroud and eldest son of the former Speaker, was interviewed by Gladstone and Spencer on 4 Feb. and urged to jon the government. Refusing, Brand pointed to the difficulty of accepting office in view of the anti-home rule speeches he had delivered to his constituents 'from which I have gone back not one iota'. Brand to Hartingon, 5 Feb. 1886, CP, 340. 1930.

[60] E. Heneage to J. Wintringham, 25 Jan. 1886, Heneage Papers, 2 HEN 5/13/4.

[61] See The Red Earl, i, ch. 9.

[62] J. R. Dasent, Memorandum for Lord President, 25 Feb. 1886, Cranbrook Papers, HA 43 T501/59.

[63] Spencer to Playfair, 24 Nov. 1888, Playfair Papers, 637.

years later, Spencer stated the reasons why these reforms were not carried out: 'We knew we were probably in office for a very short time, and it was no good stirring the mud unless we could settle the business completely.' The scheme was later rejected by Cranbrook, his Conservative successor.[64]

The Lord President was also responsible for initiating legislation. One bill which Spencer was pleased to pilot through the Lords was the Medical Acts Amendment Bill in April 1886. More than 20 such bills, aimed at reforming the medical profession, had been unsuccessfully presented to Parliament since 1870, some during Spencer's first term as Lord President.[65]

Of much greater cause for concern at this time, however, was the settlement of the Irish crisis. Spencer was quite clear on the best way of proceeding. In an important letter to Lansdowne on 2 February he wrote, 'We must come to terms with the National Party in Ireland, getting terms for Landlords and the minority. It is the only chance of settling Ireland ... I began this change of view thinking that guarantees could not be got, but I believe now they can be got. The Landlords must be bought out. Mr. Gladstone agrees to this. If we are able to go on I should go to the Parnellites and say if you will settle the Land Question on terms safe for the Landlords, we will settle also the question of Home Rule. We are going to form the Government on the basis of looking into the question and trying to settle it somewhat on the terms I have vaguely sketched.'[66]

Gladstone submitted his scheme to the cabinet on 13 March which consisted of a land purchase bill, worked out in some detail, and a more sketchy home rule bill. Chamberlain, who strongly criticized both proposals, thought that no one in the cabinet except Spencer was consulted on the matter beforehand;[67] in fact Spencer and Morley had seen Gladstone on the previous day in connection with the scheme. Edward Hamilton had shortly before met Spencer who felt strongly on the absence of provision for converting tenants into proprietors.[68] Spencer saw the settlement of land purchase as an essential prerequisite to home rule and he was influential in persuading Gladstone to adopt this view. Harcourt admired Spencer's independence of mind, telling Lady Spencer after a meeting with him on 14 March, 'Spencer is such a Rebel, he is sure to be hung!'.[69]

Gladstone's home rule plan provided for a separate assembly in Dublin, responsible for Irish affairs. It was to consist of two orders: the first order, composed of 28 representative peers and 75 members having property qualifications; the second would consist of the 103 Irish M.P.s then at Westminster and 101 new representatives. Excluded from these powers and reserved for Westminster were foreign affairs, defence, trade and navigation, and matters relating to the Crown and the Succession. The financial aspects of the plan were important: customs and excise control would remain in London but the proceeds arising in Ireland would be applied to Irish fiscal matters. The exact

[64] Playfair to Cumin, 21 Nov. 1888, Playfair Papers, 205d (copy).
[65] Spencer to Sir H. W. Acland, 6 Nov. 1882, MS. Acland d. 80.
[66] Spencer to Lansdowne, 2 Feb. 1886, Lansdowne Papers. No. 462.
[67] A Political Memoir, p. 193.
[68] EHJ, 12 March 1886, Add. MS. 48643 f. 37.
[69] Lady Spencer, Diary, 14 March 1886, SP.

relationship between the Westminster and Dublin assemblies were not spelled out. Irish members were to be excluded from the Westminster Parliament. This issue caused trouble within the cabinet: both Harcourt and Morley threatened to resign if exclusion were not considered as a vital part of the bill, though neither Spencer nor Gladstone took so firm a line.[70]

Spencer's main worry was that Gladstone would give home rule precedence over a land purchase measure. On both financial and strategic grounds, Spencer argued, there was a need to settle land at an early date. Financially, the Anglo-Irish landlords needed to be pacified because of the prospect of home rule. The scheme allowed every Irish landlord desiring to sell his rented lands to the State to do so. He would receive from a specially-created fund, after certain deductions, a sum equivalent to 20 years' purchase of the net rental. The majority of such land was to be made over to tenant occupiers who, instead of paying rent, were to pay the purchase money back at the rate of 4 per cent per annum. Strategically, it seemed possible that if a Local Government Bill were successful, 'the Irish members would alter their present attitude as to a Land Purchase Scheme, and would either oppose it or try to cut it down to an extent which would make it inoperative. I should like to see the acceptance of a Purchase Bill by the Irish the condition of proposing the Local Government Bill. That has always been my view.'[71]

One immediate consequence of Gladstone's proposal was that on 15 March Chamberlain and Trevelyan submitted their resignations. Gladstone considered that Spencer should try to pacify Chamberlain, but there is no evidence to show that any subsequent meeting took place. Chamberlain talked with Harcourt in the latter's room at the Commons on 15 March, hoping to persuade Harcourt to resign with him. Harcourt suggested that he should discuss the matter with Spencer, to which Chamberlain replied, 'No, certainly not. I have the greatest contempt for Spencer, who has been the origin of all the mischief. He thinks that because he could not govern Ireland no one else can.'[72] However, Edward Heneage, who was Chancellor of the Duchy of Lancaster and head of the Agricultural Department of the Privy Council under Spencer, in contemplating resignation from these posts, had a long interview with his chief on 26 March. He was told that written communications had passed between Chamberlain and Spencer and that 'Mr Gladstone was to have some more time to try and find a modus vivendi.'[73]

Gladstone introduced the Home Rule Bill on 8 April and the Land Purchase Bill eight days later. On the first bill, the debate was spread over sixteen days. The most notable feature was that the main attack on it was made by both wings of the dissident Liberals, notably Hartington, Goschen, James and

---

[70] Spencer's views were clearly expressed in a letter to Sir Bernhard Samuelson, M.P., Banbury, 'I confess that I do not share your anxiety about the consequences of the exclusion of the Irish from the Parliament at Westminster ... for I do not myself believe in the least degree that the new Irish Assembly will desire Separation.' Spencer to Sir B. Samuelson, 11 April 1886, SP (copy).

[71] Spencer to Gladstone, 24 March 1886, SP (copy). No. **466**.

[72] LHJ, 15 March 1886, HP, MS. 735 f. 216. The following month, Harcourt told Chamberlain, 'I am going down to the New Forest to hold my tongue. It is the best comment I can offer to my friends.' W. V. Harcourt to Chamberlain, Chamberlain Papers, JC 5/38/48.

[73] E. Heneage to J. Wintringham, 26 March 1886, Heneage Papers, 2 HEN 5/13/22.

Chamberlain. Many considered that, as a hostile nation, Ireland was receiving too generous treatment by the bill. A large minority in Ireland opposed the bill: many landowners felt impelled by the threat of home rule to join the Conservative ranks.[74] Despite concessions publicly and privately made by Gladstone, from the time of the second reading on 10 May, the fate of the bill was in the balance. On 28 May, Lord Richard Grosvenor, formerly Liberal Chief Whip and now a Liberal Unionist, discussed the defections from the Liberal ranks with W. C. Cartwright of Aynhoe Park, Northamptonshire, and told him, 'They are falling away like rotten sheep.'[75] The fate of the bill was sealed following the second of two meetings of Chamberlain's supporters at the end of May when they agreed to vote against the second reading. The government was defeated in the Commons on 8 June.

Much to Spencer's regret, the Land Purchase Bill could not now be proceeded with. There were many features of it which alienated both Conservatives and Liberals. Conflict would probably have arisen between the debtors of the State and the tenants of the non-selling landlords, and would have led eventually to a demand for compulsory purchase. The cost of compensation to landlords would have placed a burden on the British taxpayer and was seen as an unsound use of credit. He believed, on the other hand, that the risks involved were worth taking for the beneficial effects the provisions of the bill would have on political opinion in Ireland.[76] Speaking on the Land Purchase Bill at Newcastle on 21 April, Spencer, whilst admitting to Gladstone that the audience 'were coldest when I referred to the Land Scheme', demonstrated that home rule and land purchase were inseparable issues. 'Depend upon this,' he went on, 'if the land question is not settled there will be no peace in Ireland.'[77] Shaw-Lefevre, a former Liberal Postmaster-General and a home ruler, who had himself submitted a detailed scheme of land purchase to Gladstone in January, later wrote, 'There can be no doubt that the scheme of Land Purchase mainly contributed to the defeat of the Bill. It conciliated no one. The Irish landowners did not accept it.'[78]

Two days after the dissolution of Parliament was announced, Spencer informed Gladstone that he strongly held to his previous views on the question, adding, 'it is impossible to conceal from oneself that the Land Bill was unpopular, though I am confident that you would have carried it through had we ever reached its discussion'.[79] Spencer's insistence on legislation for land purchase with home rule reduced the latter's chance of success. Spencer conceded in a speech at Bristol on 23 June that the government was no longer bound to

[74] E.J. Feuchtwanger, *Gladstone* (1975), p. 239.

[75] W. C. Cartwright, Diary, 28 May 1886, Cartwright Papers, Box 6/16.

[76] Spencer to W. Rathbone, 15 April 1886, SP (copy). G. O. Trevelyan, who as Secretary of State, Scotland, had resigned from the government at the end of March along with Chamberlain, wrote to the latter, 'Spencer, who has a strong family feeling, is guardian to Lord Clifden, who has very large Irish estates, which Spencer has managed for the last 20 years. He would never what he would call "throw-over" Clifden and a very great number of other Irish landlords with whom he is closely connected, who used to worship him, and who now regard him with suspicion, tempered by a desire for the Purchase Bill.' Trevelyan to Chamberlain, Chamberlain Papers, JC 5/70/15.

[77] Spencer to Gladstone, 21 April 1886, GP, Add. MS. 44313 f. 69. No. **474**.

[78] Lord Eversley, *Gladstone and Ireland* (1971 edn.), p. 305.

[79] Spencer to Gladstone, 11 June 1886, GP, Add. MS. 44313 f. 76.

proceed with both bills simultaneously,[80] an admission capitalized on by Gladstone after the party's heavy defeat at the polls in July. In a final memorandum to colleagues, written on 27 July he stated:

> The relation of inseparability in which we were obliged to place it to the principal Bill has greatly, perhaps mainly, contributed to the defeat of both measures. Numbers of the enemies of Home Rule were really friendly to the Land Bill; but they kept back the expression of their feeling, or like Lord Hartington disparaged the Land Bill, or even went further than disparagement in order to stab Home Rule through its sides; the Bills having been *originally*, and for the occasion presented as Siamese Twins. On the other hand, numbers of persons really, and even warmly friendly to Home Rule, and having only a superficial acquaintance with the Land Bill, voted as opponents, or abstained from voting on account of their disapproval of the Land Bill, misrepresented as it was by such men as Mr. Chamberlain and even Mr. Bright. In this way each Bill has been fatally used against the other; and this combination has been the principal weapon in the adversary's hand for the destruction of the policy of Home Rule and of the Government. The result in my mind is that we can no longer maintain the inseparability of Bills, as it has become in a Parliamentary sense absolutely impossible to give effect to either measure under that condition.[81]

Spencer replied later, 'I admit the force of what you urge against the late Siamese Twinship of the two measures ... I agree therefore that the same connection between the Land and the Home Rule Proposals, as you established, cannot under existing circumstances so be maintained.'[82]

Perhaps the most painful consequence of Spencer's acceptance of home rule was the social ostracism and hurtful public criticism which long dogged both him and Charlotte. John Bright, who had delivered a laudatory address at the banquet given in Spencer's honour in July 1885 on his return from Ireland,[83] less than a year later wrote, 'I do not wish to appear against Lord Spencer—altho' I am astounded at his courage or his charity in whitewashing the Irish ruffians who in the last Parliament charged him with hanging men whom he knew to be innocent, which, if it be true, shows him to be a murderer of even a worse stamp than those whom he was compelled by law to hang.'[84]

Spencer was now regarded with great suspicion in Court circles. In February 1886, the Duchess of Teck confided in a friend, 'We have heard that Lord Spencer, of *all people* is a convert (*pervert* I think I ought to say!) to Home Rule.'[85] Stronger still was the verdict of Sir Dighton Probyn, comptroller and treasurer of the Prince of Wales's Household: 'I am worried over Lord Spencer. I have always looked upon him as being an honest Englishman, and a Gentleman ... But he has fallen into the traitor's clutches, and is lending a helping

---

[80] M. Barker, *Gladstone and Radicalism* (1975), pp. 57-8.
[81] Memorandum, W. E. Gladstone, marked 'Secret', 27 July 1886, SP (copy).
[82] Spencer to Gladstone, 20 Aug. 1886, GP, Add. MS. 44313 f. 92.
[83] R. G. C. Hamilton to Lord Spencer, 23 July 1885, SP. No. 414.
[84] Bright to W. C. Cartwright, 25 June 1886, W. C. Cartwright Papers, Box 6/16.
[85] Mary Adelaide, Duchess of Teck to Mrs. E. Colnaghi, 18 Feb. 1886, Vic. Add. MSS. RA C/ 14/46.

hand to a fearful Civil War ... A man of that sort advocating Communism shakes my belief in anything mortal.'[86] To a large extent, these sentiments were shared by the Queen, who pointedly no longer invited Spencer, as a leading member of the Opposition, to Windsor.[87] Hartington, his second cousin and former political colleague, waited a further twelve years before asking the Spencers to visit Chatsworth.[88]

Edward Hamilton, always a close observer of the social scene, paints a graphic picture of the snubs administered to Spencer:

> One certainly hears in Society plenty of abuse of Mr G. Whatever he does is always wrong and always done from the lowest motives—love of power and office.
>
> But the person now on whom Society to its shame mostly 'runs a muck' against is Lord Spencer. They might at any rate give him credit for honesty of purpose, however mistaken they think him and however low they estimate his capacities. His friends actually cut him and won't meet him. I hear Lord Fitzwilliam cut him in the street the other day and that the Listowels declined to be guests at Bagshot Park during Ascot week if the Spencers were to be there. Such behaviour is hardly conceivable; and it is certainly not the behaviour of ladies and gentlemen.[89]

It was not only Spencer himself who was snubbed. Lady Knightley, a near neighbour of the Spencers at Fawsley, and her husband, Sir Rainald, a long-standing Conservative M.P. for South Northamptonshire and fellow member with Spencer of the Pytchley, met them at a dinner party in June 1886. 'Saw Lady Spencer,' she recorded afterwards, 'both R. and I greeted her with *marked* coldness—publicly and privately I do feel so angry with them.'[90] Similarly, in 1888 the Duke of Westminster, with whom Robert Spencer and his wife were to dine, wrote to say that as Robert had attended the dinner given to Parnell at the Eighty Club, he could not receive them.[91] Even the Spencers' restricted social life did not escape criticism. At a political party given at Spencer House, several Irishmen were present. 'Many of his *quondam* friends,' Hamilton remarked, 'take now to pitying him for the "low" company he has to keep.'[92]

A massive defeat at the polls in July, with only 196 Gladstonian Liberals being returned as against 316 Conservatives, 74 Liberal Unionists and 83 Parnellites, was a setback to Liberal hopes. Horace Seymour wrote to Lady Spencer, his sister, who together with Spencer had gone to Aix-les-Bains, blaming the timing of the dissolution for the poor results, especially in rural counties such as Northamptonshire. 'It was very difficult in the middle of the hay harvest to

---

[86] Probyn to Sir H. Ponsonby, 4 Feb. 1886, in A. Ponsonby, *Henry Ponsonby, Queen Victoria's Private Secretary* (1942), p. 355.

[87] The only occasion on which Spencer was invited to Windsor between 1886 and 1890 was during the Queen's Golden Jubilee celebrations.

[88] Spencer to W.V. Harcourt, 2 June 1898, HP, MS. 48.

[89] EHJ, 27 May 1886, Add. MS. 48644 ff. 8–9. Spencer complained to one Liberal M.P. that 'when things were at their hottest, he did not get one invitation where he formerly got twenty'. R. Farquharson, *The House of Commons From Within* (1912), p. 183.

[90] Lady Knightley, Journal, 23 June 1886, Knightley Papers, K 2902.

[91] EHJ, 11 May 1888, Add. MS. 48648 f. 94.

[92] EHJ, 22 March 1888, Add. MS. 48648 f. 62.

get the labourers to the polls ... thousands of Liberals have abstained only from voting, and have not declared against the Government policy ... Indeed most of our County victories of last year have melted away.'[93]

The Spencers, as was their normal practice after Parliament had risen in July or August, headed for one of the European spas to recuperate. Their favourites were Aix-les-Bains, Nauheim and Homburg. Spencer preferred Aix, situated in the Savoy Alps, 'as it braces me up more'.[94] Aix was celebrated for the good results obtained in the stiffness of joints and from 'gouty affections', and attacks of eczema, to which Spencer was prone.[95] These were treated mainly by douches and baths, preferably before breakfast, together with massage, sometimes followed or preceded by a vapour bath. As there was not room at the establishment for patients to rest after treatment, they were carried on chairs from their hotels to the bath and back again to bed afterwards. Cold sulphur water was recommended for internal use, but unlike the procedure at German spas, drinking the waters played a comparatively small part in the treatment. Another difference from its German counterparts was that it eschewed customs such as the early morning promenade with music, preferring a more sober approach to health restoration.[96]

The Spencers frequented Nauheim, or Bad Nauheim, less than Homburg,[97] but its 'Sprudel' baths, which were regarded as beneficial in strengthening and stimulating the heart and circulation, attracted them. These salt baths, at a temperature of 92° to 95°F, lasted for six to eight minutes, and were followed by rest. The baths were taken in conjunction with gymnastic exercises, based on the Ling Swedish system. The effect of this course of treatment, taking up to six weeks, was said to resemble that of digitalis.

By far the most desirable of the three spas was Homburg. It attracted fashionable society, particularly from England and America, and, as one contemporary guidebook to spas remarked, 'so much English conversation is heard, that one might imagine himself to be promenading by the shady waters of an English watering-place'.[98] The centre of attraction in the town was the Kurhaus, with its large, magnificent salons, each elegantly and luxuriously appointed, a superb ballroom with marble columns, a grand dining salon, conversation rooms and two large reading rooms, one for German, the other for foreign newspapers, including most of the leading English ones. Running the full length of the building was a wide corridor, which afforded the opportunity for promenading if bad weather prevented exercise in the open air. To the north was a large terrace overlooking a well-laid park with beautiful flower beds and trees. In the afternoons, visitors, as a guide book brightly stated, may 'take

[93] H. Seymour to Lady Spencer, 12 July 1886, SP. All the Liberal M.P.s in Northamptonshire were returned with reduced majorities.

[94] Spencer to C. R. Spencer, 1 Aug. 1890, SP.

[95] Spencer to Catherine Gladstone, 27 Aug. 1894, Mary Gladstone Papers, Add. MS. 46229 f. 145.

[96] See H. Weber and F. P. Weber, The Spas and Mineral Waters of Europe (1896), pp. 213–16.

[97] Lady Spencer noted in 1892 that 'since Gambling was suppressed, Nauheim is not much frequented'. Lady Spencer, Diary, 2 July 1892, SP.

[98] E. Gutmann, The Watering Places and Mineral Springs of Germany, Austria and Switzerland (1880), p. 95.

coffee, listening to the music and eyeing each other'.[99] All five springs were in the park, the most popular spring being the Elizabethan-Brunnen. A long, shady, promenade adjoined this spring. With over 10,000 visitors a year, Homburg was seen more as a place of amusement for fashionable society than as a health resort, but the Spencers admirably combined both aspects. Bathing was much favoured, but the main part of the cure lay in the springs. These contained iron and salt as well as the sparkling muriated waters of Homburg. Water from the iron springs, either alone or in conjunction with the ordinary muriated waters, were taken, whenever possible, on a fasting stomach before breakfast.

Spencer normally began drinking the waters at 7 a.m., though different doctors prescribed different treatment from time to time. In June 1892, for instance, Lady Spencer was 'recommended to take mud baths and pine baths alternately and to drink Elizabeth (i.e. water from the spring in the Elizabeth-Brunnen) in the morning at 8 o'clock. I had a mud bath this morning at 11.30, and liked it.'[100] Spencer described the effects of a course of treatment to Granville, another frequent visitor to Homburg: 'I wonder whether you have yet had a crisis after getting rid of the effect at Homburg?' he wrote in 1889, 'My experience, last year and this, has been that one gets odd and queer after about a fortnight and then one rapidly feels the better for the cure. I have just had my week of chill and malaise, but was right again, and find my walking much improved and altogether I begin to feel the benefit of Homburg. When one has been saturated with salts and other compounds for three weeks, the sudden loss of all this in the system must affect one.'[101]

Political and social gossip abounded and at election times; news of the results as they became known was eagerly sought after. Homburg also provided an opportunity for social intercourse with members of European royal families. One luncheon party to which the Spencers were invited included the Empress Frederick, the Crown Prince of Greece and Prince Frederick Charles of Hesse and his fiancée, Princess Margaret.[102]

However much Spencer claimed that he was disillusioned with politics, preferring to be either on his Northamptonshire estate or abroad, he was happiest when involved in affairs of state. Writing from Aix-les-Bains, he admitted to Gladstone, 'I have often wondered at the apparent inconsistency of a horse, when he shows the same delight to return to his stables as he did a few minutes before when he came out of it. But I have gone through the same process for I was delighted to get away from England, but no sooner got here than wished I were home again in the midst of the stir of the present politics at home.'[103]

Now in opposition, Spencer closely followed events in Ireland and the attempts of the Salisbury government to control them. The 'Plan of Campaign' heralded a renewal of the land war of 1879-82, the suppression of the National League, a new Coercion Bill, an attenuated Land Act, and the Mitchelstown incident later the same year. Spencer was the principal Opposition speaker in

[99] Gutmann, *Watering Places*, p. 94.
[100] Lady Spencer, Diary, 21 June 1892, SP.
[101] Spencer to Granville, 22 Sept. 1889, Gr. P, PRO 30/29/29A.
[102] Lady Spencer, Diary, 23 June 1892, SP.
[103] Spencer to Gladstone, 1 July 1886, GP, Add. MS. 44313 f. 85.

the Lords on Irish affairs, criticizing particularly the introduction of the Coercion Bill. Lord Londonderry, the Conservative Lord-Lieutenant of Ireland who had to defend the government's policy against Spencer in the Lords, on being warned of the coming confrontation, replied to Lord Cadogan from Dublin Castle, 'Many thanks for your letter ... I have no doubt that I am suspicious, but much as I like Spencer *personally*, it is impossible to have been here now getting on for 2 years without distrusting him politically.'[104] Shortly after this, in April 1888, Spencer even contemplated going over to Ireland incognito, to gather information at first hand, but was dissuaded by Rosebery from carrying out this plan.[105] Earlier, an attempt was made to reunite the scattered portions of the Liberal Party, through the Round Table Conference, at which Chamberlain consented to be present. Harcourt discussed the membership with him, saying that it was necessary to have someone who was well acquainted with Ireland and the land question. He asked if Chamberlain had any objection to Spencer. 'C. pursed his mouth, looked very much displeased and was silent a long time, then said quite suddenly, "I would much rather have Morley."' Lewis Harcourt, who was at the meeting, went on, 'We were greatly taken aback at this; but W.V.H. said at once, "Oh if that is so, so would I." '[106] Spencer was kept informed of the Conference's proceedings by Morley and Harcourt and applauded the possibility of a reunion with Chamberlain. Writing from Althorp to Harcourt shortly before the first session took place, he remarked, 'We may be a convenient half way Meeting House between London and Hawarden ... Come any moment and bring anyone including the great J.C. if you like'.[107] But the failure of the Conference shortly afterwards signalled the end of any possible co-operation with Chamberlain.

Greater demands were being made on leading Liberal politicians for public speeches, particularly with the move to London from Birmingham of the National Liberal Federation in 1886. Schnadhorst, the new joint secretary of the N.L.F. and the Liberal Central Association, reorganized the metropolitan area where Liberal support was dwindling; by 1887, the N.L.F. was a national body with many affiliated Liberal associations. As Irish home rule remained its first priority, it is not surprising that Spencer's services were increasingly sought.

Speeches cost him much effort, especially as the number of invitations multiplied. 'I have lately been arranging my campaign of woe and boredom with Schnadhorst the Slavedriver,' he informed Lewis Harcourt.[108] And later, 'I will book the 10th Dec. as my next day of Sackcloth and Ashes. Pray be merciful. It is bad enough to make one speech but to screw oneself up 3 or 4 times as I had to at Guildford and Rochester is a great aggravation. I bargain for one speech at a meeting but for nothing else.'[109]

The extra burden of the chairmanship of the Northamptonshire County Council from 1889 had its effect. At Althorp for a Volunteer dinner, he told

---

[104] Londonderry to Cadogan, 23 Feb. 1888, Cadogan Papers, CAD/333.
[105] Rosebery to Spencer, 3 April 1888, SP.
[106] LHJ, 30 Dec. 1886, HP, MS. 735 f. 229.
[107] Spencer to W. V. Harcourt, 2 Jan. 1887, HP, MS. 45. No. 513.
[108] Spencer to L. Harcourt, 9 Sept. 1890, HP, MS. 429 f. 9.
[109] Spencer to L. Harcourt, 10 Nov. 1889, HP, MS. 429 f. 5.

his sister Sarah, 'I am rather headachy, not bad, but queer enough not to wish to sit through the hot dinner. It is the penalty for my Speeches and rushes to the North and back followed by heavy County Council work. I have been lucky, as I have had only this malaise, and not a bad one, out of three Speeches and expeditions. It is partly the nervous excitement of speaking, partly the hot room but more than anything the irregular meals and odd food one gets. But I am much better now than 2 years ago when I never missed a headache after a big Speech.'[110] It was only at the end of his political life that he resorted to using full notes for his speeches.[111]

Spencer never rose to the same heights of oratory as some of his colleagues, like Gladstone, Morley and Rosebery, but the majority of his public addresses, though often marred by their delivery, had the merit of being based on strong conviction and reflection. Spencer was chided by a friend, Courtenay Boyle, for refusing a speech. 'You disdain powers of speaking,' he wrote, 'I really think with greater persistence than the facts at all necessitate. What the public expect from you and what they know they will get is a straightforward statement, made without mental reservations or qualifications, of conclusions arrived at after a most careful and capable analysis of opposing difficulties. As such your speeches are valued and valuable.'[112]

Rosebery, a good judge of speakers, praised Spencer's oratory. He told Robert Spencer after attending a meeting in Edinburgh, 'I wish you could have witnessed Spencer's meeting. He spoke admirably with a dignity which charmed the audience and your humble servant. He kept 5000 well in hand for more than an hour, and scored a triumph.'[113] Spencer himself occasionally registered pleasure at a successful meeting. In June 1887, he described one as follows: 'At Bristol, I never had such a reception, they were wild. It was a splendid sight, 6,000 packed human beings in a great Hall. I got hold of them, and spoke to my own satisfaction better than I ever spoke before.'[114] Although Spencer in his correspondence frequently complained of inadequate reporting of his speeches in the press, the coverage matched that of many of his colleagues.[115]

A matter of some embarrassment and irritation to Spencer was the reluctance of the Liberal Party to make any commitment on Ireland: by 1889, the Conservatives were eagerly exploiting this weakness. A conference of Liberal leaders to review home rule policy was held at Hawarden in October 1889, though Spencer was unable to attend. It was decided not to announce any definite scheme, as no agreement could be reached on the question of Irish members at Westminster. Whilst the conference was still in progress, Spencer caused

[110] Spencer to Lady Sarah Spencer, 31 Oct. 1889, SP.
[111] Spencer to L. Harcourt, 2 Feb. 1905, HP, MS. 429 f. 89.
[112] C. Boyle to Spencer, 11 June 1887, SP.
[113] Rosebery to C. R. Spencer, 27 Oct. 1887, SP, and Rosebery, Journal, 25 Oct. 1887, f. 298.
[114] Spencer to C. R. Spencer, 25 June 1887, SP.
[115] On 3 Nov. 1885 the Pall Mall Gazette published the Central Press Agency's criteria for reporting speeches: Chamberlain, Churchill, Gladstone and Salisbury were rated 'Class I', i.e. verbatim coverage. Spencer and Hartington, in the light of the Irish question, were each worth a full column. S. Koss, The Rise and Fall of the Political Press (1981), i, p. 346.

consternation by admitting in a speech at Stockton that Irish members should be retained in the Imperial Parliament.[116]

This incident, though soon hushed over, demonstrated the lack of unity amongst Liberal leaders. Two months later, Parnell paid a long delayed visit to Hawarden to discuss future Irish policy; both Gladstone and Parnell agreed that the main difficulty lay in determining the particular form in which Irish representation should be retained at Westminster, though, Gladstone noted, 'he has no absolute or foregone conclusion.'[117] Spencer, in forwarding to Rosebery Gladstone's account of the meeting, commented, 'It is pleasant to know how affable and reasonable the uncrowned King is',[118] and to Granville, that it showed 'good temper and moderation to rule in Mr. C. S. P.'s heart.'[119] Spencer respected Parnell and acknowledged his value as the Nationalists' leader. The two men had publicly shaken hands in March 1889 at a dinner given in honour of Parnell after the revelation of the Pigott forgeries, though many could not understand Spencer's tolerance in the light of Parnell's activities during his Viceroyalty.[120] Meeting Hugh O'Donnell, a former Irish M.P., whilst on holiday in Switzerland in August 1890, Spencer defended Parnell saying, 'Well I do not know of any case where Mr. P. has been untrustworthy in his relations with our leader.'[121]

The outcome of the O'Shea divorce proceedings three months later led to a statement from Gladstone, in the form of a letter to Morley, that Parnell should resign his leadership of the Nationalist Party. The matter was fully discussed by leading Liberals on 24 November. Morley reported later that day, 'Had some talk with Spencer in the drawing-room. He was the one man who doubted whether we were right in putting any screws at all upon Parnell, and he pressed earnestly that P. was the only man who could drive the Irish team.'[122] Spencer's reasons for keeping faith with the leader were based more on a consideration of policy than personal liking. He wrote later, 'I confess that I thought Parnell, without being a paragon of Moral and Political virtue, was reliable as a statesman ... [but] it must be said that we believed in Parnell's adhesion to Mr. G.'s plans not as a man, but as a representative of the Irish majority.'[123] On 30 November 1890, when Parnell was struggling for political survival, Spencer commented to Harcourt, 'I still think it a loss that he is placed out of reach of any communication from us, for he certainly can manage the Irish and is not a Mad Separatist.'[124] He also favoured the subsequent Boulogne negotiations with Parnell in order to obtain continuity of Irish leadership.[125]

[116] Spencer explained his views more clearly to Rosebery. 'We want devolution for every part of the Empire, and development of the new Local Councils, but we do not want if we can help it to give separate Legislatures for each part of the United Kingdom.' Spencer to Rosebery, 24 Nov. 1889, RP, 10062 f. 43.

[117] Memorandum, W. E. Gladstone, 23 Dec. 1889, SP (copy).

[118] Spencer to Rosebery, 24 Dec. 1889, RP, 10062 f. 45.

[119] Spencer to Granville, 29 Dec. 1889, Gr. P, 30/29/22A/6.

[120] Sarah Spencer strongly disagreed with her brother on this matter. 'My *critical* difficulty is and will be that you can put trust in Parnell and the Irish in general after the things they did.' Lady Sarah Spencer to Spencer, 19 Jan. 1889, SP.

[121] Spencer to J. Morley, 21 Aug. 1890, SP (copy).    [122] Morley, *Reminiscences*, i, p. 261.

[123] Spencer to U. Kay-Shuttleworth, 4 Jan. 1891, Shuttleworth Papers.

[124] Spencer to W. V. Harcourt, 30 Nov. 1890, HP, MS. 45.

[125] F. S. L. Lyons, *The Fall of Parnell 1890–91* (1960), p. 229.

Spencer wrote at length to Dillon on Parnell's death in October 1891, 'I who have in bygone days been so often in opposition and sharp conflict with Mr. Parnell am quite affected at this sudden disappearance of one who was so great a power in politics, and who yet might have exercised a serious part in our political warfare.'[126] Lady Spencer agreed with her husband. 'How difficult it is when a great man dies to hit off the *juste milieu* in his praise. Poor old W. H. Smith is rapidly being turned into a hero. Parnell was really too great a man for exaggeration as to his position and intellect.'[127] Spencer's main concern was now directed to his successor. 'The danger with our Irish friends is that with no big men among them they may quarrel. He had a hold over them and they may now break out.'[128] Although Spencer's fears were not fully realized, the Nationalist Party took several years to recover from the internal antagonisms which surfaced during the events of 1890-1.[129]

Having little prospect of improvement in rents and land values in Northamptonshire, Spencer was obliged to seek a dramatic solution to his financial problem:[130] the sale of the Althorp Library, long acknowledged as one of the greatest of the European collections. Most of the Library had been collected by George John, second Earl Spencer, who succeeded to the title in 1783. Besides holding high political office—he was First Lord of the Admiralty and briefly Home Secretary—he was an avid collector of manuscripts and early printed works. By the time of his death in 1836, he had amassed over 43,000 books. The basis for the collection was the library of Count Károlyi Reviczky, a Hungarian nobleman, and it contained a large number of choice editions of Greek and Latin classics, including productions from the presses of Aldus, the Elzevirs and many Bibles. The second Earl was assisted in his collecting from 1802 by a young clergyman, Thomas Frognall Dibdin, who became his librarian and was the author of a descriptive catalogue of the fifteenth-century books, *Bibliotheca Spenceriana*. The Earl had travelled to the Continent in 1819 where he acquired the entire library of the Duke of Cassano-Serra, which included early books from Naples and Sicily, and he was constantly bidding in English auction rooms for rare pieces.

Amongst the most valuable books in the Althorp Library was the first Mainz Psalter, dated 1457, and the so-called Mazarin Bible, which was the first printed Bible, by Gutenburg, of about 1456. In 1892 the Mainz Psalter was valued at £10,000 and the Mazarin Bible at £4,000. Apart from the many printed editions of Virgil, Cicero, Sweynheym and Pannartz, there were 53 Caxtons valued at £15,900.[131] By 1892, all 43,331 books were housed in eight main rooms at Althorp: the Long Gallery, Long Library, Breakfast Room, Domenichino Room, Raphael Room, Old Book Room, Billiard Room and the Ante Billiard

---

[126] Spencer to Dillon, 1 Oct. 1891, Dillon Papers, MS. 6788/132.

[127] Lady Spencer to Spencer, 10 Oct. 1891, SP.

[128] Spencer to Lady Spencer, 23 Oct. 1891, SP.

[129] See F. S. L. Lyons, *Parnell* (1977), p. 609, for a judgment on the matter.

[130] He had also been affected by the financial collapse of the merchant bankers, Barings, in Nov. 1890. Spencer to Granville, 21 Jan. 1891, Gr. P, PRO 30/29/29A. Robert Spencer had married Margaret Baring, daughter of Edward Baring, 1st Baron Revelstoke, in 1887.

[131] 'Estimated Valuation of Althorp Library, 1892', SP.

Room. The largest and most striking of them was the Billiard Room, with a light gallery around it, with tier upon tier of shelves.[132]

Other great libraries, such as those of the Earl of Jersey and the Earl of Crawford and Balcarres, had recently been sold and Spencer now sought a valuation of the Althorp collection. E. G. Hodge, of Sotheby, Wilkinson and Hodge, the auctioneers, discussed the matter with him on 19 July 1892 and later reported that he had 'difficulty in getting Lord S. to name a price, so many opinions existed as to the price likely to be obtained at auction or from one or two wealthy Americans. One of his Lordship's advisers, a well known English Bibliographer, gave it as his opinion that the Library was well worth £300,000.'[133]

Earlier, in 1890, Spencer had offered the Caxtons to a syndicate consisting of the British Museum and Oxford and Cambridge Universities. He was anxious that the books should be kept in England and be available for scholars. Referring to the Library, Spencer had previously written, 'In one way I should be glad to see the books more available for the Public for I often lament how few people visit the Library to see the early editions and other curiosities.'[134] When these negotiations proved to be abortive, however, he agreed to put the sale of the whole Library in Hodge's hands.

For some eighteen months before this, J. Arnold Green, son of the secretary of the Religious Tract Society, had been aware that the Library might one day be placed on the market. Green had been commissioned by Enriqueta Rylands, widow of the Manchester businessman, John Rylands, to purchase a collection of books to form the basis for a theological library dedicated to her husband's memory. When Hodge arranged for an article to appear in *The Times* on 17 June 1892 stating that the Library was for sale, A. B. Railton, manager of the bookseller's Sotheran's, immediately contacted Green.[135] Railton was instructed to open negotiations with Hodge and within 48 hours, Mrs. Rylands had secured, confidentially, the first option on the Library at £220,000. On 25 July 1892, the contract was signed. It was not known by Spencer at the time that an American agent was waiting to see Hodge when Railton called; acting on behalf of the New York Public Library, he was ready to offer £300,000, the amount first suggested by Spencer.[136] After the sale more than 600 cases of books were packed and dispatched to Manchester by train in August and September, 1892. Spencer, who was at Althorp at this time, wrote to his wife, 'I certainly think we had better go to Creake [their shooting lodge in North Norfolk]. It is very trying to see the Books being packed. I don't like it at all.'[137] Nevertheless, one of his main objectives, to make the Library more

---

[132] For a good description of the Library, see 'Lord Spencer's Library', *Birmingham Daily Post*, 16 April 1870, p. 6.

[133] A. B. Railton to J. Arnold Green, 19 July 1892, John Rylands Library Papers.

[134] Spencer to E. Thompson, 7 Jan. 1890, SP. No. **597**.

[135] Railton, on behalf of Sotheran's, was also involved at this time with 'the disposal of literary rarities' from the Lamport Hall Library. A. B. Railton to Sir C. Isham, Isham Papers, IL 4610.

[136] A. Hobson, *Great Libraries* (1970), p. 176. See also correspondence, *New York Herald Tribune*, 29 Aug. and 10 Sept. 1892; and E. G. Hodge to Spencer, 6 Oct. 1892 and G. W. Smalley to Spencer, 6 Dec. 1892, SP.

[137] Spencer to Lady Spencer, 15 Sept. 1892, SP.

widely available, was achieved; the collection forms the basis of the John Rylands University Library at Manchester, housed in a building specially designed
by Champneys and described as one of the finest examples of modern Gothic
architecture in Europe.[138]

In early December 1891, Althorp had been the setting for a meeting between
the Liberal leaders, Gladstone, Harcourt, Morley, Rosebery and Spencer, to
discuss aspects of the Newcastle Programme, announced in October 1891 and
dealing with future Liberal policy. Morley painted an affectionate picture of the
scene at Althorp in his *Reminiscences*:

> After dinner, we went into what I do think was the most fascinating room
> I ever saw in a house—great or small—one of the libraries, lined with well-
> bound books on white enamelled shelves, with a few, but not too many,
> nick-nacks lying about, and all illuminated with the soft radiance of many
> clusters of wax candles. A picture to remember: Spencer with his noble
> carriage and fine red beard; Mr. G. seated on a low stool, discoursing as
> usual, playful, keen, versatile; Rosebery, saying little, but now and then
> launching a pleasant *mot*; Harcourt cheery, expansive, witty. Like a scene
> from one of Dizzy's novels, and all the actors, men with parts to play.[139]

On the second night of the conference, Spencer, at dinner, wore his red coat as
Master of the Pytchley and early the following morning, 9 December, he said
goodbye to Morley before going for a fourteen-mile ride to the meet in the
pouring rain. 'I envied such capacity for free enjoyment,' commented Morley.[140] Although no momentous decisions were taken at the conference, home
rule was one of the main items on the agenda. Differences of approach between
Gladstone on the one hand and Harcourt and Spencer on the other on the
question of the retention of members at Westminster were not resolved.

At the general election of 1892, the Liberals had a majority of only 40 over
the Conservatives, with 81 Irish Nationalists being returned. Disliking much of
the Newcastle Programme, Gladstone was determined both as a matter of
personal conviction as well as political expediency to carry a home rule measure
at an early stage. Spencer agreed with this strategy.[141]

Even before Salisbury's resignation on 11 August 1892, cabinet-building had
begun. At Mentmore, almost a year previously, Edward Hamilton and Rosebery had amused themselves by drawing up a Liberal cabinet, with Gladstone
as prime minister and Rosebery 'against his will' as Foreign Secretary: both
independently nominated Spencer as First Lord of the Admiralty.[142] It was not
immediately obvious in the following July that this forecast was correct. Shortly
after the final election results were known, Morley reported to both Edward
Hamilton and Lewis Harcourt that Gladstone, interestingly, was not contemplating that Spencer should once again be Lord-Lieutenant of Ireland. Morley
also stated that 'he was determined to have the entire responsibility for Irish

[138] H. Guppy, *The John Rylands Library, Manchester* (1906), p. 38 ff.
[139] Morley, *Reminiscences*, i, pp. 293-4.
[140] Ibid., p. 205.
[141] Spencer to Gladstone, 25 July 1892, GP, Add. MS. 44314 f. 39.
[142] EHJ, 12 Sept. 1891, Add. MS. 48656 f. 78.

affairs.'[143] The Home Office was considered for Spencer but Gladstone was anxious not to have too many peers as Secretaries of State, a point later confirmed by Harcourt and other colleagues.[144] On 9 August, Spencer, hoping for the Admiralty, believed that he would be returning to the Council Office, and expressed to Lewis Harcourt his disappointment at the prospect.[145] Five days later it seemed that he might become both Lord President and First Lord, though Kimberley finally accepted the former post. However, on 16 August, Spencer's appointment as First Lord was announced.

Gladstone once more called on Spencer to help settle some of the problems which arose in forming a ministry. The Queen insisted in July that Labouchere should not be considered for office; this caused Gladstone much uneasiness. Spencer acted as intermediary with Sir Henry Ponsonby, the Queen's private secretary, advising Gladstone on an appropriate line of action.[146] More worrying to the prime minister was the refusal of Rosebery to accept office. Spencer pleaded with him, 'Pray come and help us. Your presence and advice are much needed.'[147] Replying from Dalmeny that his political career was now over, Rosebery drew a further reply from his colleague. 'Personally I do not know what I shall do; I looked forward to serving under you in the House of Lords, and later on I hoped in the Cabinet. The future is really terrible to me if you retire.'[148] Later that day, 4 August, Gladstone asked Morley to deliver a letter personally to Rosebery at Dalmeny. However, Morley, in consultation with Edward Hamilton, decided that Spencer would be more sympathetically received and approached him about the mission. Though willing to undertake this task, Spencer believed that Morley should go, to give the lie to rumours that he and Harcourt were intriguing against Rosebery. Gladstone, puzzled at Rosebery's behaviour, told Spencer that 'From nobody in private life have I received such warm affection, such unbounded kindness, such great generosity, as from Rosebery ... But in public life he is a perfect Bismarck, so unapproachable is he and so inexplicable in his conduct.'[149] On 15 August, Rosebery consented to accept the Foreign Secretaryship.

Whilst the elections were still in progress, Spencer was in correspondence with Gladstone on the strategies to be employed in introducing a home rule bill. 'One of the principal subjects of thought in the coming weeks or months,' wrote Gladstone, 'is how far it can be done and, when the time comes, no one can speak on it with such authority as you.'[150] Spencer anticipated that it was likely that the Lords would reject the bill but nevertheless considered that the government was committed to it. He, together with Bryce, Campbell-Banner-

---

[143] EHJ, 22 July 1892, Add. MS. 48658 f. 63, and LHJ, 20 July 1892, HP, MS. 735 f. 271; also J. Morley to Spencer, 19 July 1892, SP.

[144] LHJ, 12 Aug. 1892, HP, MS. 736 f. 306. Harcourt had made this same point some years before. He wrote in 1885, 'If there is to be a new Government, we must have a clear understanding beforehand as to this *plethora* of Peers in office.' W. V. Harcourt to Chamberlain, 2 Oct. 1885, Chamberlain Papers, JC 5/38/36.

[145] LHJ, 9 Aug. 1892, HP, MS. 735 f. 302.

[146] Memoranda, Spencer, both headed 'July 1892', SP. Nos. **625** and **626**.

[147] Spencer to Rosebery, 1 Aug. 1892, RP, 10062 f. 60.

[148] Spencer to Rosebery, 4 Aug. 1892, RP, 10062 f. 64.

[149] EHJ, 4 Aug. 1892, Add. MS. 48658 f. 86.

[150] Gladstone to Spencer, 13 July 1892, SP.

man, Gladstone, Herschell and Morley, formed a cabinet committee in November 1892 to draft the bill. Once more, Spencer was sent as an emissary, now to Harcourt, to inform him that he was not to be a member of the committee. A few days later at a cabinet, Rosebery and Harcourt ostentatiously sat apart from the rest on a sofa. Spencer at one stage attempted to sit between them, but, according to Lewis Harcourt, was rebuffed by Harcourt, who said, 'Go away, you have no right here; this is the *English* Bench.'[151]

When the bill reached the Lords in September 1893, Spencer was given the unenviable task of opening the debate on the second reading. Faced with a crowded Opposition bench and with only a few supporters behind him, his speech, a plea to the Conservatives to support the bill, fell on deaf ears and it was rejected by 419 votes to 41, the hereditary peers, almost without exception, voting against it.[152]

Shortly before this, Lansdowne's term of office as Viceroy of India was coming to a close. Rosebery and Kimberley, meeting at Mentmore, agreed that Spencer would be ideal for the post but were unsure if he would wish to go.[153] Some six years previously, the Spencers had almost settled to go to India, largely for financial reasons,[154] but were persuaded by Gladstone to stay. Once more, the prime minister was reluctant to lose his services and recommended that Spencer discuss the matter with Kimberley and Harcourt, though John Morley and Rosebery were also consulted.[155] Although encouraged by Harcourt and Rosebery to accept, he finally decided to decline the offer. Gladstone rejoiced at this outcome stating, 'any other conclusion would have been nothing less than a great shock to the whole Irish policy'.[156] Spencer admitted to Rosebery, 'You would have won your 6-4 bet on my not going into a new groove. I grind on where I am.'[157] It was Rosebery who finally persuaded Elgin to accept the post.[158]

Spencer was delighted with his appointment as First Lord of the Admiralty. After a Council at Osborne on 18 August 1892, the Queen noted, 'I saw Lord Spencer who seemed pleased to go to the Admiralty, tho' all was new to him, as his father and uncle had both been in the Navy, and his grandfather First Lord of the Admiralty in Nelson's time and even had recommended him for employment.'[159] W. T. Stead, who had long taken an interest in naval affairs, congratulated Spencer on going to the Admiralty, adding, 'There are so few people on our side of the House who have any appreciation of the importance of the Navy.'[160]

As First Lord, Spencer was responsible for all the business of the Admiralty,

---

[151] LHJ, 20 Nov. 1892, HP, MS. 736 f. 356-7.
[152] For a vivid account of Spencer's speech, see H. W. Lucy, *A Diary of the Home Rule Parliament* (1896), pp. 239-41.
[153] EHJ, 11 June 1893, Add. MS. 48660 f. 95.
[154] Spencer to C. R. Spencer, 22 Aug. 1887, SP.
[155] Spencer to Gladstone, 6 Aug. 1893, GP, Add. MS. 44314 f. 81.
[156] Gladstone to Spencer, 7 Aug. 1893, SP.
[157] Spencer to Rosebery, 6 Aug. 1893, RP, 10062 f. 215 (erroneously bound with 1895 correspondence).
[158] Lord Newton, *Lord Lansdowne* (1929), p. 114.
[159] Queen Victoria, Journal, 18 Aug. 1892, RA Z 413.
[160] W. T. Stead to Spencer, 16 Aug. 1892, SP.

both within the cabinet and in Parliament. But Spencer was aware of the disadvantages of being a peer in this office. He told one of his admirals in March 1893, 'I wish I were in the House of Commons and able to defend our policy: there is a feeling in many quarters that the head of so great a spending department should be in that house, and I admit that it is desirable.'[161] He was assisted in his work by members of the Board of Admiralty, who were the four Sea Lords, the Civil Lord, and the Parliamentary and Financial Secretary. One of the important tasks of the First Lord was to decide on future naval requirements. As a part of this process, the Navy estimates were considered at the regular meetings of the Board. An innovation introduced by Spencer and continued by his Conservative successor was the retention of his professional advisers despite the change of government. This made for continuity of experience but it also increased the independence of the Board.

Spencer assumed his post at a time when there was widespread concern in Britain at the state of the Navy. The invasion scares of the 1880s fuelled the calls for adequate defence of the British Isles: the fleet would obviously play a major part if such attacks ever took place. Of more immediate consequence was the fact that other European powers were expanding their navies: Britain's long undisputed supremacy was now being challenged, particularly by France and Russia. Public doubts were expressed on the adequacy of the Navy to cope with any emergencies. As one commentator on naval policy wrote at the time, 'The truth is that in this country it is nobody's business to hold the Navy in readiness for war.'[162] However, three years before Spencer took office, a start had already been made. During Salisbury's second ministry, a Naval Defence Act, 1889, associated with the First Lord, George Hamilton, provided for a three-year building programme, consisting of eight first-class and two second-class battleships, and thirty eight cruisers as well as gunboats. At the same time, the 'Two-Power Standard' was promulgated, whereby British naval power was to be equal to the combined naval strengths of the next two largest navies. As the building programme led to similar moves by France and Russia, a further programme of new construction was outlined by the Board a few months before the Liberals were returned to power.

Apart from the numerical strength of the Navy, there were other weaknesses. Most senior naval officers were ill-educated and were lacking in the experience of fighting in modern warships in the open sea.[163] Larger ships, with powerful armament and armour, capable of firing at longer ranges, more efficient propelling machinery, and the advent of the torpedo, the mine and the submarine necessitated a reappraisal of tactics.[164] Inter-service co-operation between the Admiralty and the War Office was minimal.[165] Although a Colonial Defence Committee composed of Admiralty, War Office, Colonial Office and Treasury officials was revived in 1885 to consider the safeguarding of vital colonial posts, it was not effective.

[161] Spencer to Vice-Admiral Sir G. Tryon, 7 March 1893, SP (copy).
[162] G. W. Steevens, *Naval Policy* (1896), p. 284.
[163] See N. A. M. Rodger, 'British Naval Thought and Naval Policy. Strategic thought in an Era of Technological Change', in C. L. Symonds (ed.), *New Aspects of Naval History* (1981), pp. 148-9.
[164] B. Brodie, *Sea Power in the Marine Age* (1941), p. 161.
[165] Admiral Sir R. Vesey Hamilton, *Naval Administration* (1896), pp. 163-4.

Spencer's period of office as First Lord of the Admiralty was a taxing one. From the beginning, he communicated confidentially with each of the admirals in charge of squadrons 'on important current events', setting out his views on developments in various parts of the world.[166] These letters, written in his own hand, often ran to several pages. Remarkably, throughout his official life, Spencer conducted business practically single-handed. He explained his method of working to a hunting friend as follows. 'You mention those who have secretaries, well I am not one who has one. I have a clerk to copy important letters and put letters by, but I practically write all my letters, and they are not a few. I find that by having every letter answered the night before, starting at 8 or 7 does not bother me as I have time to write when I get home.'[167]

It is through his correspondence with the senior officers that his assessment of foreign affairs and his views on possible strategies to be employed to meet the many calls on the Navy can be best seen. In October 1893, he informed the Commander-in-Chief, Mediterranean, 'I am not much concerned at the Franco-Russian demonstration. It will fizzle off in a few weeks and leave little behind it. It amuses the French and will do us little harm.'[168] A little later, he elaborated on this. 'I do not myself fear a war. No doubt the French are excitable and were hysterical over the Russian alliance, but it may be urged that the very fact of their having found an ally will make them less sensitive and less irritable than they were when they felt the isolation of their position.'[169] Nevertheless, Spencer proposed action 'the moment we suspect the outbreak of war with France', by uniting the two wings of the Mediterranean Squadron and withdrawing the Levant Squadron to Malta.[170] Strategically, 'whatever policy we adopt in case of war, we shall always keep Malta as one of the most essential bases of our operations.'[171] Should Russia go to war with Britain, he favoured the concentration of forces in the China Seas rather than rely on a strengthening of the Esquimalt base in Canada.[172]

Following the dispatch of British troops to Egypt in January 1893 to overawe the new Khedive, Spencer reflected that 'as the line we adopted succeeded in restoring the controlling influence of this country and in quieting rising ebullitions of fanaticism, we may hope that like results may follow action, in case of a repetition of an attempt to put our influence on one side'.[173] Where action was called for, Spencer believed in firmness. 'We have some ugly fences to face with the Turk,' he wrote in 1895. 'He is playing a dangerous game as to Armenia and we can hardly allow him to laugh us to scorn. It is not improbable that we shall be left alone to enforce our demands.'[174] Spencer also discussed with his naval staff the possibility of sending an occupation force.[175] Difficulties

[166] e.g. Spencer to Vice-Admiral H. Fairfax, 23 Jan. 1893, SP (copy).
[167] Spencer to H. R. Rokeby, 3 Feb. 1898, SP (copy).
[168] Spencer to Admiral Sir M. Culme-Seymour, 12 and 15 Oct. 1893, SP (copy).
[169] Spencer to Rear-Admiral H. F. Stephenson, 14 Jan. 1894, SP (copy).
[170] Spencer to Admiral Sir M. Culme-Seymour, 14 Nov. 1893, SP copy).
[171] Spencer to Admiral Sir M. Culme-Seymour, 3 April 1895, SP (copy).
[172] Ibid.
[173] Spencer to Vice-Admiral Sir G. Tryon, 21 Feb. 1893, SP (copy).
[174] Spencer to Rear-Admiral H. F. Stephenson, 9 June 1895, SP (copy).
[175] Spencer to Admiral Sir M. Culme-Seymour, 9 June 1895, SP (copy).

with the Nicaraguans, whom Spencer called 'very irritating and very impudent', led to the ordering of a landing of a British force at Corinto in April 1895.[176] Potentially more explosive was the outbreak of war between China and Japan in August 1894. There were repercussions following the *Kowshing* affair and the victorious Japanese seemed likely to threaten the important treaty port of Shanghai. Spencer ordered reinforcements to the area, 'to strengthen Fremantle (the Commander-in-Chief) if he had to use force', knowing that seven new Japanese cruisers were in the approaches.[177]

Within two or three weeks of taking office, Spencer, with members of the Board, embarked on the Admiralty yacht *Enchantress* for a tour of inspection which included Portsmouth, Portland and the Channel Islands, the harbour at Alderney being then under the Admiralty.[178] 'Alderney is a melancholy spectacle', he wrote. 'After the thousands spent on the Breakwater, first of all the head of it was allowed to crumble away and in 1890 the Admiralty deliberately gave it up... We now have before us what we are to do. It is agreed, and as far as I can see rightly, that with Torpedo attacks and counter attacks and with the quantity of torpedo harbours on the French N. and N.W. coast, Alderney will be important for us.'[179]

Later, watching manoeuvres where torpedoes were being used, Spencer commented, 'I cannot help fearing that torpedo attack will always lead to confusion. ... From one cause or another the torpedo attack upon Fitzroy did not come off, and as far as I could make out the Torpedo commanders were in difficulties as to distinguishing between friend and foe. This would not, it is hoped, exist in real war.'[180] A few months later, the devasting series of torpedo attacks by Japan on the Chinese fleet in harbour at Wei-hai-wei[181] caused a stir in naval circles:

'You can imagine how deeply interested we have been over recent events in your command,' Spencer told Admiral Fremantle. 'The last news which you sent about the Torpedo attack on the Chinese fleet locked up in the harbour has been very wonderful. Your naval men knew what would happen with this terrible weapon of war but the outside public are amazed. The sinking of great battleships, the boldness of attack at night, the ineffectual screen of torpedo boats, the ineffectual booms or impediments at the mouth of the harbour, all are object lessons for us here which will have I expect marked influence on proposals for works which we are making for Portland, Portsmouth, Southampton Water and Gibraltar.'[182]

Two events occurred in the early part of his time at the Admiralty which caused him much anxiety. A first-class battleship, the *Howe*, commissioned only

---

[176] Spencer to Lady Spencer, 2 May 1895, SP.

[177] Spencer to Admiral Sir M. Culme-Seymour, 11 Oct. 1894, SP (copy). Spencer to Rear-Admiral H. F. Stephenson, 15 Oct. 1894, SP (copy).

[178] Memorandum, W. Graham Greene, 'Earl Spencer First Lord of the Admiralty 1892-5', Greene Papers, GEE/13 (g).

[179] Spencer to Vice-Admiral Sir G. Tryon, 15 Sept. 1892, SP (copy).

[180] Spencer to Vice-Admiral J.O. Hopkins, 25 Aug. 1894, SP (copy).

[181] For a full account of the incident, see H. W. Wilson, *Ironclads in Action* (1896), ii, pp. 128-33.

[182] Spencer to Vice-Admiral Sir E. R. Fremantle, 12 Feb. 1895, SP (copy).

two years previously, went aground off the coast of Spain in November 1892, causing much damage to the vessel. 'I am very busy, very depressed as to the *Howe*,' he informed Lord Charles Beresford.[183] While the preliminaries of the Spencer programme were being discussed, the *Victoria*, the flagship of Vice-Admiral Sir George Tryon, Commander-in-Chief, Mediterranean, was rammed by another battleship, the *Camperdown*. It sank in 13 minutes with the loss of more than 350 officers and men, including Tryon.[184] The admiral, whose home was at Bulwick, Northamptonshire, was a personal friend as well as professional colleague of Spencer. In April 1893, six weeks before the disaster, Spencer had stayed with the Tryons at Admiralty House, Malta.[185] He readily agreed that Tryon was to blame for the collision[186] but he was greatly shocked and sad-dened at his death. Rosebery informed the Queen on 23 June 1893, 'Lord Spencer was so moved in making his statement in the House of Lords that Lord Rosebery momentarily expected him to break down.'[187]

The main task of the First Lord was to prepare the naval estimates for the coming year, to be presented to and approved by the cabinet. Spencer wrote cheerfully to Harcourt, the Chancellor of the Exchequer, in October 1892, 'We are models of prudence and serenity re Expenditure, and I hope we shall be in favour when Estimates come in ... Shuttleworth [Parliamentary Secretary to the Admiralty] is a model Guardian of the Purse.'[188] In support of an increase in expenditure the following month, he submitted a return, showing the need for heavier and faster battleships, to counter the improved technology of the Russian and French navies.[189] Harcourt accused Spencer of submitting 'inflated Estimates', and threatened to resign.[190] Spencer complained that 'when I get letters from you I never quite know what they will be, whether I must expect banter, anger or serious argument.'[191] He was consoled, however, by Campbell-Bannerman at the War Office, who had received a similar fulmina-tion and had strongly protested to the Chancellor. Harcourt had replied, 'All right, you keep down your estimates and I will keep down my bile.'[192] Glad-stone, too, strongly opposed the demand for increased estimates. He considered that it would encourage militarism and have serious financial consequences for the country. It had only been in the previous year, during the 1892 general election campaign, that the Liberals had attacked the high naval expenditure of the Salisbury government.

But developments abroad during 1893 pointed towards the need for an expansion in naval strength. Russian advances in Afghanistan and continuing difficulties with the French in Egypt were given new significance with the visit

[183] Spencer to Capt. Lord Charles Beresford, 4 Nov. 1892, SP (copy).

[184] For full details, see *Admiralty, Court Martial, HMS Victoria 1893*, C. 7178 (1893) and C. 7208 (1893).

[185] C. C. Penrose Fitzgerald, *Life of Vice-Admiral Sir. G. Tryon* (1897), pp. 342–3.

[186] Spencer to Admiral Sir M. Culme-Seymour, 8 Aug. 1893, SP (copy).

[187] *LQV*, 3rd. ser., ii, p. 264. See also Spencer to Queen Victoria, 5 July 1893, RA E56/113.

[188] Spencer to W. V. Harcourt, 11 Oct. 1892, HP, MS. 46.

[189] Spencer to W. V. Harcourt, 28 Nov. 1892, HP, MS. 46.

[190] LHJ, 9 Dec. 1892, HP, MS. 736 ff. 361–2. There is some evidence to support Harcourt's contention. See, for example, S. Fortescue, *Looking Back* (1920), pp. 194–5.

[191] Spencer to W. V. Harcourt, 6 Jan. 1893, HP, MS. 46. No. 640.

[192] Campbell-Bannerman to Spencer, 10 Jan. 1893, SP.

by a Russian squadron to Toulon in October 1893. British supremacy in the Mediterranean was now threatened.[193] The Russian navy was ahead of those of both Italy and Germany in size, though in terms of first-class battleships it was well behind Britain and France.[194] It was the view of the naval advisers that the existing British overall superiority in battleships should be maintained. In August 1893 Admiral Sir Frederick Richards, the Second Sea Lord, presented a memorandum to the Board, urging that the building of more first-class battleships and destroyers was a priority. Three months later, Richards, now First Sea Lord, Fisher, the Controller, Bridge, Director of Naval Intelligence, and White, Director of Naval Construction, met to draw up two five-year programmes. The first, a 'minimum programme', asked for seven first-class battleships in order to retain equality with France and Russia, and a larger 'desirable programme', favoured by the Sea Lords to maintain the existing superiority of ten battleships.[195] Edward Hamilton saw clearly that there would be difficulties in obtaining cabinet approval for financing the programme. 'Harcourt thinks Lord Spencer's demands are in excess of real requirements; and it is doubtful if Mr. G. will even go as far as Harcourt.'[196]

A vitriolic correspondence passed between Spencer and Harcourt. At one stage, early in December, Spencer threatened, if opposition to expansion persisted, to 'retire into private life and buy hunters'. Harcourt, equally adamant, replied that 'though he has not hunting to fall back upon, he will be quite content to take himself off to Malwood and grow cabbages'.[197] Gladstone entirely supported Harcourt and refused to contemplate any further expenditure, considering that British naval supremacy was secure. On 13 December, at a dinner at Marjoribanks', Spencer gloomily reported that he was 'at loggerheads with his Board of Admirals, whose demands for new ships etc. are far in excess of what he is prepared to make, so that he is between the devil and the deep sea, with W.V.H. on one side and his Admirals on the other'.[198]

The formidable Richards had pressed large demands on Spencer. In an argument, he tended to repeat over and over again the same words and figures. In an interview with Richards at this time lasting for two hours, Spencer reported that the only words he used were '£3,126,000'.[199] On 15 December, Spencer adopted the minimum programme. Lord George Hamilton's motion calling for immediate action to increase the size of the Navy caused further embarrassment in a debate in the Commons four days later. Harcourt, during the debate, assured the House that the Sea Lords were satisfied with the present expenditure. On the following day, the admirals entirely repudiated this interpretation.[200] According to Fisher, 'We gave Lord Spencer to understand that unless Sir W. Harcourt explained we would resign ... Lord Spencer was in

---

[193] E. H. Jenkins, *A History of the French Navy* (1973), p. 307.
[194] D. W. Mitchell, *A History of Russian and Soviet Sea Power* (1974), p. 197.
[195] A. J. Marder, *The Anatomy of British Sea Power* (1940), pp. 190-1.
[196] EHJ, 14 Dec. 1893, Add. MS. 48662 f. 19.
[197] EHJ, 10 Dec. 1893, Add. MS. 48662 f. 14. See also Spencer to W. V. Harcourt, 10 Dec. 1893, SP (copy), No. **656,** and W. V. Harcourt to Spencer, 12 Dec. 1893, SP. No. **657.**
[198] LHJ, 13 Dec. 1893, HP, MS. 736 f. 434.
[199] Lord George Hamilton, *Parliamentary Reminiscences and Reflections 1886-1906* (1922), p. 223.
[200] Sea Lords to Spencer, 20 Dec. 1893, SP. No. **658.**

such distress that out of pity for him we did not really like to rub his nose in it any harder.'[201] Harcourt modified his statement the next day in the Commons.

This widely-quoted sequence of events was later hotly denied by Spencer. On the retirement of Richards in August 1899, he criticized a *Times* leader for crediting the admiral with forcing Harcourt's explanation at the risk of resignation. 'The fact was Sir Frederick never had to think of resignation for he knew that I was asking Harcourt to retract, and that I was responsible and I therefore covered him completely. The unfairness of the inferences annoyed me, but of course nothing can be done.'[202] Spencer also questioned Gladstone's propriety in attributing blame for the estimates to the Sea Lords alone. 'You must know,' he wrote to George Russell, 'that I never could or would shelter myself behind the Sea Lords: I worked with them but I, and I alone, was responsible for the proposals which I first made to the Cabinet when Mr. Gladstone was Prime Minister and second when Rosebery had succeeded him.'[203]

Towards the end of December 1893, matters looked more promising. On 26 December, Kay-Shuttleworth reported, 'He [Harcourt] is in excellent humour (bar an occasional rap at us) and told me how he should provide the money etc.'[204] Spencer quickly travelled up from Althorp and saw Harcourt at the Commons. It was not a happy meeting. Spencer put forward as an irreducible minimum an extra expenditure of £4 million for the following years for laying down seven first-class battleships, and cruisers and torpedo boats.

Harcourt had seen Gladstone who told him not to give way to Spencer[205] and once more proved to be difficult at the meeting. 'You say that I gave you no information yesterday excepting as to the 7 battleships,' Spencer wrote later. 'I was fully prepared to tell you my story, but whenever I attempted to do so, you checked me and stopped me, or you only accepted information in your own form.' He admitted, though, that he 'did not ... contemplate until the First Sea Lord submitted his statement on 22 November anything so large as what we have before us. 'But,' added Spencer, 'you fasten on what the Admirals call their desirable programme, which certainly will not have my approval and they practically will accept what they call a minimum programme.'[206] Lewis Harcourt recorded after the meeting, 'I can see that W.V.H. feels the impossibility of resisting Spencer.'[207] The latter was prepared to resign along with his Board, if the money was not forthcoming. [208] On 16 December, Spencer had discussed the estimates with Gladstone at Downing Street when the prime

[201] Fisher to Austen Chamberlain, 22 Dec. 1893. Quoted in Sir C. Petrie, *Life and Letters of Rt. Hon. Sir Austen Chamberlain* (1939), i, p. 61.

[202] Spencer to Lady Spencer, 26 Aug. 1893, SP. In the following year, Admiral Lord Walter Kerr, a Junior Naval Lord in 1893, corroborated Spencer's version of the affair. W. Graham Greene to Spencer, 7 March 1900, SP.

[203] Spencer to G. W. E. Russell, 24 May 1900, SP (copy).

[204] U. Kay-Shuttleworth to Spencer, 26 Dec. 1893, SP.

[205] LHJ, 27 Dec. 1893, HP, MS. 736 f. 439.

[206] Spencer to W. V. Harcourt, 28 Dec. 1893, SP (copy), and W. V. Harcourt to Spencer, 28 Dec. 1893, SP.

[207] LHJ, 27 Dec. 1893. HP, MS. 736 f. 441.

[208] West, p. 228.

minister 'talked in a melancholy vein about economy, now dead, eyesight and eventualities'.[209] Morley, who was closely in touch with Gladstone, told Spencer on 6 January, 'He may, I fancy, be got to go to $2\frac{1}{4}$ millions.'[210] The same day, Gladstone sent for Spencer and told him that he could not accept the estimates and would resign rather than do so. By this time, Gladstone was almost without support in the cabinet. Shortly before the vital cabinet meeting of 9 January, Spencer managed to trim the Sea Lords' demands for extra funding from £5 million to £3 million.[211]

At this meeting the prime minister, reading from notes, restated his insurmountable objections to the proposed building programme, making a final offer to sanction half the extra expenditure proposed for one year only. Lady Frederick Cavendish recorded subsequent events. 'Spencer said this was impossible as he was pledged to the Admiralty Board. Harcourt who had previously not only agreed with G.O.M. but further worked him up against the outlay (far more furious against it than was the P.M.), as soon as he saw that this line meant either resignation of P.M. or smash up the Cabinet, determined to swallow it himself, and tried to persuade him to do the same.'[212] Although the decision on the estimates was postponed, it was now fairly clear that Gladstone's resignation could not be long delayed. Gladstone placed the blame for the situation on the Sea Lords rather than on Spencer. On 11 January, he said to West, his unofficial adviser, 'It is the Admirals that have got their knife into me. Read my letter to Spencer.'[213] Two years after his retirement, however, reflecting on these events, he wrote, 'The position of Spencer was as clear as it was in my judgement deplorable. He accepted the monstrous schemes of the Admirals in a reduced form, pleased to have cut it down from something yet more monstrous.'[214] Spencer, for his part, showed no sign of yielding any further.[215] 'That Mr. G. should retire in disagreement with his colleagues, with his party and with the country would be lamentable for everyone ... [but] it is quite impossible, as far as I can see, that I should make any considerable modification of the Admiralty proposals. The fact is I scorned to resort, in a proposal to the Cabinet, to the horsedealers' plan of asking one price and being ready to take a lower one.'[216]

Gladstone, after a five-week stay in Biarritz, resigned from office on 1 March, ostensibly on account of his failing eyesight. This long expected event was a matter of some regret for Spencer. He wrote to his chief for the last time whilst still prime minister, 'I cannot conceal from myself that the policy which I proposed for the Navy has had a marked influence in bringing you to the decision of resigning at this moment. I most earnestly wish that I could have modified my proposals, or given place to someone else whose views would have agreed with your own ... This position has been most painful to me for

[209] Ibid.
[210] J. Morley to Spencer, 6 Jan. 1894, SP.
[211] F. Manning, The Life of Sir William White (1923), pp. 332-3.
[212] Lady Frederick Cavendish, Diary, 1894. CP, vol. xiv ff. 124-5.
[213] West, p. 238.
[214] Memorandum, W. E. Gladstone, 10 Nov. 1896, GP, Add. MS. 44791 f. 25.
[215] LHJ, 10 Jan. 1894, HP, MS. 736 f. 451.
[216] Spencer to Rosebery, 18 Jan. 1894, RP, 10062 ff. 139-40.

I owe my political career entirely to you, and I have always and still do admire your political principles and action and if I may be allowed to say so have a real affection and veneration for you personally.'[217] On 8 March, the cabinet under Rosebery formally approved the estimates, which provided for the construction of seven battleships, six cruisers and 36 destroyers.

It may seem surprising in the light of fundamental disagreements on naval policy that Gladstone would have been ready to recommend Spencer as his successor if the Queen had sought his views. Reflecting on the qualities of the main contenders, Harcourt, Rosebery and Spencer, in July 1894, Gladstone stated: 'My choice upon the whole would have fallen upon Spencer. Less brilliant than either he has far more experience, having entered the Queen's service over thirty years ago: he has also decidedly more of the very important quality termed weight, and his cast of character I think affords more guarantees of the moderation he would combine with zeal, and more possibility of forecasting the course he would pursue.'[218] Such a decision, as Stansky suggests, may have been governed by two considerations: that Spencer, unlike the other contenders, was still a committed home ruler, and also that he might prove to be a suitable compromise leader who would prevent animosities within the cabinet.[219]

Gladstone saw Morley on 2 March as he was setting out for Windsor, and confided that if invited by the Queen to advise on his successor, he would nominate Spencer.[220] On the following day before his final audience with the Queen, Gladstone spoke with Ponsonby on the uneasiness expressed by M.P.s of having a peer as prime minister. Gladstone did not consider that this problem was insuperable, but he did not mention a particular name.[221] Of his subsequent final interview with the Queen later that day, Gladstone told Spencer in 1897, 'You know I did not name any one as my Successor to the Queen. I was prepared to do so but she never asked me. H. Ponsonby asked who I should name but I told him I could answer that question to no one but the Queen herself.'[222]

Spencer was relieved at the outcome. He had already in February advised Rosebery that he would be foolish to refuse the prime ministership if offered it by the Queen.[223] On 20 February, Lewis Harcourt reported, 'Spencer has definitely said that he will not be Prime Minister under any circumstances.'[224] That Spencer was genuinely not seeking office can be seen from an earlier incident the previous summer when he was a candidate for the Viceroyalty of India. As mentioned earlier, Gladstone pressed him to stay to defend Irish policy, to which he agreed. Shortly afterwards, Gladstone sent for Spencer and explained that the pressure put upon him to remain was purely on Irish grounds

[217] Spencer to Gladstone, 23 Feb. 1894, GP, Add. MS. 44314 f. 110-11.
[218] Memorandum, W. E. Gladstone, 25 July 1894, GP, Add. MS. 44790 ff. 145-6.
[219] P. Stansky, *Ambitions and Strategies* (1964), p. 85.
[220] Morley, *Recollections*, ii, p. 11.
[221] Sir H. Ponsonby to Queen Victoria, 3 March 1894, *LQV*, 3rd, ser., ii, p. 369.
[222] Memorandum, Spencer, 'Notes of the conversation with Mr. Gladstone', 21 Nov. 1897, SP. No. 716.
[223] LHJ, 11 Feb. 1894, HP, MS. 736 f. 504.
[224] LHJ, 20 Feb. 1894, HP, MS. 736 f. 523.

and not with a view to succeeding him as prime minister. Spencer recalled being amazed at this statement, as no such idea had ever entered his head.[225]

On Gladstone's death in 1898, Lady Spencer reflected, 'He was always a kind friend to us—and it is 30 years since he appointed Spencer Lord-Lieutenant of Ireland at the end of 1868 and that he first served in Mr. Gladstone's Government.'[226] A few months later on the death of Bismarck, Spencer wrote, 'So the great German has soon followed Mr. G. to the grave ... They were both head and shoulders above their fellow Statesmen.'[227] But Spencer was not an uncritical admirer of his leader. In an earlier letter to his brother he remarked, 'I am glad you met Mr. Gladstone. You had not quite so much of what Rosebery calls "swinging the censer" as I had last year when I dined with the worthy Cyril Flower to meet Mr. G. They were all the profoundest worshippers, MacColl, Wolverton etc. and I confess I was a little sickened by the excess of adulation.'[228] On Gladstone's ambiguous and haphazard development of Irish policy,[229] Spencer grumbled to Harcourt, 'I often wish that more consultation took place, but we cannot change a certain person in his methods of arriving at important decisions.'[230] For the most part, though, he held his leader in some awe, contrasting unfavourably his own diffidence and lack of eloquence with Gladstone's positive qualities. A typical comment was that made to John Morley, in reporting a pleasant visit to Hawarden in 1895: 'Although we talked on Ireland I feel as I always do after seeing him that I did not make the most of my opportunity of sounding his views as to future policy, or his comments on the present.'[231]

For his part, Gladstone valued Spencer's loyalty during his four ministries particularly on the home rule issue and paid public tribute to him both on the platform and in Parliament. During Gladstone's last stay at Cannes in February 1898, Sarah Spencer, one of his favourite companions, received a letter from her brother containing a message for the ailing Gladstone, who 'was so pleased with it, and said "Ah, dear man. I have always been so fond of him." '[232] As a last act of homage, Spencer was the principal speaker at the opening of St. Deiniol's Library, Hawarden on 14 October 1902, a project which had occupied much of Gladstone's time in his closing years.[233]

During the comparatively brief Rosebery government (1894–5) Spencer continued as First Lord. He was not unduly concerned at the prime minister's pronouncement in the Lords shortly after taking office that the majority of M.P.s were hostile to home rule.[234] He did object, however, to Rosebery's plans to reduce the power of the Lords by appealing to the electorate for a

[225] LHJ, 23 Feb. 1894, HP, MS. 736 ff. 561-2.
[226] Lady Spencer, Diary, 19 May 1898, SP.
[227] Spencer to Lady Spencer, 1 Aug. 1898, SP.
[228] Spencer to C. R. Spencer, 25 Feb. 1887, SP.
[229] See J. R. Vincent, 'Gladstone and Ireland', *Proceedings of the British Academy*, lxiii (1977), p. 193 ff.
[230] Spencer to W. V. Harcourt, 15 July 1892, HP, MS. 46.
[231] Spencer to J. Morley, 22 Sept. 1895, HP, MS. 37.
[232] Lady Sarah Spencer to Spencer, 15 Feb. 1898, SP; and Catherine Gladstone to Spencer, 25 Nov. 1898, SP.
[233] See A. T. Bassett, *The Life of the Rt. Hon. John Edward Ellis* (1914), p. 198.
[234] Spencer to Gladstone, 25 March 1894, GP, Add. MS. 44314 f. 114. No. **678**.

mandate.[235] Together with Rosebery, Spencer played an important part in the formulation of foreign and defence policy,[236] though members of the cabinet expressed their disapproval of the premier's personal handling of many aspects of foreign affairs.[237]

Overshadowing all other happenings was the fierce animosity which existed between Rosebery and Harcourt during the administration. As Chancellor of the Exchequer, Harcourt put forward a plan for introducing a graduated death duty in the 1894 budget; this met with firm opposition from Rosebery. Spencer was anxious to avoid a split, and attempted to act as peacemaker, not stating his own views on the topic.[238] In July Spencer visited Harcourt, complaining of the strained relations between the Chancellor and Rosebery and begged for a *rapprochement* but without success.[239]

By the beginning of 1895 quarrels within the Liberal Party and the cabinet had taken their toll of Rosebery's health. Already suffering from insomnia, he contracted influenza and was out of public life for over a month. Spencer assisted in his recuperation by offering a cruise in an Admiralty yacht. For eight days the two men combined business and pleasure, inspecting dockyards as well as visiting Cowes and the Scilly Isles.[240]

In preparing the estimates for 1895, his last year in office, the First Lord was able to state that the shipbuilding programme far outstripped those of France and Russia.[241] Demands by Fisher for the provision of three more battleships in the 1895-6 estimates were resisted. 'People are still growling over the taxation of last year necessary in order to begin our programme,' Spencer replied. 'They barely realize that the programme of last year involved increased Navy Estimates this year. We shall have a job to get the H. of C. and country to accept that situation.'[242] Six months later, after the government's defeat on a motion in the Commons critical of Campbell-Bannerman, Rosebery resigned. In the general election which followed, the Liberals suffered a heavy defeat, the Unionists being returned with a majority of 152. 'I am sure that you will feel the blow,' Spencer wrote to Rosebery, 'I never expected a majority, but I did not think the numbers against us would be so great.'[243]

When Salisbury succeeded Rosebery as prime minister in July, the proposals for the estimates were left to Goschen, the new First Lord, to consider. In a farewell letter to one of his admirals, Spencer noted, 'I am glad that Mr. Goschen has kept all my Naval Board and even my Naval Private Secretary. That is very gratifying to me as it shows that he has nothing to find fault with in our conduct as a Board.'[244] But he admitted that 'I am very sorry to leave

[235] Spencer to Lady Spencer, 20 Nov. 1894, SP. No. **687**.

[236] M. Bentley, *Politics Without Democracy 1815-1914* (1984), p. 284.

[237] See James, pp. 347-50.

[238] Spencer to W. V. Harcourt, 22 April 1894, HP, MS. 47. No. **680**.

[239] LHJ, 13 July 1894, HP, MS. 737 f. 764.

[240] An imaginary and amusing account of the event, under the heading 'The Premier's Cruise', appeared in *Punch*, 25 May 1895, p. 246.

[241] Memorandum, Spencer, 'British, French and Russian Battleships, and Modern Cruisers'. 1 Dec. 1894, SP, and PRO CAB 37/37/42.

[242] Rear-Admiral J. A. Fisher to Spencer, 6 Jan. 1895, SP, and Spencer to Fisher, 7 Jan. 1895, SP (copy).

[243] Spencer to Rosebery, 6 Aug. 1895, RP, 10062 f. 213.

[244] Spencer to Admiral Sir M. Culme-Seymour, 3 July 1895, SP (copy).

this Office and to part with the Naval Service with whom I had been proud to work.'[245]

Spencer's naval colleagues expressed their regrets at his departure. Culme-Seymour, who described himself as 'a Unionist or Conservative', stated that 'no one could have done better than you have done at the Admiralty. It is not only my opinion but the opinion of Naval officers generally'.[246] Expressing similar sentiments, Richards, the First Sea Lord, added, 'What we want now is peace for a few years and if that can be maintained there need be no fear of the fortune of this our Empire. It will be well to have the full intent of your shipbuilding programme clearly on record here.'[247] The Queen paid her own tribute. Writing to Salisbury of her anxiety over the selection of Goschen for the Admiralty, she stated, 'Lord Spencer has been very successful not only as an Administrator but from his personal and social position which has lent prestige to what is our national service.'[248] During the Navy scare of 1893, he had succeeded in steering a middle course which avoided the resignation of both the Sea Lords and of members of the cabinet. Marder's judgement is a fair one. 'Lord Spencer left office knowing that he had not laboured in vain. His administration of the navy, if not brilliant, had at any rate, in spite of difficulties, been advantageous to the navy and the country.'[249] Spencer continued to take a deep interest in naval matters for the rest of his career, advising and encouraging the second Earl of Selborne, the Liberal Unionist First Lord (1900-5), to promote a scheme for the reappraisal of entrance requirements and training of naval officers.[250]

Out of office, Spencer quickly found himself involved in the final rupture between Rosebery and Harcourt. Early in August 1895, Harcourt, as Leader of the Party in the Commons, suggested to Spencer that a meeting of the ex-cabinet should be held at Spencer House.[251] Rosebery, in a letter to Spencer of 12 August, announced the severance of all communication with Harcourt, at the same time sending the latter a copy of it.[252] Despite Spencer's efforts at conciliation, the breach was not healed. Rosebery, now sulking, remained as Leader of the Party for a further year.

Evidence of Spencer's immense energy at this time can be seen in an account written by his private secretary at the Admiralty, Graham Greene. He had become Master of the Pytchley for a third time in February 1890 and, following his practice of never neglecting any duty he had undertaken, within a fortnight of being appointed First Lord, he paid a hurried visit to Althorp for a meet. Greene wrote: 'He took me with him, mounting me on one of his own hunters, and after a successful early morning run presented me with the mask and brush

[245] Spencer to Vice-Admiral Sir E. R. Fremantle, 3 July 1895, SP (copy).
[246] Admiral Sir M. Culme-Seymour to Spencer, 5 July 1895, SP.
[247] Admiral Sir F. Richards to Spencer, 28 June 1895, SP.
[248] Queen Victoria to Salisbury, 26 June 1895, RA C40/30/30 (draft cypher).
[249] Marder, op. cit., p. 235.
[250] 2nd Earl of Selborne to Spencer, 20 Dec. 1902, SP. Spencer to Selborne, 21 Dec. 1902, Selborne Papers, 149.
[251] Spencer to J. Morley, 9 Aug. 1895, HP, MS. 37.
[252] Rosebery to Spencer, 12 Aug. 1895, SP.

of the victim. We returned to London the same morning ready for an after-noon's work, none the worse for our strenuous exercise!'[253]

On accepting office as Master in succession to Herbert Langham, he had offered to hunt the whole of the Pytchley country for £3,800 a year or less *pro rata* if he decided not to keep a separate pack for the Woodlands.[254] During 1890, Spencer spent £5,064 10s. on horses and £4,106 14s. 4d. in 1891,[255] a financial burden which increased over the years.[256] In 1892, he was anxious to relinquish the Mastership because of his other pressing commitments but was persuaded to carry on until February 1894. A historian of the Hunt considers that it would have been better for all concerned if he had been allowed to retire at the earlier date.[257] Spencer believed that the Master should rule supreme and refused to contemplate suggestions for a Committee. He was once more offered the post in October 1900, but did not accept on the grounds: '1. Because it is not as it used to be. At 65 I cannot be out all day always. 2. The money is serious. It is not a profitable affair.'[258] Nevertheless, he continued to be an enthusiastic member of the Pytchley. He informed Lady Spencer in January 1902, 'I think I have now quite got over my hunting excesses,' but added, 'I shall be more careful in future not to have long days.'[259]

The continuing depressed state of land made the need for economies essen-tial.[260] One extra source of income was the letting of Spencer House. 'I am doing all I can to find a tenant for Spencer House,' W. S. Forster, his solicitor, wrote, 'but it is no easy matter ... Nearly everyone is so poor now, nothing seems to sell or let.'[261] In 1887, it was impossible to find a tenant. During his period as First Lord, spacious accommodation was available at the Admiralty.[262] He told his wife in May 1894, 'I don't want to go back to Spencer House this year. There is always the hope of letting it, which would be a great help, and I confess as far as my work goes I like being at the Admiralty.'[263] Un-doubtedly the strangest tenant of Spencer House was Barney Barnato, a flam-boyant East Londoner who had made a fortune in South Africa. 'I felt I ought not to refuse so good an offer as he made for 2 winters...,' Spencer confessed to Rosebery. 'He volunteered to pay the whole rent at once.'[264] The atmo-sphere of the building changed dramatically, as Barnato kept open house for

---

[253] Memorandum, W. Graham Greene, loc. cit. Spencer was described by an old friend as being 'one of the last of the fox-hunting country gentlemen who also wielded political influence'. Lord Willoughby de Broke, *The Passing Years* (1922), p. 101.

[254] Hon. H. Wyndham, *The Pytchley Mastership of the Fifth Earl Spencer* (1970), p. 20.

[255] 'Summary of Sale and Purchase of Horses, 1890-4', SP.

[256] Spencer to Lady Spencer, 30 Jan. 1894, SP. No. 670.

[257] G. Paget, *The History of the Althorp and Pytchley Hunt 1634-1920* (1937), p. 216.

[258] Spencer to C. R. Spencer, 28 Oct. 1900, SP.

[259] Spencer to Lady Spencer, 11 Jan. 1902, SP.

[260] The net receipts from rents at Althorp fell from £21,325 18s. 9d. in 1890 to £12,240 6s. 9d. in 1895. Estate Account Book, 1890-5, SP.

[261] W. S. Forster to Spencer, 20 June 1886, SP.

[262] Hicks Beach, when Chancellor of the Exchequer, commented on this arrangement, 'The salary of the First Lord of the Admiralty is only £4500 because of the house. From my point of view, it would be much better if it could be made £5000, like the other great offices, and the house given up.' Hicks Beach to Salisbury, 26 Oct. 1900, Hicks Beach Papers, D 2455 PCC/34 (copy).

[263] Spencer to Lady Spencer, 14 May 1894, SP.

[264] Spencer to Rosebery, 8 Sept. 1895, RP, 10062 f. 223.

actors, journalists, racing trainers, boxers and theatre managers.[265] According to Edward Hamilton, Spencer had a curious approach to financial affairs. In April 1902, he let Spencer House for the season, and took a large house in Lancaster Gate, both arrangements being made apparently without the knowledge of Lady Spencer.[266]

Freed from the responsibilities of office, the Spencers embarked on a world tour. 'Rents are very bad and tenants calling out for further help,' he informed Rosebery from Althorp. 'It will be a relief to shut up shop here for six months.'[267] They left England in a man-of-war for Italy on 28 October 1895, and then travelled by regular steamers to Bombay. From there, they departed with Spencer's brother-in-law, Sandhurst, for Hyderabad and Quetta, spending a month touring before returning to Bombay on 16 December. In the New Year, they visited an old palace near Jaipur by elephant. Lady Spencer noted in her diary, 'A more shaky conveyance it is impossible to find, especially going up and down hill. When the elephant gets up from his knees, it is all one can do to cling on to the howdah.'[268] At Agra, the Taj Mahal struck Spencer as 'certainly one of the most beautiful things I have ever seen'.[269] There was a meeting in Calcutta with Sir Henry Brackenbury, formerly Assistant Under-Secretary for Police and Crime at Dublin Castle,[270] and on 1 February, he attended a four-hour meeting of the Viceroy's Legislative Council at which Elgin considered cotton duties. Afterwards, Spencer wrote to 'the great Fowler', Secretary of State for India in Rosebery's government. 'He is a veritable hero in India,' he told Rosebery. 'Doubtless he was a very strong and able advocate of what your Cabinet did for India, but Kimberley had also his share in what was done and so had the Cabinet.'[271]

After short visits to Ceylon, Singapore and Hong Kong, where Spencer discussed the necessity of rectifying the Kowloon frontier with the governor,[272] Japan was reached. A month was spent studying the naval installations and ships and, as a former First Lord of the Admiralty, he was well-received. A banquet in his honour given by the Oriental Society of Japan at Tokyo on 11 April was attended by a large number of the Japanese aristocracy. Spencer expressed in a speech his admiration for that country's sea power and the recent series of naval victories.[273] There was a further interesting event later in the evening. Lady Spencer recorded, 'Just as I went to my room and was lying on the sofa, reading, I felt the sofa trembling and then everything in the room began to shake, the chandelier, doors, etc. I got up and opened the door and heard everything rattling in the corridor. It was a shock of earthquake.'[274] One other highlight of the visit was an audience with the Empress of Japan in the Palace

[265] S. Jackson, *The Great Barnato* (1970), p. 164.
[266] EHJ, 22 April 1901, Add. MS. 48678 f. 34.
[267] Spencer to Rosebery, 15 Sept. 1895, RP, 10062 f. 224.
[268] Lady Spencer, Diary, 12 Jan. 1896, SP.
[269] Spencer to C. R. Spencer, 22 Jan. 1896, SP.
[270] See *The Red Earl*, i, p. 24.
[271] Spencer to Rosebery, 12 Feb. 1896, RP, 10062 f. 227.
[272] Satow, Diary, 19 April 1896, Satow Papers, PRO 30/33/15/17.
[273] 'Notes for Speech in Japan, 1896', SP.
[274] Lady Spencer, Diary, 11 April 1896, SP.

(the Emperor had influenza). The Spencers were struck by the spacious building, which was new, a mixture of Japanese and German styles.

The last part of their voyage, across the Pacific Ocean to Vancouver, proved to be a rough one. 'Stayed in bed all day,' wrote Lady Spencer, 'discretion being the better part of valour in this instance.'[275] Landing at Victoria, Spencer inspected the fortifications and dockyards in the vicinity of Esquimalt on 29 April. The same day, a telegram was received announcing the death of Lilah, Lady Spencer's eldest sister. They travelled by Canadian Pacific Railway and saw Vancouver, Banff, and Winnipeg, where Spencer gave his first ever interview to newspaper reporters.[276] They also watched a large number of newly-arrived Russians and Austrians being registered at the Immigration Office, visited schools and had 'endless visits from Northamptonshire farmers and Irishmen'.[277] At Ottawa they stayed with the Aberdeens and, after sightseeing at Niagara, spent the remaining few days in New York, which Spencer had last visited almost exactly forty years previously. Whilst there, he took the opportunity to discuss politics with Theodore Roosevelt.[278] The journey across the Atlantic was uneventful, but Lady Spencer commented, 'Another smooth day and it is a pleasure sitting on deck—but the crowd is very disagreeable and such a motley collection.'[279] The tour had been both enjoyable and instructive, though Spencer felt 'rather ashamed at so long a holiday, but it would have been a pity not to have seen Japan'.[280] But he wrote to his brother, 'How glad we shall be to be home again!'[281]

Robert Spencer was a casualty of the 1895 general election. He had been one of the two representatives for North Northamptonshire from 1880 to 1885. When the county was divided into four single-member constituencies, he was elected for Mid Northamptonshire in 1886 and again in 1892. It was the most rural of the four divisions, the only urban district being Rothwell, with a population of under 5,000 in 1901.[282]

The Franchise and Redistribution Acts of 1884-5 dramatically shifted the hitherto landed control of county politics towards the newly-enfranchized agricultural labourers and the industrial villages in the county. The Irish home rule issue also weakened the support of county families: Spencer was the only Liberal landowner of any consequence in the county from 1886.[283] However, it was still possible to draw on the accumulated fund of goodwill which existed towards a long-established family. At a gathering of predominantly Tory farmers at Milton, Northamptonshire, in October 1885, Robert Spencer was warmly received. 'The whole meeting,' he informed his brother, 'might have been called "Spenceriana" or stories of the family.'[284]

---

[275] Lady Spencer, Diary, 19 April 1896, SP.
[276] *Manitoba Evening Bulletin*, 5 May 1896, p. 4.
[277] Lady Spencer, Diary, 6 May 1896, SP.
[278] Theodore Roosevelt to Spencer, 9 Oct. 1901, SP.
[279] Lady Spencer, Diary, 17 May 1896, SP.
[280] Spencer to C. R. Spencer, 31 Dec. 1895, SP.          [281] Ibid., 27 April 1896, SP.
[282] H. Pelling, *Social Geography of British Elections 1885-1910* (1967), p. 121.
[283] For a full analysis of the changing pattern of voting, see J. Howarth, 'The Liberal Revival in Northamptonshire, 1880-1895: A Case Study in Late Nineteenth Century Elections', *The Historical Journal*, xii (1969), pp. 78-118.
[284] C. R. Spencer to Lord Spencer, 14 Oct. 1885, SP.

Robert's majority of 1099 at the 1885 election over his Conservative opponent, Pickering Phipps, was reduced the following year to 956 against a former
Liberal, W. C. Cartwright. Liberal Party organization within the division did
not match that of the Conservatives, who exploited Lord Spencer's conversion
to home rule. Warning his brother of a possible defeat, Robert, now a Government Whip, wrote, 'The Tories are hounding on all weak Liberals to go
anywhere and do anything against you and all of us Gladstonians and the
bitterness and violence of their canvassers is sad. I have only seen it openly at
Floore, but I keep hearing of the way we are called Turncoats and hash of that
kind. Our labourers are frightened as the Primrose League and the Unionists
have flooded the place with pamphlets saying we shall swamp the labour market
with Irishmen.'[285]

Whilst not personally campaigning for his brother, Lord Spencer was able to
advance the Liberal cause in several ways. He was president of the Mid Northamptonshire Liberal Central Council and underwrote Robert's election expenses;[286] as Lord-Lieutenant of the county, he continued to infuse a Liberal
element into the magistracy;[287] and as chairman of the first Northamptonshire
County Council and a county councillor from 1889, he was able to play a
leading part in local affairs. He was in constant correspondence with Robert,
giving advice and commenting on electioneering strategies.

After the 1895 defeat of Robert Spencer by a local small landowner, James
Pender, Lord Spencer wrote to John Morley from Homburg, expressing concern at a new development in county politics. 'My impression is that we have
not lost our hold on the rural districts ... but that the frightful demoralization
of all Political sides in Northampton has taken away my brother's town
majority. Something like 1200 Socialists to have polled was enough to frighten
moderate Politicians.'[288] Spencer was convinced, however, that the cause that
most contributed to Robert's defeat was Harcourt's second Local Option
Bill.[289] A West Haddon Liberal supporter also pointed out the increasing efforts
being made by many clergymen and politicians in the division since 1892 to
bring about a Conservative victory. 'It only required 3 electors in each Parish
to vote Tory instead of Liberal to do what has been done. 2 farmers who have
Brewery shares changed in that way in one Parish... A good many Liberal
Farmers, and nearly every Tory Farmer, dislike the Parish Council Bill, as they
naturally in these times resent any increase of Rates... I also think a great many
Farmers who had been losing money, and working men who had been out of
work, were like drowning men ready to catch at straws.'[290]

Spencer advised his brother not to consider another fight for Mid Northamptonshire in the forseeable future, but, whilst keeping up registration, to seek a
seat elsewhere.[291] This advice was followed: in June 1898, he contested the

[285] Ibid., 10 July 1886, SP.
[286] During the 1900 election campaign, Robert Spencer acknowledged receipt of £1500 for this
purpose from his brother. C. R. Spencer to Spencer, 20 Sept. 1900, SP.
[287] Spencer to C. R. Spencer, 9 May 1888, SP.
[288] Spencer to J. Morley, 20 July 1895, HP, MS. 37.
[289] Spencer to Rosebery, 6 Aug. 1895, RP, 10062 f. 213.
[290] R. Parnell to Spencer, 24 Aug. 1895, SP.
[291] Spencer to C. R. Spencer, 21 July 1895, SP.

by-election in East Hertfordshire, caused by the death of the Conservative member, Abel Smith, a country gentleman, who had been returned unopposed in 1885 and 1886. With its traditional pattern of Conservative support, it was a very different prospect from Mid Northamptonshire. The Hatfield influence too was a powerful factor, particularly at the by-election, as Robert's opponent was Salisbury's grandson, Evelyn Cecil.[292] A vigorous campaign was fought with much enthusiastic Liberal canvassing. Whilst warning his brother not to shirk the challenge of home rule, Lord Spencer suggested that attention should be paid especially to the solution of foreign affairs and to education.[293] Robert failed to win the seat, but managed to reduce the Conservative majority from 1,236 in 1895 to a mere 268.

The time was ripe two years later, in September 1900, once more to contest Mid Northamptonshire when Salisbury suddenly called the 'Khaki Election'. 'I see that the tricky dissolution and the unnecessary disenfranchisement of many electors tells tremendously,' Spencer told Robert.[294] Spencer had sounded out leading Liberals in the division during July, when it was agreed that there was a good chance of recovering the Mid Northamptonshire seat.[295] During the campaign, he was able to help his brother on political issues by delivering speeches which received national coverage. Robert, writing from Dallington in September 1900, commented on his brother's speech at Derby, touching on agriculture, 'The local report of your speech was welcome reading for my day off ... some of your tenants who voted Tory last time are by way of regretting it, I heard in the market. So perhaps your remark has percolated and will do good.'[296] Robert Spencer's third and final election campaign against Pender resulted in a modest victory by 794 votes. Churchmen were now more sympathetic to the Liberals in the division, a fact which pleased Lord Spencer. 'Although I dislike Parsons and their ways, it is good to hear that more went with you, for it is very wrong for all the Church to be Conservative.'[297] John Becke, Robert Spencer's election agent, believed that 'if Labby [Labouchere] had been defeated the election might have gone wrong'. He added, 'I hope now we have secured a majority that we will hold the seat for many years but it has been very hard work.'[298] Robert remained a member for the division until he was created a viscount in December 1905.

The range of activities which Spencer undertook both at national and local levels is impressive. Combining county council with political duties made for difficulties. 'The fact is,' he mentioned to Robert, 'I have been hunted to death with two Committees of the House of Lords, and after two days at Northampton. As it gets near the Council's meetings I have also to prepare several long and difficult reports.'[299] Apart from being governor of both Harrow and

[292] *Northampton Daily Reporter*, 9 June 1898, p. 2.
[293] Spencer to C. R. Spencer, 13 June 1898, SP.
[294] Ibid., 22 Sept. 1900, SP.
[295] Ibid., 17 July 1900, SP.
[296] C. R. Spencer to Spencer, 23 Sept. 1900, SP.
[297] Spencer to C. R. Spencer, 14 Oct. 1900, SP.
[298] C. C. Becke, to Spencer, 5 Oct. 1900, SP.
[299] Spencer to C. R. Spencer, 1 Aug. 1890, SP.

Rugby Schools simultaneously for many years[300] he was Chancellor of Victoria University (later the University of Manchester) from 1892, where he had the pleasure later of bestowing an honorary doctorate on Mrs. Rylands. Entertaining at Althorp, as well as at Spencer House, was resumed on a larger scale as the animosities generated by the home rule issue faded. Spencer informed Harcourt in 1898, 'We have had a very dignified week: 2 balls, a large party of young people, 3 days' hunting and 2 days' shooting, and I survive quite fresh, but have no wish to renew these orgies!'[301] Visits to Althorp by Royalty were made by the Duke and Duchess of Teck in 1891 and the Empress Frederick in 1895.[302]

Among the guests on a previous occasion was the ailing Granville who died a few weeks later. Spencer's private tribute to him was a sincere one:

> I feel very low at the loss of so old and excellent friend as dear Lord Granville. I owe him my start in public life and his friendship has been constant and unflagging to Charlotte and me. The pleasantest episodes in our life have been with him. He was not by the public rated as high as he should have been, for he had first rate abilities, and was a genuine Liberal on principle. I never knew him falter as to which line to take and always on the Liberal side. He is one whose influence in Politics was much greater than appeared. He was certainly Mr. G.'s best adviser.[303]

One delightful episode which occurred during Spencer's time out of office arose from John Morley's activities as an author. In September 1898, he was engaged in writing a book on Oliver Cromwell and wished to see the places in Northamptonshire which had associations with him. Spencer invited Field Marshal Lord Wolseley to Althorp with Morley and after visiting Holdenby, Wolseley explained the battle of Naseby on the field itself.[304]

With a little more time available, Spencer read more widely, including Purcell's *Life of Cardinal Manning* who, he believed, sacrificed expediency to principle,[305] and he became aware of 'the wisdom and intellectual charm' of Carlyle, through his essays on Cromwell and Napoleon.[306]

A lifelong interest of Spencer's was education. Besides twice being Lord President, a post which included education among its responsibilities, he played an important part in its development within the county, serving on the County Council's Education Committee, visiting schools and providing finance where necessary. One of the Conservative election pledges was to redress the balance

---

[300] He took a close personal interest in his old school, Harrow, and was chairman of the governors for many years. Lord G. Hamilton to Sir M. Ridley, 1 Nov. 1900, Ridley Papers, ZRI 25/97/52. Spencer was also deputy chairman of the Rugby governors. *Reminiscences of Lord Kilbracken* (1931), p. 214.

[301] Spencer to W. V. Harcourt, 30 Jan. 1898, HP, MS. 48.

[302] See *NH*, 7 Feb. 1891, p. 5 and *Northampton Daily Reporter*, 19 March 1895, p. 3.

[303] Spencer to C. R. Spencer, 3 April 1891, SP. After Granville's death, it became clear that serious financial difficulties would be encountered in winding up his estate, arising from shares held in the Shelton Iron Steel and Coal Company. Spencer readily agreed to provide assistance, offering '£3,000 or if necessary £5,000'. Spencer to E. Waterhouse, 31 Aug. 1892, SP (copy).

[304] Spencer to Wolseley, 15 Sept. 1898, Wolseley Papers.

[305] Spencer to Lady Spencer, 26 Aug. 1896, SP.

[306] Spencer to Lady Spencer, 3 Sept. 1896, SP.

in favour of voluntary schools as against board schools. Extra grants were made payable to them by the 1897 Voluntary Schools Association Act; diocesan areas were encouraged to form Associations, representing schools, which could give advice to the Education Department on the distribution of grants.

Arthur Acland wrote to his father at this time, 'Lord Spencer tells me that though he is Lord-Lieutenant of Northamptonshire and owner of several voluntary schools the clergy deliberately made all the arrangements for association without his knowledge and behind his back. He is very much annoyed.'[307] The Act changed Spencer's hitherto moderate views on elementary education. 'Every year drives me away from the line which I have hitherto taken as to Voluntary Schools,' he informed one parson. 'I do not desire in small places and where no feeling is expressed against the Church School to set up needlessly a Board School. But in large centres of population particularly where the Church School has ample accommodation for children belonging to the Church, where a considerable number of persons prefer and desire a Board School, I certainly no longer intend to help directly any movement which is likely to prevent the establishment of a Board School.'[308] One solution which he favoured was a plan to bring board schools and voluntary schools together, though he opposed the notion of an elective authority to replace the former.[309] He believed that Northamptonshire, with its 363 parishes and some 50 miles in length, was too large for county councillors to supervise all its schools. Whilst in favour of religious instruction in schools, Spencer considered that it should be under the control of popularly-elected ratepayers, who could appoint teachers without religious tests.[310] It was on these principles that he led the Opposition in the Lords against the 1902 Education Bill, though without success.

The prospect of being in opposition after 1895 was not an unpleasing one to Spencer. He warned Harcourt shortly before going to the Far East that 'when I return I may be able to retire to Country Work, and look after my Estates ... This would be difficult work to commence at 60 but pleasanter than mixing up in the rough and tumble contests of Political acts among friends or foes.'[311] The immediate reason for this pessimism was Rosebery's outburst at a Liberal meeting in Scarborough on 17 October, where he reiterated his views on the House of Lords and urged that the policies of the party should be revitalized. In a letter to Spencer at the time, Rosebery remarked, 'I expect to be summarily decapitated by the Liberal Party for my Friday's speech. But it had to be spoken, and I don't care a d—!'[312] There is a curious entry in Rosebery's Journal shortly afterwards recording a meeting with Spencer, who expressed disappointment at Rosebery's refusal to patch up relations with Harcourt: 'Spencer seemed to go further than usual in saying that on a clear call of duty he might undertake the leadership.'[313]

As has already been seen, Spencer had refused to seek the highest office when

[307] A. H. D. Acland to T. D. Acland, 29 June 1897, Acland Papers, MS Eng. lett. c.100.
[308] Spencer to Rev. W. P. Hurrell, 21 May 1898, SP (copy).
[309] Spencer to F. A. Channing, 24 Oct. 1898, SP (copy).
[310] Spencer to E. E. Bowen, 12 Oct. 1902, SP (copy).
[311] Spencer to W. V. Harcourt, 1 Nov. 1895, SP (copy).
[312] Rosebery to Spencer, 20 Oct. 1895, SP.
[313] Quoted in Crewe, ii, p. 515.

Gladstone retired two years previously. In October 1896, when Rosebery formally resigned from the leadership of the party following Gladstone's speech on the Armenian question, he remarked to Spencer, 'Now I think that the eyes of many will turn to yourself as my successor. I sincerely trust that this may be the case... I believe that you are the person who would best rally the Party.'[314] In reply, Spencer protested, 'I abhor the notion of taking the position which you suggest may be pressed upon me. I have before now told you how honestly I feel my unfitness for it. I am glad to think at this moment there will be no possible question of this.' He concluded the letter, 'I dread the discussions which must follow.'[315] Writing to Gladstone, Spencer deprecated Rosebery's reason for resigning—'the Turkish question is too serious to be taken as an excuse for breaking up the party arrangements which have gone on since your retirement'—but conceded that 'I can understand any one not agreeing entirely with your mode of dealing with the question.'[316] Much to Spencer's relief, Kimberley was elected Leader of the Opposition Peers on 18 January 1897.

The resignation of Harcourt as Opposition Leader in the Commons in December 1898 and Morley's threatened withdrawal from the inner conclaves of the party were considered unreasonable by Spencer. Harcourt had claimed that Rosebery's speeches on foreign policy, especially his support of the government's handling of the French at Fashoda, could be interpreted as a challenge to his leadership.[317] As early as December 1896, Ripon reported from Dalmeny, 'I found Rosebery full of life and evidently beginning already to work for a future leadership free from the Harcourt connection.'[318] Spencer believed that Harcourt was playing into Rosebery's hands by resigning and that the position of a new Leader in the Commons would be made difficult by Harcourt acting independently alongside him.[319] In Spencer's eyes, Harcourt and Morley, as well as Rosebery on previous occasions, had 'treated the party abominably, with disloyalty and want of public spirit'. Writing to Asquith at this time, Spencer complained that Morley was 'most indignant and angry with Rosebery, and nearly as angry with you and others (including myself) for the line we had adopted on Fashoda. He was almost hysterical because I had in a speech praised the eloquence of Rosebery's language.' Dismissing Harcourt's belief that intrigues against him had been rife, Spencer attributed his action to jealousy of Rosebery's successful speeches on foreign affairs.[320] However, Harcourt remained adamant and on 6 February 1899, Campbell-Bannerman became Opposition Leader in the Commons after Asquith, whom Spencer favoured for the post, refused it on financial grounds.

That same month the Spencers embarked on a tour of Egypt visiting Luxor, Abu Simbel, Assouan and Cairo. There, Spencer had long talks with Cromer—

[314] Rosebery to Spencer, 7 Oct. 1896, SP.
[315] Spencer to Rosebery, 10 Oct. 1896, RP, 10062 f. 233.
[316] Spencer to Gladstone, 11 Oct. 1896, GP, Add. MS. 44314 f. 127. Spencer's own solution was to 'seize the Government of the Sultan by a mixed European Commission, and rule the place while Russia occupies the Armenian provinces'. Spencer to Lady Spencer, 2 Sept. 1896, SP.
[317] W.V. Harcourt to Spencer, 12 Dec. 1898, SP.
[318] Ripon to Spencer, 11 Dec. 1896, SP.
[319] Spencer to W. V. Harcourt, 13 Dec. 1898, HP, MS. 48.
[320] Spencer to Asquith, 24 Dec. 1898, AP, 9 f. 150.

'no one could have been more cordial or kinder'—and he also renewed acquaintance with Cecil Rhodes.[321] From Alexandria, they sailed for Naples where they met Harcourt and visited Pompeii together. 'A little bit of excavation was done for him,' Lady Spencer noted, 'but nothing but a frying pan turned up.'[322] After a tour of Rosebery's villas, narrowly missing him, the Spencers went on to Rome. They attended a Mass in St. Peter's at which Pope Leo XIII officiated and they had audiences with the King and Queen of Italy.[323] Harcourt was also there; an enthusiastic sightseer, he lectured the Spencers on Rome and its history. After one of several long political conversations with him, Spencer recorded: 'He says that everything which has happened justifies his recent action, that Campbell-Bannerman is in the same detestable position in which he was placed, deserted by his Whips and followers, that the whole party is rotten with no material for a Government or leaders etc. Then he declares that J. Morley and he have saved the party from ultra jingoism and Imperialism, and by this had achieved much at which they aimed.'[324]

Harcourt's boast was premature. By the summer of 1899, the government's relations with the Boers had worsened. Chamberlain, the Colonial Secretary, and Milner, High Commissioner in South Africa, had broken off negotiations with Kruger, the president of the Transvaal, at Bloemfontein in October. Spencer expressed uneasiness at the South African situation. 'We have no earthly right to use force. Whether Govt. can make out a strong case of outrages or not is another thing, I doubt it. If they cannot and they go to war, we Liberals shall be in a very uncomfortable position for I expect the Party is divided, but we must stick to what is just and right.'[325] Shortly afterwards, Rosebery reappeared in the centre of the political stage by means of a public letter of 11 October 1899 when he criticized Gladstone's handling of the situation in South Africa after Majuba Hill in 1881, and defended the need to go to war. He also stated on 26 October, 'I believe that the party of Liberal Imperialism is destined to control the destinies of this country.'[326] This policy of an imperial federation of the white colonies under an Imperial Parliament in London, opposed to Gladstonian Liberalism, also included the abandoning of Irish home rule as an unrealistic proposition. The 'Lib Imps' had attracted to their ranks young and ambitious M.P.s elected in 1885 and 1886, such as Edward Grey, Haldane, Fowler, Munro-Ferguson and later, Asquith. With the outbreak of war, the Roseberyites, who had remained relatively quiescent, now openly advanced their cause.

A schism in the Liberal ranks followed. After a government motion in the Commons on 17 October supporting Milner's policy, Horace Seymour told Lady Spencer: 'The Liberal leaders as usual were all at sea—some voting with the Government, which seems to me perfectly inexcusable, some not voting, and others voting against the Government. They might have the decency at

[321] Spencer to C. R. Spencer, 19 Feb. 1899, SP.
[322] Lady Spencer, Diary, 20 March 1899, SP.
[323] Spencer to C. R. Spencer, 3 April 1899, SP; and Lady Spencer, Diary, 8 April 1899, SP.
[324] Spencer to Kimberley, 3 April 1899, KP, 10247 f. 90.
[325] Spencer to C. R. Spencer, 26 Sept. 1899, SP.
[326] James, p. 411.

least to *appear* to act together... Many ask themselves are the leaders *Liberal* at all.'[327]

Spencer, gravely suspicious of Rosebery's motives,[328] supported Campbell-Bannerman's attacks on the government's handling of the war. 'I really believe', Campbell-Bannerman wrote to Spencer, 'that if we all go on speaking out, as you and I, and Tweedmouth have done, and as Kimberley substantially did although, as you say, his style is necessarily milder, we shall make a great impression.'[329] Campbell-Bannerman's task in the Commons was a difficult one. 'A long letter from H.C.B., evidently worried with his divided followers,' Spencer noted in February 1900.[330] The difficulties were not all on one side, however. Rosebery had told Spencer when they met at Brooks's, for a very friendly talk, 'that E. Grey went much further than he would.'[331]

Although Spencer deplored the outbreak of war, he did not lay the whole blame on the government. 'The Boers must take the consequence of their action and ultimatum,' he later commented to Campbell-Bannerman. 'Can we tolerate any state of things which will leave room if possible in the future for a repetition of this hostility towards us? I doubt it.'[332] The Khaki Election in the autumn of 1900 was a great reversal for Liberal fortunes. Spencer favoured an attempt to create unity within the party by inviting Rosebery to be Opposition Leader in the Lords in place of Kimberley,[333] though Rosebery refused. Spencer disapproved of Campbell-Bannerman's speech on 14 June 1901 condemning the government for using 'methods of barbarism' in South Africa, calling it 'an unfortunate sentence',[334] as it aggravated the split between Campbell-Bannerman and the Liberal Imperialists.

Rosebery clearly stated his position in a major speech at Chesterfield in December 1901. He was anxious to repudiate Asquith's and Grey's calls for supporting the government's conduct of the war and to revive the flagging public support for his policy. On the war, Rosebery favoured a negotiated settlement and generous peace terms. He urged the party to 'wipe its slate clean' of Ireland and abandon the obsolete proposals enunciated in the Newcastle Programme: 'efficiency' henceforth was to be the keyword. Spencer wrote to Rosebery, heartily agreeing with his conclusion as to the war, though regretting the scarcity of communication between them on politics during the previous five years.[335] To Edward Grey, he expressed regret at Rosebery's reference to the Irish question. 'The way R. put it struck me as wanting in loyalty to Mr. Gladstone... I cannot repudiate it and I wonder he can. If he does this, as some words imply, because the Nationalists are strongly against us in the war, I think that he uses an absolutely wrong argument.'[336]

Planning a campaign to counter Rosebery's speech, Campbell-Bannerman

---

[327] H. Seymour to Lady Spencer, 20 Oct. 1899, SP.
[328] Spencer to Lady Spencer, 12 Oct. 1899, SP.
[329] Campbell-Bannerman to Spencer, 19 Nov. 1899, SP.
[330] Spencer to Lady Spencer, 20 Feb. 1900, SP.
[331] Spencer to Ripon, 27 Nov. 1899, Rip. P, Add. MS. 43538 f. 73.
[332] Spencer to Campbell-Bannerman, 14 Jan. 1900, CBP, Add. MS. 41229 f. 78.
[333] Ibid., 12 Nov. 1900, CBP, Add. MS. 41229 f. 93.
[334] Spencer to Ripon, 20 Dec. 1901, Rip. P, Add. MS. 43538 f. 76.
[335] Spencer to Rosebery, 19 Dec. 1901, RP, 10062 f. 240.
[336] Spencer to E. Grey, 18 Dec. 1901, SP (copy).

agreed that his attitude towards the war was satisfactory, 'But the rest of the speech, involving a surrender of all that makes the party Liberal, is quite intolerable, and if any reconciliation took place it would have to be distinctly understood that these new ideas must be dropped. It is not only mischievious but silly, mere Sidney Webb and water.'[337] Spencer supported Campbell-Bannerman in his speeches after Chesterfield in calling for unity within the party and in defending the official policies. In February 1902, Rosebery and his followers established the Liberal League for the purpose of promoting their views. It was never an effective political base for Rosebery's challenge to the leadership.[338]

Spencer's responsibilities had increased following Kimberley's illness in 1901. It was agreed that Spencer would act as Leader of the Opposition in the Lords, though in fact Kimberley never sufficiently recovered to resume his post. Edward Hamilton recorded in his Journal in April 1901, 'Spencer has not been formally elected as Lord Kimberley's successor in the House of Lords but his lead is acknowledged by the few Peers who constitute the Liberal Party in that House and he evidently likes the position.'[339]

After the Chesterfield speech, Spencer asked Campbell-Bannerman, 'Would you work with Rosebery as Leader of the House of Lords? Recollect I am no obstacle. It would be an immense relief if the mantle of Kimberley envelop other shoulders than mine.'[340] Rosebery was sounded on the matter and replied that he hoped Spencer would remain in the post 'cum fine successionis.'[341] Following Kimberley's death in April 1902, shortly before the ending of the Boer War, Spencer was elected as his successor, carrying out the duties conscientiously for the next three years.

During the autumn of 1902, much of Spencer's energy was directed towards fighting 'the miserable Education Bill'. He told Herbert Gladstone, now the party's Chief Whip, that 'every help should be given to the opponents of the Education Bill'.[342] He agreed with Campbell-Bannerman that no compromise on the issues should be contemplated unless the establishment of popularly-elected boards of management with full powers to appoint teachers was conceded. Spencer campaigned against the bill, making speeches in Harcourt's constituency, where he was tumultuously applauded, and at the Northampton Church Congress in October, where, in contrast, his address was coolly received.[343] The divisions within the Liberal Party at the time weakened opposition to the bill. Although Spencer detested the Liberal League and its actions, he nevertheless wished that Asquith and Grey would lend their support on this issue.[344]

[337] Campbell-Bannerman to Spencer, 21 Dec. 1901, SP.
[338] See G. L. Bernstein, 'Sir Henry Campbell-Bannerman and the Liberal Imperialists', Journal of British Studies, xxiii (1983), pp. 117-21.
[339] EHJ, 23 May 1901, Add. MS. 48678 f. 34.
[340] Spencer to Campbell-Bannerman, 18 Dec. 1901, CBP, Add. MS. 41229 f. 142.
[341] Rosebery to Spencer, 28 Dec. 1901, SP.
[342] Spencer to H. Gladstone, 18 Sept. 1902, HGP, Add. MS. 46017 f. 123.
[343] Spencer to W. V. Harcourt, 22 Sept. 1902, HP, MS. 48, and J. Rennie Wilkinson to Spencer, 14 Oct. 1902, SP. See also bundle marked 'Letters received on the Education Bill', SP.
[344] Spencer to Campbell-Bannerman, 1 Oct. 1902, CBP, Add. MS. 41229 f. 174.

Liberal fortunes improved in May 1903 with Chamberlain's dramatic challenge to the government's fiscal policy by proposing imperial preference. The Conservatives' morale had already been shaken by the alienation of Nonconformist Liberal Unionists since the Education Act, by the outcome of the Boer War and by Chamberlain's policy as Colonial Secretary. Arthur Balfour, who had succeeded Salisbury as prime minister in July 1902, was now angry with Chamberlain for offending the free traders in the party and those who believed that imperial preference was unpopular with the electorate. By the summer of 1903, four members of the cabinet, Ritchie, Hamilton, Devonshire (formerly Hartington) and Balfour of Burleigh, opposed Chamberlain's policy, whilst outside the cabinet they were supported by a group which included Hicks Beach, Goschen, Hugh Cecil and Winston Churchill. Reporting on one of the many heated debates in the Commons during the session, Spencer stated, 'Hicks Beach admirable. Under very civil phrases and forms of Speech, he hit the Government fearfully hard ... [he] was tremendously cheered by our side. Ritchie made one of the worst speeches I ever heard ... His statement as to what the Cabinet decided (as all hated it) was ludicrous. It destroyed the collective responsibility of the Cabinet, and of the Prime Minister in particular. It was derided by both sides of the House.'[345]

The prospect of an imminent break up of the government led to immediate speculation on the possible candidates for Balfour's position. In a letter to his wife in early June, Spencer reported a meeting with Harcourt who 'was sure I should be sent for, not H.C.B. or R. We talked over possibilities at great length, and I left thoroughly depressed at the prospect which may shortly open out before me.'[346] There is evidence, nevertheless, that Spencer was planning realistically for the future. Among the Spencer Papers is a note, in his own hand, of a conversation with John Morley on 7 August, sketching out the composition of a Liberal ministry. In it he surmises that should the King send for Campbell-Bannerman, Grey, Asquith and Rosebery would refuse to serve and then he would be asked to form a government. Campbell-Bannerman would go to the Lords if possible.[347] Five days previously, Henry James told Devonshire that he 'had reason to know' that if the government broke up, the King would favour Spencer as prime minister.[348]

Support for him also came from the Liberal Imperialist wing of the party. Haldane argued that under Campbell-Bannerman's leadership, the cause of free trade would be lost and that therefore the real control of the Liberal Opposition should be with Rosebery, Asquith and Grey. It had been agreed at a meeting in Aberdeenshire on 30 August between Haldane and Asquith to launch a campaign at meetings throughout the country to 'decide who are to be in front, the C-B.ites or our people'. Rosebery's own position as their leader was unknown, but Haldane joined him and Grey at Dalmeny on 3 and 4 September. They were agreed that in the event of Rosebery refusing to come forward,

[345] Spencer to Lady Spencer, 10 June 1903, SP.

[346] Spencer to Lady Spencer, 6 June 1903, SP. No. **769**. Describing the meeting to Campbell-Bannerman, Spencer omitted all mention of the discussion on possible Liberal prime ministers. Spencer to Campbell-Bannerman, 5 June 1903, CBP, Add. MS. 41229 f. 197.

[347] Memorandum, Spencer, 'Notes of conversation with J.M. 7 Aug. 1903', SP. No. **773**.

[348] Journal, 30 Nov. 1903. Quoted in Lord Askwith, *Lord James of Hereford* (1930), p. 281.

then Asquith would be the most suitable leader. Both in August and in September, Rosebery drew up private memoranda setting out the reasons for remaining on the sidelines: these included his state of health, the fact that, through the Liberal League, he now represented only a tiny minority of the party and, finally, 'I cannot forget 1895.'[349] More positively, he suggested that 'We may compromise by taking Lord Spencer as a figure head, if C.B. will retire.'[350]

A few weeks later, at the beginning of October 1903, Grey and Haldane again saw Rosebery at Dalmeny. The latter confirmed that he would not be prepared to form a government. Haldane further informed Asquith, 'R. will not enter a Spencer ministry. He expresses the utmost contempt for S. R. vehemented that he is going to work with all his strength for an Asquith ministry ... He finally admitted that a Spencer compromise might be necessary to get C.B. from the H. of C.'[351] Grey, also describing the meeting to Asquith, believed that if Campbell-Bannerman were deposed, to be replaced by Asquith as Leader of the Commons, 'it would be urged upon you and your friends that it would be ungenerous and unnecessary to insist upon jumping over Spencer too.'[352] These manoeuvrings were known to Spencer, who expressed regret at the continuing animosity of the group towards Campbell-Bannerman. 'Possibly he is not a born leader,' he told Ripon, 'but he ... has been so grossly attacked and maligned that I feel we must stick to him most strenuously.'[353]

The resignations from the cabinet of Ritchie, Balfour of Burleigh, Hamilton, Devonshire and Chamberlain in September and early October appeared to weaken Balfour further. Campbell-Bannerman, after a discussion with Herbert Gladstone, informed Spencer, 'H.J.G. is busy forming the new Government—carries a list in his pocket! He is in high spirits and thinks well of our electoral preparations and prospects.'[354] The publication of Morley's *Life of Gladstone* in October, revealing that in 1894 the prime minister would have recommended Spencer to the Queen as his successor, further enhanced Spencer's claim in the eyes of his supporters, though his detractors regarded the timing with some cynicism.[355]

By October, Balfour had, for the time being at least, managed to pacify many of his supporters and confuse the Unionist free traders.[356] Chamberlain, now isolated, continued his mission to convince the electorate of his case by conducting a country-wide campaign. He was one of the very few politicians whom Spencer regarded with contempt. During the 1900 Khaki Election, Spencer, replying to a letter from Kimberley, wrote:

Chamberlain's speeches are well described by you, imprudent, arrogant and disgusting. I would add untruthful and degrading to the Nation and the Cabinet. According to him all are working for the Boers who do not vote for the Government candidate. I feel so angry that I should like to see a

[349] See Crewe, ii, p. 586, and James, p. 447.
[350] Haldane to J. St. Loe Strachey, 8 Sept. 1903, Strachey Papers, 5/8/2/1.
[351] Haldane to Asquith, 5 Oct. 1903, AP, 10 ff. 90-1.
[352] Grey to Asquith, 7 Oct. 1903, AP, 10 ff. 92-3.
[353] Spencer to Ripon, 25 Sept. 1903, Rip. P, Add. MS. 43538 f. 131.
[354] Campbell-Bannerman to Spencer, 26 Sept. 1903, SP.
[355] Margot Asquith to J. St. Loe Strachey, Strachey Papers, 5/8/2/1.
[356] See R. A. Rempel, *Unionists Divided* (1972), p. 61.

Demonstration in the House, the whole of the front bench decline to sit opposite to a Government and party which own so disgraceful, unreliable and degraded a Minister as Chamberlain.[357]

Spencer was not alone in his views. He told Harcourt the same day as he wrote to Kimberley, 'My indignation with Joe C. is only surpassed by Lady Spencer's, who would not be safe if armed in the same room with him.'[358] And towards the end of his political career, he observed:

J.C. is a very curious personality, full of inconsistencies and contradictions. A tremendous hitter himself, he is very sensitive to what is said of himself. A strong man in himself he is weak in allowing his surroundings to run away with him. He does not understand economic questions, but he is a brilliant bruiser. He is obliged to drop the subject he is weak in and have recourse to personalities.[359]

Despite the vicissitudes which followed his espousal of home rule, Spencer was generous in his opinions of most of his colleagues, extending in some cases to political opponents. 'Poor old Iddesleigh,' he wrote after that statesman's sudden death in 1887, 'I feel very much about him. He was an excellent man, too gentle for the present rough and tumble work of the H. of C. A man may lead there if he has the surpassing eloquence and experience of Mr. G., the sterling toughness of Hartington, or the brass and want of scruple of Randolph Churchill, but a mild and gentle creature like Sir Stafford will not go down or cope with the elements against him.'[360] Spencer greatly respected Salisbury, though not his nephew, A. J. Balfour, whom he considered 'a very clever and admirable debater [but] too dogmatic and logical.'[361] Rosebery, whom Spencer in later years dubbed 'The Great Sphinx', was difficult to fathom. He explained to Campbell-Bannerman, 'I do not attribute the coldness, the want of cordiality or even the apparent rudeness to malice but to the extraordinary self consciousness, shyness and awkwardness which possess him.'[362]

Of the new young men in the party who came to prominence from 1892, he always liked and admired Asquith but was 'grievously disappointed' in 1901 when he was 'pushed over the brink into the abyss of Imperialism and Milnerism'.[363] Grey's eloquence, if not his loyalty, was acknowledged.[364] Fowler, he considered, very able 'but always was a wobbler until he wobbled over to our

---

[357] Spencer to Kimberley, 7 Oct. 1900, KP, 10247 f. 108.

[358] Spencer to W.V. Harcourt, 7 Oct. 1900, HP, MS. 48.

[359] Spencer to Campbell-Bannerman, 20 Dec. 1904, CBP, Add. MS. 41229 f. 293. At an Eighty Club dinner on 9 Oct. 1903, Spencer had publicly denounced Chamberlain as 'one of the most ruthless and unscrupulous of statesmen who never hesitated to use any weapon that advanced his cause'. Three days later, he wrote to Harcourt, 'I spoke what I felt as to Joe's methods but I am half sorry that I said what I did. Truth is sometimes best kept back but I hate personalities, and should be sorry to having given the cue to personal attacks in the coming war, but anyhow I did not begin.' Spencer to W. V. Harcourt, 12 Oct. 1903, HP, MS. 48.

[360] Spencer to C. R. Spencer, 16 Jan. 1887, SP. Spencer attended a meeting concerned with erecting a statue of Iddesleigh within the precincts of Parliament. W. H. Smith to Queen Victoria, 15 Feb. 1887, Hambleden Papers, PS 10/16 (copy).

[361] Spencer to Lady Spencer, 19 Oct. 1891, SP.

[362] Spencer to Campbell-Bannerman, 27 Nov. 1903, CBP, Add, MS. 41229 f. 215.

[363] Spencer to W. V. Harcourt, 25 Nov. 1901, HP, MS. 48.

[364] Spencer to Lady Spencer, 28 Oct. 1899, SP.

weak kneed division'.[365] In 1899, the sudden death at the age of 40 of Tom Ellis, 'the Parnell of Wales' and the party's Chief Whip, greatly shocked him. 'Poor fellow,' he remarked to Robert Spencer, 'there seldom has been a more attractive, genuine, natural man, full of charity and brightness, and so honest, full of good sense and earnest.'[366] Of another young Welsh contemporary, Lloyd George, Spencer was less enthusiastic, describing his speeches as 'awfully exaggerated and violent'.[367] Harcourt's political pugnacity was not carried over into his long-standing personal friendship with the Spencers. Sending greetings on New Year's Day 1903, a year before his death, Harcourt wrote to Lady Spencer, 'We have no friends that we love and value more than you and Spencer who are so steadfast in word and deed.'[368] John Morley and Spencer found few difficulties in a friendship based on their agreement on Irish matters. Morley, a frequent visitor to Althorp and the Library, described one such visit in 1890. 'I had a delightful day with Spencer at Althorp—not a soul but ourselves and a kitchen maid and a pack of horses. We settled a Home Rule Bill before lunch, and a Land Bill after tea.'[369] Spencer's relations with Campbell-Bannerman differed from those with other colleagues. From the time when Spencer was Lord-Lieutenant in Ireland and Campbell-Bannerman was his Chief Secretary, the latter always looked up to Spencer, who in turn regarded the other as a junior. Both of Campbell-Bannerman's biographers make clear that because of his boundless admiration for Spencer, he would not advance his claim for the premiership at the other's expense.[370]

By the beginning of the present century, Spencer's colleagues in the Lords were few in number. After Granville's death in 1891, Spencer corresponded most freely, if not frequently, with Kimberley, whose moderate views and loyalty he highly regarded,[371] and with Rosebery, though mainly whilst in office. After Rosebery's resignation from the leadership in 1896, Spencer turned to Ripon as a regular correspondent, an arrangement which continued for the rest of his political career. Few of the former friendships with colleagues who were now Liberal Unionists were reclaimed. However, the painful estrangement from Hartington was coming to an end by 1891[372] and later, Spencer was once more on good terms with Northbrook. Spencer noted in November 1904: 'Poor Northbrook. I feel very much his death. He had been so long a tried and dear friend especially when we were in office from 1880 to 1885. We talked everything over, and there was no one whose opinion I valued more than his...

[365] Spencer to Campbell-Bannerman, 28 May 1902, CBP, Add. MS. 41229 f. 167.

[366] Spencer to C. R. Spencer, 9 April 1899, SP.

[367] Spencer to Lady Spencer, 9 Nov. 1898, SP. No. 721.

[368] W. V. Harcourt to Lady Spencer, 1 Jan. 1903, SP. On the night before Harcourt's sudden death, 30 Sept. 1904, he remarked to Lady Harcourt, 'Oh, I *must* write to Lady Sarah to ask after Spencer.' Typically, he wrote, 'Remind him from me that I have always told him that *exercise* is the thing which destroys everybody.' Reproduced in Gardiner, ii, p. 574. Spencer later wrote to Lewis Harcourt, 'I am sure you will believe me when I say that not only then but ever since I have mourned at the blank in my life that his death has made.' Spencer to L. Harcourt, 19 Dec. 1904, HP, MS. 429 f. 80.

[369] J. Morley to Rosebery, 18 Aug. 1890, RP, 10045 f. 192.

[370] Spender, ii, p. 179; J. Wilson, *C. B. A Life of Sir Henry Campbell-Bannerman* (1973), p. 423.

[371] C. S. Roundell to Spencer, 16 April 1902, SP.

[372] J. Morley to Spencer, 2 Sept. 1891, SP.

He was a very level-headed, clear-minded man. Latterly I had recovered my intimacy with him, so I shall miss him sadly.'[373]

During one of the most hectic spells of political activity in the autumn of 1902, Spencer was distracted by the sudden illness of Charlotte. Cancer was diagnosed and immediately a two-hour operation was performed at Spencer House, by her medical adviser, Dr. Mary Scharlieb.[374] By late November, Lady Spencer was pronounced to be out of danger and by the following January 1903, she was well enough to travel to Althorp. She recovered rapidly, convalesced at their seaside home at St. Leonards and then returned to Althorp. On 14 June, she accompanied Spencer to Northampton Station in an open landau and saw him off to London, but on her return journey she was caught in a rainstorm. As she felt unwell on the following day, she travelled up to London to see Dr. Scharlieb. Three days later, at Spencer House, she was taken ill with pneumonia and on 22 June became paralysed on her right side and was unable to speak.[375] Spencer continued with his political and county duties, but spent the majority of his free time at Spencer House with Charlotte. In September, he wrote to Ripon: 'I had another shock yesterday. I went on the River yesterday leaving Lady Spencer as I thought in her usual condition, but when I returned I found she had had a very bad day, and my sister who was here and the Doctor were very anxious ... these sudden relapses (not fresh brain trouble) are very trying.'[376] The end, however, was in sight. She lingered on until 31 October when, as Spencer recorded in a diary of Charlotte's illness, 'At 12.50, "Sorrow of sorrows." She left us in a sleep of perfect peace and beauty.'[377]

After the funeral at Althorp, Spencer spent the following two months at his shooting-box at North Creake. By the end of November, he was 'making an effort to read speeches again. For a time I sickened of them.'[378] As Leader of the Opposition in the Lords, he told Herbert Gladstone that he could not contemplate giving the January dinner before Parliament reassembled, but was prepared to take his place in the Lords at the opening: 'that will be a serious strain on me, but I think I must do that'.[379] In a letter to Harcourt, written on 30 December 1903, Spencer declared, 'My life is very much changed, but I am striving to occupy myself, and I have been out in the bracing Norfolk air a good deal, and it has done me good: I hope to be fit to get to work again in public when Parliament meets.'[380]

The importance of the part played by Spencer in negotiating with the Unionist free traders at this crucial time has not been generally acknowledged by historians of the period. In Norfolk, Spencer closely followed developments in the split in the Unionist Party between the Tariff Reformers and the Free Food

---

[373] Spencer to C. R. Spencer, 19 Nov. 1904, SP.

[374] One of the early students at the London School of Medicine for Women, later the Royal Free Hospital. M. D., 1886. Spencer admired her medical skills. See Mary Scharlieb, *Reminiscences* (1924), p. 176.

[375] F. Seymour, *Charlotte, Countess Spencer: A Memoir* (1907), p. 93.

[376] Spencer to Ripon, 25 Sept. 1903, Rip. P, Add. MS. 43538 f. 132.

[377] Spencer, 'Diary made up afterwards of Lady Spencer's two illnesses', SP.

[378] Spencer to Campbell-Bannerman, 27 Nov. 1903, CBP, Add. MS. 41229 f. 215.

[379] Spencer to H. Gladstone, 6 Dec. 1903, HGP, Add. MS. 46017 f. 134.

[380] Spencer to W.V. Harcourt, 30 Dec. 1903, HP, MS. 48.

Leaguers, headed by Chamberlain and Hicks Beach respectively. In his opinion, it was a golden opportunity for a stock-taking of Liberal policy in order to secure the maximum political benefit from the disarray of the Unionists. He advised Campbell-Bannerman that it would be necessary, in the first place, to make some pronouncement on home rule. He believed, however, that Liberals uniting to oppose fiscal changes need not necessarily agree to proposals on Irish home rule. John Morley and Spencer had pledged themselves not to support a plan for home rule until a land purchase scheme had been carried. The government's Land Act of 1903 completed the transfer of ownership of land from the larger landlords to tenants. Spencer considered that attempts at further home rule legislation could now be postponed. This conciliatory attitude would, he presumed, be sufficient to satisfy Devonshire and Goschen. It was not, however, possible or desirable to alter the party's attitude on education. 'If we did we should greatly weaken the forces in favour of free trade, for we should shake the faith and lose the confidence of Non-conformists who think much more of Education than of fiscal policy.'

Spencer, weighing up the alternative possible strategies, believed that only a few free traders would join the Liberal ranks, but that steps should be taken to secure their help at election times and in Parliament. He asked Campbell-Bannerman, 'Would not Unionist Free Traders be forced to vote with you on a resolution aimed entirely at Chamberlain's policy? ... By constant worrying Resolutions and motions you will be able to shake them and almost drive them to Dissolve.' The immediate action to take, he suggested, was to discuss possible amendments to the Address when Parliament met in February 1904. He also proposed that, with the agreement of Rosebery, Devonshire should be approached for his support.[381]

Two Unionist by-election victories in mid December 1903, which apparently vindicated Chamberlain's policy, led to speculation on the chances of a general election. 'I hope the Government will dissolve,' Spencer remarked to his brother. 'As yet and with little real knowledge I am confident we shall win. The populace to whom food and cheap food is the most important item of daily life cannot support J.C., and they can carry Elections.'[382] But the issue was not put to the test. Lacking confidence that a victory at the polls could be ensured, Balfour continued in office.

Behind the scenes, moves were being made to draw up an alliance between the Unionist free traders and the Liberals: Spencer was to play a central part in the negotiations. Devonshire had privately asked Rosebery in December for advice on initiating fiscal debates in the Commons without appearing to seek a vote of censure on the government. Rosebery, though sympathetic, took no further part in the proceedings. It is known that by 18 December Devonshire was making soundings, through friends, with a view to making contact with Spencer.[383] On 2 January 1904, Devonshire wrote to Spencer, suggesting closer

[381] Spencer to Campbell-Bannerman, 7 Dec. 1903, CBP, Add, MS. 41229 ff. 219–25.

[382] Spencer to C. R. Spencer, 23 Dec. 1903, SP.

[383] H. Cox to Spencer, 18 Dec. 1903, SP. No. 779. Spencer had himself contemplated approaching Devonshire. 'He gave me a sort of opening weeks ago and I had written to say how glad I was that he had resigned.' Spencer to Rosebery, 25 Dec. 1903, RP, 10062 f. 283.

co-operation between Liberals and Unionists. From the time of his arrival in London from Norfolk on 4 January, Spencer was engaged in negotiating with Devonshire. A meeting of the ex-cabinet the following day confirmed that the Duke's terms for co-operation should be explored by Spencer.

One visitor to Althorp at this time, on 10 January, was the young Winston Churchill. Then still a member of the Conservative Party but a strong opponent of tariff reform, he was seeking to bring about an alliance between Devonshire and the Liberals. He contemplated that Spencer, whom he greatly admired, might one day head a Liberal government,[384] and discussed fully with him the difficulties in the path of a *rapprochement*[385] as well as his wish to become a Liberal. Six months later he joined the Liberal Party.

Plans for co-operation between the Liberals and the Unionist free traders seemed a real possibility until the series of resounding anti-government by-election results indicated that the need for an alliance was diminishing. Spencer, who was unwell in January 1904,[386] wrote to Campbell-Bannerman at the end of the month, 'I have much to tell you as to the Duke of Devonshire but really there is scarcely anything for us now to decide.'[387]

The upturn in the fortunes of the Liberals renewed speculation over the headship of the next administration. Campbell-Bannerman, concerned for the health of his wife, had contemplated taking a peerage and holding a cabinet post without departmental responsibility in the event of a change of government.[388] Asquith was a likely contender for the prime ministership. John Morley told Spencer in January 1904, 'Fowler and I dined tête-à-tête on Wednesday. Rather amusing to find that section all ready with Cabinets etc. among other things in what was called by him a Spencer-Asquith base. He spoke with some asperity of the want of spirit in Lord R.'[389]

Rosebery, as has been seen, had already drawn up for himself a list of reasons, physical, personal and political, why it would be impossible for him to form a government. Isolated from old friends and with only a small band of followers in the Commons, he regarded the future with little enthusiasm. Arnold-Forster, then War Secretary in the Balfour ministry, paints a vivid picture of Rosebery towards the end of 1904:

> Went to Windsor ... I had a strange talk with Rosebery, who, by the way, came in black evening dress, and was dreadfully nervous on that account. He asked me how I was, and I said that I was very well, but that I did not know that I had any right to be alive. This he took very seriously, and with a face like an undertaker, he asked me 'Is life worth living?' I said that on the whole it was, but he was not at all content, but kept repeating

[384] Churchill to his mother, 18 Sept. 1903, in R.S. Churchill, *Winston Churchill, Young Statesman 1901-1914* (1967), ii, p. 67.

[385] The difficulties were reiterated the following day to Devonshire. Churchill to Devonshire, 12 Jan. 1904, CP, 340.3061.

[386] Spencer complained of 'a bronchial gouty ailment'. Spencer to Crewe, 29 Jan. 1904, Crewe Papers, C/46.

[387] Spencer to Campbell-Bannerman, 28 Jan. 1904, CBP, Add. MS. 41229 f. 255.

[388] S. Koss, *Asquith* (1976), p. 61.

[389] J. Morley to Spencer, 8 Jan. 1904, SP.

his question with great solemnity. He had evidently been thinking a good deal about it ... I said that meanwhile, being alive, I found my Army work very difficult but interesting; that my great hope was that his party when they came in would get on with it... I said I believed the best people in the Party would do this. 'What about Campbell-Bannerman?' growled his Lordship, and then he spoke with the most concentrated bitterness about C.B. whom he described as 'the greatest Conservative' in the House. ... We came up in the carriage with the Lord Chancellor, the Speaker and Sir H. Campbell-Bannerman. The latter unconsciously repaid Rosebery in kind by making some very 'sniffy remarks' about him and his coming in the wrong costume. There is certainly no love lost between these two great men.[390]

Spencer had been anxious at the end of 1903 to draw Rosebery into the party's deliberations on possible co-operation with the Unionist free traders. Rosebery wrote cordially to Spencer on the matter, but declined the invitation to rejoin the Opposition front bench.[391]

Spencer once more resumed his multifarious activities in the Lords. On the outbreak of the Russo-Japanese war in February 1904, he corresponded with Selborne, the First Lord, on its naval implications, concerned himself with the Chinese labour question in South Africa, condemned the Tibetan mission and criticized the government's scheme for army reform. He was evidently still cabinet-building. Kay-Shuttleworth (now Lord Shuttleworth) wrote in January, 'I have thought over what you say about the Dilke difficulty ... my view is that you have little or nothing to gain by giving him Parliamentary office, while you run great risk, to say the least.'[392] Munro-Ferguson, formerly Rosebery's private secretary and a Liberal Leaguer, reported to Rosebery in March that Tweedmouth's latest sketch for a government included Morley as Chancellor of the Exchequer, Campbell-Bannerman as Foreign Secretary, Asquith as Leader of the Commons and Spencer as prime minister.[393] When it seemed a few months later that Balfour would not be able to hold his followers together, Perks, the Liberal Imperialist, declared, 'I believe that we are on the eve of a marvellous Liberal victory, which ought to give us a majority independent of the Irish vote. I suppose Spencer and C.B. will form a ministry.'[394] Haldane had also told Perks 'that Spencer talks very freely in private about the Government he means to form, and among other things he says he shall send Sydney Buxton [Under-Secretary of State, Colonies, 1892-5] to South Africa to reverse Milner's policy: and he will have "no Imperialism at the Foreign Office".'[395] Henry Lucy, Punch's parliamentary reporter, added to speculation by forecasting in the October issue of the Nineteenth Century that Spencer would be the next prime minister.[396] But Balfour, involved in, along other matters, establishing the Committee of Imperial Defence, army reform and in renewing the

[390] Arnold-Forster, Journal, 16 Nov. 1904. Arnold-Forster Papers, Add. MS. 50341 ff. 86-9.
[391] Rosebery to Spencer, 22 Dec. 1903, RP, 10062 ff, 280-1 (copy).
[392] Shuttleworth to Spencer, 17 Jan. 1904, SP.
[393] R. C. Munro-Ferguson to Rosebery, 31 March 1904, RP, 10010 f. 190.
[394] R. W. Perks to Rosebery, 22 June, 1904, RP, 10051, f. 232.
[395] Ibid., 8 July 1904, RP 10051 ff. 236-7.
[396] H. W. Lucy, 'The Next Liberal Ministry', Nineteenth Century, liv. Oct. 1904, p. 684.

Anglo-Japanese Agreement, was determined to cling on to office until these matters were settled.

Towards the end of the session Spencer became ill and in August travelled to Nauheim to recuperate, returning to Althorp on 22 September. On the following day he suffered a heart attack. 'It is indeed vexatious,' John Morley sympathised, 'for I left you on Wednesday in a most cheerful frame of mind (my mind, I mean), and full of good hopes for the future.'[397] Spencer was advised to rest as much as possible until at least December as other aspects of his health were giving rise to some concern.[398] All political engagements were cancelled. Only one important task was undertaken during the period: the securing of the purchase of the Liberal *Northampton Mercury* in October 1904 when it seemed in danger of falling into the hands of political opponents.[399]

On New Year's Eve, Spencer wrote to his brother, 'The best of wishes for the coming New Year. How one wonders what it will bring.' He returned to London in early January, attempting once more to persuade Rosebery to give the traditional dinner for leading members of the party on the eve of the opening of Parliament, but he again refused.

Although Spencer had been away from politics for almost six months, he was still considered by many as the likely next Liberal prime minister.[400] Margot Asquith wrote to Loe St. Strachey, editor of the *Spectator*, 'I want you in your paper not to talk of a Rosebery administration now but an Asquith one. This won't mean that my husband will be P.M. Probably it will fall to Ld. Spencer, but I don't know if you will agree with me.'[401] As the chances of taking office became more realistic, the divisions between the leading Liberals continued. Haldane, a strong Rosebery supporter, congratulated the latter on a speech in which he had referred to both Campbell-Bannerman and Spencer. 'I am glad,' he wrote, 'it makes the work easier of lifting things gently out of the hands of the "over 65" leaders of the Opposition.'[402] After dining with Haldane in February 1905, Edmund Gosse recorded the situation in his Journal:

> The confusion of the Liberal Party beggars description, and if A.J.B. only knew, the most damaging thing he could do would be to dissolve tomorrow. The dissensions are still quite ludicrous. Asquith, Rosebery and Haldane have not been consulted about anything. Lord Spencer takes the position of leader and prime-minister-elect, but it is at his own invitation and he has no mandate from any section of the party, except the extreme Rump.[403]

After meeting Spencer four days later, Gosse reported: 'He told me that he dreaded the strain of the coming session. He is not strong, nor wholly recovered, and he is evidently pulling himself up towards the ambition of being Prime Minister.' Gosse also noted that Edward VII, who had succeeded to the throne

[397] J. Morley to Spencer, 27 Sept. 1904, SP.

[398] W. Mather to Spencer, 15 Nov. 1904, SP.

[399] Ripon to Spencer 21 Oct. 1904, SP. No. **803**, and W.R.D. Adkins to Spencer, 27 Nov. 1904, SP. No. **805**.

[400] Morley, in conversation with Sir Francis Mowatt, formerly Permanent Secretary, Treasury, on 13 Jan. named Spencer for the post and Campbell-Bannerman as Foreign Secretary in the Lords. EHJ, 14 Jan. 1905, Add. MS. 48683 f. 5.

[401] Margot Asquith to Loe St. Strachey, 3 Jan. 1905, Strachey Papers, 11/7/7.

[402] Haldane to Rosebery, 8 Dec. 1904, RP, 10030 f. 119.

[403] Gosse, Diary, House of Lords, MS. L32, 13 Feb. 1905, f. 30.

in 1901, had purportedly said to Haldane a few days previously, 'Who told Lord Spencer that I am going to call upon him to form a Government? I am sure *I* didn't. I am not at all convinced his health would allow it.'[404]

An unexpected turn of events in the leadership question was the publication of a 'manifesto' by Spencer in the national press on 10 February 1905, the day after a conference of Liberal leaders at which he had presided, and four days before Parliament met. It was, in fact, a letter addressed to Corrie Grant, M.P. for Rugby, stating Spencer's views on the policy of a future Liberal government. Its importance, as W. T. Stead quickly pointed out, lay in the fact that 'no other leader had been so precise in setting forth his opinions' and the letter would be 'regarded as being equivalent to a recognition by the Party of the right of Lord Spencer to succeed Mr. Balfour, and the assumption by Lord Spencer of a right to draw up a programme for the coming Election.'[405] In the document, Spencer attacked Balfour and Chamberlain on fiscal reforms and protection. Government policy on education would be reversed; schools paid for out of public money would be placed under public control. South Africa would be given full representative government and indented labour would not continue. On self-government for Ireland, Spencer cautiously stated, 'Liberals will always be ready, at the proper moment, to extend the application of the principle of self-government in that country.' At home, he favoured a revision of the whole basis of the incidence of taxation and rating, restoration of certain powers to trades unions following the Taff Vale and other recent law cases, and a promise to curb the extravagance of government spending.

The 'manifesto' was received with some cynicism. One political opponent commented:

> A portentous Radical Programme from Lord Spencer: it raises a number of interesting problems. Why for instance should Lord Spencer be protagonist, and above all why should this catalogue of promises be addressed to a personage of Corrie Grant's mental calibre? This evening's telegrams show that the manifesto is roundly repudiated by Asquith, Gladstone and so forth: poor Lord Spencer: poor ridiculous Corrie Grant.[406]

Edward Hamilton was very much more accurate in his assessment: 'It has been commonly taken as the manifesto of a leader, but I believe it is nothing more than an attempt to do duty for a speech. The way it has been received gives one a taste of the bickerings and jealousies ahead.'[407]

Herbert Gladstone immediately issued a statement to the press, explaining that as Spencer had been unable to fulfil his speaking engagements in various constituencies, the letter to Grant was intended as an equivalent to a speech. Spencer was angry at the interpretation placed by the press on the letter. He took the unusual step of writing personally to A. G. Gardiner, editor of the *Daily News*, protesting at the paper's leader as 'others might think that I had

[404] Gosse, Diary, 17 Feb. 1905, f. 32.
[405] W. T. Stead (ed.), *Coming Men on Coming Questions*, No. 2. 'Leaders in the Lords: Lord Spencer and Lord Rosebery', 20 April 1905, p. 5.
[406] Crawford, Journal, 10 Feb. 1905, Crawford and Balcarres Papers.
[407] EHJ, 11 Feb. 1905, Add. MS. 48683, f. 17.

pushed myself selfishly forward'.[408] Certainly, Spencer had been anxious to seek Campbell-Bannerman's approval of the letter before it was issued. 'I have tried to avoid a programme', he wrote, 'but my letter is rather long.'[409] The 'different passages', as Spencer called them, had been discussed and agreed with Campbell-Bannerman on 9 February before the Liberal leaders' meeting.[410] Spencer had in fact displayed some naivety in not anticipating the motives which were likely to be attributed to the letter at such a crucial stage in political affairs. Adopting a philosophical outlook, he wrote to a colleague, 'I feel much annoyed at this, but I must grin and bear it, and it will be only a one morning wonder and will be forgotten tomorrow.'[411]

Nevertheless, *The Times*' reaction to the letter was that in the event of a Liberal victory, Spencer would be offered the premiership.[412] But other alternatives were being canvassed. The Liberal Imperialists solution was for Campbell-Bannerman to accept a peerage, with Haldane, Grey and Asquith occupying the main posts in the Commons.[413] Rosebery suggested to the King, during a visit by him to Mentmore in February 1905, that he should send for Campbell-Bannerman and Spencer together and ask for their advice. Edward was attracted by this solution until it was pointed out that this touched on the royal prerogative, which gave the Sovereign absolute choice of persons: the matter was then dropped.[414]

Whilst these leadership manoeuvres were being mooted, Spencer was fully occupied with his House of Lords duties. His last parliamentary session proved to be a busy one. Though fiscal affairs were still the dominant issue, the revelation that George Wyndham, the Irish Chief Secretary, had been a party to the plans of his Under-Secretary, Sir Antony MacDonnell, to grant further powers to the Irish Executive, led to a furore in Unionist circles and to Wyndham's resignation in March. For his part, Spencer doubted if the Liberals would promise a real home rule measure during the life of the next Parliament. 'I wish heartily we could but were it put forward as part of our policy, the Tories would work it hard so as to try and override the effect of Fiscal and Education Policy.'[415]

By the time Parliament was prorogued in August, the government's chances of survival until the end of the year were slim. Balfour had written despairingly to Hugh Cecil, 'I really do not know which is worse—the right or the left wing of the Party which I have the melancholy privilege of leading! As a rule, I find myself for the first time taking the gloomiest view of the *last* speaker.'[416] Spencer, still not fully recovered from his illness, had no regrets when the

---

[408] Spencer to A. G. Gardiner, 11 Feb. 1905, Gardiner Papers, 1/3. See also Gardiner to Spencer, 11 Feb. 1905, SP.

[409] Spencer to Campbell-Bannerman, 8 Feb. 1905, CBP, Add. MS. 41229 f. 308.

[410] Spencer to L. Harcourt, 10 Feb. 1905, HP, MS. 429 f. 90.

[411] Ibid.

[412] *The Times*, 11 Feb. 1905, p. 13.

[413] Haldane outlined this plan to Gosse on 12 Feb. Gosse, Diary, House of Lords, MS. L32, 13 Feb. 1905 f. 31. See also Gladstone Memorandum, 29 March 1905, HGP, Add. MS. 45988 f. 161.

[414] EHJ, 18 Feb. 1905, Add. MS. 48683 f. 20, and M. V. Brett (ed.), *Journals and Letters of Reginald Viscount Esher* (1954), ii, p. 7, entry for 7 March 1905.

[415] Spencer to Campbell-Bannerman, 28 April 1905, CBP, Add. MS. 41229 f. 311.

[416] A. J. Balfour to Lord Hugh Cecil, 11 July 1905, Quickswood Papers, Qu I 4/3.

session came to a close. Writing to his brother from Nauheim, he confessed, 'I was so glad to get rid of my last Speech for the Session. I wonder how many I made, a sad number. It is very dispiriting to make them at some trouble and however they may affect the Lords, they have not a shred of influence elsewhere in the press or country.'[417]

Shortly before leaving England, Spencer was asked by Campbell-Bannerman to sound out Rosebery on his position in the event of a Liberal victory. At Mentmore, Spencer met Asquith and Ribblesdale, who were equally anxious to know if Rosebery would be willing to take office. In a brief conversation which, wrote Rosebery, 'I had been eluding all day,'[418] he confirmed that his active political life was over.[419] Grey, Haldane and Asquith had, when alone with Rosebery on 17 July, attempted to ascertain his position.[420] Haldane followed up the meeting with a letter, regretting Rosebery's withdrawal, adding, 'Our only course is to stick as tight as we can to our principles and keep as many people together as we can.'[421]

Rosebery's final refusal to be considered for the leadership left Campbell-Bannerman and Spencer as the main contenders. Earlier in the year, Gosse had informed Haldane that Spencer had consented to be prime minister. This 'somewhat gloomy intelligence', remarked Haldane, 'shows where we stand at all events.'[422] Haldane also confided to Gosse that he hoped to be the next Lord Chancellor. Spencer, however, according to Haldane, had received a request for the post from Lord Davey, a former Solicitor-General, which, much to Haldane's chagrin, Spencer answered favourably.[423]

Whilst Spencer was in Nauheim and Campbell-Bannerman in Marienbad, Asquith, Grey and Haldane were hatching a plot to force the leadership issue. The trio met on 9 September at Relugas, a remote fishing lodge in north-east Scotland. They agreed on a plan to accept, if necessary, a Campbell-Bannerman administration on condition that he was elevated to the Lords, thus surrendering the Leadership of the Commons. This, together with the Exchequership, would go to Asquith. Haldane would be Lord Chancellor and the Foreign or Colonial Office would be given to Grey. They agreed not to take office if Campbell-Bannerman refused these terms.

Haldane communicated the terms of the 'Relugas Compact' to Lord Knollys, the King's private secretary. After considering the matter, Knollys indicated the difficulties which would arise if the plan were pursued.

> ... If you and your friends decline to form a part of the Administration the King would be obliged (1) to accept Sir H.C.B.'s Government with the loss ... of the most able and moderate men of the Liberal Party, or (2) he would have to seek for a Prime Minister elsewhere, and where is he to be found? If Lord Spencer were to be sent for, Sir H.C.B. would be still more

[417] Spencer to C. R. Spencer, 14 Aug. 1905, SP.
[418] Rosebery, 'Betting Book', 1905, RP, 10184 f. 38.
[419] Spencer to C. R. Spencer, 8 Aug. 1905, SP. No. **820.**
[420] Haldane, Diary, 17 July 1905, Haldane Papers, MS. 5974 f. 29.
[421] Haldane to Rosebery, 19 July, 1905, RP, 10030, f. 123.
[422] Haldane to Gosse, 4 Jan. 1905, Gosse Papers.
[423] Gosse, Diary, House of Lords, MS L32, 27 March 1905, f. 38.

unwilling to leave the House of Commons, and I should doubt the former attempting to form a Government without the assistance of the latter. To whom then could the King turn? ... It appears to me therefore that unless you can suggest a way out of the difficulty, by mentioning someone besides Sir H.C.B. and Lord Spencer, the King would find himself in a very unfortunate position if you, Asquith and Sir E. Grey would not accept office.[424]

The monarch discussed the plan with Haldane at Balmoral early in October and agreed to express his doubts to Campbell-Bannerman when the latter returned from Marienbad in November. Edward VII, according to Haldane, wondered 'whether anyone but a young man can be both P.M. and Leader in the H. of C. with the increasing business.' Haldane noted, 'This leaves it open to C.B. to think that Ld. S. may be sent for, and later on will enable the K. to suggest a peerage to H.C.B.'[425]

That the plot failed and Campbell-Bannerman became prime minister in December 1905, remaining in the Commons, is now a matter of history. What emerges from the story of the political manoeuvrings during September and October of that year is that Spencer's candidature was not completely ruled out. The difference in age between the two men was slight—Spencer was then almost 70 and Campbell-Bannerman 69—and there was no question of rivalry between them. Campbell-Bannerman's case was a stronger one, and the turn of events put the issue beyond doubt.

Spencer returned to London on 18 September and, according to John Morley, 'He was in great spirits, confident that Nauheim had made him well again, keen about politics.'[426] He had outlined to his brother his plans for the rest of the year: they included the unveiling of a memorial to Gladstone in London,[427] addressing a meeting at Raith, Scotland, and leading a political rally at Manchester in December.[428] Letters exchanged with Campbell-Bannerman, mainly on the political situation at home and abroad, looked ahead to the tasks for the new Liberal government. 'Education is first,' wrote Spencer on 31 August, 'to insist on a Welsh Disestablishment Bill being in our first Session strikes me as somewhat a strong order.'[429]

At the end of September, Spencer was at North Creake for shooting, preparing himself for the hectic time ahead. He replied to a letter from Lewis Harcourt, reminding him of the Manchester meeting. 'I have begun strongly here and find heaps of birds. Oh yes, the 8 December is registered in "my book of fate".' Yet, he added, 'What a happy day it will be when I have not to enter Public meetings in the book.'[430] On 8 October, he entertained Morley, assuring him that he never felt better.[431] Three days later, whilst out shooting, Spencer suffered a severe stroke.

It is interesting to speculate on Spencer's position had not his sudden and

[424] Knollys to Haldane, 19 Sept. 1905, Haldane Papers, MS. 5906, ff. 200-9.
[425] Haldane to Asquith, 6 Oct. 1905, AP, 20 ff. 25-7.
[426] J. Morley to Rosebery, 14 Oct. 1905, RP, 10047 f. 175.
[427] Spencer was chairman of the committee.
[428] Spencer to C. R. Spencer, 22 Aug. 1905, SP.
[429] Spencer to Campbell-Bannerman, 31 Aug. 1905, CBP, Add. MS. 41229 f. 316.
[430] Spencer to L. Harcourt, 26 Sept. 1905, HP, MS. 429 f. 101.
[431] J. Morley to Bryce, 10 Nov. 1905, Bryce Papers, UB 12.

serious illness removed him from the political scene. The 'Relugas' plotters appeared, in their correspondence at least, not to have considered Spencer's role in the likely event of a Campbell-Bannerman ministry. The only negative evidence is to be found in a memorandum drawn up by Haldane the following year, recalling the deliberations with Asquith and Grey: 'The second point which we held essential was that the Foreign Office should be in the hands, not of Lord Spencer, but of Grey. This became easier to accomplish because of poor Lord Spencer's illness.'[432]

As a serious rival to Campbell-Bannerman for the prime ministership, Spencer was at a disadvantage. Balfour revealed to Lord Newton in January 1906 that he had wanted to dissolve in the previous October, but that rank and file Conservatives had objected: if he had done so 'he would not have advised the King to send for Lord Spencer, even had he been sufficiently capable, because Campbell-Bannerman was evidently the man whom the Commons wanted'.[433] More intriguing, however, is the statement made by Asquith in 1910 when he was prime minister, in a conversation with Lord Rendel: 'Asquith said that Lord Spencer fully wanted to be Prime Minister in 1906. If so he not only was unconscious of his mental incapacity but oblivious of his three years old arrangement with C.B. made before his stroke and maintained up to it.'[434] Both the Campbell-Bannerman and Spencer Papers reveal no hint of a pact between the two men in 1903 on the matter, though it can be surmised that after the death of Charlotte, Spencer may have temporarily given up his political ambitions.[435] Campbell-Bannerman fought off the challenge of Asquith, Grey and Haldane and became prime minister in December 1905. A shrewd, easygoing and at first uninspiring party leader, he would have drawn heavily on Spencer's vast political experience in office. Almost a year later, Campbell-Bannerman wrote to Robert Spencer, 'his loss has been an unspeakable blow to me, and hardly a month passes in which I do not miss his advice and help'.[436] To those within the party who regarded him as a rival, however, Spencer's illness came as a relief. Munro-Ferguson reported 'a good talk' with Haldane in November 1905. 'Our men have made great way this autumn, and the done ups are weakened by the loss of a figure head in Spencer, who, much as I like him personally, was a drag in politics. The "Party" is really taking to itself again those whom it deuced near ostracised, and we are all good friends now.'[437]

[432] *Richard Burdon Haldane: An Autobiography* (1929), p. 174.
[433] Lord Newton, *Retrospection* (1941), p. 147.
[434] 'Note of conversation with Asquith, 31 Jan. 1910', Rendel Papers, vol. 3, 79.
[435] The only evidence of any discussions having taken place between Spencer and Campbell-Bannerman on their respective roles in the event of a Liberal ministry is to be found in Campbell's-Bannerman's well-known interview with Asquith on 13 Nov. 1905. According to Margot Asquith, Campbell-Bannerman stated, 'I hear that it has been suggested by that ingenious person, Richard Burdon Haldane, that I should go to the House of Lords, a place for which I have neither liking, training nor ambition. In this case you would lead the House of Commons. While Lord Spencer was well and among us, nothing under Heaven would have made me do this! Nothing except at the point of the bayonet. Spencer and I talked it over, and he was quite willing that I should go to the House of Lords.' *The Autobiography of Margot Asquith* (1921), ii, p. 67.
[436] Campbell-Bannerman to Viscount Althorp, 27 Nov. 1906, CBP, Add. MS. 41229 f. 337.
[437] R. C. Munro-Ferguson to W. Runciman, 5 Nov. 1905, Runciman Papers, WR 11.

Spencer's stroke was accompanied by loss of speech. The Duke of Devonshire pronounced him 'politically dead'[438] and Edward Hamilton, nearing the end of his own Journal, reported a week later that 'though he is getting his speech back, I doubt if he will be much good again'.[439] He was well enough in November to return to Althorp, accompanied by his sister Sarah. She described him to Lord Rendel: 'I cannot say how sad it is to see him still so utterly unable to work, or do anything. He cannot write a line yet, only sign his name. His speech is much clearer but still *no* nouns, and he can read very little; it is piteously sad but I trust and pray he may get on still better, and be able to attend to home and county work.'[440]

Spencer soon resumed hunting, though by the end of the year his horses had been sold.[441] He was delighted at the impressive general election victory for the Liberals in January 1906. Robert Spencer had been appointed Lord Chamberlain, and was created Viscount Althorp in December. 'It has been hard to leave the H. of C.,' he told Lewis Harcourt, 'especially as the reason for my doing so was my dear Brother's condition. Happily, he thinks it is all owing to my own health.'[442]

Spencer continued to take an interest in naval affairs, receiving from Lord Cawdor, the Conservative First Lord, his Blue Book on Admiralty policy.[443] Cawdor's Liberal successor, Tweedmouth, wrote in February 1906, 'Now that I am sitting in your old chair at the Admiralty and issuing my first statement, with the annual estimates, I cannot refrain from sending you a copy ... We all missed you so much at the opening of Parliament and many were the regrets expressed at your absence.'[444] In May, he was asked for his advice by the Admiralty, in the light of his contacts with Selborne and Cawdor. 'I hear you saw Lord Tweedmouth for a short time,' wrote Graham Greene, who was still at the Admiralty. 'I hope you gave him to understand that you had approved of the main features of the policy of the last three years. It will be of much help to us that he should know this, as really the questions at issue are all those which were considered and decided upon a year ago, and I think you were placed in full possession of the facts.'[445]

During the next few years, Spencer visited the Continent though keeping in touch with political events in England. He was sad to learn, whilst in Italy in 1908, of the deaths of Devonshire and Campbell-Bannerman and of Ripon's and Tweedmouth's in the following year. Cabinet changes that year resulted in John Morley and Fowler being elevated to the Lords and he was delighted that Winston Churchill had become President of the Board of Trade.[446] One of his

---

[438] Sir A. Fitzroy, *Memoirs* (1910), i, p. 266.

[439] EHJ, 30 Oct. 1905, Add. MS. 48683 f. 83.

[440] Lady Sarah Spencer to Rendel, 8 Nov. 1905, Rendel Papers, vol. 2, 752.

[441] M. Fawcett to Spencer, 16 Dec. 1905, SP.

[442] Viscount Althorp to L. Harcourt, 22 Jan. 1906, HP, MS. 439 ff. 3-4.

[443] C. R. Spencer to Lord Cawdor, 3 Dec. 1905, Cawdor Papers, I, Box 293.

[444] Tweedmouth to Spencer, 28 Feb. 1906, SP.

[445] W. Graham Greene to Spencer, 5 May 1906, SP.

[446] Spencer to Viscount Althorp, 25 March, 11 April, 15 April, 26 April, 11 July 1908 and 16 Sept. 1909, SP.

last letters was to congratulate his old Admiralty colleague, Fisher, on becoming a peer.[447]

Spencer reluctantly relinquished the Lord-Lieutenancy of Northamptonshire in 1908, a post he had held for 37 years, on account of increasing ill-health. Apart from one visit to Windsor in November 1909 when he attended an investiture, he now remained at Althorp. On 5 July 1910, he suffered a further stroke and died on 13 August. Robert Spencer, now sixth Earl Spencer, told Gosse, 'I had the ribbon of the Garter put upon him, and later when he lay in the big hall, I covered him with the mantle of the Garter. The last service was touching, great crowds of people, but all gently sympathetic.'[448] Asquith attended the funeral at Great Brington church, motoring from Malmesbury for the service.

Many tributes were paid to his memory. Morley wrote to Lord Minto, 'I wonder whether you were well acquainted with Lord Spencer? For some ten years he and I were very close friends, and we fought the hard cause of Home Rule side by side. Without his great authority and character the cause would have been even harder than it was. He was a noble fellow, such lofty simplicity; such sovereign and steadfast unselfishness; such freedom from the horrid vice of thinking of petty personal things amid the tide of great public issues.'[449] Arthur Acland recalled that 'his personal kindnesses to me again and again are one of the happiest memories of my political associations of the past'.[450] Lansdowne too stressed 'the innumerable kindnesses of a sort which an elder public man can confer on a beginner ... There was no-one whom I more respected, and I have often regretted the recent cleavages, as political parties had the result of throwing him and me in different camps.'[451] Arthur Ponsonby stated, 'In these days of push and advertisement it is refreshing to think of a man of his type.'[452] Rosebery, from Vichy, penned a fulsome tribute: 'He was indeed the best and truest of friends ... I shall always remember him with the truest affection and respect.'[453]

The most moving and perhaps the most sincere words were from James Bryce, then ambassador in Washington:

> He always seemed to me the most beautiful, indeed, the most perfect character I have known in public life, the most admirable example of the union of courage with sweetness, of self-reliance with modesty, coupled with the strongest sense of public duty and complete unselfishness. His love of truth and his delicate honour gave him a chivalric quality that one values almost above all other merits, perhaps because it seems rare in our modern day. It was always counted by me as a privilege to know your brother ... I shall never again meet anyone like him.'[454]

[447] Spencer to Fisher, 10 Nov. 1909, Fisher Papers, FISR 3/3.
[448] 6th Earl Spencer to Gosse, 27 Aug. 1910, Gosse Papers. No. **839**.
[449] Morley to Minto, 19 Aug. 1910, Minto Papers, MS. 12734 f. 144.
[450] A. H. D. Acland to 6th Earl Spencer, 15 Aug. 1910, SP.
[451] Lansdowne to 6th Earl Spencer, 16 Aug. 1910, SP.
[452] Ponsonby to 6th Earl Spencer, 16 Aug. 1910, SP.
[453] Rosebery to 6th Earl Spencer, 14 Aug. 1910, SP.
[454] Bryce to 6th Earl Spencer, 24 Aug. 1910, SP.

Spencer's long career in public life has not so far attracted the attention it deserves. He first came into prominence in 1867, with his refusal to head a faction in the Lords opposed to franchise reform. A member of a Whig family who supported moderate Liberalism, Spencer was rewarded by Gladstone in the following year by being given office: he was a member of successive Liberal governments for the rest of the century, and a member of the cabinet in all except the first.

As Lord-Lieutenant of Ireland during the crucial periods 1868-74 and 1882-5, Spencer was given the task of carrying out the provisions of the Land Acts and, with growing agitation in Ireland, a Coercion Act. He narrowly escaped assassination at the time of the Phoenix Park murders in 1882. Whilst dealing firmly with secret societies and outbreaks of lawlessness, he believed that pacification could be achieved only by amending the 1881 Land Act as to purchase and sale of land. He was bitterly disappointed when the cabinet rejected his plan in 1884. Spencer's stubborn opposition to Chamberlain's central board scheme was crucial in the cabinet's rejection of it in May 1885.

Spencer's subsequent conversion to the cause of Irish home rule was regarded with astonishment by many members of both parties. Even in 1893 Lady Monkswell, witnessing a debate on the Evicted Tenants Commission in the Lords, could write: 'I came away in a state of double bewilderment, how two such nice men as Spencer and Herschell could in any degree take the part of these Irish thieves and murderers.'[455] In fact, Spencer's decision to adopt home rule was entirely consistent with his character: once convinced of the necessity of a course of action, he was willing to pursue it, however uncomfortable the consequences. Another example was the support given to the admirals in 1893 for the Navy estimates in spite of Gladstone's protests. He rarely courted popularity for its own sake, but he treated political opponents with courtesy and consideration, as the correspondence on home rule in this volume indicates.

Loyalty was another quality which he prized highly. It seems unlikely that Gladstone could have successfully formed a government in 1886 without Spencer's assistance. It may be the case that Spencer's insistence on a land purchase bill preceding a home rule bill dealt a blow to the prospects of a successful outcome for the latter; but for the rest of his political life, Spencer gave high priority in Liberal programmes to making home rule possible.

The Spencer shipbuilding programme, the steps taken to improve naval defences and the successful handling of crises abroad involving naval intervention marked his time as First Lord. Out of office, he proved a capable Leader of the Party in the Lords and played a significant part at the end of 1903 in efforts to bring about a reunion between the Liberals and the dissident Unionist free traders led by Devonshire. Spencer made important contributions to the advancement of education. As Lord President, he took a close interest in the work of the Education Department. During his two terms of office the great 1880 Education Bill, which promoted compulsory school attendance, was enacted, and more enlightened Codes, which affected the status and work of inspectors, teachers and children, were put into operation. He was an advocate

---

[455] E. C. F. Collier (ed.), *A Victorian Diarist, Monkswell 1873-95* (1944), p. 223.

of higher education: together with his Vice-President, Mundella, Spencer was responsible for uniting the scattered science institutions in London at South Kensington, where a school devoted to all branches of science applicable to industry was formed.[456] He encouraged the development of a national system of schools and of higher education in Wales,[457] and took a deep interest in the expansion of Manchester University, where he was Chancellor from 1892 to 1907.

Described by Edward Hamilton as 'almost the last of the *grand seigneurs*',[458] Spencer was praised by many of his contemporaries for his honesty and unwillingness to intrigue. This aspect of his character made him the obvious choice of person to attempt to smooth out difficulties when they arose between leading members of the party. He was, for example, called on to persuade Carlingford to relinquish the Lord Presidency in 1884 and for Granville to take the Colonies two years later; he also attempted to act as conciliator between Rosebery and Harcourt during the last Gladstone and Rosebery ministries.

Although Spencer was much occupied in affairs of state in London, he was able to devote time to his Northamptonshire duties. He was never happier than when at Althorp, where he was a model landlord. As a large landowner, his influence in county politics was considerable, not least as Lord-Lieutenant, and he used this to good effect in furthering the parliamentary career of his brother Robert from 1880. The majority of his estates were located in the south of the county, a traditional Conservative stronghold, and Spencer had to seek support from the Whig landowners in the North. However, he refused to bring any pressure to bear on his tenants in voting. With the growth of urbanization and changes in the franchise after 1884, the aristocracy displayed its resilience by associating itself with the growing civic pride of industrial towns from the 1880s, occupying high office and exchanging real power in the towns for social prestige.[459] It would be incorrect to interpret Spencer's election as councillor to the County Council, and his appointment as its first chairman, solely in this light. From the beginning he opposed the notion of political nominees, preferring those who, like himself, wished to advance the cause of efficient local government. Spencer's record of committee work over two decades is impressive.

The likelihood of a Spencer ministry in 1903 and 1904 if Balfour had resigned was widely accepted at the time. How successful a prime minister he would have made is worth considering. Arthur Balfour made a rare visit to the Lords in March 1905 and heard Spencer speaking in a debate. Afterwards he said to Gosse: 'What an amazing example Spencer is of what can be done in this country by a noble presence and a great hereditary position and fine personal record, assisted by no intellectual parts of any kind! It is really very remarkable. Such a sweet, and even such a beautiful character, and no ability at all.'[460]

---

[456] W.H.G. Armytage, *A.J. Mundella* (1951), p. 206.

[457] Spencer to T. E. Ellis, 19 July 1897, Ellis Papers, 1951. Spencer presented a memorandum to the cabinet in Oct. 1883 outlining a comprehensive reorganisation of education for Wales at all levels. F. R. Sandford, to Rendel, 25 Oct. 1883, Rendel Papers, 19455E 483a.

[458] EHJ, 13 Oct. 1905, Add. MS 48683 f. 81.

[459] D. Cannadine, *Lords and Landlords, The Aristocracy and the Towns 1774-1967* (1980), pp. 52-3.

[460] Gosse, Diary, House of Lords, MS. L32, 9 March 1905, f. 35.

Balfour's somewhat bitter judgment cannot be accepted as a statement of fact though Spencer himself was aware of his limitations as a politician as compared with Gladstone. He inspired few with his oratory. Ribblesdale, a Liberal Chief Whip for many years and a personal friend, described one of Spencer's speeches on Irish home rule in the Lords. 'Dignified in tone, it was unrelieved by historical or literary grace: there was very little personal about it ... One felt his speech to be collated laboriously from Blue Books and White Papers and the reports of Commissions and Committees. The speech shambled along and suffered, not only in delivery and arrangement, but from the tameness of vocabulary.'[461]

Spencer's reserved manner was sometimes mistaken for aloofness. There was some truth in this impression as Spencer himself admitted. The *Daily News* published a character sketch of him in 1892 describing his manner as 'amiable and courteous with perhaps a tinge of condescension which belongs more to the official representative of Royalty than to a Private Member of a Liberal Society'. Spencer's comment on this passage is illuminating. 'Granville once said that no one who had been a Viceroy altogether lost its effect on his manners. I always kept that before me, and tried to be natural, but there may be something in it.'[462] Nevertheless, he had a sense of fun which was rarely seen by his colleagues.[463] One such occasion, witnessed by Stuart Rendel, was after the Liberal success in the by-election at Southampton in 1888. 'Lord Spencer, after trying vainly to write "Great Liberal Victory" upon the post in front of this house, decorated his hatband with a placard announcing the majority and so carried the news along our road to Holmbury. In fact his delight is boyish and a pleasure to behold.'[464]

Though he never gained the highest office, Spencer was content to have served his party with a loyalty which both friends and foes alike acknowledged. His achievements were many and, like a true Whig, without being a leader of popular movements, he worked for changes which would benefit the country through constitutional means. George Leveson-Gower summed up Spencer in 1904 as 'si simple et tellement grand gentilhomme'.[465] As one newspaper stated after his death, 'No one recalls a bitter speech or an envious action in the whole of his career, lived, though it was, for the most part, in the fierce light of publicity.'[466] Perhaps Spencer's life is best summed up in C. P. Scott's tribute in the *Manchester Guardian*:

He was the type of men who seem made to be lieutenants, never chiefs-in-command: to command boundless respect, but never enthusiasm. Nor did he seek to lead. His ambition was to serve, and, perhaps that is the nobler, as it is the more easily and richly satisfied ambition.[467]

---

[461] Lord Ribblesdale, *Impressions and Memoirs* (1927), p. 187.
[462] Spencer to Lady Spencer, 6 June 1892, SP. No. **571**.
[463] See *The Red Earl*, i, p. 6.
[464] Rendel to A. C. Humphries-Owen, 25 May 1888, Glensevern Papers, 389.
[465] G. G. Leveson-Gower to Lord Monson, 19 June 1904, Monson Papers, MON 25/13/2/31.
[466] *Daily Chronicle*, 15 Aug. 1910, p. 4.
[467] *Manchester Guardian*, 15 Aug. 1910, p. 6.

# I

# LIBERAL DIVISIONS, 1885

*On 6 July 1885 Carnarvon, Lord-Lieutenant of Ireland in the Conservative govern-
ment, made an important statement on Irish policy in the House of Lords. He repudiated
coercion and called for a peaceful settlement of the outstanding problems between the
two countries. With a general election in prospect towards the end of the year, both
main parties were anxious to gain Parnell's support. In a speech on 24 August in
Dublin, Parnell reaffirmed the need for Irish national independence. Gladstone, whose
mind was also moving in this direction, saw his task as reconciling the differences within
the party if progress on the subject was to be made. His address to the electors of
Midlothian on 17 September was conciliatory towards Ireland, but on 10 November,
Parnell challenged him to make a more specific declaration: Gladstone declined. Fearing
that a large Liberal majority at the forthcoming election might lead to the shelving of a
home rule bill, in a speech on 21 November, Parnell directed the Irish in Britain to
vote against all Liberals and Radicals, with a few special exceptions. In the event, 335
Liberals were returned, 249 Conservatives and 89 Parnellites. Neither Liberals nor
Conservatives could govern without Parnell's support. Furthermore, the results from
Ireland clearly indicated that there was a strong wish for home rule. Lady Spencer, who
was with Gladstone in Edinburgh during the election campaign, wrote at the time to
her husband, 'Mr. Gladstone talked to me after dinner, and began on the subject of
Ireland. He thinks 80 Parnellites in Parliament necessitates some decision regarding
Ireland. He has not yet made up his mind what is to be done, but he leans to some
measure for giving Ireland her own Government.' (Lady Spencer to Lord Spencer, 22
November 1885, SP).*

*Spencer had remained at Althorp since the fall of Gladstone's government in June,
apart from making brief visits to Rosebery at Mentmore, the Duke of Grafton at
Euston, Wolverton in Dorset and the Prince of Wales at Sandringham. On 6 December, Gladstone invited Spencer and Rosebery to Hawarden to discuss Ireland. Accepting
the fact that some solution, though with guarantees to landlords, was inevitable, Spencer
agreed with Gladstone's private approach to Balfour on 15 December, offering to lend
support for a scheme of Irish home rule. The revelation of the 'Hawarden Kite' in the
national press two days later, purporting to be Gladstone's plans for an Irish settlement,
greatly shocked Spencer. His doubts on Gladstone's ability to form a government capable
of handling such plans were deepened after Hartington's visit to Althorp in late December, and on learning of Northbrook's discussions with Trevelyan and Campbell-Bannerman.*

*When Parliament reassembled on 21 January 1886, the Queen's Speech made clear
that Salisbury did not intend to introduce home rule. The government resigned and on
3 February, Gladstone became prime minister. Spencer considered the prospect of office
'very hateful'.*

**415**  LORD SPENCER TO LORD GRANVILLE[1]
*8 August 1885; Althorp, Northampton*
Gr. P, PRO 30/29/22A/5

We came here last Monday and feel odd and unsettled . . .

I went to see Mr. Gladstone and found him at home.[2]

I thought his voice decidedly better and Mrs. G. said that half of the congestion had gone. It is difficult to judge of a man's spirits when he can only whisper but like on several other occasions lately he did not seem at all lively but depressed as if absorbed in some idea.[3]

He spoke very gravely over the Irish question. He said that he considered the Central Council[4] idea dead, but that he was sure some Irish settlement would immediately be to the front when the new Parliament met.

He said that you and Derby[5] had a leaning to some plunging beyond the Central Council, and I said 'Well I am not disinclined to the same view' meaning that if any scheme were propounded once more though would perhaps be safer than that which gave a leverage for future agitation.

He scoffed at Grattan's Parliament.[6]

He seemed very vague.

I told him what Chamberlain had written,[7] and he said no doubt Parnell was anxious to get a plan adopted. I said I suppose by the Government. He replied, 'No, I think he would prefer us.'

I could not help seeing a docketted letter from O'Shea on the table which looked ominous of communications between that Arch intriguer and Mr. G.[8]

I said that I thought it would be very dangerous, if not impossible to formulate any plan before the General Election. He said Yes that no one should undertake such a responsibility.

I told him that I thought we ought not to throw ourselves into any great scheme, that we ought to try what generous reforms such as Local Government, abolition of the Lord Lieutenancy and change of the system of Boards in Dublin, together with a liberal policy on Education would do, that we did not know that Parnell would continue to hold the opinion of the Irish, that he had great difficulties before him, and that if we persevered in sound Liberal reforms we might win over a sufficient party in Ireland to be able to carry on without a Radical experiment.

In reply to something I said as to the Central Council, only leading up to greater demands, he replied, 'Yes, but that is the case with all reforms,' to which I said 'That may be, but not to give power to a very dangerous set of men.'

He said the dangerous character of the men did not affect him, for they were in the H. of Commons and they must be dealt with.

This makes me think the position very vague and uncomfortable.

He never said a word about his giving up public life.

He said that he did not think it usual or desirable to try and get a common platform. It must be left to the discretion of leaders to lay down policy, but he was going to see Hartington[9] yesterday and would give him all the ideas which he could.[10]

They will have an odd party on *The Sunbeam* packed like sardines.[11]

[1] Granville George Leveson-Gower, 2nd Earl Granville, Foreign Secretary, 1880-5.

[2] On 6 Aug.

[3] Gladstone noted in his Diary, 'Lord Spencer ... Dr. Semon 19th century treatment. A castor oil day.' Gladstone, Diary, 6 Aug. 1885.

[4] During 1885 both Parnell, leader of the Irish Nationalist Party, M.P., Cork City, 1880-91, and Joseph Chamberlain, M.P. Birmingham, 1876-1914 had put forward schemes for developing Irish local government. A central board was envisaged, with powers of direct taxation and legislation. In June, Chamberlain favoured a plan of national councils for all constituent parts of the United Kingdom to replace the central board scheme. C. H. D. Howard, 'Joseph Chamberlain, Parnell and the Irish "central board" scheme, 1884-5', *Irish Historical Studies*, viii, Sept. 1953, p. 355.

[5] Edward Henry Stanley, 15th Earl of Derby, Colonial Secretary, 1882-5. For Derby's views on home rule, see J. R. Vincent (ed.), *The Later Derby Diaries* (1981), pp. 25-6.

[6] Henry Grattan (1746-1820), barrister and Anglo-Irish Protestant, who led a movement which culminated in the securing of legislative independence for the Irish Parliament and the judicial system in 1782. The so-called 'Grattan's Parliament' was comparatively short-lived, surviving until the end of the century.

[7] 'By constantly raising our bids, we produce the impression that there is no limit to the concessions from Parliament, and accordingly all the parties concerned will wait to see if more may not be obtained ... I believe the result must tend to separation and to further agitation.' Chamberlain to Spencer, 26 July 1885, SP.

[8] Correspondence on Parnell's draft constitution for Ireland had been passing between Lord Richard Grosvenor, Liberal Chief Whip, Gladstone and Mrs. O'Shea, Parnell's mistress, during July and early August. Katharine O'Shea, *Charles Stewart Parnell* (1914), ii, pp. 23-4.

[9] Spencer Compton, Marquess of Hartington, Secretary of State for War, 1882-5.

[10] At the meeting on 7 Aug. Gladstone read out a memorandum, which included the following sentence. 'I cannot treat the people of Ireland as foes or aliens, or advise that less should be done for them than would in like circumstances be done for the inhabitants of any other portion of the U.K.' GP, Add. MS. 44769 f.218.

[11] Mr. and Mrs. Gladstone were the guests of Sir Thomas and Lady Brassey on their yacht during a visit to the Norwegian fjords, from 8 Aug. to 1 Sept.


## 416   LORD GRANVILLE TO LORD SPENCER

*14 August 1885; Walmer Castle, Deal*

I took the same view of Gladstone as you did.

My leaning to a stronger measure is merely comparative with the Chamberlain-Manning-Parnell scheme,[1] which seems at present to me to combine all disadvantages.

You seem to have talked great sense to him.

I wrote to Hartington the pith of the conversation I had with Gladstone, and he sent me an account of his,[2] which he will repeat to you.

... I am glad Hartington will speak before the end of the month.[3] It appears to me that our line should be to state our views, as our views, but not in opposition to the views of others. Chamberlain has done harm enough already.

When I heard some time ago of Dilke's mariage, I thought it foolish, but it now will be of use to him.[4]

I suppose you heard of Chamberlain asking Labouchere[5] what they said about Dilke. 'Oh, they all say that they are sorry it was not you.'

[1] On 25 May 1885, Sir Charles Dilke, then President of the Local Government Board, had sent Spencer a memorandum of a conversation with Cardinal Manning 'in which he told me that the Cardinal had seen some of the Irish Bishops including Archbishop Croke on their way to Rome, that the Cardinal had argued with them against Separation, that they had been convinced by him

and said that provided they got a scheme such as that propounded by Chamberlain and Parnell and would openly declare against a separate Parliament provided this scheme were carried and that they believed that Ireland would be pacified by this policy.' Spencer, Memorandum, 19 May 1885. No. **402**.

[2] Hartington to Granville, 8 Aug. Letter printed in Lord E. Fitzmaurice, *The Life of Second Earl Granville* (1906), ii, pp. 461-2.

[3] In his address at Waterfoot, Lancs. on 29 August, Hartington attacked Parnell, rejecting an alliance with him in order to attain office. *The Times*, 31 Aug. 1885, p. 8.

[4] News of intended divorce proceedings by Donald Crawford against his wife, citing Dilke as co-respondent, appeared in the press on 10 August. Dilke's engagement to Mrs. Mark Pattison was announced shortly afterwards.

[5] Henry Labouchere, an advanced Liberal, M.P., Northampton, since 1880.

**417   LORD SPENCER TO LORD LANSDOWNE[1]**
*16 August 1885; Bolton Abbey, Skipton*
Lansdowne Papers

I shall tell you what I can as to Politics and I can write now more freely than when in office.

I need not dwell on what the Papers and other correspondents have told you as to our exit from office.

At the time I felt very strongly that we ought to resign.

We had been time after time attacked by votes of confidence which though not carried had been supported by increasing majorities. Our Egyptian and foreign Policy had to my mind not been altogether successful, and there seemed little prospect of a change in our own attitude towards these two questions. We did not put into jeopardy any principle or action on which we placed importance, for the Tories could not reverse our policy. They could not go to war with Russia, they could not resume possession of the Soudan. On the other hand they could by adopting our lines of action strengthen the position of England by showing the practical agreement of parties on these important questions. It always strikes me that the great counterweight to the evil which our party system of Government creates is the almost invariable rule that continuity of Government is recognized.

The evil is shown by the cries of cowardice and want of Patriotism raised by the Opposition to the action of Government, these when repeated seriously endanger the position of the country. They make foreigners think for example that England will not fight and encourage a power with whom we are negotiating to resist even to the extent of going to war. They make us look hopelessly divided and weak in Parliament.

With a change of Government all this also changes. The Opposition turn into Government, they take up the same ground as their opponents, the country becomes united etc.

Of course there are and must be exceptions; most can be defended, but some turn out to be wrong. The Candahar retirement belongs to the first, the Transvaal probably, but not certainly, to the latter.[2]

Anyhow in our position there was no room for this. The Tories accepted our policy, and their freedom from attack enabled them to bring about settlements which were not easy to us with their vehement opposition.

We were able to show that when repeated opposition is made to Government, those who do this must become responsible for their action and take the consequences, however much they may dislike it. On all these grounds I still think we were right to go out.

As to Ireland I hold much the same view and though the way they have spoken has done a great deal of harm, we could not anticipate this, and I hope that permanent harm to the cause of Law and Order will not remain.

We had got (and as to this I ought perhaps to use the singular and say I) into hopeless antagonism with the Popular Party. They would not allow us to do anything without vehement opposition, I was abused and assailed in every national paper and press and though I had (I am sure) with me the bulk of loyal and sensible men, the violence of the Extreme party was not likely to moderate.

This was doing harm to the influence of the Crown, and bringing the Government of the country into constant collision with the people. Had there been a chance of long continuance in office this might have worn down but as no Government stays in for more than 5 or 6 years, the change could not have been brought about by me. Now the Irish are settling down again a bit to better relations with the Irish Government, and this is a gain.

I doubt whether our Government (had they remained in office or retaken office after defeat) would have carried any measure to take the place of the Crimes Act. Of course I should have gone as I was committed to some measure, but that would not have so much mattered, and the dropping of all Exceptional legislation has been now done with less party feeling than it would have been had we done it and the Tories opposed it as they certainly would have done.

I still think that a great mistake has been committed. The risk was too great, and I fear that if not at once before many years have gone by the necessity for some exceptional powers to uphold the Law will be proved. As it is now we shall have to bear with a great deal of crime without power of dealing with it effectually, and no exceptional legislation will be possible unless after a fresh outbreak of murders and crime.

If I am wrong I shall be very glad, and it will show that our Irish Policy has succeeded even quicker than I hoped it would.

Boycotting is what I fear most. It was barely kept in check with the powers which we had and which have now lapsed, and the Irish Press, though they denounce crime just now, advocate boycotting.

To keep order in a country with the cooperation of the people and their public opinion is what every Government should aim at, but to keep it by aid of an Association of men who represent only one party in the country is a dangerous thing. That is what the Irish Government will do if they now succeed. Whatever faults we had we kept order by our own forces, and in spite of this Association.

I am afraid that all recent events will greatly strengthen the National League and Parnell. There can be no doubt that if there was no actual compact, there was an understanding between Randolph and the Parnellites. The latter will throw their new friends over directly they see that they have got all they can out of them.

We are in a very unpleasant position as to Politics, not only as to Irish but as to other questions.

Each side is posing to catch the votes of the New Electorate, and are likely to outbid each other.

I have been so taken up with Irish work for the last three years that I find myself behind hand on general Politics but I begin to pick up the thread of what has been going on, and I do not like it.

I cannot agree with a great deal that the Radicals urge. At the same time I think it would be dangerous for moderate Liberals to break with Radicals. Whigs of old never agreed with their Radical colleagues on all their principles, and yet they went on together and the influence of each section made itself felt in the measures of a Liberal Government.

We who are moderate Liberals can do a great deal to check extreme views. It has not yet been shown that the Extreme men are dominant and the Moderate men in a hopeless minority. Possibly the New Electorate may reverse this but I doubt it.

When Mr. Gladstone leaves Public life a great change will occur. I am not sure that in foreign Policy the future Liberal Government would lose, but in Home Politics we should be in a great difficulty. Probably for a time we must be out of office so as to let parties shake down to practical ways of going on.

Just now we are entering upon something like Socialism and I do not at all like this e.g. the giving to Local bodies power to settle how Landlords deal with their land. This has already been done in Salisbury's Bill for Housing the Poor,[3] and the same principle of interference is in J. Collings' Bill for dealing with Charity Lands.[4] They want to go further and give Local bodies power to buy land to redistribute it to the Poor.

I do not like giving Public bodies these powers and I should like to draw the line between cases where public necessity as to Health and Morality arises and cases which affect distribution of property on which people differ widely.

On Irish questions we shall have Home Rule or something like it to face.

I wonder what your Canadian experience leads you to think on such a matter.

My own views are that we must give Ireland, even at risk of considerable difficulties, wide local Government such as County Boards but that we must at all events for the present keep clear of Central Boards which might assume the right to speak for the whole country. This would be very dangerous.

I would deal liberally with Ireland as to Education, reforming the Queen's Colleges and giving the R.C.s some secure claim for University Education. I would abolish the Viceroyalty, make a strong Irish Ministry, the First or Under Secretary to be generally ruling in Dublin. I would if possible reorganize the Boards in Dublin and put the Department which these Boards now govern more directly under a responsible Parliamentary Chief.

With these and other reforms we might still win over such a body of people in Ireland that an independent party in favour of Law and Order and the present Constitution would be formed and do battle with the Parnellites.

If we cannot do this we shall have to try the experiment of some form of Federal Government with Home Rule.

But I do not think the time yet come for this. It is much to be deprecated if we can do without it, but I do not see how we can for ever carry on as we are doing now, with a representative constitution in Ireland the great bulk of the Members being in direct hostility to the Government!

Many think the time has come for a radical change, that we have tried to win over the people to our English Constitution and Government and have failed so constantly that we must try new lines of Policy.

I think we are too impatient. We must give time to see what the enormous measures recently passed will do for the country.

I am not at all sure that the Parnellites elected next Autumn will hang together.

The Labourers won't pull with them and though these are a weak body in Ireland they may be enough to form a New party in alliance with Landlords of a Liberal type.

I should like to strike out an Irish Policy such as I sketched just now, do this boldly and liberally and see its effect before going into Home Rule. The danger is that the English and Scotch are so sick of the Irish in Parliament that they will press for some measure to get rid of them, and nowadays men do not look forward enough.

All this makes me very uneasy on Politics.

My pen has run on to dreadful length and I have written a long essay on Politics which will be very dull reading.

You look on calmly from Canada, and can compare Canadian institutions with our own and your views on the stage we are entering upon will be very interesting.

I won't go into the Irish Purchase Act.[5] I don't like the lengths to which it goes, but I am very glad that some Bill has been passed and I hope it will start Purchase and Sale of Land again in Ireland. It will in the North and if so the movement may spread, but to use your simile the Occupying Clauses of the Act of /81 got the most favourable terms of the Handicap, and though an enormous deal of weight has been taken off the Purchasing Clauses, I am not sure that the Race will be supplied with Runners by the new Teams.

We are enjoying a holiday.[6] I am greatly relieved by the removal of Irish responsibility but I miss the work very much.

I find however a great deal of trouble on my Estate. Last year was a very bad financial year for tenants and I shall have the lowest rent payments I have ever had excepting /81.

I am very hard up and hardly know what to do, but as I have had to change my Agent I must stay at home to look up my Estate management and possibly we shall be again in office in December.

I felt so sick of office that I longed to be out of Public life when we first came home, but I begin to take interest again and I cannot well turn back now having taken up my line of work in life.

I won't write on: forgive the length of this letter.

[1] Henry Charles Keith, 5th Marquess of Lansdowne, Governor-General of Canada since 1883. Resigned as Under-Secretary of State for India, over the Compensation for Disturbance Bill, 1880. Owned large estates in Co. Kerry and was the target of 'No Rent' campaign.

[2] Relieved by Gen. Sir Frederick Roberts in 1880, Candahar was evacuated in the following year. Transvaal was annexed by Britain in 1877 and given self-government under British suzerainty in 1881.

[3] In his first ministry Salisbury dealt with a number of measures left outstanding. The housing of the poor was one of his particular concerns and the Housing of the Working Classes Bill received the royal assent on 12 Aug. 1885.

[4] Jesse Collings, Radical M.P., Ipswich, since 1880, champion of the cause of creating a peasant proprietary, had initiated a measure in Dec. 1884 and again in March 1885 entitled The Peasant Proprietary and Acquisition of Land by Occupiers Bill. See J. Collings and J. L. Green, *The Life of the Right Hon. Jesse Collings* (1920), pp. 174-7.

[5] The Irish Land Purchase Bill, introduced in the House of Lords by Edward Gibson, 1st Lord Ashbourne, Lord Chancellor of Ireland, on 17 July 1885, greatly extended the system of land purchase. Spencer refused Gibson's request to disclose details of the proposed Liberal Land Purchase Bill of the late government. Spencer to Gibson, 1 July 1885, Ashbourne Papers, B. 140/5.

[6] A shooting party at Bolton Abbey and Danby, Yorkshire, from 15 to 31 Aug.

## 418 LORD SPENCER TO W. E. GLADSTONE

*19 September 1885; Althorp, Northampton*
GP, Add. MS. 44312 ff. 188-9

We have been away from home this week, but I got your letter on Thursday and was exceedingly obliged to you for it.[1]

I have today read with the deepest interest your Address.[2]

I like it very much and think that you have now put every one of our side who are engaged in Election work in a satisfactory position.

You do not shut out those who do not agree with Chamberlain, and you give him and his friends opportunity for asserting any of their views which do not carry all the party with them.

I am not surprised at your anxiety about Ireland,[3] and I very heartily agree in your desire that the question should be approached with moderation and without prejudice.

We cannot be sure what may occur there between this and the meeting of Parliament. I trust that the position may not be aggravated by such serious an outbreak of intimidation as may call for interference.

I need not say how glad I am to think that you are at the head of our party during the coming contest, and trust you will guide us long after the meeting of the new Parliament.

We have been in a hot Tory Camp, H. Chaplin's.[4] It was amusing to hear their views about your Address. They could not denounce it as far as I could learn.[5]

[1] Enclosing a copy of a letter to Kimberley announcing his (Gladstone's) intention to stand for re-election. Gladstone to Spencer, 15 Sept. 1885, SP.

[2] Gladstone's address to the electors of Midlothian was published on 17 Sept.

[3] In his letter of 15 Sept. to Spencer, Gladstone stated, 'Ireland has been in my own mind by far the greatest difficulty. I fear lest a new Irish question open, after the Dissolution, like a chasm under our feet. Now that the Central Board scheme is extinct, I cannot pretend to say I see my way.' SP.

[4] Lord and Lady Spencer were at Blankney Hall, Lincolnshire, from 14 to 19 Sept. as guests of Henry Chaplin, Conservative M.P., Mid Lincolnshire, 1868-85, and for Sleaford division, Lincolnshire, 1885-1906; Chancellor of Duchy of Lancaster in Salisbury's 1885-6 government. Other guests included Hartington and Randolph Churchill.

[5] Though Hartington told Spencer that 'he was afraid that the Irish party might lead to hopes and anticipations on the Parnellite part which could be dangerous'. Spencer to Granville, 19 Sept. 1885, Gr. P, PRO 30/29/22A/5.

**419** LORD SPENCER TO C. BOYLE[1]
*20 September, 1885; Althorp, Northampton*[2]

I think Mr. Gladstone's Manifesto very good and it will clear the air and support those who do not wish to commit themselves to Municipal Socialism. He is enigmatical about Ireland, but it is well that he is so just now with his inclinations. Suppose we could

1. Get security for the Landlords
2. Prevent a Civil War with Ulster
3. Make the Irish nation our friends, not enemies,

it would be worth while giving them Home Rule, but I don't see my way to the 3 conditions or any of them being secured. Yet I sometimes despair of conciliating the Irish on other lines, and it is desperate work going on as we have been for the last 5 years. I cannot shut out these ideas from my mind.

[1] Courtenay Boyle, private secretary to Spencer, 1882-5; Assistant Secretary, Local Government Board, 1885-6.
[2] Copy, SP.

**420** LORD SPENCER TO LORD HARTINGTON
*3 October 1885; Mentmore, Leighton Buzzard*
CP, 340. 1813

I came here for a night en route for Norfolk.[1]

I have had a cold and thought it would be worse by going to London or I might have gone up today to see you and Harcourt.[2]

I do not think Rosebery[3] is keen about the Municipal authorities buying land, but thinks it better to get this as an insurance against worse things.

I don't like this method of increasing proprietors and occupiers of land, though I am very keen that the object should be attained. I should not like to commit myself to Chamberlain's proposal though I should certainly back up the object he has in view.[4]

I thought Harcourt's Utopian view of every cottager owning his home and garden a great mistake.[5] It cannot be done however good it may look in a dream.

If this is so surely it is wrong to dangle before the labourers this idea. It never will be carried out, and then they will turn on those who deluded them.

What labourer has the money to buy his cottage and bit of land. Are the rates to pay? I think the ratepayers would kick at supplementing the rents of cottage tenants.

Harcourt did not commit himself to a plan but he certainly held out hopes to the labourers which are illusory.

I will in a day or so send you some papers about Free Education. I expect that will have to come on account of the difficulty of enforcing fines for non-attendance. I wish we could leave it alone, but it is not so bad as the Land proposals to my mind.

Pray don't go at Chamberlain direct.

Speak out your mind when clear on any question but without reference to him. I don't comprehend his position unless he wishes to break with the Moderates altogether.

It is very aggravating to read his Speeches very often, but it would be a misfortune if he breaks away from moderate men.

[1] Spencer had writen to Rosebery, 'May I come to you for a night? I want to talk on Politics. My Irish moss and rust are gradually wearing away and I want to compare notes with you.' Spencer to Rosebery, 1 Oct. 1885, RP, 10062 f. 12.

[2] Sir William Vernon Harcourt, Liberal M.P., Derby, Home Secretary, 1880-5.

[3] Archibald Philip, 5th Earl of Rosebery, Lord Privy Seal, 1885.

[4] From Jan 1885, Chamberlain developed a programme of reforms which included the conferment on local authorities of powers for the compulsory purchase of land to create smallholdings, a proposal popularly known as 'three acres and a cow'. See, for example, Chamberlain's speech at Warrington on 8 Sept. C. H. D. Howard, 'Joseph Chamberlain and the "Unauthorized Programme",' English Historical Review, xlv (1950), pp. 482-5.

[5] In a speech to the Dorset Liberals at Blandford on 28 September. See The Times, 29 Sept. 1885, p. 10.

## 421  C. R. SPENCER TO LADY SPENCER

*9 October 1885; Northampton*

I came down yesterday to Becke's,[1] and drove over to Kingsthorpe. He and Manfield[2] came to the meeting,[3] and we were paraded round the whole village preceded by a Voluntary Band, and a Radical banner.

It was very exciting and the tent was very full, about 600 people. It was all decorated, and there were garlands, and the platform was hung with red, and there were nosegays on the table, one large one being given to me. The enthusiasm was very inspiring, and the audience excellent.

Spoke for ½ an hour, and made a radical speech, some of it you would not like I fancy.[4] Becke was very pleased, and when I sat down Walker[5] got up and shook me by the hand, and thanked me, which was nice.

3 Tories held up their hands against me and the resolution about me was carried with much shouting and cheering. The Radicals all behaved too beautifully, and the most violent of them all, one Green who wrote a letter Spencer saw full of crotchets, made an excellent speech for me. An old man walked all the way from Hackleton four miles the other side of the town to hear me. It was almost too exciting, and I was nearly collapsing in the middle, as my voice nearly went from the heat, and having to shout so. I wish you could have been there.

[1] John Becke, solicitor and Robert Spencer's election agent.

[2] Moses Philip Manfield, one of the largest shoe manufacturers in Northampton and a member of the Town Council since 1866. A Radical, Manfield had healed the rift between the left and right wings of the town's Liberals by inviting Labouchere to accept the party's nomination in the 1880 election. See E. Royle, 'Charles Bradlaugh, Free Thought and Northampton', in Northamptonshire Past and Present, vii, no. 3 (1980), p. 148.

[3] A Mid Northamptonshire election meeting at Kingsthorpe on 8 Oct.

[4] In his speech, Spencer advocated, among other reforms, the abolition of undue restrictions on land, and the alteration of procedure in the Commons. NH, 10 Oct. 1885, p. 5.

[5] Walter Walker, solicitor, Northampton, and Clerk to the Hardingstone Local Board.

## 422  LORD SPENCER TO C. R. SPENCER
*21 October 1885; Euston Hall, Thetford*

I am trying to work up my Speech at Saffron Walden.[1]

Now I have begun I have got asked for others, first Dorchester,[2] now Fowler has asked me to Cambridge,[3] but I shall first see how I get on at these other meetings.

[1] Edward Hamilton, formerly Gladstone's principal private secretary, had asked Lord Spencer to speak on behalf of a friend, Herbert Gardner, who was contesting Saffron Walden. Spencer spoke in the constituency on 28 Oct. *The Times*, 29 Oct. 1885, p. 10. Gardner was elected and represented the division until his retirement in 1895.

[2] Spencer addressed the Dorset Liberals, mainly on the topics of land reform and free education, at Dorchester on 3 Nov.

[3] W. Fowler to Spencer, 18 Oct. 1885, SP. Spencer did not accept the Cambridge invitation.

## 423  LORD LANSDOWNE TO LORD SPENCER
*17 November 1885; Ottawa*

I owe you a letter for your long and interesting one of the 16th of August.[1] It was a great pleasure to me not only to know that my notes about Education had been of use to you, but also to read your review of the political situation.

It has not become more satisfactory since you wrote to me, and I think your anticipations in regard to the effects of the abandonment of coercive legislation have every chance of being realized. There are no doubt many plausible arguments in favour of the course which you adopted in giving up office, but I am afraid that the 'historian' whose verdict we always look forward to will say that you allowed yourselves to be driven out by the Tories because you knew that disruption from within was inevitable.

I agree with most of what you say as to the future of Ireland. I think I detect in your opinions too much of that very impatience and readiness to try experiments which you deprecate. You seem to contemplate the immediate concessions 'at the risk of considerable difficulties' of 'wide local government, such as County Boards', with a sort of understanding (among ourselves) that if this does not satisfy the people 'we shall have to try the experiment of some form of Federal Government with Home Rule'. If the powders don't produce an immediate cure, try the pills, and if the gout doesn't go within a fortnight cut the patient's leg off. The argument proceeds on the assumption—utterly fallacious, in politics as in 'therapeutics'—that there is a specific and infallible remedy for every disease, and that if you go on trying long enough you are sure to hit upon the right nostrum.

Is it not better to look round thoroughly, to redress all demonstrated grievances, and when you are able to lay your hand upon your heart and to say that no Irish individual or corporation labours under any genuine injustice or disability as compared with British individuals and corporations, to try what, not a few months, but a generation of firm and *steady* government will do for the country? That experiment has never been tried. We have tried concessions of all sorts, repression in many forms, the legislation of one year has undone that of its predecessor, and yet we are surprised that the country has not thriven under a treatment which was I believe predestined to fail, but which under no conceivable circumstances could have succeeded while we were still pouring our remedies down our patient's throat.

[1] See No. 417.

### 424  LADY SPENCER TO LORD SPENCER
*20 November 1885; Dalmeny Park, Edinburgh*[1]

I do not think any good can come in discussing Ireland with Mr. G. just now, unless you can bring a batch of facts and prove your case.[2] He is very anxious about Ireland, and the idea of the non-payment of rents seems to stagger him rather. He wants proofs of this. Do you think you can find out about it, and whether there have been any actual cases of refusal to pay rent? I think if it is so, it would weigh much with Mr. G. and he would then see more clearly the character of the National League, and the difficulty of dealing and treating with such men.

I dined tête à trois with Mr. and Mrs. Gladstone last night. He was very agreeable, talked chiefly about Plate China and old shops in London. In the evening, we took our books and newspapers. I need not say Mr. G. did not take the latter. He quite scorned the idea of *The Times* when I suggested it to him![3] I said you are not like Lady A.[4] in that respect. No! he said, she is a regular Cockney! How I wish he would read the papers a little more and know the other side of the case as well!

Hannah[5] took me on a charming drive yesterday. How pretty the views are. We went to Queen's Ferry and saw the New Bridge building.[6]

[1] Lady Spencer was at Dalmeny, Rosebery's home, from 17 to 24 Nov. where Gladstone also was staying during his Midlothian election campaign.
[2] Spencer was not anxious to join the party, as 'I do not feel that I see my way clearly enough to be of any use re Ireland.' Spencer to Lady Spencer, 19 Nov. 1885, SP.
[3] At dinner, Gladstone had said that 'if he wanted real recreation, he read Walter Scott. His 2 favourites *The Bride of Lammermoor* and *Kenilworth*.' Lady Spencer, Diary, 20 Nov. 1885, SP.
[4] Marion Elizabeth, widow of 1st Marquess of Ailesbury.
[5] Rosebery's wife, daughter of Baron Meyer de Rothschild, banker.
[6] The Forth Bridge was opened on 4 March 1890.

### 425  LADY SPENCER TO LORD SPENCER
*21 November 1885; Dalmeny Park, Edinburgh*

Your letter just expresses what I feel, *despair* but I think if *facts* can be placed before him regarding the state of the Country some good might be obtained.[1]

The House is singularly cold and after Sandringham which was too hot, the contrast is great. Last night Lord Young[2] and wife dined here. He sat near to me, he was very full of you, and spoke with great satisfaction, of the wave of disgust which was felt by all parties at the way you were treated by Sir M. Beach and Randolph.[3]

Poor Mrs. G. is in such an awful fret of anxiety over the elections that it is almost painful, and she jumps down Hannah's throat if she ventures to say she has heard that the Majority may only be 10 or 20! Altogether it will be a good thing when the elections are over...

Mr. G. does not prepare his speech at all! and Mrs. G. told me he would probably make a few notes this morning! just in the order, and on the subjects he wishes to mention. How delightful to have so little trouble about a speech in which all England, Scotland and Ireland depend so greatly.[4]

[1] In a speech at Edinburgh on 9 Nov., Gladstone warned of the need to return to Parliament 'a party totally independent of the Irish vote'. Spencer commented, 'Mr. G. evidently is thinking of nothing but the Political effect of Ireland without taking the peace of the country into account. ... Such a view as Mr. G.'s fills me with despair for I feel that he either is blind or does not know the real state of the country, and of the goings on of the Parnellites.' Spencer to Lady Spencer, 20 Nov. 1885, SP.

[2] Lord George Young, Scottish High Court judge.

[3] On the Maamtrasna debate in the Commons 17 July 1885. See No. **412**. Sir Michael Hicks Beach, M.P., E. Gloucestershire, 1864–85, and Chief Secretary for Ireland, 1874–8; Lord Randolph Churchill, M.P., Woodstock, 1874–85.

[4] Gladstone delivered his speech later that day at Dalkeith. Lady Spencer recorded in her diary: 'Drove to the Corn Exchange, where 3,000 people were assembled. Mr. Gladstone spoke for over an hour—a fair speech, but I fear it will alarm the weak-kneed Liberals.' 21 Nov. 1885, SP.

**426   LORD SPENCER TO LORD GRANVILLE**
*22 November 1885; Althorp, Northampton*
Gr. P, PRO 30/29/22A/5

I hear from Dalmeny that Mr. G. is in a very optimistic mood re Ireland. I sent him a most moderate letter from Naish[1] who gave his view about the state of the country and only indirectly alluded to the prospect of Ireland being ruled by the Parnellites which he said made all those bound up with the country say God help them.

This it was I suppose which roused Mr. G. who told Lady S. that the letter was evidently that of a man who had not been in the H. of C. but was steeped in the Castle atmosphere and had not been knocked about.[2]

He was bitten by some letter of Powerscourt's who is a fool with glimmerings of Liberal sense.[3] The only thing which staggered Mr. G. was the idea that rent was not being paid.

He was delighted at Gibson ruling Ireland: why I cannot think for it can hardly be called a success.[4]

He rather wanted me to come up to see him, but it would have been immensely inconvenient just now, and to tell the honest truth I think more harm than good would come of a talk about Ireland.

I dread the discussion which must precede the formation of a Government on this question.

I am a little afraid that as Boroughs come first and we are likely to lose ground there, that this may give the hint to other constituencies and that if it once begins our majority will go down like a pack of cards.

It will be a political disaster but personally how agreeable.

Salisbury was very affable at Sandringham,[5] very gloomy about Ireland. He plainly told me that he himself thought that strong measures would be necessary but that they were almost impossible with Parliament. He did not see how guarantees could be got. He talked of our Rosewater method of Government being unsuitable to Ireland, and our Government by consent not suiting either [sic] that country.

He admitted that we would not have put down the National League and that they could not either.

Lady Salisbury said that they would meet Parliament unless knocked into a Cocked Hat.

[1] John Naish, Lord Chancellor of Ireland in Gladstone's government, May–June 1885. Appointed Lord Justice of Appeal in Aug. that year.

[2] Lady Spencer to Spencer, 19 Nov. 1885, SP.

[3] Mervyn, 7th Viscount Powerscourt. Irish Representative Peer, 1865–1904. Created a Peer of the United Kingdom as Baron Powerscourt of Powerscourt, Co. Wicklow, 1885. Hartington had sent two of Powerscourt's letters to Gladstone on 15 Nov. GP, Add. MS. 44148 ff. 152-3. Gladstone called them 'noteworthy signs'. Gladstone to Hartington, 18 Nov. 1885, CP, 340, 1833.

[4] For Gibson's equivocal attitude to home rule, see A. B. Cooke and A. P. W. Malcolmson, *The Ashbourne Papers 1869–1913* (1974), p. xvi.

[5] The Spencers joined a shooting party at Sandringham on 9 Nov. staying until 16 Nov. Lord and Lady Salisbury arrived on 14 Nov.

**427   LORD SPENCER TO W. E. GLADSTONE**
*2 December 1885; Althorp, Northampton*
GP, Add. MS. 44312 ff. 198-201

I did not write to congratulate you on your splendid majority[1] as I knew you would believe how delighted Lady Spencer and I were without having the trouble to read an additional letter, but I must do so now when I am writing for another purpose.

I want to tell you though I fear I have nothing definite to say about Irish proposals, I am at your service any day next week if you would like me to run down to Hawarden ...

We are in great delight over my brother's large victory.[2] He deserves great credit for the hard work he has done, and done so well. The way in which he has conducted the contest has secured this large majority.

I am disappointed at the result of the County Elections. I fully expected that the newly enfranchised Voters would solidly vote for the party which gave them their votes: but the Elections seem to go very evenly in Agricultural Districts.

Out of 9,826 Votes given here only 33 were bad ones which speaks well for the intelligence of the Labourers.

Out of 11,306 Voters 1,480 did not vote, not I imagine a large number; in several villages near here all Electors voted.

I look with dismay at the Political prospects ...

The Irish Elections are dreadful. Not one Liberal! Poor Walker even defeated! I thought at all events he would have got in.[3]

[1] Gladstone received 7879 votes and his Conservative opponent, C. Dalrymple, 3248.

[2] Spencer had heard of his brother's victory earlier in the day. Lady Spencer noted, 'The Poll was declared about one o'clock. We got a telegram from Becke saying "All right, will send particulars later." and soon afterwards came another, saying Bobby was in by a majority of 1099, the numbers polled being Spencer 5446 and Phipps 4347.' Lady Spencer, Diary, 2 Dec. 1885, SP. Pickering Phipps, the brewer, had represented South Northamptonshire since 1881.

[3] Samuel Walker, formerly Solicitor-General for Ireland, was defeated at Londonderry North by H. L. Mulholland.


## 428   W. E. GLADSTONE TO LORD SPENCER
*6 December 1885; Hawarden Castle, Chester*

I am very sorry for what has happened but acting on your letter which spoke of any day next week, I had invited Rosebery for Wednesday and there is so much difficulty for me (physical as well as otherwise) in proceeding by single threads of conversation that I hope you can manage to put off your man and come then. Granville who is here today will come back from Chatsworth on Wednesday if he finds it can be of use.


## 429   LORD GRANVILLE TO LORD SPENCER
*6 December 1885; Hawarden Castle, Chester*

The situation is most extraordinary. G, will not abandon the hope (which appears to me to be lost) of being in a majority over Tories and Parnellites.[1]

He is very bilious and all for a revolution anyhow. This is contrary to the opinion of all I have heard on the subject.

I am not clear that it is not better being a little under, than a little above the requisite number.

I am pressed to meet you here but I must go to Chatsworth tomorrow, even if I come back for a night.[2] Please telegraph to Chatsworth when you come.

India is impossible now. I do not see why you should not go abroad for a *month*, if you start at once.[3]

P.S. Gladstone does not like your going away for a month even.

[1] This was reflected in Gladstone's address to the electors of Midlothian, published in *The Times*, 4 Dec. 1885, p. 7.

[2] Granville arrived at Hawarden on 5 Dec. and left for Chatsworth on 7 Dec. by the 8.10 a.m. train.

[3] Spencer asked Gladstone on 2 Dec. if it would be feasible for him to go to India. GP, Add. MS. 44312 f. 198.


## 430   LORD SPENCER TO LADY SPENCER
*8 December 1885; Hawarden Castle, Chester*

I made an excellent but cold journey yesterday.[1]

I arrived about 7.30 and found the Duke, Egerton and Eddy[2] in slippers in the drawing room ...

The Granvilles etc. and a heap of relations made up 26 to dinner.[3] I had long talks with Granville and Hartington last night and this morning and arrived here about 5.30 to find Rosebery.[4]

We had already a long talk, not to great purpose, but Mr. G. is red hot on Ireland but I am glad to say sees the difficulties.

[1] Spencer travelled from Althorp to Chatsworth via Manchester on 7 Dec. staying the night.

[2] William, 7th Duke of Devonshire, Admiral the Hon. Francis Egerton, his son-in-law, and Lord Edward Cavendish, Hartington's younger brother, M.P., Derbyshire West, 1885–91.

[3] The *Daily News* commented the following day, 'The announcement that the Duke of Devonshire is this week entertaining a large party at Chatsworth has not in itself any political import. ... The facts that Lord Hartington is at Chatsworth and that Lord Granville has just come from Hawarden are, however, circumstances worth noting.' *Daily News*, 9 Dec. 1885, p. 4.

[4] Rosebery arrived at Hawarden from London earlier that day. Hartington was unable to accompany Spencer as he was dining with the Prince of Wales in Lincolnshire. Granville also decided not to return as 'we all thought that my leaving Hawarden, rushing to Chatsworth, and then back again to Hawarden, would give rise to some foolish talk'. Granville to Gladstone, 8 Dec. 1885, GP, Add. MS. 44178 f. 269 and Ramm, ii, p. 414.

## 431   LORD SPENCER TO LADY SPENCER

*9 December 1885; Hawarden Castle, Chester*

I have just come in from a walk with Mr. G. He is very hoarse, I am afraid as hoarse as he was in London.

Rosebery has gone[1] and we have had tremendous talks.

I dread the political prospect more than ever.

Wolverton[2] comes tomorrow but I shall miss him. I shall come by the first morning train getting to Althorp Station about 1.

[1] Rosebery left shortly after noon for The Durdans, his house at Epsom, before returning to Scotland.

[2] George Grenfell, 2nd Baron Wolverton, Paymaster-General in Gladstone's previous ministry.

## 432   LORD SPENCER TO LORD GRANVILLE

*17 December 1885; Althorp, Northampton*

Gr. P., PRO 30/29/22A/5

Since we parted I have seen several important people besides Mr. W. E. G. and Rosebery.

I am much impressed and oppressed by the gravity of the position of the Irish question. Northbrook came here for Sunday and we had a very thorough discussion. He admitted that there was considerable force in my plea for a large measure, but he was very strong on the necessity of the greatest caution in procedure. ...

I was in London on Tuesday[1] and Goschen[2] sent to see me. I had a very long talk. I was very reticent as to what I knew of Mr. Gladstone's views, saying only that I knew that Mr. G. would like the Tories to settle it and that if they proposed a sufficient measure he would support them: but I spoke very freely my own views.

I perhaps put the case for a big measure more strongly than I ought. At least I argued that way and did not perhaps show how difficult I thought all the guarantees were.

What I carried away from $1\frac{1}{2}$ hours conversation was that Goschen admitted a good deal but felt tremendously the difficulty of yielding to a Pack of people like Parnell and his crew. He also laid immense stress on the difficulties of the Liberal party who including Mr. G. had fought the Election on the cry that a big Liberal majority must be got to render Mr. G. independent of Parnell. The party he thought were strongly committed to an anti Irish cry, and he dreaded the effect of the announcement of a big measure from Mr. G.

He took the same view as to Hartington's position as Northbrook. He seemed to know something about Government intentions or at all events Carnarvon's, and I fancy that Carnarvon agrees with my view. He considers things hopeless without some big scheme.

Goschen was very strong against Mr. G. taking a lead at first on the subject. He wants the Government to have time to show them Land and Parnell too. He said that the Tories would not bring in a big measure unless they knew that moderate Liberals would back them. They would not do it on the Tory Democrat lines. That would wreck their party. The only chance would be if they knew that the moderate Liberals would support them.

I fancy that he (Goschen) might go that way, but he is evidently balancing in his view, hating as we all must the idea of concession after all that has been said of the Tory alliance with Parnell etc. It is not clear however that he might not declare against the Government policy if he thought it went too far.

I am in despair at Herbert Gladstone's letter to that miserable Artist. Writen by him and from Hawarden it has set every rumour afloat. What too is the history of the *Standard* announcement today?[3] It oddly enough has in it one of Mr. G.'s oddest ideas for guarantees, viz. the nomination principle. How could they have got this. Is it a pure shot?

I am trying to see Campbell-Bannerman on whose judgment I much rely. I hear he is for a big measure. He writes to impress the necessity of doing nothing without feeling the pulse of our party. He seems to think that it may be, since the Elections, very anti Irish. All this points to the utmost care in any movement.

I trust that Mr. Gladstone will not open any communications with Parnell until he knows how we stand among the Leaders of the party and if possible among the rank and file on the question. The question involves such big national interests and also the honour of our leading Politicians who may by a false move lay themselves open to the accusation of bidding for the Irish vote, that I begin to lean to some attempt to bring about an understanding with the Tories. If anything like a fair basis could be hit upon, then negotiations might be opened with the Parnellites without sacrificing any man's political honour.

I get letters from Ireland in despair at the state of the country re Law and Order and also as to Political prospects. The difficulties of settling the question certainly increase on facing it.

In one way my talk with Goschen did not leave me so alarmed as I expected. He evidently was ready to discuss and consider the subject and saw the difficulties of remaining on the moderate lines which Hartington and I have hitherto advocated. I fancy that he was startled at my view. No wonder!

[1] 15 Dec.

[2] George Joachim Goschen, recently elected for Edinburgh East as an Independent Liberal. He had served in the Russell and Palmerston administrations and was President of the Poor Law Board, 1868–71 and First Lord of the Admiralty, 1871–4 under Gladstone. Goschen wrote to Hartington on 7 Dec. suggesting that Gladstone should be asked to explain his Irish policy before defeating the Salisbury government. A. D. Elliot, *Life of Lord Goschen* (1911), i, p. 318. In Jan. 1887, he accepted Salisbury's offer of the Chancellorship of the Exchequer.

[3] On 17 Dec. the *Standard* printed what purported to be Gladstone's proposals for dealing with the home rule question on taking office. These arose from a series of interviews given by his son, Herbert, M.P., Leeds West, 1885–1910, to the press on the previous day. Gladstone telegraphed to the Central News Agency denying their accuracy and stating that they were published without his knowledge or authority. For the background to the so-called 'Hawarden Kite', see H. Gladstone, *After Thirty Years* (1928), pp. 306–14.

**433**  LORD SPENCER TO C. BOYLE
*17 December 1885; Althorp*[1]

I cannot go with my views, but I am in a most anxious state. I am convinced that our old methods are useless and hopeless. The question is what can be done. I am, as you are, dead against simple repression. Can we take the other alternative with proper guarantees? The difficulties of this course increase as they are faced, and the idea of giving the reins to Parnell and Co. even for a time sticks in my nostrils, but the emergency is tremendous. I never felt so anxious about the line to take. Events may help us. I lean at present to some understanding with the Tories, and if a basis can be agreed on then [sic] to negotiate with Parnell, but it needs a more experienced and skilful political guide than I am to decide on how to drive the coach.

Not only are there all the questions affecting the future of Great Britain and Ireland itself, but there are questions affecting the character of our Public men. We can find now no course which is in theory perfect. Everything must be good comparatively with the present state of things and what they will, if left alone, develop into. The line taken by the Tories about Coercion and their semi alliance with the Parnellites, the new power of the League, the Elections, all have altered the situations since July. I have always been smothering a feeling that some Home Rule would have to be given, but I feel that I have nothing left to smother it with.

This is but a sketch of what I am thinking about. I am not committed, and the difficulties are such that I may have to come back to the old lines, but then I despair of the future. We shall then really have to rule by force, and you know what that is, and how impossible it is to get continuity in such a policy.

[1] Copy, SP.

**434** LORD NORTHBROOK TO LORD SPENCER
*17 December 1885; Chatsworth, Chesterfield*

I have had as you may suppose long talks to Hartington and William Harcourt on the situation.[1] Both are as gloomy as is possible.[2] Harcourt expects a strike against rent and unless Parnell gets his will the secession of his party to Dublin and his setting up of a National Convention there.

You will see E. Jenkinson's letter to Mr. G. which is to go to you from Granville by Mr. G.'s wishes.[3] Jenkinson has expressed, rather more fully than he did in conversation with me, and I believe also with you, his opinion that the only way out of the difficulty is to concede Home Rule very widely, in the trust that a party would be formed in the Irish Parliament to support the Union (or rather against total separation) which would keep the Extremists in check.

But the answer to this is what reasonable probability is there of such a party? It is admitted that the Irish National League and Irish Parliamentary party are influenced and controlled by the Clan-na-Gael and the I.R.B., the avowed object of both of which secret societies is to establish an Irish Republic by force.

What is the most likely result of giving Home Rule? That this bond should be dissolved, or that the concession would be used as a platform for further demands and lead either to separation, or to a fight to prevent it, and a fight for which our action would have strengthened our opponents.

Pushing all the probabilities home, the question seems to be between accepting Separation or refusing Home Rule, with all the consequences of having to govern Ireland absolutely.

The alternatives are simply appalling.

Hartington has argued everything out very calmly and fully. He is greatly mystified with the announcement of Mr. G.'s views in today's *Standard*, which agrees so much with your account of them that we can hardly doubt their authority. Hartington had no reason to suppose that Mr. G. intended to make any such announcement, and indeed has had no communication with him upon Irish affairs for some time.

I hear that Chamberlain is against concession. Possibly he will say so as he will speak somewhere tonight.

I am inclined to think Mr. G. has taken some steps to sound the Parnellites as to what they would accept. Do you know? I fear that he still thinks conciliation will win over the Irish.

It is just possible something will happen to clear the situation. If not, and if the *Standard* paragraph is not denied, and if Mr. G. has made up his mind to take action in that direction when Parliament meets my opinion is that he will not be followed by the Party or by the Country.

My impression is that the feeling in the Country among the Liberals is against concession to Parnell, and that even Mr. G. cannot turn it.

We examined your sine quâ non, that the landlords should have some guarantee, and cannot see what guarantee can be given them. Harcourt said 'When the Landlords are cleared out, there may be a chance of a settlement,' but I fancy more as a flash which came over his acute intellect than as intending to agree to sacrifice them.

Hartington is going to remain quiet. He has writen to Mr. G. to ask what his views now are.

My opinion is that Mr. G. as leader of the Party ought not to have gone as far as he has without full consultation with Hartington.

¹ Thomas George Baring, 1st Earl of Northbrook, First Lord of the Admiralty, 1880-5, visited Althorp on 13 Dec. There, it was agreed that when Northbrook went to Chatsworth, he would not tell Harcourt of the Althorp deliberations.

² Carlingford, Lord President in Gladstone's previous ministry, informed his brother from San Remo, 'I have had a long and interesting letter from Northbrook who had just been at Chatsworth. Evidently Mr. G.'s action is greatly condemned.' Carlingford to Lord Clermont, 28 Dec. 1885, Strachie Papers, H. 338 C. 3/686.

³ Edward George Jenkinson, formerly Spencer's asistant private secretary, Dublin Castle, and since 1884, Assistant Under-Secretary, with responsibility for Police and Crime in Ireland, wrote on 12 Dec. Hartington had also received a copy of the letter, Gladstone to Hartington, 15 Dec. 1885, CP, 340.1850. Gladstone replied to Jenkinson that he agreed 'very emphatically, in what appear to be the leading propositions of your letter'. 12 Dec. 1885, GP, Add. MS. 44493 f. 212 (copy). Jenkinson called on Northbrook on 17 Dec. and discussed home rule at length. See Northbrook to Spencer, 18 Dec. 1885, SP. and Jenkinson to Spencer, 20 Dec. 1885, SP.


**435** LORD SPENCER TO W. E. GLADSTONE
*18 December 1885; Althorp, Northampton*
GP, Add. MS. 44312 ff. 205-7

I do not know that I should have written at all to you about the *Standard* article of yesterday or even about the *Pall Mall* statement of last night¹ were it not that I had on the shortest notice to send a reply to a fishing Telegram from the Central News.

Luckily a friend coming from London brought the *Pall Mall*, so I was able to see what was said and what was more important your Telegram about the *Standard*.

I thought it necessary to reply, and I could clearly state that 'No scheme of Home Rule for Ireland had received my approval.'²

I enclose the Telegram I got.³

The mischief of these reports upon opinions like yours is very great, for even sensible men cannot throw off their belief in what is said with such audacity and apparent authority. I got a letter this morning from Charles Roundell⁴ in despair at what was stated in the *Standard*.

The extraordinary thing is that though it may be all speculation founded possibly on your visitors at Hawarden⁵ (possibly too on your son Herbert's letter to the Artist), they have one or two points which are remarkable such as the principle of nomination.

¹ Stating that Gladstone would be likely to win over leading moderate Liberals to home rule and that 'Lord Spencer is practically convinced that no other policy is possible.' *Pall Mall Gazette*, 17 Dec. 1885, p. 8.

² Spencer's disclaimer appeared in the following day's issue.

³ Not traced in GP.

⁴ Charles Savile Roundell, formerly Spencer's private secretary in Ireland. Liberal M.P., Grantham, 1880-5.

⁵ Spencer later blamed Gladstone for speaking 'more freely than I should have said was prudent for a man in his position, to men like Acland, Canon MacColl etc. Wolverton too can hardly be very discreet.' Spencer to Granville, 5 Jan. 1886, Gr. P, PRO 30/29/22A/5. Sir Thomas Acland was

at Hawarden 10-14 Dec., MacColl 12-13 Dec. and Wolverton 10-12 Dec. See letters from Acland
to his son, 11-14 Dec. in A. H. D. Acland (ed.), *Memoir and Letters of the Rt. Hon. Sir Thomas Dyke
Acland* (1902), pp. 355-7, G. W. E. Russell. *Malcolm MacColl, Memoir and Correspondence* (1914), pp.
118-23, and A. B. Cooke and J. R. Vincent, *The Governing Passion* (1974), pp. 313-14.


## 436   W. E. GLADSTONE TO LORD SPENCER

*19 December 1885; Hawarden Castle, Chester*

I am truly sorry you should be troubled on my account. . . .

The question to you I think impudent. Your answer is different from Granville's;[1] *both* be assured I have not budged from the ground described by me in
our conversations. Nothing less likely than that I should hereafter do so without
your knowledge.

Irish question urgent, big, not to be paltered with.

Our duty to think about it,

But to have no plan or instruction, as matters now stand.

Only the Government can deal with it.

I look to them. Parnell should do the same.

I might add to these scraps that I would gladly to the best of my power
support them. While, as you know, thinking over the rudiments of a plan, I
adhere to my public declaration at Edinburgh that I can supply none, and wait
(how long may be a question) to hear what the Government have to say.

Amidst a tumult of communications, I may get confused, but I believe this
will hold water.

[1] Granville was inclined to support Dilke's and Chamberlain's plan of waiting for the Salisbury
government to produce their proposals for Ireland. Granville to Gladstone, 17 Dec. 1885, GP, Add.
MS. 44178 f. 277 and Ramm, ii, p. 415.


## 437   LORD SPENCER TO LORD HARTINGTON

*20 December 1885; Althorp, Northampton*
CP, 340. 1860

I have not advanced beyond where I was when I saw you. I am hopeless as
to moderate measures, but I do not see my way over the difficulties of a bigger
one.


## 438   LORD GRANVILLE TO LORD SPENCER

*20 December 1885; Walmer Castle, Deal*

Instead of answering you this afternoon, I have been writing volumes to
Hartington[1] to implore him not to issue an announcement tomorrow, which
after a conversation with Goschen[2] he had as good as settled to do.[3] A telegram
this morning saying that he does not go to Kimbolton today leads me to hope
he is wavering.

I agree with you as to the black character of the outlook.[4] And a great catastrophe may result from either Government or opposition going in for coercion, concession or leaving things alone. In such a state of things, I should be very sorry that any friend of mine should do what might be described as one of the causes.

I still agree with you that I do not object to concession, if the minority and the landlords can be secured. Gladstone says he has discussed this with you, but I do not gather from either of you that you have come to any conclusion.

The bribe to me and I suspect to Great Britain which would have most effect would be to get rid of the Irish members from the House of Commons, into which these are introducing dry rot. Gladstone was rather yielding on this in my last conversation, but Wolverton who saw him later does not think so.

I hear that there will be no adjournment. Some of us ought to meet before the 12th.

[1] Granville to Hartington, 20 Dec. 1885, CP, 340, 1861.
[2] The Queen also approached Goschen, urging him to persuade Hartington from falling in with Gladstone's Irish plans. T.J. Spinner, *George Joachim Goschen* (1973), pp. 113-14. Hartington and Goschen met in London on 19 Dec.
[3] Hartington's letter to the chairman of his election committee at Rossendale, Lancs., dissociating himself from the Liberal Party plan of legislative independence for Ireland, appeared in the national papers on 21 Dec.
[4] The last election results had been declared on 19 Dec.

**439**   LORD SPENCER TO W. E. GLADSTONE
*22 December 1885; Althorp, Northampton*
GP, Add. MS. 44312 ff. 218-20

I was writing to Sir R. Hamilton[1] the other day, and referring to what he had said in a letter to me which showed a change of opinion, I said that as we had had so many consultations on this topic I thought it right to tell him that I had changed my opinion in so far that I thought the solution of the difficulty by the old methods which I advocated last May, was now hopeless but that I saw immense difficulties in the alternatives.

I said that I did not write to elicit his views as he might find it impossible to communicate them to me. I got the enclosed from him.[2] It is important. I consider from the last paragraph of his letter that I am justified in showing it to you in strict confidence.

I cannot agree with his views of leaving the landlords to take their chance. His suggestion as to the Constabulary is only a method of getting rid of them, for of course every local authority would speedily create a force of their own. I thought by the way in which he began the argument that he was going to find some means of keeping the Constabulary as an Imperial force which would be difficult. I wrote to him before the *Standard* and *Pall Mall* announcement. Had I foreseen the likelihood of these rumours I should have hesitated about writing to him. I had in the same way written to Monck[3] a letter fishing for his opinion. I am to hear from him in a day or two ...

I have not altered the views which I held when at Hawarden, but I see great difficulties in getting the proper guarantees for the landlords without which I do not yet see that a scheme could be proposed.

I wish it were possible for you and Salisbury to agree to the heads of a scheme which might be the basis of communication with Mr Parnell. This would avoid the danger of one party negotiating with Parnell, and laying itself open to the accusation of trying to outbid the other party.

However patriotic those might be who negotiated with Parnell without the knowledge of their opponents, the public would never be got to believe that they were not acting from selfish party motives. This of itself after what has been said at the Elections might wreck a scheme. I presume however that now, unless anything unexpected turns up, everyone must wait for the Government.

I do not write this with a view of asking your opinion or of making you write a letter, but it may be well that after our conversations you should know how my thoughts are running.

[1] Sir Robert George Crookshank Hamilton, Under-Secretary, Dublin Castle, 1882-6.

[2] In a long letter putting forward a scheme for home rule, Hamilton ended, 'This letter, confidential in the highest degree as an expression of my individual views, is confidential in no other sense.' Hamilton to Spencer, 20 Dec. 1885, SP.

[3] Spencer to Monck, 17 Dec. 1885, Monck Papers. Charles Stanley, 4th Viscount Monck, Liberal M.P. Plymouth, 1852-7, Governor-General of Canada, 1867-8 and Commissioner, Irish Church Temporalities, 1869-81. Created Baron Monck of Ballytrammon, Co. Wexford, 1866.


## 440    W. E. GLADSTONE TO LORD SPENCER

*23 December 1885; Hawarden Castle, Chester*

I thank you for your very interesting inclosures, most of all for your letter.

The spirit in which you approach the great and difficult question of Irish Government is the only spirit which gives any hope of a tolerable issue. Absolute renunciation of prejudices, calm and searching reflection, abhorrence of all passion and exaggeration, a fair, not illiberal, estimate of humanity: these are among the indispensable conditions of progress in such a case. To which I will add for the moment great reserve.

I inclose some off hand comments on main points raised by your and by Hamilton's letters.

I heartily wish we could exchange ideas and information orally from day to day.

One step in advance I have taken by two letters to Mr. A. Balfour,[1] which I inclose, and which I hope and think you will approve.[2] Please to return them.[3]

The relations of the Government to the Nationalists ought to be cleared up betwen this time and the meeting. This only they can do.

[1] Arthur James Balfour, Salisbury's nephew; M.P., Hertford, 1874-85, President of the Local Government Board.

[2] A few days earlier, (15 Dec.) Gladstone had called on his neighbour, Hugh Lupus Grosvenor, 1st Duke of Westminster, a former Liberal, at Eaton Hall, Cheshire, where Balfour was staying. Gladstone urged the government to take strong and immediate action in Ireland in the direction of home rule and sent two letters to Balfour on 20 and 23 Dec., Balfour Papers, Add. MS. 49692.

[3] Balfour told Salisbury on 23 Dec., 'He [Gladstone] gets no support from any *important* member of his late Cabinet except Spencer.' B. E. C. Dugdale, *Arthur James Balfour* (1936), i, p. 94.

**441 W. E. GLADSTONE TO LORD SPENCER**
*26 December 1885; Hawarden Castle, Chester*

I thank you very much for Monck's letter.[1] I had been longing to know what he thought: as he, and Gibson, are among the very best Irish opinions. One and the same body of cogent evidence is in many quarters bringing many minds to a conclusion, from which flesh and blood too naturally recoil on account of the various conflicts and anxieties which it threatens to involve.

Flesh and blood make *me* sigh for the earlier and smaller plan; but it is a sigh accompanied with full knowledge that its day appears to have gone by.

Granville will send on to you a Memorandum of mine, which I am just sending to him.[2]

I am glad you approve my having written to Balfour.

[1] Monck reluctantly took the view that it was necessary, if a peaceful solution to the problem was to be found, to open negotiations with the Irish. Monck to Spencer, 22 Dec. 1885, SP. In forwarding the letter to Gladstone, Spencer noted, 'It is remarkable that he should have come to the same point as others without consultation.' 23 Dec. 1885, GP, Add. MS. 44312 f. 222.

[2] The memorandum, dated 26 Dec., set out in point form questions relating to Ireland which would have to be decided before the beginning of the next parliamentary session. Gr. P, PRO 30/29/22A (copy), and in Morley, *Gladstone*, iii, pp. 270-2.

**442 H. CAMPBELL-BANNERMAN[1] TO LORD SPENCER**
*27 December 1885; Gennings, Hunton, Maidstone*

I have been thinking a great deal, of course, of all you said the other day at Althorp.[2]

I think all the difficulties of detail—police, landowners, tariffs, taxation, etc.—are capable of adjustment.

The two great points on which my doubts fasten are the finality of the scheme, and the possibility of carrying it.

As to the first, though of course we can have no certainty, yet I think we ought to have some better evidence than we possess that it would be accepted as satisfactory and final. Can we depend on the *moderates* standing firm? They would have some evil days, between the angry loyalists on the one hand, and the Fenian extremists on the other. Take for instance the very probable contingency that capital would leave the country, and thus that employment would be diminished and trade reduced, if not to a standstill, to a condition of great dullness. There would be an outcry for absolute independence so as to attract foreign money, and for relief from imperial taxation. This would come very early, before any new combinations or parties had been formed. Would this outcry not sweep away the new Parliamentary constitution, just as the National League denounces the Land Act?

Then as to practicableness. I do not imagine that public opinion would support it, unless both parties agreed.

If there is no agreement, ought the proposal to be mooted, or, at least, formally adopted? On the whole, I think not. If things are left as they are, the Government may struggle on, and opinions would ripen gradually. But with a number of prominent public men giving often support to the proposal of a separate Parliament, it would be impossible to administer Ireland, and people in this country would at once fall into one or other camp on the subject. The question would be compromised, and prematurely forced: and we might find ourselves, before we knew how, in a civil war in Ireland.

My hopes rest, therefore, more than ever, on some entente between the two parties.

The whole prospect is most perplexing and bewildering, and I do not know that my muddled cogitations are of much value. I confess that I find my opinions moving about like a quicksand!

[1] M.P., Stirling Burghs, 1868-1908, Chief Secretary, for Ireland, 1884-5.

[2] In inviting Campbell-Bannerman to Althorp for Christmas, Spencer wrote, 'You are the one person I want to talk over the Irish question with.' Spencer to Campbell-Bannerman, 16 Dec. 1885, CBP, Add. MS. 41228 f. 296. To Northbrook on Boxing Day, Campbell-Bannerman confessed, 'I have seen Lord Spencer and learned his views ... I think I am a good deal more timid that he is.' Spender, i, p. 93.

### 443   LORD SPENCER TO LORD HARTINGTON
*27 December 1885; Althorp, Northampton*
CP, 340. 1873

I do not know whether you wish me to go up to see you. I of course will do so Tuesday if you want me, but I wish instead you would come across here for a night or two. It is very easy. I have a great variety of correspondence to show you.

I do not agree that we ought to go on fighting until we are beaten into a cocked hat.[1] Well I am not sure that we are not much in that condition now, but if we are not I do not see a chance of holding our own.

If one feels that, the sooner one takes the horrible plunge the better before fresh lives are lost and much more disaster is heaped on miserable Ireland. But I get at times sick at the idea of giving up to such men!! with such a history belonging to them!!

The crisis is so serious, that I hope we may get through it better than we expect. I should like the Heads of the two sides to try and arrange a basis, and then call Parnell in.

The 4.30 from London lands you here at 6.15.[2]

[1] See Hartington to Spencer, 25 Dec. 1885, SP.

[2] Hartington arrived at Althorp at 6.30 p.m. on 30 Dec., staying until the following day. Spencer told Rosebery that they had discussed Ireland 'up hill and down dale ... but luckily there was nothing which you and he and I had not discussed at Hawarden, so H. rode off on that and all went well.' 1 Jan. 1886, RP, 10062 f. 16.

### 444   LORD GRANVILLE TO LORD SPENCER
*27 December 1885; Walmer Castle, Deal*

I have received today a suggestion from Hartington[1] (evidently against his own opinion) that I should comply with a request of Harcourt's and Chamberlain[2] that Gladstone should be pressed to call together immediately an ex-Cabinet of the late colleagues.

I have declined, giving reasons, which I am sure you would think good.[3] I have however repeated a request that he will name a day before the meeting when he will be in town.[4]

It is impulsive and exaggerated, but the feeling is violent against concession and nowhere stronger than among our late colleagues.

I presume that Gladstone has a clear idea of what he wishes. You are on the road to one. But as far as I know, Hartington, Harcourt, Chamberlain, Derby and Northbrook have none.

How is it all to end?

[1] Hartington to Granville, 25 Dec. 1885, Gr. P, PRO 30/29/22A.

[2] Harcourt left Chatsworth on 18 Dec. for Highbury, Chamberlain's Birmingham home, where he spent 19-20 Dec. with Chamberlain. Leonard Courtney, Financial Secretary to the Treasury, 1882-4, met Harcourt in London a few days later. ' "You did not find Chamberlain in a very thanksgiving state of mind I imagine," said Leonard. "No indeed", was the answer, "after the first greeting it was nothing but 'Damn! Damn! Damn!' all day long!" "What a pious Sunday you two must have spent," returned Leonard.' Kate Courtney, Diary. 23 Dec. 1885, Courtney Papers, vol. 22, p. 57.

[3] Granville to Hartington, 27 Dec. 1885, CP, 340. 1872.

[4] Granville to Gladstone, 27 Dec. 1885, GP, Add. MS. 44178 f. 285. Gladstone did not fix a meeting until 12 Jan. 1886.

## 445   LORD GRANVILLE TO LORD SPENCER
*28 December 1885; Walmer Castle, Deal*

I send you this important paper.[1] I propose answering it by saying that at so critical a moment, with so much divided or rather one-sided opinion, particularly among leaders, the greatest consideration ought to be given to every slip.[2]

That I believe he has a complete plan, though I do not know it, that I believe you have not made up your mind as to safeguards, that the safeguard question is all important, that the bribe to me and to public opinion I believe in Great Britain would be exclusion of Irish M.P.s, however illogical.

That it seems to be difficult to settle anything by correspondence until we have an opportunity of meeting and discussing.

I shall write nothing till I hear from you by telegram or letter.

P.S. I shall say nothing to other but you.

[1] See No. 441 n. 2.
[2] A counterfeit coin.

## 446   LORD SPENCER TO LORD GRANVILLE
*29 December 1885; Althorp, Northampton*
Gr. P, PRO 30/29/22A/5

Mr. G. is usually logically right and it is difficult to traverse his present Memo. The only point where I think he may be wrong is as to the Vote of

Confidence. If he could carry his party with him, it might be right to move as he proposes, but everyone will wish to look forward and see whether a Government can be formed. They will not blindly vote with him unless they see their way afterwards.

He however may say I can carry with me enough of the party to have a majority on my Irish proposals in the House of Commons, and until I make known my views no one can deny this. If the party is seriously split on this question, and that can be clearly shown, then I do not see that a Vote of Confidence is necessary for this purpose.

A serious question lies behind this. If Mr. G. and others are in a minority among leaders of the party and yet think that their views must eventually prevail, are they not bound to make known their views?

On the one hand it may be argued that no difficult question has yet been solved without considerable and bitter previous controversy, and that this question is no exception to the rule. On the other hand the mere fact that Mr. Gladstone has joined hands with Parnell will strengthen them in Ireland immensely, and increase the difficulties of Irish Government to an enormous degree.

If it is clear that the party is against Mr. G. I should be against immediate action against the Government if they are not in accord with Parnell. I should be for allowing time to develop the situation.[1] The opposition are not bound to show up their own Divisions, and if they are divided they cannot form a Government, unless the split is so small that the main body of the party can carry on Government.

Mr. G. evidently expects that the Irish difficulty need only be faced when the formation of a Liberal Government is actually under discussion and after the defeat of the Government. It is evident to me, that it will be indispensable that he should meet the leading members of the late Cabinet, or ascertain their views. I can see difficulties in having a meeting of the ex Cabinet, but Mr. G. can surely feel their pulse and see those who are the principals in this business. You, Hartington, Harcourt, Chamberlain, Derby. Knowing the views of these men he will with Dick Grosvenor's help be able to test the position.

I am not shaken in my views. I consider our old methods for governing and treating Ireland quite useless, and if the guarantees as to the protection of the minority can be got I should be for taking the plunge rather than adopting for a time stronger coercion than ever. I say for a time as we can get no continuity of such acts.

I am not at all sure that the guarantees cannot be got. Mr. G. seems of that opinion. He is moreover dead against Separation. I cannot help thinking that a great deal of the outcry arises from fear of Separation. If that were shown to be impossible, more moderate views might prevail.

While the violence of some men extends to declarations of fighting, I have evidence that other sensible men incline to Home Rule. See an article in the November number of *Fortnightly* by S. Laing,[2] a sensible man though an old Adullamite.

All points to great caution.

Mr. G. himself seems to think that no more could be made unless the condition of Ireland were in 'a state of legality', 'not substantially worse than when I left the country', and this cannot be known except by Government itself until Parliament meets.

Why should not the Address be treated as an opportunity for an armed reconnaissance without bringing the main bodies of the opposing forces into collision? The fact of passing over the Address without a vote of want of confidence would not prevent one being brought on immediately afterwards if thought necessary by an[y]one.

This is a long rambling letter with little or no point in it.

I half expected to hear from Hartington today. He said something of being in London on the chance of seeing me, and I wrote to say if he really wished I would go up but wanted him to come here. I have no reply. I doubt whether I should do any good by seeing him, and having heard so much from Mr. G. in matters which I could not refer to I should feel a bit awkward.

[1] Spencer informed Gladstone the same day, 'From what I hear in various directions, opinion is running strongly against a bold Irish measure among leading men of our side.' Spencer to Gladstone, 29 Dec. 1885, GP, Add. MS 44312 f. 242.

[2] Samuel Laing, who represented various Scottish constituencies from 1852 until his retirement in 1885. Financial Secretary to the Treasury, 1859-60.


**447** LORD SPENCER TO LORD ROSEBERY
*30 December 1885; Althorp, Northampton*[1]

I have been meditating a letter for some days, as I feel that you and I will be looked upon by ex-colleagues as co-conspirators in aiding and abetting the G.O.M. in his wickedness ...

As far as I can judge, you and I, and I know not whether you still hold the views you did at Hawarden, you might well have gone back from them, will stand alone among Mr. G.'s colleagues. Possibly Ld. G. will follow Mr. G. but I know of no one else inclined to do so. We 3 Peers and John Morley[2] could not form a Gladstone Government, and at present I see no prospect of Mr. G. getting a following enough to justify his going on.

The question then is, ought he to join the Home Rulers with his voice and support them or ought he and those who may agree with him to keep silence, lest Ireland should become ungovernable?

I cannot yet answer this to my satisfaction.

I fancy that Mr. G. would like to move an amendment on the Address clear of the Irish question, if it is shown that Government stand unsupported by the Irish.

I look on that as impossible without facing the next question, can he with his views form a government?

There is a great deal against having a meeting of the ex-Cabinet, but it is essential that Mr. G. should see and talk to leading members of that body. I hope he will move towards London next week. This is essential before he settles anything. After all the Tories may take the thing up. What a blessing if they would!

[1] Copy. Original not traced in RP.
[2] M.P., Newcastle upon Tyne since 1883.

**448** W. E. GLADSTONE TO LORD SPENCER

*30 December 1885; Hawarden Castle, Chester*

*Secret*

I understand your idea to be that in as much as leaders of the party are likely to be divided on the subject of a bold Irish measure, and a divergence might be exhibited in a vote on the Address, it may be better to allow the Tory Government with 250 supporters in a House of 670 to assume the direction of the Session and continue the administration of Imperial affairs.

I do not undervalue the dangers of the other course.

But let us look at this one.

1. It is an absolute novelty.
2. Is it not a novelty which strikes at the root of our Parliamentary Government? under which the first duty of a majority freshly elected, according to an uniform course of precedent, and a very clear principle, is to establish a Government which has its confidence.
3. Will this abdication of primary duty avert or materially postpone the (apprehended) disruption of the party? Who can guarantee us againt an Irish or Independent amendment to the Address? The Government must in any case produce at once their Irish plan. What will have been gained by waiting for it?

The Irish will know three things

1. That I am conditionally in favour of at least examining their demand.
2. That from the nature of the case I must hold this question paramount to every interest of party.
3. That a part, to speak within bounds, of the Liberal party will follow me in this respect.

Can it be supposed that in these circumstances they will long refrain, or possibly will refrain at all? With their knowledge of possibilities behind them, *dare* they long refrain?

An immense loss of dignity, in a great crisis of the Empire, would attend the forcing of our hands by the Irish or otherwise.[1]

There is no necessity for an instant decision. My desire is thoroughly to shake up all the materials of the question. The present leaning of my mind is to consider the faults and dangers of abstention greater than those of a more directed course. Hence, in part, my great anxiety that the Government should move.

Please send this on to Granville.

---

[1] Spencer, in his reply, pointed up the dilemma: 'The Irish ... will know the three things about your opinion which you name, and will work their knowledge and try and force your hand, but you run the same danger if you proceed with a vote of want of confidence.' Spencer to Gladstone, 31 Dec. 1885, GP, Add. MS. 44312 f. 246.

**449**　LORD SPENCER TO LORD GRANVILLE
*31 December 1885; Althorp, Northampton*
Gr. P, PRO 30/29/22A/5

I send you a letter from Mr. G. by his desire,[1] and the Memo. I also send as near a copy of my letter to him, to which his is a reply, as I can give. I did not copy it verbatim, and in writing it from a rough draft, I shortened and modified it.[2] I will also enclose what I wrote today.[3]

I have had very long talks with Hartington. He read me copious extracts from Harcourt,[4] Gladstone etc. I felt very awkward as I was bound not to refer to Mr. G.'s Memo. I abstained from doing so, and only read him out extracts from other letters of Mr. G. on the main question. I did not feel at all comfortable. He is I am now convinced quite irreconcilable to any plan of Home Rule.

Harcourt pours out volumes of excellent arguments both ways, but on the whole is dead against the plan. If one can guess accurately his view of the position, Derby is equally strong.[5]

I feel in despair.

Hartington is to meet Chamberlain, Dilke and Harcourt in town tomorrow.[6] If he and Chamberlain put their houses together (which he rather hopes to do) I do not see that it will be possible for Mr. G. to go on with his plan. I confess I agree with Hartington but he could not vote for a vote of confidence if he knows that he cannot agree with Mr. G. in case of the latter trying to form a Government: as you will see I put that kind of argument in my letter to Mr. G.

I am not sure that it has not had some effect, the end of his letter is not so unyielding as the beginning.

[1] No. **448**.
[2] Spencer to Gladstone, 29 Dec. 1885, GP, Add. MS. 44312 ff. 242-4.
[3] Ibid.
[4] Harcourt to Hartington, 24 Dec. 1885. Gardiner, i, pp. 553-4. Harcourt had called on Hartington on Wednesday morning, 30 Dec., before the latter left for Althorp.
[5] See Derby to Granville, 29 Dec. 1885, Gr. P, PRO 30/29/22A/5.
[6] At Devonshire House, Piccadilly, Hartington's London home.

**450**　LORD ROSEBERY TO LORD SPENCER
*31 December 1885; Lansdowne House, Berkeley Square, W.*

*Confidential*

A happy new year to Lady Spencer and yourself. I wish it with all my heart, but I never knew a political year open so gloomily.

I think I agree with every word of your letter. Infinite harm has been done by these disclosures. Like war-elephants they have trampled down our own ranks before attacking those of the enemy.

However that cannot be helped. We must face the situation as it is.

I arrived here yesterday, and, as far as I can make out, the late Cabinet is in open revolt, chiefly on account of the G.O.M.'s silence to them, which, if he was privy to Herbert Gladstone's disclosures, is certainly ill-judged. Hartington however will have told you the situation better than I can. I shall not write to Mr. G. today as I should not like to seem to be keeping back from him the meeting at Devonshire House tomorrow; while I feel that that should be brought before him in a joint note of the Powers assembled. But my purpose is to write and urge him to come to town as soon as possible and meet his late Cabinet.

The experiment of Home Rule is now inevitable. Even if the abstract principle were wrong, the practical necessity is certain: because once a man of Mr. G.'s position declares in favour of it Ireland will never be quiet until it has been tried. But in the abstract the case seems to stand thus.

1. You have given Ireland the franchise, i.e. the amplest means of putting forward her wishes.

2. The first use she makes of that power is to demand by an overwhelming majority powers of local self-government, such as

    1. we deprived her of by fraud in 1800.

    2. we give to all our colonies.

    3. we should unhesitatingly give her if she were 1000 miles away.

Moreover the chiefs of the party demanding these know that it is only by obtaining these, and soon, that they can keep the volcano of disturbance in America from overflowing.

Hartington will say 'You are then giving way to dynamite'. I reply, 'No, for I would give the same powers to Scotland if she wanted them (which she does not). But no prudent minister disregards dynamite. And a minister should have sufficient moral courage not to avoid doing the right for fear he should be suspected of fearing dynamite.'

If my view of the case be correct, the Liberal party should not in the abstract oppose this concession, nor as a concrete question will they be able to avoid trying the experiment, now that Mr. G. has pronounced in favour of it.

The Tories, not holding popular opinions, may say, 'No, we would rather govern by the sword,' (for that is the only other option). But we cannot. And indeed all the malcontents (except Hartington whose views on this I do not know) declare, I believe, that they cannot vote for another Coercion bill.

Then what, in God's name, do they propose to do as regards Ireland? No coercion: no home rule—result—chaos lit up by dynamite.

I could go on but I am ashamed of the length of this letter.

**451 LORD HARTINGTON TO LORD SPENCER**
*3 January 1886; Devonshire House, Piccadilly, W.*

The only result of our deliberations on Friday[1] was to send a rather urgent appeal to Mr. Gladstone to give the earliest opportunity first to the leader and subsequently to the party of hearing and discussing his options and intentions; especially if there were any question of a Vote of want of Confidence; and suggesting that the 12th would scarcely give the necessary time for consideration.[2]

We had of course much talk on the merits of the schemes which have been more or less definitely put forward. All are strongly opposed to them all. Chamberlain, if any Home Rule at all is to be granted, would give a more complete separation, and get rid of the Irish in Parliament. But all are in a greater or lesser degree hopeless about the possibility of governing Ireland by repression—especially after the announcement of Mr. Gladstone's opinions. The irritation against him is great and I think well founded.

I asked Mr. Gladstone to telegraph to me yesterday if he could tell me whether he was likely to accede to our request on account of my private arrangements; but I have had no answer. From what I hear from Granville, I should think it unlikely that he will agree to come up before the 12th ... I shall probably go to Chatsworth on Tuesday.

[1] The meeting on 1 Jan. 1886 was told by Hartington, reporting on his talks with Spencer at Althorp, that Spencer 'sees nothing for it but some kind of Home Rule, but he does not believe it will succeed'. Lewis Harcourt recorded, 'Spencer's attitude seems to have shaken and depressed Hartington and The Council of Four at Devonshire House came to the conclusion that Home Rule would have to be tried.' LHJ, 1 Jan. 1886, HP, MS. 735, f. 170. See also Spencer to Hartington, 5 Jan. 1886, CP, 340. 1885.
[2] Hartington to Gladstone, 1 Jan. 1886, GP, Add. MS. 44148 ff. 192-5.

**452   LORD NORTHBROOK TO LORD SPENCER**
*7 January 1886; Stratton, Micheldever Station*

*Confidential*

I have had much talk with Trevelyan[1] and Campbell-Bannerman about the position.[2]

Trevelyan is stronger in favour of resisting the Parnellites than any of us, and quite approves of Hartington's letter.

Campbell-Bannerman, although still very doubtful as I am of the ultimate success of resistance is against giving any support to the Parnellite demands under present circumstances.[3]

I come to your own position. After all our talk about it I hope you will not mind my putting it as it strikes C.B. and myself. I have been guarded with Trevelyan, as you have not opened your mind to him.

1st. If you give an opinion in favour of Home Rule it will have more weight in the country than that of any other man, but it would not carry Home Rule. Its effect would be, as you say in your letter of the 29th, to strengthen the Parnellites, and increase the difficulty of governing Ireland.

For instance, if the Government determine to ask for powers to strengthen their hands against the N.I. League, such a declaration from you would make the passing of any so called 'Coercion' Bill nearly impossible.

2nd. Notwithstanding all the consequences, is it your duty with your special knowledge to state your opinions fully?

I can quite feel your difficulty in answering this question to your own conscience. It is possible that it may even have crossed your mind that not to do so would be an act of moral cowardice.

Upon this I would observe that the duty of expressing opinions depends upon the circumstances and the subject matter.

You do not look upon Home Rule as a good thing in itself, but only as the least bad of two bad alternatives.

You think, also, that Home Rule is only to be accepted, even as the least bad alternative, provided it is coupled with guarantees against its use as a stepping stone to independence or for the spoilation of the landlords.

Therefore your inclination in favour of Home Rule is governed by a condition which it is beyond your power to secure. No one but a Minister prepared to propose such a measure to Parliament can ascertain if these guarantees can in any substantial form be obtained.

It is also to be recollected that there is no reasonable probability of Home Rule being accepted by the Parliament or the People of England, and I doubt if there is any such probability of a measure of which you would approve being accepted by the Parnellites.

You have, in short, no power of carrying a plan of which you yourself would approve.

If, therefore, the Government, as is probable, determine to produce no large scheme, I do not see how it can be your duty to propose the alternative of Home Rule.

If the measure was one good in itself, and carried along with it neither in the interim nor when passed any evil consequences you would of course be bound to advocate it, just as Parliamentary Reform was advocated for years before it passed; but in your own view it is at best a *pis aller*, and the impossibility of carrying it has heavily weighted the scale against it. If it had been good in itself you would have proposed it long ago.

If, indeed, the Government were to propose some measure of this kind with the guarantees which you think essential, you would be bound to help them. But if they do not, your course seems to me to be to give them such support as you fairly can, and not to propose the alternative. You would state your opinion with perfect truth by saying that you have seen no proposal for Home Rule from the Parnellites of which you could approve.

C.B. illustrated the position thus. A Town is beseiged—there is a question of capitulation. Some of the council of war, probably rightly, are for capitulation as the least bad of two bad alternatives. The Commanding Officer and the main part of the garrison decide to fight. Is it the duty of those who are for capitulation to hoist a white flag, and so strengthen the hands of the enemy? Certainly not.

One somewhat new point has come out in our conversations, and that is that it would be unsafe to use the general phrase—as Childers[4] has done at Edinburgh—that the same self-government can be given to Ireland as to England. In some respects, e.g., possibly Education, Ireland might have larger powers. In others, e.g., the franchise for the election of local bodies, and the control over the police Ireland could not safely be given the same powers.

If the policy of resistance is adopted we must not put arms into the hands of our opponents.

I am doubtful if it would be wise even in England to give County Elective

Boards executive power over the police. The Quarter Sessions now have practically no such power. The Chief Constable has the whole responsibility, and if there was real trouble he would, I presume, go to the Home Office for advice and assistance. Neither the Chairman of Quarter Sessions nor the Police Committee give him executive orders.

C.B. says that it would require very strong reasons indeed to induce him to take a course different from yours on the question of Ireland, and his language was even stronger than I have used as to the effect upon the H. of Commons and the country of the expression of your views.

You should if possible take an early opportunity of seeing G. Trevelyan. I have had no communication of late with Mr. Gladstone, and I do not like being the intermediary between him and Lord Selborne.[5] Shall I ask Lord S. to send him the memo?[6] You know best if it would be of any use.

[1] Sir George Otto Trevelyan, M.P., Hawick, 1868-86. Chief Secretary for Ireland, 1882-4, Chancellor of the Duchy of Lancaster, 1884-5.

[2] The meeting at Stratton was from 6 to 8 Jan. For Northbrook's own position, see B. Mallet, *Thomas George, Earl of Northbrook* (1908), pp. 226-7.

[3] Campbell-Bannerman informed Spencer that Northbrook and he took 'an identical view of the situation'. The only difference between them was that Northbrook anticipated that the government would introduce a Coercion Bill whilst Campbell-Bannerman did not. Campbell-Bannerman to Spencer, 8 Jan. 1886, SP.

[4] Hugh Culling Eardley Childers, Chancellor of the Exchequer, 1882-5, spoke on 29 Dec. *The Times*, 30 Dec. 1885, p. 4.

[5] Lord Chancellor, 1880-5.

[6] On 23 Dec. Northbrook had sent his impressions of the meeting with Spencer to Lord Selborne, Gladstone's Lord Chancellor, asking Selborne for his own thoughts on home rule. The latter drew up a memorandum for Northbrook, dated 28 Dec., which was shown to Spencer who subsequently passed it on to Gladstone. The memorandum is reproduced in Selborne's *Memorials* (1898), ii, pp. 196-201.


**453   W. E. GLADSTONE TO LORD SPENCER**
*7 January 1886; Hawarden Castle, Chester*

I go to town on Monday afternoon, and I propose to see some three or four friends, by way of beginning, at 21 Carlton House Terrace[1] at 11.30 on Tuesday morning. If you can then be in town I hope you will come, just to break ground a little.[2]

[1] Lady Frederick Cavendish's house.

[2] Gladstone saw Spencer, Granville and Chamberlain on 12 Jan. and held a long meeting.


**454   LORD SPENCER TO W. E. GLADSTONE**
*8 January 1886; Althorp, Northampton*
GP, Add. MS. 44313 ff. 4-5

It is perhaps no use troubling oneself about a phase of this subject before we have reached it; but I confess that I in my small way am troubled with what I ought to do, and of course your position on the same point is far more important.

It is this.

Supposing it is found to be impossible to carry a big measure with the safeguards which I think necessary, because public opinion is not ripe for it or is dead against it, ought those who think that such a measure ought to be carried to declare their opinion?

On the one hand no big measure is pressed until after a period of agitation and discussion and it might be necessary in order to bring opinion round to it that all those who are in favour of it should speak out.

This clearly would be the duty of anyone if the measure were one on which no doubt could exist.

But this is hardly a case of that sort. The measure is not one which I for one should advocate as theoretically the best. It is only as the safest alternative that I should support it.

On the other hand the difficulty of governing Ireland will be increased enormously if it becomes known that you and in a less degree others like myself, are in favour of a large measure of Home Rule.

I confess that I look with dismay at what may occur in Ireland, if Parnell is backed by you in a demand for Home Rule: without a measure being carried at once.

You have always said that no one out of the Government can know enough to justify his formulating a measure. Ought then a general support of a principle of Home Rule be given by you and others before the details of a measure are mentioned?

Forgive me for stating my difficulty. I have several letters from men of good sense who know my inclinations urging me strongly to hold back my opinions. I cannot yet clearly see what will be the right course to adopt.[1]

[1] Gladstone replied, 'In lieu of any lengthened answer to your letter, I send you a copy of a letter I wrote two days ago to R. Grosvenor. You will see from it, how closely we are on the same lines as to the present difficult situation. The material part of this letter may perhaps be suitable to read on Tuesday.' Gladstone to Spencer, 9 Jan. 1886, SP. The letter to Grosvenor, 7 Jan. GP, Add. MS. 56447, mentioned rumours of two contradictory plans on the part of the Irish: one, which stated that Parnell would support the Liberals and a second which gave the impression that there would be no breach between Conservatives and Nationalists on the Address. See Cooke and Vincent, p. 316.

**455** LORD SPENCER TO LADY SPENCER
*12 January 1886; 18 Carlton House Terrace, S.W.*

I was very nearly starting off for Althorp, but Hartington and Granville both rather wished me to stay so I remain.[1]

It is very interesting though awful, to discuss the position.

I dined with Trevelyan with only Mrs. T. and the two boys ... I then went on to Harcourt's and found Chamberlain there. We had a strong but very friendly argument, and he seemed very pleased to find that I received him cordially.[2]

We had a small informal talk at Mr. G.'s,[3] Granville, Chamberlain, Harcourt and Dick Grosvenor.

Opinion is so strong against a big measure that I expect nothing will be said or done in favour of Home Rule.

### 456   A. J. MUNDELLA[1] TO LORD SPENCER

*14 January 1886; 16 Elvaston Place, Queen's Gate, S.W.*

*Confidential*

I have spent a few very busy days in Ireland, very usefully I hope,[2] and have brought away with me much food for reflection. If I am any wiser, I am not any happier. I could almost wish myself in that state of bliss which is the fruit of ignorance, and which enables politicians to make up their minds as absolutely as the Duke of Westminster[3] and Mr. Lecky.[4] Unfortunately for the latter he has written a book,[5] and his teachings as an historian and philosopher are in ludicrous contrast to his conclusions as an Irish Landlord.

I had long *confidential* interviews with Sir Robert Hamilton which I have his permission to communicate to you. . . .

I dined at the Vice Regal Lodge. Breakfasted with Michael Davitt,[6] Webb[7] and others. And discussed the situation with Radicals, Tories, Whigs, Nationalists, and a real Fenian!

To tell you all will require an hour's talk. I can however honestly say that nothing could possibly give a more accurate diagnosis of the situation than your own letter to me. I am, while sharing all your embarrassments, in *entire agreement* with your conclusions.[8]

Poor Carnarvon's government excites *universal derision*. Everybody agrees that Ireland was never in so deplorable a condition as now.[9] Morris, Porter, McDonnell,[10] Hamilton and all the Banking and Commercial men are unanimous on this head.

Everybody, except the Nationalists, are praying for Lord Spencer, and even *some* of the Nationalists have said that your return would be the greatest blessing to the country. I confess I am not ready to support their prayer, unless you return to carry out your own ideas.

The League governs the country, and it is a tyranny as odious as the Mafia at Naples or the most secret societies of Italy. There is no such thing as personal freedom under it, and the Priests everywhere enjoin obedience to its behests. Business is paralyzed, confidence is destroyed, thousands are starving and a sort of white terror prevails.

The most unpopular men in Ireland today are Lord Ashbourne and David Plunket.[11] The first is in much the *worst odour*. The so-called Loyalists regard him as their betrayer.

Lord Carnarvon and Sir William Dyke are leaving,[12] and Coercion I believe is resolved upon. God only knows what will come of it. Sir Robert Hamilton and Michael Davitt however are of the same opinion, and said to me the same thing—wild and bloody revenge in Ireland. Danger and disaster in England. 'Your prisons will be too full to hold us' said Davitt.

... Until they have a Government of their own to criticize and abuse they will never realize how much advantage they derive from the English connexion. To this complexion we must come at last.

Meantime passion and prejudice are in the ascendant here. We shall go through the old routine—and then?

I repeat, you are the only man who would be listened to on the side of reason and moderation. I am *not sure* that you would prevail until further trial and failure had demonstrated the hopelessness of the Cromwellian enterprise.

[1] M.P., Sheffield, Vice-President, Committee of Council on Education, 1880-5.

[2] Mundella was serving on the Royal Commission on the Condition of the Blind, Deaf and Dumb in the United Kingdom.

[3] Westminster, speaking at Chester on 12 Jan., urged that no further concessions should be made in the direction of home rule. The Times, 14 Jan. 1886, p. 8.

[4] William Lecky, the Irish historian and essayist. In a letter to The Times published on 13 Jan., Lecky claimed that the Parnellites were 'animated by two leading ideas—a desire to plunder the whole landed property of the country, and an inveterate hatred of the English connexion in every form' (p. 12).

[5] Presumably referring to Lecky's The History of England in the Eighteenth Century, of which the first four volumes had been published.

[6] One of the founding members of the Land League in 1879.

[7] Alfred John Webb of Dublin, one of the few Protestant survivors of the 1870 home rule movement; author of Compendium of Irish Biography (1878).

[8] 'There seems nothing but a big measure, Home Rule with proper safeguards, or at no distant day, coercion stronger than we have ever had before.' Spencer to Mundella, 31 Dec. 1885, Mundella Papers, MP 6P/18.

[9] The resignation of Carnarvon, Lord-Lieutenant of Ireland since June 1885, was announced on 16 Jan., though the Standard caried the news on 13 Jan.

[10] Michael Morris, Lord Chief Justice, Ireland; Andrew Marshall Porter, Master of the Rolls, Ireland; possibly Schomberg Kerr McDonnell, Carnarvon's private secretary.

[11] Irish barrister, Conservative M.P., Dublin University, 1870-95, First Commissioner of Works, 1885-6. See G. W. E. Russell, Fifteen Chapters of Autobiography (1914), p. 297.

[12] Sir William Hart Dyke, M.P., Dartford, 1885-1906, Chief Secretary, resigned immediately after Carnarvon.

## 457  J. CHAMBERLAIN TO LORD SPENCER
*21 January 1886; 40 Princes Gardens, S.W.*

I return with thanks the extracts and reports of Parnell's speeches.

I have copied the most important. I am convinced that Mr. Parnell's demand is for Legislative Independence as a step to complete Separation. His language can hardly be twisted into any other construction.[1]

[1] On the morning of the Queen's opening of Parliament, 21 Jan., Gladstone held a meeting of ex-ministers to discuss parliamentary tactics, especially with regard to Ireland. Chamberlain presumably used Parnell's speeches in drafting the memorandum which was sent the following day to Parnell through Capt. O'Shea. In it, Chamberlain argued that Salisbury should not be turned out of office at that moment. If this proved to be necessary to assist in the settlement of the Irish question, Chamberlain suggested that Collings's amendment (see No. 459 following) would provide a good opportunity. Memorandum reproduced in Garvin, ii, pp. 166-7.

## 458 LORD SPENCER TO LADY SPENCER

*24 January 1886; Althorp, Northampton*

I dare say my speech did not suit the *Morning Post*.[1]

I quite admit that nothing could be more unsatisfactory than the position. It must remain so unless the Government take up a positive attitude re Ireland, or are defeated on a side issue and the Liberals try to form a Government. Then will be the difficulty. . . .

The Government are in a ridiculous position.

Meanwhile no one knows what will happen. The Queen must send for Gladstone but she may not like his programme and could then appeal to Hartington to form a Coalition Government.

[1] On 21 Jan., Spencer spoke in a debate on the Address, defending the late government's record in Ireland. Hansard, 3, cccii, cols. 69–73. The speech was briefly reported in the *Morning Post*, 22 Jan. 1886, p. 5.

## 459 LORD SPENCER TO LADY SPENCER

*27 January 1886; Spencer House, St. James's Place, S.W.*

Last night will be a memorable one, not only for the defeat of the Tories[1] but for the separation of Hartington from Gladstone. It was very sad.

I have always held more or less the objections urged by Goschen[2] to the adroit Bills of Jesse Collings, but the Resolution was general and did not raise the worst points of the measure.

No doubt Hartington's arguments against abstract Resolutions were generally right, but considering the impossibility for most of the new County Members to oppose the Resolution, I think he ought to have gone on for it. He did not even put it on his differences as to Ireland.[3] That was so much the better for us.

I feel very unhappy at the Division. He spoke well but evidently felt the position much. . . .

I know not what will happen but I expect Mr. G. will form a Government.[4] Opinion is going his way but the difficulties will be very great. It is very hateful.

[1] On the fourth night of the debate on the Queen's Speech, Collings moved an amendment expressing regret that no measures were announced for helping agricultural labourers in rural districts obtain allotments and smallholdings on equitable terms as to rent and security of tenure. Hansard, 3, cccii, cols. 443–8, 26 Jan. The amendment was carried by 331 to 252. 74 Nationalists voted with the government, but Hartington, Goschen and sixteen other Liberals voted with the Conservatives.

[2] Ibid, cols. 497–504.

[3] Ibid, cols. 520–5.

[4] Gladstone told Harcourt on 26 Jan. that he was prepared to form a government without either Hartington or Chamberlain. He recalled in 1897, 'I believe it was in my mind to say, if I did not actually say it, that I was prepared to go forward without anybody.' Morley, *Gladstone*, iii, pp. 287–8.

# 2

# THE IRISH HOME RULE CRISIS, 1886

In the process of forming a new government, Gladstone relied heavily on the judgement of a small band of ex-cabinet colleagues. According to Lewis Harcourt, Gladstone, just before starting for the wedding of his daughter, Mary, to the Reverend Harry Drew, called on Granville on 2 February 'and told the three, Granville, Spencer and W.V.H.[arcourt], that they were to allot the Cabinet places as they thought best and he would come in and consider them after the ceremony was over'. (LHJ, 2 February 1886, HP, MS. 735 f. 204). A major difficulty in carrying out this task was the refusal of leading members of the ex-cabinet – Hartington, Derby, Northbrook and Selborne – to join a government which would be willing to grant an Irish legislature. Spencer reluctantly acted as an emissary between Gladstone and the ageing Granville in an attempt to reconcile the latter to not being reappointed to the Foreign Office. Spencer accepted the post once more of Lord President of the Council, though much of his time was occupied with Ireland.

Two bills were submitted to the cabinet, one proposing a new Irish legislature, the other dealing with land purchase on a large scale. Chamberlain and Trevelyan thereupon resigned. The Government of Ireland Bill was presented to the Commons on 8 April by Gladstone, and the Land Purchase Bill eight days later. Spencer loyally defended these measures in public and to correspondents, whilst privately expressing doubts to Gladstone. The vital debate on the second reading of the Government of Ireland Bill in May extended over fourteen nights and encountered opposition from Irish Unionists and a strong minority of Liberals of varying states of opinion: the scheme for land purchase, unpopular with Irish landowners, also weighed against the success of the Home Rule Bill. On 7 June, the House divided: the government was defeated by 341 to 311, with 93 Liberals voting with the Conservatives.

With the announcement of the dissolution of Parliament on 10 June, Spencer journeyed to Aix-les-Bains for a health cure. He followed the progress of the elections with some misgivings. 'I don't like the look of things,' Spencer wrote to Playfair, his Vice-President of the Council. 'If we can't gain the towns we shall not do so in the country, as I fear the labourer thinks more of his 3 acres and a cow than of Ireland, and there is no enthusiasm.' (4 July 1886, Playfair Papers, 1038). He did, however, closely follow the fortunes of his brother, Robert, in defending his seat against a Liberal Unionist, W.C. Cartwright. As the local Liberal paper commented, 'to contest the seat held by the brother of Earl Spencer will bring the question of Home Rule before Mid-Northamptonshire in a more pointed manner than it could well be placed before any English constituency.' (Northampton Mercury, 12 June 1886). In the event, Robert Spencer was returned though with a reduced majority. Of the seven members elected for Northamptonshire, four were Gladstonian Liberals. Nationally the picture was somewhat different. The Unionists gained 394 members, the Liberals 191 and the

*Parnellites 85. Gladstone resigned on 20 July and Salisbury once more became prime minister.*

---

**460  LORD SPENCER TO LADY SPENCER**
*31 January 1886; Spencer House, St. James's Place, S.W.*

I was quite right to go up. I find Granville and Mr. G. both wishing to see me.[1]

I fear that Hartington has decided to keep aloof,[2] but is very friendly, and almost admits that we are right. He is strong for the attempt being made but says he is too strongly committed against it to be able to join. I had a long talk to him today. I feel very sad about it all. I can't in a letter tell you all that is going on. I think the prospect very bad and I am in despair at the turn taken in certain quarters.

Mr. G. goes to Osborne and returns to London tomorrow.[3]

I shall not move for the present. My idea is that Mr. G. will eventually form a Government but there will be great difficulties.

... I shan't know what will happen to me. Certain places are kept open; until difficulties are cleared up I can't tell where I go. It will not be to War or Navy.[4]

I hope Mr. G. will keep well. He is so now but is greatly worried.

The Queen seems as yet very reasonable.

[1] Gladstone summoned Spencer from Althorp by telegram on 30 Jan. Spencer left by the 8.30 a.m. train.
[2] Hartington told his father on 30 Jan,' 'He [Gladstone] sent for me this morning and I have declined.' CP, 340.1924.
[3] Gladstone journeyed to Osborne to accept office on 1 Feb., returning the same day.
[4] After seeing Spencer on 30 Jan. Gladstone noted, 'Lord Spencer. At my disposal for any office or none. I said, some absolutely. The rest stands over.' GP, Add. MS. 44771 f. 33. Nevertheless, Lewis Harcourt saw Spencer the following morning and found him 'anxious to have the Admiralty'. LHJ, 1 Feb. 1886, HP, MS. 735 f. 203.

**461  LORD SPENCER TO E. W. HAMILTON**
*31 January 1886; Brooks's St. James's St., S.W.*
Hamilton Papers, Add. MS. 48613 ff. 299-300

*Secret*

Mr. Gladstone told me where you were dining and that he had authorized you to speak to Mr. F. L. Gower.[1] I went over to Lord Granville's and prevented his sending at once a letter to Mr. G. and got him to say that he had no objection to Mr. F. Leveson seeing Mr. Gladstone.[2]

Mr. Gladstone had himself suggested this idea, but when I went back to him and reported (Lord Granville said I might) the purport of his letter, he rather shied away at seeing Mr. Leveson as he wanted to spare himself. He said however that you or he might come down to him after dinner.[3] You will best judge whether in prospect of the journey and the strong feeling Mr. G. has about this matter, you should see him or let Mr. Leveson see him tonight.

I hope Mr. Leveson will be able to urge Lord Granville's acceptance of the Colonies. If Lord Granville remains of his present mood, in which he says his brother agrees with him, I shall be in despair, both on Mr. Gladstone's and Lord Granville's account.

I shall be here after dinner if you would come and see me. I had a hope that this might have been settled satisfactorily before Mr. Gladstone went to Osborne. Perhaps Mr. Leveson could do it. Pray urge him to prevent this disaster.

Use your discretion as to whether you tell him what I write or not. I should not myself think it desirable, but I won't object if you think it necessary.[4]

[1] Hamilton was to dine with Edward Frederic Leveson-Gower, Granville's younger brother, M.P. Bodmin, 1859-85, that evening to persuade Granville not to insist on being appointed Foreign Secretary in the new administration. 'I was commissioned to use Mr. G's new arguments about age as well as physical infirmity.' EHJ, 31 Jan. 1886, Add. MS. 48642 f. 120.

[2] GP, Add. MS. 44179 f. 16.

[3] In fact Gladstone sent a letter to Granville at 11.30 p.m. begging him to accept another office. Gladstone to Granville, 31 Jan. 1886, Gr. P, PRO 30/29/29A.

[4] Lady Spencer went to London 1 Feb. and found Spencer 'low and worried, the difficulty just now being Lord Puss. Spencer was to go and see him about 12 o'clock.' Lady Spencer, Diary, 1 Feb. 1886, SP. Granville relinquished his claim later that day, taking the Colonial Office.

## 462   LORD SPENCER TO LORD LANSDOWNE

*2 February 1886; Spencer House, St. James's Place, S.W.*
Lansdowne Papers

*Secret*

I may not be able to write to you at length as the political crisis absorbs my time, but I want to send you a few lines[1] ...

You will be politically cursing Gladstone and all those who go with him. Your eye detected my possible leaning in what I wrote to you from Bolton. I must admit that I have changed or at all events advanced rapidly in my views since June.

Our old methods of redressing every grievance and maintaining Law and Order by coercive measures I am convinced are hopeless after the Tory surrender last July.

No stability of policy in that direction is possible. The English people will not stand coercion for long. Every time it is carried out the Irish are more and more irritated. A seesaw policy like that of 83/84 and the last 6 months is fatal. There is no alternative in my mind between coercion of the most rigid kind, including regulation of the Press, and suppression of Representative Institutions in Ireland and, as Hartington thinks, in Parliament expulsion of the Irish M.P.s and a wider concession in the direction of Home Rule than we have ever yet thought possible. No concession short of this will be allowed by the Irish party to succeed. No Land Purchase for example will be permitted to work unless some real form of Home Rule is given.

I look upon the alternative of force as hopeless and unworkable now. The English people will not tolerate it for any time; if it is tried at the end of it you are in a worse position than when you began. I therefore have come to the conclusion that we must try to come to terms with the National Party in Ireland, getting terms for Landlords and the minority. It is the only chance of settling Ireland: it is a risk, but it must be run, as the other course is hopeless. It is odious to have to deal with men who have tolerated methods of agitation such as those of the Land League, and who have not when they could exert themselves to put down outrages; but they are the chosen representatives of Ireland. I began this change of view thinking that guarantees could not be got but I believe now they can be got. The Landlords must be bought out. Mr. Gladstone agrees to this. If we are able to go on I should go to the Parnellites and say if you will settle the Land Question on terms safe for the Landlords, we will settle also the question of Home Rule. We are going to form the Government on the basis of looking into the question and trying to settle it somewhat on the terms I have vaguely sketched.

We may break down. The Parnellites may not accept what we can offer. If so there is no use in proceeding. We may find it almost impossible to get proper guarantees. We may find the social state of Ireland too bad to justify our proceeding.

If this occurs we shall be driven to governing Ireland by force and we must go on with it. After the limits of concession have been tried we shall get unanimity in Great Britain for this course which we cannot get now.

I do not however myself think that we shall be defeated by these difficulties.

If Landlords are safe my belief is that crime will drop, and that an Irish Government like any other in the world will be bound to maintain Law and Order and protect Commerce. No doubt a great shock will be given to all enterprise in the transition but in my opinion it must be done for the sake of the eventual peace of Ireland and the strength of the United Kingdom. If we had to go to Coercion now, our difficulties would be a hundred fold increased. Since July the National League has governed Ireland. No rent will be the cry, and no taxes; if these attacks on Law and Order are quietly carried out what Government can stop them?

Hartington agrees that the experiment must be tried, but is too much committed to join the Government.[2] The task is a gigantic one: I dread what you will say about it and those who have taken up this new line, but I am sure you will give me at least the credit of taking it up from a stern sense of necessity and for no love of seeking for Power or Office. To take this line is against my associations and inclinations. It would be much easier and pleasanter to follow the other path of policy.

P.S. I have written this in great haste and missed many points. Separation is out of the question and is not in my opinion desired by the Irish. If a settlement is made the Extremists will have to be dealt with by Parnell and Co. They will have tough work, but not as tough work as the English Government.

What has occurred to bring about this change?

1.  The declaration of the Tories last Summer against exceptional measures.
2.  The result of the General Election in Ireland, notably in Ulster and Dublin, which showed the weakness of the Party of Union, and the strongly expressed bias of the Irish people.

3.  The complete adoption by the whole Irish hierarchy of the National League
    policy.

[1] Lansdowne's letter of 13 Feb., congratulating Spencer on becoming a member of the cabinet,
crossed with Spencer's. Lansdowne wrote again on 19 Feb. affirming his opposition to home rule.
SP.
[2] On 10 Dec. 1885, Lansdowne had composed a lengthy memorandum for Hartington on the
consequences of home rule for landlords and tenants. Spencer received permission from Hartington
to print and circulate the memorandum for the cabinet. Hartington to Spencer, 24 Feb. 1886, SP.
It was subsequently printed on 1 March 1886. Copy in SP, and also PRO CAB 37/16/66.

### 463   LORD SPENCER TO W. E. GLADSTONE
*6 February 1886; Spencer House, St. James's Place, S.W.*
GP, Add. MS. 44313 ff. 22–3

I rarely knew a better reception than that given by the Queen.[1]

She of course stated doubts and difficulties but listened and I got 6 or 7 good
minutes on Ireland which I hope may have some effect, though I wish I could
have thrown in better arguments. Still I got in some good ones, but you know
it is not very easy with H.M. to continue a distasteful subject.

I can say this that she spoke more to me on Ireland and was more ready to
speak than during the whole of my first years in Ireland.

She was very civil otherwise and in good humour.

[1] All the ministers, except Gladstone, who had already received the seals of office, went to
Osborne on 6 Feb. Spencer had a private audience with the Queen prior to the Council.

### 464   LORD SPENCER TO LORD GRANVILLE
*17 March 1886; Spencer House, St. James's Place, S.W.*
Gr.P, PRO 30/29/22A/5

I have thought over what you said as to Mr. G.'s wish that I should talk
with Chamberlain.[1] I will do so if opportunity occurs naturally, but I fear it
will be of no use.

What might be of real use would be if Mr. Gladstone himself saw him and
took him, as far as he can, into his confidence.

I am sure that part of the difficulty is that Chamberlain does not consider
that Mr. Gladstone sufficiently values him.

I know the difficulties about consulting him. Still the attempt to reconcile
him should I think be made.

[1] At the cabinet of 13 March, Gladstone outlined his scheme for Irish land purchase. Chamberlain
criticized the proposals, contending that it was impossible to make a judgement without knowing
the provisions of the Home Rule Bill which was to accompany it. *A Political Memoir*, p. 193.
Chamberlain and Trevelyan sent in their resignations to Gladstone on 15 March, but consented to
wait until Gladstone's final scheme was submitted to the cabinet. It seems that Gladstone had
requested Spencer to speak to Chamberlain on the matter. Cooke and Vincent, op. cit., p. 385.
When Harcourt suggested to Chamberlain that Spencer should be consulted, he replied 'No,
certainly not. I have the greatest contempt for Spencer, who has been the origin of all the mischief.'
LHJ, 15 March 1886, HP, MS. 735 f. 216.

**465   W. E. GLADSTONE TO LORD SPENCER**
*18 March 1886; 10 Downing Street, Whitehall*

I would suggest your asking Kimberley[1] to join you today, if you think fit.
I hope you will be able to put into shape the remaining points of the Land
Plan.[2]

[1] John Wodehouse, 1st Earl of Kimberley, Secretary of State, India.
[2] Lady Spencer recorded in her Diary, 'Spencer brought in at luncheon Mr. Morley (Chief
Secretary), Sir H. Thring and Mr. Vernon (Irish Land Commissioner) with whom he had been
closeted for some time over this terrible Irish business.' 18 March 1886, SP. Spencer joined Granville
and Morley in Gladstone's room at the House of Commons for discussions.


**466   LORD SPENCER TO W. E. GLADSTONE**
*24 March 1886; Spencer House[1]*

*Secret*

I have been thinking over the suggestion that the Bill for Local Government
in Ireland should be introduced before that relative to Land Purchase.

As this strikes me to be a very serious matter, I hope you will consider certain
arguments before you finally decide on adopting the proposal.

1)   The opposition to the Local Government proposals will be much stronger
from the Irish Landlords and those who think that equitable terms of Sale
should be offered to them before the Imperial Government gives up control of
Law and Order in Ireland, if this measure is brought forward before a Land
Bill.

2)   If you are defeated in the House of Commons on Local Government and
dissolve, you will not be able to keep out of view the necessity of a Land
Purchase Bill, and the consequent demand on English credit; unless indeed the
two subjects are treated separately; and that would I fear be quite impossible
for many (who support your present policy) to accept. If however the two
subjects are discussed together you do not gain any advantage; for the financial
difficulty which weighs so much on the opinion of the House of Commons
would exist in full force.

3)   I am strongly of opinion that if the Local Government Bill passed the
House of Commons the Irish members would alter their present attitude as to
a Land Purchase Scheme, and would either oppose it or try to cut it down to
an extent which would make it inoperative.

I should like to see the acceptance of a Purchase Bill by the Irish the condition
of proposing the Local Government Bill. That has always been my view.

You may say that the Irish, and any Radical Supporters they might get,
would be defeated, but by this action you would start them committed to
opposition to the Land Scheme, and this would have a bad effect.

If the Local Government Bill passed the House of Commons and came up to
the House of Lords how could those who think as I do oppose a motion to
read the Bill a second time until the Land Purchase Scheme had passed the
House of Commons?

You said yesterday that though you proposed to have a clause in the Land

Bill suspending its operation until a Local Authority was created, you could not insert a Clause in the Local Government Bill suspending its operation until the Land Scheme had become Law.

I understand the difficulty, but mere resignation of the Ministry would not meet my objection, for the Local Government Bill might have been passed, or at all events such a pronouncement of opinion made in the House of Commons in favour of that measure and against Purchase, that the latter would have to be dropped.

I do not see how we could accept the one measure without the other.

Forgive my treating you in this way but the proposal seems to me so serious a step, the first in a direction from which I shrink, that I feel bound to put my views at once before you, particularly as I do not think you had decided what to do yesterday.

I readily assented the other day to inverting the order of procedure as far as the Cabinet was concerned, but I then understood that you did not think it desirable to follow the same course in Parliament.

[1] Copy. Original not traced in GP.


### 467   W. E. GLADSTONE TO LORD SPENCER
*27 March 1886; 10 Downing Street, Whitehall*

Not comprehending the cause of your uneasiness which I would gladly return, [sic] I am driven to guess, and it occurs to me you may think my idea is to carry Irish Government through the Commons before doing anything on Land. But I have no such idea; and I am inclined to think we should take the 2nd Reading of Land before Committee on Irish Government. I see no reason to doubt that before Irish Government can pass we shall pretty well know whether Land is likely to pass.

At present I do not share your apprehensions even as to the disposition of the Irish party about Land. But be this as it may I certainly agree that (barring the case of refusal by the Landlords) we are bound to strive equally for the passing of the two measures.[1]

[1] Spencer endorsed this letter 'I saw Mr. G. on this on the evening of the 27th. and on Sunday morning 28th.'


### 468   J. MORLEY TO LORD SPENCER
*28 March 1886; 95 Elm Park Gardens, South Kensington, S.W.*

*Secret*

I find that I had made the following notes of the conversation in Mr. G.'s room on Tuesday last:-[1]

'Present Lord Granville, Lord Spencer, Harcourt and me. Order of proceeding altered. Home Rule to come first.'

That was certainly my impression at the time. Pray, do not trouble to take any notice of this. But I felt rather unhappy at the unpleasant turn of things yesterday, and wished to be sure.[2]

[1] 23 March.
[2] The cabinet of 26 March agreed, with Chamberlain, President of the Local Government Board, and Trevelyan, Secretary of State, Scotland, dissenting, to ask Parliament to establish by statute a legislative body in Dublin. Gladstone later that day advised the Queen of Chamberlain's and Trevelyan's resignations which were accepted. Chamberlain was informed on 27 March. *A Political Memoir*, p. 199.

### 469   LORD SPENCER TO LORD HERSCHELL
*5 April 1886; Spencer House, St. James's Place, S.W.*[1]

*Secret*

I hope that I made some impression on Mr. G.[2]

1. He accepted our proposals as to Chambers but admitted that he had no intention of including Royal Charters under Contracts.

2. He was ready to agree to some proposal for making the first Order effective, and not leaving it to be composed practically of the same men as the 2nd Order.

He preferred a Property qualification for *the chosen* to other forms of amendment which I enumerated.

3. He is ready to consider a better Refuge for Civil Servants who may be driven out by the new Government of Ireland.

4. He begged me to put down all the methods for dealing specially with Ulster, that he might state them in his speech.

He did not see his way to put England and Scotland in a better financial position in relation to Ireland.

I confess myself that I am not afraid of this part of the question, and could not argue strongly for it.

I hope that all these things will modify your objections.

I need not say how strongly I hope that they will.

I may have omitted some points of my talk. Granville was with us: for we did all this while walking, and I could not make any notes.

[1] Copy, SP.
[2] Herschell, the Lord Chancellor, was unhappy with some aspects of the proposed legislation for Irish government which Gladstone was to introduce in the Commons on 8 April. Herschell wrote two letters to Gladstone on 5 April, in the second of which he commended Spencer's suggestions on the bill. GP, Add. MS. 44496 ff. 175-6.

### 470   LORD HERSCHELL TO LORD SPENCER
*14 April 1886; 46 Grosvenor Gardens, S.W.*

I see Mr G. has fixed Friday for the Land Bill. Surely we are to have a Cabinet before that day? It has never yet been before the Cabinet and there are vital questions to be discussed which may give rise to differences of opinion and about which as you know I am very uneasy.

I cannot be a party to such a measure without thorough discussion as to its leading points. We were hustled into a corner about the Govt. Bill.[1] It seems to promise to be worse still about the Land Bill.

[1] On 13 April, the debate on the first reading of the Government of Ireland Bill had ended after four sittings of the Commons. Gladstone, in a closing speech, stated that the exclusion of all the Irish members was not a vital part of the bill. At the cabinet the next day, Herschell, John Morley and Harcourt announced that they would resign if Gladstone gave way on this issue. LHJ, 14 April 1886, HP, MS. 735 f. 221.


## 471   LADY SPENCER
*14 April 1886*

### Memorandum of conversation with Mr. Gladstone

Mr Gladstone told me tonight[1] talking of Trevelyan, that when he went to him (when Mr. G. was forming the Government), Mr. T. said, 'I must tell you frankly that I think I am entitled to have the choice of the Admiralty or War Office. When I was Secretary of the Admiralty I had to move the Estimates. I did it in a manner which was I believe universally admitted to have been remarkable' and so on in the same strain.[2] Mr. G. told me this in proof of what he had been just saying i.e. that the Liberal party suffered from too much cleverness, and individuality in its members, and that vanity and originality seemed to go together . . .

Mr. Gladstone took me in to dinner. In the evening, I spoke to Cyril Flower[3] who gave me a tolerably satisfactory report of the way things are going in the House. Said a few words to Mr. Childers – he is hopeful . . . Sir A. Hayter told me Herbert Gladstone told him things were again going less well, and that there were several fresh seceders, Lord W. Compton,[4] Sir Julian Goldsmid[5] and others. Sir J. St. Aubyn[6] is very unhappy about Home Rule. I tried to make him see it in its true light, but he says he is pledged against it to his constituents.

[1] At a dinner given by Sir Arthur Hayter, Lord of the Treasury and Financial Secretary, War Office, in Gladstone's previous ministry, at 9 Grosvenor Square.
[2] Trevelyan saw Gladstone on 3 Feb. and accepted the Scottish Office.
[3] M. P., Luton, 1885–92, and Junior Lord of the Treasury.
[4] Lord William Compton, son of 4th Marquess of Northampton. Elected Liberal M.P., Stratford-on-Avon division, Warwickshire, in 1885.
[5] M.P., St. Pancras South, from Nov. 1885.
[6] Sir John St. Aubyn, M.P., Cornwall West, since 1858.


## 472   W. V. HARCOURT TO LORD SPENCER
*15 April 1886; Treasury, Whitehall, S.W.*

I am surprised to hear from my son that you are under the impression that I yielded my views at the Cabinet yesterday on the subject of the removal of the Irish members from the House of Commons.[1] Such a misapprehension could only have arisen from the habitually mild and moderate manner in which I put forward my opinions.

... I have written to Mr. Gladstone to say that I adhere strictly to the position I have taken up and that if I am called upon in the recess to speak to my constituents or elsewhere I must state that in my judgment and that of John Morley the provisions on that subject stated by Mr. Gladstone and contained in the 24th. clause of the Bill cannot be departed from.

[1] See No. 470 n. 1. At a party on 14 April, Spencer told Lewis Harcourt that W. V. Harcourt had withdrawn his threat. Spencer subsequently apologized to him. Spencer to W. V. Harcourt, 15 April 1886, HP, MS. 45.


**473  LORD SPENCER TO W. E. GLADSTONE**
*17 April 1886; Spencer House, St. James's Square, S.W.*
GP, Add. MS. 44313 ff. 65-6

The Chancellor as you know took somewhat of the same objection that I did to the limitation of the advance for buying Irish Estates.

He came here this morning and pointed out a passage in your Speech[1] which he said would be taken up, and in his view, took away the force of the moral obligation of Parliament to which you referred. You said among other qualifications 'if it finds that repayments are duly made in my opinion Parliament will never under-estimate the moral obligations that may be comprehended in this subject'.

That may mean that if the Irish authority are unpunctual in their payments then the rest of the Landlords who may desire to claim their right to sell their Estates may be left out to struggle with the Irish authority, as Parliament may consider it impossible to sanction further advances for the Purchase of their Estates.

I confess that I rather shudder at the interpretation which may be placed on these last sentences of that part of your Speech. I hope they are more than covered by the earlier references to the 'pledges of good faith as between us and the Irish Landlords'.

I think it right to point out this view to you, as it will be doubtless taken up. If the words are pressed, I see no answer excepting the formidable one that if the future Irish authority do not pay faithfully, we shall consider they have broken a solemn treaty, and we shall then go in to recover possession of the Government of Ireland.

[1] On 16 April, Gladstone had moved the first reading of the Sale and Purchase of Land (Ireland) Bill in the Commons. 'It was somewhat dull,' reported Lady Spencer, 'and the financial details tiresome. It created no enthusiasm, but the terms seem to be fair to the Landlords.' Spencer, who had gone down to Osborne, was back in time to hear part of Gladstone's speech. Lady Spencer, Diary, 16 April 1886, SP.

**474** LORD SPENCER TO W. E. GLADSTONE
*21 April 1886; Newcastle*
GP, Add. MS. 44313 ff. 68–70

While waiting for the Train which is to bring Lady Spencer from London and which will take us both to Edinburgh,[1] I will write you a few words, to report what took place here last night.

To begin with I need hardly tell you that John Morley is deservedly extremely popular. He was received by an enthusiastic crowd at the station, and his reception at the meeting and afterwards was of the warmest character.

The meeting made a profound impression on me.[2]

Excepting two Electioneering meetings in Essex and Dorsetshire I have never appeared at a popular meeting since 1857, and I never stood before so large an audience since I addressed (when only just 21) the Electors in the Market Square of Northampton in 1857.

The Town Hall here is a queer building in the shape of a wedge, long and angular.

It was densely packed in body, gallery and orchestra behind the Speakers.

The numbers were at the lowest computation over 3,000, and I can say without the slightest fear of contradiction that only one opinion was there, and that absolutely in favour of your Policy.

I did not get on well. I was at first bewildered but I got better as I went on, but omitted several important points.[3]

The audience however went absolutely with me, and I don't think I lost their ear for a moment, but that was because they were absolutely favourable to your schemes.

They were coldest when I referred to the Land Scheme. John Morley made an admirable Speech, and dealt forcibly with the question of exclusion of Irish Members. It made a great impression, though I could see that when he began the audience held (or many of them) the opposite view.

If all England and Scotland followed Newcastle, our Irish opponents would soon come to terms.

[1] The Spencers stayed in Edinburgh on the night of 22 April, on their way to a holiday at Loch Awe, in central Scotland. They left on 1 May for Leeds, where Spencer delivered a speech on 3 May and arrived in London on the following day.
[2] Morley and Spencer spoke on the two Irish bills at Newcastle Town Hall on 21 April. *The Times*, 22 April 1886, p. 9.
[3] Edward Hamilton called Spencer's speech 'thoroughly sensible and practical'. EHJ, 22 April 1886, Add. MS. 48643 f. 97.

**475** SIR L. PLAYFAIR[1] TO LORD SPENCER
*28 April 1886; Bedford Hotel, Brighton*

On Monday, the two Government Bills are the Budget Bill and the Medical Bill.[2] The former it is not thought will occupy long. If I miss my chance in carrying the 2nd Reading of the Medical Bill on Monday, Government will score its 23rd failure, as it is not likely another day can be got for it.

[1] M.P., Leeds South, 1885-92, and Vice-President, Committee of Council on Education.

[2] Playfair introduced the Medical Acts (1858) Amendment Bill on 5 April. Since 1870, 22 bills aimed at reforming the medical profession had failed owing to the jealousies of the many licensing medical examining boards. Spencer warmly supported the measure in the Lords. Hansard, 3, cccvi, cols. 1836-9, 18 June 1886. The bill received the royal assent on 25 June. See T. W. Reid, *Memoirs and Correspondence of Lyon Playfair* (1899), pp. 349-50.

**476    LORD SPENCER TO LORD MONCK**
*28 April 1886; Loch Awe*
Monck Papers

Your letter followed me and only reached me this morning.[1]

I am much concerned that you hold such distinct views against the Local Government Bill of Mr. Gladstone. From what you said to me some time ago I hoped that you would have been with us.

I have very carefully read your letter. I do not admit many of your objections to the Bill. You say that 'the Unity of the Kingdom is destroyed. Ireland is reduced from the position of an integral portion of the U.K. etc. and the Imperial Parliament will cease to exist.' Could our country last century be so described?

I saw a letter in some Paper the other day recalling the fact that the motto of the Order of St. Patrick was given just when Grattan's Parliament was constituted.[2]

I deny also that the Parliament will lose its character as Imperial. It will deal with every part of the United Kingdom, with Ireland as well as Scotland and England, with India with our Colonies.

It is true that we propose to delegate certain powers to a Dublin Assembly, just as she now delegates powers of making Bye Laws to Rail Road Companies. If our Bill passes, she will no doubt delegate much wider and more important powers, but the principle is the same, that delegation of powers does not destroy the law making or supreme attributes of the Assembly which gives the concession.

I admit that logically your arguments as to Taxation without representation are sound: but I am sure that at all events at present it is altogether better for Ireland and for England that the Irish should keep their energies for Irish affairs.

J. Morley put the difficulties well in his Newcastle Speech – it is a choice of difficulties, we take what is for the least objectionable way that which is preferable.

We are not ripe for a complete remodelling of our Constitution. I am disposed to think that eventually we may come to this in which case Ireland will be represented as other parts of the United Kingdom. But there is no demand for Federation or change in Wales, Scotland or England. We cannot propose what is not wanted.

You may go a little far when you say that Irishmen will be excluded from citizenship. That means that every privilege of Englishmen will be taken away from Irishmen.

No change whatever is made in these respects excepting the one, no doubt important, of having Ireland represented in Westminster.

The mere fact that we are ready to let off, if she objects, Ireland from contributing to a War Tax does not cut her off from her connections. She contributes to the Army and Navy, all of which form part of preparation for War. She gives her sons to officer and man Army and Navy.

I do not see how you can satisfy the Irish demand, and yet hold the Irish Parliament in complete subordination to the Imperial Parliament as now constituted. This to my mind is impossible.

Our plans will be no doubt much altered in Committee if it reaches that stage.

Your views will be freely and fully discussed.

I for one if a practical solution in your sense be found shall not object, but many important men will.[3]

[1] Monck to Spencer, 23 April 1886, SP.

[2] The Order was instituted on 5 Feb. 1783 and carried the motto *Quis Separabit*.

[3] Spencer sent Monck's letter to Gladstone who stated, 'There is really some refreshment in reading a temperate letter of objections such as Monck's ... I contemplate with more satisfaction that we may be able to frame proposals which will in a considerable degree remove his objections.' Gladstone to Spencer, 7 May 1886, SP.


**477**   E. HENEAGE[1] TO LORD SPENCER

*6 May 1886; 20 Upper Brook Street, Grosvenor Square, S.W.*

*Private and Confidential*

Altho' we are now on different platforms and Mr. Gladstone's Manifesto is most insulting to those who joined the Government at his request and have left on account of his Irish Policy as he does not give us the credit he accords to Lord Hartington and Mr. Bright,[2] still I cannot help giving *you* a warning note; the Whips, no blame to them, are in perfect ignorance of the probable numbers on a Division.

I have tested my own figures not only by the names of those who have been willing to tell me that they approve my resignation and shall vote against the Home Rule Bill on 2nd. division but by private lists to which I have access from the best Liberal and Radical sources[3] and you will be beaten, if you proceed with the Measure comprising its present principles by a good majority and even if you mean to condescend to 'gut' both your Bills to purchase Mr. Chamberlain's vote you would still be defeated but you would also be absolutely discredited in Parliament and in the Country.

[1] Edward Heneage, Liberal M.P., Grimsby, since 1880. Chancellor of the Duchy of Lancaster and Vice-President, Committee of Council on Agriculture, responsible to Spencer. Resigned 9 April over the Home Rule Bill. Spencer had earlier, on Gladstone's behalf, attempted to persuade him to stay in the government. Heneage to J. Wintringham, 7 April 1886, Heneage Papers, 2 HEN 5/13/27. To his letter Spencer replied, 'As to the Bill, you may be right. I have no private or special means of knowing how men will vote, but I am not disposed to accept your dictum that the Bill is doomed to defeat. We certainly shall not sacrifice what we think essential for Chamberlain or anyone else.' Spencer to Heneage, 7 May 1886, SP (copy).

[2] M.P., Central Birmingham, Chancellor of the Duchy of Lancaster, 1873-4, 1880-2, who now opposed Irish home rule.

[3] Heneage and Sir Rowland Blennerhassett, M.P., Kerry, 1880-5, had compiled the lists. W. C. Cartwright, Diary, 5 May 1886, Cartwright Papers, Box 6/16.

## 478   LORD SPENCER TO SIR H. PONSONBY[1]
*9 May 1866; Privy Council Office*
RA D38/73

I have received your letter enclosing a copy of the Queen's letter of the 6th May to Mr. Gladstone, which Her Majesty was good enough to desire you to send to me with permission to show it to the other Ministers.[2]

I am sure that I am expressing the opinion of my colleagues when I say that we deeply regret to learn that the Queen considers that the Irish measures of the Government are dangerous to the Union of the Empire. With all humility we venture to take a different view of the proposal and share with Mr. Gladstone the opinions which the Queen is good enough to attribute to him, that he is doing what is best, not only for Ireland but for the whole Empire.

I feel the serious nature of the crisis but I trust that whatever may be the issue, the strength of the Crown and Constitution will be increased.

[1] Sir Henry Ponsonby, the Queen's private secretary.
[2] The Queen expressed anxiety on the Irish measure then before Parliament and stated 'that her silence does not imply her *approval* or acquiescence in them'. Queen Victoria to Gladstone, 6 May 1886, GP, Loan 73/25.

## 479   W. E. GLADSTONE TO LORD SPENCER
*10 May 1886; 10 Downing Street, Whitehall*

I will hope our amendments[1] may do something but he [Chamberlain] gives his explanations of what he cannot defend in a more polemical spirit than I had expected from him in such a crisis of his country's fate.

[1] Gladstone, in moving the second reading of the Home Rule Bill later that day, announced the concessions he was prepared to make to obtain Chamberlain's support. Gladstone left the House convinced that his speech was satisfactory, but his advances were rebuffed. See Herbert Gladstone to Henry Gladstone, 14 Aug. 1886, reproduced in J. L. Hammond, *Gladstone and the Irish Nation* (1938), pp. 530-1.

## 480   LORD SPENCER TO SIR J. W. PEASE[1]
*15 May 1886; Spencer House, St. James's Place, S.W.[2]*

*Private*

Your letter[3] needed no apology, for its object is one of deep interest to the country and to the Liberal Party at this moment. I need hardly say that a decision upon your suggestion will not rest with me, and is sure to be carefully considered before the 2nd Reading of the Irish Government Bill. When its consideration takes place I will take care that your views are made known.

Speaking for myself I confess I see great difficulty if not impossibility in withdrawing the Bills.

1st. We knew when the Government was formed and when these Bills were prepared that we probably should not carry with us the whole party. The magnitude of the issue and the importance of it alone justified our running the risk of dividing the Liberal Party in the House of Commons. Having this before us, ought we to give up our policy now because a division of the party, and I admit a very serious one, has taken place? I doubt whether you could find a precedent for a Government withdrawing a measure of first class importance, on which their existence depended, because they find they are unlikely to carry it.

2nd. Are we sure to secure greater support next year or in the autumn for our present Bill? May not our adversaries gain strength?

3rd. No one has yet shewn us how a practical measure can be framed which would reconcile our seceding friends. If they can do this, Mr. Gladstone has stated that we are ready to consider the proposal in Committee.

4th. Will the condition of Ireland justify suspension of action?

You will notice that Lord Hartington will not alter his action, even if the Government declare themselves ready to withdraw the measures provided the principle of autonomy were adopted by the passing of the 2nd Reading.[4]

What hope then would there be of he and his friends agreeing to any measure of Home Rule which would have the least likelihood of settling the question and satisfying the Irish?

I see none and we shall be in a worse position if we postpone taking the opinion of the House until the autumn, because we shall have shown that we have not faith in our proposals, and are hesitating. Hesitation and vacillation will do us more harm than anything. I cannot but think that the best course is to go straight on and take the consequences: subject to alterations which as Mr. Gladstone announced will be considered in Committee.

[1] Liberal M.P., Barnard Castle, Co. Durham, 1885–1903.

[2] Copy. Original not in Pease Papers.

[3] Urging Spencer to use his influence in obtaining the withdrawal of the two bills. A meeting of 64 dissident Liberal and Conservative M.P.s had been held at Devonshire House on 14 May, and was addressed by Chamberlain and Hartington. *The Times*, 15 May 1886, p. 11.

[4] Hartington informed another opponent of the Home Rule Bill, Sir Hussey Vivian, an Independent Liberal M.P., Swansea, 'It is quite impossible to suggest the terms of a Resolution which I could support and which the Government could with any consistency accept.' Hartington to Vivian, 16 May 1886, Vivian Papers, C 2491.

## 481   J. MORLEY TO LORD SPENCER

*30 May 1886; 95 Elm Park Gardens, South Kensington, S.W.*

*Private*

I agree with your view of our recent tactics. The only defence for them is that if we had not adopted them, we should certainly have been beaten on 2nd Reading,[1] and then had to face a dissolution under extremely difficult circumstances. But I suspect (1) that we may be beaten on 2nd Reading even now, (2) that we shall have to face a difficult dissolution anyhow.

Therefore, I have always doubted about the recent line, and I doubt now.

[1] On 27 May, Gladstone held a meeting at the Foreign Office for Liberal M.P.s who favoured the establishment of a legislative body in Dublin to manage Irish affairs. Some 220 attended. Gladstone won over a number of waverers by promising members who voted for the second reading that amendments might be made in committee.

## 482   C. R. SPENCER TO LADY SPENCER
*31 May 1886; House of Commons*

6.50 p.m.

Chamberlain's meeting just over.[1] 45 to 48 uncertain which pledged to vote against the bill. 10 to stay away and 2 or 3 to support. So we are done I think – great feeling in the lobby.

57 at the meeting.

[1] At a meeting of Chamberlainites at the Commons on 31 May, a letter from John Bright was read out, indicating that he would vote against the bill. For its effect, see K. Robbins, *John Bright* (1979), p. 257.

## 483   W. E. GLADSTONE TO LORD SPENCER
*11 June 1886; 10 Downing Street, Whitehall*

I send you H.M.'s very proper letter, chiefly that you may consider precisely the last paragraphs and the order of steps to be taken.[1]

Please send the letter in box on to Granville.[2]

[1] After the government's defeat on the second reading of the Government of Ireland Bill by 341 votes to 311 on 7 June, a cabinet was held that day to decide whether to resign or dissolve. The Queen advised Gladstone on 9 June to take the latter course. See *LQV*, 3rd. ser., iii, pp. 144-5. Gladstone announced the dissolution of Parliament the following day.
[2] Concerning the Prince of Wales's suggestions for honours. Gladstone to Granville, 11 June 1886, PRO 30/29/29A and in Ramm, ii, pp. 451-2.

## 484   W. E. GLADSTONE TO LORD SPENCER
*12 June 1886; 10 Downing Street, Whitehall*

The whole position as to Irish Land Purchase has now been rendered most cloudy and equivocal

1. by the conduct of the Irish Landlords
2. by the action of Hartington and others who keenly wish for the Bill but have thrown dirt upon it with a view to damaging Home Rule.

Yet I think with you we ought *not* to recede from any of our positions, and not to go beyond mild intimations that time and circumstances must of course act upon this question as upon all others.[1]

The bulk of the Home Rule subject swollen by stiff contest will make the method of *pari passu* handling (I think) impossible.

I hope there need be no new difficulty on this matter now, which is really in the shade. I have great confidence in the real strength of the argument for it.

[1] See Spencer to Gladstone, 11 June 1886, GP, Add. MS. 44313 ff. 75-6.

## 485   LORD SPENCER TO W. E. GLADSTONE
*12 June 1886; Berkhamsted House, Great Berkhamsted*
GP. Add. MS. 44313 ff. 79–81

I am glad that you think that we ought not to recede from any of our positions on Irish Policy.

I am certainly of opinion that we ought not to press at this moment the *pari passu* treatment of the Government and Land branches of Irish Policy.

At the same time I do not want to put that method of action out of the question, as it may eventually be the best to adopt.

I do not consider that the conduct of the Irish Landlords have [sic] altered the circumstances, for I do not see how as honest men they could if opposed on principle to Home Rule have acquiesced in the Home Rule Bill merely to secure a measure of Land Purchase.

What I do lament about is that hardly any of the Irish Landlords or leading commercial men have had the foresight to see the necessity of Home Rule.

I do not quite recollect what Hartington said to throw dirt on the Land measure, but Finlay[1] and Trevelyan certainly tried to catch Radical votes by connecting the two measures together.

I think I may now speak without difficulty on the situation.

I shall not connect inseparably Land and Home Rule though I cannot put Land altogether in the shade, as I attach great importance to it.

Indeed I could not fight, as I hope to do, earnestly for Home Rule unless I was sure that the Government would in one form or another make a serious and resolute attempt to deal with Land Purchase.

I consider it a necessary part of our Irish Policy and I could not go in for Home Rule alone, both because of reasons of principle and because I have pledged myself deeply against such a course and could not in honour depart from what I have said.

[1] Robert Bannatyne Finlay, Liberal M.P., Inverness district, 1885–92; follower of Chamberlain.


## 486   LADY SPENCER TO LILY SEYMOUR[1]
*13 June 1886; Berkhamsted House, Great Berkhamsted*

I hardly know what to say about the Crisis. It did not surprise me that we were *beaten*, but the Majority did. I think we are right to dissolve and not to resign. I rather fear the result. I cannot believe that Scotland will remain true to Mr. Gladstone. I hear now the Tories are saying that they are not against Home Rule!! and hardly anybody speaks in favour of coercion. We know that Ireland cannot be governed without, and therefore if they are in power they must do something or the other.

Lord Carnarvon's statement was curious.[2] I think the little man's head was turned by the good reception he met with from the people, and that he fancied he alone could conciliate the Nationalists, and he means to try and meet their views. There would have been no harm in that if he had consulted the Cabinet first! but it was a great error to act off his own bat,[3] and of course Parnell was quite justified in believing they were going to get 'Home Rule' when the Viceroy, who was also a Cabinet Minister, discussed the question with him. I feel that Lord Ashbourne must have known all about it. People are quite hopelessly prejudiced on this subject, and it is maddening to speak about it!

I was at the Division. Gladstone's speech was magnificent, the end a masterpiece of eloquence.[4] Parnell's speech was excellent,[5] but nothing can avail against obstinate prejudice. I think Chamberlain's manifesto[6] extremely clever, but it has the glaring defects of proposing schemes vaguely, which will not satisfy the Irish.

We went to Dollis Hill last Sunday to see the Aberdeens.[7] The Gladstones were there. He was very well and in great spirits. People are angry with Spencer for not speaking out more firmly about the Land Bill, but he says it is impossible to pledge themselves now as to what they will do in the future now their bills are thrown out of Parliament.

[1] Lady Spencer's sister-in-law.

[2] Carnavon had secretly met Parnell at an unoccupied house in Hill St., London, on 1 Aug. 1885 to discuss Ireland. During the debate in the Commons on the second reading of the Home Bill on 7 June, Parnell informed the House of the meeting, claiming that Carnarvon had offered 'a statutory Parliament with power to protect Irish industries'. Three days later in the Lords, Carnarvon denied this. A. Hardinge, *The Life of Fourth Earl of Carnarvon* (1915), iii, pp. 222–6.

[3] Carnarvon omitted from his statement, at Salisbury's request, the fact that the meeting with Parnell was held with his (Salisbury's) full knowledge.

[4] Hansard, 3, cccvi, cols. 1215–40, 7 June.

[5] Ibid, cols. 1168–87.

[6] Dated 11 June, addressed to the electors of West Birmingham. *The Times*, 12 June 1886, p. 7.

[7] John Campbell, 7th Earl of Aberdeen, Lord-Lieutenant of Ireland. His villa at Dollis Hill, Middlesex, had been lent to Gladstone.


**487   W. E. GLADSTONE TO LORD SPENCER**
*14 June 1886; Holmbury*[1]


I am not sure from yours received today whether I quite understand your view of my last letter on land purchase.

There can be no harm I think in making any amount of argument in favour of our plan and its principle.

But as to the relation of the two subjects I think it would be a mistake either to recede from or to restate what we formerly said.

To restate at this date would be a new measure.

We ought I think to keep in our hands a perfectly [sic] liberty of rejudging the case when the proper time comes, in the measure which honour and policy may recommend. But let us, I should say, keep to the old point of departure, nothing having occurred which would justify a new one, and to say we stand in June in all points precisely as we did in April would be a new one.

I do not find fault with the landlords or say they have refused our offer. We shall probably be far better able to judge some time after the elections; all I would say is let us not prejudge but let the matter stand without adding or subtracting. Restarting with a new date would be adding.

[1] Holmbury House, Dorking, Surrey, home of Edward Frederic Leveson-Gower.

### 488   LORD SPENCER TO W. E. GLADSTONE
*18 June 1886; Privy Council Office*
GP, Add. MS. 44313 f. 83-4

I was delighted to see how enthusiastic a reception you had on your journey to Edinburgh.[1]

I am sure that this will last and increase.

I found the audience at Chester[2] as keen and enthusiastic as those which I addressed at Newcastle and Leeds some months ago.

What I wish to ask you now is merely a personal matter.

I should much like to go through a course of baths at Aix-les-Bains. This has a wonderful effect on me, and though I am very well now, I feel that I should be set up for the winter if I can get these baths.

As we may all be hard at work again in August or September I could not be sure of getting any then, and I should like to go off during the Elections.

I can be of no use then.

Do you see any objection?

[1] Gladstone left London on 17 June, delivering a speech at Edinburgh on the following day.
[2] On 16 June, see *The Times*, 17 June 1886, p. 7.

### 489   W. E. GLADSTONE TO LORD SPENCER
*19 June 1886; Edinburgh*

I must admit that you have worked with unsparing devotion and admirable effect, nor do *I* know any reason connected with the Cabinet and general operations of Government which is likely to interfere with your most reasonable plan.

On the question of your presence here during the elections, I do not like to speak, *simply* because it is not in my province. Perhaps you would not mind seeing A. Morley[1] for a moment.

All things here look well. Enthusiasm is at its topmost, if that will do the work. At my meeting last night I could manage pretty well with the names of Hartington and Salisbury. But nothing could induce them to tolerate the name of Chamberlain, invariably followed by the bitterest hooting and groaning. They evidently place *him* in a different category – and I am afraid they are right.

[1] Arnold Morley, M.P., Nottingham East, 1885-95, Chief Whip. Spencer left London on 26 June.

### 490   C. R. SPENCER TO LORD SPENCER
*24 June 1886; The Cedars, Northampton*

Things seem to be going well for me, and as far as we can judge there is only apathy to fear. Certainly there is that but as the polling day approaches I think we may rouse the people. Welford was very good only six dissentients,

Bugbrooke the same number, and the meeting was very hearty, Moulton un-animous in my favour though a small meeting.

Very few Liberals have left us and Cartwright's[1] agent is very low and somewhat annoyed as he considers he has been brought down on a wild goose chase.

Lord Henley[2] took the chair at Long Buckby last night for Cartwright and he took a few people over with him from Watford. We sent Fall[3] to keep order, at my request the bootmakers were told, and it all went off quietly and calmly.

After Cartwright's speech, one man asked if he thought he Mr. C. or you Lord Spencer knew most about Ireland. C. answered 'You did'. Then he was asked who brought him down to fight me, the Tories? he said No! the Liberals? he did not answer as he could not say they had.[4] When the vote of confidence was put to the meeting, a man rose and said that he considered Mr. C. an unfit and improper person and that he proposed that the meeting should support me.[5]

The whole meeting bar the Watford people voted for me, so only about 6 could be said to have supported Cartwright.

[1] William Cornwallis Cartwright of Aynhoe Park, Liberal M.P., Oxfordshire, 1868–85; adopted as Unionist candidate for Mid Northamptonshire on 16 June.
[2] Anthony Henley, 3rd Baron, Watford Court, Northamptonshire, Liberal M.P., Northampton, 1859–74.
[3] G. E. Fall, Secretary, Mid Northamptonshire Liberal Council, of Long Buckby.
[4] Of this meeting, Cartwright wrote, 'I have so far succeeded in not being at a loss to answer the shoemakers who have been heckling me.' W. C. Cartwright, Diary, 26 June 1886, Cartwright Papers, Box 6/16.
[5] See NH, 26 June 1886, p. 3.

### 491 J. BECKE TO LORD SPENCER

*1 July 1886; The Cedars, Northampton*

I presume you will be glad to hear something about the Elections. I think your Brother is quite safe: you know I am not of a sanguine temperament and I am aware of the danger always attendant on a split in the Party. I am not disposed to under-estimate that danger. We mean to work as if the contest was to be a very close one. Cartwright gets no support from the 'Rank and file' of Liberals. Personally he is not attractive, ungenial in manner, ineffective as a speaker. I know his agents regard his case as hopeless. The loss of the Henleys, Wakes, Langhams etc. is to be deplored, but their following is very small. Charles[1] was chaffing Fred Henley the other day and asking him whether he thought he could influence one vote. Henley said, perhaps two, but he was not sure.

Your Brother works well and makes friends everywhere he goes. I am usurping Dominion over him and protesting against his going into other Divisions. He has quite as much as he can do here, and in this great heat he must not over exert himself.

In South Northamptonshire, Charles wishes me to tell you that he is not hopeful. If that Division had been properly organized last time, Fitzgerald[2] would have been in. There is no organization now. Charles is doing all man could do to set it right, but I fear the task is beyond him, Briggs[3] utterly useless at the head of affairs is of but little utility in the second place. Channing is quite safe in the East.[4] Lord Burghley will not be opposed in the North.[5] A Tory Sheriff, with the Undersheriff Knightley's Agent,[6] prevented our having a chance in the South. One more week and I should say Carmichael would be in.

In the Borough the Tories have shown considerable skill. They have persuaded Mr. Richard Turner to start as an 'Unionist' in conjunction with Hastings Lees.[7] This was clever, the idea being that the Moderate Liberal would be bound to support Turner, who has always acted with them, and their so doing would exasperate the more advanced section, who would withhold support from Spencer. I saw at once it was a move for the County. Turner who is a man of no education and who has not the slightest idea as to what Home Rule means fell into the snare, although one of the Tory speakers was foolish enough to say in public that he was only to be a 'Catspaw'. Turner's family are all Tories, very anxious to get into Society, so he was surrounded by adverse influences. Charles and I met the move at once by saying that we thought it most unfair as against Bradlaugh, and although we had always gone against him, we should support him. Some, I think, many moderate Liberals will follow our lead, the Romanists have all agreed to do the same. So I think Labouchere and Bradlaugh will be stronger than ever, and we shall have their party as very strenuous supporters.

[1] Charles Cecil Becke, John Becke's son. He was election agent for Fitzgerald.

[2] Sir Maurice Fitzgerald, of Valencia, Co. Kerry, contested that division in Dec. 1885. He was narrowly beaten by the sitting Conservative member, Sir Rainald Knightley. See P. Gordon, 'Lady Knightley and the South Northamptonshire Election of 1885', *Northamptonshire Past and Present*, vi, no. 5 (1981-2), p. 267.

[3] Edwin Francis Ashworth Briggs, a Radical barrister, Daventry.

[4] Francis Allston Channing, Liberal, fighting his first election campaign against the Hon. Leopold Agar-Ellis, formerly M.P. Co. Kilkenny, 1857-73. See F. A. Channing, *Memories of Midland Politics 1885-1910* (1918), pp. 55-63.

[5] Brownlow Henry, Lord Burghley, Conservative M.P., North Northamptonshire, 1877-95.

[6] Thomas William Thornton, Sheriff; Richard Waters, Under-Sheriff.

[7] Turner, a Northampton shoe manufacturer and magistrate, and Thomas Orde Hastings Lees of Guilsborough House, Guilsborough, barrister. Formerly Chief Constable of the county, 1871-84, having served as Sub-Inspector, Royal Irish Constabulary, for seven years.

**492   C. R. SPENCER TO LADY SPENCER**
*2 July 1886; The Cedars, Northampton*

We in the Mid are getting on very well. If our people will only go to the Poll, it will be quite right, and the majority large. Cartwright would retire, only he is kept up by the bitterness of the Tories against us personally and cannot do as he wishes. Turner having started for the Town was simply to hurt me, but as my people have sent word to Bradlaugh's[1] Committee that they are going to support him, all the Radicals will vote for me. We shall lose some Liberals who cannot vote for Bradlaugh and so will vote for Turner and for

Cartwright. Canon Hughes[2] has signed my nomination, and would not sign Turner's, who came out as a Christian.

We have had innumerable meetings. I have been to 16 for myself and to 2 for Carmichael.[3] I fear he will not get in, the time not having been long enough. Carmichael's Election comes off on Tuesday, and mine Tuesday week ... Lord Hartington has written a letter to Cartwright,[4] which is placarded about, with one from Chamberlain to him too.

The exasperation of the Tories at the poor way Cartwright is received, is indescribable, but as many of them themselves will not do any work for him it is not much to be wondered. Va[5] came yesterday and we went to an open air meeting at Long Buckby, then to Percival's[6] for luncheon, then to West Haddon where we paid some visits, then to Harpole ...

S's letter just arrived, for which many thanks. There has been no difficulty as to any of his speeches, yet and I fancy the party supporting Leo Ellis[7] in the East will not dare mention him except vaguely: as his name always brings down the house.[8] Labby alluded to him last night at the mass meeting in the Town Hall, and the people cheered a great deal.[9]

Lady Cecily Clifton[10] is working like mad against us, and has tried to prevent any Liberal bills being put up in the village. She distributes masses of pamphlets, and has done some harm. Lord Henley and Bertie Langham[11] have done all they could for Cartwright, but as one is very unpopular, and the other insolvent they are not very dangerous.

[1] Charles Bradlaugh, Radical M.P., Northampton, 1881-91.

[2] Canon Nathaniel Thomas Hughes, rector of St. Edmund's, Northamptonshire.

[3] Sir James Morse Carmichael, Gladstone's private secretary, 1885. Unsuccessfully contested the Southern division of Northamptonshire. The meetings were at Towcester on 25 June and Stoke Bruerne on 26 June.

[4] Hartington to Cartwright, 27 June 1886, W. C. Cartwright Papers, Box 16/6.

[5] Victoria, Lady Sandhurst, Robert's sister.

[6] Charles Percival, farmer, West Haddon.

[7] On 12 June, Leopold Agar-Ellis saw Sir Rainald Knightley about standing as a Unionist against Robert Spencer. Lady Knightley noted, 'He *detests* Lord Spencer and knows the country [Ireland] from his nephew, Ld. Clifden's property there.' Lady Knightley, Journal, 12 June 1886, K 2902. He was nominated for East Northamptonshire, opposing Channing.

[8] Agar-Ellis's meeting at Wellingborough on 30 June had to be abandoned.

[9] At the meeting, Labouchere compared Lees's knowledge of Ireland with Spencer's. *NM*, 3 July 1886, p. 8.

[10] Lady Eleanor Cecily Clifton, The Grange, Guilsborough.

[11] Herbert Hay Langham, Cottesbrooke Hall.

**493** LORD SPENCER TO C. R. SPENCER

*4 July 1886; Aix-les-Bains*

I am glad to hear good accounts of you from J. Becke and from your letter to Charlotte. I have also been studying the *Mercury*, and the accounts of the meetings read very well.

I have been reading Speeches until I am sick, but really there is little in them.

I am honoured by Randolph. I wonder that Speech of mine did not turn up before. I used an unlucky word 'United Parliament'. If I had said 'Union with Great Britain' I need not unsay a word.[1] I am as strong now as I was then against Dynamiters, and those who want complete separation, and my [      ]² was directed against them really.

I was always careful not to go against some form of Home Rule. But it does not matter. I admit that up to November I hoped that we could win the Irish to our side as we won the Scotch. The Elections finally turned me to see that this was hopeless and past praying for

(1) The conduct of the Tories as to exceptional legislation

(2) The weakness of the Loyalists at the Irish Elections

(3) The complete adhesion of the R.C. hierarchy to Parnell.

These were the causes of my change of view.

¹ Churchill at Manchester on 30 June quoting Spencer's speech in Belfast in 1884: 'Lord Spencer goes as Mr. Gladstone's Lord-Lieutenant to Belfast with a solemn pledge that no British statesman ever gave up one point or one idea necessary for the maintenance of a united Parliament.' *The Times*, 1 July 1886, p. 5.

² Word omitted.

**494**   W. E. GLADSTONE TO LORD SPENCER

*4 July 1886; Hawarden Castle, Chester*

I write one hasty line to thank you for your very interesting letter and to express my fear, from the train things are at present taking, that you will hardly make out your little holiday in peace, as probably in about a week the Cabinet will have to meet and determine upon its course.

If there is to be an anti-Irish Government, the sooner it begins, the sooner it will end.

Everybody is dancing on the dead body of the Land Bill.

Whoever of us may suffer in this business your record at any rate is clear.

**495**   J. BECKE TO LORD SPENCER

*5 July 1886; The Cedars, Northampton*

I have this afternoon received your Lordship's letter. I had intended writing to you today as soon as the Poll for the Borough was declared. I have now (3 p.m.) received the figures.¹

|  | Poll 1886 |  | Poll 1885 |
|---|---|---|---|
| Labouchere | 4570 |  | 4845 |
| Bradlaugh | 4353 |  | 4315 |
| Turner | 3850 |  | — |
| Lees | 3456 | (Richards)² | 3890 |

The Tories were very exultant last night, they were sure Bradlaugh was out. Had Turner got in, it would have injured your Brother much.

So far as I can judge from what I read and what I hear, there is no feeling of enthusiasm on the part of our Supporters. John Bright's Speech has made a very strong impression.³ Next to Gladstone he has ever been the popular idol.

The impression that Gladstone has made a great mistake is steadily gaining ground in all the constituencies. The falling off of the Liberal vote is remarkable, considering the vast importance of the subject, wonderful. I take it it arises in large measure from a counterpoise between two opposing principles, on the one hand respect and gratitude towards Gladstone, on the other distrust of the wisdom of the Measure.

We shall have very many abstentions here in the Mid Division and some 100 or so have declared their intention to vote for Cartwright. On the other hand I know many Tories will not vote for Cartwright, some will vote for Mr. Spencer. His meetings are well attended, and always favourable – Cartwright's are badly attended. In the greater number of villages, he has been obliged to decline having a vote declared. In several instances hostile votes have been carried without difficulty. I adhere to my view that your Brother is safe, but I admit the difficulty of predicating what will be the result of the rupture of all party ties.

South Northamptonshire Poll will be taken tomorrow, the counting on Wednesday. All that can be said there is we have a chance. With another week's organization it would have been a certainty. On the canvasser returns we have a majority of 500 in this Division (South) but I never place faith in these.

... Your Brother is getting very tired. I have seen most of the leading men and have got them to promise me not to importune him to make speeches elsewhere. There is quite enough for him to do. I fear we shall not have the support of Lord Clifden.[4] Many ties will be broken this Election, tender party ties.

[1] Polling took place on Saturday 3 July. However, as Turner withheld his consent for counting to begin, the result was not announced until 5 July. *NM*, 10 July 1886, supp. p. 9.

[2] Henry Charles Richards, Conservative, a London barrister, who contested Bradlaugh's seat in 1884 and 1885.

[3] Bright broke his public silence on home rule at Birmingham on 1 July.

[4] Henry George, 4th Viscount Clifden, Spencer's nephew. Family seats at Gowran Castle and Ringwood, Co. Kilkenny and also at Holdenby House, Northamptonshire.

## 496  C. R. SPENCER TO LADY SPENCER

*12 July 1886; The Cedars, Northampton*

I am in great hopes now, as it has been raining hard, and the hay cannot be touched much, and if it only continues to rain, our men will poll tomorrow. Channing's majority of 1426 is good, though I confess to being surprised Leo Ellis got as many as 3042 odd votes.[1] John Morley spoke admirably on Saturday at Kingsthorpe a large meeting about 3700, and very few Tories ...[2] Morley was excellent and pleased the people though it struck me as almost above them. He left to my great relief just as I began, as he made me very nervous. I was well received ...

Holly has hired vehicles for the people at Naseby, but I telegraphed to him that it was not advisable to do so, so I hope he has stopped them. Nice of him tho' to wish for his voters to go to the Poll irrespective of politics ...

I expect from the short time this Election has lasted, and the necessity of getting to as many places as possible, that the expenses will be more than we fancied, but of course we don't know yet.

[1] In fact the final figures were Channing 4428, Agar-Ellis 3012.

[2] Morley included a passage in his address on 10 July praising Lord Spencer for his endeavours to secure an Irish settlement. *NM*, 17 July 1886, p. 9.


## 497  LORD SPENCER TO W. E. GLADSTONE
*14 July 1886; Aix-les-Bains*
GP, Add. MS. 44313 ff. 87–8

I hope to be with you at dinner on Saturday,[1] but if anything befalls us on the way you will excuse me if I do not come at the last moment.

I am very sorry at the turn of the Elections. What does Hartington mean when he says that he is disappointed as he hoped that the Liberals would have been in a position to settle the question?[2] It almost looks as if he expected that his Dissentient Liberal friends would have swept your supporters off the face of Politics.

If this was what he meant what a shock he will have had.

I fear that there is nothing for it but to make way for others, in order as you said that the period of anti Irish Government may, if it is to come, be the sooner ended.

[1] 17 July, Spencer reached London in the evening after a ten-day holiday and attended a cabinet dinner at Downing Street.

[2] At Chesterfield on 5 July. *The Times*, 6 July 1886, p. 10.


## 498  C. R. SPENCER TO LORD SPENCER
*14 July 1886; Althorp, Northampton*

We came over here for a few hours' quiet after the terrible counting. You know by now of the victory which is a real good one. 956 majority ought to stop any further attempts at this seat.[1] Cartwright was very nice indeed and kept saying 500 would be my majority, but he was the least disconcerted of our opponents when the real numbers came out.[2] Bertie Langham looked very sick indeed. Our own people must have polled late yesterday between 6 and 8, as the Tories were very jubilant because they thought the labourers would not poll. I am so pleased at the result, as it shows our people are really in earnest. 1000 less polled, but the majority only 143 less, so the proportion is very good.

Yesterday I rode for 3 hours from 7.30 to 10.30 in the morning to Houghton, Denton, Horton, Hackleton, Rode, Wootton and back. Then we posted to Duston, Bugbrooke, Floore, Long Buckby, Kilsby, Crick, West Haddon, Gilsboro, Spratton, Brixworth, Moulton, Weston Favell and so home.

When we got home, we found we must go to Kingsthorpe as the working men wanted to give Va a nosegay, so off we went and were much pleased at finding the people had just begun to poll hard, and the result was most useful.

... I am so pleased at not being beaten. I felt it was so very likely, and I could not bear to think of our own county turned against you and Mr. G. The latter's letters have done a great deal of harm, the nonsense he has written and telegraphed has been dreadful.

¹ Spencer 4887, Cartwright 3931.
² Cartwright confided his real feelings to his Diary: 'Though I did not expect to win, I was not prepared for the majority against me.' W. C. Cartwright Papers, 14 July 1886, Box 6/16.

**499   LORD GRANVILLE TO LORD SPENCER**
*28 July 1886; 18 Carlton House Terrace, S.W.*

Gladstone suddenly summoned a meeting of Ministers[1] today – Dilke,[2] Government Irish Policy, and Queen's refusal to make 3 of his proposed Baronets.[3]

We had a long talk about Dilke, and it was settled to leave to our successors[4] to take his name off the list of Privy Council, and the question of prosecution.[5] There is hardly time to ascertain whether there will be further legal proceedings against or for Dilke, and our Law officers are all concerned in the late suits.

Gladstone was evidently all for fighting against any proposed delay on question. But we were all for abusing it in debate, but not dividing.

He rather wished to yield to the Queen but we advised him to stick to his guns about the Baronets.[6]

¹ At Granville's residence.
² The Spencers dined with Gladstone at Downing Street on 23 July. 'Mr Gladstone was in excellent spirits and very well. He was very unhappy as to the terrible Dilke Case.' Lady Spencer, Diary, 23 July 1886, SP. The Crawford divorce case was heard on 12 Feb. 1886, with the charge against Dilke being dismissed with costs. At a rehearing of the case, which lasted from 16 to 23 July, the Queen's Proctor failed to establish Dilke's innocence. S. Gwynn and G. M. Tuckwell, *Life of Sir Charles W. Dilke* (1917), ii, p. 177.
³ James Kitson, president of the National Liberal Federation, Dr. Balthazar Foster, Liberal M.P., Chester, 1885-6 and John Cowan, chairman of Gladstone's election committee in Midlothian since 1879. The Queen had rejected them on 27 July. GP, Loan 73/25.
⁴ Gladstone resigned on 20 July. Salisbury undertook to form a government on 25 July.
⁵ Gladstone had sought Herschell's advice on removing Dilke from the Privy Council. Herschell suggested that the decision should be taken by the next administration. Herschell to Gladstone, 24 July 1886, GP, Add. MS. 44498 f. 276.
⁶ Gladstone wrote to the Queen after the cabinet and she reluctantly agreed to his request. Queen Victoria to Gladstone, 28 July 1886, GP, Loan 73/25.

# 3
## WAITING FOR POWER, 1886-92

*Irish affairs continued to dominate the political scene. Salisbury's government failed to disclose its plans for the future of Ireland and in September 1886, Parnell took the initiative by introducing a Tenants Relief Bill, intended to deal with the general inability of leaseholders to pay their rents. Although it received Liberal support, the Bill was defeated. There followed an organized agrarian movement, backed by Parnell, which aimed at inciting Irish tenants against landlords.*

*Following the resignation of Randolph Churchill in December 1886, a welcome olive branch was held out by Chamberlain to effect a reconciliation with his former Liberal colleagues. Gladstone accepted the offer and a meeting, known as the Round Table Conference, was held at Harcourt's London house on 13 and 14 January 1887 between Chamberlain, supported by Trevelyan, and Harcourt, Herschell and Morley. Spencer, at Chamberlain's request, was not present, but he was kept informed of the negotiations by the Gladstonian participants. After a promising start, the Conference proved abortive.*

*Since the 1885 election, Welsh M.P.s had become more vocal in pressing for disestablishment in Wales and the realization of national aspirations. Spencer was persuaded by John Morley and Schnadhorst, the party organizer, to address the initial meeting of the North Wales Federation in November 1886. This move was, as Spencer reported to Granville, 'to prevent Wales forming a separate Liberal Federation'. The uneasy Irish situation made it politic for the visit to be postponed, though a year later at Aberystwyth Spencer publicly indicated his sympathy for Welsh disestablishment.*

*He unintentionally caused a more serious stir in the Liberal camp with his Stockton speech on 24 October 1889. At a conference held earlier in the month at Hawarden, Gladstone, Harcourt, Morley and Ripon agreed to remain silent upon disputed points of Irish representation at Westminster. Unaware of this decision, Spencer upset the strategy by declaring that Irish members should be retained at Westminster. Apologizing to Gladstone, Spencer wrote, 'I confess to having been nettled at the constant jibes of our opponents as to our having no Policy.' (Spencer to Gladstone, 8 November 1889, GP, Add. MS. 44314 f. 5). Earlier in the year, Spencer had been in the public eye when he had shaken hands with Parnell at a dinner given by Liberals. This followed the exposure of a forger, Pigott, during the course of the proceedings of a Parliamentary Commission investigating Parnell's alleged links with the Phoenix Park murders. Spencer was saddened at Parnell's downfall, following the O'Shea divorce case, and at his subsequent death.*

*Within the Liberal Party Spencer's own standing was high. Rosebery told Edward Hamilton in June 1889 that 'the best solution of the difficulties connected with forming a Govt. apart from Mr. G. would be a Spencerian Administration with Harcourt as Leader of the House of Commons'. (15 June 1889, EHJ, Add. MS. 48651 f.14), a sentiment echoed by Catherine Gladstone.*

*A gradual shift from the preoccupation of the Liberal Party with Ireland towards domestic affairs found its expression in the programme of reforms endorsed by the National Liberal Federation Conference at Newcastle upon Tyne in 1891. It included Welsh and Scottish disestablishment, free elementary education, an employers' liability bill, parish councils, local option, taxation of land, reform of the franchise and of the House of Lords. This programme was aimed at recapturing the seats lost in the 1886 general election. For a time there seemed to be a real hope of the Liberals returning to power. With this in mind, the ex-cabinet met at Althorp in December 1891 to discuss the prospects before them.*

### 500   J. MORLEY TO LORD SPENCER
*14 August 1886; Frensham, Farnham, Surrey*

*Confidential*

I shall be very anxious to have a talk with you, if it is possible, before the debate.[1] We shall perhaps meet at Harcourt's on Tuesday, and could then arrange for a quiet hour on Wednesday.

There is much to depress one, I admit.

1. Even Mr. G., if I may judge from a talk with him on Thursday, now fears that a reunion of the party has ceased to be probable. Chamberlain's formal adhesion to Hartington he regards as fatal to reunion.

2. Excepting you, who know the ground thoroughly, and me, who know it partially, nobody in the party is really acquainted with the difficulties and necessities of Irish government.

3. Half the late Cabinet are sceptical and cynical, at bottom; especially Harcourt, who is naturally so important a figure among us.

4. Parnell has his own battle to fight, and he may have to fight it in a way which will never do for us.

On the other hand,

1. We know for certain that no peace is at all possible until some large and serious attempt has been made in our direction.

2. Moreover masses in the constituencies have now been educated in the question, and will not fall away.

3. Our party in the House of Commons is doubtless very loosely held together by Mr. Gladstone's name, but at the same time it now contains more than a hundred men who are as thoroughly determined and in earnest on one side, as Hartington is on the other.

In public it seems to me to be vital that we should show a bold and straightforward front, whenever, as you say, a legitimate occasion arises.

The comparison with O'Connell's time[2] is a desperately bad one.

[1] The Queen's Speech was delivered on 19 Aug.
[2] See No. **174** n.2.

**501   C. R. SPENCER TO LORD SPENCER**

*17 August 1886; Hotel Metropole, Langen Schwalbach, Germany*

I am very glad to see in the paper I got just now that the Election expenses are under £800. Becke certainly does manage wonderfully well. This is a nice place though in a hole, so not very bracing but the waters are very strong and do act as a tonic.[1]

... I dined with the Prince[2] the only night he was here, he was rather down on Lord Aberdeen, which I would not agree with ...[3] Of course the Prince anticipates brilliant results from Londonderry[4] and his money.

I had a long talk to Lord Hartington after taking the oath Monday week back,[5] and he was as nice as possible. I asked him several questions as to what he was going to do, and he said anything to keep this Government in office, and oppose any semblance of a separate legislative body in Ireland.

He told me that he had been compelled to sit on the front Opposition bench, as he would not have kept the seat below the gangway as Labouchere would be sure to want that, and the one just behind the front bench he would not have been able to to keep. He was in great spirits, but admitted that if the Tories brought in a modified Home Rule under another name he should not know what to do quite.

[1] Sir Francis Head, a leading nineteenth-century spa-fancier, thought that taking a bath at Langen Schwalbach was like 'lying with a set of hides in a tan pit'. E. S. Turner, *Taking the Cure* (1967), p. 135.

[2] Albert Edward, Prince of Wales.

[3] Aberdeen had been appointed Lord-Lieutenant of Ireland by Gladstone in his 1886 ministry at the age of 39. When Spencer saw the Queen on 8 Feb. she observed that Aberdeen was 'a weak, nervous, not clear man'. Spencer concurred, stating that 'this was better as they wished to leave it in the hands of Mr. Morley.' Queen Victoria, Journal, 8 Feb. 1886, RA C 37/280b.

[4] Charles Stewart Vane-Tempest-Stewart, 6th Marquess of Londonderry, appointed Lord-Lieutenant of Ireland on 28 July at the urging of the Prince. Sir S. Lee, *King Edward VII* (1925), i, p. 529.

[5] The new parliamentary session began on 5 Aug.

**502   LORD SPENCER TO C. R. SPENCER**

*22 August 1886; Althorp, Northampton*

I went up to London on Tuesday and remained until Friday. I expected to speak on Thursday and rose for the purpose of replying to Argyll,[1] but Salisbury rose at the same time, and after he had finished[2] it was dinner hour and the House cleared at once. I was sorry and yet relieved.

The Tories have not been unskilful in making a show to fill up time. Sir R. Buller's mission to Kerry looks like force.[3] It will answer for a time and then the country will fall back to its present condition.

The Land Commission is really absurd but if they have it in order to stop the agitation against judicial rents and allow it to lead up to some measure of ability, it will be good, but I have no faith in it and as to the Commission on Works, Irrigation, Rail Roads, Harbours etc. that is all bosh. It will cost money and catch no support.

However if they bring in a big measure in Feb. they might succeed but I doubt their bringing in anything big enough which will satisfy Irish aspirations.

Salisbury made a very statesmanlike Speech, measured and careful in language. I hear Randolph did well, but went further than Salisbury in some ways which was not wholly wise.[4] He looked ghastly ill.

We have had our domestic coup d'Etat, and given notice to all Servants not needed to take care of House, excepting Under Butler. We shall begin afresh on a small scale after a time but we shall try and do without regular establishment for 2 or 3 months.

We shall do very well and be very comfortable on a smaller scale when we get into it, but it is a bore after so many years to change, but to keep up a large establishment and not entertain is horrid. We can with a smaller Establishment do more at times.

We have as good as settled to remain in England. I find it really necessary to look after things.

Harcourt seems to have made a capable Speech on Friday.

Mr. G. is going abroad[5] and keep out of the way. He is issuing a pamphlet on the position[6] as he is not going to spout. It is good but I am not quite sure whether it is necessary. Still we must keep up our flag.

[1] On 18 Aug., George Douglas, 8th Duke of Argyll, who had resigned in 1881 as Gladstone's Lord Privy Seal over the Irish Land Bill, charged the late Liberal government with neglecting to protect life and property in Ireland. Hansard, 3, cccviii, cols. 37–51.

[2] Ibid, cols. 55–70.

[3] Maj.-Gen. Sir Redvers Buller, appointed special commissioner in Ireland in mid-August to suppress moonlighting and boycotting in counties Kerry and Clare. C. H. Melville, *Life of General Sir Redvers Buller* (1923), pp. 302–3.

[4] In the debate on the Address, warning that coercive measures might be necessary if intimidation continued. Hansard, 3, cccviii, cols. 113–33, 19 Aug.

[5] To Tegernsee, Bavaria, to visit Döllinger and Acton. He left London on 25 Aug. and returned on 19 Sept.

[6] *The History of an Idea and the lessons of the Elections* on the Irish question. For Spencer's detailed comments at proof stage, see Spencer to Gladstone, 20 Aug. 1886, GP, Add. MS. 44313 ff. 92–3.

**503  J. MORLEY TO LORD SPENCER**
*28 August 1886; Frensham, Farnham, Surrey*

*Confidential*

Harcourt's deliverance last night gives me a good deal of concern.[1]

Mr. G.'s last word to me was to urge upon Harcourt to say nothing that would prevent one having a perfectly free hand, if we were called upon to deal with the Irish question again. I did this. Harcourt was in high wrath that Mr. G. had shown you and me the new pamphlet, and never consulted him. 'He would not stand it—he would say what he liked—d - - n Land Purchase,' etc. etc.

I thought that I had prevailed upon him to leave it out of his speech. But, as you see, I was mistaken; and I hear that he was saying in the tea-room as boisterously as he could that he ought to have left the Government on the Land Bill, that the landlords would never have another chance if he could help it, and so on.

Of course, Chamberlain was very jubilant. Harcourt could not have chosen a worse moment, for C. had already scored by his own speech of Thursday,[2] and the public abandonment of the Land Bill, along with the announcement that Harcourt had cut loose from you and me, made an extra-delicious morsel for him. He asked me whether I agreed with Harcourt, but somebody interrupted, and he got no answer.

The distraction is almost complete.

*Mr. G*: 'Home Rule and Land are separable questions, but Land is an obligation of honour.'

*Harcourt*: 'Land is not an obligation of honour, and I will not touch it.'

*Lord Spencer: and J M*. 'You may separate them, if you like, for tactical purposes: but you cannot settle Home Rule without Land.'

I have not had any word with Harcourt since his speech, but of course I shall tell him that he has produced a serious embarrassment. At this moment, I do not see my way out of it. It would be painful to announce that one does not agree with Harcourt, and yet if nothing is said, it will be assumed that we have dropped an old principle.

Perhaps it is best to keep silent. There is no call for action, nor likely to be.

I shall try to stay here on Monday, and be in town on Tuesday, where a line at the Athenaeum would find me.[3]

[1] On 27 Aug., the seventh night of the debate on the Queen's Speech, Parnell's amendment, deprecating any attempt to transfer any loss likely to arise from the inability of Irish tenants to pay rents to British taxpayers, was defeated by 304 votes to 181. Harcourt stated that he would refuse to vote for Parnell's amendment. Hansard, 3, cccviii, cols. 735-6. Spencer protested to Harcourt that he was creating a split in the Liberal ranks. Spencer to Harcourt, 31 Aug. 1886, HP, MS. 45.

[2] In a bold speech in the Commons on the previous evening, Chamberlain announced that he would not attempt to turn out the government 'as long as the Government which is to take its place is committed to a Separatist policy'. Hansard, 3, cccviii, col. 614 ff, 26 Aug. 1886.

[3] Spencer annotated the letter, 'Answered and saw him on Monday' (i.e. 30 Jan.).

**504  LORD SPENCER TO C. R. SPENCER**

*18 September 1886; Spencer House, St. James's Place, S.W.*

We were to have gone up to Dalmeny today, but yesterday Granville telegraphed to me for opinions etc. on Parnell's Bill,[1] so I thought it better to come up to see him. My views are hazy. I hate the lines of the Bill but it is a very serious responsibility to refuse the demand.

It is like the Compensation for Disturbance Bill in our time.

I am not clear what ought to be done.

On the whole I incline to a temporary measure to bridge over the autumn and winter until the Government inquiry, which of itself is an admission that something may be wanted, is ready. A great deal may happen before then and just now it is right to avoid all excuse for disturbance. But it is very disagreeable to interfere again.

[1] The Tenants Relief (Ireland) Bill to allow for the admission of certain leaseholders to the Land Act, 1881. See L. P. Curtis, *Coercion and Conciliation in Ireland* (1963), pp. 142-4. Gladstone spoke on the second reading of the bill on 20 Sept., after holding a meeting of ex-cabinet ministers at Granville's in the morning. Lord and Lady Spencer went to the Commons later in the day to hear Gladstone's 'very spirited speech'. Lady Spencer, Diary, 20 Sept. 1886, SP.

## 505 C. R. SPENCER TO LORD SPENCER
*22 September 1886; Abergeldie Castle, Ballater, Aberdeenshire*

I am more thankful than ever that we are Liberals, surrounded by servile Tories of the Monty Corrie[1] style. I feel really that it is despicable to be a Tory. The Queen has twice sent for Monty, and apparently takes his advice, or at least listens to it. Bulgaria excites them all here, and Francis Knollys[2] and I are bothered to death by the shrieks and yells about Russian duplicity and poor dear Sandro's (Alexander) attempted assassination.[3] As the said Sandro is known never to speak the truth, it is all ridiculous. H.M. is rabid about him, and as Monty is a furious Russophobist I imagine that he adds fuel to her excitement. H.M. sent me a nice message saying she hoped to see me, civil but meaningless I think.

[1] Montagu William Lowry Corry, Baron Rowton, former private secretary to Lord Beaconsfield.
[2] Sir Francis Knollys, Prince of Wales's private secretary.
[3] Prince Alexander of Battenburg, elected Prince of Bulgaria in 1879. He was kidnapped in an officers' coup on 22 Aug. 1886 and formally abdicated on 4 Sept. 1886. He described his overthrow to the Queen in a letter dated 15 Sept. See *LQV*, 3rd ser., i, pp. 208-9.

## 506 LORD GRANVILLE TO LORD SPENCER
*3 November 1886; Hawarden Castle*

I am waiting for a train, and send you a hurried line.

We had 2 hours conversation, nothing very new.[1]

Morley's information was that Dillon had failed,[2] that the good Landlords were making great abatements, and their tenants were paying, that there is a percentage of tenants who would not pay, and of Landlords who will not abate, and that some outrages will be the consequence.

We were all 3 agreed that the line should be a frank adherence to our principles, (Gladstone not excluding the acceptance though not an approval of any measure that gives a central body in Dublin of any sort).

We also agreed that Morley should pitch into Stanhope[3] for preaching the doctrine that the right thing was to legislate for Ireland, quite independently of the Irish M.P.s.

Gladstone and I were at the furthest ends as to the Dissentients.

He at first much wished that by mild objurgations and courteous arguments, that they should be convinced that it was impossible for them as Christians and Gentlemen to support the Government in any delay as to Irish proposals, his theory being that there are few Hartingtonians still fewer Chamberlainites and that the mass of the dissentients are quite open to persuasion.

My view was that we should state our views and defend them, but not attempt to intimidate or cajole the dissentients [and] as much as possible to ignore them in public speaking. Harcourt and Morley agreed with me, but I am not sure that they will act upon this theory. The question of what was to be done in Parliament, when the Government propose procedures and neglect Ireland, was left for future consideration.

[1] Granville arrived at Hawarden on 30 Oct.

[2] After the rejection of Parnell's Tenants Relief Bill on 21 Sept., Dillon returned to Ireland, together with O'Brien, to organize tenants for the coming struggle through the Irish National League. The plan, outlined by Dillon in his Dublin speech of 28 Sept., appeared in *United Ireland* on 23 Oct. under the heading 'Plan of Campaign.' F. S. L. Lyons, *John Dillon* (1968), pp. 83-4.

[3] Edward Stanhope, Colonial Secretary, Conservative M.P., Horncastle, Lincs, 1885-93. See his speech to his constituents on 15 Oct. *The Times*, 16 Oct. 1886, p. 7.

## 507  F. SCHNADHORST[1] TO LORD SPENCER

*19 November 1886; National Liberal Federation, 41 Parliament St., London S.W.*

I am very desirous of meeting the wishes of the North Wales Liberals for a great meeting in December.[2] I shall be extremely glad if you will consent to go.

After careful consideration I am satisfied that we cannot do a better thing now than help the Welshmen. I have enquired what views they hold on the Land question and find them something of this mind—Fair rents by arbitration with an appeal to the County Court Judge, something like fixity of tenure and compensation for unexhausted improvements to be fixed also by arbitration. It would not be necessary to go into any of these points. The question of deepest interest is Disestablishment and with it the question of tithes. These and the question of Ireland would be the main points of interest. Something might be said about Education.

The movement in favour of North Wales Liberal Federation will be merged in our organization if I can now take the matter up and getting you to go is one of the principal inducements.[3]

I want to know now so as to give them ample time to work up an attendance from all parts of North Wales.

[1] Secretary of the National Liberal Federation since its establishment in 1877 and from 1886 also Secretary of the Liberal Central Association. See B. McGill, 'Francis Schnadhorst and Liberal Party Organization', *The Journal of Modern History*, xxxiv (1962), p. 269.

[2] At Rhyl on 14 Dec.

[3] Schnadhorst had advised Stuart Rendel, Liberal M.P., Montgomeryshire, 1880-94, and a strong home ruler, who became the first president of the North Wales Federation, to bring together the individual Liberal associations in the country. K. O. Morgan, *Wales in British Politics 1868-1922* (1980), p. 78.

## 508  LORD SPENCER TO LORD GRANVILLE

*4 December 1886; Sandringham, Norfolk*
Gr. P, PRO 30/29/29A

I shall get myself into a scrape I fear about a Political engagement, but when the Dillon prosecution was started[1] and the Government seemed to be beginning active work in Ireland, I thought that it would be very dangerous for me to speak on Ireland.

John Morley advised me to get off my engagement,[2] and accordingly I have said that circumstances have arisen which make it impossible for me to go to Rhyl.

I thought it better to offend those who got up the meeting, than run the risk of getting into a hopeless mess about Ireland. After the. trial I could not have avoided alluding to it. Whatever I said I should be told that I was backing up illegality.

I thought that John Morley steered very cleverly at Edinburgh[3] but it does not follow that I should have done the same.

[1] Dillon was to stand trial on 12 Dec. before the Court of Queen's Bench for his activities in connection with the Plan of Campaign. After a two day trial, Dillon was found guilty and the Plan pronounced illegal, but he was bound over and released. The Times, 15 Dec. 1886, p. 6.

[2] The Welsh meeting took place on the same day that Dillon's trial ended and Morley wrote to Spencer stating that 'Gladstone is all for abstaining from any public utterance if coercion seems to be to hand'. Morley to Spencer, 29 Nov. 1886, SP. Mundella took Spencer's place at Rhyl.

[3] On 2 Dec., expressing sympathy for Scottish self-government. The Times, 3 Dec. 1886, p. 7.

## 509 LORD SPENCER TO W. E. GLADSTONE
*25 December 1886; Althorp, Northampton*
GP, Add. MS. 44313 ff. 106-7

This is to wish Mrs. Gladstone and yourself the best wishes of the season. We hope you are very well. You may feel some satisfaction at not being in the midst of a Political crisis like Salisbury.

What an extraordinary collapse this is! I never expected that Randolph would throw up his powerful position so suddenly.[1] He cannot have treated his colleagues handsomely. I have no idea whether he has any real following among Conservatives, possibly enough to upset Salisbury but not enough to form a party of his own. I suppose however that he will aim at becoming Leader of a new party sooner or later.

Chamberlain seems to be playing a new part. I fear that his attitude of conciliation is not very genuine: but he may find that his former position was hopeless.[2] It will separate him I should suppose from Hartington who will be disposed to continue his support to Salisbury. Nothing can be decided until Hartington's decision is known. Without him to lead the House of Commons Salisbury will be in a very difficult position, for Beach can hardly be removed from Ireland,[3] nor can he hold the Irish Office with the Leadership with any comfort. Moreover he was not a success as leader.[4]

I cannot help thinking that this will strengthen your position. I have not much hope of immediate reconciliation with the Dissentient Liberals, but recent events must shake the cohesion of our Liberal opponents.[5]

[1] Churchill, then Chancellor of the Exchequer, submitted his resignation direct to Salisbury on 20 Dec. rather than discuss his disagreements on general policy in cabinet. Two days later, Salisbury accepted the resignation. That night Churchill broke the news to the editor of The Times, Buckle, and a statement was published on 23 Dec. See R. F. Foster, Lord Randolph Churchill (1981), pp. 304-10.

[2] In a speech to the Liberal Divisional Council at West Bromwich on 23 Dec. Chamberlain said, 'I am convinced that, sitting round a table and coming together in a spirit of compromise and conciliation, almost any three men, leaders of the Liberal Party, although they may hold opposite views upon another branch of the question, would yet be able to arrange some scheme which would fulfil the conditions which I have laid down.' The Times, 24 Dec. 1886, p. 4.

[3] Hicks Beach was Chief Secretary, Aug. 1886 to March 1887.

[4] In the first Salisbury ministry.

[5] For the reply, see Gladstone to Spencer, 26 Dec. 1886, SP.

**510** LORD SPENCER TO U. KAY-SHUTTLEWORTH[1]
*28 December 1886; Althorp, Northampton*
Shuttleworth Papers

I received your very interesting and important letter about your Irish visit[2] just as I was brewing a Speech for Leicester.[3] I intended to have taken it up immediately afterwards, but various reasons have kept your letter on my table without my writing to you upon it. I have again read it, and cannot say how much I appreciate all you write.

I wish we had approached Irish subjects in the same spirit years ago. I cannot help thinking that the study of the Home Rule question will teach many men to see that we failed even when doing good work for Ireland because we had adopted forms and methods which did not appeal to Irish sentiment and feeling, or suit Irish needs. Your comments on the Trinity College men is very true. I suppose that reliance on the strong arm of England has hardened their intolerance and prevented their solving questions which if left free to face their opponents they must long ago have settled.

... As to the Land question, we hoped that we had introduced sufficient elasticity in our Land Bill to meet the difficult cases of Western proprietorship, for we intended that average net receipts for a series of years should cover a sufficiently long time to include several years where little or no rent had been received, and we further gave discretion to the Commission to vary the terms of Purchase.

However, if our machinery was not sufficient to meet the cases to which you refer we should in any new measure remedy that defect. No doubt now some modification of judicial rents would have to be made.

It is curious by the way how people are coming round to the necessity of a land settlement.

There is great truth in the remark that there might have been danger had Home Rule been adopted too suddenly. People are every day preparing themselves for it, and my anxious hope is that even in Ulster progress towards receiving Home Rule will be made.

We see some fruits of our work in the attitude of the Nationalists about this Plan of Campaign.

The rasher spirits who rushed at it, have apparently been checked not merely by the action of the Government, but by the feeling that they had shirked the moral feeling of many of their English supporters and friends.

I wonder whether you printed any part of your letter? I hope you did.

I showed your letter to John Morley and one or two others. Morley was much struck by it.

Did you send a copy to Mr. Gladstone? He certainly should see it and if you have not sent it, I will certainly do so.[4]

---

[1] Sir Ughtred James Kay-Shuttleworth, Liberal M.P., Clitheroe, Lancashire, 1885-1902. Under-Secretary for India and Chancellor of the Duchy of Lancaster in Gladstone's 1886 ministry.

[2] Kay-Shuttleworth visited Ireland in Nov. 1886, touring reformatory and industrial schools. He also took the opportunity to seek the views of many leading figures on the political situation. He told Spencer in a twelve-page letter, 'I feel strongly confirmed in the opinion that the experiment

of legislating at Westminster on Irish affairs has proved a failure.' Shuttleworth to Spencer, 19 Nov. 1886, SP.

3 On 25 Nov. defending Gladstone's home rule plan. *The Times*, 26 Nov. 1886, p. 6.

4 The letter was printed and circulated to ex-cabinet members. In acknowledging his receipt of the letter, Gladstone replied, 'Nothing would be more healthful for the English people than to walk them in a long file through Ireland, of which they know nothing; as people are walked through a Palace where someone lies in state.' Gladstone to Kay-Shuttleworth, 1 Dec. 1886, Shuttleworth Papers.


## 511 LORD SPENCER TO J. DILLON[1]

*1 January 1887; Spencer House, St. James's Place, S.W.*

I had much pleasure in meeting you last week at Sir W. Harcourt's and I hope I may again before long see you as I feel that it is an excellent thing to be brought into contact with you Irish leaders. The want of this has done much harm in the past.

I should not however feel that I were quite honest if I did not say something on parts of the interesting information which you gave us.

I did not express my opinions at the time, as I did not wish to begin what might have led to a long discussion, but on reflection I think that I ought to have shown that I did not agree with some of your views, as my silence may have been misconstrued by you.

I refer to two methods practised in the land war in Ireland, which have your approval.

The Plan of Campaign and Boycotting. Now as to the Plan of Campaign, I have not infrequently in speeches stated that I could not approve of it though I have always said that the action of the Government in the H. of C. and in Ireland to a great extent justified the adoption of some combination of the kind.

I confess however that I feel differently about a system of Boycotting which is used as you stated the other night by the National League for preventing Tenants in certain cases selling their interests in their farms, or of taking farms even where they did so of their own accord.

I must frankly say that I do strongly object to a system of this sort.

I do not go to the length of Bishop O'Dwyer's denunciation,[2] for I believe that if in the past Boycotting may have led to outrage, it does not now do so, and it has taken the place of outrage which I admit is a great gain.

I know that loyalty inflicts cruel sufferings on those who do come within its reach, and I should still wish to stop it just as I tried to stop it (but with small success) when I was in Dublin.

I shall not now further discuss these points.

I realize more than before, not so much the existence of Boycotting and its occasional sanction by the League, but the systematic adoption of it by leaders like yourself, and I confess that I grieved at so marked a difference existing between us in one method of getting Home Rule.

This does not for a moment slacken my desire to get Home Rule, nor my determination to do what I can to promote it, but it makes it clear to me that on some parts of the question I fight on different grounds to those occupied by you and your friends.

In some ways it is better that this should occur, for in a large body of people supporting a general Principle there must be great variations of opinion, and in my humble and feeble way I may influence men who could not be influenced by your more striking and powerful arguments and methods of carrying on the agitation.

But as I hope I may retain your good opinion I wish to make my position clear to you, so as to have no misunderstanding when we meet in private, or no surprise on your part if when I speak in public I express (as is sometimes absolutely necessary for supporting my arguments) in what will be I hope moderate but distinct terms my disagreement and disapproval of such a thing as systematic Boycotting. You I feel sure have no difficulty in justifying your adoption of this method of warfare. I cannot do so.

We differ on this, but it will not prevent our agreement on the main question, that the solution of Irish difficulty is to be found in giving Ireland Home Rule.

[1] Headed 'Not sent. Kept to show my views after dinner at Harcourt's.' SP.

[2] In Dec. 1886, Dr. Edward O'Dwyer, Bishop of Limerick, and Dr. John Healy, Bishop of Clonfert, had supplied information on the activities of Irish priests to the Prefect of Propaganda in Rome.


**512   W. V. HARCOURT TO LORD SPENCER**
*1 January 1887; 7 Grafton Street, W.*

*Confidential*

I think you ought to know what has been passing in our camp during the present crisis. On reading Chamberlain's speech[1] I wrote to him at once expressing my satisfaction at its conciliatory tone and my desire to co-operate with him in any reasonable scheme of reunion.[2]

To this he replied in the most friendly spirit[3] and at my request came up to London to see me on Thursday.[4] I of course informed Mr. Gladstone of what I was about and received his entire assent to our communications.[5] His phrase was to me that 'Chamberlain's speech ought to lead to a *modus vivendi* in the Liberal Party'. The result has been that Chamberlain made a definite proposal that he should meet some of us to discuss the Irish Question and particularly '(1) Land and (2) The Local Government.' I insisted as a *sine qua non* that the discussion should include (3) a *Legislative Body for Ireland*. To this not without reluctance he agreed. The object was to be to seek some common ground of agreement on which the Liberal Party could reunite. The suggestion on his part is that he and G. Trevelyan should meet Herschell, John Morley, myself and H. Fowler,[6] the last introduced as a financial expert for the Land Question. It is proposed that the above-mentioned should meet together in a friendly way without binding authority and endeavour to settle a common platform for the united Liberal Party. I have been in London for the last three days and in constant communication with Chamberlain and John Morley. John Morley and I are completely satisfied of the sincerity and *bona fides* of Chamberlain in the matter. It is needless to speculate on the motives of this venture on his part—it is sufficient that it is made.

In my opinion we shall be deeply responsible for the final ruin of the Liberal

Party if we reject this attempt at accommodation. If it succeeds it will be an immense gain. It it fails we shall be no worse off than before. In any event it will remove the spirit of bitterness which has prevailed. If we are the parties to decline it Chamberlain will have the advantage of casting the whole blame upon us. J. Morley and I are quite at one in accepting this proposal and urging it to the utmost—indeed if it is rejected I for one shall wash my hands of the whole affair. We have sent the proposal in this shape to Mr. Gladstone. We have informed him of course that the whole discussion on our part will be conducted under his auspices and instructions. I am a good deal disappointed not to have received an immediate acceptance on his part. I cannot but fear that he is still a good deal under the influence of such evil counsellors as Labouchere and others who are the principal causes of the mischief that has been already done.

I hope sincerely that you will employ your great influence with him to induce him to come in to this most reasonable proposal and I should be glad if (as I hope) you agree in our view that you will write to Mr. Gladstone to support it, I shall send a copy of this letter to Granville.[7]

[1] See No. 509 n. 2.

[2] Harcourt to Chamberlain, 24 Dec. 1886, Chamberlain Papers, JC 5/38/55.

[3] Chamberlain to Harcourt, 26 Dec. 1886. Reproduced in Garvin, ii, p. 281.

[4] The two men met at Harcourt's London house in Grafton St. on 30 Dec.

[5] Harcourt to Gladstone, 'Xmas Day', 1886, GP, Add. MS. 44200 ff. 195-8. and Gladstone to Harcourt, 27 Dec. 1886, ibid, ff. 207-8 (copy).

[6] Henry Hartley Fowler, Liberal M.P., Wolverhampton, 1880-1908. Financial Secretary to the Treasury in Gladstone's 1886 ministry.

[7] See Spencer to Gladstone, 2 Jan. 1887, GP, Add. MS. 44313 ff. 108-9. Granville's view was that 'the bridge is difficult even for the Prince of Opportunists to pass'. Granville to Spencer, 3 Jan. 1887, SP.

## 513   LORD SPENCER TO W. V. HARCOURT
*2 January 1887; Althorp, Northampton*
HP, MS, 45

*Confidential*

Well done! as your first Political move of the year has been, so may the rest of your acts during the year contribute to the Reunion of the Liberal party and I will add to the settlement of the Irish question.

I entirely agree in all you write about the Chamberlain proposal. It may lead to excellent results, and if it fails it will smooth over rough places, and relieve us of the responsibility of maintaining disillusion in our ranks.

An open discussion must do good but one cannot hide from oneself the difficulties which will meet you.

If Chamberlain really wishes for Reunion, some *modus vivendi* ought to be found which would be accepted by Parnell and Co. It will not do to alienate Parnell, but if the plan of compromise is skilfully framed, so as to be one which Parnell could recommend to his party without appearing to sell the Pass, he will see the advantage of getting the question, if not actually settled, put on the high way to settlement.

The position is deeply interesting, and I shall be very anxious to hear how the discussions progress.

I have written to Mr. Gladstone stating shortly how glad I am at the decision you have arrived at,[1] although I heard from Morley (who wrote after you)[2] that you had received an approving Telegram from Hawarden.

I don't know whether Labouchere has Mr. Gladstone's ear just now or not, but from what John Morley told me I was afraid that Mr. Gladstone was disposed to grovel in the dust to bring about a fusion, so I should have had no doubt as to his views on your letter, particularly after your carrying No. 3 of the points to be discussed.

P.S. We may be a convenient half way Meeting House between London and Hawarden: Mr. Gladstone kept open an invitation to come here until we knew when Parliament met.

Come any moment and bring anyone including the great J. C. if you like.

[1] Spencer to Gladstone, 2 Jan. 1887, GP, Add. MS. 44313 ff. 108-9.
[2] Morley had been to the theatre with Chamberlain on 31 Dec. The next day, Morley told Spencer, 'I believe that J. Chamberlain finds himself in a great fix and will do much in order to extricate himself.' Morley to Spencer, 1 Jan. 1887, SP.

### 514   J. MORLEY TO LORD SPENCER
*3 January 1887; 95 Elm Park Gardens, South Kensington, S.W.*

I admit that I dislike the constitution of the conference.

Herschell is weak on the question, Fowler is weaker,[1] and Harcourt is apt to fly off at a tangent. If Chamberlain captures them at any point, he will be able to denounce me as stubborn, etc. etc. I am writing to Harcourt on this.

We do not meet until the 13th., and I should much like to talk to you before then. If you do not come to town, I will gladly come down to you, whether Mr. G. be there or not.

[1] Spencer considered that Fowler was 'perhaps not as sound on Home Rule as many others' with 'a strong Chamberlain leaning.' Spencer to Gladstone, 20 Jan. 1887, GP, Add. MS. 44313 ff. 110-11.

### 515   W. E. GLADSTONE TO LORD SPENCER
*3 January 1887; Hawarden*

I received your letter with particular pleasure for it shows me, I think, that we are in identity of view on all the points of delicacy and importance involved in the present situation of affairs so far as it regards us.

I estimate that in three days of last week I had 1300 arrivals by the post and though my family staff is good and worked hard you may judge that I have had a heavy time for conducting a political correspondence.

I dare not send you the letters I have written to Harcourt because I want them for reference but I will mention a point raised outside them.

Labouchere has written me a letter (now with J. Morley) urging that the two subjects of Home Rule and Land Purchase should be severed, and proposing what seems to me an impossible alternative plan for getting rid of Land Purchase altogether.[1]

Now my natural answer is that by public declarations so far as I am concerned I have severed them already but hold myself free to treat each on its merits. But as he made a reference to Morley I thought it right to send him the letter before replying.

The fact is that on very practical grounds and with high objects we made a Parliamentary *tack*. To renew this would be quite another affair.

I rather think you are cognisant of my language and have not disapproved it, no departure from our old opinions on the subject of Land Purchase itself being involved.

[1] For Gladstone's reply, see Gladstone to Labouchere, 29 Dec. 1886, GP, Add. MS. 44499 ff. 304-5 (copy).


**516   J. MORLEY TO LORD SPENCER**
*15 January 1887; 95 Elm Park Gardens, South Kensington, S.W.*

*Very Secret*

The Conference[1] has so far been rather a surprise. The limitation of topics broke down at once, and we were very speedily in mid-ocean. One of the interlocutors might just as well not have been there—so weak, irresolute, and shadowy: you have good reason, I daresay, to know who that is.[2] But there is no real fight in J. C. either. He is tired, and even heartily tired, I am quite sure, of his present 'leader', and only wants a decent way of escape.

We meet again when the session opens. It would be absurd to be too sanguine of a *modus vivendi*.[3] Only one really formidable difference is in the air, so far. It is important that I should have a talk with you before we meet again. All next week I shall be busy with my second article in reply to Dicey,[4] but the week after, I should be glad if we could meet. Meanwhile, I wish you could collect your ideas together about *Ulster*, and the best way of meeting that difficulty.

Please to regard this as most secret, and not to be mentioned to Lord Granville or anyone else...

J. C.'s *tone* is elaborately friendly and civil.

Hartington speaks at Newcastle on Feb. 2: so I have taken the Town Hall for Feb. 4,[5] so as to pluck up the tares out of my field at once. J. C. is very annoyed, or seemed so, at this step of Hartington's. Both J. C. and G. O. Trevelyan were pressed to go down with Hartington, but declined.

[1] The Conference consisted of three Gladstonians, Harcourt, Herschell and John Morley with Trevelyan supporting Chamberlain. The first meeting began at 4 p.m. on 13 Jan. at Harcourt's house in Grafton St. and continued next day at noon. An account of the proceedings appeared in *The Times*, 14 Jan. 1887, p. 9. See also M. Hurst, *Joseph Chamberlain and Liberal Reunion: The Round Table Conference of 1887* (1967), p. 202 ff.

[2] Trevelyan.

[3] One more meeting only of the Conference was in fact held, on 14 Feb. at Trevelyan's house in Grosvenor Square. Gardiner, ii, p. 32.

[4] 'The Government of Ireland (Part I): a reply' (to Dicey's book on home rule), appeared in the *Nineteenth Century*, Jan. 1887. Part II was published in the Feb. issue.

[5] Morley's meeting, at which he accused Hartington of inconsistency in his attitude towards Ireland, was postponed until 9 Feb.

## 517   W. E. GLADSTONE TO LORD SPENCER
*28 February 1887; 21 Carlton House Terrace, S.W.*

I incline to believe that all questions connected with the Round Table are for the present effectually hung up in consequence of Chamberlain's most recent, and most ill-advised, utterance.[1] Land Purchase therefore may stand for a future consideration.

Harcourt had been fighting Chamberlain's battle, but he is now indignant and has told C. a piece, and more than a piece, of his mind.[2]

[1] Letter by Chamberlain to the *Baptist* and reproduced in national newspapers on 25 Feb., accusing Gladstone of obstructing the claims of Welsh Nonconformists, Scottish crofters and English agricultural labourers.

[2] Harcourt to Chamberlain, 25 Feb. 1887, Chamberlain Papers, JC5/38/68. Harcourt told Edward Hamilton five years later, 'We had practically come to an agreement at the Round Table Conference ... when all of a sudden, nettled by something that J. Morley said (not very discreetly) at Newcastle, Chamberlain fired off his famous letter to the Nonconformists ... we had to choose between giving offence to some of our best supporters and bringing the Conference to a close.' EHJ, 8 Jan. 1892, Add. MS. 48657 ff. 23-4.

## 518   C. R. SPENCER TO LORD SPENCER
*25 March 1887; 28 St. James's Place, S.W.*

That letter in yesterday's *Times* was beastly, and its innuendoes about you nettled me.[1] I spoke to John Morley about it, and he said of course *you* would not answer it, as I well knew; but it struck me that (unless answering it gave it undue importance) Dasent or Courtenay might. However today it has become absorbed, in the interest of last night's debate. Mr. G. was quite perfect, not as rhetorical as he is sometimes, but debating, as only he can.[2] Full of spirit and humour and his compliments to Smith were delightful, a good deal of sarcasm in them. His praises of Buller were very amusing, some irony in them, giving the 'bite'.

Joe was intensely funny, full of repartee and banter, and he crushed old Anthony John.[3] When the latter said to him 'You did not hear the speech', Joe turned right round to A. J. who was sitting next to him, and said very blandly, 'But I *can* read.' His chaff about John Morley was capital fun. Some seem to have thought he scored in the passage he read out.[4] I don't think so, though no doubt for the moment he did.

[1] Headed 'Parnellism and Crime. signed 'X, Kildare St. Club, Dublin', one passage read, 'I can hardly believe that Lord Spencer was not aware of the *personal* relations which existed between Mr. Parnell and that previous crew, though I can well believe that owing to the exigencies of the Kilmainham Treaty, he was not anxious to know more than he could possibly help.' *The Times*, 24 March 1887, p. 6.

[2] Hansard, 3, cccxii, col. 1354 ff. 24 March 1887. Two days previously, W. H. Smith, the Leader of the House, announced that the Criminal Law Amendment (Ireland) Bill would take priority over other legislation. The 'closure' or 'guillotine' was used to ensure its passage through the House on 10 June.

[3] Mundella.

[4] Chamberlain read out a passage 'if great social disorder has spread over a country from whatever cause, every Government, exactly because it is a Government, is bound to do its utmost to restore order temporarily, even while it is removing the more permanent causes which have made disorder natural and justifiable.' He then revealed that Morley was the author when editor of the *Pall Mall Gazette*. Hansard, 3, cccxii, col. 1418.

**519   J. MORLEY TO LORD SPENCER**

*10 April 1887; 95 Elm Park Gardens, South Kensington, S.W.*

*Confidential*

I have had a long talk with Chamberlain on Tuesday. He is very low: thinks that we (Harcourt and I) have used him ill in driving him on to the rocks of Coercion.[1] If we had not broken off the Round Table, he would have brought Hartington round (I don't believe that), and there would have been no Coercion Bill. He kept saying, 'I cannot join the Tories': that the things which he had hoped for would come in his son's time, not in his own, etc. etc. Was quite sure that if *we* came in, we could not carry on.

[1] A.J. Balfour moved the first reading of the Criminal Law Amendment (Ireland) Bill on 21 March 1887. The debate on the second reading lasted until 18 April.

**520   LORD SPENCER TO LADY SPENCER**

*16 April 1887; Truro*

I had a severe time on Thursday. I had to speak from the window[1] at Exeter, was met at Teignmouth by people, and at Newton I had another interview.

I saw in the Plymouth paper that some big affair was contemplated but did not fully realise what it was until I got to my room ... When I looked out, I saw in front towards the sea a dense mass of heads, and it turned out I had to speak to them in the open air.[2]

I had not a word ready, and when I got down it was the most extraordinary scene. There were it is said from 20,000 to 25,000 people there.

Electric light was to have been turned on but did not arrive in time. Instead they put up two lines of lights close to me. I was so to speak illuminated and stood blinking before this huge mass of people. It was I suppose like a fairy feels in a transformation scene on the stage. I was quite bewildered but I managed to hammer out a speech which went down well.

[1] Of the train taking Spencer to Plymouth, where he was to stay the night before continuing to Truro the next morning.
[2] Spencer arrived at the Grand Hotel, Plymouth, at 9.15 p.m. His impromptu speech was delivered from the balcony overlooking the Hoe. For full details, see the *Western Daily Mercury*, 15 April 1887, p. 5.

**521   LORD SPENCER TO LADY SPENCER**

*18 April 1887; House of Lords*

I am waiting to go to the House of Commons to hear the debate and Row.[1]

I lunched with John Morley yesterday and did a lot of work over my speech at Truro.[2] I then went down to Durdans. It was so hateful in London and I wanted to talk with him.[3] They kept me for the night.

We have had a meeting today re Land Bill.[4]

Parnell's letter is a great sensation.[5] It may be a forgery. We don't know. If it is not it is very ugly but it really is not much worse than before.

I shall be at work tomorrow on the Bill.

[1] The adjourned debate on the second reading of the Criminal Law Amendment (Ireland) Bill ended that night. The second reading was carried by 370 votes to 269.

[2] The speech, dealing with the government's Irish policy, was given at Truro on 15 April under the auspices of the National Liberal Federation. See the *Royal Cornwall Gazette*, 22 April 1887, p. 7. Spencer wrote to his wife afterwards. 'I will send you a copy of my Speech. It was I fancy badly reported in *The Times*.' Spencer to Lady Spencer, 16 April 1887, SP.

[3] Edward Hamilton was with Rosebery at The Durdans when Spencer 'turned up unexpectedly.' For an account of the discussions, see EHJ, 17 April 1887, Add. MS. 48646 f. 24.

[4] The Irish Land Law Bill, to amend the Land Law Act of 1881 and the Land Purchase Act of 1885, was presented by Cadogan in the Lords on 31 March.

[5] Parnell's purported letter to Egan, dated 15 May 1882, stating that he had been obliged, as an act of policy, to condemn the Phoenix Park murders, appeared in facsimile in *The Times*, 18 April, p. 8.

## 522 LORD SPENCER TO LADY SPENCER

*22 April 1887; Spencer House, St. James's Place, S.W.*

I did not write yesterday as I was kept up to the very last moment at my Speech.[1] It went off very well, I think, infamously reported. Granville was very complimentary. I dare say we shall get a roasting from Argyll tonight who opens the Debate. . .[2]

There is a most amusing description of my style, in a West Country paper. It talks of imperfect enunciation, in fact a kind of aristocratic lisp though I always was quite distinct and made myself heard.

[1] In moving the second reading of the Irish Land Law Bill in the Lords on 21 April, Spencer expressed his support for the measure. Hansard, 3, cccxiii, cols. 1355-67.

[2] Spencer interrupted Argyll's speech, stating that the report in *The Times* on 22 April misrepresented him. Hansard, 3, cccxiii, col. 1555, 23 April 1887. For a contemporary account of this incident see Sir R. Temple, *Letters and Sketches from the House of Commons* (1912), p. 324. The bill received its third reading in the Lords on 4 July and the royal assent on 27 Aug.

## 523 J. MORLEY TO LORD SPENCER

*18 September 1887; 95 Elm Park Gardens, South Kensington, S.W.*

*Private*

I had a long talk with Parnell on Tuesday. He was rather melancholy; evidently Dillon and O'Brien are forcing the pace faster than he likes,[1] and also he professes (sincerely, as I believe) to apprehend revenge from the violent men both in Ireland and America, for coercion. Communications (no doubt of an informal and unauthorised kind) were made to him three weeks ago from the other side as to the amount of Home Rule that would satisfy him.

[1] Prosecutions had been initiated against William O'Brien, secretary of the Irish National League, and John Mandeville, a leader of Tipperary tenants, for inflammatory speeches. They were to appear at Mitchelstown, Co. Tipperary, on 9 Sept., but O'Brien did not appear. Dillon, accompanied by several English M.P.s, addressed the crowd. The police clashed with the crowd, killing three men and wounding six others. Lyons, *John Dillon*, pp. 88-9.

**524  J. MORLEY TO LORD SPENCER**
*29 September 1887; 95 Elm Park Gardens, South Kensington, S.W.*

*Private*

I have thought a good deal from time to time about your departure.[1] Crisis, in the sense of the Government going out, I cannot think at all likely for some months at any rate. It would be impossible for them to allow any amount of internal difficulty to make them hand over the reins to Mr. Gladstone. Nothing will affect them for some time to come except a series of hostile by-elections. Don't you agree?

But then your departure to such a distance as India would certainly tend to damp our friends and encourage the enemy. They would argue 'It shows that Lord S. at any rate does not expect any speedy result from the fulminations of W. V. Harcourt, John Morley, etc; it shows too that he cannot think the prospect in Ireland particularly critical.' Such is my view, offered in all diffidence. It is not as if you were the first man in the street. You are next to Mr. G. on this question.

There is *another* contingency, a remote one, I hope and trust, which might make your absence at an inaccessible distance very unfortunate.[2]

[1] The Spencers were planning to go to India.
[2] Gladstone was approaching his 78th birthday.

**525  LORD SPENCER TO LADY SPENCER**
*30 September 1887; Althorp, Northampton*

I send you John Morley's letter. I will not settle until I hear from Granville and you, but I should not like going against the wish of Political friends if my doing so throws a damper for the moment on them.[1]

I fear there is something in it. If we give it up I don't know what we can do. For economy it would be well not to set up at Althorp for Xmas etc. I think we should be, or perhaps I ought to say I, be bored if we live on the Riviera.

We might visit, if we have invitations, in November and stay at Fen Place[2] and settle in in December. The Royal visit[3] will make it all the more necessary to be economical.

[1] Lady Spencer replied, 'I have read Mr. Morley's letter, and to my mind it carries no weight. At least there was no argument against your going which did not exist before.' Lady Spencer to Spencer, 1 Oct. 1887, SP.
[2] South-west of East Grinstead, Sussex.
[3] Prince Albert Victor, eldest son of the Prince of Wales, visited Althorp on 17 Oct., 'The last time postillion and outriders were used here.' Lady Spencer, Diary, 17 Oct, 1887, SP.

**526  LORD SPENCER TO LORD GRANVILLE**
*1 October 1887; Spencer House, St. James's Place, S.W.*
Gr. P, PRO 30/29/22A/6

I don't like the Gladstone-Hartington controversy. Moreover I was driven into a corner yesterday morning by Mrs. G. and had to tell her that I did not quite approve of what her husband had said as to previous differences with H.

I certainly shall say nothing. My wife sat by Harcourt last night at dinner and found him raging against Mr. G. and his late colleagues, and loud in praise of Hartington.

## 527  LORD SPENCER TO LADY SPENCER
*3 October 1887; Spencer House, St. James's Place, S.W.*

I send you Granville's letter.[1] I am going to see John Morley this afternoon and I will let you know what my final inclination is. If we give up India we must settle it this week.

I am not clear in my own mind though wavering.

Don't tell this, as it may be altered ... It might be well to consult an Indian Doctor or authority as to what he thinks of Cholera. The best is Sir Robert Phayre.[2]

[1] Not traced in SP. Lady Spencer replied, 'I got your letter all right with Lord Granville's. It is somewhat difficult to decide.' Lady Spencer to Spencer, 5 Oct. 1887, SP.

[2] Lt.-Gen., serving in India from 1839 to 1887. In fact, Lady Spencer telegraphed Lord Reay, Governor of Bombay 1885-90, who confirmed that it was safe to make the visit. Lady Spencer to Spencer, 7 Oct. 1887. SP.

## 528  LORD SPENCER TO LORD GRANVILLE
*10 October 1887; Althorp, Northampton*
Gr. P. PRO 30/29/22A/6

I was interested in what I saw in Wales.[1] I listened to the businesslike 10 minutes Speeches at the Conference. There is no doubt as to the Welsh determination to get Disestablishment, and from what I heard myself and from what I picked up from others who know the country, there will be some real danger if we do not adopt Welsh disestablishment as part of our programme *after* Ireland.[2]

There is a tendency to a strong Cave of Ultra Radicals, who want to nationalize all tithes whether in lay or clerical hands, who want a Land Bill like the Irish ones and even a Welsh Parliament.

The moderate men with leaders such as S. Rendel want support from the party in England, and if they can show that we are ready to meet special Welsh grievances, they will keep them in hand.

I was glad to see that S. Rendel had been elected Chairman of the United Welsh Council.

I was so impressed with all this that I went further as to the Church than I had decided to do before I got to Wales. I myself would have gone even further than I did, but from something you once said to me on this matter, I thought it right to wrap up a little my step in advance of Mr. Gladstone.

I hope you won't be wrath.

I was well received, and I hope got through my Irish arguments fairly well.

I was infamously mangled in the Press, and what I said against defiance of the Law was, as far as I could gather, left out by the *Times*[3] and London papers.

... It is dreadful to hate as I do the preparation for a Speech, which is part of one's profession in life. The thoughts of my Welsh campaign (small as it was) quite spoilt my pleasure in life for 3 weeks before it came off.

The absence of Speeches will make up for and prevent any fidget I might get when far away over Politics.

[1] Spencer spoke at Aberystwyth on 7 Oct. at the inauguration of the Welsh National Council.

[2] At the Nottingham meeting of the National Liberal Federation on 18 Oct. Welsh disestablishment was formally adopted as part of the party's programme.

[3] See *The Times*, 8 Oct. 1887, p. 10.

### 529   J. MORLEY TO LORD SPENCER
*11 October 1887; Hawarden Castle, Chester*

I opened the matter of your journey.[1] He [Gladstone] said that we all owed so much to you, that it would be most ungrateful to put on even an appearance of pressure. His fear is that

1) The Tories will attack *you* by way of recrimination when we denounce them.

2) You are the only *authority* we have on the points now coming up.

[1] On 7 Oct. Spencer had again discussed with Morley his plans to go to India. Morley, who was due to visit Gladstone at Hawarden on 10 Oct., promised to find out Gladstone's views on the matter.

### 530   LORD SUFFOLK[1] TO LORD SPENCER
*18 October 1887; Charlton Park, Malmesbury*

I am greatly obliged to you for sending me the Scheme and first Report of your Co-operative Farm at Harleston,[2] also for the trouble you have taken, busy as you must be, in writing to me.

I suppose the experiment must be deemed *fairly* successful as far as it has gone. The persons most to be congratulated being the parson who has got so good a tenant for his glebe, and the labourers; but as you seem to have been already hampered by this farm on your hands and to have been losing more at it than is here represented you also must have slightly improved your position. At the same time I do not quite make out who pays the annual loss if you do not.

Of course I see that 127£ of this loss of 207£ is represented by depreciation of value of horses, and this is only a paper loss, for as I remember Mr. Clare Read[3] once said. 'My horses are in happy ignorance of this diminution of their value and do my farm work as well as ever.' Still there remains 80£ to be paid by someone.

As far as one can judge without knowledge of your locality your valuation of stock is on the modest side of fair; I should have fancied your tegs[4] perhaps a trifle dear, but your pigs and cattle within the mark. However the prices of these things fluctuate so much and so often that one has no right hardly to express an opinion.

As to your name appearing so often in the Scheme, that is expressly provided for in the preamble. You might had you chosen, have called yourself the Capitalist, the Lessee, the Tenant or the Boss, only it happened to be simpler to call yourself by your own name.

I sincerely hope that you may reap the reward you deserve for your kindness and enterprise. At the same time, as kicks rather than half pence are the usual guerdon of philanthropists, you will probably meet the result, whatever it may be, with philosophic composure.

¹ Henry Charles, 18th Earl of Suffolk, a contemporary of Spencer at Harrow. Liberal M.P., Malmesbury 1859-68; a Liberal Unionist.
² A farm of 300 acres founded by Spencer in 1887 for eight co-operators and a manager. He provided the working capital, the net profits being carried to a reserve for repayment of the original capital; a quarter of the profits were to be set aside, to be divided according to the proportion of wages earned by co-operators during the year. The experiment proved to be a failure, because of bad prices and the general agricultural depression. The loss on the first balance sheet was £207 9s. 7d. and on the second £672 13s. 5d. As a result, the co-operators once more became labourers, drawing their weekly wages. An observer also recorded, 'Outside the question of financial success, the scheme does not appear to have led to any great harmony among the co-operators themselves. On the contrary, jealousy is stated to have crept in where formerly there was none.' Royal Commission on Agriculture. Report by R. Hunter Pringle, Assistant Commissioner in the counties of Bedford, Huntingdon and Northamptonshire, 1895, P.P. 1895 xvii, pp. 32-3. The balance sheet for 1887 is given in Appendix C. ibid, p. 133.
³ Clare Sewell Read, a large-scale tenant farmer in Norfolk and writer on agriculture. Conservative M.P., Norfolk East, 1865-8 and Norfolk South, 1868-80.
⁴ Sheep in their second year.

## 531   J. MORLEY TO LORD SPENCER
*28 October 1887; 95 Elm Park Gardens, South Kensington, S.W.*

Let me congratulate you on your Edinburgh speech.¹ I felt when I read it in the *Scotsman* that you handled both the Police and J. C.'s Land Scheme in a most masterly manner. This morning I have a letter from Rosebery. He says, 'Spencer spoke admirably to a splendid audience which hung on every word. He never made nearly as good a speech, I think.' I had the same feeling in reading it.

Hartington's speech² must mean that he has definitely done with us. A pity, a pity—but it was inevitable, I fear.

When you are at Hawarden, I hope you will be kind enough to lock up a certain G. O. M., and bring the key away in your pocket.

¹ Spencer was the principal speaker at a rally in Edinburgh on 25 Oct. Rosebery was chairman. *Scotsman*, 26 Oct. 1887, p. 7. Rosebery considered the speech to be a great success: 'He [Spencer] held 5000 completely for the 65 minutes during which he spoke and never consulted a note.' EHJ, 30 Oct. 1887, Add. MS. 48647 f. 50, and Rosebery, Journal, 25 Oct. 1887, f. 298.
² At a Liberal Union meeting at Nottingham on 24 Oct. attacking Gladstone's two speeches on Ireland, delivered at Nottingham on 18 and 19 Oct. *The Times*, 25 Oct. 1887, p. 6.

### 532 J. BRYCE[1] TO LORD SPENCER
*5 November 1887; 35, Bryanston Square, W.*

I cannot refuse myself the pleasure of thanking you once again, now that the success of the volume of Essays on Home Rule is secured, for the Preface you wrote, and of telling you how highly it has been appreciated by every one whom I have talked with regarding the book.[2]

I venture to take some credit to myself for having urged you[3] to proceed with it when you doubted your own literary experience, and for having felt, as soon as I saw the first draft, that it was just the thing we wanted, simple, calm, judicial, far more likely to command attention and respect than rhetorical vehemence would have been. It seems to have been exactly what was needed to strike the keynote of the book, and to affect the minds of moderate men.

When I last saw the publishers, three days ago, nearly 8000 copies had been sold; and they expect to sell 15,000.

[1] James Bryce, Liberal M.P., Aberdeen South, 1885-1907, Regius Professor of Civil Law, Oxford University, 1870-93.
[2] The second edition of *Handbook of Home Rule*, edited by Bryce, was published in Oct. 1887. Besides Spencer's spirited piece in defence of home rule, there were articles by Gladstone, Morley, Thring, MacColl, Bryce, R. B. O'Brien and E. L. Godkin.
[3] See Bryce to Spencer, 18 June 1887, SP.

### 533 W. E. GLADSTONE TO LORD SPENCER
*7 November 1887; Hawarden Castle, Chester*

I do not know where you mean to move, but, before going, please to determine with Morley whether anything and how much if anything should be done on Balfour's speech.[1]

I went over the points with Granville last night,[2] and I inclose a note.

How grievous is the manner in which our concerted recommendations to Wolverton[3] have been frustrated. Man appoints, God disappoints. A right loyal man is gone to the land where there is only loyalty.

P.S. *The Times* pays you the greatest compliment in villainously cutting down your speech.[4]

[1] Balfour spoke at Birmingham on 4 Nov. on Ireland, calling Gladstone's speeches 'spiteful'. *The Times*, 5 Nov. 1887, p. 7.
[2] Both Granville and Spencer arrived at Hawarden on 2 Nov. Spencer left on 4 Nov. for Scarborough.
[3] Died 6 Nov.
[4] *The Times* devoted one column to Spencer's speech at Scarborough on 4 Nov. Balfour's Birmingham speech appeared on the same page and occupied four and a half columns, p. 5.

### 534 LORD SPENCER TO W. E. GLADSTONE
*9 November 1887; Spencer House, St. James's Place, S.W.*
GP, Add. MS. 44313 ff. 126-7

I received your letter at Althorp yesterday, and saw both John Morley and Granville in the course of the evening.

A. Balfour's speech struck me as singularly weak, his only new points were small ones and he did not go beyond details or reach principles.

I do not see how you can with any advantage answer him. If you were about to speak you could easily dispose of his attacks, but there seems to be no necessity to have a speech on purpose, nor do I think a letter would be desirable; special notice from you would give importance to the speech and it really has carried no importance with it.[1] At Hanley, Granville dealt generally with the attack, and the others have done the same with effect.[2]

No doubt when Parliament meets many of Balfour's points will be revived, when you will effectively dispose of them.

These are the views of both Morley and Granville. I went over your notes separately with each of them. I entirely share your views about our excellent friend Wolverton. I was sure you would be greatly shocked. We can ill spare so loyal and generous a supporter just now.

Our plans are all upset, but we shall not move this week, and probably shall stay in England making London headquarters.[3]

[1] Spencer's view, as expressed to Edward Hamilton, was that Gladstone 'must be careful not to alarm the waverers. There is indeed no necessity for strong language—the steam is well up.' EHJ, 10 Nov. 1887, Add. MS. 48647 f. 63.
[2] On 7 Nov. The Times, 8 Nov. 1887, p. 10.
[3] Spencer mentioned in his Scarborough speech that he was postponing his intended visit to India 'to be within the call of his party'.

**535   LADY FREDERICK CAVENDISH[1] TO LORD SPENCER**
*18 December 1887; Hawarden Castle, Chester*

*Private*

I have a confession to make to you, which I fear may displease you, but which I feel it would not be right to withhold.

This morning at breakfast I was telling Uncle William[2] of two or three converts (very dowdy ones!) I hoped I had made to Home Rule; and I said 'I reserve to both them and myself the permission to scold you on occasions' or words to that effect. He knew I had in mind certain things he has said of late, and he immediately took up the cudgels for himself, (with all his usual good-nature, but still energetically); and said 'What do you say to Spencer's opinion?—he goes further if anything than I do.' He meant, in condemning police illegalities in Ireland.

Well, when I saw that (as always would be the case) he attached the greatest weight to your opinion on the Irish question, and considered you were entirely with him at this moment, I thought I *must* tell him of the way you wrote to me, in answer to my comment on the first Nottingham speech. Those words, you may remember, were 'While I admired much that Mr. G. said, there was much that I could not myself have said, and which laid him open to Harting-ton's able reply.' These are very nearly the words you used. I need not say, I should never have quoted them to him, had you marked the letter 'private' or otherwise shown that I was not to repeat them.

He took it very well, but as I was not able *exactly* to say to what particular points in the speech your words referred, he made not much of a reply. But I cannot tell you how earnestly I hope, that when you are with him, you will never shrink from expressing disagreement upon matters of real importance.

Mr. Roundell breakfasted with Alfred[3] and me the other day, and spoke most strongly of the need of all moderate and temperate action and word just now, in aid of the great cause. And another friend said to me lately (it was I think Sir Reginald Welby)[4] that the loss of so large a section of the Moderate Liberals left the G. O. M. minus much of the wholesome check and balance which was always largely present in the party before this miserable split. I know Mr. G. himself is conscious of this to a large extent and deeply deplores it. But old age *does* tell even upon him, and chiefly in making him less clear in judgment upon minor but yet important points. A want of proportion—a tendency to give undue weight to incidents (the Dopping business is an awful case in point!)[5] this was always a weakness in him; and one notices it more now.

Now that he has pretty nearly survived all his contemporaries, the number of *friends* who feel in a position to 'stand up to him' and criticize anything he says or does, is terribly small. And this is a great calamity for any public man, a calamity in proportion to the influence he exerts. Moreover, he takes criticism, (when it is made use of at the right moment, and with clearness and terseness), as well as anybody in the world. You will believe this when I tell you how patiently he lets *me* scold him, who am only an ill-informed woman.

[1] Lucy Caroline, widow of Lord Frederick Cavendish, who had been assassinated in Phoenix Park, Dublin on 6 May 1882 shortly after becoming Chief Secretary, Ireland.

[2] i.e. Gladstone. Lady Frederick's mother, Mary, daughter of Sir Stephen Glyn, was Catherine Gladstone's younger sister.

[3] Hon. Alfred Lyttelton, her younger brother.

[4] Permanent Secretary of the Treasury, 1885-94, and great admirer of Gladstone.

[5] In his Nottingham speech of 18 Nov., Gladstone, as reported in the national press, accused Lt.-Col. J. H. Dopping, an Irish land agent, of pointing a rifle at a young boy during an eviction at Gweedore, Co. Donegal. Dopping threatened legal action but finally Gladstone claimed that he had been misreported. See his letter, *The Times*, 23 Nov. 1887, p. 10.

**536**  LORD SPENCER TO C. R. SPENCER

*23 December 1887; Spencer House, St. James's Place, S.W.*

The Trade now is in a bad way. Nothing will be settled until after Xmas. The men never work much these 2 weeks, and as the Union men get 12s. a week they are really better off than when they were not on the Union.[1]

The dispute is very complicated. Becke seemed to think that the men were wrong. I fear that many families are in great distress. It is very difficult to know what to do. I have been asked to subscribe but I refused to give to a general relief fund, as it seemed like taking sides with the men. I said that the thing to be aimed at was to stop the dispute. Meanwhile I would put in C. C. Becke's hands something to help starving children and women.

[1] On 22 July 1887, some 40 lasters employed by Cove and West's boot and shoe factory, Northampton, took strike action as a protest against low wages. This led to a lock-out. After arbitration, agreement was reached between the employers and operatives at a meeting on 30 Dec.

The men returned to work on 2 Jan. 1888. See J.H. Porter, 'The Northampton Arbitration Board and the Shoe Industry Dispute of 1887', in *Northamptonshire Past and Present* iv, no. 3 (1968), pp. 149-54.

### 537   LORD ROSEBERY TO LORD SPENCER
*3 April 1888; Hotel de la Grande Bretagne, Naples*

... With regard to the Local Government Bill, I hope our people will support it in the main with ardour.[1] We cannot, it seems to me, shew too much enthusiasm for the democratic parts of the measure as I understand it. I do not say this in the cynical belief that no course would cause more annoyance to the Tories. But I say it because in principle it seems a measure such as we should have wished to carry, though of course the House of Lords would have thrown it out. If my views be correct we are bound as honest men to promote the bill. Secondly, as regards expediency, it seems to me clear that this bill lays a basis for the Liberal party in England such as it has never had before; while it makes Home Rule in Ireland a topical necessity in addition to being a political necessity which it was before.

[1] The first reading of the Local Government (England and Wales) Bill was given in the Commons on 19 March. It received the royal assent on 13 Aug.

### 538   LORD HERSCHELL TO LORD SPENCER
*14 October 1888; Walmer Castle, Deal*

I think it would be better for you to take charge of the Oaths Bill after what passed with Bradlaugh.[1] But it would be well that you should put Hobhouse[2] or Monkswell[3] or both of them to attend to the legal part as the Chancellor may raise some points. You might get some M.P. say Asquith to come to the bar of the House while the Bill was in Committee so that he might be consulted.[4]

[1] The Oaths Bill, allowing Members of Parliament to affirm, had been sent from the Commons to the Lords on 9 Aug. Herschell, who was in charge of the bill, was going abroad and explained details of procedure to Spencer, 11 Oct. 1888, SP. Spencer moved the second reading of the bill on 13 Nov. Hansard, 3, cccxxx, cols. 1013-17.

[2] Arthur, 1st Baron Hobhouse, barrister, an advanced Liberal, and member of the Judicial Committee of the Privy Council since 1881.

[3] Robert, 2nd Baron Monkswell, barrister, a Liberal; briefly Under-Secretary for War, Jan-July, 1895.

[4] The bill received the royal assent on 24 Dec. For full details, see W.L. Arnstein, *The Bradlaugh Case. A Study in Late Victorian Opinion and Politics* (1965).

### 539   W. V. HARCOURT TO LORD SPENCER
*17 October 1888; Malwood, Lyndhurst*

*Confidential*
We really must make some mutual arrangements not all to speak at once. Last week Rosebery, G. Trevelyan and I were all off in a volley into the crowd.[1]

Considering how few we are we ought to distribute ourselves better. I have spoken to Schnadhorst to keep a register at Parliament Street and show who speaks and where and when, so that we shall send in our engagements and be able to fix them with some regard to other discourses. It is idle to bid against one another in the speaking auction.

[1] Rosebery at Leeds and Trevelyan at Hull on 9 Oct. Harcourt at Oldham on 10 Oct.


**540   LORD GRANVILLE TO LORD SPENCER**
*27 October 1888; 14 South Audley Street, W.*

The Selborne Controversy[1] does not seem to me to stand very well.

Harcourt dissuaded Gladstone from publishing, on account of some awkward expressions against Irish M.P.s.[2]

Gladstone joyfully availed himself of the Queen having only given permission to divulge in Parliament, not in periodicals and newspapers,[3] and having delayed for some days answering a further application; and slipped out of the publication.

I asked him but in vain to consult with you and Harcourt before he gives his explanation, which is now to be asked for.

I am afraid that his announcement that on further consideration he thinks it better to rest upon his declaration will be interpreted by friends as a hint that the Queen had refused, which will not be *absolutely* fair to her, and his enemies will conclude that the documents do not bear him out.[4]

[1] Gladstone reviewed Wemyss Reid's biography of W. E. Forster in the Sept. 1888 issue of the *Nineteenth Century* in an article entitled 'Mr. Forster and Ireland'. In it he claimed that Parnell's release in April 1882 was because the cabinet believed that he was no longer suspected of being implicated in crime, and that Forster's resignation as Chief Secretary of Ireland on 2 May was due to disagreement with this decision. Selborne, Lord Chancellor at the time, publicly challenged Gladstone's version of events (see *The Times*, 21 Sept. 1888). Spencer wrote at length to Gladstone on the matter, but stated that 'my memory will not aid the controversy as to what took place at Cabinets'. Spencer to Gladstone, 23 Sept. 1888, GP, Add. MS. 44313 f. 144.

[2] Harcourt was at Hawarden with Rosebery and Gladstone on 11 Oct. The latter contemplated writing to the Queen for permission to consult contemporary cabinet documents and then possibly publish the results. Harcourt, when shown the Selborne correspondence, 'put an *absolute veto* on it (i.e. Gladstone's proposed action) for reasons which I don't like to write but will tell you when we meet'. Harcourt to Spencer, 17 Oct. 1888, SP. Spencer commented, 'I had no idea that Harcourt would have had such an influence. Whether he took the same line as I did in criticism or a different line I know not.' Spencer to Granville, 22 Oct. 1888, Gr. P, PRO 30/29/29A. Spencer himself went to Hawarden on 1 Nov. 'where I had two or three successful talks with the Great Man'. Spencer to Lady Spencer, 2 Nov. 1888, SP.

[3] Queen Victoria to Gladstone, 30 Sept. 1888. See P. Guedalla, *The Queen and Mr. Gladstone* (1933), ii, p. 430.

[4] See B. Hawkins, 'Gladstone, Forster and the release of Parnell 1882-8', *Irish Historical Studies* xvi, (1969), pp. 417-45.

**541   LORD SPENCER TO H. SEYMOUR**[1]

*11 March 1889; Althorp, Northampton*

Many thanks for your pleasant letter which cheers me up and makes up to me for the collapse and nausea (actual and metaphysical) which I have for two days after a big effort for a Speech.

It is one of the first Speeches which *The Times* has reported in full and no doubt the occasion was a remarkable one.[2] The 80 Club are very representative, the cream of young Liberalism and they mustered with their friends in great force. They were very candid and kind to me, and that must always gratify the recipient.

I am glad you liked what I said. I of course missed out points etc. but I never looked at my notes from start to finish. I was rather anxious about it, for though my mind had been fermenting over the Speech, I did not quite like the arrangement of it, and altered it at the last moment.

Parnell's presence was of course a great feature. I have never met him since 1874. I am glad to have done so, and the moment was propitious. It would have been better at the close of the Commission provided the judges clear him of all serious charges.[3]

[1] Horace Alfred Damer Seymour, Lady Spencer's brother. Gladstone's private secretary, 1882-6, Commissioner of Customs, 1885-9, Deputy Chairman, Board of Customs, 1890-4, Deputy Master of the Mint, 1894-1902.

[2] On 8 March shortly after the exposure of the Pigott forgeries (see No. **553** below) by Parnell's lawyer, Sir Charles Russell, Parnell had been invited to a dinner at the Eighty Club, Willis's Rooms, St. James's. Spencer in his speech admitted that he had changed his opinion on Ireland after the 1885 general election and later the two men shook hands. Rosebery, chairman at the meeting, claimed that it 'was the hand-shaking of two nations across St. George's Channel; it was the burying of the historical animosities of England and Ireland.' *The Times*, 9 March 1889, p. 12.

[3] The Parnell Commission found conclusively that the Pigott letter was a forgery in its report of 13 Feb. 1890.

**542   LORD SPENCER TO C. R. SPENCER**

*15 March 1889; Althorp, Northampton*

I thought I might have seen you Tuesday at Rugby and so did not write. Many thanks for your letter. I am glad you thought I got on well in my Speech. I got into trouble over 'miserable and despicable'.[1] I laid myself open to attack though I think everyone ought to have seen that I referred to the Election of '85 only. Hartington pitched into me very nicely however,[2] not so James McCalmont in a letter which I had to answer.[3]

[1] In his speech at the Eighty Club, Spencer, in alluding to the loyal minority in Ireland, called them 'a most miserable and despicable body'.

[2] At Islington, London, on 13 March. *The Times*, 14 March 1889, p. 7.

[3] Capt. James Martin McCalmont, Unionist M.P., East Antrim, 1885-1913. Letters were exchanged between 11 and 21 March; the correspondence was published in *The Times*, 26 March 1889, p. 8.

**543   LORD SPENCER TO W. V. HARCOURT**
*18 August 1889; Villa Hammelmann, Homburg*
HP, MS 45

We are very happy here, with a strong Home Rule contingent—Rosebery, C. Russell,[1] W. Beaumont,[2] F. and G. Leveson[3] and others, and tomorrow the Granvilles arrive...

Royalty smiles on us in many shapes from the Prince of Wales, who after all your lectures is economising here under the shelter of Reuben Sassoon's[4] hospitality. ... The Duke of Cambridge[5] in desperate love with a fair Yankee dame, the Grand Duke of Mecklenburg[6] in sorrow at his slim fair Helen not being here, and the Empress Frederick with 3 daughters and the Crown Prince of Greece.

So our Society is confused and flurried by all these Royal personages seeking dinners and entertainment.

... We stay here another fortnight and then move somewhere for a short time before returning home.[7] I want to go to Heligoland[8] to add a qualification for the Colonies to any I may have got, but I don't think Lady S. will agree, and tries to pull me towards Paris which won't agree with reduced rents.

I hear poor accounts of crops, so many seem to have been laid flat by the storms: but Norfolk gives excellent account of itself.[9]

[1] Sir Charles Arthur Russell, Liberal, M.P., Hackney South since 1885 and Attorney-General in Gladstone's 1886 government.
[2] Wentworth Blackett Beaumont, Liberal M.P., Northumberland South, 1852-85 and Tyneside division, Northumberland, 1886-92.
[3] Edward Frederic Leveson-Gower, and his son, George Granville Leveson-Gower, Gladstone's private secretary, 1880-5, Liberal M.P., N.W. Staffordshire, 1885-6, Junior Lord of the Treasury, 1886.
[4] The Prince had become friendly with three members of the Sassoon family—Albert, Arthur and Reuben—in the late 1880s. P. Magnus, *King Edward the Seventh* (1964), p. 247.
[5] George, 2nd Duke of Cambridge, Commander-in-Chief of the Army, 1856-95.
[6] Frederick, Grand Duke of Mecklenburg-Strelitz. For his earlier adventures, see R. Fulford (ed.), *Dearest Mama* (1968), p. 307.
[7] Spencer arrived at Homburg on 9 Aug., returning to England on 11 Sept.
[8] Island in North Sea off the West German coast, at this time a British possession.
[9] See article 'The Harvest of 1889', *The Times*, 12 Aug., p. 7.

**544   LORD SPENCER TO C. R. SPENCER**
*10 September 1889; Hotel de la Plage, Ostende*

Rosebery was in very good case at Homburg. I saw a good deal of him. I was the serious friend among several others...

I think that Balfour's Irish University policy will give him a good deal of trouble.[1] I don't know what note we shall sound, but as far as I can see we shall not go in hammer and tongs for Catholic University Endowment.

We cannot do that. We may admit that with Home Rule the Irish would do it, but that is different to its being done by us and out of Imperial funds. But if you are to govern Ireland according to Irish views from London, it is difficult to refuse them this.

We burnt our fingers in 1871 or 72 over Irish University Education. I dare say they will do the same and sincerely hope they will.

Randolph's speech in Wales as a stern Churchman is amusing.[2]

Hartington's proposition for a Policy of Obstruction is also a good card for us and shows what he expects is coming.[3]

My speaking I am glad to say does not now begin until the 15th Oct.[4]

[1] On 28 Aug. Balfour announced in the Commons a scheme to establish a Roman Catholic college which would be built and maintained by the state. Hansard, 3, cccxl, cols. 754-9. For subsequent history, see B. E. C. Dugdale, *Arthur James Balfour* (1936), i, pp. 168-70.

[2] At Newtown, Montgomeryshire, on 6 Sept. *The Times*, 7 Sept, 1889, p. 10.

[3] Hartington at Ilkley on 7 Sept. *The Times*, 9 Sept. 1889, p. 7.

[4] Speeches at Bury, 15 Oct., Stockton-on-Tees, 24 Oct., Lanark, 28 Oct. and Newcastle upon Tyne, 3 Nov.


### 545   H. SEYMOUR TO LADY SPENCER
*19 September 1889; Board Room, Customs*

I dined with Hamilton last night. He told me that he had seen you, and that you had gone to the play with Rosebery. He also referred to the regard which the Roseberys have for you and Spencer. He said Lady Rosebery had talked to him most warmly of you, and that Rosebery would be quite content to serve under Spencer's leadership in the House or elsewhere, which is more than could be said of him with regard to others.[1]

[1] Hamilton dined with Lady Rosebery on 15 Sept. at Berkeley Square, where they discussed politics. 'The Roseberys had seen much of the Spencers at Homburg,' Hamilton noted afterwards, 'It is pleasant to see how loyally the two men and likewise the two ladies work together: neither is jealous of the other.' EHJ, 15 Sept. 1889, Add. MS. 48651 ff. 95-6.


### 546   LORD SPENCER TO W. V. HARCOURT
*20 October 1889; North Creake, Fakenham*
HP, MS. 45

I was more than ordinarily interested to see what you said and how things went at Carnarvon,[1] for one day not long ago, S. Rendel poured forth a tremendous account of what he was thinking of writing or saying to you. Indeed his monologue lasted without interruption from South Audley St. to the Travellers' as we walked together.

I thought that the Welsh were going to resolve unanimously for violent resistance to tithe, and under such circumstances I agreed to his idea, that you could not identify yourself with this. But I see the violence disappeared and I am sure that it is of immense moment that the Welsh Liberals should be kept in good humour with Liberal leaders.

I was much impressed with their earnestness and seriousness of purpose when I looked in at the Conference at Aberystwyth, and I felt that if we neglected them and their big question, they might become very unruly and really dangerous in a Political sense.

I am delighted with your excellent argumentative Speech. It must do great good and was just what was wanted. I expect you are right as to Free Education, but it will be a very costly affair to carry, and will be extremely difficult to deal with; but let that pass.

The Disestablishment of the Church in Wales must come. What fools the Church people are to resist it.

Tell Loulou[2] I was not the least depressed as to Politics, but I feel ready to cut my throat when a Speech is hanging over me, so I shall be very near to distraction for some weeks to come.

[1] Harcourt addressed the annual meeting of the Welsh National Council of North Wales Liberal Federation at Carnarvon on 17 Oct. 1889, supporting the demand for Welsh disestablishment, free education, and Sunday closing. *North Wales Observer and Express*, 25 Oct. 1889, p. 6.
[2] Lewis Harcourt.


**547   LORD GRANVILLE TO LORD SPENCER**
*22 October 1889; Eaton, Chester*

I left Hawarden yesterday. I met there Ripon and John Morley.[1]

I told Gladstone that I was going to write to you. He asked me to tell you that he had not done so, because although Parnell has promised to pay him a visit he has heard nothing from him directly or through Morley.

I was relieved to find that not only Gladstone, Ripon and Morley were against announcing any definite scheme,[2] but that Harcourt was strongly of the same opinion.

With regard to the Irish M.P.s, Gladstone was at first inclined to the admission of all to the Imperial Parliament but only on Imperial subjects, but he came round to the opinion that it would be better not to limit the questions.[3] He, Ripon and Morley are for diminishing the number.

Harcourt is for no diminution either in number or subjects, he believing that we shall want them for a Liberal majority.[4] It is not clear that Parnell would consent to a diminished number, though he does not object to their total exclusion.

[1] Morley arrived at Hawarden from Ireland on 18 Oct; Granville and Ripon came later in the day.
[2] On the possibility of reaching a fresh agreement with the Nationalists, especially on the question of Irish representation at Westminster.
[3] For details of the conference, see M. Barker, *Gladstone and Radicalism* (1975), pp. 67–8.
[4] 'I am myself very strongly of opinion that they must remain and *remain just as they are in all respects and to all intents and purposes.*' Harcourt to Spencer, 25 Oct. 1889, SP.


**548   LORD SPENCER TO LORD GRANVILLE**
*27 October 1889; Althorp, Northampton*
Gr. P, PRO 30/29/22A/6

I feel that I may have seemed to transgress what you laid down at Hawarden with my Speech at Stockton:[1] but unless on one point I believed that I agreed on your lines.

I tried to show that though (which as you say is a truism) the Bills of '86 are dead, their principles are alive, that the Bills contain the principles for which we now fight.

That we have renounced some of them, for I do not consider the Exclusion of Irish M.P.s was laid down as fundamental in '86, I illustrated a further argument by taking certain principles of the Government Bill of '86, and I showed that the Bill proved that it was practicable to carry out the Principles which we now advocate, but I further argued that once agreed on Principles there were few of them which might not be carried out in different ways. For this reason it was futile to argue on details until the Principles were agreed upon.

I could not avoid the question of Irish M.P.s, retention or exclusion, and I may have gone a step too far here,[2] but I showed that this might have been dealt with in two ways, and that at the outset of the discussion we did not assume that the M.P.s must be excluded.

I let out my belief that if as seemed inevitable, they are to be retained there was no middle course and they must be retained as they are now. As you know I have always been against limitation of their numbers, and I am sure it will never work to call them in for some purposes and exclude them for others.

I shall not try the same line again for I felt I was on the thinnest of ice all the time, close to questions on which we colleagues might differ.

I had a long and kind letter from Harcourt, who evidently thought I had said more than I ought, but I agreed in the main with his arguments.[3]

I was really much riled at the constant jibes that we had given up Home Rule, and I tried to show by the same illustrations that we had a practical Policy and yet one which might be carried out in several ways.

I was in favour of arguing principles and not details.

I go to Lancaster tomorrow and relax next day. I finish up next week at Newcastle and shall be thankful.

[1] 24 Oct. See *The Times*, 25 Oct. 1889, p. 8.

[2] '... it would not do to exclude the Irish from the Imperial Parliament. It seemed, therefore, inevitable that the Irish must be retained in the English Parliament.'

[3] Harcourt expressed himself more strongly to Morley on Spencer's indiscretion: 'He is one of those children of light who has all the innocence of the dove, and but little of the craft of the serpent.' 27 Oct. 1889, Gardiner, ii, p. 148. Morley also remarked on Spencer's 'impatience under the queries of our foes'. Morley to Spencer, 28 Oct. 1889, SP.

## 549   LORD BRAYE[1] TO LORD SPENCER

*4 November 1889; Stanford Hall*

So to speak you are the hereditary Grand Master of the Pytchley. If you do not convoke a meeting your non interference prevents others doing anything to set matters straight ... There is no doubt that the Pytchley is now in a condition which is scandalous and it is very disagreeable to hunt with other packs (as I do) when such a stigma is cast rightly or wrongly in one's own country. Surely a meeting in January (say) would not be precipitate action when you might propose the question of a new Management, for Langham[2] I imagine must retire in the spring.

[1] Alfred Thomas Townshend, 5th Baron Braye of Stanford Hall, near Rugby.

[2] Langham was Master of the Pytchley, 1878–90. See G. Paget, *The History of the Althorp and Pytchley Hunt 1634–1920* (1937), pp. 207–11. Shortly after Spencer accepted the Mastership of the Pytchley for the third time, a member wrote, 'It is the saving of the county and ... I know how popular it will be with the farmers.' W. F. Dawnay to Spencer, 25 Feb. 1890, SP.


## 550 W. E. GLADSTONE TO LORD SPENCER
*9 November 1889; Hawarden*

Though I am sorry you should have had the trouble of putting on paper so full an exposition[1] I am very glad to be put in possession of your full and exact meaning especially as to the delicate and difficult point of the *manner* in which an Irish membership should (if at all) be retained.

The leanings of the different minds vary a good deal. The grand rule is I think that no one should bind himself absolutely but that all should retain plenty of elbow-room. I lean on the whole to limitation not of voting but of numbers: so do a good many men. But it is a choice of difficulties. My main anxiety is to do that which shall least prejudice the main question.

I think the Irish would be unworthy of their cause and country if they consented to go on without a settlement of account, in view of the abominable manner in which they were swindled both before the Union and before the consolidation of the Exchequer. It is another question whether their share of Imperial expenses might if they remain be fixed by a percentage.

I have heard nothing of the probable time of Parnell's coming here. Though I wish it, yet, if he is closely engaged in the endeavour to push on his suit (the excuse for the postponement by the Judges seems a poor one),[2] I quite feel that that matter is of greater importance than his coming a little sooner or a little later to compare notes with me.[3]

I do not understand that you have tied up your own hands as to the manner of retention, though you have indicated what you think the likeliest form of the solution.

I am much inclined to think that one of us should bring in a Bill to open the Irish Vice Royalty to Roman Catholics; and that the best way would be to do it in the Commons on the first night of the Session. What say you?

P.S. Whatever your enemies may say to you about speeches to come, your friends never have reason to complain of the result.

[1] Spencer wrote a nine-page letter defending his Stockton speech. Spencer to Gladstone, 8 Nov. 1889, GP, Add. MS. 44314 ff. 5–9.

[2] The Parnell Commission continued until 22 Nov.

[3] Parnell visited Hawarden on 18 Dec., staying the night.

**551  LORD SPENCER TO LORD GRANVILLE**
*20 November 1889; Althorp, Northampton*
Gr. P, PRO 30/29/22A/6

Wonderful weather. I don't know when I have enjoyed myself so much as I have for the last 14 days, since my Speeches ended.[1] I don't ride as straight as I used, but on an occasion think I could, and shall see enough of the Hounds to enjoy myself thoroughly.

[1] The last two of the autumn speeches had been at Lancaster on 28 Oct. and Newcastle upon Tyne on 5 Nov.


**552  LORD SPENCER TO LORD GRANVILLE**
*22 December 1889; Althorp, Northampton*
Gr. P, PRO 30/29/22A/6

We are settled in my sister's house next door to Spencer House, which you know we let to a Yankee...

We shall therefore do nicely with our own stables and laundry at the back, and we shall get a small nest egg which will be useful for cleaning up rooms etc.


**553  LORD SPENCER TO J. MORLEY**
*21 August 1890; Munich*[1]

I write to you and have a little political news to record. It is not worth much—indeed you may say it is worth nothing but still it is a small index of certain opinion on the Irish Question, possibly only one man's opinion but a few men are absolutely alone.

We were staying at that loveliest of all spots in the world, Beau Rivage, only for two days and one evening.[2] I recognized that strange being, once M.P. for Dungarvon, Hugh O'Donnell.[3] I never knew him but I thought I would speak to him and accordingly went up to him and spoke to him claiming to have often heard him from the Gallery of the House of Commons. He was quite agreeable and he said he should be glad to talk to me as he knew certain things on the Irish Question so we agreed to meet next morning.

He said he had broken down in health, a nervous collapse followed leg and spinal disorder; he had been living abroad for some time and would not be fit for any work for two years to come. He looked very shaky but said he was getting better and had a little yacht which he had brought overland from Paris at only a cost of 800 francs; on this he had hoisted a Home Rule flag. We had seen it and wondered what it was, green with the Union Jack in corner, and a large harp on the green ground. In this he sailed about and found much benefit from it.

In the morning I went on board for a talk and we had a short sail.

Who would have thought that Hugh O'Donnell would have taken me a sail on the Lake of Geneva? Well we had a long Irish talk. I will try and jot down what I recollect.

He said that he never expected to be well enough for the Imperial Parliament again but he hoped in two years to be fit for something etc. then go back to Ireland and work hard there.

He evidently is heart and soul a Home Ruler, but he is a strong Roman Catholic. He said 'I am called an Ultra Montane but I am not that. I am', and he hesitated, 'I am a strong Catholic.'

He said that he had been cruelly used over his trial with *The Times* but that he consoled himself by thinking that he had caused the final exposure of *The Times* and the vindication of the Parnellites from accusations of crime. He said that after he had started the case he worked with Parnell and that at one time Parnell and he were to have had a counsel on the case; that the whole programme had been arranged with Parnell that he (O'Donnell) was to have been called last but that eventually he found that Sir C. Russell had pledged his counsel not to call him at all (he was rather vague on this) and had squared him. The consequence was that he could not without a regular scene have got into the witness box and that as he was in sadly broken health he did not dare do this. His counsel had the tears in his eyes when he told O'Donnell how he had been persuaded by C. Russell and O'Donnell said that evidently Sir Charles was afraid of what might have been then disclosed and not believing how absolutely free from crime the Parnellites were. The judge being a Parnellite[4] thought that O'Donnell was in league with *The Times* and summed up strongly against him. This is what he told me.

Davitt he says was indignant with the way he (O'Donnell) had been treated and, although what he said might have been a rhetorical phrase, declared that the Nationalists had been too long dragged at the chariot wheels of a 'liar and coward' (meaning Parnell).

However he seemed delighted with the upshot of the whole affair.[5]

He spoke oddly about Parnell. He praised him exceedingly in many ways, said that when he began in Parliament he never cared as long as he had Parnell beside him; he was always ready, fair, and bold and a most adroit debater.

He said he was a delightful companion, gentlemanlike, kind, pleasant and courteous; he was not a very able man but he suited the Irish for he ruled them with a light hand, did not mind what they did as long as he led in Parliament. He liked sitting on the stile as long as he could and then started with the winning side.

O'Donnell seemed behind with news of the trial:[6] if it went against Parnell he said it would do harm but would not upset P. in his leadership. If P. disappeared he was sure that a Leader would be found, either Justin McCarthy[7] or Arthur O'Connor,[8] the latter he thought very able and somewhat of a trimmer, not a bad quality, he said for a leader. He thought that though McCarthy was timid he had a mature instinct for going for advice to the right man. O'Donnell did not seem to care for Dillon. He liked Sexton, said little about O'Brien.

[1] Copy, SP. Spencer left London for Aix-les-Bains on 1 Aug. travelling via Lausanne, Zurich, Munich and Oberammergau.

² The celebrated Hotel Beau Rivage at Ouchy, Lausanne.

³ Frank Hugh O'Donnell, a former member of the Council of the Home Rule League, M.P., Galway City, 1874, but unseated on petition, and Dungarvan, 1877-85. Brought unsuccessful action for libel against *The Times* in July 1888, arising out of a series of articles entitled 'Parnellism and Crime'. As a result of this case, Parnell asked for a Special Commission, composed of three judges, to investigate charges made by the newspaper.

⁴ John Duke, 1st Baron Coleridge, Lord Chief Justice of England since 1880. Gladstone's Solicitor-General, 1868-71, Attorney-General, 1871-3. There is no truth in O'Donnell's claims of Coleridge's favourable disposition towards Parnell.

⁵ For O'Donnell's later version of events, see his *History of the Irish Parliamentary Party* (1910), ii, p. 224 ff.

⁶ The Special Commission was set up by the government in Sept. 1888 to investigate charges levelled at Parnell by *The Times* that he was linked with the Phoenix Park murders in 1882. The newspaper's case rested largely on a series of letters, which proved to be forgeries. Richard Pigott, the perpetrator of the forgeries, made a full confession before the Commission on 23 Feb. 1889 and committed suicide six days later. The Commission met for the last time on 22 Nov. 1889. See T. W. Moody, '*The Times* versus Parnell and Co. 1887-90', in T. W. Moody (ed.), *Historical Studies*, vi (1965), pp. 147-82.

⁷ Historian and novelist. Vice-chairman of the Irish Nationalist Party under Parnell from 1879; M.P., Longford Co., 1879-85 and for N. Longford, 1885-6. From Oct. 1886, when also returned for Londonderry City, he chose that seat.

⁸ A London Irishman and expert on parliamentary procedure. Secretary of the Irish Parliamentary Party; M.P., Queen's Co., 1880-5, and E. Donegal, 1885-1900.

## 554   J. MORLEY TO LORD SPENCER

*16 September 1890; Dublin*

The enclosed is rather heartbreaking.¹ I was with Dillon when it arrived, and he is convinced that, if true, it will give a frightful shock to the party here, and destroy us at the election.² It is the nasty *detail* in these things that is fatal. Please destroy the letter. I shall not speak of it to anyone else.

I had a note from Parnell himself this morning, offering to see me in London whenever I like.

¹ Not in SP. Obviously refers to the news of the O'Shea divorce case to be heard on 15 Nov. 1890 before a London jury.

² Dillon, on the other hand, told Morley at the meeting that proof of the charge against Parnell would make no difference to his authority in Ireland '*provided* there was no disclosure of nauseous details'. F. S. L. Lyons, *The Fall of Parnell 1890-91* (1960), p. 82.

## 555   J. MORLEY TO LORD SPENCER

*17 November 1890; 95 Elm Park Gardens, South Kensington, S.W.*

*Private*

I would give much for a chat with you today.

In default thereof, I enclose you

1) a copy of my letter to Mr. G., on my interview with P. at Brighton last Monday.¹

2) At Mr. G.'s request, a memo. by him. Please return both by next post.²

I have a very full memo. of my conversation with P., which I should like to show you, but I think it better not to trust it to the post.³

It is a sad mess, isn't it? P. is going to stand to his guns, as if nothing had happened, and I don't see that he has any choice, save total disappearance.[4] Mr. G., however, thinks that *now* the Pope may come down upon him more effectively than before.

[1] Morley to Gladstóne, 13 Nov. 1890, GP, Add. MS. 44256 ff. 63-7. The meeting took place on 10 Nov.
[2] Not traced.
[3] Reproduced in Morley, *Recollections*, i, pp. 251-6.
[4] On 18 Nov. O'Shea was granted a decree nisi.

## 556  W. V. HARCOURT TO LORD SPENCER

*29 November 1890; Park Hotel, Park Place, St. James's Street, S.W.*

*Confidential*

I am sure you must be revelling in the latest development of your *dear friend*.[1]

The most serious mischief which will be done is by the statements of proposals by Mr. G. which P. affirms to have been made to him as the result of 'the *unanimous opinion of his colleagues* after careful consideration of the alternatives' this particularly applies to the proposal to reduce the Irish M.P.s to 33.

I suppose this refers to a certain conclave held at Hawarden in November last year of which I was allowed to know nothing until it was mentioned accidentally to me by J. Morley.[2]

You will remember that I at once wrote a letter to Mr. G. to Granville and to yourself protesting against the reduction of Irish M.P.s and saying that I could never be a member of a Government which made such a proposal.

I should be very grateful to you if you could let me have that letter to you, in order that I may refresh my memory as to its contents.[3]

Of course the revelation that such a scheme was decided upon will have a very injurious effect on the minds of our friends. It will look like an unworthy evasion of the pledge that the Irish M.P.s should remain at Westminster. They did not mean by that 33 any more than they meant ½ dozen members.

And further they will justly complain that if such a decision were taken by us it should have been intentionally concealed from the country.

The other point which will also produce a bad effect will be that Mr. G. 'intimated that he was prepared to introduce a Land Purchase Bill on the lines of the Bill of 1886.' This is the very thing which beat us at the last Election and will infallibly beat us at the next and that Mr. G. should be supposed to have given such a promise to P. will be most disastrous. It remains to be seen what comes of it all.

Mr. G. has sent a denial to the Press this afternoon. In my judgment it is too long and detailed not that is *more suo*.

I have just seen J. Morley. His denial will not be out till Monday.[4]

[1] In response to Gladstone's publication of a letter written to John Morley of 24 Nov. stating that Parnell's continuance as leader of the Irish Party was a great embarrassment, Parnell issued a manifesto which appeared in the press on 29 Nov. In it, he claimed that at the Hawarden meeting with Gladstone the previous Dec. the latter had put forward the proposal to reduce Irish representation in Parliament from 103 to 32 'with the unanimous opinion of his colleagues'. *The Times*, 29 Nov. 1890, p. 9.

[2] Harcourt had left Hawarden before Granville, Morley and Ripon.
[3] Harcourt to Spencer, 29 Oct. 1889, SP.
[4] Both Gladstone's and Morley's denials appeared in *The Times* on 1 Dec., p. 6.


## 557  LORD SPENCER TO H. SEYMOUR
*29 November 1890; Althorp, Northampton*

I am so glad you approve of my Bromley speech.[1] It was not easy, particularly as the bent of my mind was exactly yours; but I was bound to back Mr. G., and certainly from what I hear the opinion in the Constituencies was overwhelming and conclusive.

The letter was probably necessary, but I doubt the wisdom of rushing it to the front in public until more conference had been held with the Irish.

My belief is that Parnell will sit still in the Saddle and after what may be a long race come in triumphant. Probably *The Times* will settle Home Rule with him.

I cannot but admire his indomitable will and pluck, though I dislike his morality, and the shiftings of his words and actions in this affair.

I have so long argued for measures and not men in Irish policy that I was not much moved by the long anticipated verdict, but I was amazed at the strength of feeling against Parnell. It is creditable when it does not reach cant.

[1] On 27 Nov., stating that Parnell should withdraw from the leadership of the Irish Party. *Daily News*, 28 Nov. 1890, p. 5.


## 558  W. V. HARCOURT TO LORD SPENCER
*1 December 1890; 10 Park Place, S.W.*

Many thanks for the letters. You will note that before Mr. G. made his communication to P. at Hawarden he had received your dissent and my strong protest against the diminution of Irish Members.[1]

On the whole I am not dissatisfied with the situation. It is well we should have found out in time what sort of man we had to deal with in case the responsibility of action had ever devolved on us. We may have better men to deal with hereafter. We can't have worse.

I was with Mr. G. yesterday when he saw Justin McCarthy[2] who poor man was the bearer of a message from P. proposing that Mr. G., J. Morley and I should sign a letter containing certain terms to be binding upon us in the final settlement of Home Rule which he P. undertook to keep an inviolable secret!!

This was to be a condition of his surrender. Can you imagine that impudence could go further? You may imagine the answer which was given to this inconceivable proposal.

I feel great sympathy with the unhappy Irish Members who have had the courage to stand out. This position is no doubt a most painful one as P. will wage war to the knife against them in Ireland.[3] Everything is possible in that unhappy country and that the Nationalist party there will be hopelessly split up there can be no doubt, but I do not agree with you that it is by any means certain that P. will prevail. He has already had to ransack the byways and ditches to find candidates even for his late party. Now every man of credit or influence in that party with the exception of the two Harringtons and Redmonds[4] have declared against him.

With Davitt, Healy, Dillon, O'Brien, T. D. Sullivan and Sexton against him[5] as well as Archbishop Walsh and Croke[6] what will he have to rely on? His impudent attempt to rally the campaigners will fail in the presence of the opposition of Dillon and O'Brien whom it is well known he has always cold shouldered and thrown over on the subject of the campaign. The disgust of his own friends at the Manifesto and its shameless treachery is satisfactory.

What will be the future of the Nationalist party is dark enough but it is plain that we have saved the English Liberal Party which was the paramount consideration. My belief is that Mr. G. is stronger today in Great Britain than he was before the row.

The Bassetlaw Election will be an interesting fight.[7]

[1] See No. 556.
[2] Gladstone's memo of conversation with Justin McCarthy, 30 Nov. 1890, GP, Add. MS. 56446.
[3] Parnell left for Cork late on 30 Nov. arriving there in the early hours of 1 Dec.
[4] Edward Harrington, M.P., Kerry West; Timothy Charles Harrington, M.P., Dublin Harbour division; John Edward Redmond, M.P., Wexford North; William Hoey Redmond, M.P., Fermanagh North.
[5] Timothy David Sullivan, M.P., Dublin College Green division; Thomas Sexton, M.P., Belfast West. Dillon and O'Brien telegraphed from America on 30 Nov. deprecating Parnell's continued leadership.
[6] Joint action, following the appearance of Parnell's manifesto, took the form of a telegram from Archbishop Croke of Cashel to Justin McCarthy, vice-chairman, Irish Parliamentary Party, urging Parnell to retire, whilst Archbishop Walsh of Dublin gave an interview to the Central News Agency, warning that the document could bring 'potential disaster' upon Ireland.
[7] The result of the by-election at Bassetlaw, Nottinghamshire, declared on 16 Dec., showed an increase in the Conservative majority from 295 in 1885 (there was no contest in 1886) to 728 in 1890. Sir F. Milner, Conservative, 4381, J. W. Mellor, Liberal, 3653.

### 559  J. MORLEY TO LORD SPENCER
*1 December 1890; House of Commons*

... The moment is certainly a trying one, but my nerves are good. I cannot say that my spirits are the same. The loss of Parnell is irreparable, but I am more than ever sure that it was absolutely inevitable after the trial. Ireland had better have stuck to him, I daresay, as the man most likely to unite all factions both there and in America. But this would have been the ruin of their cause in England.

His conduct, in reporting confidential talk from Mr. G.'s dinner table and mine, reveals an infamy of character which I never suspected.

At last the holy men seem to have plucked up courage.

Once more, thank you for writing to me. We are all in high tension here, waiting for the break-up of the Irish meeting (5.40).[1]

[1] The Irish Parliamentary Party met in Committee Room 15 in the Commons on 26 Nov. to elect its leader, and subsequently adjourned until 1 Dec. At a further meeting two days later, Parnell was beaten, 44 votes to 29, but still refused to resign. After receiving assurances from Gladstone on any future home rule bill, the majority of delegates on 6 Dec. proceeded to organize the National Federation under McCarthy's leadership, in place of the National League.

**560  LORD SPENCER TO U. KAY-SHUTTLEWORTH**
*14 December 1890; Althorp, Northampton*
Shuttleworth Papers

Have you studied the methods by which Free Education can be given?

I suppose the Tories will promise it, and perhaps produce a measure, but I doubt whether they will succeed.[1]

It strikes me that we ought to see our way a little and formulate general principles upon which to deal with the question.

Have you any plan?

Morley and Mundella were said to have arranged a compromise with Sexton, but I never could follow it.

At the outset there seem several questions to settle.

1) Are the fees to be paid out of Rates or Parliamentary grant or Consolidated Fund?

2) Are they to be paid without representative local control?

3) Are they to be actual fees paid or averaged, if so on what scale?

4) If no grant is taken for Free Education by certain schools, are present public contributions to continue?

I am going to communicate with Mundella (but I fear his wife is very ill[2]), A. Acland, Playfair and one or two others, and when we have put some ideas together I would write to John Morley.

[1] At a speech to the National Union of Conservative Associations at Nottingham on 26 Nov. 1889, and much to the surprise of his colleagues, Salisbury pledged his party to a measure for 'assisted education'. See G. Sutherland, *Policy-Making in Elementary Education 1870-1895* (1973), p. 284 ff.
[2] She died on 14 Dec.

**561  LORD SPENCER TO U. KAY-SHUTTLEWORTH**
*4 January 1891; Althorp, Northampton*
Shuttleworth Papers

I am much obliged to you for your long and interesting letter.[1] I do not intend to answer it at length but should like to touch on one or two points.

I went through doubts about Free Education. You put well the arguments of weight in favour of fees,[2] but you do not put the reasons why it is impossible for us to oppose it.

The great argument in favour of Free Education is the difficulty of thoroughly applying the principle of compulsion if fees are kept up. Exceptions and remissions are not satisfactory, they may be applied wisely in one district but harshly and badly in another.

I was prepared to adopt it on this account, but the arguments of expediency come in as well, after the Scottish concession. The principle is conceded, and must be worked out in England as well as in Scotland. Unfortunately Scotland is so differently organized for Education that we cannot apply the same process which succeeds there to our Country.

The Roman Catholic question seems to be solved in Scotland, merely because

it is so small a question. The same principle will be claimed for Roman Catholics here, and I cannot see how in principle they can be separated from Extreme
Church of England Denominationalists.[3]

[1] Kay-Shuttleworth to Spencer, 19 Dec. 1890, SP. His father, Sir James Kay-Shuttleworth, was
the first Secretary of the Committee of the Privy Council on Education, 1839-49.

[2] In the same letter, Kay-Shuttleworth wrote, 'I will confess to you in confidence that I have
never liked the "Free-School" cry. I do not think school-fees an unreasonable burden on parents.'

[3] For background, see V. A. McClelland, 'The "Free Schools" Issue and the General Election of
1885: A Denominational Response', *History of Education*, v (1976), pp. 141-54. The Elementary
Education Bill received the royal assent on 5 Aug. 1891.

### 562   J. MORLEY TO LORD SPENCER
*8 February 1891; 95 Elm Park Gardens, South Kensington, S.W.*

*Secret*

I have been so occupied by this harassing business, and it has so changed from
day to day, that I put off writing. Even now I have nothing definite to tell you
as to the acceptance of our assurances on Land and Police by the men of
Boulogne.[1] They (no doubt at the instigation of P., who was over there last
Monday) pressed for small changes. Mr. G. most wisely stuck to it that we
would not alter a comma.[2] When I parted from Justin and Sexton on Friday,
they had not got authority from Boulogne to convey their acceptance of our
declarations as payment in full. All this is easily summed up, but I can assure
you that it has involved endless talking, telegraphing, and other forms of time
wasting. How it will end, I don't know, but it is clear to me that we ought not
to budge from our position deliberately taken up in Mr. G.'s room on January
29th.[3]

On Thursday next, Justin will call his men together,[4] will tell them that he
perceives that the party can best be united, or only united, under a man who
was not mixed up in the quarrels of the Committee Room; and therefore that
he resigns. The next step will be to call a meeting of the whole party (both
sections) under the presidency of one of the Whips; and then Dillon will be
elected chairman.[5]

They all swear to me that Parnell means to retire; but whether this is retirement for good, or only from the leadership, they either don't know, or won't
tell. Our assurances, if Mr. G. gives them, will not be mentioned at these
meetings. Perhaps they won't ever come to anything as Dillon may be afraid
of accepting them fully. He is not half the man that I thought him, tho' one
must allow for immense difficulties.

Parnell will no doubt crow; but we cannot help that. It will soon be over.

Mr. G. was inclined to dissuade Justin from his mode of resigning; but I
persuaded him that it was no business of ours to give advice, unasked, as to
leadership.

It is a trying time, and I daily wish that you were accessible. One cannot
write fully and precisely; and even if one could, there is an incessant shifting of
shoals and currents from hour to hour almost.

[1] Negotiations took place in Boulogne towards the end of Dec. between O'Brien and Parnell on
the terms proposed by O'Brien for Parnell's retirement from the leadership.

[2] A meeting of Liberal leaders on 28 Jan. to determine guarantees for the next home rule bill

were agreed upon. These related to land and the police. Besides Gladstone, there were also present Harcourt, Morley, Ripon and Spencer. See Lyons, *The Fall of Parnell 1890-91*, p. 234.

[3] Parnell had returned to Boulogne on 3 Feb. for a further conference with Dillon and O'Brien, but the negotiations broke down. Dillon's and O'Brien's statements announcing this appeared in *The Times*, 12 Feb. 1891, p. 9. On the same day the two men landed at Folkestone and were arrested.

[4] On 6 Dec. a meeting in Committee Room 15 resulted in the splitting of the Irish Party. McCarthy was elected by 45 members; the remaining 26 stayed with Parnell.

[5] McCarthy gave up the leadership of the National Federation to Dillon in 1896.


**563   LORD SPENCER TO H. SEYMOUR**

*6 April 1891; Althorp, Northampton*

I do feel very much poor Granville's death.[1] He was quite our staunchest and oldest friend. I owe all my introduction to Politics to him and he has been my closest Political ally. Everything almost most pleasant in our early life was connected with him.

I don't think he had failed in mind in the least. He was from failing health less vigorous in action and sometimes in Political thought. But he remained as he always was a strong sturdy Liberal.

He had a great horror of big funerals and begged me once to prevent any swell from attending his funeral.

His public services deserved every Public recognition, and he was a greater man than many who have received services at Westminster Abbey.[2]

He was greatly altered when here in February. He had lost his go, and was I could see much weaker than I had ever seen him.

[1] On 31 March.

[2] Granville was buried at Stone, Staffordshire, on 4 April. Spencer attended the service.


**564   LORD SPENCER**

*Memorandum of conversation held at Spencer House, St. James's Place, S.W.
on Tuesday afternoon 28 July 1891*

*Secret*

Mr. Gladstone began the conversation by referring to the Land Act just passed.[1]

He said that he and other Liberals in the H. of Commons considered that the present Parliament was pledged not to use the Imperial credit for the purpose of Irish Land Purchase.

I said that personally I could not have gone so far and he admitted that but it did not affect his main argument.

He considered that we should when in office have to deal with the Act, for we should in our proposals for Home Rule remove the only substantial and practical Security namely the payments which we make for Education and Police to Ireland.

He said however that Parliament being pledged British credit, it would not be possible to alter such a Settlement, and it would have to remain, but we should have to find other Security.

He considered that no repetition of the Loan for Purchase of the 30 million which might go on as the Government proposed for 120 years, ought to be made without direct authority of Parliament; he also thought that the desire in the Bill of 1886 of appointing a Receiver-General through whose hands all Irish resources should pass and who should be responsible for the payments due to clear the British Exchequer in cases of default of payment of annuities would be the proper mode of dealing with the question: and I understood him to say that all the complicated arrangements for rating counties and impending Probate duties etc. should be swept away.

He thought that this work should be done in the Second Session after Home Rule had been disposed of and established, which should be the work of our first Session. He distinctly said that no attempt to couple the 2 measures as in 1886 should be made.

He strongly favoured the idea that for two years after the establishment of Home Rule *all* Irish members should remain in the Imperial Parliament in order to give an opportunity of settling the Land question. If it were not settled during that time it must be left to the Irish Parliament.

He thought that this arrangement might overcome difficulties and smooth the way for subsequently dealing (as I suppose) with the numbers of the Irish M.P.s to be left for Imperial purposes in Westminster.

On this point I gathered that he distinctly desired to reduce, for the permanent arrangement, their numbers.

I put to him what I had said on the H. of Lords that I considered that Balfour's Purchase Act would be probably the last large Act of the kind, although amendments in it would probably be necessary.[2]

He assented.

I said 'Your proposed measure will not be a first class measure, not "a figure head" in party Programmes.'

He said 'Certainly not.'

I understood him distinctly to say that it must follow the Home Rule measure.

He said he had sounded McCarthy and Sexton about the Receiver-General and found that they had no objection.

He was of opinion that Land Purchase in Ireland would not proceed at a more rapid rate than heretofore and this he calculated at about one million or one and a quarter million a year.

He listened with attention to my assertion that I thought it likely that now that something like finality in big land Legislation had been arrived at, there might be expected large foreclosures of mortgages. He said 'But is not interest paid regularly?' I said 'Yes' but I did not think a state of things would continue when over 900,000£ p.ann. rental was in the hands and under the management of receivers in the Court of Chancery.

He said that I might be right, and that in that case this would bring about a fall in prices. I agreed for a time at all events.

He referred to opinions held by certain members of our party which he considered very objectionable[3] on the Home Rule question.

He said that next to the Parnell crisis the greatest danger we have run was that of 'The Round Table Conference'.

I alluded to the idea that if all Irish M.P.s remained in Westminster it would not be necessary to breach the financial arrangement with Ireland. He considered an arrangement as essential, that probably that the Irish must be asked for a smaller contribution than that asked in 1886. He was inclined to a proportionate and not a fixed contribution.

I said that might be right but it would increase the Irish contribution in time of War.

He answered that Dr. Dale had refused his support to his Home Rule plan because in time of war Ireland would not contribute.[4]

Anyhow he thought the Irish would not grudge an extra contribution and it would not be serious.

He seemed to have some difficulty or hesitation about Customs and Excise, because we allow our Colonies to tax us. At the same time he admitted that to alter this part of the plan was not possible and to do it would increase our difficulties.

He said that Parnell had the sagacity to see that to try and modify this arrangement would have been so difficult, that it was a case of taking it as offered or not at all.

He was very emphatic on making certain questions in the Settlement vital, and making this clear to the Irish, that if they would not accept the proposals we must abandon dealing with Home Rule at all, for no plan could be proposed or carried which had not the full approval of the bulk of the Irish members.

He indirectly alluded when referring to bias of certain persons to the impossibility of proposing any small measure, retaining the appointment of Judges and R.M.s and the control of the Police, but we did not go into detail on these points as Mrs. Gladstone came in. He said however that such a settlement with no financial arrangement would not amount to more than Chamberlain's Council scheme which had been rejected in 1885. He considered the control of the Military and Naval forces by the Imperial Government as of vital importance.

I referred to Parnell's last programme where any control of Measures by the Imperial Parliament was put on one side, and nothing left of Union but the Link of the Crown with its veto direct or through the Lord Lieutenant. He added 'Yes on the advice of Irish Ministers.'

He placed no confidence in Parnell but he remarked on this part of the subject that if the Westminster Parliament had the power of interference it would be extremely rare that it would exercise it.

I think however he placed this question as to the Supremacy of Parliament among those treated as 'vital.'

---

[1] The Purchase of Land and Congested Districts (Ireland) Bill was read for the third time in the Commons on 15 June and agreed to by the Lords on 31 July. Spencer, Kimberley and other peers indicated their general approval of the measure. It received the royal assent on 5 Aug.

[2] Hansard, 3, ccclv, cols. 1147-52, 14 July 1891.

[3] Spencer noted in the margin, 'Not his actual words.'

[4] Dr. Robert William Dale, a leading Birmingham Congregational minister and friend of Gladstone. The latter was strongly affected by Dale's irreconcilable attitude on the question. A. W. W. Dale, *The Life of R. W. Dale of Birmingham* (1902), p. 738.

## 565  J. MORLEY TO LORD SPENCER
*28 July 1891; Overstrand, Cromer*

*Secret*

By the time you get this, you will have seen Mr. G. and had a talk with him.

I did my best to press on him the difficulties in the way of tinkering [with] the Land Bill.[1] It is true, as he says, that the finance of the Land Bill affects the general finance of a future Irish Government, but it would be a frightful danger to our friends to find themselves struggling once more with the Serbonian bog of the Land Question.

Then the postponement of Home Rule for two years! At his age! At the same time there is no room for the raging hurry of 1886.

I raised the point of repealing the Crimes Act. He thought, and I fully concur, that we might leave that alone. We need not use it. Its rèpeal would follow the passing of H. R. But I expect that W. V. H. will press for making this the first business, because his policy is to send as many bills as possible up to your House, which they are likely to reject. On the fatal crux of the Irish members at Westminster, I neither gave nor received much daylight.

I ventured to say a few words on the future Irish administration. I said our Irish friends would look for some change of personnel at the Castle, and that for my part I thought W. R.[2] ought to go. He agreed decidedly and talked of the recall of R. H.[3] I told him I was not quite sure of this being good, as he will have lost touch of the Resident Magistrates etc. We ought to have an Irishman.

Then I said 'I think you will have to secure an *effective* Viceroy this time. Lord A.[4] would never do, as the Chief Secretary, *whoever he may be*, will have plenty to do in the House of Commons.'

He made no remark as to my fishing little parenthesis about the Chief Secretary, but at once assented about A., saying, moreover that he did not think the Viceroy could be in Cabinet: that it had only been tried once, with you and Forster; and that it exploded in 24 hours. I did not think the time had come for going further, as he was in this frame of mind.

He evidently thinks it not impossible that a certain big friend of ours may quarrel with us about H. R. I told him that all would depend on the feeling in the party at the time.

He may have gone over these secondary points with you, and so I may be wasting your time with repetition.

---

[1] Gladstone was staying at Lowestoft with his daughter, Mary. Morley met him there on 27 July. A heavily-edited version of the conversation is given in Morley, *Recollections*, i, p. 278.

[2] Sir West Ridgeway, Under-Secretary, Dublin Castle, 1887-92.

[3] Robert Hamilton. In Oct. 1886 he told Edward Hamilton that he had 'practically been given notice to quit', having received the offer of the governorship of Tasmania. EHJ, 28 Oct. 1886, Add. MS. 48645 f. 19. He accepted the post and left England on 27 Jan. 1887.

[4] Aberdeen, the former Viceroy.

## 566   LORD SPENCER TO W. V. HARCOURT
*14 September 1891; Althorp, Northampton*
HP, MS. 45

I expect that Homburg did Hartington great good.[1] He grunted and groaned but all the same was not really bored and admitted he felt wonderfully better ... He was as pleasant with us as ever. It was the first time since 1886 that we had even seen anything of him. So we were very glad to get back for at any rate a time to our old friendly relations.

[1] The Spencers were at Homburg for a month, returning to England on 27. Aug.


## 567   LORD SPENCER TO L. HARCOURT
*18 October 1891; Althorp, Northampton*
HP, MS. 429 f. 21

I had a rough and tumble week in Scotland, and what with Speeches, travelling and a heavy cold, I am surprised at being so fresh and well.

Better meetings than the Home Counties.[1] One was in a Church! and a man was so drunk I had to sit down while he was carried out cursing and blaspheming like a Demon. It does not sound well to ears of strict Religionists.

A first rate meeting in Dumbarton[2] where drunkards did not appear. In S. Lanark the meeting was the day and night of the storm, and I really hoped no one would appear but the church was nearly full to my disgust.

[1] R. C. Munro-Ferguson, Liberal M.P., Leith Burghs, 1886-1914, informed Rosebery that Spencer's meeting at Lesmahagow 'went off very well. He seems very hopeful about Ireland'. 18 Oct. 1891, RP, 10018 f. 69.
[2] On 15 Oct. See *The Times*, 16 Oct. 1891, p. 4.


## 568   J. DILLON TO LORD SPENCER
*13 October 1891; 2 North Great George's Street, Dublin*

I read with very great pleasure your letter. It was so kind and sympathetic and showed how thoroughly you have been able to enter into our feelings in reference to Mr. Parnell's death.[1] His qualities were rare and of a kind badly needed amongst our people. And in spite of the deplorable events of the past few months he did a work for the Irish people, the effects of which will, I firmly believe, not pass away for generations.

It has been a very sad and painful time for all of us. And we have a good deal of trouble before us still. But the common sense of the Country is solidly with us. And our only difficulty lies with a section of the people in Dublin, Cork, Waterford and Limerick, who are under the influence of that peculiar personal attachment to an individual who has always had so strong a hold on Irish Nation. I am convinced however that their bitterness will steadily die away. The tone adopted by you and Mr. Morley has helped us enormously in combating this feeling.[2]

[1] Spencer had written privately to Dillon following Parnell's death on 6 Oct., 'I who have in bygone days been so often in opposition and sharp conflict with Mr. Parnell am quite affected at this sudden disappearance of one who was so great a power in Politics, and who yet might have exercised a serious part in our political warfare.' 11 Oct. 1891, Dillon Papers, MS. 6788/132.

[2] Morley spoke at Cambridge on 21 Sept. and Spencer at Buxton on 29 Sept., pledging support for home rule.

## 569  LADY SPENCER'S DIARY
### 5–9 December 1891; Althorp

On Saturday, the 5th December, Sir William and Lady Harcourt arrived from Derby where he had been speaking.[1] He was in great force though with a cold in his head which obliged him to go early to bed.

### Sunday 6th December

There were many strangers in Church hoping to see Mr. Gladstone.[2]

### Monday 7th December

Mr. Gladstone arrived about 3.30.[3] Spencer had gone out hunting but Bobby came from London in time for luncheon and went down to our Station to meet him. I received him on the Staircase where he sat talking for some time with Sir William, Lady Harcourt, Bobby and myself. He had come from Liverpool where he had been staying since Saturday with 4 nephews, all unmarried, and looked after by an old nurse aged 87 and now an invalid and attended by another nurse, who was with Mr. Maybrick when he died of supposed poison.[4]

Mr. Gladstone said, (the conversation having turned on Lord Melbourne) that there were 3 men he regretted always not having made acquaintance with—Lord Melbourne, Sir Walter Scott, and Dr. Arnold. He had sat at the same dinner table with Lord Melbourne but had never been introduced to him. Mr. Gladstone went upstairs to write letters.[5] It was such a wet afternoon with a heavy gale blowing that he did not go out. At 5 o'clock Mr. Gladstone came down to tea in the Old Breakfast Room. The conversation turned on Lord Rosebery's Life of Pitt. Mr. G. said he had written to Lord Rosebery when he had read the first half and he was able to praise it warmly.[6] He did not agree entirely with the views Lord R. took of Pitt in the War policy in the second half. Sir William Harcourt said the only thing that was new to him was that Pitt had brought on a Socialistic Bill on behalf of the poor and that it was to be found in Eden's *Rights of the Poor*.[7] I found them the latter book which they wanted to refer to. At 6.30 Lord Rosebery,[8] Mr. J. Morley,[9], Sandhurst[10] and Horace arrived from London. I had never seen Lord Rosebery since his wife's death.[11] I thought him much altered and with an expression of great sadness. Lady Harcourt had not seen him either and I think he felt sad seeing us both for the first time.

Our dinner party was Mr. Gladstone, Lord Rosebery, Sir W. and Lady Harcourt, Mr. J. Morley, Sandhurst, Horace. We sat at a round Table in the new dining room. Mr. G. took me in and was on my left, Lord Rosebery on my right. Next Mr. G., Mr. J. Morley, Sandhurst, Lady Harcourt, Spencer, Sir William and Horace, next Lord R. Mr. Gladstone was in great spirits and talked much on all sorts of subjects.

After dinner we sat in the Long Library. I was sitting on the large red leather sofa near the fire place, Mr. Morley next to me, Lady Harcourt in the armchair. Mr. Gladstone took possession of a little Austrian chair near the fire and remained sitting there the rest of the evening. Lord Rosebery and Sir W. joined our circle and we had a most agreeable evening, Mr. Gladstone discussing most pleasantly.

I was loth to go to bed but as it was 11.15, I felt I ought not to let Mr. G. sit up late and knew if Mrs. Gladstone had been here she would have packed him off before 11.

### Tuesday 8th December

Mr. Gladstone, Spencer, Lord Rosebery, Mr. Morley and Sir William Harcourt held an ex Cabinet meeting in the Old Book Room at 11.30, which lasted till 1.30[12] when they joined us at luncheon and Lord R. left us for Mentmore at 2.20.[13]

Mr. Gladstone took a walk with Mr. Morley and Spencer, Horace and I and the Harcourts walked up the kitchen garden.

Mr. and Mrs. Guthrie and Mr. and Mrs. Cecil Bingham[14] arrived to dine and sleep. Sandhurst left by an early train this morning.

### Wednesday 9th December

Spencer went off hunting at 9.30. I came down at 10.30 to say goodbye to Sir W. and Lady Harcourt and Mr. J. Morley, who left us by the 10.55 for London. Mr. Gladstone was in the hall eagerly discoursing with Morley. After the guests were gone Mr. Gladstone went to his room to write letters, and I after taking leave of Mrs. Guthrie and Mrs. Cecil Bingham who left by the 11.10 train for Rugby went to the Billiard Room to try and see if we had a pamphlet of 16[ ]4[15] containing the liturgy psalms and morning prayers, corresponding to two pamphlets Mr. Gladstone had become possessed of and of which they have no duplicates in the British Museum. I was unsuccessful in my search. Bobby arrived from London soon after one o'clock.

We lunched at one thirty, Mr. Gladstone full of anecdote. He inveighed against Mrs. Smith having been made a viscountess[16] and put on the same level with Canning's widow![17] He said Smith was an excellent man of business, a kindly upright man, but a wretched debater, and his position in this respect in the House was absolutely absurd. We again got on the subject of Lord Melbourne and I said his language I supposed according to the fashion of his day was very much interlarded with oaths.

Mr. Gladstone said undoubtedly so, and proceeded to tell us a story of the old Duke of Cambridge who coming out of Berkeley Chapel one day put his arm on his son and said 'My boy, that was a d---ed good sermon.'

... Coming down dressed to start for Northampton, I suddenly bethought that I had forgotten to ask Mr. Gladstone to plant a Tree as I had intended. I met Bobby and told him I was in despair. I rushed into the Garden—not a Gardener to be seen. Bobby ran for me and opened the gate into the backyard.

He saw an underling, and told him to come and speak to me. I said, Are there any shrubs about? Yes, three, waiting to be put in in the bed we had turned for the new road. I said Get a spade, quickly. I looked frantically about to see where to plant the Tree. I chose a spot, told the man to dig a hole as quick as he could. Bobby had gone to fetch Mr. G. The three shrubs were a box, a laurel and a ragged thuja. I chose the latter. [sic] The hole was tolerably deep. We put in the shrub, and Mr. Gladstone seized the spade, and with the greatest vigour shovelled in the earth. He said, 'I like to put in plenty of earth,' and did so. Before he had finished the servant came to say the carriage was at the door, and hurried off as Mr. Gladstone was going to receive addresses at Northampton[18] before starting by the 3.20 train to Mentmore. The whole transaction, digging and planting, had occupied about 5 minutes.

We drove in the landau to Northampton. As we neared the Town there were a great many people about who cheered Mr. Gladstone vigorously. He responded by taking off his hat and waving it. On the Bridge was a dense crowd. We had some difficulty in getting through.

[1] Harcourt's speech, in his own constituency, was on 3 Dec. He told Spencer on being invited, 'A visit to Althorp would be very pleasant though you are not able to mount men. But the library would console me in place of the Meet.' Harcourt to Spencer, 24 Nov. 1891, SP.

[2] Gladstone left Hawarden on 5 Dec. for Liverpool.

[3] For an account of Gladstone's arrival at Althorp Station, see *Northampton Daily Reporter*, 7 Dec. 1891, p. 3.

[4] On 6 June 1889, Florence Maybrick, widow of a wealthy Liverpool cotton broker, was found guilty of murdering her husband with arsenic. She was sentenced to death, but as a result of public agitation, the sentence was commuted to penal servitude for life. I. Butler, *Murderers' England* (1973), pp. 51-2.

[5] See Gladstone to his wife, 7 Dec. 1891, headed '4¼ p.m.' GGP, 30/2.

[6] The book was published by Macmillan in Nov. 1891. Gladstone, in acknowledging a copy sent by Rosebery, called it 'the ablest monograph of the kind that I have ever read'. Reproduced in Crewe, ii, p. 476.

[7] Sir Frederick Morton Eden, *The State of the Poor. A History of the Labouring Classes in England* (1797).

[8] Rosebery had been reluctant to join the conclave at Althorp. Edward Hamilton, who with Rosebery was staying with the Sassoons at Brighton, telegraphed to Spencer on 6 Dec., to persuade Rosebery to come to Althorp. Hamilton to Spencer 6 Dec. 1891, SP, and EHJ 6 Dec. 1891, Add. MS. 48656 f. 156.

[9] Morley had made a speech at Oldham on 5 Dec.

[10] Spencer's brother-in-law.

[11] Hannah Rosebery died on 18 Nov. 1890.

[12] Later that day, Gladstone wrote to his wife, 'We have had a long and harmonious talk on affairs ... The wealth of this house, useless in money, is wonderful.' GGP, 30/2.

[13] Rosebery's account makes clear the wide-ranging nature of the agenda. 'One persuaded to stay till after luncheon. So a long palaver in the old book room of Spencer, Harcourt, Morley and self presided over by Mr. G. We discussed every imaginable subject from a list brought down by Mr. G. Egypt, as to which I said that the Government which *simultaneously* gave HR to Ireland and evacuated Egypt would be a bold one, finance, probable dissolution, Goschen's one pound notes, the navy. Harcourt copious on each, and at length Ireland. There was only time for a short discussion between Harcourt and Mr. G. as to the reduction of the Irish members, and as to an Irish second order on them.' Rosebery, Journal, 8 Dec. 1891, f. 342. Spencer agreed with Harcourt that Irish M.P.s should remain at Westminster, but pointedly remarked, 'But you don't say what you are going to do with the Irish peers!' Morley, *Recollections*, i, pp. 294-5.

[14] David Charles Guthrie of East Haddon Hall, Liberal M.P., Northamptonshire, Southern division, 1892-5. Lt. (later Maj.-Gen. Sir) Cecil Bingham, 2nd Life Guards, and a relative of Spencer.

[15] Figure missing.

[16] Emily, widow of W. H. Smith, former Leader of the House of Commons, had become Viscountess Hambleden on 10 Nov. 1891. Viscount Chilston, *W. H. Smith* (1965), pp. 359-60.

[17] Created Viscountess Canning in Jan. 1828.
[18] At Castle Station, Gladstone received two addresses, one from the Mayor and Corporation, the other from the Northampton Liberal and Radical Association.


## 570  LORD SPENCER TO LORD BRAYE
*14 February 1892; Althorp, Northampton*[1]

I thank you and those who delegate to you the petition to ask me to reconsider my decision as to the Mastership, for your confidence and kindness.

I do not feel justified in altering my views: it is but a day or two since the meeting and I am strongly desirous of being relieved from the duties of Mastership.

It strikes me that as there is little or no prospect of my ever continuing for any long time Master, it is better for the Committee to face the position at once and deal with it.[2]

[1] Copy, SP.
[2] Nevertheless, Spencer was persuaded to continue as Master of the Pytchley until Feb. 1894.


## 571  LORD SPENCER TO LADY SPENCER
*6 June 1892; Althorp, Northampton*

Did you see a sketch character of me in the *Daily News*? I am not sure what day,[1] but it was copied in to the *Mercury* Saturday.

It is flattering, too much so, in some respects, but rather scathing in others under a soft covering. I feel to some extent true, but not wholly so, and I felt a bit riled at it, probably I ought not to have minded it at all.

'A greater dab at riding than reading', an indirect comparison with Lord Melbourne and uneducated Pagets.[2]

A reference to my work at the Council Office all left to Mundella which is not true, for I did as much or more than any Lord President; the Vice-President always doing the bulk of the work, but it happened that I took a leading part in some of the very important Education questions when I was there and all the Agricultural work which was heavy.[3] Then it ends with manners 'amiable and courteous with perhaps a tinge of condescension which belongs more to the official representative of Royalty than to a Private Member of a Liberal Society' or some such words.

I dare say there is truth, or something of truth in all this, and a writer must show or try to show his impartiality, but though not learned or literary I have never been idle in School or College work or without a love of reading, and in other points I do not feel very guilty.

Granville once said that no one who had been a Viceroy altogether lost its effect on his manners. I always kept that before me and tried to be natural, but there may be something in it.

Anyhow I have unburthened my internal grumblings to you, and I cannot complain, as public men must be criticized even by their friends.[4]

[1] 31 May, headed 'Our Public Men'.

[2] The passage read 'Lord Melbourne, perhaps the most omnivorous reader of his time, declared that he did not believe in education because "the Pagets got on so devilishly well without it".' This reference was to Henry William Paget, 1st Marquess of Anglesey, an Army general, appointed Lord-Lieutenant of Ireland by Wellington in 1828 and dismissed the following year. Reappointed by Grey in 1830, he served until 1833.

[3] See *The Red Earl*, i, Introduction, p. 15.

[4] Lady Spencer replied, 'I do not wonder you *smarted* under some of it!—really it is written by someone who does *not* know anything of you till '88 evidently, so much is ignored! and your life up to '88 is said to be singularly uneventful! I felt the more annoyed that Mrs. Gladstone told me of it and thought I should like it!' Lady Spencer to Spencer, 8 June 1892, SP.

# 4

# FIRST CHAIRMAN OF THE
# NORTHAMPTONSHIRE COUNTY COUNCIL,
# 1888-92

*The 1888 Local Government Act which brought into being a new unit of administration, the county council, transferred the work of governing the counties from the Court of Quarter Sessions ro elected representatives. How this was achieved varied from county to county.*

*An interesting feature of the electoral register was that, unlike those for parliamentary elections, it contained the names of peers of the realm, and women were eligible to vote by virtue of being ratepayers. Elections were fixed for 17 January 1889. Spencer, who was Lord-Lieutenant of the county, announced his candidature in November 1888, though he emphasized that he was not standing as a party candidate. He hoped to minimize the political element in the county councils, thus encouraging other candidates to come forward. However, as in most other counties, the campaign in Northamptonshire was fought on party lines. Of the 51 divisions in the county, 18 were uncontested, including Spencer's, but in the remaining 33 divisions, 65 candidates offered themselves, with the labels of Conservative, Liberal or Independent.*

*The results declared on 18 January showed a nice balance between the parties on the Council: 25 Conservatives, 25 Liberals and 1 Independent. After the meeting of the Provisional Council, S. G. Stopford Sackville, the deputy-chairman of Quarter Sessions, was elected provisional chairman after tying with Spencer; the issue was settled by lot. At the next meeting, Spencer was elected as permanent chairman for the life of the Council. The work was time-consuming and onerous. A leader in the Northampton Mercury commented, 'As Chairman of the County Council, Lord Spencer is also chairman of the Finance Committee, and to the function of Prime Minister for the county he is called upon to add, therefore, that of Chancellor of the Exchequer. Entering upon a new and untried field, under circumstances totally unprecedented, the task devolving upon him was no light one.'* (Northampton Mercury, *6 April 1889,* p. 5).

*The next task of the Council was to choose aldermen. The Act gave councils the option of drawing aldermen either from existing councillors or from leading men in the county. Spencer hoped to avoid a purely political approach to the issue by offering to meet Stopford Sackville and present to the Council an agreed list of suitable candidates. This suggestion was rejected and both parties compiled their own lists. On 30 January 1889, 17 aldermen were elected by the Council, 11 Conservatives and 6 Liberals, none of them drawn from the ranks of councillors. Overall, it was calculated that of the 68 members, 34 would vote as Conservatives, 29 as Liberals, 3 as Liberal Unionists and 2 as Independents. In spite of the fine balance between the parties, the Council was soon commended by the* County Council Magazine *for its 'thoroughly business-like manner' and Spencer was congratulated 'on having his Council so well in hand'.* (County Council Magazine, i, 3, 1889, p. 186).

When the Liberals were returned to power at Westminster in August 1892, it was obvious that Spencer could not fulfil his ministerial duties and continue to act as chairman of the Council. He relinquished the latter post at the end of 1892, but continued to take an active part in Council affairs, retaining his councillorship until 1907.

---

### 572   LORD SPENCER TO C. R. SPENCER
*19 January 1888; Althorp, Northampton*

In the County the chief business has been with the Boundary Act of last Session which appointed Commissioners to see what could be done to bring together the boundaries of various jurisdictions such as County Quarter Sessions areas, Poor Law Unions etc.

Our Committee[1] made a sad muddle of what they presented to Sessions, and we went over all the work again last Monday.

Every County almost in England agree that we should not alter our County boundary, and we have taken that view and have suggested alterations of Unions instead.[2]

[1] Under the Local Government (England and Wales) Act, 1888, the Courts of Quarter Sessions appointed a committee to divide Northamptonshire into 49 electoral divisions, having regard to the requirements of each district as well as to actual population.

[2] At the meeting of the Committee of Justices at Northampton County Hall on 16 Jan., it was agreed that there should be an attempt to make County and Union boundaries conterminous. Spencer, in a speech to the Brixworth Guardians on 19 Jan. recommended that it would be better to retain the existing County boundaries and rearrange Union areas accordingly. *NM*, 21 Jan,. 1888, p. 5.

### 573   LORD SPENCER TO C. R. SPENCER
*23 September 1888; Althorp, Northampton*

I was in Northampton yesterday and hope the Electoral Divisions will do. They are made strictly according to Principle, and so any attempt to say they are 'Jerrymandered' won't hold.[1]

[1] The Report of the Committee on Electoral Divisions for the County was considered and approved at the Quarter Sessions meeting on 17 Oct. *NM*, 20 Oct. 1888, p. 6.

### 574   C. C. BECKE TO LORD SPENCER
*29 October 1888; Northampton*

We had a long discussion about the County Council on Saturday. It was felt that unless something was done to stir up the electors, they would treat the matter with entire apathy and that any candidate would get so, so we determined that a meeting should be called by our association in every district to consider what should be done it being understood that contests were to be avoided as far as possible and that when good men were put forward they were not to be opposed merely on political grounds, that is to say that the association would not assist in so opposing.

The Conservatives are strongly urging us to make the contest non political and at the same time are putting forward a party candidate in every district. This is so like them. It is clear that if we do not bestir ourselves a little, 9/10ths of the Council will be Conservatives which I do not think is to be desired on any ground. If on the contrary we take the matter up we shall win more than $\frac{1}{2}$ the seats. I shall hope to talk the matter fully over with you when you return to Althorp.[1]

[1] It was possibly at this meeting that Spencer's name was put forward for the Council. The *NM*, 3 Nov. 1888, p. 5, carried the news that 'it is understood that Lord Spencer is willing to become a candidate, but not as a party candidate'.

## 575 LORD SPENCER TO LORD WILLOUGHBY DE BROKE[1]
*9 December 1888; Althorp, Northampton[2]*

I agree with you that it is not a question of party Politics, and although I think it more than likely that in the future party Politics will come into the County Council Elections I certainly wish to avoid them at the first Election.

This being my view I feel it would be absurd for me to mix myself up in the Election without any knowledge to guide me as to the Candidates and what is wanted for a good representative body.

I certainly hope to see the working men of Quarter Sessions elected, and I dare say you are one of them in Warwickshire, in addition to being a large Proprietor and a constant resident, but I also hope good representative men, not necessarily Magistrates, will be elected so that all classes may be represented as far as possible.

[1] Henry, 18th Baron Willoughby de Broke, Kineton House, Warwickshire, wrote to Spencer on 8 Dec. informing him of his intention to stand for the Kineton district of Warwickshire, which included Wormleighton, SP.
[2] Copy, SP.

## 576 LORD SPENCER TO SIR E. LODER[1]
*9 December 1888; Althorp, Northampton[2]*

I have been asked as one of the Candidates for the County Council to join in a representation to you as to Polling Places...

I am of opinion Polling Places should be within easy reach of those who have the franchise, and that Electors should not be put under any disability owing to their residence being some distance from a Polling Place, or made to depend on conveyances being offered to take them to the Poll.

As far therefore as I can see I should be favourable to the view which I understand is to be put before you, viz: That there should be a Polling Place in every Village where the Electorate numbers 100 or over, and also that a Polling Place should be provided within two miles of every village however small. These principles seem generally just, though they might have to be modified in carrying them out.

¹ Sir Edmund Giles Loder, of Whittlebury, Northampton, High Sheriff, 1888.
² Copy, SP.

## 577 SIR E. LODER TO LORD SPENCER
*13 December 1888; Floore, Weedon, Northamptonshire*

The arrangement of polling places has had my earnest attention for some time past and I quite agree that it is extremely desirable that there should be no difficulties in the way of electors wishing to record their vote.

But at the same time the ratepayers have to be considered.

If I were to arrange the polling places as desired by the Petitioners I should be putting the County to £1000 additional expense.

I have arranged for 12 additional polling places in villages containing over 100 electors.

Every village of over 100 electors will now have either its own polling place or else a polling place within two miles. It is only in a few instances that electors will have to go over three miles.

## 578 LORD SPENCER TO C. R. SPENCER
*21 December 1888; Althorp, Northampton*

I had my County Council Meeting at Little Brington,¹ and J. Brambley² and your other swells were there. They were very civil and quiet and J. Brambley only asked one question about Polling Places. I was dull with figures, but J. B. seemed pleased.

¹ The meeting was held on 19 Dec. at Little Brington National School. It attracted an attendance of about 100 people. *NM*, 22 Dec. 1888, p. 6.
² John Brambley, Harleston, of a farming family.

## 579 LORD SPENCER TO LORD ROSEBERY
*14 January 1889; Althorp, Northampton*
RP, 10062 ff. 39–40

I must tell you how much I admired not only the Speeches which you have delivered as a candidate for the London Council, which are singularly excellent in matter and form of words, but your courage in holding going against making the question one of party.¹

As so injurious an effort has been made in London to decide the issue entirely on party lines, it was courageous of you to go against the popular tide.

In my humble way I have tried to do it here, and only succeeded in preventing every seat being contested on party lines by the Liberal Association and in mitigating the contests which could not be avoided. I have myself stood as you did, but I expect in every contest and there are a majority of seats contested, the fight turns on Politics. This seems inevitable, and men who have started as non political have dropped into the other line because their opponents have done so. In some cases seats will be lost by good men who pledged themselves not to be Political, but whose opponents have fought as strict partizans.

In one case a Liberal who refused to be Political will be defeated by another Liberal who has gone the whole hog.

[1] Rosebery stood as an independent candidate for one of the four City seats allotted to the London County Council. In a speech at the Memorial Hall, Farringdon St. on 10th Jan., he had urged the need to abstain from party politics in local elections. Elected on 18 Jan., Rosebery became the first Chairman of the Council. He replied to Spencer, 'I thought it very important to try and keep out the political element at first, in London at any rate. But in the vast majority of cases I know this to be impossible.' Rosebery to Spencer, 24 Jan. 1889, SP.

## 580   LORD SPENCER TO LORD MONSON[1]
*16 January 1889; Althorp, Northampton*
Monson Papers, MON 25/13/2/30

My impression is that few Councillors will like to create fresh Elections in order to become Aldermen. I feel myself that I shall prefer to remain as Councillor for 3 years rather than be possibly tied down for 6 years and where there has been a contest the chance of losing the seat with another candidate will have to be taken into account.

On the whole I should be disposed to select for Aldermen the best available men irrespective of the question of their having been defeated.

Oddly enough in this county though party has not been strongly brought in, 3 of the best J. P.s and most useful men for the Council have contests, and will I think be all defeated. If they are so defeated I should certainly like to see 2 or all three of them made Aldermen.

[1] William John, 7th Baron Monson, Viscount Oxenbridge, formerly Liberal M.P., Reigate, 1858–62, and one of the Deputy Speakers in the House of Lords, 1882.

## 581   LORD SPENCER TO S. G. STOPFORD SACKVILLE[1]
*20 January 1889; Althorp, Northampton[2]*

At Sessions the other day you referred to the election of Aldermen and what you said leads me to write this letter to you.

The election of Aldermen will be a complicated and difficult affair, and if 51 Elected Councillors are left to their own devices to draw up a list of 17 Aldermen, confusion will be great and the most suitable men for the position may be overlooked. In any case it is certain that consultation and arrangement will be made by groups, large or small, of those who are to vote.

However much we may all deprecate party Political action it is certain that those accustomed to act together in Politics will consult together to some extent.

It seems however very important that they should not do this in such a way as to make their election solely on party lines; and I write to you to ask you whether you would co-operate with those who have the same object in view to try and hit off a list or ticket to which all, or the great majority of Elected Councillors would agree. I was informed yesterday that a considerable number of Liberal County Electors desired to meet and discuss this subject, and I was asked to call a meeting of them. I declined to do this as I thought that as that explanation could not be made, in summoning a meeting my doing so would not seem consistent with my declarations as to the desirability of keeping out strict party Politics from the Elections. I agreed however, to attend the meeting which they settled to call on three conditions

(1) That it should not proceed to select candidates for Election of Aldermen solely on party lines.

(2) That I should be at liberty to announce to you or some other County Councillor who did not take part in this meeting of the conditions on which I agreed to take part in the meeting.

(3) That when this meeting or a Committee of the several meetings convened (for there were to be separate meetings in 3 or 4 Divisions of the County to collect information and names) had made their list, a Deputation should be appointed to meet you and any other Councillors acting with you and endeavour to come to an understanding as to a list to which all Councillors would agree, or at any rate the great bulk of them. I hope all may agree.

I presume that there may always be some men who will not be actually bound by an arrangement of this kind.

The meeting for Northampton is to be on Friday next, and I therefore at once write to you

(1) to tell you what is being done, and my part in the arrangement.

(2) to ask you whether you will be willing to co-operate in the proposal to meet early next week and try and settle a list.

I would propose to meet you and 3 others, bringing with me 3 others, appointed to represent the meeting to which I have referred.

I cannot but think that this arrangement will be of Public service and will enable us to reduce to a minimum if not to exclude altogether strict party Politics from this important business for constituting the Council: I hope therefore you may see your way to agree to may proposal. If we could meet to talk this over I should be very glad.

¹ Sackville George Stopford Sackville of Drayton House, Thrapston. A leading Conservative in the county, M.P., North Northamptonshire, 1867-80, who unsuccessfully contested the Bosworth division, Leicestershire, in 1885. Deputy Chairman, Northamptonshire Quarter Sessions. He had been returned unopposed as Councillor for Brigstock.
² Copy, SP.

### 582   S. G. STOPFORD SACKVILLE TO LORD SPENCER
*21 January 1889; Drayton House, Thrapston*

I am much obliged to you for your letter, and quite agree with you that some forethought and consultation are necessary before the Provisional Council meets to elect Aldermen, nor do I see any objection to the two parties holding separate Conclaves on this subject. I do not feel sure however that there would be any advantage in endeavouring afterwards to arrange a joint Meeting which might be productive of misunderstandings and unpleasantness.

I believe my object is the same as yours, viz. to get the best men possible elected as Aldermen, without much regard to party considerations, but I am bound to add that after thinking over as impartially as possible the names of all those who appear qualified for the position I find a very preponderating majority in the Conservative ranks. If therefore I were to enter into conference with those whom you represent I should be virtually pledging myself to accept as Aldermen some gentlemen who in my judgment would not be so eligible as others who have been conspicuous in their devotion to County business. I am deterred from attempting to do this 1st by seeing how often those who try to bring about compromises burn their own fingers, and 2ndly by the reflection that no action of ours can affect the elections of 1891, or prevent the party majority of that day (on whichever side it may be) using their power.

I expect we shall have a Meeting before the end of the week, and as you are to do the same I do not anticipate that the actual election of Aldermen will be very complicated or difficult. I will put it to the Meeting (if held as I anticipate), whether or not they would wish to appoint a few of their number to meet you as you propose, but without their consent. I should not feel authorized to do so, and the only pledge I can personally give at this moment is not to vote for any one as Alderman who has not shown some capacity for public business, and not to object to any one *solely* on party grounds.


### 583   LORD SPENCER TO C. R. SPENCER
*25 January 1889; Althorp, Northampton*

We had a preliminary meeting of your Division Liberal County Electors. A very difficult affair it was, as we had to keep out of pure party lines and yet to keep Liberalism in view.

We had to select 6 for consideration tomorrow by a Committee consisting of 2 representatives from each Division . . .

It is an open question whether we have a majority of one, or are in a minority of one.

We shall therefore have to vote one ticket if we are to expect to carry many voters. We shall I think select 9 or 10 Liberals and 8 Tories. We shall probably get more votes by the mixed ticket. If we had a pure Liberal ticket the doubtfuls would not like our list at all.

**584   S. G. STOPFORD SACKVILLE TO LORD SPENCER**
*27 January 1889; Northampton*

*Private*

We had a Meeting today, and I read your letter and the draft of my reply, but the Councillors were so eager to discuss the names of possible Aldermen that it was not until the close of a protracted Meeting that I was able to gather from them that they preferred that I should not talk over the names of those that approved themselves to the Conservatives with the representatives of the Liberal party. I confess I do not regret their decision, as I think it might have been difficult to know on what basis to try and arrange a compromise, and disgreeable, if either party had raised personal objections to suggested candidates. Now we have agreed upon a certain number of names which we shall support, and they are, I hope, open to no objection on the ground of unfitness for the important position.

**585   LORD SPENCER TO S. G. STOPFORD SACKVILLE**
*27 January 1889; Althorp, Northampton*[1]

*Private*

I must thank you for both your letters, and especially for the frank reception of my communication. From what you said in your first letter I rather expected the decision made by your friends yesterday against the endeavour to attain some concerted action. I regret it for though I admit that there are such as you describe I believe that such difficulties might have been got over. I have seen the leading men of the Liberals, and although their selection of some of the candidates for Aldermen may be made on different lines to those on which you may have gone, a spirit of moderation has prevailed and they readily agreed to the terms of my letter to you. I do not know how far the knowledge that you and your friends have rejected my proposal may modify their views, and desire to press their own people more decidedly than they agreed in order to meet you.

[1] Copy, SP.

**586   LORD SPENCER TO C. R. SPENCER**
*31 January 1889; Althorp, Northampton*

We had a disastrous day. We began by having to elect the provisional Chairman who will act for the two meetings before the Council is complete.[1]

Sackville was put up by Markham[2] and I forget who seconded. Northampton[3] proposed and Henley[4] seconded me. 25 voted for each of us (Sackville and I voting for each other). One man[5] a Tory Democrat from Kettering would not vote. It is believed he had promised both sides. So it had (as by Law prescribed) to be settled by lot, and the lot fell on Sackville.

Then came the election of Aldermen 17.

We went in for our mixed ticket. The Tories went in for a ticket of 12 including Grafton[6] and Wake[7] and left I suppose the others blank. They carried all theirs and we got 4 in or 3 I am not sure, Braye, Smeeton, S. Dunkley of Creaton and Woolston.[8] The Tories could not have voted for one of these. John Becke was defeated. Henley behaved I hear scandalously. He waited to hear how votes were going, and hearing that J. Becke had a good many votes he voted the Tory ticket having promised to vote ours.

The Tory Democrat voted against us I presume, and John Gee[9] occasionally for us.

The Tories behaved to my mind very badly. They stuck in some Tory farmers like H. H. Atterbury.[10]

The election of Chairman is to be on this day fortnight.

[1] The first meeting of the Provisional Council was held at County Hall, Northampton, on 31 Jan. 1889. For a full account of the proceedings, see NM, 2 Feb. 1889, p. 6.
[2] Henry Philip Markham, Clerk of the Peace, elected Clerk of the County Council.
[3] William Compton, 4th Marquess of Northampton, Liberal, Councillor for Yardley Hastings.
[4] Councillor for Braunston.
[5] Henry Frederick Henson, builder.
[6] Augustus Charles Lennox, 7th Duke of Grafton.
[7] Alderman, chairman of the Northampton Divisional Bench and a Liberal, 'with supposed Unionist proclivities', of Pitsford House. NM, 2 Feb. 1889, p. 2.
[8] Lord Braye, Stanford Park; John Smeeton, Theddingworth, farmer; Samuel Dunkley, Creaton, farmer; Charles Joseph Woolston, Wellingborough, corn merchant and maltster.
[9] John Gee, Crick, gentleman 'yeoman', described as a 'a very moderate Liberal'.
[10] Henry Herbert Atterbury, West Haddon.

## 587   C. C. BECKE TO LORD SPENCER
*10 February 1889; Northampton*

I did my best to learn what was being done about the chairmanship yesterday. There were a number of Conservatives present in the town and I fancy they held an informal meeting.

My father spoke to Drury Wake who told him nothing had been determined, that he hoped you would be appointed. He thought it was best not to see any of the Conservatives but to leave them alone as there was a feeling amongst a number of them which if allowed to work would end in your being selected. He said he should probably know by Thursday what was going to be done and would let us know. I then met Lord Exeter[1] who began to talk about it. He said he had a high opinion of Sackville and that he considered that the Lord Lieutenant should not be Chairman for which reason he had refused to be chairman himself of the Soke of Peterborough. He admitted you would be the best man except for this objection.

The Duke of Grafton is taking up the matter very warmly. He has prepared a memorandum setting forth the great importance it is for the county to secure your services and has given it to Chettle[2] to shew to the Conservatives and get as many as possible to support you. The Duke looks upon your election as certain.

Walker[3] has called a meeting for 11 on Thursday which the Duke has promised to attend. I trust you will do so also.

P.S. John Gee writes that Sir R. Knightley[4] told him he thought you ought to be chairman.[5]

[1] William Alleyne, 3rd Marquess of Exeter, alderman, Conservative.
[2] John Chettle, Councillor, Conservative member for Paulerspury, farmer, friend of the Duke of Grafton.
[3] William Walker, J.P. Councillor, Liberal member for Hardingstone, farmer.
[4] Sir Rainald Knightley, of Fawsley, alderman. Conservative M.P., South Northamptonshire, 1852-92.
[5] Spencer was elected chairman at the second meeting of the Provisional Council on 14 Feb. with Stopford Sackville as vice-chairman. *NM*, 16 Feb. 1889, p. 6.


**588   LORD SPENCER TO LADY SPENCER**
*10 October 1891; Althorp, Northampton*

I have been all day at Northampton, a heavy Education Committee, which sat, lunch excepted, from 11 to 3.45.

We are going to have an enormous number of Cookery Classes. They have begun in several divisions very well ... We shall be ready to have 160 lectures.[1]

[1] The Technical Instruction Act 1889 allowed local authorities to supply technical or manual instruction out of the rates. A Technical Education Scheme for women was established in Northamptonshire, with emphasis on cookery classes for labourers' wives. Lady Knightley to Lady Spencer, 3 Oct. 1891, SP.


**589   W. R. D. ADKINS[1] TO LORD SPENCER**
*20 March 1892; Springfield, Northampton*

We had an interesting meeting yesterday[2] ... I may tell your Lordship the feeling was ... that in the event of your Lordship's Parliamentary duties conflicting with your Chairmanship of our Committees, the whole machinery of County Government would be left under the guidance of Sackville, Monckton, Pell, Smyth and Pearson,[3] all Tories, all Quarter Sessions men, and all unpopular with our party.

[1] William Ryland Dent Adkins, barrister, of Springfield, Northampton. Author of *Our County* (1895).
[2] The first meeting of the new County Council, at which aldermen were elected, took place on 10 March. The first full meeting followed on 24 March.
[3] Edward Philip Monckton, J.P., Fineshade Abbey; Albert Pell, J.P., Haselbeach Hall, Conservative M.P., S. Leicestershire, 1868-85; Christopher Smyth, J.P., Little Houghton; George Hooke Pearson, J.P., Market Harborough. In the 1892 Council all except Sackville and Monckton were aldermen.


**590   LORD SPENCER TO C. R. SPENCER**
*25 June 1892; Villa Hammelmann, Homburg*

I doubt whether the County Council casting Vote made the difference of a contest, for they could hardly have avoided one, and I take it that a great many

Tories saw there was some reason in my vote, and admitted the true answer to their attacks which was that if they attached such importance to Knightley they ought to have secured him for they could have easily done so having a clear majority of votes.[1]

I hold that I was right, but notwithstanding that it was as disagreeable a thing as I ever had to do, as Knightley was such a very old friend. But in County Council Elections friendship ought not to curry everything, and if I had given my vote to a former member of the Council, I should certainly have had, on account of service due, to have given it to Dr. Roughton of Kettering who did a great deal of Council work, whereas Knightley did next to nothing.

What would the Tories have said if I had voted for Roughton?

[1] At the first meeting of the new County Council on 10 March, when Spencer was re-elected as chairman, elections took place for nine aldermanic vacancies. Eight were elected, but three candidates for the ninth place all received 24 votes each—Sir Rainald Knightley and T. Wallis, J. P., Kettering, Conservatives and Dr. J. J. Roughton, J. P. Liberal. Spencer was given the task of using his casting vote, choosing the Liberal candidate. *NH*, 11 March 1892, p. 7. He was subsequently attacked by his opponents, being accused of unfairness. See, for example, article entitled 'Fairplay', *NH*, 18 March 1892, p. 9.

## 591 DUKE OF GRAFTON TO LORD SPENCER
*22 September 1892; Euston Hall, Thetford*

I thought it well to sound some of the Council in case you really resigned and I now write urging you to think well over it again and try if you could not continue as our Chairman. There is but one beginning to all the answers on sounding out members of the Council 'Must Lord Spencer resign? Could not he be persuaded to continue as no one will be acceptable to all as he is?'

## 592 LORD SPENCER TO LORD GRAFTON
*25 September 1892; Balmoral Castle*[1]

I have very carefully considered what you say. I feel that the wish which you and others express that I should continue Chairman of the County Council is very flattering to me and it gratified me much: and I should be glad to accede to your wishes but at the same time I feel that I ought to give up the Chair. The Admiralty work is heavy and continuous and any additional work even if it only comes occasionally would be a strain on my strength and would often take up a day's holiday which is of great help when one is in severe official work.[2]

[1] Copy, SP.

[2] Although Spencer tendered his resignation as chairman at the Council meeting on 13 Oct., he agreed, after representations, to delay it until the end of the year. Grafton was responsible for presenting Spencer with an address from the Council on 12 Jan. 1893. *NM*, 13 Jan. 1893, p. 5. For Spencer's reply, see Spencer to Grafton, 3 Feb. 1893, Northamptonshire County Council MS. Minute Book, 1892–5.

**593   LORD SPENCER TO LADY SPENCER**

*16 July 1897; Althorp, Northampton*

I had a very long day yesterday. We sat until past 3 in the County Council. We were on the whole very successful. The Redistribution of Seats was carried, the Lights for Vehicles was carried, but was marred by the old Duke, who I fancy hears nothing, and moved a most idiotic amendment which the opponents of the Lights jumped at, making the necessity of having Lights apply only in winter, as if there were not very often dark nights in Spring and Summer.[1]

The big thing as to the Medical Officer of Health for the County was carried as well.[2]

I had to be very stern as to amendments, for even Ryland Adkins wanted to concede to carry it, and I refused, and we won all down the line. It was unexpected; R. Adkins had worked very hard for it, and deserves much credit, but he seemed to founder a bit at the last.

[1] A Special Committee of the Council recommended that vehicles should carry lights from the end of the first hour after sunset until the beginning of the last hour before sunrise. The Duke of Grafton's amendment was opposed by Spencer. *NM*, 16 July 1897, p. 7.

[2] Spencer had previously made inquiries in other counties where Medical Officers of Health had been appointed. Spencer to Lord Harrowby, 10 Feb. 1897, Harrowby Papers, liv, f. 271. The first Medical Officer for Health, Charles Paget, was elected on 14 Oct. from 48 applicants. *NM*, 15 Oct. 1897, p. 7.


**594   E. KENNARD[1] TO LORD SPENCER**

*3 November 1900; The Barn, Market Harborough*

Autocarists as a body owe you and Lord Northampton a great deal of gratitude for opposing the Northampton County Council when seeking to restrict the maximum speed of motors to ten miles an hour.

On open roads we can do no possible harm to anybody, but where control should undoubtedly be most properly maintained is in populous places and while our cars are passing restive horses any infringement of this very salutary precaution should certainly be rigorously punished, but for a harmless motor to be stopped, and the owner fined, when she can be of no conceivable danger to any body is quite unreasonable.

In France and Germany as you are aware there is a big trade in horseless vehicles, which some silly nervous magistrates are now vainly trying to stamp out in England. For example last week the clever Lutterworth Bench imposed an absurd fine upon me when I could not possibly have been exceeding the legal limit as nobody out of Bedlam would think of bumping over a level crossing faster than seven or eight miles an hour . . .[2]

Hoping we shall soon meet in the happy hunting fields where our pace is not regulated by timid J.P.s.

[1] Edward Kennard, J.P., Monmouthshire and Northamptonshire. A keen motorist with six years' experience. Owner of the first Napier ever built. 'Considers motoring combines the pleasures of

steeple-chasing and a fast run to hounds; and that it is bound to be the locomotion for all in the near future.' *The Motoring Annual and Motorist's Year Book for 1904* (1904), p. 58.

² The police alleged that Kennard went over the level crossing at North Kilworth on Oct. 13 at between 18 and 20 m.p.h. thus exceeding the speed limit stipulated in the County Council's by-laws. He was fined £2 and 12s. costs. *Midland Times and Rugby Gazette*, 27 Oct. 1900, p. 8.

# 5

# SALE OF THE ALTHORP LIBRARY, 1892

*From the beginning of 1889, Spencer contemplated selling part of the famous Althorp Library, those books kept in the Old Book Room. This room, measuring 26 ft. by 20 ft., housed some 4,000 books including the most valuable of the whole collection. Among them were many fifteenth- and sixteenth-century volumes, the Gutenberg Bible, two copies of the Mainz Psalter, 57 Caxtons and 600 Aldines. After some hesitation Spencer offered the Caxtons to a syndicate, consisting of the British Museum and the Universities of Oxford and Cambridge, but this venture was not successful.*

*Lord Charles Bruce, Spencer's librarian, consulted Gladstone, who recommended that Quaritch, the London bookseller, should be approached. As Spencer was not on good terms with Quaritch, he consulted instead E.G. Hodge of Sotheby, Wilkinson and Hodge, the auctioneers, who took the matter in hand. Hodge arranged with Humphry Ward of The Times to write an article, which appeared in the paper on 17 June 1892, announcing the sale of the Library and describing its contents of more than 40,000 books.*

*The article immediately attracted the attention of Mrs. Enriqueta Rylands, widow of John Rylands, the Manchester millionaire. She wished to found in the city a library for theological students and instructed Dr. D. Green, secretary of the Religious Tract Society, to purchase appropriate volumes. His son, J. A. Green, who was delegated to carry out this task, was acquainted with A. B. R. Railton, manager of Sotheran's in the Strand. Railton sent The Times cutting to Mrs. Rylands, who encouraged him to call on Hodge and make an offer. Railton's valuation of the Library was £193,127 though Spencer hoped for a higher price. A sum of £210,000 was in the event agreed, to be paid in two instalments.*

*After payment of the second instalment on 8 August, Mrs. Rylands, Railton and Green travelled to Northampton, staying at the George Hotel. Railton, later describing the event, noted that 'next morning I went alone to Althorp, arranged a number of the gems for Mrs. Rylands and her friends to inspect, which inspection took place in the course of the forenoon; as the party drove away Mrs. Rylands took my hand, remarking she was well pleased with all she had seen and immediately the packing began.' (Memorandum, n.d., Papers relating to the Spencer and Crawford Purchase, 1892– 1901, John Rylands University of Manchester Library MS.) The secrecy surrounding the purchase was so well maintained that it was not until 6 August that Spencer was aware that the buyer was a woman.*

*One final stumbling block remained before the transaction was completed. There was an understanding that Spencer could withdraw any books he wished to retain, to be paid for at a reasonable valuation. Lady Spencer particularly wanted the Mordaunt Manuscript, a history of the Poyntz family, but she objected to its price, £300. At this point it was learnt that Spencer had presented a copy of a painting of the founder of the Althorp*

*Library to the new John Rylands Library; in return, Lady Spencer was allowed to retain the Mordaunt Manuscript.*

*On 6 October 1899, the day after the opening of the Library in Manchester, Spencer, as Chancellor of Victoria University, bestowed an honorary degree on the Library's benefactress.*

---

**595** LORD C. BRUCE[1] TO LORD SPENCER
*31 January 1889; Travellers' Club, Pall Mall, S.W.*

Altho' you had in some degree prepared me for the announcement contained in your letter, it has nevertheless come upon me as a blow. To think of such an unrivalled private collection being broken up and scattered throughout the world, no one can tell where, fills me, as it will many a man who has far greater pretensions to literary knowledge than I have, with dismay. They will regard such an event as I do in the light of a national disaster.

I have but a lingering hope that you have not fully made up your mind on the subject, and have you entertained the idea, which I suggested, of first disposing of the China? I went to see Sir G. Dasent[2] at the Athenaeum today, as you suggested, and I put that point before him. He told me that lately he had seen a Dealer in China in the Strand who informed him that good Sèvres at this moment sells like diamonds. Is not this worth while enquiring into, before you make your final decision?

In my conversation with Sir George, he suggested that, if the Old Book Room is to be sold, Sotheby would be by far the best man to employ; that a year's interval would be required between the commencement of cataloguing the books and the day of sale which should take place in March; that Sotheby should be consulted as to the desirability of selling all the books in the Old Book Room, or only a part at first. This would depend much on the state of the book market. In all these suggestions I quite concur.

Sir G. thinks that the whole of the books would fetch £150,000. Without a doubt they are fully worth that, but considering the number of book sales which have taken place during these last years, I should put the figure at £100,000.

I told him of my small work on the Library, which is now nearly ready to put into the printers' hands, and he strongly advised me to push it forward as quickly as possible, which I will do. It will probably bear the title of 'The Treasure of the Althorp Library' which will be arranged and described so as to give an account of the Origin and Progress of the Art of Printing[3] ... I will only add that if the Old Book Room *must* go, I will do all I can for you in the matter.

[1] Lord Charles William Brudenell-Bruce, Liberal M.P., N. Wiltshire, 1865-74 and Marlborough, 1878-85.

[2] Sir George Webbe Dasent, Scandinavian scholar, author and Civil Service Commissioner. One of the original Commissioners of Historical Manuscripts, 1870.

[3] Not traced. Bruce had earlier published a full description of the books in two articles entitled 'The Althorp Library' in *Book Lore*, Jan. 1885, pp. 33-8 and Feb. 1885, pp. 65-71.

## 596   LORD SPENCER TO LORD C. BRUCE
*16 September 1889; Althorp, Northampton*[1]

I had a long talk with Mr Hodge[2] and settled not to think of a Public Sale until at least the spring of 1891.

I have thought over the question a good deal, and the only new point which suggested itself to me was the possibility of selling the Old Book Room to one purchaser so as to keep the collection together. My own feeling would be very strongly towards this, and I should be willing to sacrifice some possible profit if it could be achieved. The Government are out of the question. They might desire to buy some books but as they have most of the best books they would not entertain any idea of buying the Old Book Room en bloc.

There may be some millionaire desirous of having some out of the way treasure who might however purchase.

Hodge was to think it over. He did not expect that we should find such a purchaser in England nor yet in America where it might be more likely. He was to think over the question as to whether the attempt as unostentatiously as possible would injure a Public Sale.[3]

[1] Copy, SP.
[2] Edward Grose Hodge, employed by Sotheby's since 1847. Became partner in 1863 when the firm adopted the style Sotheby, Wilkinson and Hodge. F. Herrmann, *Sotheby's, Portrait of an Auction House* (1980), p. 49.
[3] Hodge offered to 'commence the endeavour to sell by private contract'. Hodge to Spencer, 1 Oct. 1889, SP. However, Spencer was dismayed at the large percentage be charged and told Hodge to suspend any action. Spencer to Hodge, 10 Nov. 1889, SP (copy).


## 597   LORD SPENCER TO E. THOMPSON[1]
*7 January 1890; Althorp, Northampton*[2]

No arrangements have been made for a Sale of the Library here. It would be a matter of much concern to me to be obliged to deprive this House of the books which have such a great reputation, and are a monument of the book learning and collecting industry of my Grandfather. But I cannot deny that the heavy depression in agriculture which has for many years prevailed makes it extremely difficult for me to keep locked up the large amount of capital which the books here represent.

In one way I should be glad to see the books more available for the Public, for I often lament how few people visit the Library to see the early editions and other curiosities.

I should if I sold the Library like to see the choice part of the books go either as a whole or in Divisions to large centres of Industries in the Kingdom or our Colonies, but at present I have not put this idea forward.

[1] Edward Maunde Thompson, palaeographer, Principal Librarian, British Museum. For a full account of his activities and character see E. Miller, *That Noble Cabinet. A History of the British Museum* (1973), pp. 258–62.
[2] Copy, SP.

**598   E. THOMPSON TO LORD SPENCER**
*23 September 1891; Fair Meadow, Mayfield, Sussex*

Your letter of the 21st. inst. has reached me. I will at once prepare the ground. The Trustees meet on the 10th October, when I will bring your letter before them...

I hope we may succeed in keeping the best of the Althorp Library in the country, and Your Lordship may be sure that I shall do all I can, although I too, in spite of being a national collector, am truly sorry that a great historic library should be dispersed.

**599   LORD C. BRUCE TO LORD SPENCER**
*26 October 1891; Mayfield, Sussex*

I enclose a letter from Thompson whom I saw yesterday. Nothing could be more satisfactory he says than the way in which the two Universities have responded to the proposal of the Syndicate.[1] A list of the Caxtons has been sent to each of the Librarians, in order that they may note what they would each like, Thompson having first marked thereon what the Museum would wish to acquire. With such a good start I should feel disposed to throw in other books. Evidently the Museum would like to have more than is in the Caxton list, and, as Thompson rightly says, the chances of your disposing of other books to the nation would be far greater if the Museum were to go to the Treasury for the larger sum at once which would enable them to make further purchases from Althorp than the Caxtons, than if they were to ask for help twice.

If too the Museum were to come forward with a large amount the Universities would be likely to respond in a generous spirit. If each of the 3 components of the Syndicate put down £10,000 the result would be very satisfactory. Of course I don't know whether if you obtain a good price for the Caxtons you would still feel obliged to part with other portions of the Library. I hope not. If you were to do so, you might in the first instance only deal with the English Early Press of which have so many remarkable specimens besides the Caxtons viz. Wynkyn de Wordes, Pynsons, Oxford and Cambridge Books—but at all events Mr. Garnett the Keeper of the Printed Books will send me a list of the Althorp books other than the Caxtons which the Museum would like to have, and then you might settle what should be done.

As regards the prices I have been able to arrive at some kind of conclusion having data before me of the prices given at various times during this century for 43 out of your 57 Caxtons. These of course have much varied e.g. your Grandfather gave for 14 of them an average per volume of only £146, and the following are the average per volume given at some of the greatest Caxton Sales which have taken place during the last few years

| | |
|---|---|
| Osterley (Lord Jersey) | £877 |
| Lord Crawford | £196 |
| Buccleuch and Hopetoun | £417[2] |

The first and last of these are very exceptional.

Taking all the prices I have of the 43 vols., I find that the highest average per vol. was £364 and the lowest £176.

All this required very careful looking into, and Mr. Thompson thinks the best way of arriving at a valuation will be by consulting the various Caxton sale catalogues. This I shall be able to do thoroughly at the Museum when in town next month. In the meantime it would be helpful to me if I might have the volume of the Spencer Dibdin MS.[3] correspondence which is in the Old Book Room, and also, if you have it, a copy of the Roxburghe Sale[4] if it contains the prices given.

As regards Oxford and Cambridge a fair price could be arrived at by ascertaining what the Museum gave for such Caxtons as they may desire to have and which are in the B.M.

P.S. Quaritch[5] in 1884 was asking for 4 Caxtons which you have at an average of £626 a volume.

[1] Of the 57 Caxtons at Althorp, the British Museum already possessed copies of all but 13 of them. At a meeting between Bruce and Thompson earlier in the month, the latter suggested that Oxford and Cambridge should be contacted with a view to forming a syndicate with the British Museum to purchase the Caxtons. Bruce to Spencer, 6 Oct. 1891, SP.

[2] The Osterley Park Library, owned by 7th Earl of Jersey, was sold in May 1885 by Messrs. Sotheby, Wilkinson and Hodge for £13,000; the Haig Hall Library belonging to 25th Earl of Crawford raised £26,000 in two sales held in June 1887 and June 1889; and the Hopetoun House Library of 7th Earl of Hopetoun was sold in Feb. 1889 for £6,117.

[3] Rev. Thomas Frognall Dibdin, who popularized the taste for rare books and author of *Bibliotheca Spenceriana* (1814-15) 4 vols. *Aedes Althorpianae* (1822) 2 vols. and a catalogue of 15th cent. books from the Library of the Duke of Cassano Serra in Spencer's collection (1823).

[4] Dibdin kept detailed notes of the daily sessions of the famous Roxburghe Sale in May 1812, when the 2nd Earl Spencer, against stiff opposition, successfully bid for five Caxtons. See Dibdin's *Reminiscences* (1836), pp. 345-71.

[5] A leading London bookseller. See 'Bernard Quaritch and his Clients', in S. De Ricci, *English Collections of Books and Manuscripts* (1930), pp. 158-67.

**600** LORD SPENCER TO E. THOMPSON

*24 February 1892; Althorp, Northampton*[1]

Some time has elapsed since I had the honour of offering to the Trustees of the British Museum for the Nation the Caxtons belonging to the Library at Althorp.

I stated that I would leave the price of these books to 3 gentlemen, Lord Charles Bruce, Sir Geo. Dasent and Mr. Tedder[2] [who] kindly consented to put a value on them. I have now received their decision. They value the Caxtons, 57 in number, at £15,510 and I now offer them to the Trustees at that price.

I understand that possibly the Universities of Cambridge and Oxford might combine with the Trustees in the purchase. I shall have no objection to that arrangement as any books which they might take remain in the Country in the possession of one of the great Universities of England.

[1] Copy, SP.

[2] Henry Richard Tedder, Librarian of the Athenaeum from 1875 and Secretary from 1889, combining both posts until his retirement in 1924. F.R. Cowell, *The Athenaeum* (1975), p. 69.

## 601 LORD SPENCER TO E. THOMPSON
*28 February 1892; Althorp, Northampton*[1]

I wish to add what I forgot to say in my last letter that it is right to inform the Trustees that I have quite settled to sell the best part of this Library and if the Trustees of the British Museum do not accept my offer the Caxtons will be sold with the rest of the books.

As it is nearly certain that no individual will be found to buy the books as a whole they will in all probability be sold by public auction.

[1] Copy, SP.

## 602 LORD C. BRUCE TO LORD SPENCER
*6 April 1892; 77 Pall Mall, S.W.*

I have seen Thompson at the British Museum today, and the present position of the Syndicate is this. Oxford and Cambridge can only each put down £2000 and the Trustees would ask the Treasury for £4000.[1] It is possible that more may be coming from Cambridge.

Thompson asked me whether you would be willing to enlarge the Syndicate by adding thereto certain book collectors, such for instance as Christie Miller,[2] who are in no way connected with the trade.

I told him that I would let you know this at once.

It is evident that the Syndicate as constituted will be unable to come to terms.

[1] Bruce later corrected this statement as the Trustees had not, in fact, approached the Treasury. Bruce to Spencer, 11 April 1892, SP.
[2] Wakefield Christie-Miller, book collector, who inherited the Britwell Court, Bucks., collection in 1889 from Samuel Christy, who was better known as S. Christie-Miller, M.P., Newcastle under Lyme, 1847 and 1852-9.

## 603 LORD SPENCER TO E. G. HODGE
*19 May 1892; Spencer House, St. James's Place, S.W.*[1]

I have, for several reasons, been obliged to suspend all operations connected with the sale of Althorp Library but I am at last quite free to deal with the matter.

Since my interview with you I have abstained from communication with any other firms who might undertake the sale. I have carefully considered all you said. I cannot admit the force of all your arguments. I concede that the sale of a Library as well known as that of Althorp can hardly be compared with other library sales.

I should prefer that you should manage the sale and if you undertake it with a 9 per cent charge I will at once put the business into your hands and make no other inquiry from others who might perhaps undertake the sale for a lower charge.

[1] Copy, SP.

### 604   E. G. HODGE TO LORD SPENCER
*21 May 1892; 13 Wellington Street, Strand, London, W.C.*

I deeply regret your Lordship thinks 9 per cent a sufficient commission, but I will not trouble you with a long letter. I accept the terms and undertake the sale of the Althorp Library at a Commission of 9 per cent.

### 605   E. G. HODGE TO LORD SPENCER
*24 June 1892; 13 Wellington Street, Strand, London, W.C.*

We have duly received your Lordship's letter of the 21st inst.

Mitchell[1] of New York whom we know well has not telegraphed to us. He is by no means likely to find a purchaser for the library.[2]

We have a Gentleman who has means and who appears to be really inclined to purchase *en bloc* if, as he says, we will sell the library at its fair market value. The difficulty is to arrive at this value. We are of course asked to say what price will be accepted, and if we can have in perfect confidence your Lordship's idea of the lowest sum that should be accepted, our cause will be much simplified. We of course should not communicate this, our duty being to get the largest sum possible.

Finding your Lordship had gone on the Continent we wrote on Thursday to Lord Charles Bruce on this subject, but have had no reply. He has probably written to your Lordship. To sell the library *en bloc* would be such an enormous advantage to your Lordship in point of time (always assuming we get a fair value) that 'tis important to strike whilst the iron is hot. The person in question has proposed to go to Althorp early next week to inspect the library. If he continue serious [sic] doubtless we shall have to make a valuation. We would wish him to make an offer, then if we know of your Lordship's feeling as to the price we should be in a good position to negotiate.

[1] John J. Mitchell and Co., booksellers, established 1879.
[2] Spencer's intention to sell the Althorp Library was announced in *The Times*, 17 June 1892, p. 9.

### 606   LORD C. BRUCE TO LORD SPENCER
*3 July 1892; 77 Pall Mall, S.W.*

I have been so busy this last week that I have not had time to write to you as to the negotiations *in re* Althorp Library, of which you have heard from Hodge. I saw him yesterday, and he showed me your two letters. He is of opinion that should an offer of £150,000 be made, it would be unwise to refuse it. He is so afraid, that at the rate at which old books are selling, the Library would not realise its proper value at a public Auction. The best chance of its doing so would be by the sale covering 3 years.

The party who is now making enquiries about the Library lives in England, and evidently means business. He has been I believe at Althorp, and he has sent down two experts to report to him what they would consider a fair price, and of course he cannot have this valuation without paying for it, probably largely.

He quite understands that you intend reserving part of the Collection. He has been advised by his Solicitor not to make an offer, but first to hear what you would accept. I think that £250,000 is somewhat too high and that £200,000 would be nearer the figure. Hodge very rightly pointed out to this intending purchaser that a high price would be asked on account of the prestige which is attached to such a library.

Altho' I hope to see you soon I thought you would like to have this information without delay.

**607** LORD SPENCER TO C. R. SPENCER
*26 July 1892; Spencer House, St. James's Place, S.W.*

*Confidential*

I am rather depressed and I daresay you will be when I tell you that the negotiation for the sale of the Library has been all but concluded.[1]

I feel it much, now that it has come, but I do not alter my view that it was my duty to do it. I could not have gone on as I have been for the last 12 or 13 years.

I do not know who the purchaser is, but I am glad to say that he is an Englishman, and that he intends to place the Library in a building where it will be available for public use. He won't allow the price to be known.

I am sorry in one way at the turn negotiations have taken. I began by hoping that he would buy the Old Book Room and a few choice books scattered about in other rooms, but in the negotiation he has made an immense point of getting practically the whole Library. I reserved the right to keep back some books, but I fear that more must go further than I like at all. But that point remains still open for negotiation.

I intend to have a thoroughly good readable and reference Library, and probably may get a better collection of Books for that purpose than we have at present. Still we shall lose the character of the rooms, and I do not like it: but I could not when it came to the point refuse the offer, which only would have been made on conditions of almost entire sale, and there is this to be said that the whole will probably be kept together, and be available for the public in a better way than if at Althorp.

It will make a vast difference to my financial position, and relieve me of what at times was intolerable, the feeling that I had no right to go on even in the very reduced way which we have adopted for some years past: and I saw no way out of the difficulty.

[1] The contract was effected on 25 July. Hodge to Spencer, 25 July 1892, SP.

**608   LORD SPENCER TO LADY SPENCER**
*29 July 1892; Althorp, Northampton*

I was very sad over the books I confess. I have gone through all the manuscripts etc. in the Old Book Room and took them out, together with your
Portland Book and a good many others but there will be opportunity to deal
with the books only in the Old Book Room. I must have the rooms photo-
graphed.

It is a great thing that they should be kept together and for the Public, and
this would not have been done unless the lot had gone together. I should have
got a great deal less and they would have been scattered to the four quarters of
the world. We can get any number of the books we want. But I feel it is a
great pity.

**609   C. R. SPENCER TO LORD SPENCER**
*5 August 1892; Dallington House, Northampton*

I waited till 4.15 before seeing the photographer,[1] and as I had heard nothing
from you then, I gave the order for the Old Book Room to be done, and
showed him what was wanted. ... Mr. Humphry Ward had been sent down
by *The Times* for another article,[2] so I showed him round. He was immensely
struck by the Murillo.[3]

When I was leaving Sotheran's[4] son, a lady and a gent. appeared. The son
knew who the purchaser is, so we talked on about the books all being together,
and I said after some time, 'I hope *she* won't alter their positions.' He stammered
a little, and then said nothing would be altered, and seemed rather surprised at
my saying *she*. So it struck me that very likely it is Mrs. Rylands after all. The
man said we should not know for a long time but that a place was to be built
especially for the books, and was to be called the Bibliotheca Spenceriana.

A covered truck is ordered at the station for Tuesday for the books, but
nothing is known of its destination.

[1] Charles Katterns, Mercers' Row, Northampton.
[2] Thomas Humphry Ward, journalist, leader writer for *The Times* in art and literature. He was
the author of two unsigned articles on the sale of the Library which appeared in *The Times* on 17
June and 8 Aug. 1892.
[3] A self-portrait.
[4] Henry Sotheran and Co., booksellers, 136 Strand, London, Mrs. Rylands' agents. The firm had
written to *The Times* on 29 July informing the public that the library had been purchased 'on
behalf of the at present unknown "English gentleman" '.

**610   LORD SPENCER TO C. R. SPENCER**
*6 August 1892; Spencer House, St. James's Place, S.W.*

Thanks about the Photographs.

As to the Purchaser I never heard until last night at dinner of the rumour
about Mrs. Rylands when a Tout sent in a slip to ask me about it.

I should not have liked to have tried to find out indirectly the Purchaser by speaking of 'She', as I felt bound to respect the incognito, and should have been afraid that any attempt to find out would make them think I doubted the genuineness of the proceedings, and the goodness of the cheque which is to come so soon: but of course you could do what you liked, and I daresay your conversation will not be traced to me in any way.

I am still and so is Sotheby in complete ignorance about the Purchaser.

Newspaper 'touts' bother in every direction about the matter, but they get nothing from me, as I plead absolute ignorance and inability to mention or hint at the price.

### 611  LORD SPENCER TO C. R. SPENCER
*6 August 1892: Spencer House, St. James's Place, S.W*

Since I wrote to you I have seen the notice in *The Times* about Mrs. Rylands[1] and I went straight up to Sotheby's.

They did not insert the paragraph and knew nothing of it, but went across to Sotheran and complained of the announcement. Sotheran said that they had had nothing whatever to say etc. as to his action and were not authorized to disclose the name of the Purchaser. From what they said however Sotheby & Co. feel sure that Mrs. Rylands is the Purchaser, and she has been buying through a Mr. Green[2] son of a partner in Longmans.

It is typical of the age that I should be told of the Purchaser of the books through *The Times*. I told Sothebys to say that I was considerably annoyed at the announcement, which must have come out owing to indiscretion of some of their people: and that I certainly expected that I should be told the name of the Purchaser before the public.

I dare say it does not really matter. I wonder where you heard of it, for until 9.20 last night I never heard a rumour of Rylands.

[1] Briefly announcing that Mrs. Rylands was the purchaser and that she intended to present the Library to Manchester. *The Times*, 6 Aug, 1892, p. 9.

[2] John Arnold Green, son of Rev. D. Green, secretary of the Religious Tract Society.

### 612  E. G. HODGE TO LORD SPENCER
*10 August 1892; 13 Wellington Street, Strand, London, W.C.*

I spent yesterday at Althorp. On arriving there I found the Purchaser Mrs. Rylands her Agent Mr. Green and Messrs. Sotheran's Manager and men who are to pack the books.[1]

I received there your Lordship's letter and have fully instructed our cataloguer Mr. Daniel whom I have left to remain during the packing and removal of the books.

I think everything will go on rightly and smoothly now that I have shown them that your Lordship will not except from the sale any books but those especially connected with the family.

The money (instalments) has been paid to our Bankers to whom I have given notice that on Thursday we shall draw a cheque for £130,000 which will on that day be paid to your Lordship's 'Purchase and Sale' account at Messrs. Hoare's, Fleet Street.[2]

[1] The first instalment of £130,000 was paid on 12 Aug and the second, £60,772 8s. on 3 Sept. The commission amounted to £18,867 12s. SP.
[2] The *Northampton Mercury* reported that 'the authorities are flooded with applications for permission to pay a last visit to the library while photographers are here in force'. 12 Aug. 1892. p. 5. The first instalment of the Library, the volumes from the Old Book Room, arrived in Manchester on 16 Aug.


### 613   LORD SPENCER TO LADY SPENCER
*27 August 1892; Admiralty, Whitehall*

I have settled about most of the books. Two only remain. The Lady Lucan Shakespeare is valued at £200. The most difficult case is that of the Mordaunt Genealogy valued at £300. I shall look at it today and settle on Monday.[1]

[1] One part of the agreement of the sale was that Spencer could withdraw any books which he wished to retain at a 'reasonable valuation'.


### 614   E. G. HODGE TO LORD SPENCER
*30 August 1892; 13 Wellington Street, Strand, London, W.C.*

On reading your Lordship's letter this morning I felt very desirous that the Mordaunt Genealogy should continue in Your Lordship's possession, and Mrs. Rylands' agents calling on me just now on the subject of the retained books, I spoke of it and said I considered it harsh to have to pay £300 for a Family Manscript and offered to pay £100 for it, but the value being fixed at £300 by the Arbitrator, they could do nothing.

I then mentioned (and I trust your Lordship will not think me wrong) that I had heard your Lordship say you felt disposed to give Mrs. Rylands a copy of the portrait of the Earl[1] who formed the library if she would like to hang it in the library when in its new home. They were struck with the courtesy of this and immediately expressed hope that Mrs. Rylands may thankfully accept the portrait and beg your Lordship to retain the Mordaunt MS. They will write to her on these subjects.

[1] i.e. 2nd Earl Spencer.


### 615   LADY SPENCER'S DIARY
*[June] 1893*

When the Books were sold there were 7 rooms with empty shelves, mostly from floor to ceiling, common deal shelves, with only the edges painted white. It was absolutely necessary to do something with these rooms. We settled that only the Long Library, which was the original Library of the House, should be re-planted with Books and remain the Library. The Raphael Room I turned into a China room. The Old Breakfast Room, which we had for some time used as a sitting room, I did up in green damask pattern and hung it with pictures taken from the picture gallery or bedrooms. The Domenichino Room or Marlboro' Library as it used to be called we threw into the Old Book Room and made it the Billiard Room.

The Ante-room and Billiard Room built by Frederick Lord Spencer were pulled down. They were a great eyesore outside the House and not particularly good rooms. The Billiard Room was a very large room with a gallery running round it. It was lit by 2 large windows at the north end and west side and contained below splendid Folios magnificently bound. Above the Gallery were chiefly modern books except at the end where there was a large collection of tracts in white vellum which belonged to the House. This Billiard Room took the place of the Gothic Library which had to be pulled down. It faced east, the new room due north. The Rooms now became the Billiard Room, running north with 2 windows to the east, opening into the Green Drawing Room with north windows, China Room, (Raphael Room) and Long Library. The books I collected. I bought them chiefly in Norfolk at sales and old shops in Norwich, and a great many from Catalogues in various towns – London, Dublin, Cambridge, Brighton, Birmingham, Portsmouth, Southampton – in short – wherever I went, I made for a 2nd hand Book shop. I had nearly finished filling the Library in 4 months after the Books were taken away,[1] with the help of *Edinburgh* and *Quarterly Reviews* which were in the Picture Gallery, and which were well bound in light calf with tooled backs. These books were not wanted and were left when the other Books were sold.[2] There were also some old novels and a large number of Sermons.

When the Old Breakfast Room was being done up and the shelves removed, Smith of Northampton told me the inner wall was composed of large stones, which proved again that it must have been an outer wall of the Court Yard which was said to have been covered in by Dorothy (Sacharissa), wife to Henry Lord Spencer, created Earl of Sunderland,[3] and the Stair-case was made then.

[1] The last books were removed from Althorp on 1 Nov.

[2] In Oct. Spencer told his wife, 'The Book people have discovered that it will cost more to pack and carry a good many more books than they are worth, so they propose to leave books like Annual Registers, R. Agric. Soc. Reports and similar books, also all Novels. They hardly know yet how many volumes but probably 2,000. I am very glad of this.' Spencer to Lady Spencer, 3 Oct. 1892, SP.

[3] See No. **128** n. 5.

## 616   LORD SPENCER TO MRS. E. RYLANDS
*19 July 1893; Admiralty, Whitehall*[1]

I hope you will accept a picture of my Grandfather which I have had painted for you. It is copied from one of the best portraits which I have of Lord Spencer by Clint[2] and which hangs in the largest Library at Althorp.

As I was obliged to part with the Books it was a matter of great satisfaction to know that my Grandfather's Library although no longer at Althorp, would be kept together and placed by your Liberality in a great centre of Population like Manchester for the benefit and teaching of large numbers of people.

If you are good enough to accept my proposal, the picture will be placed in the midst of the Books which my Grandfather collected and to which he was so devoted.[3]

[1] Copy, SP.

[2] George Clint, R.A. It was painted in 1829.

[3] Mrs. Rylands replied, 'I am proud to accept it, and to feel that the Portrait of the great Collector of so many wonderful and rare books will by your kind thoughtfulness accompany them to their destination.' Mrs. E. Rylands to Spencer, 21 July 1893, SP.

# 6

# GLADSTONE'S LAST ADMINISTRATION, 1892-4

At the end of June 1892 Salisbury dissolved Parliament and the election campaign was opened. Gladstone counted on a large majority, though in the event the Liberals were dependent on Irish members. At the election, 273 Liberals were returned, 81 Irish Nationalists and 1 Labour member, with a small majority of 40 over 269 Conservatives and 46 Liberal Unionists. Rosebery, who was host to the Gladstones at Dalmeny during the elections, reported to Spencer that Gladstone 'was very depressed' at the results but was 'convinced that in his present frame of mind he would form a government with a majority of five'. (Rosebery to Spencer, 8 July 1892, SP). Salisbury, however, continued in office until the new Parliament met on 4 August. A week later, the government lost a vote of confidence and the prime minister resigned. On 13 August, Gladstone received the Queen's commission to form his fourth administration.

Spencer was appointed to the post of First Lord of the Admiralty, and shortly afterwards acted as intermediary between Gladstone and the Queen over the claims of Dilke and Labouchere for office in the new government. One of the difficulties facing Gladstone was the need to fulfil an election pledge to introduce a home rule bill, with the knowledge that the Lords were likely to reject it. Spencer was a prominent member of the cabinet committee charged with drafting the bill. After a difficult passage through the Commons, the bill was defended by Spencer in the Lords in September 1893, but as expected it was resoundingly rejected by 419 to 41 votes, and the subject was subsequently shelved.

During 1893 there was growing public concern at the possibility of an alliance being formed between France and Russia. A visit by the Russian Fleet to Toulon in October fuelled fears, and calls were made to increase British naval strength. An Opposition motion in the Commons by Lord George Hamilton, Spencer's predecessor at the Admiralty, supported such an expansion. Edward Hamilton accurately forecast that 'Lord Spencer will have his work cut out for him ... he will have no easy task in steering between Scylla (the British public or a sector of it) and Charybdis (an impoverished Exchequer).' (EHJ, 6 Nov. 1893, Add. MS. 48661 f. 116). Harcourt was presented with two programmes for shipbuilding, a minimal one and a more ambitious one favoured by the Sea Lords. Spencer had the uncomfortable tasks of pacifying Harcourt and obtaining an agreement with the Sea Lords for a modification of their demands, both of which he successfully accomplished.

By the end of the year cabinet support for Spencer's naval estimates was unanimous except for Gladstone himself and Shaw-Lefevre. To the former, the estimates represented a threat to the foundations of Liberalism and would end in a race to bankruptcy and war by the leading European powers. He later told Stuart Rendel that Spencer's proposal was 'the worst ever submitted to Parliament'.

Gladstone, now isolated, went to Biarritz in January 1894, returning five weeks

*later. He held his last cabinet in 1 March, when he informed his colleagues of his
intention to resign. Shortly afterwards, he went to Windsor for his final audience with
the Queen. Gladstone later recorded that, despite his differences with Spencer over naval
estimates, if his advice had been requested, he would have recommended Spencer as his
successor, but the Queen did not consult him on the matter. On 5 March Rosebery was
summoned by the Queen, and consented to be prime minister.*

---

**617**  LORD SPENCER TO C. R. SPENCER
*8 July 1892; Homburg*[1]

I don't like the look of things, except in London, where we have already
won more seats that I expected. That is very good especially Ritchie's defeat[2].

But Craig's defeat[3] is ugly. John Morley ought to have been able to carry
him in with himself.[4] We seem to have lost several seats from local candidatures.

The Labour candidates have had heavy falls, but they will I suppose find
future strength in having brought defeat at Newcastle, Perth etc. That is not
pleasant ...

The excitement here is very great. The Duke of Rutland[5] gets more detailed
telegrams than I do, but mine confirm numbers, and give some details. He is
most kind and considerate and lets me have all his news.

We leave tomorrow and either stay at Brussels until Monday morning or go
over Sunday night.

[1] The Spencers left London for Homburg on 18 June, returning on 11 July.
[2] Charles Thomson Ritchie, Conservative, President of the Local Government Board, 1886-92,
was defeated by John Williams Benn, Leader of the Progressive Party, London County Council,
and a home ruler, in the St. George's division, Tower Hamlets, which he had represented since
1885. Benn, 1661, Ritchie, 1263.
[3] James Craig, a strong supporter of home rule, M.P., Newcastle upon Tyne, since 1886. Charles
Hammond, Conservative, 13823, Morley, 10905, Craig, 10686.
[4] Morley was M.P., Newcastle on Tyne, from 1883-95.
[5] John James Robert Manners, 7th Duke of Rutland, whose last office was the Chancellorship of
the Duchy of Lancaster, 1886-92, wrote to Salisbury from Homburg on 15 July 1892 when a
Liberal victory seemed likely, 'Your forebodings are being realised. Nothing remains for us but to
wrap our togas decently round our moribund forms.' C. Whibley, *Lord John Manners and His
Friends* (1925), ii, p. 256.

**618**  LORD SPENCER TO C. R. SPENCER
*9 July 1892; Hotel de l'Europe, Brussels*

I am delighted at Guthrie's victory.[1] A small majority but there he is M.P.
for South Northamptonshire. It must have been a tremendous fight. Our other
6 County victories are good. I am very angry at the Irish running Candidates
here, they have no chance and splitting the vote to let a Tory in.

[1] Guthrie, 3930, T. L. M. Cartwright, 3882.

**619**   W. E. GLADSTONE TO LORD SPENCER
*13 July 1892; Dalmeny Park, Edinburgh*

*Secret*

I was indeed angry with myself for not having obtained an opportunity of full conversation with you before you left London. But as matters have thus far turned out the loss is not so great, since the conversation would on my part have been conducted under anticipations which have not been verified.

The argument from the by-elections[1] and the computations of our skilled and sober-minded friends at headquarters appeared to justify the expectation of a minimum majority of 80 or 90, probably rising into three figures. With such a majority we should have been very strong, and could have carried Home Rule into the House of Lords with a voice and impetus somewhat imperative. Our majority is now placed by Marjoribanks at 30, and though I do not abandon the hope of its coming near 40, yet it is not homogeneous throughout and much reduces the scale of our immediate powers, as compared with our hopes ten days ago.[2]

I have meditated much on the proper line of policy to adopt, in the event of our coming in, which I suppose the party hardly can avoid.

One consideration to be borne in mind which I think is true, and if true I am sure is vital, is this, that if we had thrown British questions into the shade we should have had no majority at all. And supposing now we were on coming in so to arrange matters as to *appuyer* on Home Rule alone for the Session, we should run a most serious risk with the constituencies which might I think amount to a great deal of temporary sacrifice if they saw us conducting a Parliamentary movement for Home Rule so strong as to have a chance of overawing the House of Lords, but who if they saw immediate Home Rule to be out of the question would feel with some justice that we ought not to postpone all their wants with no hope of an equivalent.

All this looks like some degree of shifting of our polarity and the whole Irish department of our case will require anxious consideration. Postponement of the whole subject of Home Rule over the new Session does not seem to be possible. But if we are not strong enough to carry it at once we shall have to consider our subject mainly under two subjects.

1. What we can do for Ireland, in a situation which forbids simple postponement of the main Irish issue, and also forbids carrying it.

2. What satisfaction we can give to other wants, English, Welsh and Scotch.

In this view I think we should study the husbanding of our strength for a decisive movement: and I do not despair of its being so husbanded if we address ourselves to those subjects of Liberal legislation which would be both *concise* and telling, in the various divisions of Great Britain.

In Ireland we might repeal Coercion: we might (this is Morley's) make some provision in favour of the evicted tenants; but a main portion of our plan must we both suppose evidently be to *Drummondise*[3] (so to speak) the administration of Ireland. The operation of this method under the Melbourne government was wonderful. I dare say you remember a declaration of Hartington's when he was propounding alternatives, and before he had hardened into practical Toryism, to the effect that 'Dublin Castle' must be fundamentally recast. This would require a strong hand. One of the principal subjects of thought in the coming weeks or months is how far it can be done; and, when the time comes, no one can speak on it with such authority as you.

¹ During 1891, the Liberals gained five seats at by-elections: The Hartlepools, Stowmarket, Harborough, Wisbech, and South Molton. In Jan. 1892, Rossendale, Lancashire, was also won by the Liberals.

² This letter was written on the day his own poll in Midlothian was declared. After being unopposed in the 1885 and 1886 elections, Gladstone was returned with a majority of only 690 votes. Morley, who saw him on the following day reported that he was 'a good deal dazed' at the outcome of the election. Morley to Spencer, 19 July 1892, SP.

³ Thomas Drummond, appointed Under-Secretary, Dublin Castle, by Melbourne in 1835 on the recommendation of 3rd Earl Spencer. Indefatigable worker, reorganizing the Dublin constabulary and formulating scheme for a national system of railways. His health broke down under the strain and he died in 1840. W. M. Torrens, Memoirs of the Rt. Hon. William 2nd Viscount Melbourne (1878), ii, p. 127. On this point, Spencer wrote to Harcourt, 'I agree with you, that the situation is very different now to what it was in the Melbourne period. Something may be done, but without radical change which will need Parliamentary action, I doubt whether much can be done that will strengthen the position ... To Mr. G.'s letter my reply (14 July) was absolute coolness. I said that I would carefully think over what he said, and await further consultation.' Spencer to Harcourt, 18 July 1892, HP, MS. 46.


**620  LORD SPENCER TO W. V. HARCOURT**

*15 July 1892; Spencer House, St. James's Place, S.W.*

HP, MS. 46

I found Bobby,¹ as was to be expected, tired but very well. His diminished majority² is attributed to the necessity of sending 5 or 6 of the best organizers in Mid Northamptonshire to take charge of parts of Guthrie's division, which would certainly have remained in the hands of the Tories, had not this been done. The consequence was many villages in Bobby's Division were neglected, and voters did not go to the Poll.

My own opinion is that although this cause drew down his figures, constant Primrose leaguing for 5 years had the most effect. They had 'habitations' in villages altogether belonging to me, and of course I could say nothing to tenants who took this line. In the heart of my property, where at former elections there were only 4 or 5 votes in the Polling boxes, there were 50 this week. People have had little or no personal consideration in the fight, and we Liberals cannot object, even if we regret to lose votes.³

¹ Robert Spencer.

² Spencer 4731, Pender, 4300. In 1886, his majority was 956.

³ In a speech at Reading on 6 Feb. 1889, Spencer accused members of the Primrose League of 'exclusive dealing and social isolation of individuals against political opponents'. Lord Harris, chairman of the Grand Council of the Primrose League, initiated a correspondence with Spencer on the topic, 15-21 Feb. 1889, SP. See also J. H. Robb, The Primrose League 1883-1906 (1942), p. 98.

### 621   W. R. D. ADKINS TO LORD SPENCER
*17 July 1892; Springfield, Northampton*

I have been impressed during the Election that unless something is done for the agricultural labourer *pari passu* with Home Rule or even before it we cannot keep our hold on the Counties in this part of the Country.[1] I mentioned this to your Lordship some months ago and you were so kind as to agree with me: but events of the last few weeks have strengthened my feeling that this matters very much. Both in the South and in the Mid[2] the Tory programme was very taking and the *Rural World* which echoes the contentions of Jesse Collings is being pushed assiduously in parts of our County.

[1] Joseph Arch, the champion of agricultural workers and a supporter of home rule, declared in the *English Labourers' Chronicle* in Jan. 1889 that Liberals must be 'determined that our Irish brethren shall be delivered at once and for ever out of the hands of the uncircumcised Tory Philistines.' P. Horn, *Joseph Arch* (1971), p. 187.
[2] i.e. two of the four county divisions. The others were East and North Northamptonshire.

### 622   W. E. GLADSTONE TO LORD SPENCER
*23 July 1892; Hawarden Castle, Chester*

I send you a Memorandum seen by no other eye, as yet, and intended to work out the best method of fixing a most difficult question, namely the just relation for 1893 between Irish and British claims. Please to let me know whether it strikes you favourably.

### 623   LORD SPENCER TO W. E. GLADSTONE
*25 July 1892; Spencer House, St. James's Place, S.W.*
GP, Add. MS. 44314 ff. 38-9

*Secret*

I am rather doubtful as to dealing with the Irish question next Session by Resolution, for I fear that our opponents will say that we desire to shelve the question, and we lay ourselves open to the same attacks which we made against the Government last Session in regard to the obvious desire to cover their pledges by introducing an Irish Local Government Bill and then to drop it.

We might meet the question of dropping our measure but I fear we should be considered as faint-hearted, if we did not bring in a Bill, and send it up to the H. of Lords. We do not moreover know what the Irish will say.

I am however diffident about opinions on procedure, and I am altogether with you on your main contention that we are bound to deal with Home Rule in our first Session by pledges, by action at Elections and by the necessity of keeping the Irish with us, which we can only do by showing them that we are earnest in our desire to[1] deal in a comprehensive and satisfactory way with the Irish difficulty.

I also cordially agree that we must push forward a few important measures which will satisfy British demands.

Next Session must necessarily be a long one; you ought to be able to carry a Home Rule Bill through Committee of the House, and if the H. of Lords rejects it and other British measures, you will be able to present them again to Parliament in the Session of 1894 with great effect.

¹ Spencer added here 'carry Home Rule' and then deleted it.


**624   LORD KIMBERLEY TO LORD SPENCER**
*29 July 1892; 35 Lowndes Square, S.W.*

*Private*

I wrote a short note to Mr. G. telling him I would not add to his troubles by calling on him unless he wanted me for anything, and I had a note from him telling me briefly what is going on. From Ripon,[1] whom I saw today, I gathered that Harcourt is pressing for postponement of the Home Rule Bill.[2] I hope this will not be attempted. Whatever the difficulties of carrying a Home Rule Bill and they are manifest enough, I feel sure that we should gain nothing, but much the contrary, by postponement. I won't go into the arguments, because they are perfectly familiar to you, and I am sure you will be for facing the question next session. Of course *if* the Irish Nationalists were themselves convinced that postponement was the best policy and cordially agreed in it, the case would be quite altered, but this I regard as quite inconceivable, and therefore not worth discussing. You know our friend well enough to feel pretty certain that if Mr. G. puts his foot down he will in due time get calm and very probably fully convinced of the wisdom of not following his present advice. Ripon says why not have another important measure in the same session as Home Rule, some measure which would give satisfaction to the English and Scotch Liberals? I agree with him: why not? In 1870 we carried both the Land Act and the Education Act both measures of the highest importance. All this will no doubt have occurred to you, but I thought you might like to know my opinion. I feel very conscious that Mr. G. should not now be worried to death with this preliminary controversy: meantime I put my trust in you and J. Morley.

¹ George Frederick Samuel Robinson, 1st Marquess of Ripon, Lord President of the Council, 1868–73, Viceroy of India, 1880–4, First Lord of the Admiralty, 1886.
² Harcourt, though not against dealing with Ireland, believed that in view of the new government's small majority, the best way of holding the party together was by devising a strong Radical programme. Gardiner, ii, p. 179.


**625   LORD SPENCER**
*July 1892*[1]

*Memorandum*

I saw Sir H. Ponsonby only last evening, and referred to a previous conversation which I had with him, and also to what he said recently to Sir W. Harcourt.

# MR. GLADSTONE'S NEW CABINET.

(1)
Mr A. J. MUNDELLA
President of Board of Trade

(2)
EARL OF KIMBERLEY
Secretary for India and Lord President of Council.

(4)
LORD HERSCHELL
Lord Chancellor

(3)
EARL SPENCER
First Lord of Admiralty

(5)
THE MARQUIS OF RIPON
Colonial secretary

(6)
SIR GEORGE TREVELYAN
Secretary for Scotland

(7)
MR BRYCE
Chancellor of the Duchy of Lancaster

(8)
MR JOHN MORLEY
Chief Secretary for Ireland

(9)
MR W. E. GLADSTONE
First Lord of the Treasury
and Lord Privy Seal

(10)
SIR WILLIAM HARCOURT
Chancellor of the Exchequer

(11)
MR H. H. ASQUITH, Q.C.
Home Secretary

(12)
MR H. H. FOWLER
President of the Local Government Board

(13)
MR ARNOLD MORLEY
Postmaster General

(15)
EARL OF ROSEBERY
Foreign Secretary

(14)
MR SHAW LEFEVRE
First Commissioner of Works

(16)
MR CAMPBELL-BANNERMAN
Secretary for War

(17)
MR ARTHUR ACLAND
Vice President of the Committee of
Council on Education

1　Gladstone's fourth and last administration, 1892–4

2  Charles Robert Spencer, *c.* 1906

**"FULL SPEED AHEAD!"**

*Britannia (to Lord Spencer).*

To "HEAR OLD TRITON BLOW HIS WREATHÈD HORN,"
MY SPENCER, IN *THIS* CLEAR DETERMINED MANNER,

IS SPIRIT-GLADDENING; SHOWING YOU WERE BORN
TO BACK MY POWER AND UPBEAR MY BANNER!

3   'Full Speed Ahead!' *Punch*, 23 March 1895. The 1895 Estimates provided for a large
increase in cruisers and destroyers

4   The Old Breakfast Room, Althorp Park, shortly before the sale of the Library.

5 'The Sinking of HMS Victoria 23 June 1893', *Illustrated London News*, 8 July 1893

6   The Painted Room, Spencer House, London, decorated by James 'Athenian' Stuart. *c.* 1765. View of *c.* 1900

7 The South Front, Althorp Park, c. 1901. The building was remodelled by Henry Holland in 1786

8 'A Modern Bluebeard', *Truth*, 25 December 1904. Lord Spencer is unmasking Joseph Chamberlain. Campbell-Bannerman stands behind them

He says that he was authorized in writing to tell anyone to whom he might think it desirable to speak, that no consent would be given to the admission of Sir C. Dilke and Mr. Labouchere into a new Government.

There was no distinction made as to Cabinet and non Cabinet offices.

His written authority went no further than this.

He added that he believed others had said to the person in question that there was an idea that some other office might be offered to Labby, which would not involve Cabinet.

She repeated this it seems to Sir Henry without expressing or threatening a *non possumus*.

He said that in his opinion she would not have Mr. Labouchere brought into contact with herself, and as Sir Henry understood, kissing hands.

She stated that she had heard that Mr. L. did not himself press for office, but that he was moved by his wife[2] who expected that if her husband got office she would be received at Court.

The objections urged would not be Political, but connected with Mr. H. L.'s moral character, and by the constant attacks, if not lately on herself, on every member by turn of her family in *Truth*.[3]

My impression from my conversation was that if an office could be found for Labby which would not bring him into contact with the Queen, the objections to him would be overcome.[4]

[1] Headed 'Cabinet Meeting 1892'.

[2] Henrietta Hodson, an actress who made a considerable reputation in burlesque, especially in boy parts. Already married, she lived with Labouchere from 1866 and later became his wife. H. Pearson, *Labby* (1936), p. 63.

[3] Labouchere, owner of *Truth* since it began publication in 1877, and a mouthpiece for his advanced Radicalism. As recently as 1891, Labouchere, as a member of a committee to investigate the question of Royal grants, drafted a report stating that 'under no circumstances' should they be increased. A. L. Thorold, *The Life of Henry Labouchere* (1913), pp. 374-5.

[4] On this point, Ponsonby's letter to Spencer written from Osborne on 8 Aug. is of interest. 'The Queen observed to me "I hope you heard nothing more about proposals on behalf of Mr. Labouchere in London?" I replied that I heard an enquiry whether she would object to his having any office in which he would not come into personal contact with her. She replied that all leading appointments must be in contact with her, but as to minor places—where the appointment was made by the Minister and not by The Queen—the responsibility would rest entirely with whoever made it and she would certainly not approve, but would express no opinion upon it.' SP.


**626    LORD SPENCER**

*July 1892*

> *Notes of conversation with Mr. W. E. Gladstone on my interview with*
> *Sir Henry Ponsonby touching C. W. Dilke and Henry Labouchere*

The points to be considered are

(1) C. W. Dilke

There is no question of his being in a position to be considered for office. That may be dismissed from discussion.

(2) The aspiration of Mrs. H. L. to be received at Court need not be con-

sidered. If the husband takes office, the wife is not of necessity received at Court.

Nothing can diminish the absolute discretion of the Queen to decide upon the question as to who is received at Court.

(3) If H. L. were offered office, he would be obliged to sever himself from all control of *Truth*, as to writing, or managing, or editing the Paper.

His financial investment in the Paper might remain.

There are precedents for ministers having a financial interest in Newspapers.

(4) 'The moral objection to H. L.' Whatever may be the facts as to his past relations with his wife, they are not recorded by judgment of the Courts of Law, or in any Public manner.

That being the case, is it right, that supposing he is by influence or ability or by any other cause himself entitled to office, he shall be excluded for a cause which is known from private and not public information? and which has for many years ceased to exist?

If the strictest rule on this point had been always laid down, would it not have excluded many able men from office; and further where is the proof of guilt which is thus to operate against a man to be found.

(5) 'The attacks made, if not recently on the Queen, on other members of the Royal family.'

Objections of this character should be specific, and should be actually traced to particular articles, in order that their weight may be taken into account.

Mr. G. seems to think that of these 5 objections, the three first are disposed of. The last two remain open for further consideration.[1]

---

[1] Gladstone informed Labouchere on 22 Aug. that 'there were incidents in your case which ... appeared to me to render it unfit that I should ask your leave to submit your name to Her Majesty for a political office which would involve your becoming a servant of the Crown'. This line of action was settled upon at a meeting of Gladstone, Harcourt, J. Morley and Spencer, in the Commons on 11 Aug. A large rally at Northampton Town Hall, held on 25 Aug., protesting at Labouchere's exclusion from the government, ended in uproar. *NM*, 26 Aug. 1892, p. 5.

### 627   W. E. GLADSTONE TO LORD SPENCER
*2 August 1892; 1 Carlton Gardens, S.W.*

*Secret*

My means of oral communication on serious matters are at present sadly limited: but I have been desiring to see you for the purpose of saying a few words which are due to you.[1]

Meanwhile I take a sanguine view of the vital question how *in principle* business is to be shaped for the Session, when the time comes, should the great task devolve upon us. And I have drawn out the sketches which I now inclose, which is pretty full, and which as far as I know is in consonance with all the general leanings, as far as they have yet been developed.

Morley has just seen it and seems to view it with general favour.

Provisional outline of work
for the Session of 1893[2]

I    Bills to be worked by the Government in the House
II   Bills to be worked through Grand Committee
III  Bills of Private members to be supported by the Government
IV   Executive Rule


I

1. Bill for the Government of Ireland
2. County Councils Bill
3. Budget
4. One man one vote
5. Transfer of Election charges to rates
6. Miners
7. Repeal of Coercion
8. Licensing by Local Option?


II

1. Registration
2. Employers' Liability
3. Law of Conspiracy Amendment


III

1. Welsh Church Suspensory Bill
2. Scotch Church Bill to provide for the cessation of all stipends from public sources when present incumbencies shall terminate: and for other purposes.
3. Bill to put an end to the representation of Univ. (?) in Parliament
4. The admission of evicted Tenants


IV

1. Welsh Land Commission
2. England Poor Law Commission
3. Labour Department
4. Ireland. Gradual reduction of Constabulary and reform of Judgeships and administration generally.

*Added by Spencer*
County Councils Bill.
1. Control of Police
2. Control of Licensing
3. Compulsory powers to take land for small holdings
4. London C.C. Enlargement of Powers
5. Parish Councils for the purpose of small holdings

---

[1] Gladstone was laid low with a bad cough. Spencer came up from Althorp to London on 1 Aug.
[2] Copy in Spencer's handwriting.

### 628 LORD SPENCER TO W. E. GLADSTONE

*2 August 1892; Spencer House, St. James's Place, S.W.*
GP, Add. MS. 44314 f. 41

I return the paper of outline of Work.

I like generally the ideas of Dividing the work into the several Heads which you enumerate.

I dare say the measures may be to some extent after discussion distributed differently.

I see a query to Miners' Eight Hours Bill being among Government measures. It would remove a difficulty if that could be left to private introduction.

There will also be some necessary discussion about the County Councils Bill.

The abolition of Standing Joint Committees with transfer of all their powers to the Councils would be a simple and effectual way of transferring the control of the Police, and doing away with several features of the present system.

I need not now enter into further details.

### 629 J. MORLEY TO LORD SPENCER

*14 August 1892; 95 Elm Park Gardens, South Kensington, S.W.*

Mundella called last night, loud in his expectation of going back to the Board of Trade.[1]

Of course, I told him nothing, but preached the doctrine of charity, and doing what the Prime Minister thinks best.

I did not drop a hint even as to Acland.[2]

But when I hear Mundella's account of the duties of the B. of T., it strengthens my misgivings as to Acland being President.

Anyhow I've taken the liberty of asking Mundella to call on you this forenoon. I think you ought to hear his case. Don't let him stop longer than you like.

[1] The following day, Mundella, according to Lewis Harcourt, was 'in a great state of excitement, disappointment and rage at hearing he was to go back to the Education Office and not to the Board of Trade.' LHJ, 14 Aug. 1892, HP, MS. 736 f. 308. He was appointed President of the Board of Trade on 18 Aug.

[2] A. H. D. Acland, son of Sir Thomas Dyke Acland, M.P., Rotherham division, West Riding of Yorkshire, since 1885 was given the post of Vice-President, Committee of Council on Education, with a seat in the cabinet on 25 Aug. Of this he wrote, 'It was with an enormous sense of relief that I was sent on by Morley to Lord Spencer ... then had a delightful talk with him and appeared to convince him gradually. Then I went back to Morley ... Morley went up to the meeting at 1 Carlton Gardens at 3 where my fate was decided and I suppose the Cabinet settled.' A. H. D. Acland, Diary, 26 Aug. 1892, Acland Papers.

### 630 J. MORLEY[1] TO LORD SPENCER

*15 August 1892; 95 Elm Park Gardens, South Kensington, S.W.*

*Confidential*

I assure you that I have seldom passed so painful an evening as yesterday, looking back on the events of the day.[2] I won't go over them now.

We shall meet to-morrow. On the merits and from the point of view of expediency, I believe that H. and I were right. But I equally believe that the manner of it was *on every side* not by any means all that could be desired.

I had already had a ferocious battle with Harcourt—in which I stamped my foot, beat the table, and so frightened him, that he rose and craved mercy. I was bouncing out of the room, when he begged me to stay. He, at any rate, has now become impracticable.

With Berkeley Square[3] I am altogether out of patience.[4]

[1] Appointed Chief Secretary for Ireland on 22 Aug.

[2] Disagreement amongst leading Liberals, particularly Gladstone, Harcourt and Morley, on the proportion of high offices to be given to colleagues in the House of Lords. See Harcourt to Gladstone, 14 Aug. 1892, in Gardiner, ii, pp. 182-3. At a conference held at Arnold Morley's that morning, Spencer told them, 'I warn you that we peers this afternoon shall have to fight for what we consider the members of our Party in the House of Lords have a right to in the way of offices.' LHJ, 14 Aug. 1892, HP, MS. 736 f. 310.

[3] 38 Berkeley Square was Rosebery's London home.

[4] Rosebery, with a great show of reluctance, had agreed that day for his name to be submitted to the Queen as Foreign Secretary. Edward Hamilton went to Spencer House to announce the good news 'at which Lord Spencer was overjoyed'. EHJ, 15 Aug. 1892, Add. MS. 48658 f. 103.


**631   PRINCE OF WALES TO LORD SPENCER**

*21 August 1892; Villa Imperiale, Homburg*

Nothing has given me greater pleasure than to know that you have been appointed First Lord of the Admiralty,[1] and I know it is a popular one in the Navy. That it is pleasing for yourself I can easily imagine as your Grandfather held the same post and your Father was an Admiral ...

[1] Spencer's appointment was announced in the Court Circular on 16 Aug.


**632   LORD SPENCER TO W. E. GLADSTONE**

*2 September 1892; Portsmouth Harbour*
GP, Add. MS. 44314 ff. 46-7

I am greatly interested in my work, but appalled at the large questions involved in the administration of the Navy. I shall do my best to do justice to the position, but feel my own ignorance of the great subjects involved.


**633   SPENCER LYTTELTON[1] TO LORD SPENCER**

*21 September 1892; 10 Downing Street, Whitehall*

I fear the quiet of the political world is not likely to continue ... And then there is Uganda which has suddenly become a most burning question demanding instant action. The Chancellor of the Exchequer has burst out in a very long—and illegible—letter[2] in which he takes a very strong line in favour of evacuation and therefore against Rosebery who, while he will have nothing to do with the Mombasa Railway,[3] is averse to evacuation—but you have his Memorandum.[4]

Mr. Gladstone has just got Harcourt's letter which is being circulated. It would be ruinous I fear to the Govt. if any catastrophe should happen because of the evacuation, and such a thing seems highly probable, as it would arouse great feeling especially in Scotland where the Central African question has taken great hold.

Rosebery told me the Church Missionary Society have spent £200,000 on the Uganda mission: that shows how much the public is interested. It is not impossible that the Cabinet will have to meet. At present the members are scattered to the winds.

¹ Private secretary to Gladstone.
² Harcourt to Gladstone, 20 Sept. 1892. Reproduced in Gardiner, ii, pp. 131-3.
³ I.e., plans by the British East Africa Company to build a railway from Mombasa through Uganda to Lake Victoria.
⁴ Memorandum circulated to the cabinet on 19 Sept., PRO CAB 37/31/23.

**634   LORD SPENCER TO LORD ROSEBERY**
*23 September 1892; Balmoral*
RP, 10062 ff. 66-7

*Confidential*

I read with great interest your Uganda Memo. It seems a very unpleasant business. I am too ignorant of what the Company expect to do even if they succeed,¹ or what Government can do to be a good judge of how far we are justified in risking lives and treasure in keeping the position at Uganda.

You brush away the defence of the Nile, very wisely. But are we justified for the upholding of Imperial interests to incur more responsibilities which will increase year after year? Ought we not for putting down Slave trade to be satisfied with our Naval means of checking it? They may be imperfect, but we know the limit of this responsibility.

I am sorry for Lugard Williams and Co. and it is always disagreeable to retreat from any undertaking. In this case the retreat seems to have been settled before we came into office.

This is not I suppose the rescue of a mission, such as we had to attempt at Khartoum, but the continued defence of a colony: a prolonged responsibility.

Of course I do not know what your alternative to letting withdrawal take place would be.²

¹ The Church Missionary Anti-Slavery Society, which had been in Uganda since 1877, supported the British East Africa Company in their occupation of that country. A deputation from the Society met Rosebery on 23 Sept. expressing the fear of the consequences of withdrawal from Uganda. See *The Times*, 24 Sept. 1892, p. 12.
² 'I have had a really terrible time,' Gladstone told Spencer, 'Rosebery has I think been quite carried off his legs by the Jingoes of the Foreign Office and its agents and correspondents ... and wants us to interfere with the coming *evacuation* which even the late Govt. had accepted.' Gladstone to Spencer, 26 Sept. 1892, SP.

## 635   LORD SPENCER TO LORD KIMBERLEY[1]

*5 December 1892; Althorp, Northampton*
KP, 10247 ff. 47–8

*Private and Confidential*

I hope that we made good progress the 5 days that we met before Mr. G. went to Hawarden,[2] and last Thursday[3] I happened to see Jenkyns[4] at the Club, and he told me he had sent a proof of the Bill to John Morley.

So we might had we had a younger Chief, have discussed the Bill this week. As it is I really think we shall do very well if we begin early in January with it.

... I had 3 hours with Harcourt[5] and 2 Admirals last week on our ships. H. had every sort of theory, and wished to ignore Russia altogether. He seems to have long had a craze about ships. He was very odd and extravagant at times, but kept his temper admirably, and did not trample on us to any extent. He said that it was the most interesting 3 hours possible to him. I got rather exhausted as did the Admirals.

[1] Lord President of the Council.

[2] The cabinet committee on the Home Rule Bill, consisting of Gladstone, Spencer, John Morley, Bryce, Campbell-Bannerman and Herschell, was appointed on 19 Nov. 'to sit *de die in diem*'. LHJ, 17 Nov. 1892, HP, MS. 736 f. 356. The committee deliberated from 21 to 25 Nov., Gladstone returning to Hawarden on 26 Nov.

[3] 1 Dec.

[4] Sir Henry Jenkyns, Treasury draftsman.

[5] Chancellor of the Exchequer.

## 636   LORD SPENCER TO W. V. HARCOURT

*9 December 1892; Admiralty, Whitehall*
HP, MS. 46

*Private*

You may be sure that I enter fully into your position, and desire to assist you considerably with what I consider my absolute duty.[1]

As a matter of warning I must tell you that the sketch estimate prepared by the Accountant-General is about 400,000£ over that of 92–93. The Financial Secretary has reduced it by 200,000£ and I hope we may reduce it further. The utmost that I think is possible, (and it will be very difficult to attain that) will be to ask for the same amount as that in the Estimates of 92–93.

You may depend on my using my best [sic] to do this.

[1] Spencer had lunched with Harcourt that day and discussed naval estimates. Harcourt threatened to resign if 'inflated Estimates' were agreed to by the cabinet. According to Lewis Harcourt, 'Spencer left, much frightened at the prospect.' LHJ, 9 Dec. 1892, HP, MS. 736 f. 362.

**637**  J. MORLEY TO LORD SPENCER
*10 December 1892; Hawarden Castle, Chester*

*Private*

I got the message from A. West[1] this morning, and did the best that I could;[2] but things move slowly, that is decisions are slowly formed. Mr. G. has an invincible aversion to Cabinets, and will do almost anything to have as few as possible.

Now, matters stand thus. Mr. G. and I have worked through the draft bill today.[3] There are still two or three points on which I ought to see the Irish. So what is proposed is that the Cabinet Committee should meet on Friday,[4] to settle about the new points that have been raised. Then the draft bill would be ready for circulation ...

Anyhow, I have got to this point, that the Cabinet will have the Bill by about Dec. 20. That will no doubt be the signal for certain winds blowing great guns. However, we must live from hand to mouth.

[1] Sir Algernon West, Gladstone's private secretary, 1868-7, Commissioner, Board of Inland Revenue, 1872-92. Unofficial adviser and secretary to Gladstone during his fourth administration.
[2] Morley, who arrived at Hawarden from Newcastle on 9 Dec., was asked by West to persuade Gladstone to hold a cabinet that week. Morley to West, 10 Dec. 1892. Reproduced in West, pp. 89-90.
[3] See Gladstone to Spencer, 10 Dec. 1892, SP.
[4] 16 Dec. Gladstone left Hawarden for London in the morning and was joined at Chester by Morley, who was returning from Ireland.

**638**  LORD SPENCER TO LADY SPENCER
*16 December 1892; Admiralty, Whitehall*

A dreadful day, but nearly over. Settled the Admirals[1] affair, Court Martial.

Mr. G. came up looking very well.[2] He goes off Tuesday, and I believe only stops away until January 10th.

[1] Vice-Admiral Henry Fairfax, Senior Officer, Channel Squadron, was court-martialled at Devonport on 29 Dec. 1892, as a consequence of the grounding of the battleship *Howe* off Ferrol, Spain, in Nov. See Spencer to Queen Victoria, 3 Nov. 1892, RA E56/70. After a nine-day trial, Fairfax was acquitted. For fuller details, see Hammill Papers, HMM/5. Spencer found the court martial personally 'extremely painful.' Spencer to Fairfax, 23 Jan. 1893, SP (copy).
[2] The cabinet committee on the Home Rule Bill met for four hours and a full cabinet lasting two hours followed on 17 Dec. The committee considered franchise, local government and the aged poor, *The Times*, 19 Dec. 1892, p. 6. Of the two meetings, Gladstone told his wife, 'both went perfectly well: plenty of serious matter but nothing sharply contentious or critical as among ourselves'. 17 Dec. 1892, GGP, 30/2.

**639**  W. V. HARCOURT TO LORD SPENCER
*19 December 1892; 11 Downing Street, Whitehall*

*Confidential*

A thousand thanks for your 'state of the Navy'. It is exactly what I wished and is more satisfactory than I had ever hoped.

I think now the best thing we can do is to declare war against all the world at once and conquer it off hand. Then we shall have no further trouble and there will be no minor questions of annexations and protectorates.

All that will be requisite will be that the *five Peers*[1] shall be placed in command of five fleets to occupy the four seas with me in reserve, and Britannia at length will really rule the main.

[1] I.e. the five peers in the cabinet, Herschell, Kimberley, Ripon, Rosebery and Spencer.

## 640 LORD SPENCER TO W. V. HARCOURT
*6 January 1893; Althorp, Northampton*
HP, MS. 46

*Confidential*

When I get letters from you I never quite know what they will be, whether I must expect banter, anger or serious argument. Whatever they are they always point to friendly conclusions in the near or distant future. Your letter received yesterday has indications of all these phases of your mind.

Poor Mr. G. his small joke as to his return was not well directed to you![1] I don't think you properly realized the position of affairs when we were in London in November.

No member of the Cabinet wanted to stifle fair discussion upon the Irish Bill, and we wanted Mr. G. to get forward with the work of preparing the measure. No doubt he shrank from it; possibly (this is entirely my own idea) he dreaded the well-known opposition which was sure to be given to the measure in whatever shape it was produced from the most prominent person in the Cabinet, but we all wanted to get this feeling of his, and we should have done it in one way or another without the somewhat strong ebullitions which we had on more than one occasion in the Cabinet.

We felt bound as we had enlisted under so old a General to try and spare him unnecessary anxiety, and yet get what was essential.

I cannot see that we are now driven into difficulties owing to short time for discussion. The Bill is in the hands of the Cabinet and we have 22 days to discuss it before Parliament meets, and as it will not be introduced for days after the meeting of Parliament, we have more time still. This ought to be ample for the consideration of this and the measures which have been prepared in addition to the Irish Bill.

It is a serious inconvenience in many ways that our Chief is so old, but we must make the best of that and in many ways he will still be the best man alive to introduce the Irish measure for which alone some of us continue in Politics, and which we put before every other measure which has to be brought forward in Parliament.

I know that you take the exactly opposite view to this, but the Liberal party as it now exists was formed on these lines, and those who have thrown themselves in with the Liberals cannot work in a different direction.

Enough as to Mr. G. and his little joke with you.

Now as to the two Heads of the fighting Departments who according to Mr.

G. would like to be backed up against their oppressors. Well, the line you take as to that is right as far as I am concerned.[2] I have done my utmost to avoid unnecessary outlay, and to keep within bounds the Estimates of the coming year, and having gone as far as I think it right, I should not be relieved by any pressure from the higher authorities of the Government but shall feel that they are needlessly wasting their powers. For I shall be responsible for what we demand, and once responsibility is assumed, there is no further question of oppression by others.

I shall be extremely surprised if there is an excess of expenditure this year over the Naval Estimates. Shuttleworth and I have used our utmost endeavours to impress on the officials the necessity of keeping within their Estimates and I am assured that we shall not exceed. I say this even with expenditure like that for saving the *Howe*. You can hardly agree with the old Generals at the United Services Club in saying that this disaster was obviously the result of having a d--- set of people like us at the Board of Admiralty ...

I know nothing of War Office expenditure but I imagine people there were committed by the last Government to various heavy enterprises.

I have been steadily refusing to put on the Estimates every kind of expenditure which I do not think essential, and it might be thought a little hard when one has done one's best, to be charged with every kind of enormity as to warlike extravagance ...

I have run on to great length and so will stop. I cannot banter like you, but I fear I can be angry but am not so now, and I do not pretend to argue against you although I can be obstinate when I think I am right.

[1] Harcourt, writing to Spencer on 4 Jan., quoted from a letter received from Gladstone the same day, 'he hears that I shall not return to London till the 18th, and that therefore he should follow my example instead of coming back sooner as he intended'. Harcourt commented, 'Pretty cool this, considering the indignation with which he and the rest of you received my suggestion of early meetings to discuss important matters.' Harcourt to Spencer, 4 Jan. 1893, SP.

[2] Harcourt had replied to Gladstone, 'I would do my *level best* to support both the heads against their professional oppressors.' Ibid. Gladstone's view was that Campbell-Bannerman at the War Office and Spencer at the Admiralty needed to be protected against the demands of generals and admirals.

**641**   C. R. SPENCER TO LORD SPENCER

*31 March 1893; Dallington House, Northampton*

Our Foreign Office meeting did good,[1] and gave our people great confidence. Of course our not having passed the 2nd. Reading of any of the big Bills will give the enemy great joy in the recess speeches, but one hopes the country will understand the reason.

John Morley went to Ireland on Wednesday night after speaking on the Irish Bill as to Evicted Tenants, which was talked out.[2] On the whole it is very remarkable how much stronger we are now than anyone would have thought we could be at Easter considering we were to go out on the Address.

[1] A meeting of Liberal M.P.s was held on 27 March to consider strategies on legislation, particularly the Irish Home Rule, Local Government and Parish Council Bills. Gladstone announced the government's intention to introduce the Irish Bill on 6 April.

[2] For Morley's speech on the second reading of the Evicted Tenants (Ireland) Bill, see Hansard, 4, x, col. 1453 ff. 29 March 1893.

## 642   LORD SPENCER TO SIR H. PONSONBY
*19 April 1893; Malta*
RA Add. A/12 2061

We got here on Monday morning after stopping Sunday at Syracuse,[1] and we leave for Gibraltar tonight as I hear I need not be in London on the 24th. Our stay away is longer than I wanted it to be, but being out here, I think it best to see what is wanted.

We found Naples detestable, a storm of dust with a piercingly cold wind. It is delightful here and we have been much struck with the beauty of the harbour and its semi Eastern town.

I have been very busy inspecting, and I hope what we have seen will be useful.

The Tryons are most hospitable, and his activity is more like that of a light youth of 10 stone instead of the massive block of 19 stone in weight. He seems to be quite the Commander in Chief, and I should think a very good one, and has the full confidence of the fleet.

[1] Spencer was the Minister in Attendance on the Queen, who had arrived at her residence in Florence on 23 March. King Humbert of Italy paid a visit to discuss naval matters and on 13 April, Vice-Admiral Sir George Tryon, Commander-in-Chief, Mediterranean, was summoned from Malta. Spencer then went to Naples, Malta and Syracuse on the way home. Greene Papers, GEE/13 (g).

## 643   LORD SPENCER TO LORD ROSEBERY
*26 May 1893; Althorp, Northampton*
RP, 10062 ff. 85–6

I will let you have a paper showing our strength compared with other nations.

Actual present strength is not enough. We must note what ships are building. Harcourt who takes great pride in his naval knowledge shows me always, and says that he tells you, that Xmas next will be the time when we shall stand strongest. That is true for we have some very powerful new ships, battleships and cruisers, just ready for commission, and at the end of the year we shall compare best with France. If we go on a year or two to '96, France and Russia will by then have more ships and we shall only be about equal to them in power.

I do not know that you will care to wade through the tables; if not I will have marked and sent to you a speech I made in reply to Brassey[1] some 6 weeks ago or more in the House of Lords.[2] I gave an epitome of present ships and also what were building here and elsewhere.

Harcourt in discussions will not hear of Russia, but she cannot be ignored and she is building a great deal notwithstanding financial difficulties: as you know, France is doing a great deal in the same way and is spending as much or a little more than we are in new construction. If you care to see this I can send you some papers which have been to Harcourt.

H. is always hinting that he expects us to cut down Estimates, but I very much fear that the difficulty will be *not* to increase them, for new and additional ships to the Navy mean more men, larger docks etc. etc. We are rather proud of ourselves this year, in keeping up building and adding to the men, and yet remaining at the figure of G. Hamilton's last year (100£ less).

I am sure that it will not do to stop new construction.

[1] Thomas, 1st Baron Brassey, formerly Civil Lord of the Admiralty, 1880-4 and Secretary to the Admiralty, 1884-5. Naval reformer and originator of *Brassey's Naval Annual.*

[2] Hansard, 4, ix, cols. 1569-78, 10 March 1893. Spencer's statement was made during a debate on the condition of the Navy.


**644**   LORD SPENCER TO QUEEN VICTORIA
*23 June 1893; Admiralty, Whitehall*
RA E56/95

Earl Spencer presents his humble duty to Your Majesty and thanks the Queen for her kind and sympathetic letter. Lord Spencer knew how shocked Your Majesty would be at this terrible disaster involving the loss of such a large number of officers and men of the Navy and marines and including the distinguished Admiral Sir George Tryon.[1]

Although the loss is a few less than in the case of the *Captain* in 1870[2] the catastrophe is even more appalling, as one to a large extent was beyond human control and of those in command of the Ship and the other was, it is difficult to avoid thinking, under the control of some officers whose responsibility cannot be determined now. Mr. Gladstone made a statement in the House of Commons and Lord Spencer in the House of Lords, and great feeling was shown in both Houses.

It was impossible to hazard an opinion upon the cause of the disaster, but it is surmised at the Admiralty that in the manoeuvres the Ships having been in two lines the one led by the *Victoria*, Sir G. Tryon's flagship, the other led by the *Camperdown*, Admiral Markham's[3] (Second in Command) temporary flagship, they made a movement which involved the wheeling of one line and its passing parallel but in the reverse direction of the other, and that somehow no one knows how and why the *Camperdown* collided with the *Victoria* in a nearly parallel direction.

If each Ship was moving at the speed of 10 knots, this force would be doubled in the collision, and the ram with a force of about 20 knots would tear out as it were nearly the whole of one side of the *Victoria*. This is the idea to account for the *Victoria* turning over at once as is supposed to have been the case and then sinking. The almost total loss of engineers and the large number of midshipmen drowned incidentally bears out this view on account of the position in the Ship where they would be usually placed.

Lord Spencer thinks the Queen may like to hear this possible explanation of the accident. Had the *Camperdown* rammed the *Victoria* more directly, the watertight compartments would in the opinion here have saved the Ship from sinking.

[1] On 22 June the *Camperdown* collided with Tryon's flagship, the *Victoria*, in a perfectly calm sea five miles off Tripoli. More than 350 officers and men were lost.

[2] The vessel, a six-gun turret ship of 4272 tons, capsized in a storm off Finisterre in Sept. 1870 with a crew of 500. The disaster showed that the rigging was not compatible with reducing freeboard to a minimum above the waterline.

[3] Rear-Admiral A. H. Markham.


**645   U. KAY-SHUTTLEWORTH[1] TO LORD SPENCER**

*3 July 1893; House of Commons*

*Private*

My mind is and shall remain open. But this is passing through it:—

If Tryon were alive, he would undoubtedly be the person to be court-martialled first. But as he is dead I cannot see any particular reason for at once court-martialling the officers and crew of the *Victoria* or any of them.

The question seems to me to arise whether the first and possibly the only inquiry should be on the questions:

Why did the *Camperdown* sink the *Victoria*?

Why did Admiral Markham not carry out his intention of pointing out to Tryon the danger of obeying his signal?

Why did he sink the *Victoria* and hazard the *Campderdown* by obeying without pointing out the danger?

Some of these would be the charges. His defence and the judgment of the Court Martial would very likely dispose of them.

A Court Martial on Markham might clear up and end the whole matter.[2]

[1] Parliamentary and Financial Secretary to the Admiralty, 1892–5.

[2] A court martial of the surviving officers of the *Victoria* was held from 17–24 July. Capt. the Hon. Maurice Bourke, Tryon's flag captain, to whom Tryon explained his proposed action, was exonerated from all blame. Markham, on the other hand, was exonerated, but in an Admiralty Minute three months later was blamed for accepting Tryon's orders without enquiry and for then executing them. Markham accepted full responsibility for the conduct of the *Camperdown*. M.E. and F. A. Markham, *The Life of Sir Albert Hastings Markham* (1927), p. 245. Markham's own detailed defence, which was never used, is to be found in Markham Papers, MAK/41. One witness to the event, Capt. (later Admiral) J. W. Brackenbury, told his wife, 'The fault was entirely the Commander-in-Chief's as we were all obeying his signal.' 23 June 1893, Brackenbury Papers, BCK/13/136. For an analysis of the verdict, see J. R. Thursfield, 'The Loss of HMS Victoria', *The Naval Annual* (1894), pp. 168–71.


**646   U. KAY-SHUTTLEWORTH TO LORD SPENCER**

*28 July 1893; House of Commons*

Admiral Fisher[1] came to see me today, and proposed to circulate papers putting our Programme for the rest of this year and for 1894–5 on a new footing, by postponing both the big Cruisers, and beginning close upon 50 more Torpedo-boat Destroyers.

I at once advised him to see you before circulating any such new proposal, as after the announcement made by you in the Estimates and in Parliament, it would be for you to consider whether so sweeping a change of ship building policy should be mooted: it would obviously need much consideration from many points of view.

The idea seems to have grown out of Sir Frederick's[2] strong desire for a prompt and large increase of T. B. Destroyers, and has been worked out by Fisher with White.[3]

The D.N.I.[4] and I have just had a good interview with Mundella and Messrs. Firth.[5] Of this more when we meet.

[1] Rear-Admiral J. Arbuthnot Fisher, Junior Naval Lord and Controller.
[2] Admiral Sir Frederick Richards, Second Sea Lord. Succeeded Hoskins as First Sea Lord in Nov. 1893. It is clear that Richards was the dominant figure in pressing for a large shipbuilding programme, with Fisher as his right hand man. R. F. Mackay, *Fisher of Kilverstone* (1973), p. 209.
[3] William White, Director of Naval Construction, Admiralty.
[4] Rear-Admiral C. A. G. Bridge, Director of Naval Intelligence Admiralty. He was appointed by Spencer to command the Australian Station in autumn 1894. See his *Some Reminiscences* (1918), p. 307.
[5] Steel manufacturers and gun-forgers, Sheffield.


**647   LORD ROSEBERY TO LORD SPENCER**
*29 July 1893; Foreign Office*

*Secret*

You must I am afraid increase your Mediterranean strength. Bridge's information confirms much else that I have heard, and the present disposition and ethics of the French make anything possible.[1]

Please resolve this. We will talk it over whenever you like.

I would rather you weakened your Pacific and Channel Squadrons than failed to add strength in the Mediterranean.

[1] On 6 Aug. information was received in England that France had granted Russia's request for a squadron of ships to visit Toulon in Oct. and that some of them would remain permanently in the Mediterranean.


**648   LORD SPENCER TO C. S. ROUNDELL**
*14 August 1893; Admiralty, Whitehall*[1]

My idea[2] is to begin with a kind of review of the position of Ireland under existing regime, showing how out of all touch with the people the Irish Government is. Then review the chief measures passed within the last thirty years or so, their effect and why they have been played out. Touch on the aspect of the Irish question in Westminster, the instability of any one policy, the hopelessness of really meeting Irish views, the obstruction of all Parliamentary legislation, then deal with what we propose. State the conditions under which Home Rule is possible.

I should only dwell on leading principles of Bill. I should avoid allusions in an opening speech to obstruction and generally try and leave on record the reasons for the policy, and a clear exposition of the policy itself. Then I am more doubtful whether I should take some of the chief objections to it such as the oppression of Ulster and the minority, the fear of Home Rule, the fear of separation etc.

Let me have your criticism on the sketch, really the first attempt of a sketch I have made on paper and what your idea of such a speech should be.

I ought not to assume that the House will reject it but appeal to them as if I could persuade them. After speeches of out and out opposition have been made other speakers will appropriately deal with the results of rejection as they can deal with obstruction in the other House.[3]

[1] Copy, SP.

[2] Spencer was to move the second reading of the Home Rule Bill in the Lords on 5 Sept. See Hansard, 4, xvii, cols. 2-24. The Duke of Argyll afterwards congratulated Spencer. 'It was so dignified, so courteous, so candid! But, alas, in all this you do not represent the Government or its methods! In all this you seem to stand alone.' Argyll to Spencer, 6 Sept 1892, SP.

[3] Added later 'Alternative to Home Rule Local Government in England and Scotland.'

### 649   H. CAMPBELL-BANNERMAN[1] TO LORD SPENCER
*5 September 1893; House of Commons*

*Private*

Rosebery is pressing about the Joint Committee on Naval and Military Preparation[2] when the Russian Fleet comes into the Mediterranean.

[1] Secretary of State for War, 1892-5.

[2] A Royal Commission was appointed in 1888 under the chairmanship of Hartington to inquire into 'the civil and professional administration of the naval and military departments and their relations to each other and to the Treasury'. The report two years later recommended that a naval and military council should be created.

### 650   LORD SPENCER TO H. CAMPBELL-BANNERMAN
*17 September 1893; HMS* Enchantress, *Dartmouth*
CBP, Add. MS. 41228 f. 335

Rosebery spoke to me again, and asked whether any scheme was ready in case of War, Russia being joined to France. I sent for the Head of our Intelligence Department and find that such a scheme is on paper. It will probably need revision, but still there it exists, so that this may console him a little.[1]

[1] A joint meeting of Admiralty and War Office representatives was held on 29 Sept., but Spencer was absent on departmental business. Rosebery chaired a conference of the two services at Downing Street in Nov; both Campbell-Bannerman and Spencer attended.

### 651   LORD SPENCER TO LORD ROSEBERY
*3 October 1893; Admiralty, Whitehall*
RP, 10062 ff. 109-10

While on our tour I settled 2 important matters.

We have our powerful battleships and cruisers, but we have no protection for them when at anchor at home. Formerly they anchored at the Downs, Spithead, Portland and Plymouth Sound. No warships can do that now as all these places are exposed to sudden Torpedo attack. They must take refuge with Portsmouth and Hamoaze[1] at Devonport, and Portland if protected. Even Portsmouth and Devonport are now open to a bold officer in a Torpedo boat which skims harmlessly over mines.

I settled and ordered to be made a boom at Portsmouth which is movable and yet effective against Torpedoes and also a larger work at Portland which will protect a large fleet lying there. We shall probably do the same thing to protect the entrance of the Hamoaze harbour at Devonport and the Medway.

The French long ago have done all this at their ports, but we were absolutely unprotected. We go back at Portsmouth to what was done by Queen Elizabeth and are repeating what the Greeks did at Syracuse.[2]

[1] The estuary of the River Tamar, an extensive anchorage long used by the Royal Navy.

[2] In 413 B.C., an Athenian fleet anchored in the Great Harbour of Syracuse to lend support to the seige of the town. The defenders closed the entrance to the harbour by anchoring a medley of boats across it, leaving only a narrow gap secured by chains. In trying to force an exit, the Athenian fleet was utterly defeated. The event is described in Thucydides, *History of the Peloponnesian War*, Book vii, Ch. 59.


**652**   LORD SPENCER TO LADY SPENCER

*5 November 1893; Admiralty, Whitehall*

I have had my Royal interview, and I am bound to say that H.R.H.[1] was very courteous and said nothing nasty, indeed he could not have carried on a disagreeable conversation more pleasantly.

I am really sorry for him. I don't think it ever occurred to him that he would have to leave the Navy, and he is fond of his profession.

But Lawyers are clear and decisive that the 2 positions are incompatible with each other.

He cannot be an independent Sovereign Prince of a foreign country, and also an Admiral on the active list in this country.

What would happen in case of war with Germany? and it could not be left open until a war broke out for no one could have their officers ready to serve at one moment and not at another.

[1] Alfred, Duke of Edinburgh and Duke of Saxe-Coburg and Gotha, Admiral of the Fleet, second son of Queen Victoria and Prince Albert. On succeeding his father's brother in Aug. 1893 as Duke of Saxe-Coburg and Gotha, the questions were raised whether he could retain the privileges of an English peer, his naval rank, and his grant of £25,000 a year. On 23 Nov. 1893, an Order in Council settled that the Duke would surrender his seat in the Lords but could retain his position as Admiral of the Fleet. See Spencer to Gladstone, 9 Nov. 1893, GP, Add. MS. 44314 ff. 95-6. After much cabinet discussion, Gladstone announced on 21 Dec. that the Duke would be allowed to retain an annual grant of £10,000 given to him on his marriage.

**653   C. W. DILKE TO LORD SPENCER**
*17 November 1893; 76 Sloane Street, S.W.*

I had a hint yesterday (that the Naval Estimates are being prepared, and) that this was the only moment at which an expression of opinion could be useful. You very probably know my view that the Navy is at the present moment dangerously weak, and I speak with the same knowledge of Toulon that Laird Clowes[1] has lately obtained. Like all who know the present position of the French fleet I rate very high their force of material and men, the strategical efficiency of their admirals, the tactical efficiency of their captains, their artillery and new projectiles, their torpedo craft, and above all their rapidity of mobilisation. I wish I felt more sure than I do that even as against France alone we possess a sufficient superiority to have for certain the undisputed command of the seas.[2]

[1] W. Laird Clowes, naval writer, then a special correspondent of *The Times* in Toulon, in an article published on 31 Oct. compared the preparedness of the French warships at the base with the inadequacy of British naval forces in the Mediterranean. Clowes followed up this theme with four more articles in Nov., urging a new British naval programme.

[2] In his reply, Spencer, whilst agreeing with Dilke, expressed the hope that a debate on the Navy at that moment could be avoided as it might be harmful. Spencer to Dilke, 19 Nov. 1893, Dilke Papers, Add MS. 43891 f. 181.


**654   U. KAY-SHUTTLEWORTH TO LORD SPENCER**
*18 November 1893; Admiralty, Whitehall, S.W.*

*Confidential*

The difficulties of equalising New Construction charges (especially for armour) over the next 4 or 5 years are enormous. They must be faced.

In order that the Controller[1] and I may work out a scheme with this object it is necessary that we should know what programme for 1894–5 and what programme for 3 or 4 succeeding years you are prepared provisionally to approve.

Fisher asks 'could the Board meet and discuss programme say on Tuesday?' I think the Sea Lords will ask for the *Terrible* to be advanced, as well as 2 contract Battleships, early in 1894. About the latter nothing must ooze out till the Contracts for *Powerful* and *Terrible* have been let.

The idea of the Sea Lords (at least this is Fisher's rough impression) is a Programme of New Construction totting up to 22 millions. They wish to do this in 4 years. But I hope, if any such sum is entertained, that it may spread over five.

That would be an expenditure of £4,400,000 a year, or a trifle more than the average under Naval Defence Act[2] (the total of which was £21,500,000). These figures of course including armaments.

Fisher impresses on me that the above total of 22 millions is a 'pure shot' of his. But it is an indication, I think, of what will be pressed upon us.

[1] Fisher.
[2] See Introduction, p. 25.

### 655   W. V. HARCOURT TO LORD SPENCER
*9 December 1893; 11 Downing Street, Whitehall, S.W.*

You must allow me again to repeat what I have so often said, that I do not consider the Admiralty are acting fairly towards the country in allowing 'panic to be created with reference to the condition of our Naval Defences by false statements circulated by persons interested in getting up a scare without any official statement of the true facts of the case.[1] ... I cannot think it right that a responsible Govt. should allow the nation to be deliberately deceived as to its actual situation. This has become with me a very vital question and I can no longer consent to be a party to withholding from the public the true facts of the case.

[1] Spencer sent the latest information on the dates of launching, expected completion, displacement and speed of Russian and French ships some days earlier. Spencer to Harcourt, 2 Dec. 1893, HP, MS. 46.


### 656   LORD SPENCER TO W. V. HARCOURT
*10 December 1893; Admiralty, Whitehall*
HP, MS. 46

I do not know what you and Mr. Gladstone and the Cabinet will say to our programme which I admit is a very serious one and will I fear meet with your opposition. Until we know how we stand in regard to the future it would be very unwise to make a statement which would lay us open to all sorts of criticisms and attacks, which we could answer if we knew what we were to do in new ship construction manning and works in the next few years.

When the serious question is settled by the Cabinet it may be desirable to make an authoritative statement. I have been working very hard to get to the bottom of what we think necessary and I propose if possible to send round for the Cabinet a statement as to the position.[1]

I of course shall wish to meet your wishes as to how this is to be done, but I see no chance of doing as we did last year, viz. of coming to a mutual agreement, and indeed the circumstances of this year are such that I think it is due to the Cabinet to have some statement of the views of the Admiralty.

I fully realize the gravity of the position.

I do not know what your 'no longer consenting to be a party to withholding from the public the true facts of the case' means. It cannot I hope mean that independently of the Admiralty you are going to make or write a statement.

That of course would relieve me of any responsibility and I shall set to work to buy some horses and enjoy myself to the end of March.

[1] Kay-Shuttleworth reported to Spencer that he had spoken to Harcourt, who was 'inclined to be restive on one point—the necessity of an authoritative statement from *you* as to the satisfactory *present* relative strength of our Navy ... he began angrily by declaring that, if you do not make the statement, he will'. Kay-Shuttleworth to Spencer, 9 Dec. 1893, SP.

**657   W. V. HARCOURT TO LORD SPENCER**
*12 December 1893; 11 Downing Street, Whitehall, S.W.*

*Secret*

I received your letter on my return from Sandringham yesterday.[1] On one point I quite agree with you, and that is that the sooner the Cabinet make up their minds whether with the prospect of a deficiency of at least £3,000,000 in the coming year they propose to add largely to the Military and Naval Expenditure of the country the better.

This Government has thoroughly proved itself to be the most extravagant and reckless in its expenditure of any which has existed for many years and if it is resolved to be still more extravagant in the future the sooner it retires in my opinion the better ...

I took the Admiralty lists with me to Sandringham and at the Prince's desire showed them to him, the Duke of York and Hedworth Lambton,[2] a very ardent sailor. They seemed to me to be very well satisfied with the superiority of our present position as indeed would any man of common sense who was allowed to know the facts which are so studiously withheld.

What I intended to say in my letter was that when I speak to my constituents I shall tell them what appears to me to be truth. Of course if the Cabinet wish it I shall be ready, I might say I shall be very well pleased, to do so in a private and not an official capacity. Though I have no hunters I can always plant cabbages.[3]

[1] The Prince of Wales arrived at Sandringham on 5 Dec. and the Harcourts on 9 Dec.

[2] Capt. the Hon. Hedworth Lambton, Spencer's private secretary at the Admiralty.

[3] On receiving this letter, Spencer called on Harcourt to discuss the matter, but they came to no conclusion. Spencer told Lewis Harcourt that his admirals said to him, 'If there is any financial difficulty, why don't they cut off 3 or 4 regiments of the line?' LHJ, 12 Dec. 1893, HP, MS. 736 f. 433.

**658   SEA LORDS TO LORD SPENCER**
*20 December 1893; Admiralty, Whitehall*

At the last meeting held in the First Lord's room on November 22nd at which Sir William Harcourt was present, after discussing very fully the tabulated lists of British and Foreign Battle Ships, and the localization of the French and Russian Squadrons (particularly the latter) the First Naval Lord (Sir F. Richards) in clear and unmistakeable terms expressed his conviction, and that of his naval colleagues, that at least 7 Battleships of the First Class ought to be laid down in 1894. Even if this were done, the British strength in Battle Ships in the years 1896-97 would not be satisfactory, that is to say France and Russia combined would probably have a numerical superiority in those years.

Further Sir F. Richards urged most strongly the absolute necessity for creating a force of at least 80 Torpedo Boat Destroyers in the shortest possible time, and no matter at what cost. Apart from such a force he considered the English Channel untenable in view of the French Torpedo organization.

Attention was also directed to the unique requirements in Cruisers of the British Navy owing to the magnitude of our commerce and Colonies. The existing number of modern cruisers, although exceeding the total numbers of similar vessels possessed by France and Russia was undoubtedly insufficient and needed speedy increase.[1]

Having regard to the above statement of fact, it is not understood on what grounds Sir William Harcourt in the debate yesterday (December 19)[2] made the following statement, under which we are unable to rest.

'When we say that the existing condition of things with respect to the British Navy is satisfactory we ... speak the opinion of the responsible professional advisers of that Department (Admiralty). The Right Honorable gentleman talks of experts! Well, who are the experts if they are not the professional sailors who advise one Government and another?'[3] *Times* Newspaper.

> F. W. Richards
> Walter Kerr
> J. A. Fisher
> G. Noel

[1] The details were set out in a document entitled 'Memorandum of Meeting to discuss Programme of New Construction, April 1 1894 to April 1 1899, drawn up by the First Naval Lord, the Controller, and the Directors of Naval Intelligence and Naval Construction, 21 Nov. 1893, HP, MS. 183.

[2] In a naval debate in the Commons on 19 Dec. raised by Lord George Hamilton, the previous First Lord, introduced a motion urging 'that a considerable addition should at once be made to the Navy. This House, therefore, calls upon Her Majesty's Government to make before the Christmas recess a statement of their intentions in order that immediate action may be taken thereon.' Hansard, 4, xix, col. 1771. The motion was defeated by 240 votes to 204.

[3] Ibid, col. 1877. Spencer observed the debate and 'feared that his Admirals might kick at being so prominently quoted'. LHJ, 19 Dec. 1893, HP, MS. 736 ff. 436-7.

**659**   LORD SPENCER TO LORD ROSEBERY
*20 December 1893; Admiralty, Whitehall*
RP, 10062 ff. 130-1

*Secret*

I do not think that I can go as far as you do as to the Debate.[1]

I did not hear the bulk of Mr. G.'s Speech.[2] What I did hear, the end, I did not like. He fell into arguments which I implored him not to touch and I thought the key note of what he was saying was not in tune with the feeling of the House, or with the views which you and I hold about the future of the Navy.

I heard Harcourt, and I think his assurances as to the future were satisfactory, and I cannot regret his outburst as to the present strength of our battleships. Surely it is very wrong to show a weak front when we are really strong.

Of course this statement is open to the criticism which I made at the last Cabinet,[3] that a partial statement is misleading, and that we have weak points which cannot be hid from sight, and which are sure to be brought forward.

I do not think we shall get a Cabinet, or if we did could settle the matter at one meeting.

[1] Rosebery complained to Spencer after the debate on Hamilton's motion: 'What I deplore is that at the moment when a clear and decisive note should have been sounded in Europe, which

would have anticipated many evils and guaranteed peace, we had something, abominable perhaps from the point of view of House of Commons tactics, but ambiguous, obscure, and therefore disastrous. You do not seem to take in that what was wanted quite as much as new naval strength was the moral effect of a timely if general declaration.' Rosebery to Spencer, 20 Dec. 1893, SP.

[2] Hansard, 4, xix, col. 1790 ff. 19 Dec.

[3] 14 Dec. where it was settled to treat Hamilton's motion as a vote of want of confidence.

## 660   LORD SPENCER TO LADY SPENCER

*21 December 1893; Admiralty, Whitehall*[1]

You will be glad to hear that all ended well after some struggle and correspondence.[2] W. V. H. volunteered to make a statement in the House and to my joy my Admirals agreed to accept it . . .[3]

I have to go up Wednesday to try and settle Estimates with Harcourt, but I shall go up and down in a day.[4]

I shall have Greene down on Saturday as I must discuss the Estimates.

[1] Annotated by Spencer 'Important. 24.12.98'.

[2] See Spencer to Harcourt, 21 Dec. 1893, and L. Harcourt to W. V. Harcourt, 21 Dec. 1893, HP, MS. 46.

[3] Hansard, 4, xx, col. 112, 21 Dec. 1893. Campbell-Bannerman and Lewis Harcourt had earlier taken the draft statement to Spencer at the Admiralty for approval, who in turn showed it to Richards and the other Sea Lords. Spencer arrived at Downing Street with the paper at 3.30, just in time to reach Harcourt in the Commons after Questions. LHJ, 21 Dec. 1893, HP, MS. 735 f. 438.

[4] Edward Hamilton, then at the Treasury, discussed Budget prospects with Harcourt a few days later, in the light of probable demands. Hamilton admitted that naval estimates would need to be increased by about £3m. EHJ, 28 Dec. 1894, Add. MS. 48662 f. 28.

## 661   LORD SPENCER TO LORD ROSEBERY

*2 January 1894; Admiralty, Whitehall*
RP, 10062 ff. 132–3

I have heard nothing from the Chancellor of the Exchequer today. I sent to him first and to Mr. G. later the proof of my Memorandum[1] and know not the result.

I hear that one day the Chancellor of the Exchequer abuses me and the Admirals roundly, and I expect in highly improper terms when addressed to officials under me here, and next day is full of smiles arranging how to find the money.

I heard that Mr. G. was very cross over it yesterday,[2] but was also talking over ways and means.

I hope to circulate my Memorandum tomorrow. I hope it won't stagger you by its length. I do not think you need read the papers by White unless you are deeply interested in details of ships. The Appendix as to distribution of cruisers and Torpedo boat destroyers will be more your line.

. . . J. Morley is charming about my difficulties, but is circular as to whether he can swallow it all. However my impression is that he will.

[1] Spencer returned to Althorp for Christmas to draw up a memorandum for the cabinet of the first year's estimates for seven battleships, six second-class cruisers and small craft. W. Graham

Greene, his private secretary at the Admiralty, who was with his chief when the finishing touches were made to the memorandum in the early hours of New Years's Day, wrote later, 'The Memo. did not concede all that the Naval Lords wanted, but it went beyond what Mr. Gladstone could accept.' Greene Papers, GEE/13 (g).

² Gladstone, when he saw Spencer on 3 Jan., stated that he would resign rather than agree to the demands. LHJ, 6 Jan. 1894, HP, MS. 736 f. 445.

## 662 LORD SPENCER TO LADY SPENCER
*4 January 1894; Admiralty, Whitehall*

A quieter day.¹ I have overtaken my arrears of work, and I feel much fresher
. . .

I had a long talk with John Morley, very satisfactory and I hope things are mending with Mr. G. but I do not know. I fear the worst.

Evidently before the end of the year even if he is well, he will be out of Politics. The most we can hope is that he will give his blessing to the party on the eve of a General Election.

. . . I dine with A. West tonight² to meet Asquith and Acland.

¹ On the previous day, Spencer had written, 'A dreadful day, poor Mr. G. finds it very difficult to swallow the proposal. I do not know how it will end.' Spencer to Lady Spencer, 3 Jan. 1894, SP.

² West was taken by Herbert Henry Asquith, Home Secretary, 1892-5, to Spencer, 'who I found happier than last night, and in some hopes of reducing his first year's estimates, which we discussed'. West, p. 234.

## 663 J. MORLEY TO LORD SPENCER
*4 January 1894; House of Commons*

*Secret*

I had an hour and a half with Mr. G.—*not promising*. But he would like you and me to meet him tomorrow at *12* at Downing Street, to discuss one or two points. So will you come?

The maximum to which he would assent is the same addition for the first year as was made under the Defence Act; so at least, I understand. So be prepared with some answer as to this.

He is *extremely* angry with W.V.H.¹

¹ Harcourt by now took a more realistic view of the situation, believing that Spencer and Rosebery would resign if the estimates were rejected. P. Stansky, *Ambitions and Strategies* (1964), p. 25.

## 664 U. KAY-SHUTTLEWORTH TO LORD SPENCER
*8 January 1894; House of Commons*

Meeting at 5 in J. Morley's room (present J.M., C.B., Asquith, Acland and self.)

Morley asked whether increase over '93-4 Estimates could be reduced from 3 millions to 1 million, which would be 2⅜ million more than what have been called the 'Normal Estimates' of '88-9, or 1¼ million more than those of the first year of Naval Defence Act (1889-90).

The answer was in the paper which you and I signed today:— viz. that we could not see our way to a less increase than 3 millions on Total Estimates of '93-4.

They quite agreed with me that the fair comparison was with the Estimates of the 5 N.D. Act years, with 2 millions added to each year for N.D. Act Contract Ships and Armament, and a million for Imperial Defence Act Ships.

They prefer (Asquith especially) to include Armaments in all cases ...

But I promised that you should have with you for the Cabinet tomorrow a statement of how the New Construction demand for 1894-5 is made up, how much on liabilities under various heads (3 battleships, T. B. Gunboats, 32 + 10 T.B. Destroyers in hand and being ordered, *Powerful* and *Terrible*, other Cruisers and smaller ships,) and how much on ships of your Programme (i.e. 7 Battleships proposed.)

... I told them my personal views as to even distribution of expenditure over the 5 years, and gave them arguments, C.B. supporting me, and explained that it was only since I found from you that in high quarters so large a step up in the 1st year was not liked that I had abandoned my own preference for an increase of 3½ millions the 1st year and a more even distribution of burden over 5 years.

They saw that my plan would be less vulnerable in debate, and a better plan for meeting and defeating the cry for a Defence Act.

I have now told you pretty well all. I hope the talk did good and will help them to overpersuade our Chief tomorrow.


**665   J. MORLEY TO LORD SPENCER**
*9 January 1894; 95 Elm Park Gardens, South Kensington, S.W.*

*Secret*

Things were dreadfully black last night. He [Gladstone] kept me until 8, and it was then too late to come over to you.

He is to make a speech to the Cabinet[1]—not less than an hour, I should say, judging from notes which he showed me.

I feel it will be hard to discover a *modus vivendi*, for he now won't argue as to figures but only policy.

[1] At midday at 10 Downing Street, at which Gladstone 'harangued the cabinet for 50 minutes about his infirmity, inability to swallow Admiralty proposals, etc'. Only Shaw-Lefevre, First Commissioner of Works, supported him. EHJ, 9 Jan. 1894, Add. MS. 48662 f. 49.


**666   LORD SPENCER TO LADY SPENCER**
*9 January 1894; Admiralty, Whitehall*

Still in suspense. I hope it will be settled before Friday, but matters look bad.[1]

I have got on better here but even here things are not quite satisfactory[2] . . .

Mr. G. delightful in his manner towards me, and we have no rough words.

[1] According to West, Gladstone, nettled by Harcourt, said at the cabinet, 'Of course I can go if you wish it', but when asked by Rosebery to decide, refused to do so. West, pp. 236-7. Apparently Gladstone was surprised that his threat to resign had not quailed the cabinet.

[2] Spencer met the Board on the morning of the cabinet and asked for a postponement of a large increase on vote 8 (shipbuilding) until the next financial year. With great difficulty, the Board reduced the £4m. increase to £700,000. A.J. Marder, *The Anatomy of British Sea Power* (1940), p. 201, and Spencer to Rosebery, 14 Jan. 1894, RP, 10062 ff. 134-5.

## 667   LORD SPENCER TO W. E. GLADSTONE
*12 January 1894; Admiralty, Whitehall*
GP, Add. MS. 44314 f. 105

I write a line to say that I was unable to satisfy the Admirals with the provisional Estimate, and the permission to tender for a Battle Ship.[1]

I made it quite clear that both matters were provisional.

I hope you will have a good journey and pleasant stay at Biarritz.[2]

I feel very vexed that I should have been responsible for bringing before the Cabinet proposals to which I quite understood you objected strongly.

It was only what I considered the necessity of the case which made me do it.

[1] Spencer called on Gladstone on 11 Jan. but did not make any concessions, explaining that he had already reduced the admirals' estimates for the next year by £1m. On the following day, Spencer returned to find that Gladstone had withdrawn his assent, previously given to the Admiralty, to invite tenders for two new battleships and some torpedo boats. However, Spencer managed to extract an unwilling assent from Gladstone for the issue of these tenders. LHJ, 12 Jan. 1894, HP, MS. 736 f. 467.

[2] Gladstone left London for Biarritz on 13 Jan.

## 668   W. E. GLADSTONE TO LORD SPENCER
*12 January 1894; 10 Downing Street, Whitehall*

Secret

You were justly cautious and reserved when I raised the question yesterday whether I might not without inconsistency be a party at any rate to asking tenders for *one* Battleship. But (writing with imperfect information) I am under the impression that if the number of battleships to be laid down were largely reduced *all* would be executed in the Dockyards. I fear therefore that the 'one' would involve me in difficulty while it would not answer your purpose and *might* cause a misinterpretation of your intentions.

## 669   LORD SPENCER TO REAR-ADMIRAL H. F. STEPHENSON[1]
*14 January 1894; Admiralty, Whitehall*

We have been very much before the public. The Naval scare has caught hold of the Press and its readers. I regretted it for although I entirely assent to the necessity of maintaining and carrying out the policy of strengthening the Navy, a scare is apt to raise false issues and to set a certain number of people against treating the question with sobriety and common sense. I was all along ready to do what I think the Service and the Country wanted. After the way in which it was taken up, I am sorry to say, by my predecessor, we shall be in this position, that whatever we do will be claimed as the result of the scare, and our opponents will claim the credit for it while we had all the work and worry ...

As to foreign politics I do not myself fear a war. No doubt the French are excitable and were hysterical over the Russian alliance, but it may be urged that the very fact of their having found an ally will make them less sensitive and less irritable than they were when they felt the isolation of their position ...

I do not know what you would say to the policy to be pursued in war. It is not an uncommon thing to find it urged that we should not have a force at Esquimalt to thwart a possible Russian outbreak but should concentrate our forces in the China Seas, and deal with the Russians from that Station. It is not thought likely that the Russians if we are strong in China would come down to the Canadian port.

[1] Commander-in-Chief, Pacific.

### 670   LORD SPENCER TO LADY SPENCER
*30 January 1894; Admiralty, Whitehall*

I wrote yesterday to give up Hounds. It is a bitter thing to do as it is what I care most for as amusement in the world. But I dare not face the cost ... In '93 I spent £5,000 more than I received.[1]

We have diminished Household expenditure from £16,000 a year to which it rose in '81 to £9,000 but last year it rose to £12,000 or £11,500. We really did very little.

Furniture, flowers £118, all rose and there was a general rise. Eating and drinking were under £4,000.

I don't know what we are to do.

If we can keep Household this year to £9,000 and remain in office I shall have a surplus, something to pay off debt of last year. It makes me very unhappy after all the effort to meet the emergency Sale of Books, etc.

We shall have to keep every cost down this year very sharp.

If rents go up and I have not to make large reductions, we should of course be at comparative ease again, but I feel inclined to try and recoup what I have overspent.[2]

[1] Another reason advanced by Spencer for this decision was the likelihood of another general election, with its attendant cost, within a year. Spencer to C. R. Spencer, 6 Feb. 1894, SP.

[2] Spencer calculated that in 1893 he received about 50 to 55 per cent less net rent than in the period between 1870 and 1884. Spencer to Dufferin, 25 Feb. 1894, DP, D 1071 H/B/F.

**671   LORD SPENCER TO H. CAMPBELL-BANNERMAN**
*4 February 1894; Admiralty, Whitehall*
CBP, Add. MS. 41229 ff. 5–6

*Confidential*

We have had our turn of night work. I escaped as Kimberley, Ripon and Herschell were more than enough to cope with opponents, but I had to be ready, and the Bill[1] was a tough morsel to get up in addition to other work.

It is impossible to make out what is going to happen. A. West was most positive that nothing could be done, and that we should give up trying to induce him to remain and turn our efforts to his not remaining in the H. of C.; but since then, there has been inquiry and some request for information on details, and certain points urged seem to have produced impressions.

Recollecting a former announcement in the old *Pall Mall Gazette* I could not help wondering whether this too was a kite.[2] I suppose not, but I am not so sure. Considering that Mr. G. told his secret to over 16 persons 7 of whom were women it is a marvel that more has not got out. As it is I hear of Rustem Pasha[3] and others having asserted that Mr. G. was shortly going before the big type *PMG* affair. Next week we shall know the worst.

He was quite ready for a Cabinet this week, but we here, Rosebery, Kimberley, Ripon, Fowler[4] and I could not see the need of one, however much we may think more frequent Cabinets desirable, but under existing circumstances there was nothing of a new nature needing one. We are to have a Committee of the Parish Council amendments this week.

Possibly Monday week Mr. G. may want a Cabinet to settle what is done re Employers Liability, but Asquith had before to settle by himself what was to be done. This however is the final stage; possible compromise *or* loss of Bill has to be faced.[5]

---

[1] The second night of debate in the Lords on the committee stage of the Local Government (England and Wales) Bill. Monkswell, Ripon and Spencer met on 2 Feb. to consider the amendments. Ripon to Spencer, 30 Jan. 1894, SP.

[2] See No. **432**, n. 3.

[3] Turkish ambassador in London, 1885–95.

[4] President of the Local Government Board.

[5] The *Pall Mall Gazette* published the news of Gladstone's resignation on 31 Jan. West, from Biarritz, issued a statement of denial. *The Times*, 1 Feb. 1894, p. 3. Replying to Spencer's letter, Campbell-Bannerman's opinion was that 'however much he may wish to go, *he cannot do it*'. He argued that the estimates would take a longer time than usual to be approved in the Commons. Campbell-Bannerman to Spencer, 7 Feb. 1894, SP.

**672   J. MORLEY TO LORD SPENCER**
*9 February 1894; Chief Secretary's Office, Dublin Castle*

*Secret*

When I saw yesterday the letter to Marjoribanks, with the astounding new proposal,[1] I really felt as if all was indeed over. I telegraphed to Murray[2] that in my judgment it was more impossible than any other course whatever.

This morning brings me a letter from Mr. G., which shows that the idea is well lodged in his mind. It is really terrible.[3]

[1] Gladstone wrote to Edward Marjoribanks, the Chief Whip, on 5 Feb. claiming that the recent rejection or mutilation of important measures pointed to the need for a dissolution. West, pp. 269-70. On 11 Feb., Marjoribanks told Lewis Harcourt that 'Gladstone is still determined to have a dissolution if he can manage it'. LHJ, 11 Feb. 1894, HP, MS. 736 f. 501.
[2] George Herbert Murray, Gladstone's private secretary since 1892.
[3] Gladstone's plan was rejected by other members of the cabinet.

## 673   LORD SPENCER TO LADY SPENCER

*11 February 1894; Admiralty, Whitehall*

I was a bit drowsy this morning. I went to the Chapel Royal and went to sleep during part of a good sermon by the Bishop of Winchester (Thorold).[1] I dreamed that I viewed a fox over a ride and woke with a jump. I had a fear I might have given a view halloe but looking at my neighbour I hope I did not.

Mr. and Mrs. G. were there.[2] I walked home with them.

He rather low but talked about all sorts of things, except the crucial things.

We have a Cabinet tomorrow and a Committee at 11.

[1] Anthony Wilson Thorold, Bishop of Winchester, 1890-5.
[2] The Gladstones had arrived back from Biarritz on 9 Feb.

## 674   LORD ACTON[1] TO LADY SPENCER

*23 February 1894; Windsor Castle*

There has been leakage in so many quarters—Devonshire House, Churchill, Margot[2]—that it is high time the Queen should be informed. She has twice spoken to me about Mr. G.'s eyesight, of which she has no exact particulars, and I gave her none; but confirmed her misgivings generally. So that he would find his chosen ground prepared. So far, I can discover nothing else.

[1] Acton had been appointed as Lord-in-Waiting to the Queen by Gladstone in 1892.
[2] Margot Tennant, who married Asquith in May 1894, and a leading light in fashionable London society. She was greatly admired by Gladstone. D. Bennett, *Margot. A Life of the Countess of Oxford and Asquith* (1984), p. 39.

## 675   LORD SPENCER TO W. E. GLADSTONE

*23 February 1894; Admiralty, Whitehall*
GP, Add. MS. 44314 ff. 109-12

*Confidential*

I do not like to let the concluding words which you spoke at the Cabinet,[1] pass without writing a few lines to you.

I hesitated whether I should say anything at the moment, but I did not like to single myself out for the purpose of representing to you what I know to be the universal feeling of all your Colleagues.

We all have the deepest and sincerest sorrow that you are to cease to be our Chief.

We keenly feel what an irreparable loss you will be in Council, and we are convinced that no one can fill your place towards the party. [sic]

If we form a new Government it will lose the force and vigour which your Government possesses.

And I fear the cause of Irish Self-Government, which I and others have so much at heart, will suffer a grievous blow.

I have possibly more reason than anyone else to lament your decision, for I cannot conceal from myself that the Policy which I proposed for the Navy has had a marked influence in bringing you to the decision of resigning at this moment.

I most earnestly wish that I could have modified[2] my proposals, or given place to someone else whose views would have agreed with your own.

But I have been unable to recede from the proposals which I made and which I still think are right, and had I resigned I do not know that the majority of our colleagues would have adopted a Naval policy differing from that which it was my duty to submit to the Cabinet.

This position has been most painful to me for I owe my Political career entirely to you, and I have always and still do admire your Political principles and action and if I may be allowed to say so have a real affection and veneration for you personally.

I can never forget your invariable kindness to me, and I shall always cherish the recollection of the support and help which you so constantly have given to me, sometimes under very trying and difficult circumstances.

Even now I hope that I may not altogether forfeit the generous confidence which you at various times have placed in me, except of course on the unfortunate subject as to which I find myself now at such serious variance with you.

I hope you will not mind my writing this letter to you. It very imperfectly expresses what is in my mind, but I could not bear the idea that possibly silence today might be confounded with coolness or indifference towards you.

Please do not write a reply to this.

[1] At the cabinet that day, Gladstone made no definite announcement of his resignation, but stated that the time had come 'to end his co-operation with the members of the Cabinet'. Morley, *Recollections*, ii, p. 9. As this occurred at the end of the sitting when everyone was leaving, there was no chance of discussing the matter and Gladstone's words were received in silence. EHJ, 23 Feb. 1894, Add. MS. 48662 f. 128.

[2] In his draft letter, Spencer wrote 'modified or withdrawn'. SP.

### 676  W. E. GLADSTONE TO LORD SPENCER

*23 February 1894; 10 Downing Street, Whitehall*

*Secret*

While I gladly and thankfully receive your letter, let me assure you without reserve that I have all along felt assured that you entertained every kind warm and manly sentiment it expresses, though I am indeed aware that some of them are much beyond my desert. I beg you to believe that nothing which has happened, and nothing which can happen, will alter my estimate of your character, or reduce it by one jot or tittle from the high place which all who know you assign to it.

My convictions indeed on the policy which the Cabinet have adopted are very strong, so strong that no words can go beyond them. And so strong that it is to me a great solace, in such circumstances to reflect, that I do not deem it my duty to express them. On the contrary I deem it a very distinct duty to refrain from expressing them both at the present moment and in any circumstances I can now foresee as probable, though of course no one can in public affairs account for the unforeseen.

And I am most glad to believe that as between us personally everything will continue as before; and I wish you from the bottom of my heart a long happy and distinguished life in the service of your country, which has no son more worthy to serve it.[1]

[1] Gladstone had audiences with the Queen on 28 Feb., 2 and 3 March. On the latter occasion, his formal letter of resignation was accepted.

# 7

# THE ROSEBERY ADMINISTRATION, 1894-5

Spencer remained as First Lord when Rosebery became prime minister. Harcourt, who was disappointed at not gaining the premiership, became Leader of the Commons whilst Kimberley took Rosebery's place at the Foreign Office. The rivalry between Rosebery and Harcourt distracted the cabinet from the beginning, weakening its deliberations. Rosebery, for his part, was determined to supervise closely Kimberley's conduct of foreign affairs whilst Harcourt was equally determined that the authority of the Commons should not be diminished in this sphere. A further source of dispute was Harcourt's Budget of 1894. Part of it was to cover the cost of the extra ships included in the Spencer Programme, but the most contentious aspect was the introduction of graduated death duties. Rosebery feared that such a revolutionary tax would alienate the propertied class from the Liberal Party. Spencer, who was not opposed to the tax, attempted to act as conciliator in the matter.

A further source of friction within the cabinet was Rosebery's plan to attenuate the powers of the House of Lords. In July 1894, Spencer called on Harcourt upon hearing of rumours that he intended to resign. In September, Spencer, together with Morley, again pleaded with Harcourt to act more responsibly within the cabinet. The breach was not healed until the end of the government when, as Rosebery recorded, 'Harcourt came to see me spontaneously before dinner: the first time since I have been PM.' (Rosebery, Journal, 23 June 1895 f. 174). Spencer earlier had received equally churlish treatment. At the end of a cabinet meeting in November, Harcourt's son noted, 'W.V.H. asked Spencer as he was leaving what the Navy Estimates are to be for the next year and he replied "about £2,000,000 more than this year." W.V.H. said, "I will not be responsible for such estimates, so when you present them to the Cabinet you may present my resignation at the same time".' (LHJ, 9 Nov. 1894, HP, MS. 736 f. 837). However, the matter was satisfactorily settled in January 1895.

The Franco-Russian Alliance, signed at the beginning of 1894, aroused concern as to Britain's naval position. Spencer and his advisers were much preoccupied with the deployment of the Mediterranean and Far Eastern Fleets.

Disagreements between ministers on domestic and foreign policies increased in frequency. Spencer reported in November 1894, 'A very unpleasant Cabinet, the nearest approach to a stand up fight I have seen since Chamberlain's and Trevelyan's secession.' (Spencer to Lady Spencer, 21 Nov. 1894, SP). Abroad, Rosebery's African policy proved to be a failure, particularly in relation to the Congo and Uganda and the deterioration of Anglo-French relations. Further difficulties were presented by the Armenian massacres and the Nicaraguan incident in April 1895. At home, the results of by-elections held during 1894 demonstrated public dislike of Rosebery's policy; in the following year, more safe Liberal seats were lost. Rosebery's promise, in October 1894, that the next general election would be fought on the issue of the House of Lords, *appealed neither to the electorate nor to the cabinet. The chief bill for 1895, that for disestablishment in Wales, received only lukewarm support in the Commons.*

*The end of the government came in June 1895 when a Conservative motion for the reduction of the salary of Campbell-Bannerman, the War Secretary, for failing to supply the Army with sufficient cordite, was carried. At the cabinet on 22 June, Rosebery, Harcourt, Ripon and Tweedmouth favoured resignation rather than dissolution. In this they constituted a minority of the cabinet. Nevertheless, this view prevailed. Later the same day, the Queen invited Salisbury to form a government.*

---

**677**  LORD SPENCER
*8 March 1894*

### Memorandum

The Cabinet[1] approved of the proposals in regard to the Navy which I submitted in a Memorandum dated 1 Jan. 1894.[2]

This includes the minimum programme of the Naval Lords, subject to a reduction of 10 cruisers as recommended by me.

The question as to the number of cruisers may be raised after next year, and it is to this extent left open for future consideration.

The whole programme contained in the Memorandum is not to be announced at once.

In presenting this year's Estimates it would be stated that the proposals contained in them were part of a larger programme of ship-building which would be carried out in the next five years, and which had been agreed to by the Cabinet.[3]

It was understood that the Estimates for new construction would be larger next year and the following year than this year.

The proposals in the Memorandum included manning and victualling works and armaments.

The total net naval Estimates proposed amounted to £3,126,000 more than the Estimates of 1893/94.

[1] Rosebery's first cabinet, held at the Foreign Office on 8 March.

[2] 'Navy Estimates, 1894-95', Spencer, 13 Dec. 1893, SP. Reproduced in PRO CAB 37/34/59.

[3] Spencer wrote 'Omit' at the side of this paragraph. Rosebery had annotated in the margin, 'I am not quite sure if this was the exact agreement. But the point does not affect the orders you have to give.' Spencer added, 'I agree and omit the paragraph.' SP. See also Spencer to Rosebery, 8 March 1894, RP, 10062 f. 152. Both Spencer and Rosebery initialled the Memorandum on the same day, 8 March. Spencer left a record of the cabinet's decision on the programme of naval construction. Memorandum, 16 March 1894, SP.

**678**   LORD SPENCER TO W. E. GLADSTONE
*25 March 1894; Althorp, Northampton*
GP, Add. MS. 44314 ff. 113-15

I do not write to draw a letter from you, but merely to say that I was very sorry to miss you last week when you came up from Brighton[1]...

We have had a somewhat exciting beginning of Rosebery's premiership. His sentence about England in the House of Lords was very unfortunate,[2] and I really believe arose from his having recently spoken so little. It was not diplomatic. We have got over it well, and the unlucky division on Labouchere's motion in the House of Commons[3] may have a chastening effect on young Liberals who do not reckon the effect of their votes when in opposition to the Government which they support.

My own impression is that we shall not have a repetition of this incident. If we have I should be anxious as to the effect which it might produce on Rosebery who is extremely sensitive, and might throw down the cards. He was exceedingly good about the incident, humble without false humility and very considerate for Harcourt and the Members of the House of Commons.

We have Asquith here and Miss Margot. She has genuine admiration and respect for him, and well she may have these feelings, and he no doubt is warmly devoted to her. It will be a curious problem to put together for life two such natures, but I have little doubt that it will work out satisfactorily for their mutual happiness.[4]

I have a great liking for him, he ought to have a great political career before him. He is earnest, and acts under principle with plenty of backbone, and certainly has a great gift of expressing his views in public so as to make an impression on those who hear or read his Speeches.

[1] Gladstone was in London on 21 March to visit his eye specialist and to prepare the move from Downing Street.

[2] On 12 March in the debate on the Queen's Speech, Rosebery, in replying to Salisbury's taunts concerning home rule stated, 'The noble Marquess made one remark on the subject of Irish Home Rule with which I confess myself in entire accord. He said that before Irish Home Rule is conceded by the Imperial Parliament, England, as the predominant Member of the partnership of the Three Kingdoms, will have to be convinced of its justice and equity.' Hansard, 4, xxii, col. 32.

[3] Deploring the powers of the House of Lords. It was carried by 147 votes to 145. Hansard, 4, xxii, cols. 194-202, 13 March 1894.

[4] Spencer was unable to attend the wedding, which took place on 10 May 1894 at St. George's, Hanover Square, London, as he was on Admiralty inspection.


**679**   W. E. GLADSTONE TO LORD SPENCER
*27 March 1894; Brighton*

I think your start as a Government is good. The critical time will be when you have to find the money. The new plans have been received with a marvellous quietude, the quietude, in my mind, of death. I was glad however that you are spared present annoyance and labour. Kimberley will I think do well at the F.O. He has I trust no hankering after permanence or ceaseless prolongation in Egypt.[1]

[1] Kimberley's appointment to the Foreign Office on 11 March 1894 in succession to Rosebery had been supported by Spencer, who assured John Morley that Kimberley 'belonged to the old-fashioned school on foreign policy'. Morley complained some months later to Edward Hamilton that 'Lord Kimberley proved to be as malleable as clay in the hands of R., and R. was practically Foreign Secretary himself as well as Prime Minister'. EHJ, 5 Nov. 1894, Add. MS. 48665 f. 37.

### 680   LORD SPENCER TO W. V. HARCOURT
*22 April 1894; Admiralty*
HP, MS. 47

*Secret*

I do not pretend to be able to enter upon the arena myself, but I do not think that I could take the view put forward in Rosebery's papers.[1] Still, as he held them he was right to put them before you, and although it gave you trouble he paid you the compliment to bow to your judgment and views, by not desiring the argument to be laid before the Cabinet.

On the other hand you showed your wish to be moderate by modifying your graduation.[2]

Pray do not look on R. as your enemy. You two should have confidence in each other to work properly together. I do not think you have any solid ground for what you said in regard to him this morning to me.

[1] Harcourt's Budget speech on 16 April announced the abolition of probate, account and succession duties, to be replaced by a single duty entitled estate duty. Rosebery, who did not favour this change, became involved in an exchange of correspondence with Harcourt on the matter. For full details of the dispute see Gardiner, ii, pp. 280–9.
[2] In a memorandum to Rosebery written on 4 April, Harcourt agreed to mitigate the scale of graduation of death duties so far as exigencies of the Revenue would permit.

### 681   LADY SPENCER TO LORD SPENCER
*12 May 1894; Admiralty, Whitehall*

I hear the Duke of Devonshire[1] says that if the new death duty had been law when he succeeded he could never have lived at Chatsworth. I suppose when there are such magnificent collections of pictures, books and works of art, it will go very hard with the successors.

[1] Hartington became 8th Duke of Devonshire on his father's death on 21 Dec. 1891.

### 682   LORD SPENCER TO LADY SPENCER
*8 June 1894; Balmoral Castle*[1]

The Queen very gracious at dinner. I sat by her. She launched on Politics, was rather sorry Rosebery joked so much in his Speeches. I told her my view of the Academy Speech[2] but admitted that people thought it too jocose. She said 'Oh, Lord Salisbury joked and sometimes said unlucky things.' She said 'I think I shall say something to Lord R. He doesn't mind my saying anything to him.'[3] I said I thought he was quite aware of his inclination to joke and of course neither encouraged nor actually discouraged the idea.

[1] Spencer, as Minister in Attendance, arrived at Balmoral on 8 June.
[2] On 5 May. The Prince of Wales and other members of the Royal Family attended. For full report see *The Times*, 7 May 1894, p. 7.
[3] The Queen wrote that same day to Rosebery, 'Lord Rosebery is so clever that he may be carried away by a sense of humour, which is a little dangerous.' Crewe, ii, p. 457.

### 683    W. V. HARCOURT TO LORD SPENCER
*21 September 1894; Malwood, Lyndhurst*

*Confidential*
Loulou and I are off to Venice next Monday.

Politics are to me *tabula rasa*. I agree with you that the prospects of the Government are gloomy enough, but that is not my affair. You have made your own beds and you ought not to complain if you find them hard to lie upon. It is unreasonable that you should complain, but I accept with patience the part which you have assigned to me and that I do not desire to assume a lead for which I am judged unfit. It has always been my habit not to force myself where I am not wanted. If I have anything worth saying on political affairs it will be to those who trust me and not to those who have no regard for my opinion. As you say I joined the Ship but I have sailed *before* the *mast* and it is not for me to mount the *bridge*.

### 684    LORD SPENCER TO W. V. HARCOURT
*26 September 1894; North Creake, Fakenham*
HP, MS. 47

What you say on Politics is sad, and I hope your mood will change.

You embarked on the Ship and are too important to be anything but an active Leader of the Crew. How can you stand by when important questions have to be considered?

If something like cordiality cannot be established between you and Rosebery and others, it is a gloomy prospect which we have before us.

These are but my reflections not intended to draw you further.

### 685    LORD SPENCER TO LORD ROSEBERY
*1 October 1894; North Creake, Fakenham*
RP, 10062 ff. 173–4

*Private*
I went over to Kimberley on Friday, and we had a good many little things going on between F.O. and Admiralty. The Foreign Secretary was in one of his most talkative moods, and I felt really as if we had not had time to discuss Jap and China war,[1] Nicaragua,[2] etc.

K. will have written to you about orders to C. in C. China to be ready in case Japan wants to break engagement as to Shanghai. It is important that Fremantle should be prepared, but I hope the Japs exulted as they are will not be so silly as to try and break with us.[3]

The *Kowshing* affair is very ugly,[4] but of course we have not got Law Officers report; anyhow Japs seem inclined to do what is right.

The Portuguese quarrel and row at Delagoa Bay was referred to.[5] I know not what the quarrel between the Portuguese and natives is. We should I presume be careful to ascertain this before rushing in to help Portuguese, merely to keep Transvaal Boers out.

I told K. that we could help with Marines, but I trust we shall be able to be clear of the affair. These African fights are most disagreeable, lives lost and risks of failure with no honour gained.

... I wrote to ask the Chancellor of the Exchequer why he had come home so soon,[6] and made some general remarks on politics, and the prospect of speeches. I had a rollicking letter back, but no sign of cordiality in politics. They are a *tabula rasa* with him etc. etc. I made a stiff reference in return which got back a good tempered letter, but still harping on his being outside politics etc. I had no time to hear of his effusions to Kimberley.[7]

[1] Japan declared war on China on 1 Aug. 1894 after China had sent troops into Korea to suppress an uprising.

[2] Serious disturbances in the Mosquito reservation led to the landing of a party of British marines to protect lives and property there.

[3] The Chinese were defeated on land at P'yung-yang on 15 Sept.; at sea, the Battle of Yalu between the two fleets on 17 Sept., though not decisive, gave the Japanese supremacy at sea. Hulbert's *History of Korea* ed. C. N. Weems (1962), ii, pp. 256-61.

[4] On 25 July 1894, the *Kowshing*, a British steamship being used as a Chinese transport, was sunk off the west coast of Korea by Japan with a loss of 1500 lives. Spencer ordered Vice-Admiral Sir E. R. Fremantle to keep a watching brief over both navies. For Fremantle's assessment of the situation see 30 July 1894, PRO ADM 1 7199. 'I entirely share your views,' Spencer wrote, 'as to the anomalous position to which we are placed in the case of merchantmen under a flag being seized as European nations have ... The Law Officers opinion ... will leave heavy responsibility upon you and your officers, which we cannot relieve.' Spencer to Fremantle, 10 Oct. 1894, Fremantle Papers, FRE/141a.

[5] An inlet of the Indian Ocean on the south-east coast of Mozambique awarded by arbitration to Portugal in 1875. The Governor of Mozambique telegraphed to Lisbon on 29 Sept., warning that the natives intended to attack Delagoa Bay. Reinforcements of troops and artillery were sent on 28 Oct.

[6] Harcourt had returned from Switzerland because of the worsening situation in the Congo.

[7] See Harcourt to Kimberley, 12 Sept. 1894, in Gardiner, ii, pp. 321-2.

**686  J. MORLEY TO LORD SPENCER**
*26 October 1894; Chief Secretary's Office, Dublin Castle*

*Secret*

I won't attempt to cover all the ground of your epistle. We shall meet next week, and can then discuss everything. My suspicion is that we shall find ourselves in troubled waters pretty early. W.V.H. is almost sure to insist on a good place for the Liquor Bill.[1] You see what a strong line Caine[2] is taking. But how we are to squeeze it in, even if we agreed that it is the right Bill, I do not at all know. If W.V.H. wants to go, he'll find some way of going on that, and it would be a very awkward question for us who were left.

I had some talk with Mr. G. the other day at Hawarden on our friend. 'He won't go', said Mr. G., 'unless there is some crisis in the party, in which he can be sure of taking a section with him.' He can possibly make such a situation with the Temperance men. That seems to be a doubtful point. The Temperance men won't put us out, in order to put Brewers and Compensation in. Or at least they ought not.

I have just been reading Rosebery's speech at Sheffield.[3] I dare say it is not very well reported in the Irish papers, so I shall read it again. As it stands, I dislike the tone of it intensely, and I am perfectly sure that many men in our party will dislike it as much as I do.

You will remember the Sunday when the Government was made. I was converted by your argument that Kimberley would be a strong and independent Foreign Secretary. So I should have expected. But it is clear that we were mistaken. I don't think the F.O. can go on as it is, and if Harcourt chooses to take a strong line in this quarter, I shall be bound to go with him.

As for 'sweeping the country', I don't think there is any chance of it, not the smallest. My expectation is that the Tories will win, but by no great numbers. I don't see, however, why we should not weather next year, and all sorts of things may happen in the meanwhile. Our real difficulty will be to hold together among ourselves. Jingo speeches won't make that very easy.

In what shape we are to prevent Home Rule in a dissolution I am puzzled to know or to think. But I don't look beyond the session.

[1] Harcourt introduced a Liquor Traffic (Local Control) Bill in the Commons on 27 Feb. 1893. The Bill ran into much opposition and was withdrawn on 18 Sept. 1893.

[2] William Sproston Caine, Liberal M.P., Bradford East, 1892-5, author of *Local Option: A Handbook.*

[3] On 25 Oct. dealing with foreign policy, especially the Sino-Japanese war and Madagascar. *The Times,* 26 Oct. 1895, p. 10.


**687   LORD SPENCER TO LADY SPENCER**

*20 November 1894; Admiralty, Whitehall*

I went down with Rosebery and Kimberley to Windsor.[1] R. looked awfully fagged and lined, not having slept in the night's journey nor had he had any breakfast. K. had to stop to introduce the Belgian and Mexican Ministers at 3.

... So R. and I returned together and we had a great deal of talk. I am afraid that I did not ease his mind for he gathered that I did not like the House of Lords proceedings;[2] he said that he wished he could have had a Cabinet but Harcourt was away and he always had understood that a Resolution had been agreed to and talked about at Cabinets.[3]

He was very pleasant and easy to talk to.

[1] For a Council at 1.30 p.m.

[2] Rosebery's plan to seek a mandate to reduce drastically the powers of the Lords was put to the cabinet on 9 Nov. but no decision was taken. The cabinet of 26 Nov. signalled the failure of Rosebery's attempt to persuade his colleagues to support him.

[3] A meeting of the cabinet was held on the following day.

**688**   LORD SPENCER TO LADY SPENCER

*29 November 1894; Admiralty, Whitehall*

I got through my little Speech better than usual to a very small audience on Allotments.[1]

I think my audience approved, and I had a great compliment as to cottages and allotments on the Estate from one who had been inspecting for a Commission and got up and volunteered that the cottages and allotments of mine in Brixworth were a revelation to anyone who had not seen them and that the accommodation and arrangements in many of the cottages on my Estate would satisfy the needs of Middle Class families.

I hope we are getting on well here as to Estimates. I am in better heart.[2]

[1] At the annual meeting of Allotments and Small Holdings Association at the National Liberal Club on 29 Nov. Spencer's speech was reported in *The Times*, 30 Nov. 1894, p. 11.

[2] According to Lewis Harcourt his father and Spencer were 'having a battle royal again about Naval Estimates for next year. Lord Spencer threatens a further increase of two millions, but Harcourt insists that the increase must depend on the amount of revenue which he can spare the Admiralty.' EHJ, 28 Nov. 1894, Add. MS. 48665 f. 69. A cabinet committee, consisting of Campbell-Bannerman, Fowler, Harcourt, Spencer and Ripon, was set up on 28 Nov. to examine the naval estimates.


**689**   W. V. HARCOURT TO LORD SPENCER

*10 December 1894; Malwood, Lyndhurst*

The conceptions of the members of this Government of their obligations in respect of public business are perfectly new.

In all former Governments with which I have been acquainted it was considered to be the business of the heads of departments to be continuously available in London from the beginning of November till the meeting of Parliament with an interval of a week or two at Xmas.

Now it seems quite enough for each to say it is not convenient for him to come to town as he has married a wife or bought a yoke of oxen or wants to go on the stump – all excellent things in their way, but which ought not to stand in the light of more important business. In the late Government as you know they had a Standing Committee of the Cabinet sitting *en permanence* on naval affairs consisting of the Prime Minister, the Chancellor of the Exchequer, the First Lords of the Treasury and Admiralty and Secretary for War in order to consult upon an expenditure not near as great as ours.[1]

However after all it does not much signify for there is no prospect of our surviving to lay the Navy Estimates upon the table.

[1] The naval committee of the cabinet had been fixed for 11 Dec. but two of its members, Campbell-Bannerman and Fowler, had sent their apologies for absence on 7 Dec., SP. Spencer subsequently informed Harcourt that the meeting would have to be postponed until 14 Dec. Spencer to W. V. Harcourt, 8 Dec. 1894, HP, MS. 47.

### 690 LORD SPENCER TO H. CAMPBELL-BANNERMAN
*19 December 1894; Admiralty, Whitehall*
CBP, Add. MS. 41229 ff. 44-5

We had a most characteristic sitting at the Chancellor of the Exchequer's last Friday,[1] no one there but Ripon[2] and myself.

We had 1 hr. ¾ by the clock solely and exclusively on the table of relative strength of the navies of this country, France and Russia. I scarcely differed from his figures, and he could not upset the tables, but he insisted on going through each Class of things nation by nation and then the same process with Great Britain and France and Russia.

I got so weary that I could hardly follow him at last, and poor Ripon barely kept awake.

When he had done this he complained I had furnished no Estimate, and it then appeared that he had never read my table of Estimates etc. at all.

This brought him up, and he admitted his error.

He was in good humour all the time.

He ended by asking me what the addition to the construction would be. I said 1 million and a quarter, and he said he thought he could give me that, and also volunteered that as he had some surplus the Estimates of next year might be relieved by a Supplementary Vote in February or March of 200,000£ or 300,000£. So I think all this is hopeful.[3]

I fancy his surplus this year will be very large: more than he chose to admit that day.

[1] Spencer had written to his wife from Bedford that morning, 'I go up to London for Harcourt's Committee which I dread.' Spencer to Lady Spencer, 14 Dec. 1894, SP. For an account of the naval committee of the cabinet on 14 Dec, see LHJ, 15 Dec. 1894, HP, MS. 737 f. 886.

[2] Colonial Secretary, 1892-5.

[3] At the cabinet on 10 Jan. 1895, Harcourt undertook to place an additional £1½ m. at Spencer's disposal.


### 691 LORD SPENCER TO W. V. HARCOURT
*23 December 1894; Althorp, Northampton*
HP, MS. 47

I send you my Publican's profit, very poor.[1] I have lately had £33 instead of £16 profit beyond my salary to the Manager. So beer has not been drunk so extensively in my rural Northamptonshire as you seem to have had it drunk in the United Kingdom.

I hear however that Phipps Brewery Co. have had a roaring trade. They have declared a dividend of 15 per cent, have given their manager £1,000 in addition to his ordinary salary of £2,000, and they say have had a profit of nearly 25 per cent ...

I am glad to have roused the ire of the Tory or Liberal Unionist Russells by my Bedford Speech.[2] G. Russell[3] pretends to be shocked. I told him that I thought it was an excellent sign that the younger Liberal Unionists do not like to be engrossed among the Tories.

[1] At Chapel Brampton in 1882, Spencer had tried the experiment of placing a manager at a fixed salary in the only public house in the village, the *Spencer Arms*. The net profit for 1894 was £16 2s. 6d. whereas the previous year, was £33 11s. 2d. See Spencer's own account of the experiment in *Short Report and Statement of Accounts for the 'Spencer Arms' Inn*, 20 June 1897.

[2] On 13 Dec. in support of S. Howard Whitbread, candidate for the borough. Spencer claimed, 'The Government believed that the disparity of opinion between the two Houses was not temporary but an increasing one, and they were determined to make a change, if possible, and put an end to it.' *The Times*, 14 Dec. 1894, p. 11.

[3] George William Erskine Russell, Radical M.P., Aylesbury, 1880-5, N. Bedfordshire, 1892-5. Under-Secretary of State, Home Department, 1894-5. Russell gave the opening speech at the Bedford meeting.

## 692 LORD SPENCER TO ADMIRAL SIR M. CULME-SEYMOUR[1]

*7 March 1895; Admiralty, Whitehall*[2]

Estimates just out. I have told them to send you at once my statement. We shall have an enormous lot of ships building. You will see that this year, we are going on with Cruisers and torpedo boat destroyers. Probably the Works are the most prominent feature in the Estimates ... Gibraltar is being pushed on, the Mole prolonged.

[1] Commander-in-Chief, Mediterranean.
[2] Copy, SP.

## 693 LADY SPENCER'S DIARY

*26 March 1895*

Dinner at Lord and Lady Breadalbane's.[1]

Mr. Gladstone said across the table to Sir F. Lockwood, Solicitor General, that he considered Lord Beaconsfield the most remarkable character in the History of the House of Commons. For a long time he had thought Mr. Pitt was but he had come to the conclusion that Dizzy was the most extraordinary character. I asked him what he thought of Lord Beaconsfield and he answered that it had been his unhappy fate to have to propose that a grant should be given for a monument to Disraeli, and that he hoped he had got out of his difficulties without saying anything that was not the truth in his favour, and by suppressing truth this would have undone the object of the monument for which he was speaking. He said that he considered Lord Beaconsfield's career had been fatal to the true interests of the *Country*.

He said the one thing that had been confirmed in his opinion during his long Parliamentary life was the danger of men with a certain amount of talent imagining that by making themselves prominent, by speaking against their friends, and gaining a cheap popularity with their enemies, mistaking the cheers as a proof of success and fancying themselves of importance, where in reality they remained nobodies. He said that would be the advice he would give a young man and avoid all this danger. He gave Mr. Fawcett[2] as an instance increased by his blindness, for hearing only the cheers that greeted his utterances, he fancied he had the support of all and imagined himself to be of the greatest importance.

He said Bob Lowe[3] also shared in this mistake, that at one time (the Reform Bill of '67) he stood very high in the House of Commons. He said he was admirable in attack, but no use at all in defence.

I asked him about the Speakership and he said he did not wish to make mischief and therefore did not like to give his opinion, but he was very glad that Mr. Courtney was not the Speaker.[4]

[1] Gavin Campbell, 1st Marquess of Breadalbane, Lord Steward of the Household, 1892-5.

[2] Henry Fawcett, Liberal M.P., Hackney, 1874-84, Postmaster-General from 1880 until his death in Nov. 1884.

[3] Robert Lowe, Liberal M.P., Kidderminster, 1852-9, Calne, 1859-68, and London University, 1868-80. Chancellor of the Exchequer, 1868-73, and Home Secretary, 1873-4. Created Viscount Sherbrooke, 1880.

[4] Leonard Courtney, Liberal Unionist, M.P., Bodmin, 1885-1900, and a formidable opponent of home rule. After Courtney twice refused the Speakership on the retirement of Arthur Peel, William Gully, Liberal M.P., Carlisle, was appointed in April, 1895. See G. P. Gooch, *Life of Lord Courtney* (1920), pp. 316-28.

**694**　LORD SPENCER TO ADMIRAL SIR M. CULME-SEYMOUR
*3 April 1895; Nice*[1]

Last night the Queen had Admiral Gervais[2] from Toulouse to dinner to meet me. What a fine fellow he seems. He must have been very young in the Crimea. He was very pleasant and cordial. I alluded to the little cloud and said that I thought it only required a little sun to clear it up, and he said reasonable men ought never to have difficulty in allaying misunderstandings, in which I heartily agreed, and added that he must know how many of us in England only wished to be on the best of terms with France.

... My own impression is that whatever policy we adopt, in case of war we shall always keep Malta as one of the most essential bases of our operations. Gibraltar is, of course, of the greatest importance also and the deficiencies there for war of the present day are so glaring that we must press on the works for a closed harbour for our fleet and some dock accommodation.

[1] Copy, SP.

[2] Admiral Alfred Gervais, French Commander-in-Chief.

**695**　LORD SPENCER TO W. E. GLADSTONE
*29 April 1895; Admiralty, Whitehall*
GP, Add. MS. 44314 f. 120

In Politics we rub on in Parliament with varying majorities. Our defeat has been prophesied by the Leader of the H. of C.[1] for many a month, but we begin to distrust the Prophet in these utterances.

We do not on other topics find ourselves in smooth waters, but I see little prospect of any change, and we shall jog on as we are until the Session is drawing to a close. Rosebery is decidedly better, but we see very little of him.[2]

I often wish I had a chance of a good talk with you. Possibly before the summer is old I may have an opportunity of meeting you.

[1] Harcourt.

[2] Rosebery, who was in a poor physical condition, had suffered a severe bout of influenza. He remained at The Durdans during the whole of April.

## 696   LORD SPENCER TO LADY SPENCER
*30 April 1895; Admiralty, Whitehall*

We have a Cabinet on Thursday. We did very well last night. The Whips up to a short time before the Division thought that we should only win by 2, but Tories and Parnellites were away, up to 27 of the former so Bobby says, and this gave us the majority.[1]

We did very well on the Naval Estimates.[2] Robertson[3] made an admirable speech. Forwood was very offensive to the Admiralty,[4] and Lord George[5] did not dissociate himself from him.

[1] On sending the Chelsea Water Bill to a Select Committee. Ayes, 163, Noes, 129.

[2] Committee of Supply on Navy Estimates 1895-6. Hansard, 4, xxxiii, cols. 70-111, 29 April 1895.

[3] Edmund Robertson, Liberal M.P., Dundee, 1885-1908, Civil Lord of the Admiralty. Ibid., col. 99 ff.

[4] Arthur Bower Forwood, Conservative M.P., Ormskirk division, Lancs., 1885-98, a former Financial Secretary to the Admiralty, who unsuccessfully moved to reduce the vote on account of the Admiralty's failure to supply sufficient and efficient boilers. Ibid., col. 70 ff.

[5] Hamilton. Ibid., cols. 107-11.

## 697   LORD SPENCER TO LADY SPENCER
*2 May 1895; Admiralty, Whitehall*

Rather a stormy Cabinet but all passed off well.[1] The Nicaraguan business was settled by the intervention of a neighbouring State.[2] I was very glad of it as I was not clear how we should get our Ships away.

W. V. H. was very cross about this, and at one moment got up to walk away, but he came back. He was brewing his Budget Speech.

I wrote to Mr. G. about our trees and the Gale, but I have not heard from him.[3]

[1] The cabinet had met earlier that day.

[2] In April 1895, an outcry had followed the expulsion of the British vice-consul from Nicaragua. A demand for £15,500 was made to settle the matter but the Nicaraguans urged that the matter be put to arbitration. Kimberley, backed by Rosebery, refused this request though Harcourt favoured this solution. On 18 April, Spencer ordered Rear-Admiral H. F. Stephenson to proceed with warships to land at, and occupy, Corinto. Stephenson to Spencer, 18 April 1895, SP. Forces landed on 27 April and re-embarked on 4 May. For an account of the occupation, see PRO ADM 1 7252. On 5 May, the Minister of Salvador in London conveyed Nicaragua's agreement to pay the indemnity on the evacuation of the British from Corinto.

[3] Gladstone expressed his sorrow at the loss of many fine trees at Althorp on the following day. Gladstone to Spencer, 3 May 1895, SP.

**698   W. E. GLADSTONE TO LORD SPENCER**
*3 May 1895; Hawarden Castle, Chester*

Perhaps you will be prompted by your desire for a conversation to come and see [me]: and of course not to come *singular*, though to a tranquil house and I fear a dull abode. I see little likelihood of my moving southwards though my wife might be tempted to a short run.

You may depend in any case on my speaking, if you invite it, with great openness. To do otherwise would manifest a want of appreciation of your character, such as would be inexcusable after my long and happy experience. I am afraid I am not wholly at peace with present tendencies. As to expenditure you are aware that I fall back upon the dead, for I think all the living mad. Never did a human being have such a timely cataract for the avoidance of scandals. There is some flavour in the Welsh Bill that is rather too sharp for my taste.[1]

I suppose there is nothing in the attempt to make out of Harcourt's words last night an epitaph upon himself or upon Rosebery or upon the Government.[2]

[1] The Established Church (Wales) Bill was introduced in the Commons by Asquith on 25 Feb. 1895. It proposed that from Jan. 1897, the Church of England in Wales should cease to be an Established Church. The Bill was at the committee stage when the government fell in June. Spencer had rightly forecast Gladstone's attitude to the legislation: 'I expect he will be up and rather strong against parts of the Welsh Bill.' Spencer to Lady Spencer, 2 May 1895, SP.

[2] Towards the end of the Budget debate on 2 May, warning M.P.s against increasing national expenditure, Harcourt startled the House by saying, 'It may be, and probably will be, the last occasion on which, from a responsible position, I shall be able to address these words in the House of Commons, or to the country.' Hansard, 4, xxxiii, cols. 363. However, Spencer pointed out that 'We have had so many threats of resignation and defeat from the same quarter that we do not take serious alarm.' Spencer to Gladstone, 4 May 1895, GP, Add. MS. 44314 f. 121.

**699   C. S. ROUNDELL TO LORD SPENCER**
*5 May 1895; 16 Curzon Street, May Fair*

The political future, or rather the future of politics, is one I look forward to with some want of heart. Mr. G. marks the close of a political era. It will be not only new men, but new ways of looking at things, which will mean unsettlement of men's minds, and an uneasy and troubled fermenting of ideas until they take new shape.

Things point to a reconstruction of parties, and to an entirely new view of things. Land, Church, Parliament, the relations of labour, our whole social system seems to me to be in the crucible.

**700   LORD SPENCER TO LORD ROSEBERY**
*10 May 1895; Admiralty, Whitehall*
RP, 10062 f. 207-8

If the *Enchantress* is not ready on Monday, the *Fire Queen* will be, at least so they tell me here. If neither are available you will receive a telegram tomorrow.[1]

I shall have to be here on Monday morning, but the yacht will be ready for you any time you like to go on board. I expect that I shall get down about 5.45, and we can go out to sea at once or have our dinner and go out later.

Do not expect a very excellent cook. Our Maltese *cordon bleu* is decent but no more than that can be said.

[1] Rosebery was Spencer's guest on the Admiralty yacht *Enchantress* from 13 to 20 May. 'R. is in very good spirits but is rather feeble,' Spencer wrote to his wife on 14 May 1895, SP. Starting from Portsmouth, the yacht called at Cowes, Plymouth, the Scilly Isles, Milford Haven and Dartmouth, then returning to Portsmouth.

## 701  LORD SPENCER TO LADY SPENCER
*22 June 1895; Admiralty, Whitehall*

*Secret*

Two long Cabinets.[1] Much difference of opinion, agreement that we must either Dissolve or resign: because the vote last night was only the indication of the growing weakness of Government.[2]

At first 11 (of whom I was one) were in favour of dissolution and 4 against, but Rosebery and Harcourt were among the four.[3] After long discussion a good many of the 11 altered their opinion or modified it. I did not[4] but still could not under the extreme difficulty resent Rosebery recommending resignation.

He and Harcourt very strong for it, but as others came round Harcourt seemed to modify his view.

R. has gone to Windsor. He seemed to wish me to be here tomorrow so I stay.

I need not say how secret this is. Perhaps the Queen will jib at our resignation as she wants us in to settle the Duke of Cambridge business.[5]

C. Bannerman resigned but Rosebery refused to submit his resignation in face of decision of Cabinet.[6]

P.S. I dine with Asquith.

[1] One in the morning at 11 and at 1.15, the second adjourned until 4. Rosebery, Journal, 22 June 1895, f. 173.

[2] In a debate in the Commons on 21 June, William St. John Brodrick, Conservative M.P., Guildford, 1885-1906, moved for a reduction in the salary of the Secretary of State for War, Campbell-Bannerman, on the grounds that the supply of cordite for the army was insufficient. The Government Whips were deceived by an apparently thin House, and the motion was carried by 132 votes to 125. Hansard, xxxiv, cols. 1690-1, 21 June.

[3] The other two were Ripon and Tweedmouth.

[4] Spencer listed the arguments for dissolution and resignation in a brief note, presumably at one of the two cabinets. He concluded 'Favour Dissolution'. Memorandum, n.d., but 22 June 1895, SP.

[5] Campbell-Bannerman had announced in the Commons on 21 June that the Duke of Cambridge, Commander-in-Chief of the Army for 39 years, had resigned. Pressure on the Duke from the Queen and Campbell-Bannerman had to be brought to bear. J. Wilson, *C.B.* (1973), pp. 190-201. The cabinet met on 24 June and decided that the government should dissolve.

[6] Campbell-Bannerman had sent in his resignation the previous evening but the cabinet agreed that he could not resign alone: either they all resigned with him or dissolved. LHJ, 22 June 1895; HP, MS. 737 f. 1170-1.

### 702 LORD SPENCER TO LORD ROSEBERY
*2 July 1895; Admiralty, Whitehall*
RP, 10062 ff. 209-10

Still in office.[1]

Queen's pleasure not yet received and so no patent prepared.

I have however conceded my official room, but by Goschen's leave[2] remain in the Admiralty until Thursday morning, when I go off to speak for T. A. Brassey at Bournemouth.[3]

I saw Mrs. Labby yesterday about a meeting of the Midland Liberal Federation at Althorp on Saturday. I told her that I knew that Labby and I differed especially as to my political leader etc. She said 'Oh I always have pitched battles with him about Lord Rosebery - I am all in favour of Lord R.'!!

[1] Spencer had earlier written to his wife 'Dreadfully busy. Dissolution on Monday.' Spencer to Lady Spencer, 2 July 1895, SP.

[2] George Goschen, the new First Lord, received the seals of office on 29 June. The first cabinet meeting of Salisbury's new government was held at the Foreign Office on 2 July.

[3] Brassey was candidate for Christchurch, Hampshire. Spencer, in his speech, told the audience that the bills rejected by the Lords would remain at the forefront of the Liberal programme, together with the Welsh Bill, Local Option and one man one vote. *The Times*, 5 July 1895, p. 6.

### 703 U. KAY-SHUTTLEWORTH TO LORD SPENCER
*5 July 1895; 28 Princes Gardens, S.W.*

Harcourt drew me aside in the House of Commons Lobby yesterday and talked very gravely about the Cordite business.

He had got some exaggerated or erroneous impressions, which I did my best to remove, though he kept (*more suo*) asserting that they were facts stated to him *by you* ...

Harcourt evidently thinks we are all in for a great attack on the subject from the new Government. He became most pleasant and friendly at the end of the talk, discussed the coming election, and the absurdity of despair, also the line to take, asked after my health, wished me luck, and said Good-bye *most cordially*!!

If you wish it I will write to him a few facts ... You may like however to tell him of *your* action on April 2 and 14 May as well as of the letter to the War Office of 3 July.[1]

[1] Spencer had approved of 'emphatic letters' to the War Office in April, May and July on the quantity and quality of cordite supplied. Spencer to W. V. Harcourt, 7 July 1895, SP (copy).

### 704 REAR-ADMIRAL SIR J. A. FISHER TO LORD SPENCER
*5 July 1895; 18 Somerset Street, Portman Square, W.*

I did not say to you what I wished yesterday as I was afraid of my feelings being too much for me because my regret and sorrow is really very great at parting company with you. I beg you not to trouble to answer this but I am desirous of expressing to you how very deeply I feel all the great kindness and confidence you have shown towards me.[1] I am confident you will live in the annals of the Navy as amongst the best and greatest of First Lords and it was no joke when I said there ought to be another 'Spencer Monument'.[2] I sincerely hope I may yet be able to serve under you again.

[1] Spencer recommended Fisher for a K.C.B. in May 1894. On receiving the Queen's approval Spencer wrote 'It is always a great pleasure to me to have you in so important a position to work with.' Spencer to Fisher, 20 May 1894, Fisher Papers, FISR 1/1. He also named one of his horses after the admiral.

[2] A monument to Spencer's uncle, Capt. Sir Robert Cavendish Spencer, (1791-1830), had been erected on Corradino Hill at the edge of the cliffs overlooking the Grand Harbour at Valletta, Malta. It was removed in 1893 to a spot between Valletta and Citta Vecchia. Vice-Admiral Sir G. Tryon to Spencer, 23 Feb. 1893, SP.

# 8

# LIBERALS IN SEARCH OF LEADERSHIP, 1895-8

*At the 1895 general election the Liberals suffered a heavy defeat, the Unionists being returned with a majority of 152. Relations between Rosebery and Harcourt further deteriorated after the latter's provocative suggestion in August 1895 that the Lords and Commons should meet at Spencer House to hear the Queen's Speech and decide on Liberal policy. Spencer acted as intermediary to patch up the affair. Rosebery's decision to resign as Leader of the party was announced in October 1896. Spencer condemned the move, which Rosebery claimed was motivated by Gladstone's attitude to the Armenian massacres in Turkey. 'Sooner or later this unfortunate state of affairs [between Harcourt and Rosebery] must have brought about a scandal,' Spencer wrote to Gladstone, 'at the same time the occasion and way of evading the difficulty seem to me unfortunate.' (Spencer to Gladstone, 11 Oct. 1896, GP, Add. MS. 44314 f. 126). Kimberley, who had briefly led the Liberals in the Lords after Granville's death, now resumed the post.*

*Harcourt, Leader of the party in the Commons, conscious of Rosebery's active political presence and aware that the party was rent by disputes, resigned two years later. Spencer, on being informed of Harcourt's move, admitted, 'I have been groaning in spirit over the folly of the Liberals who have been demanding the immediate settlement of the question of the Leadership of the Party. I have done what I could to stop the movement.' (Spencer to Harcourt, 13 Dec. 1898, HP, MS. 48). Morley also withdrew from the counsels of the Liberal Party. Now only four leading members of the party's Commons' front bench remained; one of them, Campbell-Bannerman, took Harcourt's place.*

---

**705** C. R. SPENCER TO LORD SPENCER
*19 July 1895; Dallington House, Northampton*

I feel that my defeat[1] will be a trial to you, after all that you have done for the County and your tenants. Local Veto[2] did it entirely and the wave of reaction that has swept away so many of our friends. I know that you will feel it keenly, the first time one of our family has been beaten.

... The County polled on the whole for me, but the Town against. The Socialists wrote things on the voting papers to disqualify their votes. A rest will be pleasant, though I wish that it had not come in this way. 282 was the majority against me so there has been a turn over of seven hundred votes nearly.

---

[1] In the Mid Northamptonshire election declared on 18 July, Robert Spencer polled 4802 votes and his Conservative opponent, James Pender, 5084 votes. *NM*, 19 July 1895, p. 8.

[2] Harcourt had declared in a speech at Derby on 5 July that Local Option was one of the main

issues of the election. Against the advice of his party managers, Harcourt had introduced a bill dealing with the subject on 8 April 1895. As C. C. Becke remarked on its effect, 'in rural constituencies, if you have a popular cry against you, a great risk is run'. C. C. Becke to Lord Spencer, 19 July 1895, SP.

## 706   LORD SPENCER TO C. R. SPENCER
*19 July 1895; Homburg*

I cannot tell you how sorry I am for you and Margaret in particular, for the cause and I must also confess for ourselves altogether.

But in the general rout I feared the worst, but did not I confess expect it after all you had reported.

But it is no use conjecturing the cause. In other places it is clear that the Church and the breweries have done the mischief.

I confess I trembled for you when I saw what a huge poll the Socialists and I.L.P.[1] candidates had at Northampton.[2] Such things as that frightens many moderate men who do not weigh properly the effect of special votes, nor can they see the greater need to rally to sound Liberals.

It is no use saying what we shall do. We must weigh every thing.

[1] The Independent Labour Party, founded in 1893.
[2] The results were declared on 16 July: Henry Labouchere 4884 and C. G. A. Drucker (Conservative) 3820 were elected. The unsuccessful candidates were Edward Harford (Radical and Labour), 3707, Jacob Jacobs (Conservative), 3394, F. G. Jones (Socialist), 1216 and J. M. Robertson (Independent Radical), 1131. *NM*, 19 July 1895, p. 6.

## 707   LORD SPENCER TO LADY SPENCER
*13 August 1895; Spencer House, St. James's Place, S.W.*

*Very Secret*

I am in a peck of troubles ... A crisis has occurred.

Rosebery wrote when I told him of the proposal that Lords and Commons Front Benchers should meet,[1] that he could not again co-operate with Harcourt, and by the same post sent a copy of this letter to Harcourt.

So I had to see Harcourt and discuss the position.

We settled that under the circumstances the H. of C. Front Bench should meet alone, and not here but at Bryce's.

H. was very quiet over it, but I expect a storm will come on. He means to disregard the letter altogether, and for the moment I encouraged that idea.

Nothing crucial could be done unless at all events other H. of C. colleagues met together.

It is very unpleasant, and I am sorry to be in the thick of it.

R. need not have taken this step on my letter. He could have said either let each House meet separately, or meet together but I shall be kept in Scotland and would not be present.

[1] Harcourt, as Leader of the party in the Commons, requested Spencer to call a meeting of front bench members to discuss the Queen's Speech which was to be presented on 15 Aug. Harcourt to

Spencer, 6 Aug. 1895, SP. Two days later, Harcourt provocatively suggested that a meeting of ex-cabinet members should be held at Spencer House on 14 Aug. Rosebery had not been consulted by Harcourt on these moves. See Stansky, pp. 180–93.

## 708   LORD SPENCER
*16 August 1895; Althorp, Northampton*

### Memorandum

The letters from Lord Rosebery of the 12 & 13 August were not answered by letter.[1] On the 13 I sent him a Telegram to the effect that the H. of C. ex colleagues would meet on Wednesday at Mr. Bryce's and not at Spencer House and without any Lords.

I saw him on Wednesday morning.

What occurred was that Sir Wm. Harcourt met me on 13 Aug. at Spencer House at 11.30 not having yet received Ld. Rosebery's letter.

I gave him the original to read and we then settled about the separate meeting of ex colleagues.

He declared that Lord Rosebery's letter meant that either he or Lord R. were to retire from the Liberal party, and that he (Harcourt) had no intention of retirement.

Ld. Rosebery admitted that such an interpretation would naturally be placed on the letter.

It was subsequently settled that the tone of Lord Rosebery's letter of Aug 13 sh: be adopted, and that only ex Cab. colleagues should be told of the Ultimatum for the present.[2]

Sir Wm. Harcourt at first said that he would take no notice of Lord Rosebery's communication.

He called it to me a damned piece of impertinence the only bitter words used by him in the 3 or 4 interviews I had with him.

Subsequently he wrote a short note to Lord Rosebery expressing the surprise and pain with which he had received the letter.

Kimberley (informed by letter by me) Ripon, Tweedmouth, Asquith were told what had occurred by me and Bryce was told by Rosebery.

R. and H. did not meet but I negotiated generally the sort of line to be taken in the Address debate.

Harcourt assumed the air of absolute ignorance that any serious disagreement had existed between him and R.

Personal differences he deprecated as far as they interfered with Political action. In old days as in case of Canning and Castlereagh these ended in a duel. The letter would have had this effect and he might have been shot in the buttocks!!

[1] Rosebery wrote two letters to Spencer on 12 Aug., and 'a supplementary line' the following day. SP.

[2] Spencer also saw Rosebery and Harcourt again on 14 Aug. and consulted with Ripon and Tweedmouth. Spencer to Lady Spencer, 14 Aug. 1895, SP.

**709   LORD SPENCER TO C. R. SPENCER**
*20 December 1895; Bombay*[1]

... We return here and then finally leave for Ahmadebad, Jaypore, Delhi, Agra, Lucknow, Cawnpore, Benares, reaching Calcutta about the 24th. Jan. We make an expedition from there to see the Himalayas, and on our return start off for Ceylon; we stay there about a week and then go to Singapore, Hongkong, Shanghai and Japan. We hope to stay a week in Japan and then take Canadian Pacific for Vancouver and after seeing Niagara and the Aberdeens[2] come straight home. A tremendous round. If the rest is half as pleasant as the first month has been, we shall be amply repaid.

What a nasty state Foreign affairs are in. The U.S. President very impertinent and bumptious,[3] and the East in a state of general turmoil.

Things will settle down in America, I feel sure. If they don't we shall have to alter our plans, as Charlotte will not like being chased by a Yankee cruiser and if taken shut up in 'Frisco or Cincinnati.

[1] The Spencers left London on 25 Oct., arriving at Bombay on 17 Nov.
[2] Governor-General, Canada, 1893–8.
[3] On 17 Dec. President Cleveland delivered his famous message to Congress concerning the Venezuela boundary dispute.

**710   J. MORLEY TO LORD SPENCER**
*13 February 1896; The Athenaeum, Pall Mall, S.W.*

*Confidential*

The difficulties between two high personages have been in a fashion got over for the opening of the session: that is to say, they did not meet for formal interchange of views, but the discreet Asquith was intermediary. R. had a gathering at Mentmore on Sunday before Parliament met, most of the late Cabinet, except Harcourt and me, who are of no particular consequence. Lady Fanny[1] had an evening party, and R. insisted on making his way up to W. V. H., and shaking his hand with much *empressement*. The party looked on, and held its breath. I am not sure that the great man did not regard it as 'd – d impertinence'.

[1] Tweedmouth's wife and Randolph Churchill's sister, whose London home was Brook House, Park Lane. Edward Marjoribanks had succeeded as Lord Tweedmouth in 1894.

**711   LORD SPENCER TO H. SEYMOUR**
*12 March 1896; Government House, Hong Kong*

You ask my impressions on the East, but to give these is a big order for we have seen a mighty deal and have learned a great deal, too much I fear to retain in one's mind. I wish I had come out years ago, the knowledge to be got would have been most interesting to oneself if not useful in a Public way ...

I saw a good deal of the ways of Government when with Sandhurst,[1] and I was struck with the ability and devotion of the Indian Civil Service. As a rule they govern for the people of India as well as for the British. This is in broad contrast to the view of the British civilian in India and I regret to say to that of the Military, who talk as if every Indian interest must bow to the Britisher, and the native only exists to minister to his wealth, pleasure and convenience. There are doubtless exceptions but that is the ordinary tone of these circles especially among the young men ... It is very wrong, for we cannot forget that we have seized the natives' country and are governing it for them.

[1] Governor of Bombay, 1895-1900. See S. Gopal, *British Policy in India 1858-1905* (1965), p. 203.

### 712 LORD SPENCER TO C. R. SPENCER
*27 April 1896; RMS.* Empress of China, *at sea off Alaska.*

What ages since we heard of Europe and America or Africa! We left Japan on the 17th. April ...

We do our 354 or 330 knots a day and tomorrow we are to land at Victoria.[1] I go to see Esquimalt which Hedworth[2] and the *Warspite* used as Headquarters, and Charlotte will go on and wait for me at Vancouver.

Then we have 2900 miles by rail to Ottawa. This we look forward to as the Rockies give scenery of wonderful splendour. The Aberdeens put us up and after a visit to them and to Niagara we shall go to New York where we hope to see Cecil Baring.[3] We do not yet know the day of departure from New York but the 24 May ought to be the latest.

How glad we shall be to be home again!! but we have enjoyed our travels immensely; Japan is delightful, lovely scenery at places with wonderful Parks of trees such as we never see. Then the people are wonders of energy, and ability, swilling wholesale the newest of our ideas of Government and civilization. They are ahead of us in many ways, some very odd ways.

We were fêted at Tokio where we stayed with our Minister Sir E. S.[4] a delightful man. We were very comfortable, and had every variety of dinner and amusement. The Emperor was ill and could not see me, but we had a State audience with the Empress, a dear dignified little woman ...[5] The Palace was fine, many very beautiful Japanese things in it.

[1] Capital of British Columbia.
[2] Capt. Hedworth Lambton.
[3] Director, Baring Brothers. His sister, Margaret, had married Robert Spencer on 25 July 1887.
[4] Sir Ernest Mason Satow, minister in Tokyo, 1895-1900, and a distinguished Japanese linguist. See B. M. Allen, *Sir Ernest Satow* (1933), pp. 102-10.
[5] For a full description of the visit to the palace, which took place on 13 April, see Lady Spencer, Diary, 13 April 1896, SP.

### 713 C. S. ROUNDELL TO LORD SPENCER
*23 May 1896; Northern Counties Hotel, Portrush*

You will find everything, politically, as different from what it was when you went away, as if a generation had passed - not only in the showing of the hand, or rather the cloven hoof, of the Tory Government, but in our relations towards the Nationalist Party, and in our foreign relations, and warlike undertakings.

**714   LORD SPENCER TO C. R. SPENCER**
*12 October 1896; North Creake, Fakenham*

*Confidential*

The weather is very stormy and trying, nearly as bad as the Political atmosphere. I am vexed and annoyed beyond words at what has occurred. I knew that some day or another Rosebery would escape his more prudent colleagues, and take some step to create a crisis by himself. I little thought he would have selected the present moment for this.[1]

I think that a man in his position ought not to act precipitately, and I am afraid that what he calls the last straw namely difference with Mr. G. will put R. in a bad position.

The fact is the present difficulties could easily have been overcome. There is no serious difference of principle between R., Mr. G. or anyone of his late colleagues as far as the Eastern question is concerned, but the old standing difference with W. V. H. is at the bottom of it all. I at one time hoped that might have been overcome but it is hopeless to reconcile R. with H. and therefore one of the two must go to the wall. I fear that R. will be that one for he has played into H.'s hands.

All this is very annoying. What the next step can be I know not. My impression is that H. must lead, but I know nothing of what passed at Edinburgh[2] with the considerable band of old colleagues who were there.

[1] Rosebery's letter to T. E. Ellis, Chief Liberal Whip, announcing his decision to resign as Leader of the Party, because of differences of opinion with Gladstone and the majority of Liberals on the Eastern Question, was published on 8 Oct.

[2] At a rally under the auspices of the Scottish Liberal Association on 9 Oct., Rosebery gave public support to the Government's attitude towards Turkey. *The Times*, 10 Oct. 1896, p. 6.

**715   LORD SPENCER TO LORD ACTON**
*16 January 1897; Althorp, Northampton*
Acton Papers, Add. 8119/1/s168

As far as I know everything will be straight sailing on Monday.

We shall elect Kimberley as our Leader, and very little else will be said or done.[1]

[1] Kimberley was elected as Leader of the Opposition in the Lords at a meeting held at Spencer House on 18 Jan. EHJ, 19 Jan. 1897, Add. MS. 48670 ff. 103-4.

**716   LORD SPENCER**
*21 November 1897; Hawarden Castle*

*Notes of the conversation with Mr Gladstone*[1]

*Secret*

I think some of our party have made a great mistake in deciding that no member of the House of Lords should become Prime Minister.

In a matter of this sort you want and ought to have Elbow room and plenty of it, and this idea limits the party and prevents the necessary Elbow room being kept.

I am very glad to hear you are going on the Stump.

I hear that Rosebery and Harcourt are both likely to be making Political Speeches soon, which will be taken as rival speeches for the Leadership.

I think that it is very important that a third person should at this moment be before the Public, and I am glad that you are going to be on the Stump as you are the only third person who can be thought of.

It will distract attention from the rival claims of the other two.

I said that Morley and Asquith had been speaking. He said 'Yes, but their speeches are over and Morley will never do for the Leader.'

I then said that I regretted that Kimberley would not speak. He said 'Oh K., admirable though he is has never risen beyond Departmental success in Politics and the management of the House of Lords which he does so very well. Kimberley too is over 70.'

He then mentioned Ripon as a man of good ability and excellent in every way but he would be no use for this purpose.

He expressed his deep regret or sorrow at differing so seriously with me on a fundamental principle viz, the expenditure on the Navy.

He deplored this, and he said the Tories will add to your expenditure etc. Nothing had made him alter his views on this.

Then he said he deplored this Imperialism.[2]

I asked him whether he was not surprised at Chamberlain's attitude on this. He said not in the least ...

He said he had for the last 3 months been struggling for existence, nothing seriously wrong, but such pain and discomfort preventing his work.

He said 'You must take me as I am, unfit to see anyone, as I am broken down in health.'

One thing he said as to Ireland.

'The first time I had any serious conversation with Lady Londonderry,[3] she asked me "What was it made you take up Home Rule at the particular moment you did?" I said "I very easily can answer that, it was because on the first occasion when they could declare themselves, the Irish by such overwhelming numbers at the Polls had declared in favour of it." '

He denounced Redmond and said he was tempted to say that his conduct deserved a rope round his neck.

He was bitterly disappointed with Healy of whom he thought better things. He heard that the line he had taken was forced on him by the inadequate action as Leader of Dillon.[4]

### 2nd conversation with Mr. G. on Sunday 21 Nov '97

I was rather reluctant to see him again, for after my first talk I feared that it was a painful exertion to him to converse with any one.

However after luncheon Mr. G. said he wished to see me again, and I was to go in 30 or 45 minutes. After about 40 I went in and found him placidly but fast asleep. Twice or thrice I went in with the same result, and a servant rattled coal and coal ash about and told me that Mr. G. was still asleep.

I remained in the Drawing room or Library, but about 4.30 he came through his door and went out into the garden and walked about with a shawl up to his mouth.

It was thought better that I should not try a visit until after 5 o'clock Tea.

He came to tea and was very pleasant.

We were speaking of what men felt when they were to speak.

I said to him 'I suppose you never disliked the thought of a Speech?'

'Yes sometimes before it came off, but I am bound to say that in the H. of C. when an opportunity arose in debate and I threw in a sharp debating speech, I enjoyed it very much.'

I asked him 'Did you ever fall asleep in the House?'

'Oh yes and very pleasantly before I had to reply.'

'But did you then rely on what your colleagues told you?'

'Oh' he said, 'I used to recollect some things and guessed what otherwise my opponent would have said.'

He recollected when the Speaker as he left the House for Tea pointed at Lord Palmerston reclining but no one rose to object. It was found that Pam had fallen asleep.

He said that he had trained himself never to think of business after he had laid down in bed. Once when forming the 1880 Government he woke with every kind of change of men and offices. He rose, went to his study, wrote down his ideas, and returned to bed to sleep at once.

Mrs. Drew[5] said that he had not slept after the Phoenix Park murders, but had written a poem for Lady Frederick.[6] This she added to 2 instances Mr. G. had told me of formerly (1) when the Belgian guarantee in the Franco-German war was in question (2) when some difficulty as to Mr. Bright existed.

After Tea I went to his room and he talked for nearly an hour.

He began 'You began public life at a very early age.' I said 'Well yes' but I was unluckily only a few months in the H. of C. We then spoke of my first real work the Cattle Plague Commission to which Lord Palmerston appointed me just before his death.[7]

'Ah' he said 'how old we then said Lord Palmerston was to be in office and yet I have been in office and was 8 years older than he ever was!'

I said 'Well Mr. G. I am within a year or so now of the age when you retired in 1875.'

'Yes' he said 'and I fully intended to retire. I took no part as a Leader for a long time. To show you this I will tell you how when G. Trevelyan brought up some motion on County Franchise, I went up to support him from here and on my reaching the House the official Liberals through the Whips begged me not to take any part in the debate.[8] I acquiesced and returned though thoroughly disgusted to Hawarden. It was only the Eastern question which brought me out.'

We discussed men – U. Shuttleworth, Trevelyan, Forster, Hartington, Rosebery, Harcourt.

He said that he had had 4 Cabinets, and that he had had from 60 to 70 colleagues in these Cabinets. He considered far the worst colleagues were Rosebery and Harcourt, and next Forster and Hartington.

To Harcourt and Rosebery he did not attribute any dishonourable action, far from it. They were most honourable men. They were of great ability but they gave him infinite trouble.

He said that Harcourt was a warm-hearted man with many merits but he never would forget what he called 'the blubbering Cabinet'.[9]

Rosebery was a man of immense ability but he never could prove to himself that Rosebery had any common sense in Politics.

He did not consider he had all the qualities necessary for Prime Minister.

He dreaded his Imperialism to which he attributed his unfortunate action as to Uganda, also his jingoism with which he was partly imbued.

He gave him infinite trouble as Foreign Minister although he admitted that he Mr. G. had pressed him to become Foreign Minister, not realizing his Imperialism, as to which John Morley had been mistaken for it was between John Morley and Rosebery that much had passed as to Rosebery's foreign policy.

He never knew his position in regard to himself as Prime Minister although he heard when Rosebery was Prime Minister he had stood much between Kimberley and Foreign Ambassadors.

He alluded with some warmth to Rosebery's views on Mr. G.'s interview with Waddington.[10]

He referred to our resignation. He heard when on board the *Tantallon Castle* of the defeat of the Government and neither he nor any one on board dreamed of same occurring. On reaching the Thames on the Monday forenoon some one told him of the resignation and he said it was a hoax.[11]

We ought at once to have got the H. of C 'to rescind' the resolution, laying stress as he said Peel would have put it on the last syllable. If we did not do that it would have been better to have Dissolved before resignation.

It was as it seemed to him a fatal mistake. This arose from reference to Campbell-Bannerman and the Speakership which he said H. C-B. had, even [if] we had been a Moribund Government, a right to insist on.

He had a very high opinion of Asquith's speaking but said he had never shown breadth of General Statesmanship. I argued this but he seemed piqued at Asquith's speech at Edinburgh[12] after Rosebery's and would take no excuse for it.

I said something as to my wish at times to fall out of Politics and work at County Council and other matters but I said his example always kept me in the Political career. 'Ah' he said 'you have more obligation to do this than I had for you must remain in the H. of Lords.'

He said 'You know I did not name anyone as my Successor to the Queen. I was prepared to do so but she never asked me. H. Ponsonby asked who I should name but I told him I could answer that question to no one but the Queen herself.'[13]

He had told me once before that he was prepared to name me . . .

Hartington was a difficult colleague but in some respects a good one.

He said he would never have been a Liberal had it not been for his allegiance to family traditions.

Mr. G. was much better than in the morning.

He however said that a life 'of fluctuation', that I think was his expression, was not possible for him. He had always done so much to do nothing and be able to do nothing was hateful to him.

He spoke in the keenest way of the degradation of the country in Eastern Europe.[14] He deplored having lived to see it. Lord Salisbury 'was not true', I almost think he said, 'was a coward in Politics.'

He scorned the idea that we should have invoked war if we had used force alone.

We were bound by our Cyprus Convention[15] to act for the Armenians.

He was not surprised at Chamberlain's action.[16]

He feared that possibly Rosebery's Imperialism might lead him to break the principle of Free trade.

In speaking of my continuing in Politics, he said 'It was only yesterday that J. Morley spoke of the high standing which you had in the country. No one at all in the present Political world came up to it for this.' I hesitate to repeat this but for those after me I do so.

He said 'It will take years to counteract the poison introduced into the country in Politics by Lord Beaconsfield.'

I recalled when I first went to Windsor in 1868. 'My friend G. Wellesley, Dean of Windsor[17] told me "You will find some difference in the Queen." I did not find this, she was then open, candid and frank, impartial, unprejudiced. The change came later, it took Dizzy time to work it.'

He spoke of G. Balfour as a real friend of Ireland.[18] As to the other Balfour Arthur he always detested his administration as Irish Secretary ...

He considered his last Cabinet too large, he was pressed and could not resist the introduction of several men.

It was the worst Cabinet of all his four, it never worked well as a Cabinet, the essential foundation of a Cabinet being that all its members should throw their minds in a common stock, and work not for an individual idea but for a common cause.

His Cabinets were best in order of their formation.

He was astonished to hear that lately Hartington[19] a usually moderate man had said that it would be necessary to strengthen the army as we had had to strengthen the Navy which had been done to maintain our Supremacy but he did not use the word superiority at sea. This expression was most offensive to other powers.

I said that I had not noticed it, I did not say that I expected I had been guilty of the same expression.

---

[1] The envelope containing these notes was marked *Very Secret* by Spencer. On it, he wrote, 'Original notes kept by me of probably the last and certainly the fullest conversation I ever had with Mr. Gladstone at Hawarden on 21 Nov. 1897, part 1 before luncheon. Spencer, 26 April 1903.'

[2] Three days after this interview, Edward Hamilton called on the Gladstones, who were passing through London. Denouncing 'the spirit of Jingoism under the name of Imperialism,' Gladstone added, 'It was Lord Spencer with his naval programme who had begun it.' EHJ, 24 Nov. 1897, Add. MS. 48672 f. 57.

[3] Theresa Helen, whose husband Charles Stewart, 6th Marquess of Londonderry, was Lord-Lieutenant of Ireland, 1886-9.

[4] Justin McCarthy, leader of the Anti-Parnellite Party, announced his resignation on 3 Feb. 1896.

Dillon was elected in his place. Healy, with Redmond's support, established in Jan. 1897 a People's Rights Association dedicated to preserving the liberty of constituencies. Some parts of the programme, particularly the right of constituences to a free choice of candidates and payment of their members and changes in the system of electing the party chairman, were diametrically opposed to Dillon's views. Divisions within the party followed. F. S. L. Lyons, *The Irish Parliamentary Party 1890-1910* (1961), pp. 61-7.

   [5] Mary Drew, Gladstone's third daughter.

   [6] A copy of the poem, headed 'May 6 1882', is in GP, Add. MS. 44766 ff. 93-5. See also L. Masterman (ed.), *Mary Gladstone. Her Diaries and Letters* (1930), p. 249.

   [7] See No. **39**.

   [8] On 7 July 1875 Trevelyan proposed that the Household Franchise (Counties) Bill should be read a second time. The motion was defeated, 268 votes to 166. Hansard, 3, ccxxv, cols. 1094-1108.

   [9] Lewis Harcourt, quoting Rosebery on Gladstone's last cabinet (1 March 1894), wrote of the occasion, 'Gladstone was obviously disgusted ... [and] always referred to this Cabinet as "the blubbering Cabinet".' LHJ, 28 Feb. 1894, HP, MS. 737, ff.580-1.

   [10] William Henry Waddington, French ambassador in London from 1883, concerned at the deteriorating relations between Britain and France since Rosebery's appointment as Foreign Secretary, approached Gladstone direct at the beginning of Nov. 1892 without Rosebery's knowledge to discuss Egypt. On hearing of the interview, Rosebery instructed Dufferin to complain to the French government and Waddington was recalled from London in June 1893. James, p. 273.

   [11] In June 1895, Gladstone was a guest in one of Sir Donald Currie's ships visiting Hamburg, the recently-opened Kiel Canal and Copenhagen. Charles Cooper, editor of the *Scotsman*, who was with Gladstone, recorded the reaction to telegrams received on 22 June telling of the government's defeat. 'All the rest of the day there was uneasiness among the Ministerial section of our party. They could not talk of anything but the defeat.' C. A. Cooper, *An Editor's Retrospect* (1896), pp. 394-5.

   [12] Supporting Rosebery's views on the Eastern Question at the meeting held on 9 Oct. 1896.

   [13] See Ponsonby to Queen Victoria, 3 March 1894. *LQV*, 3rd ser., ii, p. 369.

   [14] Lady Frederick Cavendish told Roundell after a visit to Hawarden in Sept., 'I think I never saw him as miserable as he is over the "disgraceful humiliation" over the Greek and Turkey business.' C. S. Roundell to Spencer, 22 Sept. 1897, SP.

   [15] Signed in Constantinople, 4 June 1878, with the Ottoman Empire.

   [16] During a visit to the United States in autumn 1896, Chamberlain's plan for co-operation between England and America to stop the Armenian massacres was well received by Richard Olney, President Cleveland's Secretary of State, Garvin, iii, pp. 165-8.

   [17] Gerald Valerian Wellesley, Dean of Windsor, 1854-82.

   [18] Gerald Balfour, Chief Secretary for Ireland, 1895-1900.

   [19] Devonshire was chairman of the Defence Committee of the Cabinet, 1895-1902.

## 717   C. R. SPENCER TO LORD SPENCER
*8 June 1898; 143 Piccadilly, W.*

Have been very much pressed to stand[1] and I made 2 stipulations one that you should not have to find the whole money, the other that Becke & Co agreed.

Gilbey[2] out of love for you has come down most handsomely £500, his partners have also sent promise of 300, the Central Office gives 400 and 200 is to be got from 2 Liberals in the Division. 1500 is the limit, so I hope if I stand not to cost you much if anything.[3]

The undesirable man has been got rid of who would have split the party. Honestly I don't think there is much chance, but it was hard to resist all the Office. The meeting at Hertford tonight is to consider the question of candidates and I am to be approached tomorrow.

Went to see Harcourt who was most cordial and much pleased at the idea of bearding the Cecils in their own den.[4] The people in the H. of C. had had an inkling of it, and had been more than nice so Causton[5] told me.

The majority in '92 was over 1,400. Now a new register of which 6,000 have not voted. I hope I have not done too foolishly to consider it, but when the offer came for party's sake I confess I panted to fight, knowing the hopelessness of it all the time.

[1] By the East Hertfordshire Liberal Association to contest the by-election caused by the death of Abel Smith, the Conservative member for Hertfordshire intermittently from 1854 and for East Herts. since 1885.

[2] H. W. Gilbey, president of the Association.

[3] Robert Spencer wrote to Tom Ellis, the Liberal Chief Whip, 'I am rather ashamed of taking so much money from your attenuated party purse but it was unavoidable, as I will explain later.' C. R. Spencer to T. E. Ellis, 12 June 1898, Ellis Papers, 1955.

[4] His opponent was the Hon. Evelyn Cecil, grandson of 2nd Marquess of Salisbury and the 3rd Marquess's assistant private secretary, 1891-2 and 1895-1902. Hatfield House lies some eight miles west of Hertford.

[5] Richard Causton, Liberal M.P., Southwark West, 1888-1910, and a Whip. His father-in-law, Sir Thomas Chambers, had been member for Hertford, 1852-7.


## 718   C. R. SPENCER TO LORD SPENCER

*23 June 1898; Wimbledon Park House, Wimbledon*

You will have received a telegram announcing the poll in East Herts.[1] It surpassed my wildest dreams. Our people were mad with excitement, and I really am enchanted. Never did I expect to win but I hoped to run them close, and the Tories' faces when the numbers were declared were very low and depressed.

For many reasons, most of which you know,[2] I am rejoiced at the result though of course I should have liked to have beaten the Tories. Still we made a big battle of it, and the diminished majority is very gratifying.

We had a tremendous ovation, and when Margaret and I left the crowd at the Railway Station sang Auld Lang Syne. The pressure that the Tories put on yesterday was terrible, but the Cowper interest was extremely quiet.[3]

[1] The result, declared on 22 June, was Cecil 4118, C. R. Spencer 3850. At the 1892 election, Smith, on a similar poll had a majority of 1458. *Northampton Daily Reporter*, 23 June 1898, p. 4.

[2] William Allard, Secretary, Home Counties Liberal Federation, reported to Spencer that 1444 of the 2000 electors canvassed were said to be 'doubtfuls'. '1444 of this class is an extraordinary number ... the time is too short, unfortunately, for us to accomplish what we aim at and ardently wish done.' W. Allard to Spencer, 19 June 1898, SP.

[3] Hon. Henry Frederick Cowper, brother of Lord Cowper, who was Spencer's predecessor as Viceroy of Ireland, 1880-2, had been the Liberal M.P. for Hertfordshire, 1865-85; defeated by Smith in the 1885 election. Lord Cowper became a Liberal Unionist in 1886.


## 719   LORD SPENCER TO LADY SPENCER

*6 August 1898; Kaiserhof, Bad Nauheim*

My only regular fellow walker was Sir Charles Cameron[1] who walks up and down with daughter and lady friend Mrs. Peter Rylands[2] (not our Library Lady). We talked of elections and I gave him the good news of Launceston,[3] Fletcher Moulton's success softens the blow dealt by Doughty.[4] The Doughty blow will be made to resound by the Tory blasts all over the country and the walls of Jericho will be expected to fall and Home Rule to disappear, but they are all wrong. What I think will happen will be that this may hasten the chance of proceeding for Home Rule, it will show the Irish that they cannot fight and quarrel among themselves. It will postpone for the present any notion of a long Home Rule measure.

It may bring about rows in Ireland, but I don't expect that. What has been done in Reforms and Policy in the past has no doubt told in Ireland. The forces of disorder are weaker than they were and the American War[5] as one factor in the sum has helped the Government to keep order this year when the Irish Americans intended trouble for the War has kept them back. But sooner or later Home Rule will be demanded in a severer form than it has taken of late years.

The financial relations between the countries will not be allowed to continue without a fight which will unite men in Ireland and we shall see the working of County Government there on a Popular basis.

The Grimsby Election cannot be compared with ordinary Elections. It is a question of Personal influence. If a Member going over on Politics is strong and popular, he is sure to carry a lot of his former supporters with him, and with the side to which he goes, he may get a large turn out of votes.

It is unlucky that this has taken place on Home Rule but it is just such a question on which men wobble, and Home Rule now carries with it the demand for a huge Financial payment from G. Britain, so it is no wonder that it needs strong convictions and strong faith to keep its supporters together.

I have been hesitating over accepting a big meeting in Scotland, the Grimsby Election has decided me to accept. Convinced Home Rulers cannot retire now from Politics and so I shall go on until Lord Salisbury goes out and we come in. Then will be the moment to go out of Politics, and sit on the cross benches or back benches.

[1] Liberal M.P., Glasgow, College division, 1874-85 and later for Bridgeton division, Glasgow, 1897-1900.

[2] Wife of managing director, Rylands Bros. Ltd, iron and steel manufacturers.

[3] The result of the Launceston, Cornwall, by-election, announced on 3 Aug., was John Fletcher Moulton, Liberal, 3951, Sir F. Wills, Conservative, 2863.

[4] George Doughty, first elected as Liberal M.P. for Grimsby in 1895, joined the Liberal Unionists three years later, resigning his seat in July 1898. He was re-elected on 2 Aug. with a greatly increased majority.

[5] The Spanish-American-Cuban war, April-Dec., 1898. See J. A. S. Grenville, Lord Salisbury and Foreign Policy (1964), pp. 214-17.


### 720   LORD SPENCER TO LADY SPENCER

*6 September 1898; Althorp, Northampton*

J. Morley has agreed to edit the Publication of Mr. G.'s papers. It is not to be talked of. He only allows me to mention it to you.[1] He is quite the best man for it, even with his peculiar views on religion, for he will conscientiously edit Mr. G.'s views without comment. Mr. G. had supreme confidence in him. Of course the public will, until they see Morley's work, criticize his having to do this, but I am sure that when the work appears no one will find fault. Even Stephen Gladstone[2] quite endorsed the offer.

He says that it will take him two years work and that it will practically withdraw him from active Politics, but he won't give his seat up and after two years, which may not be eventful years, he will be again available.

I talked a good deal with him about it. I was against his doing it if it meant his leaving Politics, but as it did not I quite thought he would be better than Bryce, G. Trevelyan[3] or anyone else.

[1] Morley wrote to Herbert Gladstone on 3 Sept. accepting the commission. He told Spencer, 'many questions will arise as to which I shall look to you for counsel. I do not propose to consult other people very much'. J. Morley to Spencer, 4 Sept. 1898, SP.

[2] Rev. Stephen Gladstone, W. E. Gladstone's second son.

[3] In fact Bryce was asked to undertake the writing of the biography, but he declined. H. A. L. Fisher, *James Bryce* (1927), i, p. 337. Trevelyan was engaged in preparing a six-volume history of the American Revolution. G. M. Trevelyan, *Sir George Otto Trevelyan* (1932), p. 140.


### 721  LORD SPENCER TO LADY SPENCER
*9 November 1898; Wood Hill, Prestwich*

It [the meeting] was in the big Free Trade Hall.[1] It was not crammed but still there was an enormous audience, some thousands.

They received me wonderfully and I think my Speech made a very good impression. All the best men applauded my moderation.[2]

We had a very eloquent and amusing speech from a Welsh M.P. Lloyd George, but awfully exaggerated and violent.[3] I am sure it will do immense harm. He did not of course fall foul of me in any way. All the other speakers were solid and good.

[1] Manchester, 8 Nov.

[2] In his address to the Northern Counties Education League, Spencer urged all sects to discuss educational rather than religious issues. *The Times*, 9 Nov. 1898, p. 4.

[3] Elected Liberal M.P., Caernarvon Boroughs, at a by-election in 1890, Lloyd George attacked the 1897 Voluntary Schools Act which gave preferential treatment to denominational schools.


### 722  LORD SPENCER TO H. SEYMOUR
*15 December 1898; Althorp, Northampton*

*Confidential*

The interpretation which you put on the letters of Harcourt and Morley are very natural.[1] I heard from H. himself and replied to him the day before the letters were published viz. on Tuesday. But as generally occurs in such cases my letter reached him on the day when the letters were published.[2]

I remonstrated with him for what he threatened to do basing my arguments on what I knew, but urging that other circumstances might be known to him.

In his letter to me there were no 'ifs' and 'buts', but simply the announcement that he intended positively to retire from the Leadership of the Liberal Opposition in the House of Commons.

In my view this fresh resignation is most unfortunate. Not only does it give ground to our enemies to blaspheme, but it will not advance our unity as a party one bit. It may strengthen Rosebery's position which I confess I regret, as I think he is much to blame and responsible for a great deal that has happened and is now happening within our ranks.

It may moreover force forward personal recriminations which will be very damaging to the reputation of Rosebery, and possibly of Harcourt. *The Times* article today deprecating further disclosures looks as if they knew that they were being contemplated. *The Times* would of course be on Rosebery's side as to this.

Of course the reference to 'proscription' gives a handle for anyone to work upon to get hold of the personal details.[3]

I do not really see what specially new facts call for the action of Harcourt. No doubt Rosebery has been coming to the front as though bidding for leadership again, and the threatened resolution from Nottingham is another awkward thing,[4] E. Grey takes the right view of this; to mind neither of these things are enough to justify Harcourt's course.[5] As to Rosebery, Harcourt is playing into his hands by resignation. As to the Resolution it would have died a natural death at Birmingham.

I agree with you that the position of a new Leader in the House of Commons with Harcourt probably allied with J. Morley on his flank would be hopeless.

I really do not know who will lead our bench. J. Morley won't do it now I feel certain. Asquith cannot, I fear, do without his practice and with his practice he cannot lead. H. C. Bannerman would in many ways be good but he is far from strong.[6] Fowler would not do, E. Grey[7] is too young.

[1] An exchange of letters between the two men setting out the reasons for Harcourt's resignation from the Leadership of the Party in the Commons was published in the national press on 14 Dec. Morley announced his withdrawal from the conclaves of the Liberal Party on 17 Jan. 1899.

[2] Harcourt to Spencer, 12 Dec. 1898, SP; Spencer to Harcourt, 13 Dec. 1898, HP, MS 48. Spencer told Asquith, 'My gun was useless for it was fired after the battle had ended.' Spencer to Asquith, 24 Dec. 1898, AP, 9 f. 147.

[3] In his letter dated 8 Dec., Harcourt wrote, 'It has been whispered by men who neither know nor care to know the truth that I have allowed personal considerations to influence public action. No man knows better than yourself the falsehood of these unworthy insinuations. If personal proscriptions have been insisted upon, as a ground for refusal of common action in the general cause, they have not proceeded from me.' *The Times*, 14 Dec., p. 8.

[4] The National Liberal Federation met at Birmingham on 16 Dec. A motion from the South Nottinghamshire Liberal Association to consider the question of party leadership was withdrawn after discussion. *The Times*, 17 Dec. 1898, p. 12.

[5] Speech at North Shields on 14 Dec. questioning Harcourt's decision to publish his letter.

[6] Campbell-Bannerman was elected Leader on 6 Feb. 1899.

[7] Sir Edward Grey, Liberal M.P., Berwick-on-Tweed, since 1885. Parliamentary Secretary for Foreign Affairs, 1892-5.

# 9

# THE SOUTH AFRICAN WAR AND AFTER,
## 1899–1902

The outbreak of the South African War in 1899 deepened the divisions in the Liberal Party. A group of leading members, including Asquith, Fowler, Grey and Haldane, known as Liberal Imperialists, had formed under Rosebery's leadership. The latter supported Milner's policy in South Africa and urged the country for the duration of the war to 'close its ranks and relegate party controversy to a more convenient season.' Campbell-Bannerman adopted a central position over the war, and aimed at securing conciliation between the two sides; for this, he was denounced by the Liberal Imperialists as a pro-Boer.

Spencer, who from 1901 acted as Leader of the Opposition in the Lords, supported Campbell-Bannerman. He wrote to Kimberley shortly before the war, 'Kruger and his people thoroughly distrust us, and I believe that we wish at all cost to swallow up the Transvaal, and if the Orange Free State have the same feeling, they will fight, as in honour bound, to save their independence.' (Spencer to Kimberley, 26 September 1899, KP, 10247 f. 94). Spencer was incensed by Rosebery's speech at Chesterfield on 16 December 1901, where he advanced the notion of a 'clean slate' in Ireland by abandoning home rule. To Spencer, it indicated 'his unfitness for a Leader ... It puts him at once into the position of a Liberal Unionist'. (Spencer to Campbell-Bannerman, 27 December 1901, CBP, Add. MS. 41229 f. 147).

With Rosebery still on the sidelines, Spencer was elected Leader of the Opposition in the Lords after Kimberley's death in April 1902. The South African War was concluded in May and Salisbury invited Spencer to preside over an inquiry into the conduct of the war, but he refused the offer. (Spencer to Salisbury, 25 June 1902, SP). Public interest now turned to home affairs. Strong feelings had been roused amongst Free Churchmen with the introduction of an Education Bill in March 1902 by Balfour, who became prime minister in July. Spencer led the opposition to the bill in the Lords. 'I always wish our church had more courage to express opinions,' he told a correspondent. 'I also maintain that every strong advocate of dogmatic teaching in schools could get all they desire if they fell in with sound views on popular control and management, and the absence of political tests on teachers.' (Spencer to Rev. W. Martin, 17 October 1902, SP (copy) ). After a bitter battle in the Lords, the bill became law in December.

**723** LORD SPENCER TO C. R. SPENCER

*2 March 1899; Assouan*

We got to Luxor by train, a long journey by day but not very hot, the dust of course peppered us all over. ....[1]

We had expeditions to Carnac, to the Tombs of the Kings, and to Medinet Abu, where we saw Newberry[2] who works for and with Lord Northampton.[3]

I never saw such a change as there has been since 1863 and 1864. Temples are now scrupulously clean, the enormous excavations and removals of soil show the splendid aisles and halls in their proper proportions, instead of which when we were last here we scrambled over rough stones and earth with the columns to $\frac{3}{4}$ of their height covered up.

[1] The Spencers were in Egypt from 14 Feb. to 15 March, mainly sightseeing. At Assouan, Spencer went on an expedition to see the barrage, accompanied by some of the directors. Lady Spencer, Diary, 1 March 1899, SP.

[2] Percy Edward Newberry, Liverpool Institute of Archeology, long resident at Thebes.

[3] Newberry published, with William George, 5th Marquess of Northampton, a report on the excavations of the Theban Necropolis (1908).

**724** LORD SPENCER TO LORD KIMBERLEY

*12 March 1899; Cairo*

KP, 10247 ff. 84–8

*Private*

I was much interested in what you told me about Politics, and the recent incident about the Soudan.[1] I agree very much with you, and regret that H.C.B. voted with J. Morley, particularly as his Speech threw his weight to the other side. No doubt, he was in a very difficult position after the former vote under Harcourt. Still he has done very well, and time soon cures political wounds, and in a few weeks the incident will only be referred to in political speeches and will quickly be forgotten.

I have had two good talks with Cromer.[2] He seems to care little about what passes in the Parliament, and had hardly looked at the Debates.

I put to him the case as it presents itself to my mind as to the Soudan and he told me distinctly that he considered one of the best things done by the Gladstone Government was the insisting that Egypt should withdraw from the Soudan. He strongly felt this at the time and he has in no degree changed his view.

Directly Egypt was set up in funds and had a reliable army, he wished to reconquer the country. His own opinion was a short time ago that that day should be postponed until the new irrigation works had amply enlarged the finances of Egypt.

He was against the first Dongola expedition.[3] He said it was settled by the Cabinet in 10 minutes. Since then everything has worked to favour the policy of prompt action. It was somewhat accidental and not foreseen but, as things had turned out, he considers that he was wrong in his desire to put off the movement. Italy at Kassala, the French pressing towards the Nile, the Abyssinian intrigues with France made it necessary to act, and action was taken as he thinks now in the nick of time.

I put this to him, starting from the supposition that we should not interfere with any power coming to the Upper Nile, could the French have maintained themselves there? He was not so decided as on many points, but he distinctly thought that they could, that they intended to remain, to take Khartoum, and he was convinced that Abyssinia intended to work with France.

He was emphatic as to the impossibility of allowing any other country to occupy the Upper Nile country.

I said what about Uganda? He oddly as I thought did not connect that with the Nile policy. I said but does not Uganda bound part of Lake Victoria the highest water on the Nile? He said if it does then we must keep Uganda. He did not seem enthusiastic as to the Cape to Cairo railway.

As to the future, he says that they must have time. The Khalifa[4] exists with a considerable force, and proves the vitality of the Mahdi's movement. He is not now dangerous and as Col. Maxwell told me at present he need not be interfered with, and if he comes to the Nile can easily be defeated, but Lord Cromer said that some day he must be got rid of, for as long as he is in the Darfur-Cordofan country[5] he will stop the development and settling down of the people. He hopes that the Khalifa will some day lay himself open to an easy attack, but he is strongly against any serious aggressive movement now. The native army has had a severe time of it, not only in battle but by sickness. It has lost large numbers (the Duke of Connaught told me that the Sirdar had lost about 2,000 men on the Blue Nile and elsewhere from sickness), the recruits from the Dervishes need drilling, and the force is not in a state for active and difficult operations. Everyone speaks of the devastation of the country ruled by the Khalifa. There are left scarcely any men, all cultivation gone to ruin, and trade gone. All this needs time. I gather that the navigation of the Nile south of Fashoda towards Lake Albert becomes very difficult what with 'Sudd'[6] and swamps. It is not the easy waterway which between the rapids carried our people to Khartoum and Fashoda . . .

Cromer was altogether very interested in his keen interest in his work. He longs to get joint control abolished . . .[7]

It is wonderful what he does. He controls every department, with no distinct power but that of moral force, unless he chose to call in British troops to make the Khedive a prisoner.

P.S. Cromer significantly said that he should prefer a war with France over joint control rather than over the Bahr El Ghazal country. He said he thought the boundary question would soon and easily be settled.

[1] In his new capacity as Leader of the Party in the Commons, Campbell-Bannerman had spoken critically in a debate on 7 Feb. on government policy in the Sudan. Later, on 24 Feb. Morley put forward a motion attacking the occupation of the Sudan, though Campbell-Bannerman, now steering a middle path, did not make his position clear on the issue. Finally, much to Harcourt's and Morley's satisfaction, he reluctantly supported Morley's motion.

[2] Evelyn Baring, 1st Viscount Cromer, agent and consul-general, Cairo. The first meeting was on 18 February, the second on 11 March. On the second occasion, Spencer also met the Khedive. Lady Spencer, Diary, 11 March 1899, SP.

[3] On 12 March 1896, the decision was taken to reconquer the Sudan by an advance on Dongola.

The forces, under Major-General Herbert Kitchener, were dispatched to take Khartoum in Jan. 1898 and decisively beat the Dervishes at Omdurman in Sept. An acute Anglo-French crisis followed the meeting of Kitchener with the Marchand mission at Fashoda, where the British insisted on a French evacuation. On 3 Nov. the French government agreed to abandon Fashoda. See D. Bates, *The Fashoda Incident of 1898* (1983), pp. 151-9.

4 Khalifa Abdullah el Taashi, successor to the Mahdi.

5 South-west Sudan..

6 An impenetrable mass of floating vegetable matter which obstructs navigation on the White Nile.

7 An Anglo-Egyptian condominium known as the Sudan agreement was established over Sudan on 19 January 1899. The agreement had been drafted by Cromer. J. Marlow, *Cromer in Egypt* (1970), p. 219.


**725   LORD SPENCER TO J. BRYCE**

*22 October 1899; North Creake, Fakenham*

Bryce Papers

*Confidential*

I am very sorry that we Ex Cabinet are so divided about the War.[1] Probably our Divisions are not of very serious moment. They are Divisions of opinion as to which side most failed in the negotiations which have ended in war.

As you know, I agreed with you more than with any other of our colleagues the other day, but probably Ripon and H. C. Bannerman (if he had given us the fall of his mind) agreed with you too. The Debate with Chamberlain's speech[2] and Clarke's reply[3] confirm me in this view.

If Chamberlain intended to accept the Boer 5 year proposals, and was surprised at the Boers not so interpreting the Cabinet answer, he and the Cabinet were very wrong not to make their meaning clear. He admits further that it is only now at the last moment that he has become convinced that Kruger all through intended war or to shake us off altogether. If so, Chamberlain showed as negotiator very little foresight from his point of view.[4]

I have lately come to the conclusion that if the Government could show conclusively that Kruger never intended peace on reasonable terms, the Government would be greatly justified, but I cannot see that this contention is proved, on the contrary Chamberlain's Speech points in the other direction.

I am very glad that none of our own Front Bench spoke on opposite sides to each other. At the same time I am afraid that our attitude looks weak, and the Debate shows clearly that a more decided line in your sense could with perfect decorum and propriety have been taken.

1 The South African (Boer) War began on 12 Oct. 1899 and the ex-cabinet met on the following day. Of the principal members, Asquith and Fowler sided with the government on the main issues in the Transvaal dispute with Bryce and Campbell-Bannerman opposing them.

2 Chamberlain, in the debate on an amendment to the Address which expressed 'strong disapproval of the conduct of the negotiations with the Government of the Transvaal', successfully defended the government's actions. The amendment was rejected by 362 votes to 135. Hansard, 4, lxxvii, col. 254 ff. 19 October 1899.

3 Sir Edward Clarke, Conservative M.P., Plymouth, Solicitor-General, 1886-92. Ibid., col. 300 ff.

4 For Bryce's account of the debate, see Bryce to Spencer, 24 Oct. 1899, SP.

## 726 LORD SPENCER TO LORD KIMBERLEY
*2 November 1899; Althorp, Northampton*
KP, 10247 ff. 58-9

I was in a very tight place yesterday. Late on Friday I got a letter from Wilfrid Lawson[1] who is a local magnate in Cumberland, regretting that the meeting[2] was to go on, and not knowing my views asked whether I should like him to absent himself.

I replied by telling my views and leaving him to settle his own action, but I also tried on hearing his opinion to stop [the] meeting. That was of course impossible, and on Sunday I got 2 proposed Resolutions, which were hopeless, going further than Stanhope's or Dillon's,[3] and quite impossible for one to accept, so I had to try and frame one. I send it to you. It was an attempt to formulate the attitude which you in the House of Lords and H.C.B. in the House of Commons took up.

To my joy my Resolution was accepted,[4] and it was carried practically but not enthusiastically. There were murmurs and questions at first but I took the warlike side first and got the meeting in excellent humour and I never was better listened to. There were all the elements of a row, 40 returned miners from the Transvaal, a lot of Irish and a band of rowdy people there. But all went well. I was very half reported, still it is a great relief to me that you take so kind a view of what I said, so does Ripon who has written to me.[5] Asquith took no exception. I saw him in town and several others liked it.

I am convinced that as this affair cannot destroy the Liberal party as H. Chaplin[6] would wish, that some meetings must go on, and if they are held it will never do to be silent as Rosebery suggested. We cannot leave the talking to Tory jingoes (and possibly to some Liberal jingoes) and to the extreme sentimentalists like Wilfrid Lawson and Channing[7] etc. on the other side.

[1] Sir Wilfrid Lawson, of Isel Hall, near Cockermouth, a Pro-Boer Radical M.P., Cockermouth, 1886-1900.

[2] At Cleator Moor under the auspices of the West Cumberland Liberal Association on 30 Oct.

[3] Proposing independent arbitration for settling the South African War. Hansard, 4, lxxvii, 17 Oct. 1899. Dillon, col. 93 ff., Stanhope, 18 Oct., col. 181 ff. Philip James Stanhope was Liberal M.P. for Burnley, 1893-1900.

[4] '... that the differences which exist between this country and the Transvaal ought to have been settled without war'.

[5] Ripon to Spencer, 1 Nov. 1899, SP.

[6] Chaplin spoke on the war at the Manchester Conservative Club on 31 Oct. *The Times*, 1 Nov. 1899, p. 7.

[7] For Channing's views on the war, see his *Memories of Midland Politics* (1918), pp. 214-19.

## 727 LORD SPENCER TO H. SEYMOUR
*28 November 1899; 100 Marina, St. Leonards-on-Sea[1]*

I was glad to get your letter, and I agree generally with your criticism of Asquith's Speech.[2]

Knowing what his views were, for he is I believe an intimate friend of Milner's,[3] and under the influence which Milner seems strongly to exercise over certain people, I was not as surprised as you were, but I differ much with what he says as to what led up to the War. I thought him better than Fowler but that is not saying much.

I agree with you that the argument of equal rights promised to the Government before the Convention of 1881[4] is not sound, for the reason which you give, and further that if such a point had been made or was intended to be made, proper conditions to carry this out would have been inserted in the Conventions.

On the first of your points our rights to interfere were (1) under the Conventions but that did not include internal Government excepting as to the natives under the Convention of 1881, (2) under International Law which certainly never has included Franchise or qualification for Franchise.

Your third point is good against Asquith, late Home Secretary, but I do not go so far as to say that there were not people permanently settled in the Transvaal who had grievances. I feel sure that the Government of the Transvaal was very bad. Whether we could have formulated a case sufficient to justify our using force to get redress, is a matter difficult to establish.

We have never put forth our case but I think it is possible that we could have established a case.

No doubt what you say is true that the people who flocked to the Transvaal for mining knew to what Government they were going, and I also believe that the grievances of the Uitlanders have been exaggerated, and are the kind of grievances which men settled in a new country crammed with immigrants of the worst character always have to encounter.

As to the future I thought that Asquith seemed sound. Anyhow it is on that we must hope and try to rally the Liberal party.

E. Grey's speech[5] today was worse than Asquith's.

It makes me despair to find our leaders taking different lines, as though they each were playing their own hand and not trying to make common cause amongst themselves.

Now that Massingham has left the *Daily Chronicle*[6] there is not a single morning paper in London (at least to my knowledge) which does not support the policy of the Government.

I have corrected the local quasi verbatim report of my Cleator Moor speech[7] and mean to put it in a separate form, as I want my views left on record clearly. Ripon made a very good Speech the other night. I did not quite like C. Bannerman's Birmingham Speech, and oddly enough both he and Kimberley said some imprudent things.[8]

What K. said as to the settlement after Majuba was only partially correct and had better have been kept back from a Public Speech. No doubt men like K. and others who could not rise to Mr. G.'s 'bloodguiltiness' argument relied on the knowledge that we might have all the Dutch in S. Africa in arms, but the main argument was that the Rebellion proved that the annexation of 1877 had been made against the popular wish of the Boers and was not therefore just, and that being so it was wrong to shed more blood for what the Government considered an unjust cause.

Both these views brought about the final recession, but not one of them alone. If one alone had the greater weight it was that of 'bloodguiltiness' which Kimberley, Hartington (?)[9] and others would not swallow.

[1] A recently-acquired house on the Sussex coast.

[2] At Ashington, Northumberland, on 25 Nov. For his views, see J. A. Spender and C. Asquith, *Life of Herbert Henry Asquith, Lord Oxford and Asquith* (1932), i. pp. 133-4.

[3] Alfred Milner, Governor of Cape of Good Hope and High Commissioner for South Africa since 1897.

[4] The treaty of Pretoria, signed on 5 April 1881, arising out of the Boers' desire for freedom, gave independence to South Africa whilst remaining under the suzerainty of Great Britain.

[5] At Alnwick, Northumberland, on the conduct of the war. *The Times*, 28 Nov. 1899, p. 8.

[6] Henry William Massingham, editor of the *Daily Chronicle* since 1895, resigned on 21 Nov. in protest for being 'prematurely required to maintain absolute silence on the policy of the Government in South Africa until after the conclusion of the war'. Quoted in A. F. Havighurst, *Radical Journalist: H. W. Massingham* (1973), p. 107.

[7] See No. **726** n. 2.

[8] Ripon at Bolton, Lancashire, on 21 Nov., Campbell-Bannerman on 24 Nov. and Kimberley at Newcastle upon Tyne on 14 Nov.

[9] Spencer's question mark.


**728** H. CAMPBELL-BANNERMAN TO LORD SPENCER

*8 January 1900: Belmont Castle, Meigle*

*Private*

　... Politically also it seems to me the whole situation has changed, for the success of the Boers makes annexation in any form impossible even if we beat them in the end.[1] The whole world would cry shame on us. But if we don't annex, then for what have we been fighting, and what will the Rhodes party have gained? The whole policy presumed an early collapse of the Boers.

　[1] Reverses in the war were suffered at Magersfontein on Dec. 10-11 1899 where Gen. Piet Cronje frustrated efforts to relieve Kimberley, and at Colenso on Dec. 15, in an attempt to raise the siege of Ladysmith.


**729** LORD SPENCER TO H. CAMPBELL-BANNERMAN

*14 January 1900; Althorp, Northampton*
CBP, Add. MS. 41229 ff. 77-8

　I quite agree as to the lamentable position in which we are placed.[1] This powerful country within 3 months of declaration of War with 2 third rate Republics, to be driven to use all our Home Defence forces for colonial defence, and to have recourse to Scottish gillies and hunting men to fight our battles. One admires the pluck and patriotism of those who respond, regardless of other home duties, to the call of Government, but one must stand aghast at the revelation which the War has made of our helplessness.

　What is clear, particularly after A. Balfour's speeches,[2] is that the Government never contemplated war and never saw two inches before their noses, and consequently could not be ready for what occurred. It is surely the business of statesmen to know more than the men in the street, and to see through the attempts to throw dust in their eyes, which our opponents made and so successfully ...

　I see the point you make as to the change of Policy, but I am not sure that I agree. The Boers must take the consequence of their action and ultimatum.

Can we tolerate any state of things which will leave room if possible in the future for a repetition of this hostility towards us? I doubt it. Gallantly as the Boers have fought, that does not alter the internal danger towards us. But all this cannot be settled yet.

[1] See No. 728.

[2] In speeches delivered in different parts of his constituency, East Manchester, on 9 Jan., Balfour admitted that greater and more rapid success had been anticipated in South Africa. *The Times*, 10 Jan. 1900, p. 6.

### 730   LORD SPENCER TO LADY SPENCER
*16 February 1900; Althorp, Northampton*

I am not altogether satisfied with either Rosebery's or Kimberley's Speeches.[1] They are thoroughly alarmist in character. Is it wise to stir up a feeling of panic? I doubt it. What does it lead to? Conscription, and are we prepared for this? Clearly not according to Government and the views we hear about. It is all very well to speak of conjecture, but unless we have conscription the numbers we get must be conjectured.

Lord Salisbury was thoroughly unsatisfactory, but he is in difficulty. He had to answer Kimberley who is very alarmist and he had not a free hand to do so.

I should have been disposed to avoid the panic line and press home questions as to what forces we have to send out to South Africa, if wanted. If Lord Roberts[2] has enough all we can do is to be ready with more troops in case he wants them. I should have tested all the War Office proposals and as Rosebery did approve of calling out old Soldiers and finding out how many of the 170,000 available were officers. I expect that with the Auxiliary forces the great amount will be officers.

Luke[3] telegraphs that French has relieved Kimberley. I somehow doubt it. How with only cavalry can he have defeated the investing forces and he will not have had time to take up infantry and field batteries. If he has, the Boer army in the middle will be cut off from its base and it will have to surrender. This of course would be a grand victory but I fear it cannot be true.[4]

[1] In a debate on Army proposals in the Lords on 15 Feb., Rosebery referred to the inadequacy of the armed forces to deal with any crisis. Kimberley, in the same debate, warned of Russia's possible hostile intentions towards India. 'I found,' wrote Spencer, 'that he had caught a little of the spirit of a great man's Speech before him: for what he said as to Russia, Soudan, etc., although no doubt perfectly correct and good, rather fanned a Panic flame and might be a little inopportune.' Spencer to Campbell-Bannerman, 18 Feb. 1900, CBP, Add. MS. 41229 f. 85.

[2] Lord Frederick Roberts with Field-Marshal Kitchener as his Chief of Staff, replaced Gen. Sir Redvers Buller as Commander-in-Chief in Jan.

[3] Luke White, Lady Spencer's great nephew.

[4] In fact Major-Gen. Sir John French, under Roberts' orders, successfully relieved Kimberley on 15 Feb. Sir G. Forrest, *The Life of Lord Roberts* (1914), pp. 210-19.

**731  LORD SPENCER TO LORD KIMBERLEY**
*22 September 1900; Reform Club, Pall Mall, S.W.*
KP, 10247 ff. 104-5

I have been taking a small share of work, as I felt bound to do, on the announcement of the Dissolution, and I was at Derby last night where our friends are very keen and very sanguine ...[1]

I asked Asquith whether R. agreed with him or with C. B. and Asquith said he thought more with him but that anyhow he was intensely hostile to Government, and wished that they would be turned out.

Now this has occurred to me, no individual or group of individuals can say who is to be Leader of the party, but it certainly appears very desirable that we should present as united a front as possible on the eve of the Election.

Could this not be made clear to Rosebery, and could he not be asked to declare his views if possible in complete agreement with C.B. or in general agreement with him in a letter to you or to C.B. wishing the party success?

I should like any communication to R. to make it clear that he is in no way to interfere with your Leadership in the House of Lords or C.B.'s in the House of Commons, otherwise I could not agree to the proposal ... Herbert Gladstone[2] is strongly for it and I don't think that Asquith dissented but hardly expected that R. would do it.

---

[1] Parliament was prorogued on 8 Aug. and the dissolution announced early in Sept. Spencer spoke in Derby to an audience of 3,000 on 21 Sept. in support of local candidates. 'It went off better than any Speech I ever made.' Spencer to C. R. Spencer, 22 Sept. 1900, SP.

[2] Chief Liberal Whip in the Commons since the death of T. E. Ellis in 1899.

---

**732  C. R. SPENCER TO LADY SPENCER**
*28 September 1900; Dallington House, Northampton*

We are working hard and the meetings are encouraging, but I am very doubtful of success.[1] Pender has said that he is certain of keeping the seat and in some parts he is not doing anything at all, which looks like real confidence. We heard at the Horse show at Althorp yesterday that Lady Pender is beside herself with excitement.

I have 3 meetings each night, and one lives somehow. Some of S.'s tenants have volunteered to support me, and have admitted that they voted against me in '95. Becke is working well, and is really in earnest ... The organization is not at all bad, and the Town is being well looked after. I am rather afraid that the Temperance people will be lukewarm, they don't like my answer about the Child Messenger Bill.[2]

The big meeting at Kingsley Park was very thrilling.[3] The socialists came and heckled me, but did not hold up their hands either for or against me. Grove[4] has terrified the Tories in the South. Adkins told me today that such is their fear that they are at their wits' end to get speakers down.

It is quite odd how flat the War has become. Quite a short allusion to it suffices now, the people don't care to hear more.[5] I go to Walgrave, Old and Rothwell tonight, a hideously long drive, Little Bowden tomorrow afternoon,

Clipston, Welford and Naseby in the evening. My strongest point seems to be that the electors are sorry that I was rejected last time and that they are disappointed with Pender.

[1] Robert Spencer was adopted for the Mid Northamptonshire division on 5 Sept.
[2] The Sale of Intoxicating Liquors to Children Bill (No. 2) was introduced in the Commons on 9 Feb. and read a second time on 9 March. Hansard, 4, lxxx, cols. 517–34.
[3] Wed. 26 Sept. Report in NM, 28 Sept. 1900, p. 9.
[4] Thomas Grove, Liberal M.P., West Ham North, 1892–5, adopted as the candidate for South Northamptonshire on 22 Sept.
[5] Nevertheless, Robert Spencer's election address, issued on 25 Sept., devoted half the space to this issue.

### 733   LORD SPENCER TO C. R. SPENCER
*28 September 1900; North Creake, Fakenham*

I write a few lines to say that I keenly look out for news of you. I like the prospect very much. Our side is fighting with great keenness, and the other side seem alarmed.

Labby's adoption[1] seemed to me a foregone conclusion. His Speech seems moderate enough. Old Tonsley will not do himself much Political good, but it is better than running for the seat himself.[2] I confess that I detest Labby's ways and Politics, but his independence and cleverness wins votes in a place like Northampton. Anyhow I am partizan enough to prefer him to a Tory.

[1] At Northampton on 24 Sept. together with Dr. J. G. Shipman.
[2] Francis Tonsley, J. P., confectioner and landlord of the Angel Hotel, Northampton. Chairman of the National Liberal and Radical Association, he resigned as candidate over disagreements with Labouchere. Mayor, 1898.

### 734   C. R. SPENCER TO LORD SPENCER
*30 September 1900; Dallington House, Northampton*

I cannot say what the result will be of this Election. I hear today that the Brewers agreed yesterday to recommend Pender not me, but I am not sure whether that means that they are going to work against me ... If it were not for Becke, I should have no hope, but he has pulled the organization together very well ... The most hopeful news is that the large body of voluntary workers for me in the Town is doing splendid work, and I fancy that we shall get a lot more votes amongst the Freeholders than we have ever had before. 25 voters in Brington went against me last Election, they now say they will support me ...

I have spoken 18 times this week and my voice at Naseby last night, the fourth meeting I went to, was very bad. John Gee was at the Welford meeting but fell asleep during my speech – shows how dull it must have been ...

Jim Manfield works the town: he is chairman of the voluntary committee for me there. I spoke to them for 10 minutes in the Town Hall. Men were there keen to work who had not taken part in politics for years. Becke thought it the most encouraging sign. There were people in quite a small way sitting by the magnates like Adnitt,[1] Hickson,[2] etc. and all of them more than nice to me.

# TO THE ELECTORS OF THE
# MID-DIVISION OF THE COUNTY OF NORTHAMPTON.

GENTLEMEN,

By the unanimous vote of the Liberal Association, I have been invited to fight your battle in Mid-Northamptonshire—a battle that we have often fought and fought victoriously before.

The fact that I was for ten years in the proud position of your representative makes it unnecessary for me to declare that I am a Liberal, and that if elected I should deal with all political questions on Liberal lines.*

Our opponents want to fight the election on one issue only, ignoring the large number of important questions which vitally affect your interests, and which demand the immediate attention of Parliament.

On the question of the War, to which the Government are anxious to limit the issue, and without entering into the questions of the negotiations preceding the War and the manner in which they were conducted, I would say this—that in view of the fact that our territories were first invaded and great hardships inflicted on our fellow subjects, and after the heavy sacrifices which the Country has cheerfully made in carrying on the War, the annexation of the two Republics became an absolute necessity. At the same time, as soon as it is possible to do so, I would give to the people of the two recently incorporated Colonies such equal civil and political rights as are consistent with the supremacy of the Crown, granting them such a full measure of liberty as will obliterate, as far as possible, all racial animosities, and will secure to all the inhabitants of South Africa freedom under the British Flag.

I hope to have many opportunities of renewing my old acquaintance with you, when we can discuss the many domestic and social questions that confront us, such as Education, the proper Housing of the Working Classes, and others; and which have been so grievously neglected by the present Government, notwithstanding their reckless promises which gained them such a large majority at the last Election.

I am, Gentlemen,

Your faithful Servant,

## C. ROBERT SPENCER.

25TH SEPTEMBER, 1900.
DALLINGTON HOUSE,
NORTHAMPTON.

Printed and Published by Jos. Tebbutt, King-st. and Silver-st., Northampton.

9   Election Address, Mid Northamptonshire Division. Charles Robert Spencer,
25 September 1900

Labby is sure to get in now, but there is in reality a strong under current against him. Our people are all going to vote straight for him and Shipman,[3] but they don't like him. Adkins was told that if he signed Labby's nomination paper, Grove would lose 300 votes at once in the South ...

Rothwell is the only place so far where the war interested the people. At all the other meetings it falls very flat ...

Margaret and Delia went to the Harlestone meeting last night, many Althorp people were there. The extract from your letter to Morley was excellent, so generous and fair. I think that several of the Tenants will vote for me this time ...

The nomination is at 11 tomorrow. I speak at 1 at St. James' End, drive to Floore (where they had an enthusiastic meeting for me on Thursday), and speak at Roade, Milton, Weston Favell and Moulton in the evening, Kilsby, Crick, Yelvertoft and West Haddon on Tuesday, besides spending the morning at Wilbarston a good long way off.

[1] Frederick George Adnitt, draper. Mayor, 1900.
[2] William Hickson, shoe manufacturer.
[3] Dr. John Greenwood Shipman, J.P., barrister, of Dallington. A Radical and home ruler. Unsuccessfully contested Gravesend in 1892. Both Shipman and Labouchere were elected.


**735   C. R. SPENCER TO LORD SPENCER**
*5 October 1900; Dallington House, Northampton*

I wished for you so much to see the joy of our people when the majority of 794 was declared.[1]

I know that you will be as pleased as anyone, and I wanted so much to win quite as much for your sake as mine.

It was an awful time of suspense, but when the end came, every one including Tories were most nice. Pender quite touched me by his warm congratulations to Margaret ... Bringtons and Harlestone were splendid. Buckby gave a majority of over 150.

[1] On 5 Oct. Spencer 5399, Pender 4605.


**736   C. R. SPENCER TO LORD SPENCER**
*13 October 1900; Dallington, Northampton*

I am amused now at hearing that I was safe all the way through. When I went into the counting, Becke said that I was in, but with a very narrow majority. Jackson and Adkins *hoped* that I was. Anyhow I was quite prepared to be beaten. The Tories now say that they did not work, which is a slightly imaginative statement as they worked as hard as possible ...

In the Market Harborough district we did extremely well, but again at Rothwell the box was not quite as good as we had hoped. We had a clear majority of 200 at Long Buckby, and there were apparently hardly any Tories at all in Harlestone and the Bringtons. Eady at Market Harborough worked splendidly for me. He was always ready to do anything that was necessary. One E. Herts friend Pawle came to us with his horse and dogcart and worked at Brixworth all day. I hear that he certainly got over 20 votes which had been doubtful.

Harcourt's unfortunate reference to Local Veto[1] rather upset some of our people, and it was not necessary for him to make it as Lord Peel's report[2] clearly postponed it for 7 years in England. Asquith spoke very well at Rugby,[3] but he is a cold speaker for such an audience. I enjoyed his speech immensely.

The South was lost entirely from want of organisation.[4] When I went to Blisworth last Tuesday I was sure that the game was up. Grove did extremely well, but meetings really are the last things that count.[5]

[1] Addressing his constituents of West Monmouthshire at Tredegar on 28 Sept. *The Times,* 29 Sept. 1900, p. 7.
[2] The Royal Commission on the Licensing Laws, with its chairman, Arthur Wellesley, 1st Viscount Peel, sat from 1896 to 1899.
[3] 10 Oct. *NM,* 12 Oct. 1900, p. 7.
[4] Hon. Edward Algernon Fitzroy, Conservative, 4174, Grove 3166.
[5] Except for Guthrie's period as M.P. for the constituency, 1892–5, South Northamptonshire had been represented by Conservatives for more than 40 years.

**737  LORD SPENCER TO LORD KIMBERLEY**
*8 November 1900; 100 Marina, St. Leonards-on-Sea*
KP, 10247 ff. 111–13

*Private*

Many thanks for your letter.[1] I fully intended to have written to you after your Wymondham Speech.[2] I thought what you said excellent especially as to the ticket of Imperialism: I detest this special cabal. Oddly enough I had a conversation with Lord Brassey[3] about this on Saturday and Monday.

I told him that I heard he joined the League to moderate etc. but expressed myself clearly as to my dislike to these sectional splittings of the party and to the term Liberal Imperialist. He did not disagree much and was very indignant because the Manifesto of the Imperial Liberal Council of which he is President had been issued without his sanction.

He is now dragged into a dinner much after the same fashion and he volunteered in speaking to me that he feared young London lawyers had taken the bit into their teeth and acted without consultation, and that if this went on he would retire altogether.

I am like you in fear of considerable trouble before and when Parliament meets.[4] From what I learned in London there is some idea that difficulty in our ranks will arise about Milner. Milner no doubt is a man who strongly carries friends with him, and his influence is powerful. He I expect has great power over Asquith, Grey and Haldane.[5] I am not thus inspired. At the same time I cannot see that he need be so bad a man at the post where he is, that he should be removed. He is doubtless very able and although in many respects he seemed to throw himself in line with and support of extreme War men at the Cape, I do not think that the special cry against him is altogether destructive of his character for good Government in South Africa.

I at present at all events should not be prepared to vote for a motion condemning him altogether. I am however not fully acquainted with all there is to be said about him. I know of his negotiations with Kruger and on these, I hardly should say that he was unyielding or pugnacious. His famous 'Helot' despatch[6] was of course a strong denouncement of Kruger's methods. He was not responsible for the publication of it, which always seemed to me very wrong.[7] Then there is Milner's interview, but what he said was denied. He also appeared to work with Schreiner[8] and at any rate did not discuss him.

You may know what the best and most Liberal people in Africa, e.g. de Villiers,[9] say of Milner.

I have dwelt on this, as from what Herbert Gladstone said and what H.C.B. says[10] in a letter received whilst writing this, a Milner difficulty seems imminent directly Parliament meets. I wonder what Harcourt thinks. He was hand in glove with him over the Death duties so has a leaning for him rather than a prejudice against him.[11]

As to Rosebery, I know not what to think. If he fell into line (without disturbing you in the House of Lords or H.C.B. in the House of Commons, conditions which I should say must be indispensible) Harcourt and J. Morley would jib and perhaps refuse support. As you say, Harcourt now professes, and I think this is genuine, loyalty to both you and H.C.B. but would he work with R. if he fell into the ranks for the time? and would R. fall into work and into the ranks if H. and J.M. were also doing the same?

I fear that there is the difficulty. It is to my mind wholly a personal one, and personal enmities or differences (to use the milder word) ought not to weigh in Politics, when the good of the party is in question. The only exception to this should be when there is a difference amounting to a question of honour. I cannot think that the R. and H. or R. and J.M. difficulty ought to amount to that. But how is this chasm to be bridged over? I do not see how, and yet between now and the meeting of Parliament some effort should be made to do this.

Whatever one may feel about R. as Prime Minister, and personally I do not feel admiration or confidence in him in that capacity, one must admit that he is a considerable power in the country, and we cannot afford to lose his help. As long as he remains in the selfish, miserable attitude which he has assumed he indirectly fans and encourages cabals and the formation of sections in the party. There is this moreover to be remembered: R. has done nothing but harm to the party since he retired. H. and J.M. have worked strongly for the party.

You are I know more tolerant about him than I am, but I look upon his conduct in resigning the leadership as the cause of all the party troubles which have been so very serious of late years. I am generally an optimist and wish to see a silver lining to every cloud, but just now the clouds are black, deep black, and the black hides any light beyond.

[1] Kimberley wrote to Spencer on 3 Nov., 'I should very much like to know what you think of the condition of our party. I hear of intrigues going on which bode no good.' SP.

[2] On 30 Oct.

[3] Thomas, 1st Baron Brassey, as President of the Imperial Liberal Council, had addressed its first public meeting on 22 Sept.

[4] The new Parliament was to meet on 3 Dec.

[5] Richard Burdon Haldane, Liberal, M.P. Haddingtonshire, since 1885, wrote to Milner on 3 March 1901, 'You may absolutely rely on Rosebery, Asquith and Grey – the only people who really count with us – to carry through what has been begun.' C. C. Headlam (ed.), *The Milner Papers* (1931) ii, p. 187.

[6] Milner's dispatch of 4 May 1899 to the government represented the grievances of the Uitlanders. 'The spectacle of thousands of British subjects kept in the position of helots, constantly chafing under undoubted grievances and calling vainly on Her Majesty's Government for redress, does steadily undermine the influence and reputation of Great Britain and the respect for the British Government within its own dominions.'

[7] The dispatch was subsequently published, with minor amendments, as C. 9345 No. 78.

[8] Will Philip Schreiner, barrister, leader of the Afrikander Bond in the Cape Parliament. Prime minister and Colonial Secretary, 1898–1900.

[9] Sir Henry de Villiers, Chief Justice, Cape Colony.

[10] 'He (Milner) will be attacked when Parlt. meets. Now I can hardly conceive myself voting confidence in him. Yet we have Grey & Asquith – &, of outsiders, Haldane – bound to his chariot wheels: more concerned to save him than for the Liberal party or anything else.' Campbell-Bannerman to Spencer, 6 Nov. 1900, SP.

[11] Milner was chairman of the Board of Inland Revenue, 1892–7, playing a leading part in shaping Harcourt's ideas for the 1894 Budget, when the new form of death duties was introduced.

## 738   LORD SPENCER TO LADY SPENCER

*6 December 1900; Spencer House, St. James's Place, S.W.*

I have had a hard day. Harrow Governors from 11–1, then Rugby Governors from about 2.20 after I had been to the House of Lords to be sworn in to past 4, and then the House of Lords. Kimberley made a safe and undistinguished Speech, lacking a lot in fight and fire.[1] Salisbury was very poor,[2] unusually poor even for his last year's performance.

Then Rosebery made a slashing party Speech on the Dissolution, the methods employed in it, the Financial Directorships of Members of the Government, etc. Devonshire most feebly replied and all was over except that Tweedmouth[3] spoke but hardly anyone heeded what he said with an emptying House.[4]

[1] In a debate on the Queen's Speech, Kimberley dealt with South Africa and China. Hansard, 4, lxxxviii, cols. 23–32.

[2] Ibid., cols. 32–8.

[3] Edward, 2nd Baron Tweedmouth, Lord Privy Seal and Chancellor of the Duchy of Lancaster in Rosebery's government.

[4] Ibid., Rosebery, cols. 38–49; Devonshire, cols. 49–52, Tweedmouth, cols. 53–4.

## 739   LORD SPENCER TO LORD KIMBERLEY

*3 February 1901; Spencer House, St. James's Place, S.W.*
KP, 10247 ff. 119–20

I was very sorry that you did not feel up to going to Windsor yesterday ... The ceremony[1] was very grand and impressive, but the Choir and the upper stalls where nearly all of us K.G.'s sat was exactly like a cellar with strong cold draughts and anyone who had a cold, or was liable to cold would have run a tremendous risk.

Salisbury was wrapped up all the time in heavy coat and skull cap, and at one period took a pull at a flask ...

St. George's was a wonderful sight with all the Foreign Kings and Princes and the music was admirable. The German Emperor bore himself with splendid dignity, not stiff or stuck up, but I don't think he moved his head once during the service.

[1] The funeral of Queen Victoria on 2 Feb. at Windsor.

## 740 H. H. ASQUITH TO LORD SPENCER
*22 June 1901; 20 Cavendish Square, W.*

*Private*

I hasten to send a word of acknowledgment of your kind letter.[1] Friends as good as you and I can afford to be frank with one another, and there is no one from whom I differ with greater distrust[2] or regret.

My speech[3] was not intended to be and was not in any sense a pronunciamento or an ultimatum. It was a declaration, rendered necessary in my opinion by recent occurrences, of the view of those Liberals who have not felt able to denounce the war; a protest against any attempt to rule them out of the party; a frank recognition that the so-called 'pro-Boers' may be excellent Liberals and have just as much right to be in the party as we have; and an appeal to all sections not to smuggle away their differences in ambiguous and unreal pretences of unity, but to show a spirit of 'mutual tolerance and reciprocal respect'. What is there to object to here?

You apparently think that what I said was at any rate inopportune and unnecessary. I am sorry to be obliged to differ.

It is not a question of temper; a man who got through five years of Rosebery *plus* Harcourt, and of Harcourt pure and simple, without any public explosion of ill-temper (as I may fairly say I did) is not likely to be provoked into a tantrum by J.M. Nor is it a question of 'front bench' squatter. If the whole front bench were annihilated to-morrow, it would not substantially alter the situation.

The plain fact is that our anti-war friends have been for some time past avowedly engaged in an organised attempt to make the Liberal party their instrument. They have many advantages: money, enthusiasm, taking speakers like Lloyd George, and a singularly unscrupulous press. I don't blame them; they believe that they are in the right, and that, both morally and politically, we who differ are hopelessly wrong. Look at some of the incidents of the past week. Lloyd George, who is far their best speaker and not at all to be brushed aside as a negligible person, in a 'humanitarian' speech in the H. of Commons suggests that Milner has been made a peer as a reward for his cruelty to the women and children.[4] Massingham, their principal journalist, describes the complacent smile with which Balfour and Chamberlain hailed Brodrick's 'triumphant' statistics of the mortality in the camps.[5] And C.B. himself (who of course is in no sense privy to their designs) says in effect that the war on our side is not war at all, but organised barbarity.[6] Harcourt tells us that we are 'aping' our opponents,[7] and J.M. that we are out of the 'main stream'![8] I could easily add to the list; but these are a sample of the spirit which is at work. Is every Liberal to sit by, in silence and apparent consent, while views such as these are put forward to the world as those of his party? I can assure you that you have no conception of the indignation and resentment which has been aroused in the rank and file. If it had not found a safety valve thro' me or some other leader, I am certain there would, before long, have been a rupture at least as serious as that of 1886.

I have been inundated by letters during the last 2 days from representative Liberals in all parts of the country ... Most of them say that the great bulk of the rank and file hold the views I expressed about the war; in this they may be wrong. But all agree that our party was steadily losing ground in the country, and that such a protest as I have made would have the effect of reassuring and rallying some of its best elements.

I fear I am unrepentant. I have always worked, as you know, for concord, but it is possible to pay too high a price for the semblance of unity.

I hope you will reconsider what you say at the end of your letter about your own future. Politics at present is a thankless business, from which one is often tempted to long for release, and one cannot but doubt at times whether after all the Liberal party, such as we see and know it, is worth preserving. But, as you say, and as you have shown by your own example, it is a question of duty.

[1] Not traced in AP.

[2] Asquith obviously intended to write 'distress'.

[3] On 20 June at Liverpool Street Station Hotel, Asquith dissociated himself from Campbell-Bannerman's 'methods of barbarism' speech to the National Reform Union on 14 June. See n. 6 below.

[4] In a Commons debate on mortality in detention camps in South Africa, Lloyd George stated, 'No doubt what has happened since in these camps and elsewhere has entitled him [Milner] to his peerage.' Hansard, 4, xcv, col. 574, 17 June 1901.

[5] See Daily News, 18 June 1901, p. 5 in his column 'Pictures in Parliament', headed 'The Cry of the Children'. Massingham attacked Asquith's speech of 20 June, quoting one M.P., 'I have only one objection, and that is, it had better not been spoken.' Daily News, 22 June 1901, p. 4.

[6] Campbell-Bannerman during the course of his speech on 14 June had said, 'When was a war not a war? When it was carried on by methods of barbarism in South Africa.' The Times, 15 June 1901, p. 12.

[7] The dinner given by the National Reform Union was to honour jointly Campbell-Bannerman and Harcourt.

[8] Morley also spoke at the dinner. For his views on the war, see D. A. Hamer, John Morley, Liberal Intellectual in Politics (1968), pp. 326-7.

## 741   LORD SPENCER TO H. CAMPBELL-BANNERMAN

*3 October 1901; North Creake, Fakenham*
CBP, Add. MS. 41229 ff. 118-21

... Yes Politics are as usual with us in a muddle. The feeling against the Government seems to rise and increase in volume, and it certainly is unaccountable that with most anxious news from the War arriving every other day, the Cabinet should be scattered over the world. But I fear that in one sense our position as a party is bad.

I do not fancy this Autumn campaign of the Imperialists to which I suppose you refer.[1] Asquith led off in his own constituency[2] which is natural enough but if without any concert with the authorized and legitimate officials of the

Opposition that is continued by him and others, it will be unpleasant. With Asquith's Speech there is no fault to find excepting on one point to which I shall presently refer.

His reference to the origins of the war was not new and was to be anticipated. His criticisms on the Government action were excellent. As to the future of the War, I do not think anything like a 'stop the War' policy can be sharply defined. In so far as that miserable and wicked proclamation pretending to close the War on the 15th Sept.[3] is concerned, it cannot be too strongly denounced, for that and similar paper proclamations must tend to harden the enemy and making them desperate to encourage and strengthen blind resistance. However vain and useless such action on the part of the Boers may be, one cannot but honour the sturdy love of independence and patriotism which inspires it.

It is difficult to judge whether the Government have done all they can to strengthen Kitchener's hands.[4] No doubt their effort to send out Yeomanry was a ghastly failure, for if it is true that out of 400 officers, 100 were sent home as totally inefficient and not likely to become so [sic] and if the rank and file were in the same proportion inefficient the Government are open to the greatest censure. Have they furnished all the efficient reinforcements which they can lay hands on? I cannot say. No doubt with the length of railway communications on which supply depends, most of the enormous army out there are occupied in defending the line of railways, but there ought to be a mobile force at the General's disposal to throw here and there wherever he can hope to overwhelm a Botha, or De Wet or De la Rey.[5] But they are far too slim and agile for our forces ...

The Concentration Camps carry with them their terrible toll of death. I look on them as the dire consequence, it may be, of the farm burnings, but if they were a necessity, surely the authorities never provided what was essential for keeping them efficiently, by way of food, nurses, doctors, tents, etc. The mortality which still continues is appalling.

I have wandered on without intending to touch these subjects.

[1] Campbell-Bannerman, writing from Salzburg, discussed possible tactics with Spencer, adding 'Until, however, our "friends" have spoken there is little material for deciding what line to take.' Campbell-Bannerman to Spencer, 27 Oct. 1901, SP.

[2] 28 Sept. 1901 at Ladybank, East Fife. *The Times* called it 'the first considerable pronouncement made by an Opposition statesman of Cabinet rank since the close of the Session'. 30 Sept. 1901, p. 7.

[3] A proclamation was issued in London on 7 Aug. demanding unconditional surrender before 15 Sept.

[4] Kitchener succeeded Roberts as Commander-in-Chief in Dec. 1900. For an account of the military situation at this time, see P. Magnus, *Kitchener* (1958), pp. 186-7.

[5] Gens. Louis Botha, Christian de Wet and Jacobus De La Rey, whose masterly commando tactics inflicted much damage on British troops and resources.

## 742 LORD SPENCER TO H. SEYMOUR

*14 October 1901; North Creake, Fakenham*

*Confidential*

I do not wonder at Campbell-Bannerman being low as to Political prospects. I fear that Asquith[1] and E. Grey[2] are acting quite on their own account. It is disagreeable for they do not seem to consult any but a very small clique.

Whenever I meet either of them they are most cordial and forthcoming but I hear from neither by letter on Politics.

I wrote to Asquith about what he said re Irish,[3] as I thought him quite wrong to pledge himself, as it were, never to take office unless we had a majority independent of the Irish. I do not think that at this moment an active alliance between Liberals and Irish is possible, but to ban any future co-operation seems to me quite wrong, and unstatesmanlike. Whether Asquith thinks that to announce this independence will help to build up a majority in Great Britain or not I know not, but it clearly will not secure this, and one never knows what may occur in Politics. It may be essential for the Liberal Party to take office even if at first in a minority (a very hateful thing to do but one which at a crisis may be necessary) but still exigencies of a Public character are sometimes very imperative, and even if we are not agreed with the Irish there is no gain in proclaiming a desire to be quit of them. I know that the Irish may be awkward as supporters on many questions at home as well as abroad, but we must face such difficulties when they arise, and they may be met perfectly and honourably without sacrificing any vital principle.

I suppose at some time the Liberals may have had a majority independently of the Irish. Was this so in 1880? but I do not think any of the big measures passed by the Liberals last century were ever gained without Irish help. No doubt the Irish since the ballot and the last Reform Act are different to the Irish before those measures were carried when they were more easy to manage, but the difference does not justify the assertions of Asquith and Grey. Haldane whilst assuming complete agreement with Asquith put the case much better.[4]

I noticed what Robson said.[5] You are right. I as well as others have shadowed out a policy of free cities (so to speak) for Johannesburg and Pretoria that will have to be considered but it is not free of difficulty. I do not know whether I shall speak. I much prefer to keep silence as I am not posing for any personal lead, and just now everyone who speaks is thought to be playing a game of some sort, probably a personal game for one's own advantage; but I may have to speak, and if I do I shall try to lay down clearly what we want both as to S. African settlement and as to Ireland. I shall certainly not back down as to Home Rule, but of course Home Rule when it comes may take a new shape and not what it took in 1886 and 1892.

I feel very isolated in Politics. In many things I still agree more with J. Morley than with others. Kimberley is now I fear getting out of the running. I did not much like what I heard as to his health when I went to see him 2 weeks ago. Ripon can take no active part again.

I expect as to the origin of the War I used to think I agreed and could work better with Asquith than anyone else but now I feel doubtful. As to Campbell-Bannerman I like him and we agree very generally, but I do not feel somehow that he carries weight enough for his position as leader in the House of Commons. Up to a certain point Tweedmouth and I get on well together, but I have not implicit confidence in his judgment. He has however come on a good deal in speaking etc., and is sure to keep a forward post amongst Liberals in future. I am sickening of Politics. I have not the power to stir up the country as a big leader, and although I might at times manage to keep the party together, I don't think any demand will be made on me to lead, and I certainly shall make no bid for the lead. I should shrink from it although I should be bound to try and do my best if a distinct call were made on me to come forward.

I have done my share of work for country and party, and I shall not shirk duty and responsibility if I gave up Politics, but after all the retirements we have had, I cannot retire until the party stands in a stronger position.

[1] In his speech of 28 Sept., Asquith also stated his views on the future relationship between the Liberal Party and the Irish Nationalists.

[2] At Newcastle upon Tyne on 11 Oct., associating himself entirely with Asquith's sentiments. *The Times*, 12 Oct. 1901, p. 6.

[3] Not traced in AP.

[4] Haldane addressed his constituents at East Lothian on 3 Oct. See *The Times*, 4 Oct. 1901, p. 8.

[5] William Robson, Liberal M.P., South Shields, 1895–1910, in a speech to his constituents on 11 Oct. advocated a settlement on lines similar to Spencer's, i.e. to give the Boers a constitution in the agricultural portion of the annexed states and to bring the goldfields and foreign element under British sway. H. Seymour to Spencer, 13 Oct. 1901, SP.

## 743 LORD SPENCER TO C. R. SPENCER
*24 November 1901; Althorp, Northampton*

I was very glad indeed to hear from you, as I wanted to know how Politics struck you.

I was boycotted in London papers over my Banbury Speech,[1] probably owing to local mismanagement. I took some pains with my Speech, setting out for the Banbury Liberal Club a connected but short account of South African affairs during the last 5 or 6 years.[2] It went off well, and I have corrected a Northampton report of it,[3] as I rather wanted to leave on record that I took the line I did before Campbell-Bannerman spoke at Plymouth.[4]

I was amazed and horrified, as were staunch Liberals in Oxfordshire, when I heard that Perks[5] would be there. He had come for a big Wesleyan meeting in the town. He was however, (excepting in one sentence, when he referred to the man on the fence, in terms which I really did not understand), quite sound.

He agreed absolutely with me!! He said that he was a Dissenting Radical and a Liberal without an adjective!!! I nearly tumbled out of my chair when he said that. Afterwards he declared that Rosebery would speak on the same lines as I had taken, excepting that he would attack strongly Lord Milner.

I told C.B. this,[6] and I suppose this led to what he said re J.C. and Milner.[7] You may have seen how I dealt with it less severely, hoping 'that a Durham or Elgin[8] might be found to settle the future of the two States' etc.

This I said at Newport.[9]

... I was aghast about Allard, and I heard that Herbert Gladstone was rabid, and denounced the plot to E. Grey. Whether his explosion caused the retreat I do not know, but it is an excellent thing.[10]

I saw H.C.B. at Bristol, he was in the up train and I had just landed to change trains. He was in great spirits and gave a splendid account of Scotland and of his Plymouth meeting. I thought his Speech at Plymouth of the highest order, far the best Speech he ever made.

[1] On 12 Nov. It was however fully reported in the *Banbury Guardian*, 14 Nov. 1901, p. 7.

[2] Of the speech, the *Pall Mall Gazette* commented, 'The Red Earl would have us offer the Boer terms of peace short of independence. Can he not understand that so long as he and his friends talk in this way the enemy will continue to struggle?' 22 Nov. 1901, p. 2.

[3] *NM*, 15 Nov. 1901, p. 7.

[4] 19 Nov.

[5] Robert William Perks, Liberal M.P., Louth division, Lincolnshire, 1892-1910, leading Rose-beryite in the Imperial Liberal Council and a Vice-President. Treasurer, Liberal League, 1902-10. See D. Crane, *The Life Story of Sir Robert W. Perks* (1909), pp. 200-3. His country house was at Wykham Park, Banbury. Lord Crewe described him as 'not a bad sort of fellow, though has become rather a political Tartarian, which is likely to happen to a respectable solicitor who is inspired by warlike ideas'. Crewe to Spencer, 18 Nov. 1901, SP.

[6] Spencer to Campbell-Bannerman, 13 Nov. 1901, CBP, Add. MS. 41229 f. 134.

[7] Dealing with South Africa after the war and the alienation of the Dutch population from Britain, Campbell-Bannerman declared, 'For my part I despair of this peril being conjured away so long as the present Colonial Secretary is in Downing Street and as long as the present High Commissioner is at Pretoria.' *The Times*, 20 Nov. 1901, p. 6.

[8] Durham was appointed Governor-General of British North American provinces in May 1838: his lenient treatment of the rebels led to his resignation in Oct. In the following year his *Report on the Affairs of British North America* was published, which proposed the union of Upper and Lower Canada. The principle of responsible government was not established until Elgin became Governor-General, Canada (1846-54).

[9] Newport, Monmouthshire, on 21 Nov., where he referred to Campbell-Bannerman's Plymouth speech. *The Times*, 22 Nov. 1901, p. 4.

[10] The Imperial Liberal Council changed its name to the Liberal Imperialist League in Oct. 1901, Grey replacing Brassey as President. William Allard, a leading Liberal agent, was appointed secretary but after angry representations from Herbert Gladstone he withdrew until Feb. 1902. H. C. G. Matthew, *The Liberal Imperialists* (1973), p. 75.

## 744  LORD SPENCER TO C. R. SPENCER

*18 December 1901; Althorp, Northampton*

I studied the Chesterfield delivery yesterday.[1] I do not like his references to general policy especially discarding the policy of 1886 and 1892. It is not loyal to Mr. G., it is unfair to his own policy and that of his colleagues. If he means that because the Nationalists are strongly against us on the War, that action of theirs is on all fours with what they have done before. We had to bear violent abuse on this very score for years. The great argument was, they will be hostile to every British interest as long as they do not get Home Rule, and if we were to notice what they say beyond protecting ourselves against it, Home Rule would never be supported in England. It is a hateful necessity but necessity it is, and the offence is not new but of long standing.

As to what he says on the War, excepting in some passages where there is a want of enthusiasm and a leaning to meet the Asquith-Grey party, I can subscribe to nearly all he said. Indeed in my Speeches in feebler terms I used many of his arguments. No doubt I laid more blame on Government than he did, say as to Concentration Camps, but the difference is more that of statement than of principle.

He was very outspoken on many points going far beyond the pro Government speeches of Asquith and Grey, e.g. as to the Proclamation re Sept. 15, and Milner in a way.

There is of course no strict connection between the Speech itself with the surroundings of it, and the Campbell-Bannerman position, but I fear that it will (though not the actual Speech) aggravate the difficulty of the Leadership of C.B.

What moreover will R. do? Will he lead in the House of Lords? Will he work in harmony and in communication with Liberal leaders?

I certainly shall stick to C.B., and I suppose if he leads and goes on leading, I shall have to go on as I did last year in the House of Lords, disagreeable as it was, and will be with R., independent, on my flank. But if C.B. is driven to resign which is not beyond possibility, I shall certainly obstinately refuse to go on leading.

However I did not mean to run off on this.

I had a letter from E. Grey on another matter in which he refers to the Speech and says that they had no idea what R. would say, but that he entirely agreed. He speaks however strongly against C.B. He expects that I do not agree with R.'s Speech.

I shall write to him today.[2]

[1] Rosebery's speech at Chesterfield contained his views on South Africa. He made clear that the war must be pushed vigorously; that concentration camps were necessary and that Milner should be retained. On Ireland, Rosebery stated, 'The primary duty of the Liberal Party is to wipe the slate clean.'

[2] Spencer told Grey, 'I fear that the surroundings of Rosebery at Chesterfield will, although in one sense they need not be so interpreted, strongly increase the split amongst our Front Bench Leaders and increase R.'s difficulties.' 18 Dec. 1901, SP (copy). Spencer also wrote to others on the Chesterfield speech: Spencer to Campbell-Bannerman, 18 Dec. 1901, CBP, Add. MS. 41229 f. 142; Spencer to Rosebery, 19 Dec. 1901, RP, 10062 ff. 248-9; Spencer to Ripon, 20 Dec. 1901, Rip.P, Add. MS. 43538 ff. 76-9.

## 745 LORD KIMBERLEY TO LORD SPENCER

*23 December 1901; Kimberley House, Wymondham*

*Private*

I have received a letter today from Ripon strongly urging me not take any steps at present to resign the leadership of the House of Lords.[1] I feel the force of his arguments, and I have written to him to say that I will take no steps at present to resign.

When I wrote to you, I under estimated the use which might be made of Rosebery's speech to undermine C.B's position, and the last thing I should wish to do would be to further any intrigue against him.

He has done his part well and manfully, and deserves all the support we can give him.

[1] Spencer had twice attempted to persuade Kimberley, who was ill, to continue nominally as Leader, himself offering to act in his place. Ripon was asked by Spencer to press Kimberley, 20 Dec. 1901, Rip.P., Add. MS. 43538 f. 78. Ripon agreed to do so, adding, 'To open that question now would be in the highest degree inadvisable. It might lead to an attempt to hurry matters disastrously, and to force Rosebery upon the Party without conditions and without securities for C.B.' Ripon to Spencer, 22 Dec. 1901, SP. See also A. F. Denholm, *Lord Ripon* (1982), p. 234.

## 746    H. CAMPBELL-BANNERMAN TO LORD SPENCER

*23 December 1901; Lord Warden Hotel, Dover*

*Private*

I lunched in Berkeley Square today.[1] I called yesterday but he [Rosebery] was out and he asked me to lunch. We had a frank talk of an hour or more.

One object of mine in going was that it is alleged that we (perhaps I must say I) stand in the way of a grand conciliation: the truth being that he is the impediment, though his speeches do not disclose it. I told him that this was what I wanted to clear up.

He said that on the war he had taken his own line; had not read a word of what Asquith or I had been saying or anyone else; had gone diagonally across every one's line. Never meant any such importance to be attached to meeting or speech, but merely to speak out what he thought.

Is wholly against the present sullen policy, against all severities, against Milner. Agrees that Milner will not negotiate successfully. Said 'I believe I could make peace tomorrow.'

Will he join and co-operate since we are so greatly agreed? Impossible. Has been five or 6 years out of the party; is not (in ecclesiastical phrase) 'in communion' with it. Besides is debarred by Irish policy. Is against Home Rule in any form. Country won't have it, especially now that Irish have proclaimed enmity. Might give councils but never a parliament of any kind. This vital. If spoke again would devote speech to Ireland.

As to general policy his phrases such as clean slate, shibboleths etc. only meant that Newcastle programme must be sunk. Principles remain, to be applied discreetly according to circumstances. If his words, and theory of 'efficiency' etc. coincided with recommendations of Sidney Webb, pure accident.[2]

What did he mean when he offered his help to utmost of power? This was offered not to Party but to country. He is ready: has no more to say: his cards are on the table.

Is he not going to play the cards? Had he seen *The Times* saying a speech not enough, must have action? Does not read newspapers: has no more to do or say, but his further action will be in House of Lords *where he will be active.*

This is the gist of it. We were entirely friendly, and I did not at all urge him, only enquired and asked for explanation. The great point is that *he won't join in.* I never thought he would, but I have it flat from him.

I thought I had better let you know at once. I think it would be most desirable somehow to let the world at large know. It is very unfair that we should be blamed for being irresponsive to his seductions, when it is he that won't play![3]

---

[1] Campbell-Bannerman, urged on by Tweedmouth and others to explore with Rosebery the obstacles to unity, (Tweedmouth to Spencer 22 Dec. 1901, SP.) called on him on 22 Dec. but Rosebery was not there. The meeting took place the following day. Campbell-Bannerman sent accounts of the meeting to Harcourt on 23 Dec., Bryce on 25 Dec., and Ripon on 31 Dec. Rosebery's own account of the meeting recorded immediately afterwards differs in many ways from Campbell-Bannerman's. Crewe, ii, pp. 573-4.

[2] Haldane first brought Rosebery and Beatrice and Sidney Webb together at a select dinner party in London in March 1900. Later, they urged on Rosebery the idea of a 'national minimum of health, education and efficiency'. G. R. Searle, *The Quest for National Efficiency* (1971) p. 123.

[3] Spencer replied, 'The position is excepting as to the War policy, eminently unsatisfactory ... His attitude is not pleasant for me, for if he is active and independent in the H. of L., I must stand up for the line which you and others among us lay down on general policy.' Spencer to Campbell-Bannerman, 27 Dec. 1901, CBP, Add. MS. 41229 f. 147.

## 747 SIR E. GREY TO LORD SPENCER

*25 December 1901; Falloden, Chathill, Northumberland*

I haven't yet thanked you for sending me your speech,[1] which I was very glad to have the opportunity of reading at length. If C.B. had spoken in the same tone, we shouldn't have this trouble, but his charge of 'barbarism' has done untold mischief to the Liberal party at home and much harm abroad.

I think Rosebery's reference to the Irish was harshly put, but I am afraid the statement he made is true, as to the present position.

I have heard nothing as to his intentions for the future and have not had any opportunity of discussing things with anybody, except by letter, since Chesterfield; nor have I heard what C.B.'s attitude is towards the Chesterfield speech; he would no doubt approve the suggestions for peace and settlement, but Rosebery went flatly against him on four points on which he has practically asked the Liberal party to concentrate – Martial Law, 'barbarism', stating terms and 'making overtures' to the Boers, and recall or supersession of Milner, and here is the difficulty ahead of us[2]. Apropos of the Irish question, I enclose a report of what I said this Autumn.[3]

[1] At Banbury on 12 Nov. See No. 743.
[2] Grey wrote to Rosebery on 17 Dec. sending his 'unqualified congratulations' adding that there was not 'a single conclusion in your speech to which I don't give a whole-hearted assent'. K. Robbins, *Sir Edward Grey* (1971), p. 95.
[3] See No. 742 n. 2.

## 748 LORD SPENCER TO SIR E. GREY

*27 December 1901; Althorp, Northampton[1]*

I have read your speech on Ireland. I should warmly approve of most of what you said, were it not for the opening where you explain your agreement with what Asquith said.[2]

I think that quite wrong, and I wrote to A. about it when I read his Speech.

As to K.[3] not his actual words 'I do not think that any leading politician should pledge himself to such a statement, in that he would not wish Liberals to accept office again unless they could rely on an independent Liberal majority in the House of Commons, for no one can forecast what will happen in the future. A crisis may come when a Party in opposition may be called upon and be obliged from Political motives to take office, and you cannot beforehand say that that party must refuse to take this step, because it has not a majority independent of the *Irish*.'

I felt this very strongly and nothing which Asquith said in his late Speeches (he did not answer my letter) has in the least altered my view which agrees with what Lord K. propounded.

I admit that you put forward reasons why a Liberal majority with Irish may be awkward [sic], I can't say dangerous, for if the Irish tried to make a Liberal Government do unpatriotic things the Liberal Government would indeed have degenerated from its true traditions if it allowed itself to be driven from the line which they think the right one in the general interests of the Empire.

As to the rest I am satisfied that C.B. would be perfectly ready to work on the lines of R.'s speech as to S. Africa. I am glad to say that he has seen R., and they had a long and very friendly conversation. It showed that they were 'greatly agreed' and I am sure that H.C.B. would act not on R.'s lines as laid down at Chesterfield; but also he made it clear that 'he would not join in' with H.C.B. and others.

Agreement apparently could be made on everything excepting Ireland, as R. seemed against Home Rule in any form. When his attention was called to *The Times* writing that a speech was not enough, they must have action, he replied that he did not read newspapers! and has no more to do or say, but his further action will be in the House of Lords where he will be active.

I am very sorry about all this.

Of course just now we must work, at all events if I have anything to say I will do so, for union on the South African position and this may lead to a better understanding on other questions . . .

As to my position in the House of Lords, we shall probably agree as to the War, but if he takes a line on Ireland I cannot be silent.

As to your point of difference between C.B. and R., I have already told you that I thought the words 'methods of barbarism' were unfortunate as they could be distorted by antagonists as they have been into charges against the soldiers, a charge repudiated time after time by C.B.

As to Martial Law I cannot think that C.B. differs about that. He only dwells on the disastrous effect that Martial Law must have on people in the Free Colony. I don't think he asserts it should not have been resorted to at all. As to terms I have never read his speeches as defining terms and certain terms only.

As to recalling Lord Milner he evidently would accept R's views as to Lord M.

'There are some details differing from what we have been advocating, but the differences are not vital' and what R. stated 'relating to the War and the Settlement is pronounced by all satisfactory and likely to make for peace.'

These are quotations from a letter I received from C.B. written on 21 Dec. after he had seen several leading men in London.[4] I have not seen him nor anyone except Tweedmouth but I hardly agree as to the effect which R.'s speech on the War etc. has had.

[1] Copy, SP.
[2] At Bristol on 11 Dec. *The Times*, 12 Dec. 1901, p. 7.
[3] Kimberley to Spencer, 17 Dec. 1901, SP.
[4] SP.

### 749   A. H. D. ACLAND TO LORD SPENCER
*13 January 1902; 2 Weaponness Park, Scarborough*

I was glad you spoke out at Manchester.[1] I entirely agreed with what you said. I am deeply concerned with what you say about politics. I had hoped that there was some chance of an attempt at unity to start with this session. Can you tell me why it is supposed to be impossible? Does Asquith of whom you speak specially say that he cannot take counsel with C.B. in future or does C.B. say that he will not invite A. to take counsel with him or how is it?

I suppose what one may call the wreckers or wirepullers on both sides are trying to make unity impossible. That always happens and can only be remedied by the men at the centre refusing to be wirepulled. I fear that perhaps neither C.B. on whom I suppose Harcourt with others brings all his influence to bear, nor Asquith whom Haldane, Grey etc. seem to have captured are quite powerful enough to snap their fingers at the wirepullers and really try for unity.

There is not really enough fundamental cause in principle to make a split. And yet when Grey was staying here a little while ago before Chesterfield he seemed to me, as I told him, to be trying to manufacture a split as hard as he could. If Asquith persists in being led by Grey I am afraid it can only have one result. Grey is the most charming of friends. He always is to *me*, but he seems to have in his *blood* a tendency to magnify differences.

It is all very sad. But I do most earnestly hope you will *insist* on seeing Asquith.

[1] As Chancellor of Victoria University, Spencer presided at a meeting to consider *inter alia*, the establishment of separate university colleges at Liverpool and Manchester. See Spencer to Lady Spencer, 11 Jan. 1902, SP.

### 750   H. H. ASQUITH TO LORD SPENCER
*2 March 1902; Cold Overton, Oakham*

*Private*

I just send you a line to say that I hope you will read in the same spirit in which it is written a letter of mine which will appear in the papers tomorrow.[1] I have been anxious all through these recent events to do what I can for peace – within such limits as one's own convictions, and the disquieting action of other people, would permit. This, as you know, is not an easy matter.

I don't know that you will agree with all I say in my letter – especially about Home Rule:[2] but I trust you will find that, for practical purposes, the area of common ground is infinitely wider and clearer than the borderland of possible differences.

[1] Following Rosebery's repudiation of Campbell-Bannerman's leadership on 21 Feb., Asquith explained his own position to his constituents in an open letter dated 1 March.

[2] Asquith stated that an Irish home rule bill introduced by the next Liberal government would be a mistake. R. Jenkins, *Asquith* (1967), pp. 144-5.

**751  LORD SPENCER TO H. H. ASQUITH**
*3 March 1902; Spencer House, St. James's Place, S.W.*
AP, 10 ff. 74-5

I am much obliged to you for writing to me.

As usual with all that you do your letter is very able, and it is also moderate.

I do not wish to pronounce finally on it now.

I will however notice 3 points.

(1) You say that you dismiss personal questions as wholly irrelevant.

I think that they ought to be irrelevant and I notice and accept what you say that no considerations of the kind have influenced your judgement or conduct, but to my mind personal considerations have started and all along influenced the sad differences in the party which have existed since Mr. Gladstone's resignation.

(2) As to Ireland.

I will not enter upon that; you know my views, I have not altered them and cannot alter them.

They ought to have been capable of adjustment with yours and with the views of others, but I very much fear that the recent utterances on the subject will separate me from you on this.

(3) I altogether dissent from your view that practical matters on which Liberals ought to be agreed (and as to this I have always even up to last Tuesday hoped for agreement) will be helped by the new organization.[1]

I dislike extremely groups in the Liberal ranks, and this last group is not one to promote one special policy, such even as Imperialism, but to lay down the whole policy of the Liberal Party which I for one do not wish to remodel, and I therefore cannot possibly approve of the formation of the new Liberal League even with its eminent leaders among whom I regret to think you are one.

Alas! I feel more than anything and have felt for many months past, the increasing separation in Politics between us, for I always looked on you as one of my most trusted Political friends, with whom I could always frankly and sympathetically discuss every political subject, even if we did not always agree.

Your note possibly reopens the possibility of this. I wish it could be so, and although I have plainly given you my first impressions on three points of your letter, I hope that nothing I have said will turn back into the region of silence and want of communication with each other.

[1] The Liberal League was formed on 24 Feb. following Rosebery's Chesterfield speech. Asquith, Grey and Fowler were Vice-Presidents with Rosebery as President. See Matthew, pp. 86-7.


**752  H. H. ASQUITH TO LORD SPENCER**
*4 March 1902; 20 Cavendish Square, W.*

*Private*

I was delighted to get your kind and friendly letter. Far from resenting, I welcome your criticisms. May I rejoin in the same spirit?

(1) Personal 'cross-currents'. I agree that these things have had a real and vicious

influence. I won't try to apportion the blame. But I said the truth when I disclaimed them for myself.

(2) Ireland. I tried to make it clear that I have not in any way renounced principles or ends; it is a question of means and methods, steps and degrees.

(3) Organisation. I think the new proposal a cheap price to pay for the avoidance of what was otherwise inevitable: a 'definite' and open split. The National Liberal Fedn. has become little more than a cockpit, in which after much subterranean preparation the factions make a periodical exhibition of themselves. Nothing can excees the assiduity and ingenuity with which Loulou and his friends are trying to capture for their own purposes our regular organisations, e.g. Eighty Club. It is not so much a question of reprisals as of selfprotection.

## 753  LORD SPENCER TO C. R. SPENCER
*27 March 1902; Althorp, Northampton*

I was glad that you heard that my National Liberal Speech was a success.[1] As far as I can judge Politics are settling down, and the Liberal League is not pushing itself forward or receiving much support.

I heard of Margaret[2] at the Station from W. Churchill[3] and D. of Marlborough[4] ... We had a pleasant and interesting talk over Politics last night. I was surprised to find how sound and liberal Sunny[5] was about the War, and so is Winston.

[1] On 19 March, at the second annual house dinner of the National Liberal Club, Spencer urged self-government for the Boers and commented on the Liberal League 'he believed he had sufficient confidence in his principles not to want the support of a league or an association.' *The Times*, 20 March 1902, p. 10.

[2] Robert Spencer's wife.

[3] Conservative M.P., Oldham, since 1900.

[4] Charles, 9th Duke of Marlborough, Paymaster-General, 1899–1902, and staff captain, Imperial Yeomanry, in the South African war. He was Churchill's uncle.

[5] Marlborough's nickname.

## 754  LORD RIBBLESDALE[1] TO LORD SPENCER
*14 April 1902; Gisburne Park, Clitheroe*

Thank you for your letter: I quite recognise the difficulty you are placed in and the ticklishness of unity to Ld. R. on the question of leadership in the Lords having regard to Ld. R.'s attitude to Sir H.C.B. in the Commons, but *if* Ld. R. is to be consulted in any special way I assumed that it must be on this question of leadership,[2] as otherwise all that is necessary is a summons or rather invitation to attend a meeting of the Party peers at your house.

Until I had seen and talked the position over with Tweedmouth[3] I was personally inclined to this latter course, and to recommend the proposal of your name as Leader at the meeting as a matter of course, but there is force in the considerations which T. brought to bear in our conversation.

First, he pointed out that if Ld. R. on your invitation were to accept the Leadership in the Lords, he *ipso facto* brings himself into line and union with C.B. and the official Liberals and the party at large; and secondly, if on your invitation he again declines, he strengthens your position from any point of view, morally and practically, and proclaims *urbi et orbi* his fixed intentions of standing aside and of doing nothing which would tend to join up the fissures in the party.[4]

[1] Thomas, 4th Baron Ribblesdale, Liberal Whip.
[2] Kimberley died on 8 April.
[3] Ribblesdale and Tweedmouth met on the morning of 11 April to discuss the leadership position. They both agreed that Rosebery should be advised of, not consulted on, the position. Tweedmouth to Spencer, 11 April 1902, SP. Ribblesdale to Spencer, 12 April 1902, SP.
[4] Rosebery declined to participate in choosing Kimberley's successor. Spencer to Rosebery, 16 April 1902, RP., 10062 ff. 254-5, and Rosebery to Spencer, 20 April 1902, SP.


## 755   J. MORLEY TO LORD SPENCER
*27 April 1902; 57 Elm Park Gardens, South Kensington, S.W.*

I heard from my wife your political cares and difficulties. I wish that I could suggest any remedy. But I see no daylight in a scene such as the Liberal party now presents and is long likely to do. It is a mixture of ineptitude and bad faith, from which I for one am glad to be detached.

As for the Education Bill,[1] I have not studied it, nor do I intend to meddle. The corn duty[2] is pure mischief, but I can only say that it is what I foretold as the certain result of the war, and it serves John Bull right for his folly and iniquity. So you see I am out of it.

[1] Balfour introduced the Education Bill in the Commons on 24 March 1902. Hansard, 4, cv, cols. 846-86. It was opposed by Liberals since it granted rate-aid to denominational schools.
[2] As part of the Budget, Hicks Beach, Chancellor of the Exchequer, announced that an import duty of 3d. per cwt. on corn and 5d. on flour would be imposed. Hansard, 4, cvi, col. 180 ff. 14 March 1902.


## 756   LORD SPENCER TO H. CAMPBELL-BANNERMAN
*19 May 1902; Althorp, Northampton*
CBP, Add. MS. 41229 ff. 161-3

I had heard nothing as to Leeds, but I wondered what Herbert G. would do in his own constituency.

That R. should go there is very unfortunate, but I cannot see what H.G. can do if he goes to the meeting except one of two things or both. 1st. Get R. to declare his willingness to co-operate cordially with you and work for the views adopted by Liberals.[1]

2nd. Or himself declare that though glad to co-operate with every Liberal he, H.G., stoutly supported you and your Policy.[2]

The situation is damnable. I found myself at a very staunch friend's house,

F. Cawley's,[3] on Thursday but with Emmott[4] I took occasion, as I suspected E.'s leanings, to express myself very strongly as to the N. Lib. League, and the odious position of Politics with the Lib. party in groups, each group struggling for its own advancement.

I also expressed myself re Perks.

Perks tried to get me to the Education Meeting.[5] I refused. I did not at the moment declare that I could not be on the same platform as R., but I said that I abhorred meetings with a circle of speakers, one being enough, that I had done my part at Bradford on the Education Question,[6] and would not come to a London meeting. Asquith, who was walking with us, it was in the Lobby, agreed with me, but he told me going down to Manchester[7] that he had been obliged to consent to go. Since then R.'s declaration at Colchester has come.[8]

If I were applied to now I should be disposed to speak out.

I draw a distinction of going to a meeting for one subject on which we all agreed, as it is of importance to unite on big questions like the Bread Tax and Education, but it is quite different where the whole Policy can be and should be discussed.

I am shocked at Birrell, but I confess I have always had doubts as to his staunchness.[9]

I have been hoping that as things went on if co-operation on special subjects were followed, the distinction of the N.L.L. would gradually disappear and that eventually there would be no group of that hue. But if they intrigue in Constituencies and try and run separate meetings, and worse than anything assume different views on big subjects such as Education, these possibilities disappear, and a crisis is inevitable.

I get very cross and indignant about all this.

At Manchester when Asquith mentioned Rosebery, quite a fair reference, there were cheers but not at all unanimous or strong. When J. Morley's name was mentioned there was a perfect storm of applause and Scott, *Manchester Guardian*, had a tremendous ovation.[10] The meeting was clearly very strongly our way of thinking, but I thought it wise to make no special references to elicit this.

I should were I in your place be silent as to the differences at Darlington.[11] Let the Robites show their hand first.

[1] Rosebery spoke at Leeds on 30 May agreeing with government policy and calling for unity on South Africa. The Boer leaders accepted the British terms at Vereeniging on 31 May.

[2] In fact, Rosebery gave the Liberal leaders the advice 'that they should postpone the production of a programme until they see a more immediate prospect of being able to carry it into effect'. *The Times*, 31 May 1902, p. 9.

[3] Frederick Cawley, Liberal M.P., Prestwich division, South-East Lancashire, 1895-1918.

[4] Alfred Emmott, Liberal M.P., Oldham, 1899-1911.

[5] Perks, chairman of the Nonconformist Parliamentary Council and a bitter opponent of the Education Bill, persuaded Rosebery to preside at a large protest meeting in London in May. Other speakers were Fowler, Asquith and Lloyd George. Matthew, p. 96.

[6] On 7 May. *The Times*, 8 May 1902, p. 10.

[7] Spencer and Asquith spoke at a meeting in the Free Trade Hall, Manchester on 15 May condemning the corn tax. See also Spencer to Rosebery, 17 May 1902, RP, 10062 ff. 257-8.

[8] On the occasion of the bestowal of the freedom of the borough on 15 May, Rosebery stated his approval of the provision in the Education Bill which would establish the county council

education committee as the authority for primary and secondary education. *The Times*, 16 May 1902, p. 12.

[9] Augustine Birrell had been defeated at Manchester North-East in 1900. He agreed to attend this one meeting only in Leeds. Birrell later claimed that his role during the war was to prevent a schism in the Liberal Party. A. Birrell, *Things Past Redress* (1937), p. 176.

[10] Charles Prestwich Scott, editor, 1872-1929 and Liberal M.P., Leigh, 1895-1906. The paper supported Campbell-Bannerman during the War. J. L. Hammond, *C. P. Scott* (1934), p. 80.

[11] Campbell-Bannerman devoted most of his speech at Darlington on 24 May to an attack on Chamberlain. *The Times*, 26 May 1902, p. 12.

## 757   LORD SALISBURY TO LORD SPENCER

*16 July 1902; Hatfield House, Hatfield, Herts*

Your very kind words, both in your letter and in the House, have affected me very deeply.[1] Since I first served under you on the Commission of 1865[2] your attitude and conduct towards me have been constantly marked by the greatest consideration. It is impossible that sincere political antagonism – and very effective antagonism – could be carried on in a more agreeable and chivalrous manner. I earnestly trust that you will long adorn the Leadership for which you have been so wisely selected.

[1] Salisbury resigned as prime minister on 11 July. See Spencer's letter to Salisbury, 14 July 1902, Salisbury Papers, and his speech in the Lords on the same day. Hansard, 4, cxi, cols. 73-5. He was succeeded by his nephew, A. J. Balfour.

[2] See No. 39.

## 758   J. MORLEY TO LORD SPENCER

*17 July 1902; Ridgeways, Hindhead, Surrey*

I had a long and free conversation with R. a few days ago, of which I will tell you more, if you want to know, when we meet. No daylight, but I think he knows that he and his men have made a mess of it . . .

R. thinks that nothing would be easier than for *you* to make an administration. Does the prospect at this moment please you?

## 759   H. GLADSTONE TO LORD SPENCER

*23 September 1902; Gosford, Longniddry, N.B.*

*Private*

Thanks for your letter. I am glad you are going to Derby. I don't suppose there is any chance of the Education Bill being in the Lords by Nov 14th.[1] In this case I understand you are going to Birmingham. I hear that Chamberlain thinks he may lose a seat or two there if the Government makes no concession.

I have knocked up against a good many notabilities interested in the Bill. Brodrick[2] is here. Today I met A. J. Balfour and the Bishop of London[3] playing golf at Mirfield. Arthur Lyttelton (Bishop of Southampton) was also there. The

Speaker I met at John Penn's[4] at Archerfield. Winston and Percy[5] and Haldane were at Guisachan.[6]

In one way or the other it seems to me that the Government are most uneasy. Balfour is being strongly pressed by Church leaders to *stiffen* the Bill in their direction.[7] They think that they have made a mistake in supporting the Bill as it is. On the other hand there is great discontent among the rank and file because of the unpopularity of the Bill, and the P.M. is between two fires. But I hear the clerical side are giving him most trouble now. I believe he is much harassed – he looks it – and he thinks the Government may be beaten in the Autumn Session.

In connection with these rumours I don't want to be quoted for what I have heard comes through 'delicate' channels. It may be that considerable changes will be made, but nothing is yet settled.

P.S. The Bishop of London is a very indifferent Golfer, and the Prime Minister is 'off his drive'. He complains I believe that this worry added to the Education difficulty makes his position very difficult.[8]

[1] The bill reached the Lords on 2 Dec.
[2] Secretary of State for War, 1900–3.
[3] Arthur Winnington-Ingram, appointed in 1901.
[4] Conservative M.P., Lewisham, 1891–1903.
[5] Possibly Henry Algernon Percy, eldest son of 7th Duke of Northumberland, Conservative M.P., Kensington South, 1895–1909, and Parliamentary Under-Secretary for India, 1902–3.
[6] Tweedmouth's home in Inverness-shire.
[7] Balfour admitted to a colleague that 'there will be a good deal of panic in the air when we meet in October... To create in the face of immense opposition a body of managers with a denominational majority, and then to leave the Anglican parson or the R.C. Bishop in uncontrolled supremacy over all that pertains to denominational teaching appears to me to be a very clumsy contrivance.' Balfour to Lord Hugh Cecil, 15 Sept. 1902, Quickswood Papers, Qu.I 1/80.
[8] In agreeing with Gladstone's assessment of the situation, Spencer wrote, 'I can well believe the difficulties which surround A.J.B. We must not ease them for him.' Spencer to H. Gladstone, 25 Sept. 1902, HGP, Add. MS. 40617 f. 125.

**760** SIR F. KNOLLYS TO LORD SPENCER
*6 November 1902; Sandringham, Norfolk*

The King is very much distressed at what I told him and he sincerely feels for you in your anxiety.[1]

He trusts however that matters may turn out better than you fear and that the result of the consultation may have the effect of reassuring you.

His Majesty says that of course he would not wish you to come here and leave Lady Spencer while you must necessarily be in such a great state of anxiety about her.[2]

[1] A report on Lady Spencer's health received on 6 Nov. was in Spencer's words 'very unpromising'.
[2] Spencer had been invited, as Leader of the Opposition in the Lords, to Sandringham from 9 Nov., where the German Emperor was to pay a private visit. Knollys to Spencer, 4 Nov. 1902, SP.

**761 LORD REAY[1] TO LORD SPENCER**
*7 November 1902; Laidlawstiel, Galashiels, N.B.*

I was delighted to see from your last speech, of which the *Scotsman* had a much fuller report than *The Times*, on what lines you intend to attack the bill in the House of Lords.[2] The bill is extremely confused; it does not show any grasp of the problem. The Act of '70 is much more original.

I suppose you wish to move its rejection and to have a debate of more than one day on the Second Reading.[3]

Will it be of any use after an exhausting Second Reading debate to move amendments which the Government have opposed in the Commons or any new ones?

We shall have I think to oppose any amendments directed against concessions made by the Government such as the Cowper-Temple Clause[4] for Secondary education and the Kenyon-Slaney amendment . . .[5]

The Tory party in the Lords is not less Protestant than the Tory party in the Commons and I should think that we might appeal to it and not attack the Church as a whole, but only the clerical elements as represented by the Bishop of Worcester.[6] If the Bishop of Hereford[7] moves his compromise, we might support him although it is illogical.[8]

[1] Donald James, 11th Baron Reay, Under-Secretary of State for India, 1894-5, chairman, School Board for London, 1897-1904.
[2] Speech at Derby on 31 Oct. on the Education Bill. *Scotsman*, 1 Nov. 1902, p. 10.
[3] The debate on the second reading of the Education Bill in the Lords took place on 4-5 Dec. 1902. An attempt to reject the bill was heavily defeated by 147 votes to 37. Hansard, 4, cxvi, 5 Dec. 1902, col. 122.
[4] William Cowper-Temple, Liberal M.P., Hampshire South, 1868-80, successfully promoted an amendment to the 1870 Elementary Education Bill which stated that 'no religious catechism or religious formulary which is distinctive of any particular denomination shall be taught in the school' (i.e. a school provided by a school board).
[5] Col. William Kenyon-Slaney, Conservative M.P., Shropshire North, 1886-1908, had introduced an amendment during the closing stages of the 1902 Education Bill which dramatically shifted the balance of power within denominational managing bodies away from the clerical element. In order to appease Nonconformist opposition to the bill, Balfour accepted it. See P. Gordon, *The Victorian School Manager* (1974), pp. 264-5.
[6] Charles Gore, Bishop of Worcester, 1902-5.
[7] John Percival, headmaster of Rugby, 1887-95, Bishop of Hereford, 1895-1917.
[8] Percival envisaged a system of compulsory attendance at continuation classes for those up to 17 who no longer received full-time instruction. The amendment was not carried. W. Temple, *Life of Bishop Percival* (1921), p. 185.

**762 LORD SPENCER TO LORD SELBORNE[1]**
*21 December 1902; Spencer House, St. James's Place, S.W.*
Selborne Papers, 149

I received your letter and the Memorandum last night.[2] I have read it with profound interest. If I may be allowed to say so I think you have dealt with a very difficult problem which called out badly for reform in a very broad and comprehensive spirit.

There was nothing which gave me more anxiety when I was at the Admiralty than the relative position of the officers of different branches employed in the

Fleet. By ordinary methods it seemed almost hopeless to attempt a change without stirring up serious objections of a formidable kind. This proposal of yours gets over this by covering the difficulty by a great fundamental change. It is a bold and fine effort and I wish it very hearty success.

I have no doubt that there will be difficulties of class and of technical knowledge which will arise, especially in the intermediate transition period. Of course looking at the change by the light of the men now in each branch of the service, it may be difficult to conceive Executive officers studying deeply the technical part of Engineers' duties, and Engineers being placed in the position of Executive officers, and the same will apply to the marine officers. But if you can effect the change of Education which you propose, you will raise the class and character of all the three services, and when once this is effected, you will find old professional jealousies and difficulties disappear.

I very heartily congratulate you on the proposal.

[1] William, 2nd Earl of Selborne, First Lord of the Admiralty since 1900. Selborne to Spencer, 20 Dec. 1902, SP.

[2] The so-called Selborne Memorandum placed navigation, gunnery and other executive officers on the same footing of social equality as engineering officers by means of a common entry system into the Navy. The scheme, which Selborne called 'revolutionary', was issued on Christmas Day 1902 and came into effect in Sept. 1903.

# 10

# THE DEFENCE OF FREE TRADE, 1903-4

*Chamberlain's speech at Birmingham on 15 May 1903 advocating imperial preference was a blow to the Balfour administration. It divided the cabinet between those such as Devonshire, Balfour of Burleigh, Lord George Hamilton and Ritchie, who opposed Chamberlain, and the protectionists among the Unionists. Outside the cabinet, there were the 'free fooders' ranging from Goschen and Hicks Beach to younger members, particularly Winston Churchill and Lord Hugh Cecil, leaders of a group who were popularly known as Hughligans for their active oppostion to imperial preference in the House. The split became more serious in July when the Tariff Reform League was established by Chamberlain and the Unionist Free Food League was formed. By the end of the session, it seemed unlikely that the government could continue in office much longer. John Morley, discussing the political situation with Haldane in August, 'spoke of the inevitable advent of a Liberal Government' (Haldane to Rosebery, 10 Aug. 1903, RP, 10030 f. 74). Three days before, Morley had sketched out a possible Liberal cabinet with Spencer, surmising that the latter might well be prime minister.*

*The free traders in the cabinet under Devonshire's leadership pressed Balfour for a decision on the tariff controversy. The final break occurred when Chamberlain tendered his resignation on 9 September, though Balfour delayed accepting it until five days later. Balfour agreed with Chamberlain that if there were support for tariff reform in the country, he would follow this course. Ritchie, Hamilton and Balfour of Burleigh immediately resigned; three weeks later, Devonshire joined them after Balfour's Sheffield speech which was strongly in favour of fiscal change.*

*The death of Lady Spencer at the end of October after a long illness led to Spencer's temporary withdrawal from politics. Meanwhile, Devonshire had accepted the presidency of the parliamentary committee of the Free Food League. At their executive meeting on 10 December, the League advised Unionists not to vote for tariff reformers at the pending by-elections and to make common cause with the Liberals where the constituencies were held by Unionist free traders.*

*Dismayed at the Unionist victories in the by-elections at Dulwich and Lewisham in London, where the free trade issue would be expected to favour the Liberal candidates, Campbell-Bannerman now considered that Devonshire should be sounded out on two points: future possible co-operation with candidates and M.P.s who were Unionist free traders, and on the action to be taken when Parliament met. 'Do you think you could find out what the Duke's view is and what his instructions are?' Campbell-Bannerman asked Spencer. 'We do not wish to compromise any of our opinions, but we wish to deal loyally with him and his friends.' (23 Dec. 1903, SP). Spencer was willing to sacrifice home rule in order to effect an agreement, but stood firm on the education issue as this would have jeopardised Nonconformist support, upon which the Liberals relied. As Spencer explained to Devonshire, 'If we tried to meet you ... on some questions other than fiscal we might be accused of betraying those with whom we have acted. In that way we might lose a great many votes at an election.' (Spencer to Devonshire, 7 Jan. 1904, CP, 340. 3056).*

Shortly before the new parliamentary session was due to begin, Spencer and Devonshire devised a plan of co-operation. The Unionist free traders would support a Liberal amendment to the Address condemning taxes on food and the Liberals would thereafter give such assistance to Devonshire as was required. However, during January and February 1904 the Chamberlainites suffered a series of heavy defeats in by-elections and the need no longer existed for co-operation with the Unionist free traders. The negotiations between Spencer and Devonshire ceased in mid-February.

---

### 763   LORD SPENCER TO LADY SPENCER

*25 February 1903; Spencer House, St. James's Place, S.W.*

I went to my meeting and then on to the House of Lords and Commons.

I was sorry to miss Winston Churchill who made I hear a brilliant Speech.[1]

I heard part of H. C. Bannerman who was heavy and without fire. Reading it I find much knowledge and good sense.[2]

I went down after dinner and heard John Sinclair,[3] very sensible and good, and then Asquith,[4] very concise and well argued with brilliant passages.

Then came Arthur Balfour,[5] very forcible and well put was his argument, but he badly hesitates and repeats words. It was very telling and well received.

The Division was not good but if the Irish had been as usual on our side the Government majority would have been very small.[6]

Asquith said well that the Debate was more important than the actual Division which represented party absolutely.

A good many young Tories walked out.

[1] Adjourned debate on the King's Speech, on the Amendment, directed at Brodrick's army reforms, regretting 'that the organisation of the land forces is unsited to the needs of the Empire, and that no proportionate gain in strength and efficiency has resulted from the recent increase in military expenditure.' Hansard, 4, cxviii, cols. 682-9, 24 Feb. 1903. See H.W. Lucy, *The Balfourian Parliament 1900-1905* (1906), pp. 231-4.

[2] Ibid., cols. 702-16.

[3] Liberal M.P., Forfarshire, 1897-1909. Ibid., cols. 757-63.

[4] Ibid., cols. 765-74.

[5] Ibid., cols. 775-88.

[6] The amendment was lost by 261 votes to 145.

---

### 764   LORD SPENCER TO LADY SPENCER

*6 March 1903; Spencer House, St. James's Place, S.W.*

This is a hurried line. . . . We had the most miserable Debate in the House of Lords[1] Carrington was deplorable[2] and gave a bad start to the debate. Bedford broke down[3] as did Lord Lorne,[4] and excepting a rather interesting Speech from Harris[5] and a good Speech from Monkswell[6] who never rouses or flares the House, until Selborne spoke there was really nothing worth listening to. Hardwicke was very bad indeed,[7] long and pompous. The Debate was absolutely collapsing. Rosebery had bolted, Burghclere would not speak,[8] so I was obliged to speak. I think that my Speech told and helped with Selborne to lift the Debate out of the Mud.[9]

They had an awful fiasco with C.B. in the H. of C.[10]

[1] On army reforms, Hansard, 4, cxviii, cols. 1479-1538, 5 March 1903.
[2] Charles Robert, 1st Earl Carrington, opened the debate for the government.
[3] Herbrand, 11th Duke of Bedford.
[4] Marquess of Lorne, John, 9th Duke of Argyll.
[5] George, 4th Baron Harris.
[6] Robert, 2nd Baron Monkswell.
[7] Albert, 6th Earl of Hardwicke, Under-Secretary for War, 1902-3.
[8] Herbert, 1st Baron Burghclere of Walden, Essex, formerly Herbert Gardner, Liberal M.P.
[9] Ibid., cols. 1520-9. The House was almost empty when a division was called at 8.50 p.m. Only 15 Opposition peers were present against the government's 51.
[10] In a debate on the need to establish a Committee of Defence. Ibid., col. 1586 ff.


**765 LORD SPENCER TO LADY SPENCER**
*22 March 1903; Spencer House, St. James's Place, S.W.*

I enjoyed my dinner very much.[1] On arriving I went straight up to Joe C. to greet him. He is wonderful, he looks younger by 5 or 6 years then he did,[2] slim and active with a most healthy look, He at once said 'I hope you did not mind my reference to you.' I said 'Oh dear no, I was not sure that you referred to me but I thought it possible. I was flattered by your referring to it, and you put the right interpretation on what I said as to "peripatetic Secretaries of State".'[3] We then talked of the tour and climate and of his power of doing it without exercising etc., but did not touch on Policy.

I sat on the left of the Prince of Wales.

I got on very well. We talked of Naval Debates etc. and he let me speak on without minding it.

The King looked very well, and was very gracious shaking hands with us all on arrival and on his going to bed.

He talked to nearly if not every one. He was very kind to me, anxious to hear of you etc. and spoke about the coming Irish Land Bill,[4] hoping that it should be a settlement and that we should not oppose. I said that we all wished for a settlement but much depended on what they asked G. Britain to pay. He spoke highly of G. Wyndham.[5] He asked about Bobby, and his family etc. He complimented me on keeping so much hair on my head.

I could not help poking a dart at Asquith, who was speaking of Mrs. F. Thomas[6] as an admirable canvasser. I said I hope not on Perks' behalf.

He grunted and half laughed.

[1] On 21 March, the King gave a dinner party at Buckingham Palace.
[2] Chamberlain was then 67.
[3] At a reception on 20 March to mark his return from a tour of South Africa, Chamberlain said, 'While I was abroad I saw an abbreviated report of a speech that had been made by a distinguished critic of mine - I think, on the whole, not an unkindly critic—in which he expressed his opinion

that there were many disadvantages connected with what he called peripatetic Secretaries of State.'
*The Times*, 21 March 1903, p. 8.
    [4] Introduced in the Commons on 25 March.
    [5] George Wyndham, Chief Secretary for Ireland, 1900–5.
    [6] Marie Adelaide, Lord Brassey's daughter and wife of Freeman Freeman-Thomas, Liberal M.P.,
Hastings, 1900–6, and a joint secretary of the Liberal League.


**766   LORD RIPON TO LORD SPENCER**
*30 May 1903; Studley Royal, Ripon*

*Confidential*

We are in for a fight now. It is the greatest political struggle of the last 50 years. . .

Chamberlain's proceedings seem to me in the highest degree mischievous from an Imperialist point of view.[1] Nothing can completely remedy the mischief which he has already done. If we at home reject his scheme, as I honestly hope we shall, the Colonies will be alienated and disgusted. If it is accepted now they will be jubilant for the moment; but when the inevitable reaction comes, and the people of Great Britain and Ireland refuse to be taxed and starved for the supposed benefit of the Colonies, the danger of a real breach with those dependencies will be very great indeed.

If Rosebery could be got to take that view he might fall naturally and consistently into line with us. Now you are the only person that can approach him on this matter. The crisis is so grave that no self-respecting public man can decently hold aloof. There is a great opening for R. Let him throw himself into this battle and with his eloquence and his talents he may come out of it our unquestioned leader.

I would follow anybody. I would unite with anybody who would take the right side now. That the great interests at stake should be sacrificed to personal considerations and individual selfishness is intolerable. This is no mere Party question. It is a vast question of national policy. We *must* unite, and towards that union the first step is to get hold of Rosebery. Can this be done?

    [1] Chamberlain's speech at Birmingham on 15 May outlining a programme for tariff reform and
proposing the imposition of duties on many imported goods. 'Wonderful news,' Asquith told his
wife the following day, 'and it is only a question of time when we shall sweep the country.' *The
Autobiography of Margot Asquith* (1922), ii. p.53.


**767   LORD SPENCER TO LORD RIPON**
*31 May 1903; Althorp, Northampton*
Rip. P, Add. MS. 43538 ff. 112–13

*Confidential*

I was very glad to hear from you, for I always feel that you are the one friend in our H. of L. on whose judgment and opinion I place faith.

I quite agree that there has not been for years such a principle in Politics thrown out by a leading Statesman, or must we put it in the plural, by Statesmen, for Balfour seems to agree with his Col. Sec.[1].. It is most mischievous, most wicked and what you say about it must be true.

I don't know what can be done as to R. He is likely to pronounce his view at [the] City Liberal Club the week after next.[2] No action by speaking can now take place before C.B.'s resolution on the Finance Bill.

I know that R. refused to come to the Cobden Club dinner which is to be held on July 1. I told them that I hoped R. would take the Chair if he preferred doing so to my taking the Chair, or that I would keep clear altogether if he preferred that. Asquith for very cogent reasons declined such as that that he had already spoken on the subject and before July 1 will have spoken many times again, and that he cannot speak again.

I hardly know what action to propose to R. but I am always ready to urge his active co-operation, but he won't agree to any meeting, e.g. when after the Ayr and Edinburgh meetings suggesting co-operation I invited him to see C.B. and bring Asquith, he declined to come.[3]

I should like much to see you. I might write to R. to say much what you suggest, that this question is so large and of such importance to the Nation, that it is of the utmost importance that we should oppose it, and in such a way as to show the union and agreement of the whole party and invite him to suggest how this could best be demonstrated!!

[1] Joseph Chamberlain.

[2] Rosebery, as president of the City Liberal Club, spoke at the dinner on 11 June, but did not touch on political issues.

[3] At a meeting at Ayr on 29 Oct. 1902, addressed by Campbell-Bannerman, a resolution was passed calling on Liberal leaders to meet and unite in forming and pursuing a policy against the government. Shortly afterwards in a speech at Edinburgh on 1 Nov. Rosebery endorsed this. Spencer approached Rosebery with a proposal for an informal gathering to talk matters over, but the latter refused. Spencer to Rosebery, 30 Nov. 1902, RP, 10062 ff. 266-7, Rosebery to Spencer, 1 Dec. 1902, SP.

## 768   W. V. HARCOURT TO LORD SPENCER

*2 June 1903; 22 Grafton Street, W.*

*Secret*

I have seen and heard a great deal in the last four days which I think is very important you should know and I wish much to see you. At present the Liberal Party is absolutely derelict as regards all Leadership. I had an interview a day or two ago with C.B. and was sorry to find him very much broken and shaken, not only by his own illness but still more by his worthy anxiety about his wife.[1]

I have also seen Hicks Beach, Asquith, Bryce and John Morley. Nobody can tell what a day may bring forth. Everyone even their leading supporters concur that the crisis is imminent and that though there can be no adverse division the internal dissensions of the party and the Cabinet will bring about the collapse of the Government who are rather willing to resign but have resolved not to dissolve.[2]

I am disposed to think that when the crisis arrives the principal responsibility will fall upon you. I can give you reasons for this opinion, which I must not write but these are things which should be well meditated beforehand and not left to a hasty decision. Asquith is abroad, Bryce is away and there is really no one as able to take charge of the ship. Besides all the mess that Chamberlain has made for them I can understand that the Government are at their wits' end about their Irish Bill[3] as the Landlords are standing firm on the minimum rent and the Irish do not dare accept it so that for all reasons the Govt. will be glad to take refuge in flight.

Finding that Hicks Beach acting in concert with Winston and Hugh Cecil[4] is prepared to take the lead in opposition to Chamberlain[5] it is now arranged that Chaplin's Amendment will come first and Hicks Beach will at once support the repeal of the Corn Tax and open fire upon the Government.[6] There will of course be an overwhelming majority against Chaplin and the Corn Duty. This of course is far the most advantageous way of opening the campaign and giving a signal defeat to a Protectionist motion.

It also affords a happy escape from the maladroit opposition Amendment which would have been equally defeated and have been represented as an overwhelming blow against Free Trade. C.B. and Asquith concur in this view. Any other course would have been a fatal error in strategy.

[1] Lady Campbell-Bannerman had been in ill health since the previous summer. 'We have lived like hermits,' he wrote to one correspondent. She died in Aug. 1906.

[2] The Duke of Devonshire asked Ritchie, 'What do you intend to do in these difficult circumstances? I presume that you will be supported in resisting any change in the Budget which Balfour's and Chamberlain's speeches may encourage Chaplin and Chamberlain to propose ... What I do not intend however is to be committed by silence or aquiesce to a policy as to which I have the gravest doubts.' Devonshire to C.T. Ritchie, 29 May 1903, Ritchie Papers, Add. MS. 53780 f. 18.

[3] The Irish Land Bill, accepting the principle that dual ownership must end, was favourably received by Irish and Liberal M.P.s. The second reading on 7 May was approved by 443 votes to 26.

[4] Lord Hugh Richard Heathcote Cecil, Conservative M.P., Greenwich, 1895-1906.

[5] Churchill, on his way to Blenheim, had a long talk with Hicks Beach 'who was quite ready and determined to fight'. Churchill to Hugh Cecil, 30 May 1903, Quickswood Papers, Qu. I 63/8. He told Loe St. Strachey, editor of the Spectator, 'You will see that some of us have quite taken our political fortunes in our hands "by forming a League" to counter Chamberlain's impending campaign.' Churchill to Strachey, 30 May 1903. Strachey Papers, 4/10/1.

[6] On the second reading of the Finance Bill, 9 June, Chaplin, formerly President, Local Government Board, submitted an amendment for reducing the tea tax by 2d. with the intention of forcing Ritchie to abandon the attempt to abolish the shilling corn duty. Hansard, 4, cxxiii, cols. 330-2. Hicks Beach, on the same date, violently attacked Chamberlain's policy, claiming that it 'will destroy the Unionist party'. Ibid., col. 356.

## 769   LORD SPENCER TO LADY SPENCER
*6 June 1903; Milton, Peterborough*[1]

I had a long talk with W.V.H.[2]

He was full of preparation for immediate break up of the Government, and was sure I should be sent for, not H.C.B. or R.

We talked over possibilities at great length, and I left thoroughly depressed at the prospect which may shortly open out before me.

Conceive if I am sent for and I am obliged to take up the matter, what difficulties I should have in regard to R., W.V.H., J.M., Fowler, etc...

I find Harcourt overpowering as to being ready and as to the Liberal Ship lying derelict without any leader. He appealed to me to go to him today, but

I refused as I had enough talk with him and should see no one before Monday.[3] To appease him I said I should come Monday evening, so I shall either go home by Motor tomorrow afternoon or by early train Monday.

[1] Milton Park, the home of William, 7th Earl Fitzwilliam.
[2] On 4 June in London, where Harcourt was recovering from an operation.
[3] 'The prospect is hateful if W.V.H. is right and will need much consultation.' Spencer to Campbell-Bannerman, 5 June 1903, CBP, Add. MS. 41229 f. 197.

## 770    W. R. D. ADKINS TO LORD SPENCER
*7 June 1903; Springfield, Northampton*

I saw your manifesto in the *Daily News*[1]. Your additions at the end to the draft as discussed at Althorp strengthened it a good deal I thought. It would be very exciting next week but I doubt if you and Sir Henry will succeed in forcing them to declare their policy or dissolve.

[1] Quoting opinions of Liberal leaders which were to appear in the June issue of *Liberal Magazine*, Spencer urged that Chamberlain's policy should be submitted to the judgement of the electorate without delay. *Daily News*, 5 June 1903, p. 7.

## 771    LORD SPENCER TO LADY SPENCER[1]
*11 June 1903; Spencer House, St. James's Place, S.W.*

The debate was very interesting yesterday.[2] Asquith made one of the most brilliant Speeches I ever heard[3], only 8 or 10 minutes, raking the Government with the most cutting and rousing fire.

Sir Edgar Vincent spoke very well.[4]

Balfour was brave in sticking to his guns but made no substantial defence,[5] and he is now shown as strongly favouring Chamberlain's Policy, which his previous Speeches have not disclosed.

We shall have a debate on Monday and I must speak.[6]

It seems clear that the Government intend to muddle on with a Divided Cabinet.

It is a most humiliating and unprecedented position.

C.B. was not vigorous or greatly good last night. He struck me as jaded and his Speech had no concentrated fire which such a Speech should have had after the debate. No doubt he made some good points.[7] He was not, it seemed to me, well received by the Party. There was a good deal of talking while he spoke.

Chaplin only got 28 Protectionist supporters.[8]

A poor nucleus for Chamberlain's new fiscal party. I don't think that the battle is over, a fresh attack will be made. No one knows to which side a Unionist belongs.

Today and tomorrow Rosebery speaks, and will make his position clear.[9]

... I think that I shall be home tomorrow coming up probably Sunday, but I shall see today how things look.

[1] Spencer's last letter to Lady Spencer.

[2] The debate on the second reading of the Finance Bill, Hansard, 4, cxxiii, 10 June.

[3] Ibid., cols, 481-7.

[4] Conservative M.P., Exeter, 1899-1906. Ibid., cols. 495-7.

[5] Ibid., cols. 557-76.

[6] In a debate in the Lords on 15 June on fiscal policy, Spencer put the case for free trade. Ibid., cols. 898-906.

[7] Ibid., cols. 576-84.

[8] Chaplin's amendment was defeated by 424 votes to 28 on 10 June and the bill was read a second time on 12 June.

[9] Commenting on Chamberlain's fiscal proposals at a Liberal League meeting at the Hotel Cecil on 12 June, Rosebery stated, 'if that does not unite the Liberal party, the Liberal party is past all hope.' *The Times*, 13 June 1903, p.8.


**772**   LORD SPENCER TO C.R. SPENCER

*17 June 1903; Spencer House, St. James's Place, S.W.*

Many thanks for your approval of my Speech. It went off fairly well, but I omitted many good points.[1]

Goschen's and Devonshire's Speeches[2] were admirable as Free Trade pronouncements. Of course D. had to defend the Cabinet concordat, but all he said on Free Trade or Free Import as he called it, even surpassed Goschen in excellence.

It made quite a sensation.

Asquith had H. Chaplin between him and Joe. When the Duke was speaking Asquith said to Harry 'That is splendid, we shall circulate it broadcast as a leaflet.' Harry told this to Joe who replied 'Let me do it and be damned.'

He [Chaplin] also asked Asquith whether it was possible that D. had been called a 'Rip van Winkle!!!'[3]. He was very angry.

[1] See No. **771** n. 6.

[2] Hansard, 4, cxxiii, 15 June 1903. Goschen, cols. 837-53. Devonshire, cols. 906-21.

[3] A reference to Chamberlain's speech at Warrington on 8 Sept. 1885, where he had likened Hartington to Rip van Winkle. 'There is not a single Liberal candidate who has not accepted some one or more points of the Radical programme. It is therefore perfectly futile and ridiculous for any Rip van Winkle to come down from the mountains on which he has been slumbering, and to tell us that these things are to be excluded from the Liberal programme.' See Garvin, ii, p. 63.


**773**   LORD SPENCER

*17 August 1903*

*Memorandum*

Secret

Notes of conversation with J.M. 7 Aug. 1903[1]

S. (John Poyntz 5th Earl Spencer) from J.M. (John Morley)

1.  That Arthur Balfour and Joe Chamberlain are sure to keep together; that they are dreading the loss of the D. of Devonshire; that if he leaves them, it may lead to a break up and resignation, but the chances are that the Govt. will struggle on.

    J.C.                                    Chancellor of the Exchequer

    Lord Milner                             Colonial Secretary, etc.

2. That the King now is likely to send for Sir Henry Campbell-Bannerman. The idea is that Grey and Asquith and Rosebery would not serve with him and then ——————[2] may be sent for.

Harcourt wishes for office.

So does Dilke; wants Chancellor of the Duchy and representing Foreign Office in the House of Commons with Cabinet rank. J.M. evidently would accept Office but not Foreign Office; this I surmise but might take the Chancellor of the Exchequer. E. Grey for Col. Office.

H.C.B. if possible to the House of Lords.

Bryce not strong enough for Colonies.

Herbert Gladstone for Chief Secretary of Ireland.

(?) whether Dilke would go down with staunch Non-Conformists!![3]

[1] Morley, who was writing his *Life of Gladstone*, visited Edward Hamilton on 12 Aug. to consult the latter's earlier Journals. Discussing the political crisis, Morley 'presumed that Lord Spencer would be sent for, and he thought he might form a Government without Rosebery, who would be sure to decline to take office'. EHJ, 12 Aug. 1903, Add. MS. 48681 ff. 37-8.

[2] Written in a different hand, 'The dash evidently means Lord Spencer himself.'

[3] For similar speculation, but from a Conservative viewpoint, see Lord Hugh Cecil to Winston Churchill, 31 Aug. 1903, printed in R. S. Churchill, *Winston S. Churchill II: Companion*, Pt. 1 1901-1907 (1969), pp. 222-3.

**774** LORD SPENCER TO H. CAMPBELL-BANNERMAN

*22 September 1903; Spencer House, St James's Place, S.W.*

CBP, Add. MS. 41229 ff. 205-6

I must write a few lines to you as to the exciting topic of Politics, but I am overwhelmed with Private and other letters today.

I will not dwell on what is so obvious to every good Liberal, that the Govt. have pursued a tricky dishonest course.[1]

Balfour agrees in principle with Joe and wishes him success, but cannot join the campaign for Taxation of Food because it is inopportune. He holds the fortress whilst Joe with a free hand careers about the country and does battle for Colonial Preference etc.

How anyone with a shred of common sense and who opposes Joe can support Balfour under the circustances beats my comprehension.

The departure of Joe from the Cabinet seems to have taken all opposition out of Michael H. Beach and the Duke etc.

I went for the day to the New Forest yesterday, W.V.H. in capital spirits but I thought less vigorous than of old...

He had heard from Beach who says that neither Ritchie nor G. Hamilton knew of Joe's resignation until after theirs were accepted, and I heard afterwards that even the Duke had not been informed.

The Duke remains it is said out of good nature, and from inability to resist Balfour's appeal to him to stay in the Cabinet!!!

[1] On 9 Sept. Chamberlain suddenly offered to resign so that Balfour could retain Devonshire's support. After the cabinet meeting of 14 Sept. the free traders, Ritchie, George Hamilton and Balfour of Burleigh, decided to resign at the cabinet the next day. The three men were astonished

to learn that Devonshire had withdrawn his resignation on learning of Chamberlain's offer. Balfour on 16 Sept. now accepted Chamberlain's resignation as well as Ritchie's and Hamilton's. See A. Sykes, *Tariff Reform in British Politics 1903–1913* (1979), pp. 48–54. On 20 Sept. Balfour of Burleigh and Arthur Elliot, Financial Secretary to the Treasury, also resigned.


**775** LORD SPENCER TO DUKE OF DEVONSHIRE

*6 October 1903; Spencer House, St. James's Place, S.W.*

CP, 340.2996

*Private*

I must write to you a few words after reading your letter to Balfour and your resignation.[1]

I am sure you will not think I am writing to you for Political reasons, but I have always either as your Colleague or opponent in Politics had such a very high admiration for your action and hearing that I cannot refrain from saying how glad I am that with the views you hold on the fiscal policy of the U. Kingdom, you have left the present Government. I do not see how you could have acted otherwise after Balfour's Sheffield Speech.[2]

I quite understand that after your association with Balfour and others of the present Government, this action on your part must be very disagreeable to you. All the many friends you have will I feel sure applaud what you have done. In some ways I dare say you will be glad to be a free man, for a time at any rate, whatever your future in Politics may be.

[1] On 5 Oct. For the texts of the letters, Devonshire to Balfour, 2 Oct. and Balfour's reply, 3 Oct., see B. Holland, *Life of the Duke of Devonshire*, (1911), ii, pp. 361–6.

[2] At a meeting of the National Union of Conservative and Unionist Associations at Sheffield on 1 Oct. Balfour asked for support for a policy of imposing tariffs to be used in negotiating lower foreign customs duties.


**776** H. CAMPBELL-BANNERMAN TO LORD SPENCER

*24 October 1903; Belmont Castle, Meigle*

You and I have done well in taking the bull by the horns and speaking out against the devious ways and questionable practices of our opponents.[1] Our people would have been utterly disappointed and flattened out if this had not been done and if we had had the air of not venturing to say what everybody is thinking. Philosophical disquistions and fine-drawn arguments are well enough, but they let down the temperature of the Party.

Some of our prominent friends are lié with A.J.B. and tender of his feelings: others have a hanker for Joe. Thank goodness I am not troubled with either.

[1] Campbell-Bannerman at Bolton 15 Oct. and Stirling on 22 Oct. on Chamberlain's attitude towards tariff reform as well as aspects of social, economic and foreign policy. Spender, ii, pp. 123–4. Spencer had spoken at the Eighty Club on 9 Oct. on the fiscal question. See Spencer to Campbell-Bannerman, 11 Oct. 1903, CBP, Add. MS. 41229 ff. 209–10.

## 777 LORD SPENCER TO H. H. LANGHAM

*3 November 1903; Spencer House, St. James's Place, S.W.*
Langham Papers, 685

One line in my desolation and unhappiness to thank you for your very kind letter.

I appreciate what you say very much. My future looks really bleak before me.[1]

---

[1] Lady Spencer died on 31 Oct.

## 778 W. R. D. ADKINS TO LORD SPENCER

*25 November 1903; Reform Club, Pall Mall, S.W.*

You may like to know about last night's 'Free Food' meeting at the Queen's Hall.[1]

The place was crowded, and the platform very strong in prominent men. No one was cheered more loudly on entering than Winston Churchill. There were a number of Chamberlainites present; I should think perhaps 1/10 or 1/12 of the whole; and a large number of Liberals. The Duke began very dully and weakly, but improved all the way through. Towards the end he was very impressive and full of energy and feeling. He is evidently opposed whole heartedly both to the Prime Minister and to Mr. C.

Sir Michael Hicks Beach looked wretched during most of the speech.[2] Lord Goschen was much hampered by want of time, and his speech as a work of art was greatly spoiled, but his figures and details were very well received, and his description of the Protectionists as not 'taking it lying down' or standing up 'but crouching behind a wall' roused tremendous cheering. I was struck with the vigorous stand made by 'Freddie' Smith in moving the vote of thanks, and Mr. Schuster the head of the Union Bank of London who seconded was very emphatic as to the evil done to banking and to the City of London by anything like Protection.[3]

I dined at Kemp's[4] before the meeting to meet Lord Goschen, and he was as vigorous in private as in public about Free Trade. Today everywhere people are interpreting the speech of the Duke as a plain resolve to fight Chamberlain hard, and the talk of any early Dissolution in the Spring is revived.

You probably know that Dickson-Poynder has resolved to join the Liberals, and his secession I hear will be announced in two or three days.[5]

It is very nice to think that the Duke means business. He gave quite the impression that Chamberlain's sneer about 'the drag on the wheel' had rankled.[6]

---

[1] The first meeting of the Free Food League where the leading Unionist free traders appeared together on one platform. See *The Times*, 25 Nov. 1903, pp. 10-11.

[2] Hicks Beach had been won over by Balfour in Nov. by the assurance from the prime minister that he did not intend to go further than the policy enunciated in his Sheffield speech. Beach reserved the right after the meeting 'to express my dissent from any comments made the speakers on Balfour's policy with which I disagreed'. Hicks Beach to Lord Hugh Cecil, 19 Nov 1903, Quickswood Papers, Qu. I 1/136.

³ William Frederic Danvers Smith, Conservative M.P., Strand, 1891–1910, son of W.H. Smith. Felix Otto Schuster, governor, Union Bank of London, 1855–1918, and an advocate of free trade.

⁴ George Kemp, Unionist M.P., Heywood division, Lancashire, since 1895. Free trader, joined the Liberal Party in Aug. 1904.

⁵ Sir John Dickson-Poynder. Conservative M.P., Chippenham division, Wiltshire, since 1892, joined the Liberal Party in April 1904.

⁶ In a speech at Cardiff on 20 Nov. Chamberlain remarked that Devonshire had intimated that 'he was not opposed to the Government, but he hoped to be a drag upon the wheel.' That is a curious ambition' (laughter). *The Times*, 21 Nov. 1903, p.8. Lady Gwendoline Cecil reported to 4th Marquess of Salisbury a conversation with Balfour on 19 Nov. Balfour accused Devonshire of intriguing with others behind his back 'saying he was a passive centre round whom others buzzed'. 4 Dec. 1903, Salisbury Papers, S(4) 54/101.

**779**   H. COX¹ TO LORD SPENCER
*18 December 1903; 6 Raymond Buildings, Gray's Inn, W.C.*

A friend of mine, who sees a good deal of the Duke of Devonshire on political matters,² made a point of telling me the other night that the Duke is gravely alarmed at Chamberlain's progress, and thinks the time has come to consider whether some fusion between the Liberals and the Unionist Free Traders is not possible.

The Duke is naturally shy of opening direct negotiations, but your name was specially mentioned. I thereupon felt that the least I could do was to offer to bring the matter before your notice.

I infer from the conversation that the Duke of Devonshire would be very glad if he could find some opportunity of having a friendly conversation with you upon the whole situation.

¹ Harold Cox, secretary of the Cobden Club and a county court judge.

² Devonshire was informed by a colleague that Cox, who had been staying with the Ripons, knew that Ripon and Spencer 'are both in favour of negotiations being opened with us for common action on the Address.' Devonshire to James, James Papers, 23 Dec. 1903, M45/1301. For an account of Cox's conversations with Ripon, see Ripon to Spencer, 20 Dec. 1903, SP.

**780**   LORD SPENCER TO H. CAMPBELL-BANNERMAN
*23 December 1903; North Creake, Fakenham*
CBP, Add. MS. 41229 ff. 231–4

*Confidential*

It seems to me that you will realize the reasons for my writing to you best by reading the letters which started with me the question on which I am now writing and those which followed the first letter of H. Cox.

I touched on some of the issues in my rambling letter to you¹ upon John Sinclair's letter to you. I mean the question of trying to form one line with the Unionist Free fooders.

I should much like to have your views.

I think the possibility of Union should be freely and fully discussed, but as yet I retain the views which I wrote to you. I don't see that we can modify our views on Education and I doubt if the Duke of D. and his friends would accept our views. I wrote to Harold Cox and Ripon strongly in this sense.[2]

I am sure that in the interests of Free Trade it is essential that we should carry Non Conformists with us on Education, and if we do, then we secure them for a Free Trade vote. If we offend the Non Conformists we strike a serious blow at Free Trade.

Whilst feeling strongly in this sense, I see the great importance of getting into close touch with Unionist Free fooders on fiscal policy. I should therefore be disposed to agree with Ripon as to H. of L. amendments on Address;[3] but then we must know what you will do in the H. of C. Our action may affect your position: for if the Duke and the Lords Free fooders vote and support an amendment against J.C. or against J.C. and A.J.B. and Govt., the Unionist Free fooders would be driven to support and speak for you on the same issue in the H. of C.

This question of amendment to Address[4] really opens up the whole subject which is of the highest moment, and embraces the question as to Rosebery, Asquith and Co.

I do not well see how the Duke of D. can be sounded, until we decide on all the big issues involved. What are they?

(1) I assume that the Old Liberal party as it was formed in the last Gladstone and Rosebery Governments is now united. Possibly this is too great an assumption and as yet we have had only on fiscal Policy practically united action. My letter asking R. to give the Parliamentary dinner to the United Liberal peers is not yet answered.[5]

(2) Can a union of parties be made between us and the D. of D. and his Lib. Unionist Free traders, also with the Conservative Free traders like W. Churchill, J. Poynder, Hugh Cecil etc? It involves agreement on (a) Education (b) Irish Policy (c) Temperance Legislation (d) Army reform and Elgin Report[6] (e) Other less important questions.

(a) and (b) are vital. On (a) you know my views. On (b) I do not wish to renounce my views on Home Rule, but I am willing to postpone action for a time. This might even be accepted by the Irish party who will be important when we come to votes and should not be overlooked, nor if possible made hostile to us.

We must not forget that Irish Policy may soon include the Irish University question, on which Non Con.'s may take strong views against concession to R.C. claims.

We should know how these 2 questions, or assuming that 1) is settled, how 2) can be settled.

My view is that with every desire for a strong fighting line, we shall not be able to unite as one party. But I should not nail my views on this to the mast until further discussion.

Supposing we agree that Union is impossible.

We must consider how we can unite on the fiscal question. Would not an informal sounding of the D. of D. help that? But I could not do it, without not only your concurrence but without Rosebery.

It will be difficult to settle these questions on paper and by correspondence.

Would it advance the position if I met you and any others who should be consulted, about the 4th or 5 Jan or 6th Jan? I had a letter from my brother this morning who went to the Liberal Office and saw J. Herbert[7] etc. I do not feel that this Office gets very reliable information. Still my brother reported that J.C. lately told a friend of his to be ready for a General Election in January, and that he J.C. was confident that he would get a majority.[8] If so confident he and A.J.B. may think it wise to Dissolve at once.

If this rumour were true we really should lose no time in meeting or settling what can be done.[9]

[1] Spencer to Campbell-Bannerman, 7 Dec. 1903, CBP, Add. MS. 41229 ff. 219–25.

[2] Spencer to Ripon, 19 Dec. 1903, Rip. P, Add. MS. 43538 f. 145.

[3] Ripon suggested 'that Devonshire should be asked by you whether he and his friends would support a Free Trade Amendment to the Address in the House of Lords'. Ripon to Spencer, 20 Dec. 1903, SP.

[4] Moved on 2 Feb. 1904.

[5] Spencer told Rosebery on 17 Dec. that it would be very 'painful and distressing' to give the peers' dinner in view of Lady Spencer's death. RP, 10062 f. 278. Rosebery declined on 22 Dec., SP.

[6] A Royal Commision to inquire into the miliary preparations for the South African War was established in Sept. 1902 under Lord Elgin. It reported in the following July.

[7] Jesse Herbert, Treasurer, Liberal Central Association.

[8] C.R. Spencer to Spencer, 23 Dec. 1903, SP.

[9] Spencer's letter crossed with one written by Campbell-Bannerman 'but they were identical in purpose.' Campbell-Bannerman to Spencer, 25 Dec. 1903, SP.

**781   H. CAMPBELL-BANNERMAN TO LORD SPENCER**

*26 December 1903; Lord Warden Hotel, Dover*

*Private*

This morning's post brings me the enclosed from Herbert G.[1] Rather a hopeless bargain, I fear.

We are to withdraw all our candidates (if our people will allow it) in order to save the skin of the Free Fooders. But Free Fooders are to support the Govt. on any division on the Address! This is a nice quid pro quo! We are to be dealt with as it were with a pair of tongs; but we are to consign our electoral interests to a joint committee on which the 53 Free Fooders are to be represented equally with the whole Liberal Party.[2]

This points more and more to the urgency of our conclave. I think the days we were speaking of are none too early, and I prefer them on the 12th. I am writing to Asquith and asking whether I can see him before he leaves the country.

I also think that James's[3] idea of the usefulness of a debate without a division is feebleness itself.[4] There must be a division and it will show who are earnestly with us and who not, out of this regiment of 53.

Further, a mere amendment of congratulation that the Speech said nothing about tariffs would be utterly inadequate. And finally, while it may be right for us to condemn delay as disturbing to trade etc. (which is true) I am by no means sure that an early dissolution just when Joe has been mafficking about the country and rousing everybody's cupidity would be good for the Free

Trade cause, and whether it would not be better to wait till people had better realized what is involved. This is at least arguable.

[1] Gladstone to Campbell-Bannerman, 24 Dec. 1903, CBP, Add. MS. 41217 ff. 59–60.

[2] Spencer replied, 'I do not quite read the idea as you do. I do not think that they mean our candidates to withdraw for Free fooders. The action would be reciprocal and the weakest candidate might withdraw [from] either side, but that of course I admit is difficult to achieve without modifying or appearing to modify our principles.' Spencer to Campbell-Bannerman, 28 Dec. 1903, CBP, Add. MS. 41229 f. 239.

[3] 1st Baron James of Hereford, Liberal M.P., Taunton, 1869–85, Solicitor-General, 1873, Attorney-General, 1873–4 and 1880–5. Opponent of Irish home rule, Liberal Unionist M.P., Bury, 1885–95. Created a peer by Salisbury in June 1895, James served as Chancellor of the Duchy of Lancaster, 1895–1902.

[4] At a meeting with Asquith on 21 Dec. James, on behalf of the Unionist free traders, suggested a high level meeting to discuss possible co-operation in constituencies. James also warned that in a division in the Commons on a fiscal amendment, few Unionist free traders would vote against the government. 'Memorandum of Conversation, 21 Dec. 1903', James Papers, M45/1299. Copies were sent to several people, including Campbell-Bannerman, CBP, Add. MS. 41217 ff. 61–2.

**782   DUKE OF DEVONSHIRE TO LORD SPENCER**

*2 January 1904; Chatsworth, Chesterfield*

*Private*

There have been some indications on both sides of a desire for close co-operation between Liberals and Unionists who are opposed to Chamberlain's policy,[1] and the opinion seems to be growing that without it the chances of successful opposition to him are diminishing.

The difficulties in the way of more united action are very great,[2] and I have at present no authority from Unionist Free Traders to enter upon any negotiation on their behalf as to possible arrangements. But it may be worth while for some of us to exchange ideas on the subject.

There are I think two main points to be considered.

The first is whether any consideration would be shown, in regard to their seats at the next election, to Unionist Free Traders in the House of Commons, who might by their votes place themselves in opposition to the majority of their party and perhaps to the Government itself. This, even if the Leaders were favourable to the principle, could only be discussed in detail by the Party Managers.

The second question is in what form the issue can be raised in the House of Commons so as to secure the best prospect of united action. There are great disadvantages in any amendments on the Address, as the Government can and must treat any amendment on the Address as a vote of want of confidence, which most of our men would be unwilling to support, even if they had any assurance of consideration such as I have indicated.

Is there any other way of raising the question which has been or may be considered? Last Session I do not suppose that the Opposition would have thought of a motion for enquiry in any form, but Chamberlain has made a good deal of progress since then, and such a motion might now meet with a good deal of support. This is only my own idea and I have scarcely discussed it with anybody. But though the question of procedure does not come first in point of time, it is that perhaps on which communications between the leaders may be most easily opened, and if you have already or are likely soon to consider it with your colleagues, I should be glad if you should find it possible to give me some information with regard to it.[3]

[1] Devonshire had received another letter from Rosebery 'urging that something should be done, but what?... I think I shall write a short letter to Spencer merely asking him whether they have considered the question of an amendment to the Address... This will not commit anybody, but may open the way to further negotiations.' Devonshire to James, 30 Dec. 1903, James Papers, M45/1308.

[2] Devonshire had told Arthur Elliot, 'now we can only operate in agreement with the Opposition; and if our association does that, more than half our M.P.s would leave us'. Elliot, Diary, 4 Dec. 1903, Elliot Papers, 19526 f. 81.

[3] James informed Lord Hugh Cecil on 3 Jan, 'The Duke becomes more enthusiastic every day.' Quickswood Papers, Qu. I 2/1. For Spencer's reply on 4 Jan. see CP, 340. 3053.

**783**  LORD SPENCER TO DUKE OF DEVONSHIRE
*7 January 1904; 28 St. James's Place, S.W.*
CP, 340.3056

We had a meeting here on Tuesday[1] of 9 or 10 ex official Liberals. Rosebery would not come.[2]

I laid before them the points which you put in your letter of Jan 2.

The first point 'Whether any consideration would be shown in regard to their seats at the next Election to Unionist Free Traders in the House of Commons who might by their votes place themselves in opposition to the majority of their party and perhaps to the Government itself.'

It was thought that to carry this out on a broad general principle would be extremely difficult, but we all thought that it was most desirable to see whether in some cases an arrangement could be made, and with that in view we should be very glad that two of your friends should meet two of us to discuss the question and report to you and to us what they thought was possible.[3]

The second question as to the form in which the issue can be raised in the House of Commons was very fully discussed.

It was thought impossible to avoid some fiscal amendment on the Address, which would raise directly the question of Free trade as against Protection. The country and Free traders in particular would demand this, but the breadth and words of the amendment could not be settled without some communications with you and your friends.

I can assure you that we all are anxious to co-operate as far as possible with Unionist Free traders, but at the same time we felt that great difficulties had to be met. If we tried to meet you and your friends on some questions other than fiscal we might be accused of betraying those with whom we have acted. In that way we might lose a great many votes at an Election and because of Free trade would thus suffer heavily.

[1] On 6 Jan. at his sister Sarah's house, to decide attitudes towards Unionist free traders. The meeting settled that Spencer should be the channel of communication with the Duke. H. Gladstone to Asquith, 7 Jan. 1904, AP, 10 f. 130.

[2] Stating that 'my attendance would be, in appearance at any rate, a renewal of those official relations which I deliberately severed when I resigned the leadership in 1896'. Rosebery to Spencer, 4 Jan. 1904, SP.

[3] Commenting on this letter, James wrote, 'Spencer's communication is not very satisfactory. As you say, he does not meet in any way the crucial difficulty you refer to—and there will be great difficulty in anyone doing so.' James to Devonshire, 12 Jan. 1904, CP, 340. 3061A.

## 784 DUKE OF DEVONSHIRE TO LORD SPENCER
*11 January 1904; Chatsworth, Chesterfield*

Thanks for your letter. James has also heard from H. Gladstone, and I am asking him (Ld. James) and G. Hamilton to meet Asquith and H. Gladstone for the proposed discussion about seats.

The Conference should I think be strictly confidential and without prejudice, and at present confined to the cases of those of our men who we are sure would desire it. For instance any discussion of the case of Hicks Beach's seat might if it should come to his knowledge do more harm than good, and there may be others.[1]

I am not sure that you see all the difficulties about an amendment to the Address. Of course it may be necessary for you to raise the issue at the earliest moment which will be on the Address. But you cannot expect more than a very few of our men to vote for what will be want of confidence in the Govt. Not many will even abstain. This may not preclude another resolution aimed directly at Chamberlain, for which our men could vote even if approved by the Govt.

A motion for inquiry need not necessarily be for a Royal Commission, though that would have a good deal of support on our side.[2]

[1] Hicks Beach had written to his son on 11 Dec. 1903 that 'when the general election comes, the Unionist party may be simply Chamberlainite—in which case I should retire from Parliament, for even I should have no chance as a Unionist Free-trader, and I can't join the other side'. Lady V. Hicks Beach, *Life of Sir Michael Hicks Beach* (1932), ii, p. 200.

[2] Spencer assured Devonshire in his reply that Liberals would possibly support a proposal for an inquiry 'if Free traders were in great difficulty'. 12 Jan. 1904, CP, 340. 3061.

## 785 LORD SPENCER TO H. CAMPBELL-BANNERMAN
*12 January 1904; Althorp, Northamptonn*
CBP, Add. MS. 41229 ff. 241–2

Here is the Duke of Devonshire's reply. There is not much in it, but anyhow the conference as to possible arrangements of seats will come off.

I had Winston Churchill and Ivor Guest[1] here on Sunday.[2] Very keen and evidently the former is quite ready after a gap in his Parliamentary career to become a Liberal.

His line was for us to strike a bargain with Free trade Unionists, that if they voted for our amendment on the Address our Leaders would engage to do all they could to get them a seat somewhere.

He said that the pressure brought on Constituencies after '86 by Salisbury was very great to get Conservative support of Liberals who had voted against Home Rule, and that this was the cause of the defeat of Mr. G. on the question.

He said that a turnover of 33 votes might be effected!![3]

I am only giving his views not my arguments with him.

One thing he said which I think is true, that if once a Unionist votes against his party, his only chance with Elections is to vote Liberal on various questions and that he is on this account sure eventually to become wholly Liberal.

No wonder the D. of D. does not choose W. Churchill as one of his delegates, for he had to deal with men like Hicks Beach and G. Hamilton who are much more Tory than W. Churchill.

W.C. says that there can be no doubt that Joe has the Tory party at his back, that the party with only [      ]⁴ exceptions were always inclined to be if they were not altogether Protectionists.

What a nice smash up of the Liberal Unionists as we have known them.⁵ My impression is that the Duke will be heavily defeated by Joe at their L.U.C. conclave.⁶

Do you think we ought to circulate the Duke's letter? I could have 9 copies made and divide the Meeting into 3.

¹ Ivor Churchill Guest, Conservative M.P., Plymouth, since 1900. He was a cousin of Churchill, as his mother was the eldest daughter of 7th Duke of Marlborough. Guest joined the Liberals with Churchill in April 1904.

² Afterwards, Churchill wrote a full account of his conversation with Spencer to Devonshire. 'Lord Spencer was most friendly to me and would like to help our people, but he dwells a great deal on the obvious difficulties, some people could be arranged for, others no.' 13 Jan. 1904, CP, 340.3063. Reproduced in full in R.S. Churchill, *Winston Churchill. Young Statesman 1901–1914* (1967), ii, p. 75. On receiving Spencer's letter, Campbell-Bannerman commented to Herbert Gladstone; 'Winston and Guest have been at Althorp, which is good.' Campbell-Bannerman to H. Gladstone. 14 Jan. 1904, HGP, Add. MS. 45988 f. 81.

³ Spencer's scepticism was shared by Devonshire. 'W. Churchill thinks that 35 or more will vote for an amendment, but I do not believe it for a moment.' Devonshire to Lord Hugh Cecil, 24 Jan. 1904, Quickswood Papers, Qu. I 2/4.

⁴ Word(s) omitted.

⁵ On 11 Jan. an edited version of earlier Chamberlain-Devonshire correspondence was published, It clearly showed that Chamberlain had captured the Liberal Unionist Association. The correspondence is reproduced in J. Amery, *Joseph Chamberlain and the Tariff Reform Campaign* (1969), pp. 574–84.

⁶ Chamberlain summoned a meeting of the Liberal Unionist Council for 3 Feb. at which he presided. Three resolutions passed by the conference—to maintain the existence of the Central Unionist Association, to assist Liberal Unionist candidates without regard to their views on fiscal reform and authorization to prepare new rules for the Council—weakened Devonshire's position. After the annual meeting of the Council on 18 May 1904, which confirmed the February resolutions, Devonshire resigned from the Association.

## 786  H. CAMPBELL-BANNERMAN TO LORD SPENCER

*14 January 1904; 6 Grosvenor Place, S.W.*

I do not know that the Duke carries the thing much further, but it is all in the right line. He seems in a terrible fright of Michael!¹

Our people would laugh at an enquiry resolution. But would it do for *them* to move it after ours, and we should vote for it as a *pis aller*. I hardly think it would.

It would be a good thing to circulate the letter as you propose.

Herbert G. has had 2 hours ('quite satisfactory') with Winston and letter from James in friendly spirit.[2] I doubt if the seats can be bartered as suggested. The Tories are much more subservient and disciplined than our people.

Two bits of gossip I heard yesterday. That the Duke has said there is nothing for it but to join the Liberals. That five members of the Govt. headed by Gerald[3] told A.J.B. that they would go if he did not slacken off from his partnership with Joe. Hence the speech at Manchester . . .[4]

I had had many indications of suspiciousness among our stalwarts that they may be sold in an alliance. So I went against any compromises last night.[5] It is absolutely necessary that that line should be taken by some one, amidst all our colloquings! and I thought I had better do it. Winston and Co. may not like it.

[1] Hicks Beach.
[2] James to Gladstone, 12 Jan. 1904, HGP, Add. MS. 46018 ff. 66-9.
[3] Gerald Balfour.
[4] 11 Jan.
[5] In a speech at Maidstone on 13 Jan., emphasizing that the Liberals would make no compromises with the Unionist free traders. Campbell-Bannerman's motive was to reassure radical Liberals such as Lloyd George. Sykes, p. 75.

**787  H. CAMPBELL-BANNERMAN TO LORD SPENCER**
*15 January 1904; Lord Warden Hotel, Dover*

*Private*

Herbert G. is very keen and a little impatient or at least urgent for an arrangement with the Duke and his men.

(1) He urges me to consult the Speaker as to a Free Trade amendment. This I will do.

(2) He finds the Education question embarrassing and delicate, and suggests that Bryce should feel the pulse of the Non Cons. Bryce some time ago offered to me to do something in this way and I will now write to him to do so. He has their confidence and is quite sound as well as well-informed. H.J.G. says 'If the Non Cons are inconvincible it will mean loss of seats and damage to Free Trade *and* Education, whereas if they would consent in certain places to back the Unionist Free Traders and to give latitude in other places to men who are faced by heavy Church and R.C. odds, we could strengthen the general position, e.g. Ritchie, to fight him is an absurdity, but the local men want to fight him *on Education*.

(3) He (very respectfully) suggests if possible a meeting between you and the Duke. Leisurely letters may find the Address on us unprepared. Is there not some force in this?[1]

(4) He says 'Personally I am all for a Royal Commission for certain specified points, e.g. the basis of our statistics, the methods and details of international exchange, fuller inquiry into invisible exports, the consular system from the commercial side, how far our manufacturers are really hit by foreign as distinct from home competition etc. It would take the wind out of the Spoils Commission sails.[2] It has been suggested by Schuster and many of the City folk.'

...I am not sure about this Royal Commission but I am sure that we must have our fling against the whole thing first.

[1] Herbert Gladstone had written to Campbell-Bannerman, 'The Address is likely to be on us with nothing done. My difficulties are two—I can't act as I should wish because the seats position turns on (a) the position which is slowly being considered by the Duke and Lord Spencer, and (b) the education position which is a very delicate one. Could not Bryce or Asquith be asked to feel the pulse of the Free Church bosses?' H. Gladstone to Campbell-Bannerman, 14 Jan. 1904, CBP, Add. MS. 41217 ff. 77–8.

[2] In the United States, 'spoils' means the patronage exercised by an incoming administration after an election victory. Gladstone may have been referring to possible patronage in the diplomatic and consular services.

**788**  LORD SPENCER TO H. CAMPBELL-BANNERMAN
*16 January 1904; Althorp, Northampton*
CBP, Add. MS. 41229 ff. 244–6

*Private*

Your letter of the 15th is very interesting...

Now I will slightly discuss some points in your letter.

I am glad to hear what you say as to Herbert G.'s keenness and views.

An arrangement with the Duke and his men cannot be settled until we know the result of the Conference between James of Hereford and G. Hamilton with Asquith and H. Gladstone.

Directly they have made their report, I should strongly advocate an attempt to see the Duke of Devonshire. H.G. will probably be able to say when the report of the Conference will be ready, whether it be verbal or written.

I certainly see great advantages to be gained if some arrangement can be made, for no doubt notwithstanding the splendid result of the Election at Norwich,[1] we must fight with our utmost strength to increase this strength if we are to win.

It will be quite right for you to consult the Speaker as to Free Food amendments. On this point in regard to what the Duke wrote, I replied by return of post off my own bat that I could not see why on a question of supreme National importance like this, men who are warm Free traders should not vote against their government. The Confidence appeal cannot be so sacred as to prevent this on a rallying fire.

Then as to the Education question.

Bryce is quite the best man to sound the Non Cons.

He and I after you left the conclave talked pretty freely on this very point, and he is quite ready to put this before the Non Cons., that without making the slightest withdrawal of our views on Education, it would be folly on their part at every possible Election to fight a Unionist on Education when by doing so we are likely to lose a Free trade seat.

There must be cases where nothing but the empty assertion of a principle is gained by fighting the Education question as against Free trade, and it is obviously in the interests of Non Conformists that the Government and Chamberlain should be defeated, and they should not therefore press rigidly the Educational Test where it is impossible to carry it.

Some of my Non Conformist friends begin to realize this, and I hope that Clifford and Co. will also.[2]

As to Royal Commision or inquiry I wrote also to the Duke as to that and answered his argument as to the Committee on the existing Tariff in 1840 or thereabouts, on whose report his Tariff changes were made.

I said that it was a very different thing to have a Committee upon an existing Tariff to having one on a hypothetical one.

But I said that in my letter although we should not wish to propose an inquiry, we might at the last moment support a proposal for one, but I personally deprecated any such proceeding as an indication of weakness in our case.

I confess I still am opposed to the R. Commission, but I should think we should not shut out the possibility of our having to agree to one if sorely pressed.

[1] The defeat of the Conservative candidate, E. E. Wild, by Louis John Tillett in the by-election on 15 Jan. This was the second of four by-elections fought between 7 Jan. and 12 Feb., in all of which the Conservatives were decisively beaten. At Norwich, according to one of Spencer's correspondents, the education question was almost as important an issue as tariff reform. Spencer to H. Gladstone, 19 Jan. 1904, HGP, Add. MS. 46017 f. 137.

[2] Dr. John Clifford, a leading Baptist, who bitterly opposed the 1902 Education Act. Bryce sounded out Clifford as to the possibility of formulating propositions on education which, if accepted by Unionist free traders, would have enabled Liberals to support Unionists in the constituencies. Clifford, in a reply to Bryce (2 Feb. 1904), discouraged any further explorations. See R.A. Rempel, *Unionists Divided* (1972), pp. 83-4.

**789**  LORD SPENCER TO DUKE OF DEVONSHIRE

*29 January 1904; 28 St. James's Place, S.W.*

CP, 340.3067

I laid before my Colleagues today the suggestions which you and your friends desired to bring before us,[1] to the effect that Campbell-Bannerman in his speech at the commencement of the Debate on the Address,[2] should ask Mr. Balfour to give time after the Address to a Debate on the Fiscal question, stating that if Mr. Balfour would promise this, Campbell-Bannerman would undertake that no fiscal amendment should be moved to the Address from those over whom he has control.

As I anticipated no one supported this proposal, and the opinion which I reported to you before prevailed, that it was impossible to avoid having an amendment upon the Address raised by a leading member of the Opposition.[3] The draft amendment which I showed you was adopted in substance but slightly altered in words.

If you desire to have it I can get it for you.

I am very sorry to see that Lord Goschen has pronounced in favour of a Royal Commission.[4] It will be a very grave thing to have this question hung up until a Royal Commission reports.

It may prolong the lease of life of the Government, which personally I should not deplore, but it will be a serious disaster to commercial and industrial industries.

Unless we had an overwhelming defeat hanging over us, I should be very loth to support such a proposal.

[1] A 'very amicable conclave' of leading Liberals was held on 26 Jan; all were present except Grey. Spencer then went to Devonshire House for a long talk with its owner. Spencer to C.R. Spencer, 26 Jan. 1904, SP. Devonshire later called on Spencer for a second interview.

[2] 2 Feb.

[3] In the debate on the Address on 8 Feb., John Morley moved an amendment stating that 'any return to protective duties, more particularly when imposed on the food of the people, would be deeply injurious to our national strength, contentment and well being.' Hansard, 4, cxxix, col. 623 ff.

[4] In a speech at Halifax on 28 Jan. Goschen declared, 'It would be an immense relief to the country if a Royal Commission could be appointed to bring the figures of all the various parties together and hear both sides.' The Times, 29 June 1904, p.8.

**790   LORD SPENCER TO LORD CREWE[1]**
*29 January 1904; 28 St. James's Place, S.W.*
Crewe Papers, C/46

We have settled not to have an amendment on the Address in the House of Lords. This is the Duke of D.'s wish, and it would be useless to have a vote without his concurrence. We shall announce that we shall endeavour to raise as soon as possible debates on the subject.

I shall try and draw the Government on their position in my Speech, but there are so many topics to touch upon that I may not go at great length into any of them.[2]

I quite agree with what you say as to Retaliation.[3] I touched the points you name in my 80 Club Speech. No Govt. can expect us to agree to invest the Privy Council or Govt. with power to raise duties in order to deal with a hostile tariff. They hold the power of introducing a special Bill if they need it, and we know they did this as to sugar last session.

I do not believe in the practicality of retaliation at all, but I do not see how it could be carried out unless you have an extensive Tariff in force and that means or will produce Protection...

I have seen the Duke twice. He is very friendly but I doubt whether much close co-operation will follow. So many of his friends are afraid of any blow which would hit the Govt. and he seems much of their mind.

The Duke admits that Balfour dare not separate himself more than he has from J.C., as he cannot throw J.C. over, and any action pointing that way would make J.C. turn at once on Balfour and turn Balfour out neck and crop.

[1] Robert Offley Ashburton Crewe-Milnes, 1st Earl of Crewe, Lord-Lieutenant of Ireland, 1892-5.

[2] Spencer's speech in the debate on the Address in the Lords of 2 Feb. dealt largely with foreign policy. On the fiscal question, Spencer stated that an election should be held to settle the issue. Hansard, 4, cxxix, cols. 19-37.

[3] 'If the Govt. admit that an Act of Parlt. is necessary in each case, they will retain the platonic support of the Duke, Lord Goschen, etc... But if the Govt. on the other hand, state... that a retaliatory policy can only be carried out by an extended use of Orders in Council, I should expect the Duke and the others to draw back.' Crewe to Spencer, 24 Jan. 1904, SP.

**791**  DUKE OF DEVONSHIRE TO LORD SPENCER
*31 January 1904; 8 King's Gardens, Brighton*

I received your letter of the 29th. yesterday after I had written.

I should be rather glad to see your amendment before our meeting tomorrow afternoon in case we should have any suggestions to make which would reconcile any of our men to it. But as I told you, I do not expect that many will vote for any amendment to the Address.[1]

I think there is a good deal to be said for Goschen's Royal Commission or any Committee,[2] but no one seems in favour of it, and it is probably too late for it now. From what the City people tell us, the suspension does not seem to be doing so much harm as one would have expected. It is too far off to affect business seriously.

I dare say you will be able to defeat Protection by yourselves at the next election which no doubt will suit you, but what I fear is that the majority of the Unionists will be pledged to Protection, and it will become a purely party question.[3] This might perhaps have been avoided by an enquiry.

[1] At Devonshire's request, Spencer called on him at 12.50 p.m. on 1 Feb. to discuss John Morley's proposed amendment. Devonshire wished to show it to his colleagues at a meeting that afternoon, but did not expect many Unionists to vote with the Liberals. Spencer to Campbell-Bannerman, 1 Feb. 1904, CBP, Add. MS. 41229 f. 258.

[2] The Liberals had won a spectacular victory at the Ayr Burghs by-election on 30 Jan.

[3] In a critical vote of confidence in the Commons on the Morley amendment on 15 Feb., the government had a majority of 51. 26 Unionist free traders voted with the Liberals, 14 with the government and 12 abstained. Hansard, 4, cxxix, col. 1446.

# 11

# LIBERAL REVIVAL, 1904-5

*Developments abroad occupied Spencer during his last two years in the House of Lords. During 1904, he strongly attacked Milner's policy in South Africa of employing Chinese labour in the Transvaal mines; he also condemned the British expedition against Tibet. The outbreak of the Russo-Japanese war might, he feared, lead to China joining forces with the Russians. Spencer admitted to Ripon, 'I have always been a strong Philo Jap' (1 Jan. 1904, Rip. P, Add. MS. 43538 f. 158), and welcomed the new Anglo-Japanese agreement signed on 12 August 1905. In the same month, when the power struggle between Curzon and Kitchener ended in the former's resignation, Spencer regarded the affair as 'very melancholy and deeply damaging to the position of the Viceroy of India'. (Spencer to C. R. Spencer, 28 Aug. 1905, SP).*

*At home, the fortunes of the Unionists continued to decline. The free trade controversy remained unsettled and the Army reforms proposed by Arnold-Forster, the new War Secretary, ran into much opposition. Rosebery's position within the Liberal Party continued to exercise the minds of many of its leading members. Spencer declined to accept that his retirement was definite, though Rosebery for 'physical and mental causes' did not wish to take office again.*

*Spencer had attempted to lure Rosebery back into the Liberal fold in January 1904 by inviting him to give the dinner to Liberal Peers before the opening of Parliament and to return to the Opposition front bench in the Lords. Rosebery refused both offers. One last effort to persuade Rosebery to join the next government was made by Spencer in August 1905, but he was rebuffed.*

*In the autumn of 1904, Spencer suffered a heart attack and was unable to resume his duties until the beginning of the following year. This did not dispel rumours of the probability of his appointment to the highest office with the likely advent of a Liberal ministry. In January 1905, Edmund Gosse reported to Haldane 'the somewhat gloomy intelligence' that Spencer had consented to be prime minister. (Gosse to Haldane, 4 Jan. 1905, Gosse Papers). Further, in February, Rosebery, entertaining the King at Mentmore, advised him to send for Spencer and Campbell-Bannerman together. (18 Feb. 1905, EHJ, Add. MS. 48683 f. 20). Much speculation had been aroused by the appearance in the national press a few days before of Spencer's so-called 'manifesto', in the form of a letter to a fellow Liberal, Corrie Grant, setting out a programme for the party. Spencer protested in vain at the interpretation placed by both politicians and the public on the letter.*

*Although Balfour's government was defeated in the Commons on the Irish estimates in July 1905, it was not until December that the prime minister resigned. Meanwhile, Spencer had been recovering at Nauheim, after a hectic parliamentary session, preparing himself for the likelihood of taking office. Whilst shooting at his Norfolk retreat in October, he suffered a stroke. 'Poor Lord Spencer,' wrote Winston Churchill on hearing the news, 'it was rather like a ship sinking in sight of land.' (Churchill to Rosebery, 19 Oct, 1905, RP, 10009 f. 171).*

---

## 792 LORD SELBORNE TO LORD SPENCER
*24 February 1904; Admiralty, Whitehall*

There is beyond question an evil influence abroad which is trying to influence Russian opinion against us especially in connection with the Navy.[1]

It has been stated in the press that we have broken the letter or the spirit of neutrality.

1. In allowing the Argentine Cruisers bought by Japan to leave Genoa under the red ensign.
2. In supplying naval officers to command these cruisers.
3. In escorting these cruisers in the Mediterranean by H.M. ships.
4. In not allowing certain Russian destroyers to dock at Malta.
5. In allowing the Japs to use Wei-hai-wei[2] as a base for an attack upon Port Arthur.

Every one of these statements is false, but they have all been swallowed greedily in St. Petersburg 'as an explanation of the Japanese successes' and public opinion is dangerously excited against us in consequence.

It is true that each of these statements has been denied publicly but in a case like this, to use a favourite phrase of Fisher's, 'reiteration is the secret of conviction', and if you or one of your colleagues could ask me a question on Thursday I think it might possibly do some good.[3]

[1] The outbreak of the Russo-Japanese War was on 8 Feb.

[2] A seaport in north-east China, occupied by the Japanese, 1895-8, leased to Great Britain since 1898 and used as a naval base.

[3] Spencer put these five points to Selborne in the Lords on 25 Feb. asking for further information. Hansard, 4, cxxx, col. 940; for Selborne's reply, see cols. 941-4.

---

## 793 C. R. SPENCER TO LORD SPENCER
*22 March 1904; 28 Bruton Street, W.*

Your peers last night debated till quite late.[1] I only heard Camperdown[2] who was poisonous. They would quote your phrase about Chinese Labour, twisting it to try and show that you knew that it was cant to call it slavery.[3] However the Govt. only had 72 majority. In our House Alfred[4] spoke better than I have yet heard him. He began on a false note twitting C.B. with reading his speech. But it was not a bad speech at all.

C.B. made capital points,[5] but reading always spoils a speech in delivery. Fletcher Moulton was very powerful.[6] Arthur B. was thin, and not very effective. Asquith was a sledgehammer crushing A.J.B.'s thin dialectics. There was nearly a row, as the Tories would not let Jack Seely speak.[7] Winston jumped up and appealed to the Speaker as he could not hear owing 'to the vulgar clamour of the Tory Party', these were his words. Ivor Guest engaged in a violent altercation with the men behind him.[8]

Then the Irish would not let Arthur Balfour speak. They yelled and shouted 'Why didn't you let Seely speak.'[9] J. Morley agreed with me that it was unpleasant. We divided at 12.15 and only had 57 majority against us.[10] Not at all bad. What with the shortened hours, and the endless time the front bench men on either side take up, the rank and file on both sides are shut out.

[1] On an Order of the Day disapproving of importation of Chinese labour in the Transvaal allowed under a recent ordinance. Hansard, 4, cxxxii, cols. 117–211.

[2] Robert Adam, 3rd Earl of Camperdown, Liberal Unionist from 1886. Ibid., cols, 133–9.

[3] The employment of the Chinese in the gold mines and their working conditions aroused much public concern. See P. Richardson, Chinese Mine Labour in the Transvaal (1982), p. 5. The Opposition motion was lost by 97 votes to 25.

[4] Alfred Lyttelton, Secretary of State for the Colonies, 1903–5. Ibid., col. 273 ff.

[5] Proposing a Chinese labour (Transvaal) motion. Ibid., col. 252 ff.

[6] Ibid., cols. 289–382.

[7] John Edward Bernard Seely, Conservative, M.P., Isle of Wight, 1900–4. Disagreeing with government policy on the fiscal question and Chinese labour, Seely resigned his seat in March 1904. He was returned unopposed in April and accepted the Liberal Whip in May. See his Adventure (1930), pp. 106–8.

[8] See H. Lucy, The Balfourian Parliament 1900–1905 (1906), pp. 309–10.

[9] Balfour, ibid., col. 343 ff. Hansard does not mention this incident.

[10] The motion was lost by 299 votes to 242.


**794**   LORD SPENCER TO C. R. SPENCER
25 March 1904; Hotel West End, San Remo

I was delighted to get your letter. Your short account of the Debate interested me much. Camperdown never speaks honeyed words and is always dry and arid.

If my speech had stood by itself I was right to say that I would not use the word 'Slavery' for of course 'Slave' cannot be applied to a man who voluntarily enters into an engagement, however bad, and therefore to impress the House and to be quite accurate I rather enforced my opposition to the whole business by saying what I did, but as many Liberals by article or Speech had used the expression, I dare say I had better not have said this.[1] I was abominably, nay I should say unfairly reported, for my best points as to the Ordinance in the most Liberal sense were not reported, my comparison with the Fugitive Slave Law rules which in Ward Hunt's time had to be revoked,[2] and my question to Sunny, who said that the Ordinances were penal. I said if humane they were not consistent with freedom and very strong attack on the whole thing etc. etc.[3]

[1] In his speech on 21 March, Camperdown quoted from Spencer in a previous debate of 18 March. 'The noble Earl ... said it would be an exaggeration to call the condition of this Ordinance slavery.' Hansard, 4, cxxxii, col. 134.

[2] In 1875, when Ward Hunt was First Lord of the Admiralty, the Admiralty issued a circular about the surrender of fugitive slaves on board British ships to owners. There was an outcry and the circular was withdrawn. A second circular was issued and also much criticized. In 1876, the Admiralty issued new instructions to the effect that slaves were not to be given up.

[3] Hansard, 4, cxxxii, col. 33, 18 March. The Duke of Marlborough was Under-Secretary of State for the Colonies, 1903–5.

**795   LORD SPENCER TO C. R. SPENCER**
*3 April 1904; Hotel West End, San Remo*

Your letter was splendid, full of interesting political things.

I have little to say except to groan almost cry over the Thibet affair.[1] What horrid bloodshed of these miserable creatures who would not fight a cadet corps of schoolboys. And for what and how is it to end? Why did they not 2 months ago order them to occupy the Thibetan territory close to our frontier, and hold it until redress for the small injuries done us had been made?

Is it right to force our presence in a country which refuses to admit Christians? Surely not. Is it Russia at the back? If Russia occupied Lhasa which is impossible, if she acquired dominant influence there, what possible harm could it do us? Thibet has hardly any lands, its climate is impossible and our frontiers are strong and easily defended.

I am in despair.

We have made our protest, and now if we demand recall of troops, we shall be accused of helping the enemy, but hardly is this possible as the Lama and his people cannot know what goes on in Parliament.

[1] George Nathaniel, 1st Baron Curzon of Kedleston, then Viceroy of India, convinced of Russia's plans against weak neighbours Afghanistan and Tibet, decided to impose British control. In Dec. 1903, he sent a mission under the command of Francis Younghusband into Tibet, when several thousand Tibetans were massacred after they had agreed to surrender. Younghusband entered Lhasa on 3 Aug. A Convention with Tibet was signed there on 7 Sept. A. Lamb, *Britain and Chinese Central Asia: The Road to Lhasa 1767 to 1905* (1960), pp. 175-96.

**796   LORD SPENCER TO C. R. SPENCER**
*14 April 1904; Chateau de Thorenc[1]*

I found your letter on my arrival here this afternoon. It interested me very much.

Look at what I say about the Thibet expedition on the Address.[2] I pressed Lansdowne as to the necessity under Act of Parliament of consulting Parliament if Indian troops were used outside India, I forget the words, but as a hostile act. He deliberately said that on the best advice they were assured that this friendly mission did not come under the Act.[3]

It is a climb down of significance, and justified what I said on the subject.

I suppose that C.B. said the same in your House.

[1] Rendel's villa at Cannes where Spencer stayed on a number of occasions.
[2] Expressing anxiety on the mission to Tibet. Hansard, 4, cxxix, cols. 26-7, 2 Feb. 1904.
[3] Ibid., cols. 43-4.

**797   LORD SPENCER TO C. R. SPENCER**
*8 July 1904; Spencer House, St. James's Place, S.W.*

I confess the election of Bingham did not surprise me.[1] I hear there was a terrible pamphleteer on our side, one Allen Upward (or some such name) who did much harm putting the Chinese Labour question into hymns etc.[2]

... I saw C.B. this morning and we had a long talk. He is very pleased with his flock. They were burning for extreme measures, like refusing to move etc.,[3] but on his sending a message to them through J. Woodhouse[4] they at once gave it up.

Harcourt was very good and sound about it all.

C.B. thinks that the Government are in a great mess still about their Army Scheme, and that they may even now be wrecked on it.[5]

I expect a good deal will be made of Nevy's Speech on Conscription.[6] Quite contrary to all traditions for the Army Council is part of the Government. Fancy if I and the Cabinet had decided against a great number of cruisers and old Richards or Hoskins had made a Speech for them. The one who made the Speech or I would have had to go.[7]

...I hear that J. Morley's speech[8] though excellent to read was almost a failure in the House, so badly delivered but he was very pleased with making it. C.B. goes to Marienbad early in August.

[1] Lord George Bingham. Convervative, was elected for the Chertsey division of Surrey in a by-election on 7 July though many Unionist free traders supported the Liberal candidate, Thomas Sadler. Bingham, 5425. Sadler, 4876.

[2] A Liberal paper, the Chertsey Elector, especially produced for the election, gave offence by publishing parodies on two well-known hymns.

[3] Balfour had announced in the Commons on 1 July that the guillotine would be used in the debate on the Licensing Bill. Hansard, 4, cxxxvii, col. 319 ff., 1 July 1904.

[4] Sir James Thomas Woodhouse, Liberal M.P., Huddersfield, 1895–1906.

[5] Later, Spencer in the Lords effectively criticized the government's plans for army reform. Arnold-Forster, Journal, 21 July 1904, Add. MS. 50339 f. 63. See Hansard, 4, cxxxviii, cols. 738–43, 21 July 1904.

[6] Lt.-Gen. Sir Nevill Lyttelton, Chief of the Imperial General Staff and First Military Member of the newly-formed Army Council, spoke at the South African dinner in London on 7 July. He indicated that he favoured a form of conscription, though he subsequently denied it. The speech was fully reported in the Standard, 8 July 1904, p. 3. Lyttelton was Spencer's second cousin.

[7] Spencer reiterated these sentiments in a debate on the Militia in the Lords. Hansard, 4, cxxxvii, cols. 1171-4, 11 July 1904.

[8] On the committee stage of the Licensing Bill (Procedure) on 4 July. Hansard, 4, cxxxvii, col. 490 ff.

### 798   LORD SPENCER TO C. R. SPENCER
*21 August 1904; Nauheim*

I wonder whether you read A.J. Balfour's address to the British Association.[1] I had a great struggle but did it, and have recurred to it since. I am not learned enough to appreciate the scientific part but I think I can appreciate some of his general conclusions, which come to this: experience is little good, we live and have lived in illusions, and we must be sceptical about every doctrine laid down. In another Speech[2] he is likewise most destructive in his criticisms on the degeneracy of a race physically, and leads up to general confusion of thought. He was not nearly as practical and sensible as first.

I do not think A.J.B. is sufficiently versed in science as to claim a right to lay down the law to scientists. Other men not learned should follow his views, and as a statesman much more as Prime Minister his Address should not only have been addressed to scientific men but to the outside public who though not scientific can form their own conclusion on general principles put forward by great men of science and by good speakers like himself. Of course it was very clear and agile as he usually is.

[1] As President, Balfour gave the opening address at Cambridge on 17 Aug., entitled 'Reflections Suggested by the New Theory of Matter.' *The Times*, 18 Aug. 1904, p. 9.

[2] Balfour attended Section A, Anthropology on 19 Aug. where the proceedings were devoted to anthropometry. He opened the discussion on the question of heredity. *The Times*, 20 Aug. 1904, p. 9.

## 799 LORD SPENCER TO C. R. SPENCER
*31 August 1904; Nauheim*

... Yes, Londonderry's Speech was deplorable for the Tories,[1] unluckily so very true, but he does not seem to realize A.J.B.'s position and what the Sheffield Speech without explanatory notes of any kind means, viz. nothing but waiting on Providence for the time when Joe's policy for which A.J.B. has such warm sympathy can be carried. I suppose Londonderry's Coal people[2] have been at him and kept him up to Free Trade.

... Channing and his agricultural reform is no good,[3] but I should like to know whether any real reform for the future is possible. I am all for small holdings, but they continually fail, yet they may possibly come about eventually.[4]

[1] At a Primrose League Habitation at Wynyard Park, Co. Durham, on 27 Aug., Charles, 6th Marquess of Londonderry, Lord President of the Council, 1903–5, told the audience that with regard to fiscal policy, the Unionist Party 'should insist upon him (the Parliamentary candidate) adhering to the only constitutional policy before the country, and that was the policy laid down by Mr. Balfour at Sheffield in August last.' *The Times*, 29 Aug. 1904, p. 10.

[2] Londonderry was deputy Lord-Lieutenant of Durham and was himself a great coal-owner.

[3] Channing was president of the Land Law Reform Association, established in 1904, which issued a 'Rural Programme'. Channing, p. 294.

[4] For Spencer's detailed views on this issue see his nine-page memorandum entitled 'Lord Spencer on the Small Agricultural Holdings Bill [1892]. General line to be taken on the 2nd reading by the Front Bench.' SP.

## 800 LORD SPENCER TO C. R. SPENCER
*11 September 1904; Nauheim*

I went to lunch with the Duke of Devonshire at Homburg yesterday ... He was very nice and chatty like old days. After lunch we went over the manuscript of one of E. Fitzmaurice's chapters in which he came in chiefly, and I was often quoted.[1]

Then we began to talk about modern politics, and had just broken the ice as we walked down to the Lawn Tennis, when his Private Secretary came up and our confidential talk was broken off. I was sorry.

I did not get much from him but he seemed interested about our side, and although he protested he would never take office again, I am not quite sure but we hardly got to the core of that ... I was very glad to have spent 3 hours with the Duke.

[1] Lord Edmond Fitzmaurice's two-volume *The Life of Lord Granville* appeared in 1906. Both Devonshire and Spencer had made correspondence available to Fitzmaurice. See Preface, p. vii and Fitzmaurice to Spencer, 1 May 1904, SP. Spencer also read the proofs of the book dealing with home rule. Fitzmaurice to Spencer, 5 Jan. 1905, SP.

### 801 LORD SPENCER TO LORD ROSEBERY
*12 October 1904; Althorp, Northampton*
RP, 10062 f. 294.

I am still under doctor's orders, but in the Gallery, and mending every day. I had a very bad time of it, not thinking of a chill and looking forward to renewed strength etc. for never did I feel better.[1]

Poor old Harcourt! We all knew his faults, but I was really fond of him.[2] What a strange mixture, so different as the Public man in the H. of C. to what he was in political conclaves out of the House. He would have had a greater career had he lived up to his H. of C. standard. The public know this and not the other side of him.

I fear I must lay by for sometime. I don't personally mind as I hate public speaking, but I feel rather like a political impostor.

[1] Spencer was taken ill on 23 Sept, the day after his return to Althorp, and was confined to bed for eleven days. *NM*, 7 Oct. 1904, p. 5.
[2] Sir William Harcourt died on 1 Oct. 1904.

### 802 H. GLADSTONE TO LORD SPENCER
*16 October 1904; Sandicroft, Littlestone-on-Sea*

C.B. may have written to you direct. He tells me that he would like a consultation before he begins his campaign. I hope, from newspaper accounts, that you are rapidly recovering your strength but I don't know whether you are likely to be in London in the near future. Would it be possible for you to meet him on Monday the 24th or Tuesday the 25th? The 24th would suit him better I think. I am writing to Asquith to find out which days would be possible for him. To save time I am asking him to telegraph and perhaps you will telegraph also...[1]

It appears to me that concentration on certain leading questions other than fiscalitis is necessary. Joe's campaign this year is so far a great fizzle, and our programme lacks at present both clearness and attractiveness.

The Irish question is urgent and I believe our men are coming to see that a definite scheme is inevitable. West Ridgeway's letter is most significant.[2]

[1] Spencer was unable to leave Althorp, so the meeting with Gladstone, Asquith and Campbell-Bannerman did not take place. Instead Campbell-Bannerman, who urgently wished to see Spencer about his Norwich speech on 26 Oct., visited Althorp alone on 22 Oct. staying the night. Campbell-Bannerman to Spencer, 14 and 18 Oct. 1904, SP; H. Gladstone to Spencer, 23 Oct. 1904, SP.
[2] In a memorandum written in 1889, West Ridgeway, Under-Secretary, Dublin Castle, advocated liberal measures concerning local government, decentralization of finance and the creation of a Council, consisting of representatives of all parties, to advise the Chief Secretary. A letter in *The Times*, 11 Oct. 1904, p. 8, from Ridgeway, on behalf of The Irish Reform Association, to Lord Dunraven, expressed disappointment at what the Unionist government had achieved in Ireland.

**803 LORD RIPON TO LORD SPENCER**
*21 October 1904; Studley Royal, Ripon*

The matter upon which you ask my opinion is a delicate one, but I have no doubt as to what I should say regarding it. As you point out there are two questions to be decided. First whether you should take your share (which will probably, I should think, be a large one) in buying the Paper[1] now for sale and in saving it from falling into the hands of Harmsworth[2] or the Tories, and second whether if you buy or help to buy the Paper, you should let your name be connected with the new Proprietors.

It seems to me from what you say to be of very high importance to the Liberal Party in Northamptonshire that the Paper should remain in Liberal hands;[3] and that if it were bought by our opponents one, if not two, Liberal seats would be seriously endangered. The loss of seats in *your* county would be a greater blow than in most other parts of the country. It would be regarded, foolishly perhaps, as a blow to your political position. You are our Leader in one of the Houses of Parliament, you are the person whom most of us would desire to see at the head of a Liberal Government: and therefore we cannot afford to see a rebuff of any kind given to you. My conclusion therefore must be that it is essential that the Paper in question should be saved from the enemy and that if it can be saved in no other way it ought to be saved by you.

But turning to the second point I think that having saved the Paper for the Party you ought *not* to be in any way connected with its management. I have never thought that it was a good thing for a leading public man to have 'a Paper'. Everything that appears in such a Paper is supposed to be inspired by him; its most foolish sayings especially are attributed to him, and if this is inadvisable for a Leader of Opposition how much more so must it be for a Prime Minister. I would recommend therefore that you should keep absolutely clear of the management. As the largest shareholder, as you are sure to be, you would have a preponderating voice in the choice of the Editor, but you should not be a Director, or even a Printer, or hold any position which would enable any one to speak of the *Mercury* as 'Lord Spencer's Paper'. That you have had a hand in buying the Paper will of course become known; that cannot be helped and would not signify, but beyond that I would not go.

[1] The *Northampton Mercury*, founded in May 1720, and at this time a Liberal newspaper.
[2] Alfred Harmsworth, later Viscount Northcliffe, newspaper proprietor, together with his brother Harold, later Viscount Rothermere, acquired the *Evening News* (1894), and founded the *Daily Mail* (1896) and the *Daily Mirror* (1903).
[3] The paper had been owned and edited by Samuel Smith Campion, a leading Nonconformist, since May 1885.

**804 LORD SPENCER TO C. R. SPENCER**
*6 November 1904; Chine Hotel, Bournemouth*

I hardly know what to say to A. Ponsonby's query.[1]

My inclination is if possible not to go on the stump until I have taken part in Debates in the House. But it may be important for me to show myself, and

I feel pretty confident that though still unfit now to speak at a big meeting, in January I shall be quite myself again.

Then even when quite fit I never like spouting just before the opening of Parliament when I must speak at length. I should therefore prefer to reply that I must ask them to hold their first meeting in January without me, but that I hope before Easter to be able to speak for them.

[1] Arthur Ponsonby, of the Liberal Central Association, had asked Robert Spencer to inquire if Lord Spencer would be able to address a Liberal meeting at Wandsworth in Jan. 1905. C. R. Spencer to Spencer, 5 Nov. 1904, SP.

### 805   W. R. D. ADKINS TO LORD SPENCER
*27 November 1904; Springfield, Northampton*

You will have heard from Adnitt[1] that Holmes secured the *Mercury* for £25,750.[2] All the other members of the syndicate met at my house yesterday. Green[3] is drawing up the contract which will be signed by Wednesday we hope.

It is arranged to get the deposit advanced by the Union Bank and that that is to be our bank.

We meet again on Wednesday to consider a draft outline of the Articles of the Company which Green will submit to us and he or I will post to you on Thursday for your approval and decision. Among the matters we will then submit to you will be the salary to be offered the Manager or Editor or whatever he is to be called.[4]

[1] Not traced.
[2] Spencer had arranged to meet Adnitt and Holmes on 18 Nov. to approve the price. Adkins to Spencer, 17 Nov. 1904, SP.
[3] Thomas Green of Becke and Green, solicitors.
[4] The proprietorship was transferred to the Northampton Mercury Company Limited on 17 Feb. 1905. Arthur Adcock succeeded Campion as editor, holding the post for three years. W. W. Hadley, *The Bi-centenary Record of the Northampton Mercury* (1920) p. 47. See also Adkins to Spencer, 6 Dec. 1904, SP.

### 806   H. CAMPBELL-BANNERMAN TO LORD SPENCER
*13 December 1904; Belmont Castle, Meigle, Scotland*

*Private*

Herbert G. suggested some time ago that we should have Committees on sundry questions to prepare us for the raising of them when Parliament meets.[1] I quite agreed and I think I named certain subjects.

He sent me a list of suggested names; and the point was at once raised whether we should go beyond the late Cabinet or Government and bring in either backbenchers or outsiders not in Parliament.[2]

I said that my disposition was to restrict it to the late Govt., especially in present circumstances, for the selection of backbenchers might be taken as the foreshadowing of another kind of selection.

A Committee of the ex. Govt. could see individuals, learn their views and gain all the good of them without any more formal process.

As to the subjects, I think that

(a) Ireland does not press for the opening of Parliament. Better leave the leaven of Dunraven and Co. to work.[3] If we were to take any open step it might check that movement and do other mischief as well.

(b) Education—this also does not press: our views on the Act are well known, and the situation in Wales is such that we had better hold aloof from it for the present.

(c) Licensing—is not for this Session.

(d) Unemployed—this presses, and on it I enclose a paper by H.J. Gladstone.

(e) Poor Law will be up, no doubt. (Housing and sanitation have nothing new in them).

There are therefore only

A. Unemployed

and

B. Feeding poor school children, which last seems not so much an Education question as a Home Office or Local Government Board question.

Should we not have two committees on these two subjects? If Fowler would take one and Bryce the other with a couple of colleagues, it would not take long and would be of great help.

What do you think?

You will observe that H.J.G. wishes his paper to be circulated and it well deserves it.

Bryce (who has been here) has seen it, and I think his idea is that it would be desirable (and unobjectionable) for the State to undertake remunerative works such as reclamation, forestry, waterways, etc. and go on with them, using them in time of distress as work on which to turn men who are unemployed; but carrying them on as beneficial and reproductive works and not merely as means of employment, and not recognizing any *right* to be provided with work. I think this is sound.

---

[1] For background to the revival of Liberal interest in social reform, see H. V. Emy, *Liberals, Radicals and Social Politics 1892-1914* (1973), pp. 127-40.

[2] H. Gladstone to Campbell-Bannerman, 10 Dec. 1904, CBP, Add. MS. 41217 ff. 145-6.

[3] Windham Thomas Wyndham-Quin, 4th Earl of Dunraven and Mount-Earl, an Irish peer and chairman of a conference held in Dec. 1902 of eight representatives of landlords and tenants. It issued a unanimous report, recommending a general policy of land purchase. This report was the basis for the 1903 Land Bill. Dunraven explained his actions in a letter. 'Being a member of the Conservative and constitutional party I should of course have preferred to see the exertion of reform in Ireland taken up by that party but it is a matter of such local and Imperial importance that the means whereby it is accomplished is really a matter of indifference.' Dunraven to Sir. A. MacDonnell, 6 Oct. 1904, MacDonnell Papers, Eng. hist. c. 350, f. 112.

**807**   LORD SPENCER TO H. CAMPBELL-BANNERMAN
*16 December 1904; The Toft, Manor Road, Bournemouth*
CBP, Add. MS. 41229 ff. 286-90

Your very interesting packet of papers could not be disposed of by return of Post.

(1) I think that Herbert G.'s Memo˙ is very good, and in many ways most cogent in its reasoning.

I go heartily with the necessity (as safeguarding Public interest against the serious evils which may arise if nothing be done to deal with the question of 'the unemployed') of tackling the subject and on the meeting of Parliament making a serious demand for some settlement of the question.

I also admit the force of the argument that relief should not be left completely to Local bodies, many of which are already overburthened with rates and unable to cope with the 'unemployed', on account of local requirements, which other and richer localities are entirely free from.

But the difficulty is enormous of securing the conditions, attaching to National relief, which H.G. puts so clearly and tersely towards the end of his paper.

What are the National works to be? Where are they to be placed? How are the unemployed to be brought to them? How are we to prevent the inrushing of destitute to places where relief is given?

I need not enumerate more difficulties but no doubt they exist, nor do I say that they cannot be overcome, but the subject is one which cannot be settled without very serious discussion.

It involves several other big questions, that of the Reform of the Local Govt. Board and probably of all bodies which it controls such as Boards of Guardians.

Does it not also involve a very big and important question which is not mentioned, as far as I can see in your papers, viz. the Incidence of Local Taxation, and the whole subject which a Commission over which Balfour of Burleigh presided dealt with in a very powerful way as specially brought out by a minority report made I think by Murray, E. Hamilton and B. of B. himself.[1]

I attach immense importance to this subject being comprehensively dealt with by a Liberal Government when it comes in. It affects all classes not least the Agricultural Class, and the question of Division of Rates comes in here, as well as that of Land Values in towns, which G. Trevelyan wrote so stiffly to you upon last year.[2]

If the cost of finding work for the unemployed is taken off the shoulders of the Ratepayers, their position in relation to Taxpayers etc. must be broadly dealt with.

All this will give great employment to clever and experienced financiers etc.

I only touch the fringe of the subject ... [section (2) *omitted*]

(3) As to other subjects and what you say.

I agree as to Ireland, but all the same it would be an advantage if quietly and without public declarations some men worked up the subject.

(4) Education.

I quite concur with you.

We had better let that simmer.

We cannot with the present Parliament carry what we want, and we had better reserve ourselves until we have the weapons for successfully dealing with the subject. There are sure to be some developments of the subject next year.

(5) The feeding of famished children who are forced to school certainly should be considered.

I should therefore be all for having 2 committees to deal with (1) and (5), your A and B.[3]

Fowler would be admirable on the first including Taxation and Local Government Board.

Bryce would be good for no. 2. I am all for the actual Committee consisting of colleagues of the ex Govt...

I think I have now touched on all the points raised.

I do not see Ed. Robertson's name on any of the lists of H.G.[4]

If it is only to humour him it would be well that he should be consulted but I do not see exactly on what subject unless Licensing when that is dealt with.

I suppose you will be moving up towards London.[5] The Bryces come here next week and J. Morley the week after Xmas.[6]

[1] Royal Commission on Local Taxation and Financial Administration chaired by Balfour of Burleigh, issued its final report in May 1901, Cd. 638. The minority report pointed out that local taxation falls on persons rather than on property.

[2] Trevelyan to Campbell-Bannerman, 5 Oct. 1903, CBP. Add. MS. 41231 ff. 40-1.

[3] Spencer had agreed earlier with Gladstone on the necessity of establishing two informal committees of leading Liberals to examine outstanding social issues. H. Gladstone to Campbell-Bannerman, 14 Nov. 1904, CBP, Add. MS. 41217 f. 135.

[4] He became Parliamentary Secretary to the Admiralty, Dec. 1905-April 1908.

[5] Campbell-Bannerman delivered a hard-hitting speech at Limehouse on 20 Dec. on the effects of Protection on the people of London. See Spencer to Campbell-Bannerman, 21 Dec. 1904, CBP, Add. MS. 41229 f. 294.

[6] Spencer discussed politics with both men, particularly the ramifications of the Limehouse speech with Bryce and the possible date of a dissolution with Morley. Spencer to C. R. Spencer, 26 and 29 Dec. 1904, SP.

## 808   LORD SPENCER TO C. R. SPENCER
*31 December 1904; The Toft, Manor Road, Bournemouth*

The best of wishes for the coming New Year. How one wonders what it will bring. I trust not illness and family sadness, possibly political changes which may affect us all very much. In some ways they may be changes which I may have to face but which I should rather avoid at my age.

## 809   H. CAMPBELL-BANNERMAN TO LORD SPENCER
*13 January 1905; Belmont Castle, Meigle, Scotland*

I received your letter and telegram yesterday and your letter this morning enclosing R.'s, which I return.[1]

I conceive that there are serious objections to a R. party taking the place of ours at this particular juncture. You won't I know think I am in any sense 'irreconcilable'; but we have to consider the impression upon our fighting stalwarts who have won our bye elections. They will say 'There we are; sold again; the reins handed over just when *we* have put the coach in the position to start.' It is nonsense. The thing might even please some important people, but that is what they (the mass of stalwarts) would think.

Nor is it better if the ticket of Free Trade is put on it.[2] There is great nervousness about the fruits of victory (as is thought) being put into the hands of the Duke and his people who are (or have been) against us on so many subjects—war, Ireland, Education etc. I do not say that it may not come to a fusion of some sort, but our Party must have the first place and the first turn. We should collapse if it was not so, I am certain.

Now this Speech party is essentially a *Party party*; and it should be in the hands of the Party and not of any one who has been outside of it ostentatiously and declaredly.

I think therefore that (at the risk of being thought, by those who know what has happened, rather a curmudgeon) I had better give the party myself, if my new house can be got ready, which with this extra fortnight I hope may be possible. It would be confined to the members of the Party in the two Houses and a few candidates: therefore as I say a Party party, not half social, half Party.

[1] Spencer left Bournemouth for London on 9 Jan. Beatrice Mary, wife of Newton, 6th Earl of Portsmouth, offered Campbell-Bannerman her house for the Opposition dinner party on the eve of the opening of Parliament. Campbell-Bannerman to Spencer, 23 Dec. 1904, SP. Spencer inquired from Rosebery whether he intended to give a party; Rosebery did not discuss the possibility. Spencer to Campbell-Bannerman, 13 Jan. 1905, CBP, Add. MS, 41229 f. 299.

[2] Rosebery told Spencer on 10 Jan., 'I am prepared to join a party on Free Trade lines.' SP.


**810   LORD SPENCER TO H. CAMPBELL-BANNERMAN**
*17 January 1905; Althorp, Northampton*
CBP, Add. MS. 41229 f. 303

Thanks for your letter of the 15 Jan.[1]

R. anticipated my letter announcing finally that you would give the party.

It is a second 'All right' letter.[2]

My position was that I preferred your giving the party, or indeed any genuine Liberal, but that if R. decided on a party it would have been inexpedient for another Liberal party to be given as one party would spoil the other.

It was on this account and at Lady Portsmouth's request,[3] that I asked R. whether he intended to give a party.

I was misunderstood by him when in my second letter I said something as to not encouraging others to give a party if he R. settled to give one.[4]

That is what he termed my phraseology and he thought I had interpreted his, R.'s, letter as thinking that I wished to encourage rivals to his party. I had to explain that.

However it has all ended right and without friction, I hope, with him.

[1] 'I am very sorry indeed to have given you so much trouble about this party.' Campbell-Bannerman to Spencer, 15 Jan. 1905, SP.

[2] Both letters from Rosebery to Spencer, 10 and 15 Jan. SP, started with this phrase.

[3] Tweedmouth encouraged Spencer to give the party. He wrote, [Portsmouth] 'is not popular with any of our sections and looked upon with some jealousy and suspicion'. Tweedmouth to Spencer, 26 Dec. 1904, SP.

[4] Letter not traced in RP., but probably written on 9 Jan.

## 811   WINSTON CHURCHILL TO LORD SPENCER

*29 January 1905; Eaton, Chester*

I have various meetings here[1] on Monday which would prevent me from getting to you that night. But I could come to Althorp on Tuesday, arriving, if you like, in time for lunch, and could stay the next day.

...I am looking forward to a talk about politics,[2] and was very sorry not to meet you at Canford.[3] I wonder what A. Balfour will say tonight. It is quite clear to me that he will not go out till he is turned out.[4]

[1] Churchill was the principal speaker at the annual meeting of the Free Trade League at Manchester on 27 Jan.

[2] Edward Hamilton met Churchill at a dinner earlier in the month. 'He has completely gone over,' wrote Hamilton, 'and has become a whole-hearted Liberal.' EHJ, 4 Jan. 1905, Add. MS. 48683 f. 4.

[3] Canford Manor, Dorset, Ivor Guest's mansion. Spencer was there to help the Liberal candidate for North Dorset, Arthur Wills, who was successful in the by-election which took place on 27 Jan. Spencer to Channing, 22 Jan. 1905, SP (copy).

[4] Balfour addressed his constituents on 26 Jan. countering the Liberal claim that the government was remaining in office without a mandate. *The Times*, 27 Jan. 1905, p. 7.

## 812   CORRIE GRANT[1] TO LORD SPENCER

*1 February 1905; 11 King's Bench Walk, Temple, E.C.*

My constituents at Rugby have been pressing me for a long time to ask you to address a public meeting there, but I have not done so, because I thought we ought not to ask so much of you. It occurs to me, now, if that is an unreasonable request (and under all the conditions, so far as I can judge, it is) that perhaps you would not mind writing me a letter which I could publish, refusing to come but expressing your own personal opinions on the present situation and giving us, and also all Liberals throughout the country a few words of encouragement and guidance. It is a difficult and critical time; electors, nowadays look further ahead than they formerly did, and it needs to be made clear to them I think that leaders cannot act in advance of public opinion as expressed at the polls. A big Liberal majority will mean big things in, for instance, Finance, Education, Liquor Laws and Colonial policy, while a small one must mean little or nothing. In other words they must save themselves.

Please excuse me if I am adding at all to your many burdens. I hope I am not, but helping to save you for a little while from speeches.[2]

[1] J. Corrie Grant, barrister. A Radical, M.P., Rugby division, Warwickshire, since 1900.

[2] Grant wrote a few days later, 'I am glad that you think well of the suggestion to deal with current questions in a letter.' 4 Feb. 1905, SP.

**813  LORD RIPON TO LORD SPENCER**
*10 February 1905; 9 Chelsea Embankment, S.W.*

*Confidential*

I have just read with great interest your letter to Corrie Grant.[1] It is an excellent exposition of Liberal Policy and I agree heartily with it though I would have wished that you could have given some hint of the exceptional position of Roman Catholics in regard to Education.[2] I feel however the difficulty of your doing so in such a letter as this and I console myself with the belief that you do not exclude the future consideration of the special case of the R.C.'s.

If you had not told me that you had spoken to C.B. about your letter I should have feared that he might not have liked it,[3] for it has certainly something of the aspect of a manifesto; as such I for one readily accept it and nail it to my mast, and if C.B. is satisfied no one else has any right to say a word. It ought to satisfy the Party as a whole and to conciliate the Irish and the Labour men.

I have got this morning a long letter from MacDonnell.[4] I have not yet read it, but I see that it is a full statement of his defence against the Orange attacks. He has probably written to you also—if not I will send his letter to me as soon as I have gone through it. He seems to think an early discussion in the House of Lords probable.

[1] Published in *The Times*, 10 Feb. 1905, p. 6 and headed 'Manifesto by Lord Spencer', the letter outlined Liberal policy on fiscal matters, education, licensing, taxation, foreign policy, child labour, trades unions and Ireland.

[2] Ripon, who had been Lord President of the Council, 1868-73, converted to Roman Catholicism in Sept. 1874.

[3] On 8 Feb. Spencer saw Campbell-Bannerman who 'approved of the difficult passages.' Spencer to L. Harcourt, 10 Feb. 1905, HP, MS. 429 f. 90.

[4] MacDonnell to Ripon, 9 Feb. 1905, Rip. P, 43542 ff. 96-100. Sir Antony MacDonnell was invited by Wyndham, the Chief Secretary, to be Under-Secretary, Dublin Castle, in Sept. 1902. An Irish Catholic, MacDonnell set out conditions for accepting the post: these included the settlement of the land question. His active assistance to Dunraven in preparing a scheme for devolution (26 Sept. 1904) was repudiated by Wyndham though he was supported by the Lord-Lieutenant, Dudley.

**814  LORD SPENCER TO H. GLADSTONE**
*10 February 1905; Spencer House, St. James's Place, S.W.*
HGP, Add. MS. 46017 f. 145.

The very last thing I desired was that my letter to Corrie Grant should be considered as a Manifesto. It was dated the 7th Feb and was written before our meeting yesterday.[1]

I got at 10.30 a Press *Central News* message, 'Will you kindly say whether you intended your letter to Mr. Corrie Grant to be a Manifesto of the Liberal Party, or merely to assist Mr. Corrie Grant in his candidature?'

I answered 'No manifesto, merely a letter to Corrie Grant explaining my views instead of a Speech.'

Will not this reply answer your Telegram? but you could certainly say that it was my individual opinion. You could say 'Lord Spencer's letter was not result of any concerted action.'

Why should they ask such questions upon a letter when they would not have done so on a Speech?

Pray act as you think best, and send it to whatever Press agency you like.[2]

[1] A private conference of Liberal leaders held at Spencer House on the afternoon of 9 Feb. Its object was to discuss the policies to be pursued by the Opposition in the coming session. Spencer presided and Campbell-Bannerman was present.

[2] Herbert Gladstone immediately issued a statement to the press: 'During the past few months Lord Spencer has been unable to fulfil his engagements to speak in various localities. In lieu of the speeches which he has been prevented from making, he wrote to Mr. Corrie Grant on the 7th instant a letter on political matters, as being the best equivalent to a speech which it was in his power to make.' *The Times*, 11 Feb. 1905, p. 11. See also EHJ, 11 Feb. Add. MS. 48683 f. 17.

### 815  LORD SPENCER TO LORD RIPON
*11 February 1905; Spencer House, St. James's Place, S.W.*
Rip. P., MS. 43538 f. 186.

I return Sir A. McD.'s letter and memorandum.

The position will be awkward, and any of us who may take part in the debate will be constrained to use the knowledge we have of his defence in surmises and probably declarations made on one side or on the other in Debate[1] as we cannot quote his letter or Memo.

His conditions on taking Office were unusual and remarkable, and apparently were cordially accepted by G. Wyndham. If any misunderstanding occurred it was as to Dunraven's proposal which in fact was Sir A. McD's.

But Sir A. McD. may claim that his conditions on taking office cover and allow of his negotiation with D.

This seems to me the weakest part of his case, and from what I gathered John Morley thought this also.

[1] In the Lords on 17 Feb. in which Spencer spoke. Hansard, 4, cxli, cols. 463-5. In the Commons debate on 22 Feb. Henry Lucy, a parliamentary correspondent for more than 30 years, declared afterwards, 'I have not seen anything exceeding the virulent passion, the personal hatred, displayed this week by respectable-looking Ulster members denouncing a Unionist Chief Secretary, accused of having trafficked with the accursed thing, Home Rule.' H. Lucy, *The Balfourian Parliament 1900–1905* (1906), p. 362.

### 816  H. GLADSTONE TO LORD SPENCER
*11 April 1905; House of Commons*

In case C.B. has not written to you this is to let you know that C.B. will ask for a day to discuss the MacDonnell case.[1]

Redmond is very anxious that this should be done, and says it will greatly help his men if they are left in some doubt after C.B.'s speech. Asquith and Fowler are quite strong for it, and so is C.B. himself. J.M. hesitates.

I have no doubt that by taking the offensive in this way we shall strengthen our position in the evening.

[1] On 12 April, Campbell-Bannerman gave notice to Balfour of a proposed vote of censure on the circumstances surrounding the resignation of Wyndham on 6 March and calling for correspondence relating to Wyndham's appointment to be made available. Hansard, 4, cxliv, col. 1412.

The debate took place on 9 May. Campbell-Bannerman's motion was lost by 315 votes to 252. See J. W. Mackail and G. Wyndham, *Life and Letters of George Wyndham* (1925), ii, pp. 97-104.

## 817 LORD SPENCER TO LORD ROSEBERY

*29 May 1905; Spencer House, St. James's Place, S.W.*[1]

I have just had (2.40 p.m.) a Telephone Message from the H. of C. that as Balfour is ill the vote of censure[2] in the H. of C. has been put off.

This being so I take it for granted that the Duke, even if he has not concurred in your views, will do the same and put off his motion in the H. of Lords.[3]

I need not go into the reasons why I agreed to having the motion to-morrow, but you will have seen that though I contributed a good deal to getting the Duke of D. to move, when once he agreed to do so, the decision as to when his interrogatories were to be moved rested with him and not with me.

After hearing your views,[4] as far as I was concerned, I should have been ready to waive my own view that Tuesday was better than any other day for action in the H. of Lords.

I do not think that you knew that this action was not to take the form of a vote of censure, for, as it was important not to show a difference between ourselves and the Free Food Unionists, when I found that they resolutely declared that they would not vote for a vote of censure I did not press for that. Therefore had I proposed a motion I should have put it in the form of calling attention to—etc., and asking a specific question: and this was what the Duke himself had prepared. But I need not now go into all this.

All I will say is that instead of my objecting to your making suggestions as to the course of business in the House, or as to any Debate which we might raise, I much regret that so few opportunities of discussing these matters with you occur.

I should gladly welcome frequent discussions on current politics with you.

P.S. I hope you have come home quite strong and well,[5] and are going to add a third Derby victory to your Turf triumphs.[6]

[1] Copy. Original not traced in RP.

[2] Grey's motion asking for a clear statement on the government's fiscal policy. Hansard, 4, cxlvii, cols. 347-8.

[3] The Duke of Devonshire's motion calling attention to declarations by ministers on the subject of fiscal union with the colonies and asking if the government intended to convene a special conference before or after the general election. The motion was introduced in the Lords on 5 June.

[4] Protesting at Spencer's action in proposing a debate in the Lords on 30 May before Balfour's statement in the Commons. 'In former days there might have been a simultaneous debate of censure. But now a division in the H. of Lords is a farce. The only value of the H. of Lords is as a court of review.' Rosebery to Spencer, 28 May 1905, SP.

[5] Rosebery had been at his villa at Naples.

[6] In 1905, Rosebery achieved his third Derby success with Cicero. He had won the Derby in two consecutive years with Ladas (1894) and Sir Visto (1895).

**818   LORD SPENCER TO LORD RIPON**
*25 July 1905; Spencer House, St. James's Place, S.W.*
Rip. P, Add. MS. 43538 ff. 197–8

I do not think that you missed much by not being at C.B.'s meeting yesterday.[1] We were practically agreed upon tactics, viz.
   (1)  That E. Grey should withdraw his Resolution.[2]
   (2)  That we should propose *no* resolution nor cause a Division which would
        enable Govt. to get a large majority.
The difficulty was how to get discussion without Division, and it was really
settled for the front bench to wait on events.[3]
   We heard that Redmond was full of fight and furious at the idea of Grey's
motion going on.
   This was all wonderfully carried out. Redmond intervened to get a motion
to enable the position to be discussed, and as far as I could learn by rules of
House no one but a Minister could propose an Adjournment. So Redmond
pressed for this and C.B. supported, and Balfour fell in with it, not thinking
that our people would not challenge the vote when put from the Chair.
   Balfour evidently was expecting E. Grey to come on.
   The Debate went through well for us. A.J.B.'s opening was very bad, long
and wanting in precision and dignity.[4]
   The subsequent Debate was brilliant, J. Redmond and E. Grey specially
good,[5] E. Grey the best H. of C. Speech I have heard for many years, courteous
yet hitting very hard, full of dignity and with admirable argument.

[1] The meeting was held at 1 p.m. on 24 July. Ripon attended a funeral that day. Ripon to
Spencer, 24 July 1905, SP.
[2] Vote of censure which Grey was to have moved on 24 July 'regretting the confusion caused by
the First Lord of the Treasury and other ministers' and stating that an election should be held before
the coming Colonial Conference.
[3] The government had been narrowly defeated by 200 votes to 196 on Irish supply on 20 July
1905. The Opposition tactics which brought about the defeat are vividly described in A.S.T.
Griffith-Boscawen, *Fourteen Years in Parliament* (1907), p. 342.
[4] Balfour, in his statement on the position of the government, quoted from a letter sent by
Gladstone to Granville in 1873, 'A Ministry with a majority, and with that majority not in rebellion,
should not resign on account of adverse manifestations, even of very numerous single constituencies.'
Hansard, 4, cl, col. 58, 24 July 1905.
[5] Redmond, ibid., col. 75 ff. Grey, ibid., cols. 112–18.

**819   DUKE OF DEVONSHIRE TO LORD SPENCER**
*26 July 1905; Devonshire House*

As to the debate tomorrow,[1] our people think that as it is our motion and
as we shall probably take rather a different line from you, it would be best if
one of our men were to wind up, and if you would get up before Lansdowne
and let him reply to both of us.
   If I begin and you finish, Lansdowne will have a right to treat us as all in the
same boat, which will not improve our discussion.[2]
   By different lines, I mean that I shall treat the resolutions as raising an issue

between two sections of the Unionists rather than one between the Government
and the Opposition.

¹ In the debate, Devonshire criticized Chamberlain's speeches at St. Helens on 3 June and in
London on 7 July and moved that the House disapprove of any proposal to establish tariffs or a
system of colonial preference based on the taxation of food. Hansard, 4, cl, cols. 471-86, 27 July
1905.
² Lansdowne, ibid., cols. 561-2; Spencer, ibid., cols. 558-61.


**820**  LORD SPENCER TO C. R. SPENCER
*8 August 1905; Spencer House, St. James's Place, S.W.*

I had a pleasant Sunday¹ at Mentmore. The E. Colebrookes, (she amusing
with her evident devotion to R. but very cordial to me), Ribblesdales, Asquith,
Percy and Neil.²

I had a Political talk with R. and at the earnest request of H. H. Asquith and
Ribblesdale asked him direct what he would do if we came into office. I
manoeuvred it pretty well for he evaded my frank query and I then discussed
all manner of men and things and finally again put the question as to what he
would do when we considered office very decidedly. He took it well but at
once said 'You must know that I am not to be considered any more in such
matters.' I give the sense rather than the very words he used.³ Asquith expected
this reply and evidently believes that he won't join.

...I was busy on my return as I had to speak on Lord James' motion.⁴

I am anxious over my Unemployment Speech tonight. I hope to get away
tomorrow night if the Navy Works Bill is up for 2nd Reading tomorrow.⁵

...I see that the Tory scare produced a large majority. I did not expect a
defeat of Government but some apparently thought it possible. The Tories
brought men all the way from Scotland. I had a talk with Herbert Gladstone
on Unemployment⁶ etc. He began rather grumpy, but got very good
humoured as we talked.

¹ 6 Aug.
² Sir Edward Arthur Colebrooke, and his wife, Alexandra Harriet; possibly Lord Algernon Percy,
aide-de-camp to the King since 1902; Neil James, Rosebery's second son.
³ Rosebery's version of the conversation, from the 1905 Betting Book, RP, 10184, ff. 37-8, is to
be found in James, p. 451. There is an interesting additional note, presumably added in 1913,
'Spender [editor of the *Westminster Gazette*], who was behind the scenes, tells me that Spencer came
on a definite mission from CB and himself, but that CB was not very anxious that it should
succeed.'
⁴ Protesting against the practice of introducing bills into the Lords without affording sufficient
time for their consideration. Hansard, 4, cli, cols. 318-23, 7 Aug. 1905. Spencer supported James.
Ibid., cols. 325-9.
⁵ Spencer was to be the main speaker in the debate.
⁶ The Unemployed Workmen Bill received its second reading in the Lords on 8 Aug. For
Spencer's speech, see ibid., cols. 555-60.

**821   LORD SPENCER TO H. CAMPBELL-BANNERMAN**
*20 August 1905; Villa Tielemann, Bad Nauheim*
CBP, Add. MS. 41229 ff. 312-4

I hope that both Lady Campbell and you reached Marienbad without over fatigue but I fear you had very hot weather for your journey for I suppose you moved when I did either the Thursday before the prorogation or on the next two days.[1]

I wish you could have been at the luncheon[2] to repeat your former success in French speech making.

I thought that the Speeches were very good, for once I could admire Balfour's Speech without reservation. He struck the right note and J.M. followed it up very well. *The Times* criticized 'the European' quotation but that was hyper-criticism, and so it would be to say he need not have repeated his 'Spark from Cowes and Portsmouth' reference.[3]

What a blessing it is that Parliament is up,[4] for much as one wanted for Patriotic reasons to see the fall of the Government, there was no hope of achieving that and one was getting sick of the Parliamentary atmosphere, and the obstinate disregard of all Parliamentary decency which A.J.B. continued to show.

You had a very successful Session and earned the gratitude of the party but I dare say you are glad to be free for a time, but for what time? I am sure that A.J.B. will wish to stick to the Government and Office, but he may have some remnant of self respect left in him, and if he has he should either dissolve or resign in Oct, or Nov. so as to give a new Government time to make ready for Parliament next year.

It is hopeless to forecast what will occur. Patriotically one must wish for the Autumn Dissolution. Personally I should prefer the beginning of next Session.

Asquith made a short and vigorous speech on the 2nd Reading of the Appropriation Act.[5] He had talked over with me his 3 points at Mentmore where I spent the last Sunday of the Session. I heard that H. Fowler had rather given an opening to A.J.B. afterwards, but H.F.'s arguments were not upset.[6] The only thing that occurred was that the Prime Minister had an opportunity of making an animated party speech which sent his people away in good heart. This perhaps had better have been avoided.

In the House of Lords, we had the usual holocaust of all Standing Orders, and regulations for securing adequate consideration of important measures, by receiving 3 or 4 big Bills from the H. of C. without any notice of them on our votes, or any copy of them in our hands. They ran through them all in a few minutes and passed them, the Chancellor saying 3 sentences on one Bill, and I making a Speech of 20 minutes on the Navy Works Bill[7] which I thought I must do after what had passed in your House and at the request of E. Robertson.

Poor Lansdowne[8] had to reply to me which he did by means of couriers to the Chief Naval Engineer who is in the House, the couriers being the fat Under Secretary of War[9] or the lean and silent Marquis Secretary for Scotland.[10] Lansdowne does not leave a Speech to any of his bench, now that Salisbury[11] and Cawdor[12] are both ill and away. But the H. of L. is very dispiriting work.

Whatever you do, you only address yourself to the House itself for your Speech is always cut down in reports of Newspapers, and no notice is taken of it at all unless on some big debate.

But it is as well not to think of public notice but to be content with trying to do one's duty where one is placed.

I suppose you will see the King.

I met him once or twice before he left London. The last time he said that after much thought he had come to the conclusion that the Lord-Lieutenancy must be abolished. It was a jimcrack thing at best and difficult now to get proper men for it. I listened but said that there might still be reasons against doing away with it, in view of possibly greater changes becoming necessary in Ireland. He laughed and said he was amused at my being so conservative.

Of course I covertly referred to possible Home Rule but did not expand the idea. I said that even with Home Rule one may say that a Viceroy is not needed, possibly not but there would be a howl in Dublin among the Nationalists, for a Viceroy living most of the year in Ireland spends more money than a King or Prince having only a short annual visit to the country.

He told me I might tell any of my colleagues and friends his view, and so I tell you as he may touch on the subject at Marienbad.

Anyhow this is not the moment to commit oneself on the topic one way or the other...

I am going to Raith for Kircaldy political gathering where I am to speak 27 Oct.[13]

I am beset with invitations before or after this, but I shall not be able to go to more than one besides Raith as I want to get to Althorp.

[1] Campbell-Bannerman left London on 11 Aug.

[2] A luncheon in Westminster Hall to celebrate the visit of the French fleet to England was held on 12 Aug. Members of both Houses attended. *The Times*, 14 Aug. 1905, p. 8.

[3] Morley stated that 'nothing would be more alien than that any sparks from the fireworks at Brest or at Portsmouth should set Europe afire'.

[4] Parliament was prorogued on 11 Aug.

[5] Hansard, 4, cli, col. 642 ff. 8 Aug. 1905.

[6] Ibid., col. 964 ff.

[7] Ibid., 10 Aug. cols. 905-12.

[8] Foreign Secretary, 1900-5. Ibid. cols. 912-14.

[9] Richard, 6th Earl of Donoughmore, Under-Secretary for War, 1903-5.

[10] John, 1st Marquess of Linlithgow, Secretary of State for Scotland, Feb.-Dec. 1905.

[11] James Edward, 4th Marquess of Salisbury, President of the Board of Trade, March-Dec. 1905.

[12] Frederick, 3rd Earl Cawdor, First Lord of the Admiralty, March-Dec. 1905.

[13] The meeting of the Scottish Liberals at Kircaldy took place on 26 and 27 Oct. Lloyd George addressed the rally on the last evening praising Spencer's work for the party. Press cutting, *Fife Free Press*, 28 Oct. 1905, Lloyd George Papers. A/13/2/8.

## 822　H. CAMPBELL-BANNERMAN TO LORD SPENCER

*26 August 1905; Hotel Klinger, Marienbad*

*Secret*

It was a great pleasure to receive your letter and I assure you it was not a bit too long—on the contrary it was most interesting. I have delayed, perhaps unduly, replying to it because I had something in view which I thought would be worth recording. The King had asked me to lunch,[1] and I thought there might be something to report: and then after the lunch he said he would like me to come to him and have a little talk some day. This came off yesterday, and I waited until I could tell you what occurred.

I enclose some notes of the conversation: which could not have been more pleasant and satisfactory both in matter and in manner. He was exceedingly friendly and frank throughout. He is looking very well and is enjoying his stay here immensely. He is also better surrounded than on some other occasions, and the little English 'society' is quieter than usual, although there is more enter-taining, dining, etc. than is quite right for the cure.[2] He will be here for another fortnight...

I take quite your view of the dissolution—it ought to be tomorrow, if possible: but personally I should prefer it in the beginning of the year. I fail to see what excuse they can find for an Autumn dissolution: they would have to eat all their recent words.

What you say of R. is most important.[3] It is a miserable mistake for him to make to cut himself off from the Party and from active public life, but he has gone so far that I presume it must be taken as final...

On second thoughts, I will send this to make sure of the post, and will send the notes of my interview later. I find it very difficult here to find time for anything, because I have nothing to do.

[1] The King, had arrived at Marienbad on 17 Aug.

[2] A few years earlier, Campbell-Bannerman commented on Edward's visit to the spa, 'Whether on account of the Prince's presence or not, the English and American Society here has contained an extraordinary number of tainted ladies—including five divorcées, and about ten others of varying degrees of doubtfulness. The decent people were almost in a minority and we thought of wearing our marriage certificates as a sort of order outside our coats.' Campbell-Bannerman to J. Campbell, 5 Sept. 1899 or 1900, CBP, Add. MS. 52517 f. 140.

[3] Spencer recounted in his previous letter to Campbell-Bannerman, No. 821, but here omitted, the conversation with Rosebery at Mentmore on 6 Aug.

## 823    H. CAMPBELL-BANNERMAN TO LORD SPENCER
*29 August 1905; Hotel Klinger, Marienbad*

*Secret*

I began writing out notes of what the King said to me, but I soon found that there were things that it would be hardly discreet to entrust to the chances of the post; and I must reserve these (there is not much) till we meet. But this is a summary.

He said he was pleased to have the chance of speaking quite frankly on affairs at home and abroad, as I had the prospect of being in Office and high Office. 1. He has great apprehensions of war between France and Germany, and in that event what should we do? He discussed the personal relations of the Royal families and also the sentiments of the peoples: the growth of the German navy etc. War between ourselves and Germany deplorable but might be inevitable.

(I deprecated contemplating it as likely—the two nations, apart from military and ruling class and press, have no desire to quarrel).

The ground of quarrel between Germany and France might be Morocco.[1]

(Incidentally, could not understand R.'s attitude on that subject. Did I understand him? did not imagine that I did.)[2]

Evidently takes very serious view of this matter.

2. Japan and Russia. Said nothing of possible treaty with Japan.[3] Discussed prospects of peace: evidently scanty sympathy with Russia.

3. Curzon and Kitchener:[4] takes reasonable view, but has high opinion of Kitchener as administrator. All the better that he is new to India: Indian army pretty much as it was left by the Mutiny.

4. Offices at home. Army in dreadful state: condemns A.F.:[5] even Brodrick better.[6]

Takes blame to himself for thinking a board would be best system.[7] Minister (i.e. A.F.) rides roughshod over board:[8] not like Admiralty where the Minister takes it with him.

Navy in splendid condition. Jack F. in *excelsis!*[9]

5. Ireland—standing difficulty: 'agitators'.

I pointed out the effect of Local Government Act and of Land Act, both Unionist measures. After these, the old line of distrust could no longer be taken. Must see how these work: but line of concession is only safe and remedial policy. No likelihood of demand for immediate advance in policy, but must work in that direction.

He assented generally, and I do not think he will be difficult to convince.

These were the principal points in a talk (mostly one-sided) of three quarters of an hour.

Today I lunched with him again. He does far too much in lunching and dining and driving: but he is well and in great spirits...

After all there is not very much in this report. The important things are the German affair and the view he takes of Ireland. He said nothing to me about the Government as a whole, dissolution, etc; and therefore was quite correct in his loyalty to them. But the salient thing is the fact of his discussing everything so frankly.[10]

[1] On 8 July, France had agreed in principle to attend a conference on Morocco.

[2] Rosebery had publicly expressed his doubts concerning the Anglo-French agreement of 1904 at the City Liberal Club on 9 March 1905.

[3] The second Anglo-Japanese agreement, replacing that of Jan. 1902, was signed on 12 Aug. 1905.

[4] Kitchener, as Commander-in-Chief, India, had been involved in acrimonious correspondence with Curzon, the Viceroy, over the system whereby the military member of the Viceroy's Council controlled many aspects of the Army's resources and had the right to veto recommendations of the Commander-in-Chief. Curzon finally resigned on 12 Aug.

[5] Hugh Oakeley Arnold-Forster, Unionist M.P., West Belfast, 1892-1906, Croydon, 1906-9. Secretary to the Admiralty, 1900-3, Secretary of State for War, 1903-5. For a summary of Arnold-Forster's failings, see W. S. Hamer, *The British Army. Civil-Military Relations, 1885-1905* (1970), pp. 228-31.

[6] Brodrick was Arnold-Forster's predecessor as Secretary of State for War, 1900-3. See his *Records and Reactions 1856-1939* (1939), pp. 119-37.

[7] The Army Council, charged with the responsibility of ensuring the efficiency of the forces, was established in Feb. 1904. It consisted of the Secretary of State, a civil member, a financial member and four military advisers.

[8] At first, there was some ambiguity concerning the division of responsibility between the Secretary of State and the military members of the Council. However, Arnold-Forster issued a secret memorandum in June 1904, declaring the Secretary for War to be directly responsible to Parliament for decisions taken by the Council.

⁹ Admiral Sir John Fisher, First Sea Lord since 1904.
¹⁰ Spencer, in acknowledging the receipt of the letter, wrote, 'It is safe under lock and key and I shall not discuss its very interesting contents by letter.' Spencer to Campbell-Bannerman, 31 Aug. 1905, CBP, Add. MS. 41229 f. 316.

**824** LORD SPENCER TO L. HARCOURT
*21 September 1905; North Creake, Fakenham*
HP, MS. 429 ff. 99-100

I got back from Germany on Monday after 24 hours at The Hague which always delights me specially the Pictures.[1]

John Morley dined with me among Tory Squires and young swells at Boodle's where Brooks's people go when renovation of the Club is going on. It is amusing to see how the Boodlites look at J.M., with great curiosity and interest, but not I expect with sympathy.

I stay here until about the 19th Oct. when I go to London for a meeting of non Political colour, and the unveiling of the Gladstone Memorial on the 21st Oct.

I am taking exercise very gently here for about 10 days after my cure, but I enjoyed 1½ hrs. among turnips yesterday.

[1] Spencer reached Bad Nauheim on 12 Aug. and arrived back in London on 18 Sept.

**825** LORD SPENCER TO C. R. SPENCER
*27 September 1905; North Creake, Fakenham*

Fancy what I did last week. I had heard a great deal about ill-feeling between Germany and ourselves and of the importance of getting fair dealing with the Germans in some London newspaper. It is much too long a story to enter upon. But I found John Morley who dined with me in London full of the same topic, C.B. by correspondence the same,[1] etc. etc.

I had written to Spender to come to luncheon at 28,[2] but he was away on Friday. I got a note from him and I immediately wrote asking him and Mrs. S. to come for Sunday. Mrs. S. was away but most grateful for the invitation, and he to my great delight came, and I never had such an ocean of Political talk from the moment he arrived to the moment he left, excepting morning service which we attended and heard the Bishop of Thetford speak.[3] It was most interesting and valuable. It is wonderful what a mass of knowledge a man like him acquires.[4]

He was not as it turned out instructed quite up to date as to the publication of the Curzon and Kitchener correspondence. Ripon (this very confidential) heard from His Excellency Lord Curzon. He advised the India Office not to publish the correspondence but was overruled.[5]

Quite monstrous.

Curzon is foaming at the mouth in regard to his old colleagues, and gushing with thanks and gratitude to Ripon and Sandhurst for their Speeches.[6]

[1] Replying to Spencer's letter of 10 Sept. Campbell-Bannerman wrote, 'I am relieved to hear that you see no cause for immediate alarm as to German relations. It was the one thing that startled me in a conversation I told you of, "probability" being the word used.' Campbell-Bannerman to Spencer, 13 Sept. 1905, SP.
[2] 28 St. James's Place, where Spencer's sister, Sarah, lived.
[3] Rev. Dr. John P. A. Bowers.
[4] J. A. Spender, editor of the *Westminster Gazette*, spent the day with Spencer on 24 Sept.
[5] Ripon to Spencer, 23 Sept. 1905, SP.
[6] In a debate on Indian Army administration in the Lords on 1 Aug., Ripon and Sandhurst defended Curzon. Hansard, 4, cl. Ripon, cols. 1075-95, Sandhurst, ibid., cols. 1110-17.

### 826   J. A. SPENDER TO LORD SPENCER
*27 September 1905; 45 Sloane Street, S.W.*

There is a point in today's publication of the Japanese treaty[1] which may illustrate what you were saying the other day about our German relations. This is the footnote to Lord Lansdowne's despatch to Hardinge intimating that a similar despatch had been sent to the British ambassador in Paris.[2]

The natural inference, but I hope not the true one, is that no similar despatch has been sent to Berlin. I suppose the treaty will be communicated, for Germany obviously has interests in the Far East, however much we may dislike her having them, and it would be a great misfortune if she could say hereafter, as in the case of Morocco, that she has no cognizance of this arrangement. But, if communication is necessary, it might as well be civil communication, as in the case of the other two Powers, and the omission of a despatch, if it has been omitted, will, I am afraid, be regarded as another pin-prick. It [will] be avenged hereafter in diplomatic encounters which will certainly, in spite of this Treaty, continue in Pekin. Perhaps I exaggerate the point, but if you have means of discovering the truth, it might be worth doing. I have just noted the point in tonight's *Westminster Gazette*.[3]

Please let me say how very much I enjoyed my day with you last Sunday. I am afraid that I most ungratefully left you bad weather, but it was kind of you to put up with so much of me and a great pleasure to me to have so much good talk about so many things.

[1] See No. **823** n. 3.
[2] Dispatch to Her Majesty's Ambassador at St. Petersburg, forwarding a copy of the agreement between the United Kingdom and Japan. Lansdowne to Hardinge, Foreign Office. 6 Sept, 1905, Cd. 2690. The dispatch was published as a Parliamentary Paper on 26 Sept.
[3] In a leading article 'The New Treaty', p. 1.

### 827   C. S. ROUNDELL TO LORD SPENCER
*27 September 1905; 32 Sussex Square, Brighton*

Your letter has interested me much, especially about Germany and the Emperor.

But why, if he means Peace, has he shown this bullying attitude towards France, exasperating France almost to war, and this strong desire to detach her from this country? Why again does he permit the aggravating and insulting tone towards us of the German Press? All this makes me rejoice at your strong assurance that, as far as you can see, he does not mean war. No doubt his main feeling, especially at this particular moment, is the sense of his isolation in Europe. Well, we have now four strong Rulers, the German Emperor, Roosevelt, Emperor of Austria, and in another way our own King.

And what you say about the hoped for non-permanence of the present relations between us and Germany is borne out by the cases of the United States and France with both of which our relations were strained but a few years ago.

I hope you saw a remarkable letter signed 'Vidi' in *The Times* 3 weeks ago.[1] The comparison between the national tone in France and here was very striking.

[1] Written by an Englishman, resident on the continent since 1892. In it, he expressed the view that whilst France had gone through a period of moral regeneration between 1893 and 1897, England was showing opposing tendencies. *The Times*, 6 Sept. 1905, p. 6.

## 828 LORD SPENCER TO H. H. ASQUITH[1]
*5 October 1905; North Creake, Fakenham*

I do not often bother you to read my bad writing, but as soon now several of us may be speaking and on the stump, I write a few lines to you as we should agree on what is said.

The leading question in the papers now is the Anglo-Japanese treaty. I saw some bad report of your September Speech[2] in which you referred to it guarding yourself as to a full declaration till you had seen the text.

You now have it, and I wonder what you feel about it.

My impression is that it was almost inevitable that the Government should renew the old Treaty or make a new one.

As to the old Treaty the line we took up when it was made was not of enthusiasm about it, but rather reserved acceptance. Harcourt made a good speech in the H. of C.[3] and I (though I really count for nothing) did the same in the H. of L.,[4] and Rosebery also spoke.[5]

The line taken was that though disposed to avoid such treaties, we could not oppose this one when made, and that we had strong sympathies with Japan, and acknowledged the common ground of policy which we had with Japan in the East on many questions.

Well we escaped the danger of having to step in in defence or alliance with Japan in the War. If as is probably the case the treaty was inevitable, I wish it could have been framed so as to promote the maintenance of the status quo and the open door in China between all great Powers without making two conditions (1) the contemplation of securing from Japan active military support for ourselves in India in the event of attack there (2) the guarantee of the integrity of the China Dominions.

As to the first, I think it objectionable that we should allow the idea to exist that we cannot defend India ourselves, and also it may lead to difficulties with our native population there to introduce Japanese soldiers into the country in time of War. I do not like the tone of some of our jingo press who seem to call for larger Naval and Military forces to carry out our Treaty obligations with Japan. In these respects the new Treaty is more objectionable than the old one.

Of course it would be out of the question to denounce 'root and branch' the

Treaty and indeed there are no doubt good points in it, but it does not seem to me to be wise to adopt it with enthusiasm, and we might point out the greater necessity of caution on our part in conducting our Eastern Policy with prudence and moderation, and not to allow ourselves to push further 'the Forward Policy' which has a school of friends here and in India, and to which our party has always been opposed.

The maintenance of the integrity of the Turkish Empire has often led us into great Political difficulties, and I doubt whether China has a really more stable and sound government than Turkey.

Her frontiers are so wide that there may be many points where she may be exposed to attack, and it would be very hazardous for us and not in the least in our interest in many instances to be obliged to use our forces in her favour on the demand of Japan.

My views are somewhat crude but I fancy that among your followers in the H. of C. there will be some active spirits who will oppose the Treaty, and although you and other Leaders certainly should not do this it would not be wise to stir them up by too much praise of it.

Forgive me for writing at all and I cannot further expand my views.

Ripon has written to me much in the sense I have now written[6] and I think that the *Westminster Gazette* upholds the same kind of opinion.

I see that you speak with Rosebery on the 21st of this month,[7] and I believe John Morley addresses his constituents before long.[8]

It is a pity that some of you could not meet to discuss the position, but everyone is separated and in different places so letters are unavoidable.

[1] Copy. Original not traced in AP.
[2] On 2 Sept. at Abercairney, near Crieff. *The Times*, 4 Sept. 1905, p. 8.
[3] Campbell-Bannerman and Harcourt regarded the alliance as an unnecessary departure from existing policy. See Hansard, 4, cii, 13 Feb. 1902. Campbell-Bannerman, cols. 1288–94, Harcourt, ibid., cols. 1298–1305.
[4] Ibid., cols. 1172–4.
[5] Ibid., cols. 1178–80.
[6] Ripon to Spencer, 28 Sept. 1905, SP.
[7] At Edinburgh on 21 Oct. *The Times*, 23 Oct. 1905, p.3.
[8] At Arbroath on 23 Oct. *The Times*, 24 Oct. 1905, p. 6.

**829**   H. H. ASQUITH TO LORD SPENCER
*8 October 1905; Raith, Kirkcaldy*

Many thanks for your letter.

You are right in supposing that, when I spoke some weeks ago of the Japanese Alliance, I reserved full liberty of judgment and criticism in regard to the new Treaty, which had not then been published. I am not at all satisfied that it has been framed in the best way, but I think it would be bad policy and bad tactics to denounce it. For (1) A renewal of the Alliance was inevitable, and (as I think) in the interests of peace and tranquillity in the East. (2) The Alliance, as defined in the new Treaty, is purely defensive, and would not extend to any forward movement, disturbing the status quo, on either side.

(3) The Treaty is a *fait accompli*, which will have to [be] adopted and carried out by the next or any Government. And, I add,

(4) The Alliance is extremely popular in this country, and people will confuse an attack on the terms of the Treaty with hostility to the Alliance itself.

All these considerations seem to me to show that we should at any rate be content with very measured criticism.

Like you, I am not fond of the 'integrity and independence of the Chinese Empire': tho' in practice this will probably come to nothing more than the maintenance of the 'open door'.

Further, I should have been better pleased if the scope of the Treaty had been confined to our interests in the Far East, and India had been left out. I am rather afraid of the effect which the inclusion of India may have on native opinion there. There is, also, a dangerous vagueness in the phrase 'proximity' to the Indian frontier. There is, I should imagine, no idea of ever using Japanese troops in the actual defence of the frontier, which would have the worst effect: the calculation no doubt is that they could give trouble to Russia elsewhere. All these are very delicate points to handle on a platform, and I am disposed to say as little as possible.

... I am glad that you are the better for your German cure.

### 830 NOTE BY MEDICAL ADVISER ON PIECE OF PAPER
*11 October 1905; North Creake, Fakenham*

Block of a small vessel in the brain producing loss of speech but no loss of power in limbs, perfectly conscious.[1]

[1] An announcement of Spencer's illness appeared in *The Times*, 13 Oct. 1905, p. 7.

# 12

# LAST YEARS, 1905–10

*Spencer took no further part in public life, but retained an interest in political develop-
ments. The appointment of Campbell-Bannerman as prime minister in December 1905
pleased him. At the general election in January 1906, the Liberals achieved a sweeping
victory, gaining 224 seats. 'He has been delighted with the Elections,' Robert Spencer
wrote to Lewis Harcourt, 'but he thinks much more of the hunting.' (Viscount Althorp
to Lewis Harcourt, 22 January 1906, HP, MS. 439 f. 4). A tragic family event a few
months later was the death of Robert's wife, Margaret, in childbirth. A number of his
political contemporaries, including Campbell-Bannerman, Devonshire and Ripon, died
during Spencer's last years.*

*Spencer retired from the Chancellorship of Manchester University and the Lord-
Lieutenancy of Northamptonshire. He travelled abroad and at home, found great pleasure
in motoring, purchasing a 40 horsepower vehicle (Spencer to A. H. Collis, 27 March
1908, SP). On 5 July 1910, Spencer suffered a further severe stroke. Robert noted,
'My Brother is just holding his own and that is about all ... His colossal strength will
keep him going for the present.' (Viscount Althorp to Gosse, 5 July 1910, Gosse
Papers). He died on 13 August, and Robert succeeded him as the sixth Earl. Spencer
left an estate of the gross value of £64,454 10s. 2d., of which the net personalty (i.e.
everything except land) was sworn at £237,851 4s. 9d. On 21 July 1933 a memorial,
in the form of a bronze bust, was unveiled in the House of Lords by one of Spencer's
former colleagues, Lord Crewe.*

---

**831   C. R. SPENCER TO L. HARCOURT**
*19 October 1905; North Creake, Fakenham*
HP, MS. 438 ff. 130–1.

Your letter was one of the nicest that I have received. I told my Brother of
it and showed it to him this morning.

He is quite conscious, and he takes great interest in all that we tell him. He
reads *The Times* for a little each day, and he walks along the passage to another
room where he spends the afternoon. Only his speech is affected. He says some
words and even short sentences. I think that there is a slight improvement in
this today. But as his general health is so good one hopes that the power of
consecutive speech will be regained eventually. Naturally the doctors cannot
say definitely about this.

My Brother suffers no pain, but of course the difficulty in his speech is very
trying to him.

**832**  C. R. SPENCER TO H. CAMPBELL-BANNERMAN
*28 November 1905; Althorp, Northampton*
CBP, Add. MS. 41229 ff. 327-8

Very many thanks for your letter, which I received this morning. I told Spencer about it, and of your kind enquiries, and he seemed pleased.

I fear that he does not read letters much, as I find that he generally gives them to me or to my sister after looking at the first few sentences. Would it be troubling you too much, if you were to write me a little letter about politics which I could read to Spencer? I think by this method one might be able to find out whether he is interested in politics or not.[1]

On the whole I confess that I do not see much change in my Brother's condition. Sometimes he seems a little better, but the improvement does not last. He has talked a little about Rosebery and his strange speech at Bodmin[2] but he cannot follow it.

May I tell you how rejoiced I was with your most useful speech. The part of it concerning Ireland and was most helpful to us Home Rulers ...

[1] Reply from Campbell-Bannerman not traced in SP.

[2] At a speech in Bodmin on 25 Nov. Rosebery startled many Liberals by stating that 'he must refuse to serve under the banner of Home Rule'. This was in reply to Campbell-Bannerman's address at Stirling on 23 Nov. promising action on the question in the near future. It was only on returning to London on 28 Nov. that Rosebery discovered that the Stirling speech was the outcome of a concordat between the four Vice-Presidents of the Liberal League and Campbell-Bannerman. Crewe, ii, pp. 592-4.

**833**  J. BRYCE TO VISCOUNT ALTHORP[1]
*14 February 1907; British Embassy, Washington, U.S.A.*[2]

These last few weeks have made me feel vividly what you felt a year ago in leaving the House of Commons, the breaking off short of that inspiriting comradeship in political life and work which had been so much to both of us since we came into Parliament together in 1880. Not many remain in the H. of C. of those who entered then, but among the newer arrivals there have been some fine, genial, earnest men with whom it has been a pleasure to fight the good cause.

It is a time now when one would have gladly stayed on to bear a part in the fight. You will have plenty of it in your House, where there will be plenty of need for both wise tactics and steady courage. How often have I been wishing we had your brother there still!

He wrote me a beautiful letter, just his old self, so that I could not have known from it of his illness: and I seemed to gather from it that he is not unhappy, even tho' he feels being cut off from the life he used to lead.[3] I do hope this is so, and that the days are not so sad, to him as they are to his friends in thinking of him. His friendship and yours have meant a great deal to me all these years, and I am sure you know that distance will not diminish it.

[1] C. R. Spencer was created Viscount Althorp in Dec. 1905 and appointed Lord Chamberlain.

[2] Bryce was appointed British ambassador at Washington in Jan. 1907.

[3] Spencer to Bryce, 1 Jan. 1907, SP (copy).

## 834    LADY SARAH SPENCER TO LORD RENDEL
*20 October 1907; Althorp, Northampton*
Ren. P., 756

I hope to get Spencer to move away from the fall of the leaf here, clay soil making it too damp for quick recovery here. . .

This week it has been discovered that the Gallery 120 feet long is all oak panelled! painted white and then canvas and paper. . . Spencer will restore it, I hope. It is very engrossing to S., just what was wanted here while he is unable to do his work or get out much.

## 835    LORD SPENCER TO VISCOUNT ALTHORP
*15 April 1908; Florence*

I am very glad that John Morley becomes a Viscount in the House of Lords and old Fowler will also become a Viscount . . . dear old Ripon remains in the Cabinet, that Elgin disappears and Crewe is to be Secretary of State of Colonies and is to be Leader in the House of Lords.[1]

Why is Edward to disappear from the 1st Lord of the Admiralty and become the Lord President of the Council? I fancy that he also had a fight with Asquith against the Vote on ships with money. I cannot believe that the letter from the Kaiser and Edward was a difficulty to change Edward's place at the Admiralty!!![2]

I like McKenna very much, and I see that poor old Robertson has to give way as Secretary of the Admiralty.[3]

[1] In Asquith's cabinet, formed in April 1908, Morley remained at the India Office, Fowler as Chancellor of the Duchy of Lancaster and Ripon as Privy Seal.

[2] Tweedmouth had corresponded privately with the German Emperor on aspects of British naval policy. He was incorrectly accused of disclosing details of forthcoming naval estimates. In the new government, Tweedmouth was made Lord President. To Spencer he wrote, 'I am absolutely heartbroken at being separated from the Navy . . . but Asquith was very strong that both War Secretary and First Lord must be in the H. of C. and that is the whole history of my misfortune.' Tweedmouth to Spencer, 13 April 1908, SP. Tweedmouth resigned his office in Sept. 1908.

[3] Reginald McKenna, previously President of the Board of Education, replaced Tweedmouth. Robertson was succeeded by Thomas Macnamara, Liberal M.P., North Camberwell, 1900–18.

## 836    LORD SPENCER TO VISCOUNT ALTHORP
*26 April 1908; Florence*

Poor old C.B. could not go on longer . . .[1] I was always very fond of him, and he did so much in Politics for the Irish Secretaryship after George Trevelyan . . .

It is not a good account in *The Times*.[2]

[1] Campbell-Bannerman died on 22 April.

[2] *The Times*, 23 April 1908, p. 4. The obituary stated that 'few would be found to say that his life offers a specially interesting subject of study to the biographer'.

**837**   H. H. ASQUITH TO LORD SPENCER
*11 October 1908; 10 Downing Street, S.W.*

It was with the most sincere regret that I received your letter announcing your wish to resign the position which you had held for so long, and filled with so much advantage to the State, of Lord-Lieutenant of the County of Northampton.[1] The King accepts your resignation with reluctance, and with earnest gratitude for the services which you have rendered him.

May I add, for myself, and for all your old colleagues in the Government, an assurance that we constantly miss your wise counsels and loyal help.

[1] Spencer relinquished the post 'with great reluctance and regret' on account of his continuing ill-health. Spencer to Asquith, 7 Oct. 1908, AP, 11 f. 205. He was succeeded by Viscount Althorp.

**838**   LORD SPENCER TO VISCOUNT ALTHORP
*18 November 1909; Althorp, Northampton*

I greatly enjoyed myself in Windsor where both the King and the Queen and many of their friends were so kind to me.[1]

[1] A Chapter held on 16 Nov. at Windsor to invest the King of Portugal with the Order of the Garter. Spencer led the procession into the Throne Room as the senior member of the Order. *The Times*, 17 Nov. 1909, p. 13.

**839**   6TH EARL SPENCER TO E. GOSSE[1]
*27 August 1910; Althorp, Northampton*
Gosse Papers
11.20 p.m.

I could not wish my dear old Brother to linger on, as his condition had become most sad. Yet the loss of him has been a heavy trial,[2] as instinctively all one's thoughts flew back to my own past happiness, and his very close connection with it.

He did not suffer at all, I think, though the fearful restlessness always to get home, driving out to get the train then awaiting the carriage to take him to the Railway Station must have been a sort of mental pain. Then the idea of hunting, actually insisting on getting up fairly early to be in time to start, and our helplessness to convince him that there was no hunting and that he was in his own house—all this was a strain. He did not speak much but seemed peaceful, and once he took great interest in a picture of Lady Caroline Lamb, telling us of her Mother[3] and calling her the right name.

He generally knew my sister, but took me for the male nurse and vice versa. At last he took to his bed, but his strength was such that even then he tried to dress on purpose to get home. I was with him when the blessed peace came to him, and he gently sighed his life away...

I had the ribbon of the Garter put on him, and later when he lay in the big hall, I covered him with the mantle of the Garter.

The last service was touching, great crowds of people, but all gently sympathetic.[4] I have been deeply touched by the sympathy shown to his memory by every one. He was so simple in his ideas that he never would have thought of the feeling of sorrow that burst out at his passing away, so that great link with my own past happiness has gone, and I feel it acutely.

[1] Edmund Gosse, poet and man of letters, Librarian; House of Lords, 1904-14.

[2] Gosse had written on hearing of Spencer's death, 'What you must have lived through in these last dreadful days!' So that the moment I saw the fatal message my one thought was "Peace at last! Peace for him, dear man, and above all peace for you".' Gosse to 6th Earl Spencer, 14 Aug. 1910, SP.

[3] Lady Henrietta Frances Spencer, younger daughter of John, 1st Earl Spencer. She married Frederick Ponsonby, 3rd Earl of Bessborough, on 27 Nov. 1780.

[4] On 18 Aug. at Great Brington Church. See the *Northampton Independent*, 20 Aug. 1910, pp. 22-3.

# Appendix

## THE PAPERS OF THE FIFTH EARL SPENCER

This vast collection of papers, which once occupied over half the shelf space in the Muniment Room at Althorp, documents in detail the life of the fifth Earl Spencer for a period of more than sixty years. The papers are now in the British Library. No cataloguing has so far been undertaken and what follows is a description of the collection as a whole rather than a chronological or subject classification. The items mentioned in each case include letters, memoranda and telegrams received by Spencer as well as copies of letters sent. At various times, items have been removed and never returned. For example, five of the ten letters from Lord Dufferin were extracted on 31 October 1880 and not replaced. In the Harcourt-Spencer correspondence there is an unexplained gap of almost four years (November 1896–May 1900). Fortunately, much of this can be filled from the Harcourt Papers, now in the Bodleian. Some parts of the collection at Althorp have been lent to biographers in the past. This has been helpful in placing on record correspondence from Spencer which now no longer exists. The political letters were originally kept at Spencer House, the family's London home.

The papers can be divided into five major headings:

1. Official letters, mainly from ministers and members of the Royal Household, 1868–1904.
2. Official papers, mainly cabinet business and correspondence, relating to the 1880–5, 1886 and 1892–5 governments.
3. Admiralty papers, 1892–5.
4. General correspondence, 1847–1910.
5. Family correspondence, 1847–1910.

The following description of the papers can offer no more than a general guide to the reader. The full richness of the collection will be revealed only when the documents have been fully and systematically catalogued.

## I OFFICIAL LETTERS 1868–1904

This series is preserved in forty-three leather-bound folders, with the names of the correspondents inscribed on the bindings. With minor exceptions, all the material relates to the periods during which the writers held ministerial or Royal Household appointments. A brief description of the contents of the letters is recorded on the envelopes in which they are kept within the folders. The official post held by the correspondent at the time is given below.

(a) CABINET MINISTERS                                                                ITEMS

| | | |
|---|---|---|
| Sir H. A. Bruce | Home Secretary, 1868–73. | |
| | 19 Dec 1868–19 Dec 1872 | 63 |
| E. Cardwell | Secretary for War, 1868–74. | |
| | 18 Dec 1868–16 June 1873 | 22 |
| J. Chamberlain | President, Board of Trade, 1880–5. | |
| | 18 Jan 1882–26 July 1885 | 21 |
| H. C. E. Childers | First Lord of Admiralty, 1868–71; Secretary for War, 1880–2; Chancellor of the Exchequer, 1882–5. | |
| | 10 Oct 1869–29 April 1870 | 9 |
| | 5 May 1882–8 Jan 1885 | 158 |
| 4th Earl of Clarendon | Foreign Secretary, 1868–70. | |
| | 14 Aug 1869–17 April 1870 | 9 |
| 15th Earl of Derby | Colonial Secretary, 1882–5. | |
| | 3 March 1883–2 May 1885 | 9 |
| Sir C. W. Dilke | President, Local Government Board, 1882–5. | |
| | 23 Dec 1883–2 Jan 1885 | 40 |
| W. E. Forster | Chief Secretary, Ireland, 1880–2. | |
| | 17 Feb 1882–18 Aug 1883 | 15 |
| C. S. Fortescue (1st Baron Carlingford, 1874) | Chief Secretary, Ireland, 1868–71; President, Board of Trade, 1871–4; Lord Privy Seal, 1881–5; Lord President of the Council, 1883–5. | |
| | 10 Dec 1868–24 Jan 1871 | 195 |
| | 4 Feb 1882–23 July 1885 | 89 |
| W. E. Gladstone | Prime Minister, 1868–74, 1880–5, 1886, 1892–4. | |
| | 4 Jan 1869–20 Feb 1874 | 263 |
| | 18 Jan 1882–30 Dec 1885 | 522 |
| | 24 Feb 1888–3 May 1895 | 39 |
| 2nd Earl Granville | Foreign Secretary, 1870–4 and 1880–5; Colonial Secretary, 1886. | |
| | 9 June 1873–16 Feb 1874 | 15 |
| | 5 Jan 1882–28 Dec 1886 | 153 |
| Sir W. V. Harcourt | Home Secretary, 1880–5; Chancellor of the Exchequer, 1886, 1892–5. | |
| | 6 May 1882–25 June 1885 | 230 |
| | 15 April 1886–14 Oct 1896 | 166 |
| | 15 June 1900–24 Jan 1904 | 30 |

| | | |
|---|---|---|
| Marquess of Hartington | Postmaster-General, 1868–71; Chief Secretary, Ireland, 1871–4; Secretary for India, 1880–2; Secretary for War, 1882–5. | |
| | 25 Jan 1870–20 Feb 1874 | 457 |
| | 16 March 1882–21 June 1885 | 64 |
| 1st Earl of Kimberley | Lord Privy Seal, 1868–70; Colonial Secretary, 1880–2; Chancellor, Duchy of Lancaster, 1882; Secretary for India, 1882–5. | |
| | 24 Dec 1868–10 May 1869 | 10 |
| | 16 March 1882–21 June 1885 | 12 |
| J. Morley | Chief Secretary, Ireland, 1886, 1892–5. | |
| | 27 Dec 1886–24 Nov 1896 | 190 |
| 1st Earl of Northbrook | First Lord of Admiralty, 1880–5. | |
| | 7 May 1882–31 May 1885 | 39 |
| 1st Earl of Selborne | Lord Chancellor, 1880–5. | |
| | 17 July 1882–18 Oct 1884 | 15 |
| Sir G. O. Trevelyan | Chief Secretary, Ireland, 1882–4; Chancellor, Duchy of Lancaster, 1884–5; Secretary for Scotland, 1892–5. | |
| | 9 May 1882–29 Oct 1885 | 962 |
| | 7 Oct 1888–9 Dec 1894 | 14 |

(b) MINISTERS

| | | |
|---|---|---|
| C. R. Barry | Attorney-General, Ireland, 1870–2. | |
| | 20 March 1870–17 Aug 1871 | 22 |
| Sir H. Campbell-Bannerman | Chief Secretary, Ireland, 1884–5. | |
| | 15 Oct 1884–25 Dec 1885 | 186 |
| 1st Earl of Dufferin | Chancellor, Duchy of Lancaster and Paymaster-General, 1868–72. | |
| | 17 Feb 1871–28 March 1872 | 6 |
| Lord R. Grosvenor | Parliamentary Secretary, Treasury, 1880–5. | |
| | 30 Oct 1882–20 July 1885 | 18 |
| J. T. Hibbert | Parliamentary Secretary, Local Government Board, 1880–3; Under-Secretary, Home Office, 1883–4; Financial Secretary, Treasury, 1884–5. | |
| | 12 May 1882–20 Dec 1884 | 6 |
| Sir H. James | Attorney-General, 1880–5. | |
| | 2 Feb 1883–2 Nov 1884 | 3 |

| W. M. Johnson | Attorney-General, Ireland, 1881-3. | |
| | 10 July 1882-2 Feb 1883 | 17 |
| H. Law | Attorney-General, Ireland, 1880-1; | |
| | Lord Chancellor, Ireland, 1881-3. | |
| | 18 May 1882-10 May 1883 | 16 |
| W. Monsell | Under-Secretary, Colonial Office, 1868-71; | |
| | Postmaster-General, 1871-4. | |
| | 24 Jan 1869-25 March 1872 | 36 |
| J. Naish | Solicitor-General, Ireland, 1883; | |
| | Attorney-General, Ireland, 1883-5. | |
| | 26 June 1883-23 March 1885 | 21 |
| A. M. Porter | Attorney-General, Ireland, 1883. | |
| | 31 Jan 1883-5 Dec 1883 | 41 |
| Sir E. Sullivan | Attorney-General, Ireland, 1868-70; | |
| | Master of the Rolls, Ireland, 1870-83; | |
| | Lord Chancellor, Ireland, 1883-85. | |
| | 31 Dec 1868-14 March 1871 | 30 |
| | 10 Dec 1883-6 April 1885 | 57 |
| S. Walker | Solicitor-General, Ireland, 1883-5. | |
| | 27 Dec 1883-20 Jan 1885 | 16 |

(c) OFFICIALS

| C. Boyle | Private Secretary, Earl Spencer, 1882-5; Assistant Secretary, Local Government Board, 1885-6. | |
| | 11 Oct 1884-13 June 1885 | 16 |
| Col. H. Brackenbury | Assistant Under-Secretary, Police and Crime, Ireland, 1882. | |
| | 15 May 1882-30 Dec 1882 | 37 |
| T. H. Burke | Under-Secretary, Ireland, 1869-82. | |
| | 1 May 1869-1 Nov 1873 | 237 |
| Sir R. G. C. Hamilton | Under-Secretary, Ireland, 1882-6. | |
| | 5 Oct 1882-18 Dec 1886 | 196 |
| E. G. Jenkinson | Assistant Private Secretary, Earl Spencer, 1882; Assistant Under-Secretary, Police and Crime, Ireland, 1882-6. | |
| | 30 Sept 1882-12 Aug 1885 | 195 |
| C. D. C. Lloyd | Resident Magistrate, Ireland, 1874-83; Inspector-General of Reforms, Egypt, 1883-4; Under-Secretary of State, 1884; Resident Magistrate, Ireland, 1885. | |
| | 4 May 1882-16 Nov 1885 | 64 |

(d) ROYAL FAMILY AND PEERS OF THE REALM

| | | |
|---|---|---|
| H.M. Queen Victoria | 7 Aug 1871–31 July 1872 | 16 |
| | 6 May 1882–14 May 1885 | 152 |
| 1st Baron Athlumney | 18 April 1870–5 Dec 1873 | 19 |
| 5th Earl of Bessborough | Lord Steward, 1869–74. | |
| | 19 Sep 1869–18 Feb 1874 | 147 |
| H.R.H. The Duke of | Commander-in-Chief, Army, 1856–95. | |
| Cambridge | 30 Nov 1869–6 Nov 1873 | 11 |
| Viscount Castlerosse | Vice-Chamberlain, 1868–72. | |
| | 14 Aug 1869–17 April 1870 | 9 |
| 3rd Earl of Charlemont | 28 May 1871–22 Dec 1872 | 12 |
| 1st Marquess of | 31 March 1871–26 July 1872 | 13 |
| Clanricarde | | |
| 3rd Marquess of | 22 Aug 1869–2 Jan 1873 | 8 |
| Drogheda | | |
| 3rd Earl of Leitrim | 25 Oct 1870–6 Sep 1873 | 6 |
| 2nd Baron Lurgan | Lord-in-Waiting, 1869–74. | |
| | 18 Aug 1870–27 Dec 1872 | 16 |
| 1st Baron Sandhurst | Commander-in-Chief, Ireland, 1870–5. | |
| | 10 Aug 1870–13 Aug 1873 | 60 |
| 1st Earl Sydney | Lord Chamberlain, 1868–74. | |
| | 19 Feb 1869–22 April 1870 | 8 |

## 2 OFFICIAL PAPERS 1868–95

This series consists of twenty-six large boxes of mainly printed materials relating to the four Gladstone ministries between the years 1868–94 and the Rosebery ministry, 1894–5. Much of it consists of documents circulated either to the cabinet or to other ministers where appropriate. There is also interesting correspondence between Spencer and his colleagues on such topics as the Irish Land Bills and Secret Service money in Ireland; a memorandum by Spencer relating the end of the 1885 Liberal administration; correspondence with Law Officers on the Irish Judicature Bills, 1884–5; and drafts of and materials for Spencer's speeches, such as that delivered on the Home Rule Bill, 1893.

Sixteen boxes are concerned with Irish affairs; a further six are taken up with United Kingdom matters and the rest with overseas business. As there was no particular ordering of the boxes in the Muniment Room, the list which follows groups the material under appropriate headings.

(a) IRELAND
  (i) *Land Bill 1869–72*
      Newspaper cuttings and speeches, 1869–70. Draft, Land Bill, 1870. Copy of correspondence and papers relating to Tenant-Right, 1869.
  (ii) *Prisons*
      Two large bundles, 1869, 1870. Papers on emigration, 1883.
  (iii) *Irish Railways 1871. National Education 1872–9*

(iv) *State of Ireland 1880–2*
Includes secret memoranda for the cabinet by Earl Cowper, W. E. Forster and others, as well as papers about the judicature.

(v) *Primary and Technical Education 1882–5*
Visit of Royal Commission on Technical Instruction to Ireland, 1882. Papers on National Education (Ireland) Bill, 1884, and Irish University Education, 1885.

(vi) *Judicial 1880–5*
Bundle marked 'Crime and Procedure for Trial, 1885'.

(vii) *Judicial 1883–4*
Includes memoranda on O'Shea and Kilmainham, 1882. Speeches, newspaper cuttings and cabinet minutes on the Maamtrasna case, 1883–4.

(viii) *Land Bill 1882–5*
Mainly printed papers.

(ix) and (x) *Land Bill 1884*
Includes correspondence between Spencer and Lord Lansdowne, documents on the Purchase Bills and Spencer's speeches (printed).

(xi) and (xii) *Government of Ireland Bills and Land Purchase Bill 1886*
Newspaper reports and speeches by Randolph Churchill, John Morley and Spencer. Spencer's notes in packet marked 'Material for speeches, 21.7.86'.

(xiii) *Government of Ireland 1886–95*
Government of Ireland Bill, 1886, secret papers. Irish Land Act, 1887. Irish affairs, 1892–5.

(xiv) *Miscellaneous*
Distress and Emigration, 1882–5. Memorandum by Spencer 'The End of Gladstone's Administration', 1885. Criminal Law Amendment Act, 1887. Resolutions against Government. Coercion Bill, 1887; printed and manuscript material.

(xv) *Home Rule Bill 1893*
Draft of Bill. Parliamentary Returns. Papers circulated to cabinet. Draft of Spencer's speech introducing the Second Reading of Bill, 5 Sept 1893. Other correspondence on this matter includes letters from C. S. Roundell.

(b) HOME POLITICS

(i) *Home Affairs 1880–6*
Mainly printed cabinet papers on such topics as Welsh Education, Municipal Corporations, Distribution of Seats Bill, Representation of the People Act, 1884 and the London Government Bill. Correspondence on Secret Service money, Spencer and H. C. E. Childers, 1880–5.

(ii) *Local Government 1883*
Envelope marked 'Papers Explanatory of County Council Bill, 1883'.

(iii) *Home Politics 1892–3*
Mainly printed cabinet papers. The bulk of them relate to the Local

Government Bill, 1893–4, but it includes memoranda on agricultural production rates on land and immigration of foreigners. There is also a manuscript memorandum by J. G. Fitch, the notable educationist, entitled 'Public Education—Recent Extensions', May 1892.

(iv) *Pamphlets on War Materials 1855–68*
Includes proceedings of the Select Committee on Military Breech-Loading Rifles, 1868. Spencer was a member of the Committee.


(c) OVERSEAS

(i) *Africa 1880–6*
Printed papers for cabinet on Tunis (Lord Tenterden), 1881. French operations in Madagascar, 1882–6, Transvaal, 1883, Zululand, 1886. Dispatches to Kimberley on Africa, 1880–1 and memorandum by same on news of General Gordon and endeavours made to communicate with him since September 24 1882, Foreign Office, 1885.
*Egypt 1892–5*
Cabinet papers and memoranda including report on the state of Egypt, 1892 (Lord Cromer) and Egypt-Sudan, 1895.

(ii) *Uganda 1892–5*
Three envelopes of memoranda 1892, 1893 and 1893–5.
*Miscellaneous 1882–5*
Cabinet papers, including relations between Great Britain and Germany, trade in Samoa, 1894 and passage of Russian ships through the Northern Straits, 1894.

(iii) *Asia 1882–6*
Dispatches on Russian advances in Asia, 1876–8 and 1879–81, France and China, 1885.
*America 1882–6*
Printed memoranda relating to Central America and West Indies, and the USA, 1884. North-Western Territories (Lord Lansdowne), 1885.

(iv) *Asia 1892–5*
Mainly dispatches from ambassadors and others for cabinet on China, Chitral, India, Japan, and Pacific Islands.
*America 1892–5*
Dispatches on Panama, 1893, Nicaragua 1894, British Guiana, 1895, Memorandum on the Ottawa Conference, 1894.

(v) *Channel Tunnel 1870–82*
Correspondence with France, 1870 and military opinions, 1882.
*France—Conference on Commercial Treaties 1881*
Proceedings, for the cabinet.

(vi) *France 1893–5*
Franco-Russian relations: dispatches for the cabinet. Training of soldiers, 1893.
*Europe 1892–5*
Includes memorandum on Austrian suffrage, 1893. Belgian electoral system, 1893. Referendum and Initiative, Switzerland, 1895.

*South-Eastern Europe 1880–6*
Memoranda on Treaty of Berlin, 1880 (Lord Tenterden), Turkey, 1880 and Greece, 1886.
*Pacific 1883–6*
Colonial Office papers on rectification of boundaries, Fiji, 1880, New Guinea, New Hebrides and other Pacific Islands, 1883 and annexation in the Pacific, 1883.

3 ADMIRALTY PAPERS 1892–5

Spencer was First Lord of the Admiralty from 1892 to 1895; these eventful years are fully documented in the papers, which comprise both letters and printed material. As this series is concerned entirely with naval affairs, correspondence relating to other political matters is to be found in the General Correspondence series (Section 5). Thus for example, letters to and from Rosebery during this period are divided between the two series according to their contents.

(a) LETTERS

The correspondence with cabinet colleagues, other ministers, Lords of the Admiralty, naval commanders and Admiralty personnel occupies thirty-one boxes, arranged in alphabetical order. It would be impossible in the space available to give a full list of correspondents, but a selection of the more important ones are here listed. The number of letters includes those both to and from Spencer.

| | |
|---|---|
| Rear-Admiral F. G. D. Bedford, 1892–5. (Cape and W. Africa) | 22 |
| Rear-Admiral N. Bowden-Smith, 1893–4. (Australia) | 11 |
| J. Bryce, 1893–4. (Chancellor, Duchy of Lancaster, 1892–4, President, Board of Trade, 1894–5) | 5 |
| Admiral Sir M. Culme-Seymour, 1893–5. (Mediterranean) | 53 |
| Rear-Admiral Sir J. A. Fisher, 1892–5. (Third Naval Lord and Controller, Admiralty) | 64 |
| Vice-Admiral Sir E. R. Fremantle, 1893–5. (China) | 42 |
| W. Graham Greene, 1894–5. (Assistant Private Secretary to Spencer, Admiralty) | 17 |
| W. E. Gladstone, 1893–5. (Prime Minister, 1892–4) | 7 |
| Vice-Admiral Sir J. O. Hopkins, 1892–4. (N. America and W. Indies) | 66 |
| Rear-Admiral C. F. Hotham, 1892–3. (Pacific) | 3 |
| Rear-Admiral W. R. Kennedy, 1892–5. (E. Indies) | 7 |
| Rear-Admiral Lord W. T. Kerr, 1892–5. (Second Naval Lord, Admiralty) | 20 |
| 1st Earl of Kimberley, 1893–5. (Lord President and Secretary for India, 1892–4, Foreign Secretary, 1894–5) | 50 |

Captain the Hon. Hedworth Lambton, 1892-4. (Private Secretary
    to Spencer, Admiralty)     32

J. Morley, 1893-5. (Chief Secretary, Ireland, 1892-5)     14

Admiral Sir F. Richards, 1893-5. (Senior Naval Lord, Admiralty)     18

1st Marquess of Ripon, 1892-5. (Colonial Secretary, 1892-5)     47

E. Robertson, 1892-5. (Civil Lord, Admiralty)     50

5th Earl of Rosebery, 1892-5. (Foreign Secretary, 1892-4, Prime
    Minister, 1894-5)     60

Sir Ughtred J. Kay-Shuttleworth, 1892-5. (Parliamentary and
    Financial Secretary, Admiralty, 1892-5)     200

Sir G. O. Trevelyan, 1893-4. (Secretary for Scotland, 1892-5)     9

Vice-Admiral Sir G. Tryon, 1892-3. (Mediterranean)     23

(b) PRINTED MATERIAL

There are six large boxes of mainly printed material devoted to naval affairs.
These boxes have no specific titles.

(i) Cabinet and Board of Admiralty papers. Strength of Navy, Naval Defence Act, Royal Navy Reserve. MS correspondence between Spencer
and W. V. Harcourt, 1892-3. Battleships, British, French and Russian,
1893-4. Naval Estimates, 1894-5. Preparations for War, 1895.

(ii) Papers on Principles of Imperial Defence, Organization of Naval Engineers, Defence of Coaling Stations and Size of Battleships. Supply of
Seamen: two deputations, 1894-5. Ships in Indian Waters.

(iii) Dockyard Workmen: pay and working hours, 1886-93. Naval Works
Bill, 1895. Naval Construction. Dockyard Labour Demarcation: deputations, Thames District: deputations in matters of contracts placed elsewhere.

(iv) Mediterranean Station: strategy, 1893. Shipbuilding programmes. Cabinet papers on the following; shipbuilding criticisms, cordite, shortage
and supply. New Construction, 1894-9. Naval Administration, Admiralty, 1892-5. Royal Dockyards. Torpedo Boat Destroyers.

(v) Official Reports:
    HM Ships and Foreign Vessels, A list: Parts I, II and III, corrected to
        April, 1891.
    Ships in Commission, 1739-1891.
    Naval Manoeuvres, 1892, 1893, 1894.
    Naval Estimates, 1892-3, 1893-4, 1894-5, 1895-6: Explanatory State-
        ments by First Lord.
    Battleships and Cruisers: Built, Building, Preparing to build, for Eng-
        land, France, Russia, Germany, Italy and Austria.
    Manning Requirements, 1895: two reports.

(vi) Index of Spencer's Admiralty Papers and Correspondence, 1892-5.
    Official Reports:
    HMS Victoria. Court Martial and Report on Loss of this ship, 22
        June 1893. Steam Ships of England, 1892.
    British and Merchant Shipping, Progress of, 1893.

Report and Minutes of Evidence of Committee on Royal Navy Executive List, 1894.

Copy of Official Procedure and Rules: Board of Admiralty, March 1889.

## 4 GENERAL CORRESPONDENCE 1847–1910

The documents so far described relate almost entirely to Spencer's political career and to those periods when he was in office. The General Correspondence series, constituting by far the majority of the Spencer Papers, whilst overlapping with the above category, contains much information on Althorp affairs as well as his involvement in London activities.

There are approximately 30,000 items kept in 384 boxes of this series, which occupied a whole wall of the Muniment Room. The boxes are arranged chronologically, varying in number according to the happenings in any particular year. For the earliest period, 1847–51, there is only one box but this is supplemented by material in the series relating to the fourth Earl Spencer (see Section 5 below). The number of boxes for each decade gives some impression of the distribution:—

| Years | Boxes |
|---|---|
| 1847–50 | 1 |
| 1851–60 | 14 |
| 1861–70 | 66 |
| 1871–80 | 57 |
| 1881–90 | 149 |
| 1891–1900 | 36 |
| 1901–1910 | 58 |
| Undated | 3 |

The contents of the boxes are arranged in alphabetical order, according to the name of the correspondent or the topic. The ordering of these papers was carried out some years ago by the seventh Earl Spencer with the help of an assistant. This comprehensive collection is an indispensable source for students of nineteenth-century political, social and economic history. Starting with Spencer's own election to the House of Commons in 1857, the papers present a detailed picture of subsequent campaigns, both locally and nationally. There is correspondence with ministerial colleagues on such measures at the Irish Land Act, 1870, the Franchise Act, 1884 and the Education Act, 1902. In some cases, letters not included in Section 1 above are to be found here, notably from Earl Cowper, 1880–3, and Gladstone, 1885–95, as well as accounts of conversations with Gladstone, e.g. 28 July 1891 and 21 November 1897. The information on Spencer's work at the Education Department as Lord President, 1880–3, as described in Volume I, is derived almost entirely from this series. The Tariff Reform Campaign, 1903–4, and the planning by Liberal leaders towards forming a new government in 1906 can also be followed here.

At a local level, such matters as church patronage, the administration of justice and the Poor Law, and the provision of education are represented. The management of the Althorp Estate, the house as the focus of social life in Northamptonshire and changes made within the house itself are also recorded. Spencer's passion for hunting accounts for the extensive correspondence relating to the Pytchley Hunt. There are Journals covering each of his Masterships of the Pytchley: Volume I, 4 November 1861-22 April 1864, Volume II, 2 November 1874-17 April 1878 and the Woodland Pytchley, 14 October 1878-19 April 1879, and Volume III, 3 November 1890-28 March 1894. Of more than local significance was the sale of the Althorp Library in 1892 and the various stages of its move to Manchester which are also documented in these papers.

Finally, mention must be made of Earl and Countess Spencer's warm relationship with Queen Victoria and the Prince of Wales, later Edward VII, which is reflected in this series. There are also interesting letters from members of the Royal Household to Spencer.

## 5 FAMILY CORRESPONDENCE 1847-1910

The General Correspondence series just described includes family letters but there are some special collections which have been little used by previous researchers. The most important one is that from *Spencer to his wife, Charlotte* between May 1858 and June 1903. These 1,120 letters, contained in eleven boxes, begin shortly before their marriage and continue until four months before her death. There are interesting pen-pictures of Spencer's colleagues, news of cabinet business, accounts of Irish visits and assessments of his own electioneering speeches. The correspondence from *Lady Spencer to her husband* consists of some 638 letters in ten boxes, dating from May 1858 to August 1900; those written in the subsequent three years are missing. Although naturally less informative on political affairs than Spencer's own letters, Lady Spencer's correspondence records conversations with many leading figures of the time and contains comments on political events.

Lady Spencer, like many of her contemporaries, kept a *Diary* from the day of her marriage, 8 July 1858. All the separate yearly diaries are now mounted in two large volumes. The main interest in the first volume, which ends at 31 December 1877, is the account of their stay in Ireland during Spencer's first Viceroyalty, 1868-74. There is comparatively little of interest written in the following years when Spencer was out of office. Volume two, beginning 1 January 1879 and ending 29 August 1902, is much fuller; for the important years 1885 and 1886 they are fairly complete, but the diaries for the period of Gladstone's last administration are almost silent. Earlier is described the return of Spencer to England from Algiers in April 1880 to receive an offer of a place in the cabinet. There are reports of conversations between Lady Spencer and Gladstone (e.g., 14 April 1886 and 26 March 1895), as well as the after-dinner talk on the occasion of the meeting of the ex-cabinet at Althorp, 5-9 December 1891. For some years no diaries remain, e.g. 1896 and 1901 and others are represented by only a page or two. Of lesser importance are the *General Letters of Lady Spencer* to a wide range of correspondents. These occupy twenty-nine boxes and amount to more than 2,000 letters. The correspondence from *Spencer* to his half brother, *Robert Spencer*, later sixth Earl, consists of 725 letters in nine boxes. It covers the period October 1870 to June 1910 and gives a full account of the latter's election campaigns in Northamptonshire and Hertfordshire. The replies from Robert Spencer to Spencer are to be found in the General Correspondence series described earlier.

Letters from *Spencer to his father, Frederick, fourth Earl Spencer*, survive in the General Correspondence series of the fourth Earl Spencer's Papers. Letters to Spencer from his father are in the earlier boxes of the fifth Earl Spencer's General Correspondence. These give a picture of Spencer's schooldays at Harrow and as an undergraduate at Cambridge. There are 112 letters in all. A small but important collection of letters (59) is that of *Spencer to Horace Seymour* dating from May 1869 to October 1901. Seymour, who was Spencer's brother-in-law, served as one of Gladstone's private secretaries from 1882 to 1884. Most of these letters, written during Spencer's second Irish Viceroyalty, (1882–5), contain unusually frank comments and opinions on political contemporaries and affairs. Seymour's replies as Gladstone's private secretary are kept with the Gladstone/Spencer correspondence in the Official Letters series, 1868–1904 (see Section 1 above). Seymour's private communications with Spencer are in the General Correspondence series.

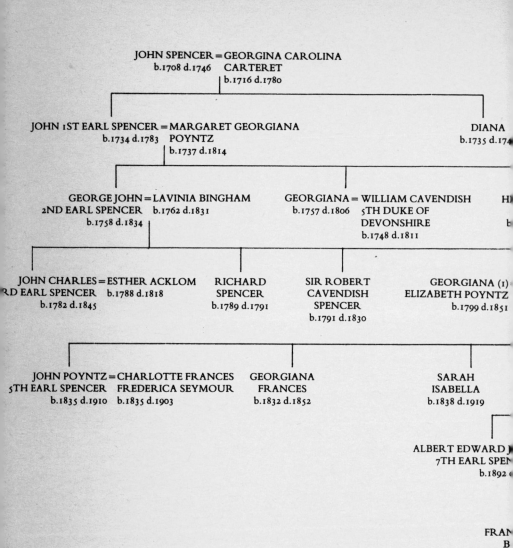

JOHN SPENCER = GEORGINA CAROLINA
b.1708 d.1746    CARTERET
b.1716 d.1780

JOHN 1ST EARL SPENCER = MARGARET GEORGIANA          DIANA
b.1734 d.1783    POYNTZ                              b.1735 d.174
b.1737 d.1814

GEORGE JOHN = LAVINIA BINGHAM       GEORGIANA = WILLIAM CAVENDISH       H
2ND EARL SPENCER  b.1762 d.1831     b.1757 d.1806  5TH DUKE OF
b.1758 d.1834                                      DEVONSHIRE                b
                                                   b.1748 d.1811

JOHN CHARLES = ESTHER ACKLOM    RICHARD          SIR ROBERT          GEORGIANA (1)
RD EARL SPENCER  b.1788 d.1818   SPENCER         CAVENDISH         ELIZABETH POYNTZ
b.1782 d.1845                   b.1789 d.1791      SPENCER            b.1799 d.1851
                                                 b.1791 d.1830

JOHN POYNTZ = CHARLOTTE FRANCES    GEORGIANA          SARAH
5TH EARL SPENCER  FREDERICA SEYMOUR  FRANCES          ISABELLA
b.1835 d.1910    b.1835 d.1903     b.1832 d.1852     b.1838 d.1919

ALBERT EDWARD J
7TH EARL SPEN
b.1892 d

FRAN
B

CHARLES EDWARD
MAURICE, VISCOUNT                                      SARA
ALTHORP
b.1964

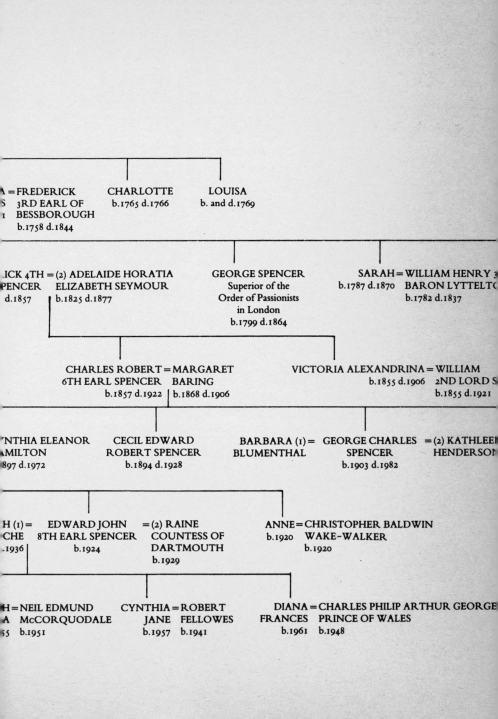

A = FREDERICK          CHARLOTTE          LOUISA
S 3RD EARL OF          b.1765 d.1766      b. and d.1769
ı BESSBOROUGH
  b.1758 d.1844

ICK 4TH = (2) ADELAIDE HORATIA          GEORGE SPENCER          SARAH = WILLIAM HENRY 3
PENCER      ELIZABETH SEYMOUR            Superior of the          b.1787 d.1870  BARON LYTTELTO
  d.1857    b.1825 d.1877                Order of Passionists                    b.1782 d.1837
                                         in London
                                         b.1799 d.1864

              CHARLES ROBERT = MARGARET          VICTORIA ALEXANDRINA = WILLIAM
              6TH EARL SPENCER  BARING                     b.1855 d.1906  2ND LORD S
              b.1857 d.1922  | b.1868 d.1906                             b.1855 d.1921

NTHIA ELEANOR      CECIL EDWARD          BARBARA (1) =  GEORGE CHARLES  = (2) KATHLEE
AMILTON            ROBERT SPENCER        BLUMENTHAL      SPENCER           HENDERSON
897 d.1972         b.1894 d.1928                         b.1903 d.1982

H (1) =    EDWARD JOHN    = (2) RAINE          ANNE = CHRISTOPHER BALDWIN
CHE       8TH EARL SPENCER    COUNTESS OF      b.1920  WAKE-WALKER
.1936      b.1924             DARTMOUTH              b.1920
                             b.1929

H = NEIL EDMUND       CYNTHIA = ROBERT          DIANA = CHARLES PHILIP ARTHUR GEORGE
A   McCORQUODALE       JANE   FELLOWES      FRANCES   PRINCE OF WALES
5  b.1951              b.1957  b.1941       b.1961    b.1948

# SPENCER
# PEDIGREE

RD          HARRIOTT          GEORGIANA = LORD GEORGE QUIN
N           b. and d.1793     CHARLOTTE    b.1792 d.1888
                              b.1794 d.1888

NDHURST

ADELAIDE = SIR SIDNEY          LAVINIA = LUKE HENRY     ALEXANDRA = HENRY MONTAG
MARGARET   CORNWALLIS          EMILY     4TH BARON      MARGARET    DOUGLAS-HOME
b.1889 d.1981  PEEL        b.1899 d.1955  ANNALY        ELIZABETH   b.1907 d.1980
           b.1870 d.1938               b.1885 d.1970      b.1906

# GENERAL INDEX

*References are to pages*